And
To i
"det
a
p

CW00351304

Encountering the Dominant Player

Encountering
the Dominant Player

U.S. EXTENDED DETERRENCE STRATEGY
IN THE ASIA-PACIFIC

WILLIAM T. TOW

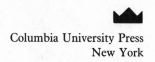

Columbia University Press
New York

Columbia University Press
New York   Oxford
Copyright © 1991 Columbia University Press

The two maps which appear on pp. 325 and 328 are from Strategic Atlas: A
Comparative Geopolitics of the World's Powers *by Gerald Chaliand and Jean
Pierre Rageau. English translation copyright © 1985 by Gerald Chaliand and
Jean Pierre Rageau. Reprinted by permission of HarperCollins Publishers.*

Library of Congress Cataloging-in-Publication Data

Tow, William T.
Encountering the dominant player : U.S. extended deterrence strategy in the Asia-
Pacific / William T. Tow.
p. cm.
Includes bibliographical references and index.
ISBN 0-231-07332-1 (alk. paper)
1. United States—Military relations—Asia.   2. Asia—Military relations—
United States.   3. Asia–National security.   4. United States–Military
relations—Pacific Area.   5. Pacific Area—Military relations—United
States.   6. Pacific Area—National security.   7. United States—Military
policy.   8. Deterrence (Strategy) I. Title.
UA23.T673 1991   90-24324
355.02'17'0973—dc20   CIP

*Casebound editions of Columbia University Press books are Smyth-sewn
and printed on permanent and durable acid-free paper*

Printed in the United States of America

c 10 9 8 7 6 5 4 3 2 1

To My Parents

Contents

Acknowledgments   xiii
Introduction   1

   The Asia-Pacific as the Focus of This Study   4
   Competing Regional Deterrence Postures   7
   U.S. Policy and Posture: The Need for Adjustment   15
   Convergent Deterrence   21

1. Extended Deterrence Strategy and the Dominant Player
Posture   23

   Comparative U.S. Dominant Player Postures: Europe and
     the Asia Pacific   28
   U.S. Extended Deterrence Strategy: Theory and Practice   32
   Bridging Extended Deterrence Theory and U.S. Policy   35
   The Dominant Player Approach to Asia-Pacific Allies   49
   Conclusion   54

2. The Dominant and Transitional Players in the Asia-Pacific:
Reconciling Global and Local Deterrence Objectives   58

   U.S. Strategy Toward Asia-Pacific Allies: Conventional Forces
     and Nuclear Ambiguity   59
   Asia-Pacific Allied Concerns: Why U.S. Allies Have Become
     "Transitional Players"   61

Policy Conflicts: Dominant Player versus Transitional Player 62
Asia Enters the Cold War: Testing Escalation Control 64
The Mutual Security Treaties and Deterrence Commitments 71
Refining the Dominant Player Posture: Maintaining Escalation
    Control 83
Extended Deterrence Commitments: Problems of Definition
    and Management 98
The Dominant Player Posture: Selected Regional Issues 119
Conclusion 143

3. Aspiring Player I: The Soviet Union 145

Soviet Doctrinal Shifts 147
Phases of Soviet Deterrence Strategy in Asia 149
Offense versus Defense: Identifying a "Balanced" Aspiring Player
    Deterrence Posture 172
The USSR's Formal Extended Deterrence Commitments: North
    Korea and Vietnam 180
The Wider Pacific 189
Conclusion 193

4. Aspiring Player II: The People's Republic of China 195

China's Strategic Interests and Its Deterrence Policies 196
China's Military History and Contemporary Deterrence
    Postures 202
The Evolution of Chinese Postwar Deterrence Outlooks 207
Ambiguity in China's Deterrence Posture 220
Linking Strategic Doctrine to China's Strategic Outlook and
    Capabilities 227
Chinese Nuclear Deterrence Capabilities: Survivability/Lethality/
    Controllability 230
Problems of Conventional Deterrence 235
China as a Regional Deterrence Actor 244
Conclusion 265

5. ASEAN as a "Reluctant Player" 269

The Dominant Player Posture in Southeast Asia 272
U.S. Extended Deterrence in Southeast Asia: Case Studies 275
Case Study Lessons 306

Alternatives to the Dominant Player Role in Southeast Asia   307
Implementing the Reluctant Player Posture: Current Problems   314
Conclusion   339

6. The Southwest Pacific: "Strategic Denial" versus "The Pacifist Player" Posture   341

Evolution of Strategic Denial   343
The Pacifist Player Emerges   350
The ANZUS Dispute: 1984–1986   355
ANZUS, Extended Deterrence, and the "Ripple Factor"   374
Threat Perceptions and the Costs of Dissent   376
Conclusion   388

7. Conclusion   390

The Outmoded Dominant Player   391
The Alternative Postures   395
Revising the Dominant Player Strategy   410

Notes   427
Bibliography   511
Index   527

Tables, Figures, and Maps

Figure 1. Competing Deterrence Postures in the Asia-Pacific:
Players and Policies 9
Figure 2. The Dominant Player Posture in the Asia-Pacific:
Factors and Applications 37
Figure 3. U.S. Extended Nuclear Deterrence 101

Table 1. U.S.-Japan Security Relations (1951–1988):
Milestones and Highlights 77
Table 2. Soviet Military Power Projection Capabilities in the
Asia-Pacific 175
Table 3. U.S. Technology Transfer Licenses Approved
for PRC by U.S. Department of Commerce 241
Table 4. Joint Exercises in the ASEAN Region in 1983–1988 334
Table 5. Key ANZUS Dispute Terms/Acronyms 356

Map 1. Strategic Oil Routes and Military Installations in
the Indian and Western Pacific Oceans 325
Map 2. Strategic Trade/Resource Routes and Military Bases
in the Pacific Ocean Area 328

Acknowledgments

THIS VOLUME is the culmination of a three year research project. The study evolved from my strong interest in how the United States would adjust postwar strategy in the Asia-Pacific at a time when its own national resource base was beginning to decline in relative terms and when the new dynamics of indigenous security politics unfolding in that region clearly required a U.S. policy reevaluation. Since 1987, the project benefited from many individuals and institutions. Space constraints allow for only a few to be cited here.

I am particularly grateful to the University of Southern California's Center for International Studies. The Center provided funding and space for writing initial drafts of the book and conducting interviews in key Asia-Pacific locales. The director of CIS, Thomas Biersteker, was always supportive and gracious. Cecilia Cicchinelli, the assistant director, read successive drafts and offered invaluable editorial advice. Richard Deck, my fellow CIS colleague, was also a major source of intellectual and emotional inspiration. Richard Smoke, a CIS Senior Fellow for 1989-90 and a major figure in international security studies at Brown University, read substantial portions of an advanced draft of the book on very short notice. For a scholar of his status to assist a colleague he had only recently met is truly extraordinary, and I am deeply grateful.

My colleagues at USC's School of International Relations were also extremely helpful. Special thanks to Peter Berton for reading an early version of the manuscript and to John Odell for his penetrating comments that made for a better Introduction. My colleagues in the inter-

national security studies field at USC, Chip Blacker and Mike Mochizuki, are always willing and able to offer perceptive comments which
inevitably strengthen the final product of any research effort. So, too,
did Hammond Rolph, SIR's "Asia hand" in-residence. Carole Gustin,
SIR's associate director, provided invaluable logistical support. Kathy
Matthes typed successive versions of the book with incomparable patience and understanding. Ryo Shimizu, Xin Gong, and Missy Yota
provided timely and enthusiastic research assistance.

I also received exceptional help from senior colleagues at other
institutions. Robert A. Scalapino read an entire draft and contributed
insights that only he, as the mentor for all those studying Asian security issues, could engender. My longtime colleague and dear friend,
Douglas T. Stuart, also provided key insights on various aspects of the
narrative. John Lewis and Serguei N. Goncharov of Stanford University's Center for International Security and Arms Control offered critical input on chapter 4. To all of these individuals, I owe much more
than I will ever be able to repay.

Finally, my wife, Leslie, and my daughter, Shannon, have endured
a number of my research pursuits beyond any reasonable expectation.
It is to my family that I extend the ultimate debt of gratitude.

Encountering the Dominant Player

Introduction

FOR A region which traditionally has been viewed by the architects of
U.S. containment policy as less important geopolitically than Europe,
the Asia-Pacific has commanded a remarkable proportion of Washington's strategic attention and resources.[1] If any single characteristic has
dominated the United States' postwar legacy in this region, it has been
one of unexpected and unwanted conflict intervention. Early in the
years following World War II, the Truman and Eisenhower administrations were convinced that the United States, historically a maritime
power, would need to maintain a land-based deterrent in Europe, and
avoid permanent deployment of American ground forces in Asia. But
Korea, and later Vietnam, resulted in by far the most significant
military interventions undertaken by the United States during the cold
war era, and the Korean War foreshadowed the permanent stationing
of limited U.S. land forces in the Asia-Pacific. Far from reinforcing
Eurocentrism as the foundation of U.S. deterrence strategy, American
involvement in these Asian wars contributed to Washington's growing
inclination for extending its strategies of containment and deterrence
beyond the NATO theater. Setting aside, for the moment, the long-
standing debate over the desirability of expanding this strategy to the
Asia-Pacific, it is nevertheless true that the United States rationalized
its extended deterrence to a more nearly global scale in the face of the
perceived communist threat.

Mired in a protracted conflict on the Korean peninsula, U.S. force
planners began viewing an "extended deterrence" strategy, supported
by a series of formal defense alliances, as the best U.S. response to a

variety of threats materializing across the world. There is no consensus among Western defense analysts about an exact definition of this concept. It is most commonly viewed, however, as the application of American military power—including strategic and theater nuclear forces, as well as conventional forces—to guaranteeing the security of the U.S. allies from external threats by positioning such forces to fight effectively at the point of an initial attack, preventing the outbreak of regional wars, or precluding the escalation of ongoing theater conflicts to global war.[2] Common use of the term "extended deterrence" by strategic analysts has encompassed two distinct meanings: a tightly defined version usually refers to countering a threat to allies with implied nuclear force; a more loosely applied interpretation is the deterring of possible adversaries in a general sense, by making alliances or by simply declaring one's intention to protect another state or geographic area, without specifying how.

However defined, extended deterrence has been the hallmark of postwar U.S. collective defense strategy, designed primarily to check the Soviet Union, as a continental power, from threatening areas perceived to be vital to American concern. Secretary of Defense Frank Carlucci summarized to Congress in early 1989 the strategic rationale for the United States pursuing extended deterrence: by forming a series of defense treaties and deterrence commitments with its regional allies, the United States can best present a defense posture representing to "potential aggressors . . . a more formidable deterrent, while enhancing our ability to defend our collective interests should deterrence fail . . . the deterrent value of our combined strength exceeds the sum of its parts."[3]

The three key regions designated by Carlucci—Western Europe, the Middle East, and the Asia-Pacific—have been the most critical theaters of potential superpower confrontation and for implementing extended deterrence. They represent, along with the Western Hemisphere, what the proponents of American containment and deterrence strategy during the cold war viewed as the vital areas of political-economic development and forward defense for containment of Soviet global military power. The North Atlantic Treaty Organization (NATO), the mutual defense accords with various noncommunist Asia-Pacific states backed by the consistent U.S. deployment of extremely powerful naval forces and the formidable U.S. offshore military presence in the Mediterranean and, more recently, in the Persian Gulf, attest to Washington's long-standing and abiding interest in maintaining its strategic access to and influence in the Eurasian landmass. So have the efforts of successive U.S. administrations to shape and refine the United States' strategic outlooks and policy approaches for each theater. These have followed specific regional crises with global ramifications: the coupling of American and West European survival following the Czechoslovakian coup and Berlin blockade engineered by Moscow in 1948, the expansion of U.S. containment strategy in the Middle East in response to Britain's global strategic recessional in the aftermath of Suez almost a decade later, and the effort to preserve U.S. global power through the pursuit of more effective strategies for defense coalition and burden-sharing expressed by the Nixon Doctrine in the waning years of the Vietnam conflict.

In responding to strategic threats confronting Eurasia, successive American presidents constantly sought means to achieve a more credible extended deterrence posture. What often materialized, however, were doctrinal inconsistencies that tended to confuse, rather than to reassure, Washington's NATO and extra-European allies about the shape and intensity of U.S. overseas commitments. President Truman's global strategy, for example, was shaped by his National Security Council's conclusions, expressed in NSC 68, that the USSR fielded sufficient military power to invade Western Europe successfully and would soon deploy sufficient nuclear weapons to deter the United States from intervening in that theater to stop any such contingency. This perceived condition, along with the fall of China to communist forces in October 1949 and the outbreak of the Korean War in June 1950, prompted the large-scale expansion of American nuclear and conventional forces.[4] By late 1953, however, the United States could deploy enough strategic and theater nuclear weapons to overcome any conventional force imbalance in Europe or Asia. Accordingly, President Eisenhower directed his Joint Chiefs of Staff to forge a "New Look" in U.S. deterrence strategy, to balance the United States' future deterrence commitments with the country's financial resources. The product of this mandate was NSC 162/2, which was forwarded to Eisenhower in October 1953.[5] John Kennedy introduced yet another revision into U.S. force planning on the grounds that "flexible response" was needed by the early 1960s to deter a wide spectrum of general and limited war threats at all levels of conflict.[6] While flexible response was gradually—albeit begrudgingly—accepted as a regional deterrence strategy in NATO Europe, it was misapplied in Southeast Asia, forcing Richard Nixon to shift U.S. global strategy from a "two-and-a-half" to a "one-and-a-half" force posture during the early 1970s.[7] President Carter sustained American extended deterrence guarantees to U.S. treaty allies on the condition that they accelerate their own defense expenditures and force buildups within the overall alliance collective defense framework.[8]

The Reagan administration reversed the trend of streamlining U.S. deterrence commitments promoted by Nixon and Carter. During his first term in office, President Reagan embarked upon the most extensive rearmament program in postwar U.S. history. His motives were clearly geopolitical in context and emphasized the importance of the United States pursuing an extended deterrence posture designed to enhance global stability.[9] By 1985, however, most expenditures tied into this force buildup had been allocated, and the U.S. defense budget began declining in real proportionate terms. By 1988, the President was arguing that earlier postwar U.S. deterrence strategies, which had focused primarily on defending Western Europe from a monolithic communist threat, needed to be supplanted by a more complex and "discriminate" approach to global strategy, one which would take into account the emergence of a number of dynamic socioeconomic, cultural, and military variables at a time when the United States was no longer so economically dominant in the world that it could afford to sustain an extended deterrent against every potential threat confronting its global security interests. President Bush's Defense Secretary expanded upon this reasoning in his 1990 annual defense posture statement, contending that the United States "must identify key technologies, weapons systems, and operational concepts that are most likely to maximize the deterrent effects of increasingly strained resources the United States devotes to national defense."[10]

THE ASIA-PACIFIC AS THE FOCUS OF THIS STUDY

A NUMBER of the United States' Asia-Pacific allies have argued that their region should be treated as a separate component of U.S. extended deterrence strategy, rather than as a mere adjunct to a Eurocentric geopolitical blueprint. This argument merits consideration on at least two grounds.

First, the strategic outlook for Europe has vastly improved. Cold war bloc politics has given way to democratic liberalization in Eastern Europe and even in the USSR, bringing into question the fundamental remises of traditional U.S. deterrence strategy extended to the NATO allies. Positive changes in the broader security environment of the Asia-Pacific, however, are less apparent. In the People's Republic of China (PRC), North Korea, and throughout Indochina, repression still outweighs political and economic reform. Serious military threats still confront American allies in Northeast Asia, and possibly Thailand, requiring some form of U.S. security guarantee. Even in some "democratic" Asian societies, however, contending forces of sociopolitical change are not necessarily allowed to coexist peacefully.

The second factor setting the Asia-Pacific apart from Europe is that the former region still constitutes a microcosm of the global strategic challenges which now confront the United States throughout most of the third world. As the twentieth century draws to a close, the Asia-Pacific will become the focal point of global development and change. China, for example, aspires to the status of a world-class power. Japan has evolved into an economic superpower and has the potential to become a first-rate military power on very short notice. A number of the region's smaller nations, such as South Korea, Taiwan, and Singapore, have recently emerged from developing nation status to assume key roles in the international marketplace. The Asia-Pacific's economic growth rate exceeds that of most of Europe (except West Germany), as well as the United States and the Soviet Union, by impressive margins. The region has emerged as a principal factor in international trade. Nevertheless, despite a clear regional shift of resources in favor of economic development, six of the seven largest standing armies in the world are still deployed on the Asian continent. Moreover, some of these have fought each other within the last two decades.[11]

The Bush administration has recently been forced to account for continued U.S. alliance commitments and force deployments in the Asia-Pacific theater under the Nunn-Warren Act, incorporated into the defense authorization bill passed by the U.S. Senate in August 1989. This legislation proposed a ceiling on the percentage of Americans among NATO troops in Europe, called on Japan to strengthen its defense and foreign aid programs, and directed President Bush to prepare a five-year plan for gradual reductions of U.S. military strength in South Korea.[12] Bush has also responded to Congressional defense burden-sharing pressures, in part, by instituting a review of Pacific strategy, formally designated as the East Asia Strategy Initiative (EASI). The resultant report was forwarded to Congress in April 1990. Leaks of the report's contents had already occurred by the first of the year. Under the EASI, the U.S. Department of Defense projected that the U.S. could withdraw 10 to 12 percent of its forward-deployed forces in the Asia-Pacific between 1990 and 1993, because of a decreased Soviet military threat in the region and improved self-defense efforts by U.S. regional allies. South Korea, in particular, would assume a "leading role" in its own defense. U.S. force deployments in South Korea would be cut from 43,000 to 37,000, and command of the U.S.-Korea military structure would be turned over to a South Korean general. Force reductions would also be made in Japan (from 59,000 to 52,000) and in the Philippines (from 17,800 to approximately 15,800).[13] U.S. defense officials, however, asserted that the rationales of strategic deterrence underlying remaining U.S. deployments would continue to be oriented toward fulfilling *global* deterrence strategy. Secretary of Defense Richard Cheney insisted, "There is no change in the commitment, and our strategic interest in the area will continue undiminished."[14]

Notwithstanding the Asia-Pacific's distinctive *regional* strategic identity, the United States continues to treat this theater as an integral component of global deterrence planning. The criteria which govern Washington's deterrence approach to NATO and the Persian Gulf still appear to underlie Pacific strategy as well. These criteria include *flexible response* to an initial enemy attack with a variety of tactics and weapons systems; *escalation control* through the measured use of manpower and firepower to keep a conflict limited in scope and intensity; *forward deployments* in host allied nations to demonstrate strategic commitment; and *force sustainability* in short-war versus long-war scenarios.

Such force priorities continue to dominate U.S. deterrence approaches but fail to sufficiently take into account the Asia-Pacific's changing political forces and indigenous geopolitical outlooks. As recently noted by James R. Kurth, East Asian states "are not cases so much of extended deterrence as of finite deterrence" because, unlike Western Europe, they are less likely to be attacked or overrun collectively and because the external threats confronting them are more amorphous.[15] In light of growing Japanese defense capabilities, rising hostility in the Philippines to U.S. global deterrence missions originating from bases in that country, Chinese strategic ambivalence, and other regional challenges, the extent to which U.S. global deterrence planning is applicable to a continued American strategic role in the Asia-Pacific has become increasingly questionable. Over much of the postwar era, the Asian frame of reference regarding Europeans has been fashioned by decolonization and, more recently, by the vagaries of international commerce. It is difficult in general for Asians to see any real connection between their own regional aspirations and the central European strategic balance. Continued American failure to adjust to the rapid geopolitical changes now unfolding throughout Eurasia could profoundly accelerate the sense of strategic isolation from each other felt by Asians and Europeans and reduce the credibility of future U.S. approaches to extended deterrence in the process.[16]

The major premise of this volume is that the United States must balance its need for strategic control over the eastern littorals of Eurasia with a heightened determination to collaborate with Asia-Pacific governments. Neither of these objectives will be realized unless the United States moves quickly and decisively to adjust its Asia-Pacific strategy, from one basically mirroring the assumptions which guide its traditional global deterrence posture to one more understanding of the alternative deterrence approaches examined here. Instead, Washington's strategic influence will decline to the point where regional power competitors such as the Soviet Union, China, India, or even a more assertive Japan, could begin to view the benefits of contesting future American strategic interests as outweighing the risks.

COMPETING REGIONAL DETERRENCE POSTURES

CURRENTLY, U.S. extended deterrence strategy in the Asia-Pacific is only one of five identifiable strategic postures which have surfaced in the area among one player or another. These are defined in this study as: (1) the U.S. "Dominant Player" posture; (2) the "Transitional Player" posture, characteristic of Washington's traditional northeast Asian allies Japan, South Korea, and Taiwan and, to a lesser extent, its Southwest Pacific ally, Australia; (3) the "Aspiring Player" posture now pursued by both the Soviet Union and the People's Republic of China (PRC); (4) the "Reluctant Player" stance, increasingly characteristic of the Philippines and historically adopted by the other members of the Association of Southeast Asian Nations (ASEAN); (5) and the "Pacifist Player" attitude recently embraced by New Zealand (see figure 1).

The "Dominant Player" Posture of the U.S.

WASHINGTON PURSUES a "Dominant Player" extended deterrence posture, maintaining formal mutual security treaties with Japan, South Korea, the Philippines, and Australia. It supplements these formal commitments with a number of selective but informal security coalitions. One such coalition, for example, was with the PRC during the late 1970s and most of the 1980s, (through military technology transfers and selective defense consultations). Another is with Thailand, through joint military exercises and military assistance conducted under the auspices of the 1962 Rusk-Thanat Communique. A third is with Taiwan, through the approval of limited defense sales of technology and equipment by American firms to strengthen Taiwan's capacity for self-defense under the terms of the April 1979 Taiwan Relations Act. A fourth example is with Malaysia and Singapore through occasional joint military exercises and military sales programs. Such a coalition also exists, albeit more distantly, with Indonesia, through arms sales and occasional joint exercises between U.S. and Indonesian forces.

The object of U.S. extended deterrence strategy in the Asia-Pacific is to preserve American strategic access to and influence within that region as part of Washington's global extended deterrence strategy. This is accomplished, ostensibly, through alliance maintenance and military power projection, even at the risk of entanglement in regional conflicts. Dominant Player strategy proponents believe that, despite the recent decline in aspects of Soviet military power east of the Urals (discussed in chapter 3), the strategic threat represented by the incremental growth of Soviet military capabilities in the Asia-Pacific over the past two decades remains sufficiently disturbing to justify adherence to its traditional extended deterrence commitments and strategies in the theater.[17]

FIGURE 1. Competing Deterrence Postures in the Asia-Pacific: Players and Policies

POLICY	Dominant	Transitional	Aspiring I (USSR)	Aspiring II (PRC)	Reluctant	Pacifist
	PLAYERS					
Alliance Relations	Global strategy erodes credibility of commit- ment at regional strategy level	More national wealth generates alliance defense burden- sharing tensions with exclusive ally	Qualified bilateral security commit- ments	Emphasizes independent foreign policy, but inter- mittently extends deterrence ties	Prefers regional neutrality but retains qualified traditional security	Retains security ties at the non- nuclear level only
Military Presence	Maintains theater- wide bases and weapons stockpiles	Growing maritime/ air power projection capabilities, but primarily self-defense oriented	Limited, but expand- ing in the region	Occasional military personnel assistance; naval expan- sion could lead to occupation of contested territories	National guards; selected naval and air exer- cises; po- tential oc- cupation of off-shore territories	Regional patrols; limited military assistance to small neighbors
Nuclear Weapons	Considered a legitimate means of establishing credibility of commit- ment	Increasingly skeptical about global nuclear- deterrence strategy, but affiliation with Dominant Player remains intact	Legitimate for homeland defense; otherwise supports regional disarmament movements	Policy of expediency; favored for strategic competition, but re- nounced for regional influence	Tolerated but not promoted	Legiti- macy denied on both moral and national security premises

Is such a belief merited? Contemporary studies on the application of deterrence to crises and wars usually dwell on unsuccessful cases of deterrence policy. However, past American successes in preventing the outbreak and escalation of general conflicts cannot be summarily dismissed in any assessment of Washington's contemporary deterrence policies and behavior.[18] Those studies which do weigh deterrence "successes" focus on instances when an attack on an ally is "prevented or repulsed without conflict between the [would-be] attacking forces and regular combat units of the major power 'defender.' "[19]

This book's initial chapter will evaluate the Dominant Player posture in the context of recent theoretical assessments of extended deterrence. It will be argued that the U.S. has had difficulty in reconciling its global extended deterrence strategy with its interests in, and commitments to, the Asia-Pacific. Chapter 1 discusses escalation control, inter-alliance transferability and commitment credibility as three links, or "bridges," between deterrence theory and how the United States applies extended deterrence as a policy. Finally, the first chapter will survey recent U.S. doctrinal adjustments to its extended deterrence strategy in the Asia-Pacific region, and the credibility of the Dominant Player posture as a result of such adjustments.

The United States and "Transitional Players"

CHAPTER 2 will assess the United States' bilateral security relationships with Japan, South Korea, Australia, and the two Chinas. The two defense treaties Washington maintains with Tokyo and Seoul conform most closely to U.S. extended deterrence strategy in NATO Europe, because they are designed to counter external threats (from the Soviet Union, North Korea and, in the Korean Peninsula, even from China under certain circumstances) and improve escalation control. The employment of a nuclear tripwire by the United States along South Korea's border certainly parallels U.S. strategy for defending its NATO partners, as does the U.S. strategic "coupling" of its security to Japan's through the Mutual Security Treaty. Unlike Western Europe, however, with its obvious avenues of access for invasion forces through Germany and the Lowlands, clear-cut lines of strategic demarcation are less common in a Pacific theater which, with the exception of the Korean demilitarized zone, reflects a more fluid geography and less obvious points of potential conflict. It is a broad and amorphous maritime theater where a great diversity of threats and contingencies can materialize. Extended deterrence criteria applicable to NATO conditions and environments, it will be argued here, are only partially transferable to Northeast Asia.

Chapter 2 will also assert that, as the Northeast Asian allies have become more prosperous and politically more self-confident, they have become more discriminate in their affiliation with and support for the Dominant Player posture. Japan, South Korea, and Taiwan have become *Transitional Players* in the regional deterrence environment, still collaborating with the Dominant Player in a formal sense because they have few other real strategic options, but nevertheless asserting greater independence within the framework of their defense relations with Washington. American-Japanese tensions were generated early in the postwar era by Prime Minister Shigeru Yoshida's refusal to adopt rearmament policies originally demanded by John Foster Dulles as a condition for alliance. More recent insistence by various U.S. political factions that Japan assume a greater defense burden in Northeast Asia and beyond, conflicts with Tokyo's long-established policy of realizing security through the exclusive pursuit of economic and marketing advantages under the U.S. security umbrella. American burden-sharing pressure also raises questions among the Japanese over the future credibility of U.S. deterrence commitments in an era when increasingly divisive trade relations are generating significant tensions in overall U.S.-Japanese ties.

Maturing of South Korean political institutions has engendered similar doubts in Seoul about the long-term value of American deterrence guarantees. Rising sentiments for reunification of the Korean Peninsula and for the expansion of Korean economic influence, regionally and globally, are powerful catalysts for resentment of Washington by younger generations of Koreans, who are already prone to downplaying the rationales which prompted the 1953 U.S.-ROK Mutual Defense Treaty. The events leading to the United States' abrogation of a similar treaty with Taiwan in 1978 understandably eroded that ally's faith in the credibility of U.S. deterrence strategy. This lesson was reinforced by the Bush administration's determination to sustain at least qualified strategic "understandings" and economic ties with the People's Republic of China (PRC) in light of Soviet power in the region and despite the bloody suppression of the Chinese prodemocracy movement in early June 1989.

After conducting a major policy review on the ANZUS alliance, Australia's Labor government reaffirmed the value to its own national security interests of extended deterrence ties with the U.S. The reasons cited for sustaining defense relations with the United States, however, varied significantly from those traditionally cited by most postwar Australian governments. Australian defense planners have concluded they can no longer rely upon strategic assurances from Washington to cover every future Southeast Asian or South Pacific contingency to which Australian forces might be committed. Canberra therefore seeks an American ally who endorses Australian efforts to achieve greater defense self-reliance in its own region, even if Australia's local deterrence agenda diverges, occasionally, from U.S. global strategy. Unlike their Tasmanian counterparts in New Zealand, most Australians realize and accept the imperative of supporting general American global strategy, even in its nuclear context, in the interest of preserving and strengthening Australian strategic influence and fulfilling their national security objectives in locales more proximate to their own shores.

The Soviet Union and China as "Aspiring Players"

A THIRD regional deterrence posture, that of the "Aspiring Player," is found in both Soviet and Chinese strategic approaches to the Asia-Pacific. The Soviet Union and China both aspire to establish a major strategic influence in the Asia-Pacific region. Both wish to see a regional order less dependent on U.S. power and more congruent with their own policy visions. Accordingly, the Soviets and Chinese are pursuing variants of the same posture in challenging U.S. interests. The USSR is attempting to move beyond its traditional Asia-Pacific military profile to develop more visible economic and diplomatic influence. China is incorporating elements of deterrence strategy reminiscent of the Dominant Player posture during the 1950s. It is building up its regional nuclear forces, while still preserving its Maoist heritage of "people's war." Neither Aspiring Player expects to supplant the United States as a regional hegemonist; both hope eventually to gain increased regional political and economic status at Washington's expense.

Throughout the 1970s, the USSR used its growing military power in the Asia-Pacific to develop greater politico-economic influence in a region where it had enjoyed almost none during the postwar era. More recently, under Mikhail Gorbachev, the Soviet Union has instituted a wide-ranging series of diplomatic initiatives. These have been designed to capitalize upon what Moscow views as waning U.S. strategic authority in the Asia-Pacific region and to soften the Soviets' image as a natural adversary to most Asia-Pacific states. The new Soviet leadership has continued to rely on the formidable Soviet military presence in the region as insurance that Moscow will retain the clout necessary to be a major actor there. It has, however, in the words of Robert Manning, established "a pattern of bold diplomatic demarches punctuated by . . . diplomatic concessions."[20] The Soviet Union's new Asia-Pacific activism is driven by a determination that its standing in the region will eventually augment its global competitiveness vis-a-vis the United States. An assessment of the effectiveness of this Soviet policy approach will provide the focus of chapter 3.

China's strategy, in contrast, is *regional* in context, more defensive than projectionist (although this is changing), ambiguous rather than distinct, and long-term rather than short-term. China strives to keep the superpowers preoccupied with each other and consequently less effective in strategic competition in Asia. It relies upon its ability to manipulate the superpowers as a means of preventing them from interfering with Beijing's quest for a Chinese version of a regional deterrence posture. At the same time, the PRC's military modernization programs and superpower arms control agreements give China increasingly important status. Chapter 4 argues that as its military modernization proceeds, China is forging a comprehensive strategic doctrine. This doctrine is based on deterrence applications similar to those found in the Dominant Player posture, but it is predicated upon a requirement to reconcile Western deterrence concepts with Chinese military thought.

The "Reluctant Players" Dilemma

THE ASEAN nations, and their stated common strategy of "peace, freedom, and neutrality," represent a fourth posture, that of the "Reluctant Player." The characteristics of this posture and its implications for Asia-Pacific affairs are reviewed in chapter 5. This strategic approach originated from the number of disappointments in their security relations with the United States which the pro-Western elements in Southeast Asia have suffered over the past four decades. Chapter 5 will discuss a quartet of policy case studies: the U.S. Joint Chiefs of Staff's effort to apply a counterattack thesis to Southeast Asian deterrence problems in 1953–1954; the 1961 Laos neutrality crisis; the Nixon Doctrine (1969); and the Reagan administration's "pillar" approach to regional security. Each of these cases illustrates specific instances in which U.S. policy planners "adjusted" the Dominant Player posture in ways which actually reinforced the tendency of Washington's Southeast Asian allies to distance themselves from American extended deterrence commitments.

New Zealand: The "Pacifist Player"

THE FIFTH and last case, that of the "Pacifist Player" is represented by New Zealand, with its policy of nonnuclear deterrence. The key aspects of this posture will be discussed in chapter 6. New Zealand's policy is not actually "pacifist" in the traditional meaning of that term, because the Labour government believes in the validity of what it regards as "conventional deterrence," as well as in the right of the state to maintain defenses against aggression. Wellington, however, rejects the validity of the Dominant Player posture's intellectual premises— escalation control, strategic commitment, and global application. New Zealand Prime Minister David Lange articulated his government's position during a nuclear policy debate at Oxford in early 1985: "There is a quality of irrationality about nuclear weapons which does not sit well with good intentions. A system of defense serves its purpose if it guarantees the security of those it protects. A system of nuclear defense guarantees only insecurity." [21]

The Pacifist Player posture has become the centerpiece of other Asia-Pacific nuclear-free zone movements. These movements are now challenging superpower nuclear strategies in the region in ways which even New Zealand may not have anticipated when it imposed its own nuclear-free zone. Most importantly, in response to Wellington's antinuclear stance, the American decision to exclude New Zealand from the deterrence network of ASEAN and Southwest Pacific states (most notably Australia) symbolizes a dramatic break in the United States' extended global deterrence strategy. Indeed, Washington's fear that New Zealand's strategic behavior will create "ripples" of dissent among other heretofore acquiescent U.S. allies was precisely why the Reagan administration adopted such a hard line in the ANZUS dispute. In chapter 6, the conceptual and political differences between U.S. and New Zealand deterrence postures are examined in some detail, as are the potential ramifications of this dispute for the Southwest Pacific's future security environment.

U.S. POLICY AND POSTURE: THE NEED FOR ADJUSTMENT

A DIVERGENCE has always existed between U.S. global deterrence strategy and those strategic objectives held to be most important by the United States' Asia-Pacific allies. Washington has been preoccupied with the nature and viability of the worldwide Soviet military threat and the challenge to the West. To most Asia-Pacific states, "security" is viewed as success in nation-building at home, the achievement of greater international influence, and the avoidance of involvement in regional or inter-regional conflicts. There may be a role for U.S. extended deterrence strategy in facilitating these regional security objectives. However, Washington must become more open than it has been thus far to understanding these alternative security approaches to deterrence and containment.

There has been no shortage of deliberation about how the United States should confront Asia-Pacific security issues during the postwar era. For this book's analytical purposes, however, three very broad policy approaches to American deterrence politics in the region can be identified. There are, of course, differences—ranging all the way from subtle to significant—among the individuals and institutions within each of the three categories. Moreover, these categories should not be regarded as covering the entire spectrum of thinking about regional deterrence problems. What follows, however, is an initial effort to delineate some key trends underlying the evolution of such thinking, to illustrate the difficulty Western policy analysts have had in separating the problem of indigenous Asian security politics from their broader preoccupation with global strategy.

Much of early American postwar thinking about the Asia-Pacific region was shaped by the *global-realist* perspective. This school of thought originated with a number of President Roosevelt's wartime advisors, including Secretary of War Henry L. Stimson and Secretary of the Treasury Henry Morgenthau, Jr. The global-realists recommended that the President apply coercive diplomacy and economic sanctions against Japan in 1940–41, believing that such policy measures would serve as effective deterrents to Japanese military action in the Asia-Pacific theater. They underestimated Tokyo's feelings that the regional status quo in 1941 would represent an unacceptable loss to Japanese national security, and instead concluded that American concepts of deterrence would automatically be applicable to Japan, as well.[22] In their efforts to merge a strategy approximating global realpolitik with democratic liberalism, the global-realists advocated an American strategic approach to the Asia-Pacific within a larger framework of global security planning, directed at preserving an acceptable international balance of power and advancing Western democratic values.

George Kennan refined the arguments of global-realism following the war. As the Soviet Union emerged as the major new threat to American security interests, Kennan sought to identify geopolitical "strongpoints" where the United States should implement a global containment posture against Soviet military power.[23] Kennan departed from the Stimson-Morgenthau school, however, in his opposition to the universalist thinking which underscored their approach and from the immediate postwar universalist foreign policy camp led by Cordell Hull, Edward Stettinius, and Henry Wallace. The universalist school envisioned a globally active UN Security Council under the joint control of the United States and Soviet Union and a rapid decolonization of the Third World which would facilitate democratic political institutions in the Western image. As John Lewis Gaddis later observed, Kennan's brand of global-realism was instead based on "a particularist rather than a universalist conception of American security interests: what was required was not to remake the world in the image of the United States, but simply to preserve its diversity against attempts to remake it in the image of others."[24]

During the later postwar era, the intellectual descendants of the global-realist group have been predominant in U.S. policymaking circles. They were especially active among the Nixon and Carter Administrations' national security planning staffs and are ascendant again in the Bush administration. Within their ranks are a number of scholars and policy analysts who have pursued an interest in Asian security matters. Such individuals, who often moved into their positions of prominence within the establishment wing of the U.S. foreign policy community from well-known American universities and research institutes, include Henry Kissinger, Lawrence Eagleburger, Richard Solomon, Michel Oksenberg, Brent Scrowcroft, and Karl Jackson. They support the continuation of U.S. politico-strategic relations with the PRC and more active strategic collaboration among U.S. allies in Europe and Asia. They have adopted an interregional outlook on U.S. security planning and have often downplayed the need to view the Asia-Pacific as an indigenous strategic region. Their viewpoints and their writings, more than those of any other policy advocates in the U.S., have influenced the projection of the Dominant Player deterrence behavior over the past two decades. They also appear to have been most surprised by the emergence in the Asia-Pacific of alternative security and deterrence postures to the Dominant Player approach.[25]

Lined up against the global realists is a loose coalition of *revisionist-idealists*. Few in number, but forceful in projecting their viewpoint, this group advocates a major retrenchment of U.S. military presence in the Asia-Pacific theater. It believes that postwar U.S. deterrence strategy has been excessively confrontational and asserts that the Dominant Player posture has been largely responsible for sustaining regional tensions and confrontation. The revisionist-idealists further believe that regional self-determination, facilitated by a strategic withdrawal of the superpowers and the winding down of their alliance relationships in the region, constitutes the best means for attaining a legitimate and enduring security order. Recent proponents of this viewpoint include William Arkin and David Chappell; Richard Barnet; the team of Walden Bello, Lyuba Zarsky, and Peter Hayes; Noam Chomsky; Bruce Cumings; and George McT. Kahin.[26]

Arkin and Chappell have argued that the Reagan administration's "forward defense strategy" (of which the Martime Strategy discussed in chapter I constitutes an integral part) triggered an unnecessary arms race in the Asia-Pacific and signaled Washington's determination to exercise unbridled strategic hegemony throughout the region. In doing so, they assert, the U.S. has actually destabilized the region by encouraging Japanese remilitarization and by adhering to "outmoded assumptions of war and peace" over the need to implement regional and global arms control measures. Arkin and Chappell conclude that: "Areas far from the Pacific will not be protected from responses to the Pacific buildup any more than the Pacific will be protected from horizontal escalation from conflicts that start in other areas."[27] Hayes, Zarsky, and Bello are even more critical of U.S. military strategy in the Asia-Pacific theater, contending that an "American strategic bias toward nuclear weapons" greatly accelerates the risk of superpower combat in that theater and of global nuclear war.[28]

Barnet and Cumings both focus on what they view as misapplied U.S. policies of alliance system maintenance through continued investment in military capabilities at the expense of the United States' own moral and economic welfare. Cumings' arguments are more sophisticated, paralleling the recent concerns advanced by the "imperial overstretch" theorists (see chapter 1). Cumings believes that by the mid-1980s the critical Northeast Asian powers—Japan, the Soviet Union, and the PRC—had all directed or reoriented their own regional policies toward economic development and away from military confrontation. Only the United States, he concludes, still resorts to "invoking the power dimension of its [Asia-Pacific] hegemony . . . trying with little success to use military means to get its way on economic matters."[29] Chomsky and Kahin have advanced essentially the same argument about the misapplication of U.S. power in the United States intervention in Vietnam during the late 1960s.

The revisionist-idealists arguments failed to convince very many key U.S. policy planners or their Asia-Pacific counterparts that either extended deterrence strategy or the selective use of military force were outdated or irrelevant to the regional security environment. Many felt that the revisionist-idealists tended to overplay nuclear weapons as policy ends rather than to treat them as legitimate tools of stability and power in the postwar era. Nor did the revisionist-idealists have any new policy alternatives to offer that were regarded by the global-realists as more promising than the dual strategy of global deterrence and arms control. Stripped of its essentials, the revisionist-idealist case appeared to American deterrence managers as little more than hyperbole, couched in the syntax of moral pretensions and lacking hard evidence to support its implementation as a long-term alternative to existing policy.

A third group concerned with postwar Asian security in the context of deterrence can be labeled as the *revisionist-pragmatists*. This school is less preoccupied than the global realists with interregional strategic linkages but is also less inclined than are the revisionist-idealists to disdain every form of U.S. power projection in the region. The revisionist-pragmatists are primarily concerned about the United States sustaining a global deterrence strategy beyond what its power or resource capabilities will allow (what Christopher Layne has labeled the "power-interests gap"). Unlike the revisionist-idealists, the revisionist-pragmatists support a continued U.S. strategic role in the Asia-Pacific, but one which is more geographically discriminate and mission-specific. The perceived reduction of the Soviet military threat in the theater, along with the lack of a coherent American strategic doctrine there to match a succession of more concrete doctrines applied to Europe (e.g., massive retaliation, graduated deterrence, flexible response), justifies the modification of U.S. traditional extended deterrence postures, according to this school of thought.

The Nixon Doctrine was the catalyst for the first wave of revisionist-pragmatist writings, most notably those of Earl Ravenal and Donald Hellman, which questioned the United States' capabilities to stabilize conflicts and control escalation of future Asian conflicts. Most of Ravenal's writings can be classified as more neo-isolationist than revisionist-pragmatist; nevertheless, his work on the Nixon Doctrine broadly fits into the latter category. In it, he described a scenario, which he believed could very likely evolve as a result of the Nixon Doctrine, under which highly trained U.S. forces disengaged in the Asia-Pacific region, leaving U.S. nuclear weapons as the only means of deterrence and response for future theater contingencies. Under these circumstances, Ravenal concluded, remaining U.S. deterrence commitments in the Asia-Pacific may well be unsustainable.[30] Hellman substantiated this reasoning by criticizing what he viewed as the Nixon Doctrine's implicit assumption that past American security commitments would be salvaged by the abrupt cessation of all military conflict in "an unstable and warprone region." He argued that while the Nixon administration viewed Japan as a regional security actor, "the dimensions of this role are left indeterminate and obscure." Japan's strategic role, Hellman speculated, ultimately would be decided by the course of Asia-Pacific politics and Japanese domestic politics, rather than by futile American efforts to "distinguish between global and more regional priorities."[31]

Recent descendants of the revisionist-pragmatist school include Christopher Layne, Donald E. Nuechterlein, Edward Olsen, and Stephen M. Walt. Layne warned against open-ended American commitments to engage in limited wars erupting in Asian or Third World conflict environments at a time when Washington's fiscal problems were becoming increasingly strained.[32] Olsen takes the defense-burden sharing arguments introduced by Layne a step further, arguing that only Japan's outright "strategic revitalization" and "reciprocity" for enjoying continued U.S. extended deterrence guarantees will allow the United States to continue effectively pursuing its own global strategic interests in and beyond the Asia-Pacific.[33] Nuechterlein largely replicates Olsen's arguments. He is even more specific about Japan's strategic "revitalization," advocating the formation of a Japanese rapid deployment force for use in Northeast Asian contingencies and removing U.S. land forces from the Korean peninsula, leaving U.S. air power as "the major deterrent to any North Korean attack."[34] Walt's advocacy of "finite containment" employs a similar line of reasoning, focused on maintaining broad U.S. security commitments to Japan and South Korea, but encouraging Japan simultaneously to increase its own air and naval capabilities. Walt concludes that the combination of greater Japanese offshore power projection capabilities and the preservation of a U.S. "defensive sea control" strategy would be enough to strategically reassure pro-Western states in the region.[35]

Revisionist-pragmatists limit their arguments to the issue of U.S. commitments versus U.S. strategic resources, leaving indigenous regional conflict factors largely unaddressed. For example, other Asian states are unlikely to accept increased Japanese air and naval power throughout the region as readily as is suggested by these writers. The revisionist-pragmatist school tends to lose sight of this fundamental reality of Asian security politics, however, preoccupied as it is by the growing U.S. strategic commitment-financial resource dilemma. Only Olsen has acknowledged possible difficulties in overcoming intra-regional barriers to a higher Japanese defense profile, but in the end, he concludes that Washington should not be prevented "from seeking Japanese cooperation by Asian protestations that it values Japan too much. For the United States, Japan is the most important country in Asia . . . Everything else in U.S.-Asian relations is a corollary of this fact."[36]

CONVERGENT DETERRENCE

WHAT SETS this book apart from the schools of thought discussed above is its argument that the United States should no longer view the Asia-Pacific region strictly in terms of traditional American global competition with the USSR. The U.S. should instead become more sensitive to its tendency to underestimate or disregard altogether the individual security interests of individual Asia-Pacific security actors. It may be that the dawn of the next century will require the establishment of an autonomous Asia-Pacific regional security order, one which meets the legitimate security needs of those actors, which prevents intraregional hegemonic competition, and which can be guaranteed by concerned external powers. For the time being, however, some form of extended deterrence offered by the United States may still be the most valid strategic approach for the region as a means of conflict avoidance or termination. The policy dilemma emanating from this is that U.S. strategic planners constantly will be faced with the challenge of reconciling inevitable and, at times, contradictory global and regional security imperatives as a result of sustaining such a posture.

This approach represents a clear departure from the global-realist, revisionist-idealist, and revisionist-pragmatist schools of thought, all of which assume that an inherent relationship exists between global and regional versions of extended deterrence. The three contending policy approaches cited above advocate either integrating global and regional strategy more completely (the global-realists); totally severing regional deterrence commitments because they encumber U.S. global deterrence objectives and missions (the revisionist-idealists); or relegating regional deterrence tasks to select allies in order for Washington to preserve a more cost-effective global deterrence posture (the revisionist-pragmatists). The argument advanced in this book calls for the United States to acknowledge the very real differences between U.S. extended deterrence strategy (i.e., the "Dominant Player" posture) and contending regional security postures. Washington must then adjust its own deterrence strategy to those differences. This book rejects the arguments of those who contend that U.S. global deterrence strategy can be readily integrated with Asia-Pacific regional security priorities or, conversely, that regional deterrence priorities can be summarily disassociated from future U.S. force planning and strategic commitments. The approach to the formulation and maintenance of a balanced U.S. global and regional deterrence policy as it applies to the Asia-Pacific is labeled here as *convergent deterrence:* the effective assimilation of changing regional security imperatives into U.S. global strategic planning and commitments.

The convergent deterrence concept will be developed more extensively in the conclusion of this volume (chapter 7). The concluding chapter will also offer some proposals for implementing the required policy adjustments and restoring greater credibility to U.S. strategy in the Asia-Pacific region. Over the past four decades, the United States has applied its Dominant Player deterrence strategy throughout most of the world. In doing so, however, the U.S. has increased the risk of losing its focus on regional security needs in favor of its global priorities. Washington's allies and friends in the Asia-Pacific theater are becoming more concerned than was previously the case about tying themselves too closely to an American extended deterrence strategy which they deem to be less than relevant to their own security needs. Concurrently, U.S. adversaries and competitors are fashioning and projecting alternative strategic postures designed to capitalize on just such doubts.

Unless American strategic planning takes such trends into account, it will be less effective in shaping the Asia-Pacific's future security environment and ultimately will fail as an instrument for war avoidance. Chapter 7's conclusions and policy recommendations are offered as an initial contribution to what should be an emerging debate on how such planning can be strengthened and implemented.

CHAPTER I

Extended Deterrence Strategy and the Dominant Player Posture

ALTHOUGH IT has been the cornerstone of U.S. and Western security policy since the late 1940s, in recent times the strategy of deterrence has gained more critics than enthusiasts. There is a rough consensus about what deterrence is: i.e., "to persuade one's opponent that the costs and/or risks of a given course of action . . . might . . . outweigh its benefits."[1] What concerns detractors are lingering uncertainties regarding how deterrence actually functions and how effective, in a multipolar strategic setting, a continued adherence by the United States to its traditional deterrence postulates can be. As more states acquire their own nuclear forces and even more procure advanced conventional weapons systems, both Soviet and American security planners, along with independent experts on international security affairs, have reevaluated the nature of strategic competition between the superpowers and the value of extending deterrence guarantees to allies as a means of exercising power and retaining influence.

Sharp disagreement has arisen over the extent to which deterrence should be regarded as a valid measurement of power and influence or as a legitimate approach to conflict management.[2] Critics of deterrence contend that its utility is hindered by the policy preconceptions and biases of its architects. They also argue that confidence-building measures and other forms of diplomatic reassurance are far more effective means of avoiding miscalculation and war than a strategy which depends upon one's ability to use nuclear weapons against an opponent if he is not deterred.[3] Proponents of the U.S. postwar approach to deterrence, however, have countered that the strategy has been applied successfully when strategic commitments have been clearly understood, were perceived to be credible, and were matched by force capabilities.[4] Inevitably, the deterrence advocates maintain, there are times and situations where a political opponent needs to be convinced *not* to challenge one's own survival or to threaten one's allies. Such arguments go on to assert that this task can be accomplished without precipitating conflict escalation in the process.[5]

Recent policy statements prepared by the U.S. Joint Chiefs of Staff (JCS) have defined the characteristics of a U.S. deterrence strategy which may be described as the "Dominant Player" posture. These include: nuclear deterrence; strong alliances; forward deployed forces; a strong central reserve; force mobility; freedom of the seas, air, and space; effective command and control; and timely and accurate intelligence. The Dominant Player posture thus "seeks to deter attacks against the United States and its allies, limit Soviet capabilities for coercion, and provide the flexibility to respond appropriately to aggression . . . U.S. forces must be capable of meeting regional challenges as well as threats of global dimension."[6] The JCS has noted that five "interrelated factors" determine the efficacy of this posture: superpower geopolitical competition, relative strengths and weaknesses of major nations, the global military balance, arms control agreements, and current regional military situations.[7] Furthermore, the U.S. Defense Department has identified four critical "operating policies" for implementing U.S. deterrence strategy: (1) the achievement of a favorable force balance for global and regional security missions; (2) the assurance of sufficient collective security, through alliance commitments, for pro-Western forces to prevail over local and regional threats; (3) the demonstration of strategic commitment through forward deployed U.S. forces, permitting their immediate integration with allied forces during wartime; and (4) the attainment of force flexibility through military planning, directed toward coping with threats across a wide spectrum of conflict.[8]

In early 1987, U.S. defense officials consolidated the second and third operating policies cited by the JCS—strong alliances and forward deployed forces—into what presently can be regarded as U.S. extended deterrence policy in the Asia-Pacific.[9] The Dominant Player posture is specifically implemented in this region by U.S. forward deployed forces which "maintain a high state of [combat] readiness through combined and joint training exercises" with various regional allies and which "serve as a strong deterrent to Soviet Pacific ambitions." By early 1990, however, American strategic planners were publicly speculating about the implications of Soviet downward "adjustments" of its military presence in Asia in deference to strengthening its political influence and economic access there. While complaining that "Soviet rhetoric has [still] outpaced Soviet behavior," U.S. officials have acknowledged that Moscow's reductions of its force in Mongolia and along the Sino-Soviet border, along with reductions in Soviet forces deployed at Cam Ranh Bay in Vietnam, may be clear signs that the Soviets are moving towards a posture of "reasonable sufficiency" and are interested in reducing tensions throughout the area. By late October Richard Solomon, the U.S. Assistant Secretary of State for East Asia and the Pacific, characterized U.S. policy as a "balancing wheel" in which Washington would play the power broker in an increasingly multipolar regional security environment. The U.S.-Japan security relationship was identified by Solomon as the linchpin of this strategy.[10]

Reflecting an apparently decreased likelihood of U.S.-Soviet confrontation in the Pacific, U.S. defense spokesmen are thus increasingly emphasizing the need to prevent *any* nation or group of nations from becoming predominant in the Asia-Pacific. They do so, however, while still insisting on placing the Asia-Pacific regional dimension in an overall global context.[11] Noting that only "16 % of our overall force structure" covers "the largest of our military theaters," they call for greater force mobility *to reinforce* the Dominant Player posture rather than actively seeking any new doctrine incorporating changing regional threat perceptions into a truly revised U.S. strategy. Consequently, a forward-deployed deterrent is still regarded as sacrosanct.[12]

Indeed, forward deployment of powerful naval and air forces, supplemented by highly mobile ground forces, more than ever constitutes the nexus of U.S. Pacific strategy. Naval and air capabilities remain designed to retain control of key sea lanes of communication and to intimidate would-be attackers from contesting the superiority of American offshore forces in the region. Over one-half of the U.S. Navy is normally deployed in this theater, as is approximately two-thirds of the U.S. Marine Corps' operational forces, and five U.S. Air Force wings. Unlike the case in Europe, where U.S. ground forces are tailored to fight wars by seizing and holding forward positions, Asia-Pacific strategy is fashioned around the principle of integrating U.S. conventional deterrence assets quickly with allied armies as the best means for waging effective coalitional warfare in the region. While army personnel comprise only one-eighth of the United States' total force strength within the Pacific Command (PACOM), the 2nd Infantry Division is deployed as the spearhead of the Eighth U.S. Army command headquartered in Seoul, in order to demonstrate U.S. strategic resolve and generate allied confidence in U.S. deterrence commitments to South Korea. The 25th Light Infantry Division (known as the "Tropic Lightning" Division) stationed at Schofield Barracks in Hawaii and the 6th Division (Light) headquartered in Alaska can be deployed anywhere within the Asia-Pacific theater in under a week.[13] In assessing the role of U.S. land forces in the Asia-Pacific, U.S. Department of Defense analysts have concluded that "the major threat to the United States and its allies in the region is Soviet naval and air power. The United States does not possess, nor does its national strategy demand, predominance in ground forces in the region, and this will remain the case."[14]

American defense officials have not developed or expanded this perception, however, into a more comprehensive outlook as to how indigenous strategic interests and regional force balances may effect overall U.S. capabilities for responding to future Asia-Pacific contingencies, given American strategic imperatives and resource limitations in other potential military theaters of operation. Critics of the Dominant Player posture point to what they believe to be a fundamental paradox in contemporary American strategy, one described by Paul Kennedy and other Western scholars as "imperial overstretch." The extent of the United States' formal alliance commitments has remained basically unchanged while its relative global power base has significantly contracted. Allies in both Europe and Asia are, as a result, increasingly prone to question Washington's capacity for defining and leading international security politics into the next century.[15] "Overstretch theorists" may now point to the Bush administration's gradual acceptance of the notion that the USSR under Mikhail Gorbachev's leadership is broadening its foreign policy approach by expanding its relations and influence to countries and regions previously viewed by Moscow as places to compete for military and geopolitical superiority with the West. A case can also be made that nuclear true-believers are becoming increasingly irrelevant in an age when the broad spectrum of possible military contingencies involves weapons mixes and conflict scenarios which often render the nuclear factor inappropriate or irrelevant to the security needs of the intended deterrence beneficiaries. The cost of deploying sufficient manpower and armaments for the United States to meet all of its overseas commitments or to respond credibly to a myriad of potential immediate deterrence contingencies has become almost impossible to sustain. It thus cannot be emphasized too strongly, the imperial overstretch theorists remind us, that the Asia-Pacific theater has become too economically and politically diffuse to preserve a regional balance of power through application of the old politics of strategic bipolarity and U.S.-dominated collective defense.

Extended deterrence advocates oppose such reasoning on the grounds that it misinterprets or distorts current American deterrence behavior in the Asia-Pacific and throughout Eurasia.[16] Most fundamentally, they argue that the imperial overstretch thesis ignores the same factor of contemporary international politics as the immediate deterrence analysts: the era of imperial wars ended with the advent of nuclear deterrence in 1945. The great powers are no longer able to play by the game of international power politics described by Kennedy and others concerned with declining hegemony because the rules simply have changed: now the risk to a would-be hegemonist of miscalculating its "grand strategy" may encompass nuclear confrontation with its adversaries. While U.S. force assets deployed in the Pacific have been employed primarily to support a "looser" form of extended deterrence than that designed exclusively for nuclear war prevention, the prospect of conflict escalation and nuclear annihilation nevertheless overwhelms what would initially appear to be even the most compelling incentives to pursue territorial and resource expansion.

The imperial overstretch concept has also been faulted as a prescription for retraction of American power without adequate cause. Supporters maintain that the Dominant Player posture has generally allowed for the evolution of a more benign international order, in which Asia-Pacific and other developing states have been able to pursue the politics and economics of self-determination under the vigilant yet benevolent umbrella of American military power. According to its adherents, the American Dominant Player is unique compared to other great powers in history, who have been intent on imperial expansion rather than on the preservation and strengthening of an existing global order. They contend that the American Dominant Player seeks to preserve an international balance of power in which conflict resolution and war avoidance are realized through both U.S. and potential adversaries' *mutual* vulnerability to nuclear destruction.

The Dominant Player approach to deterrence has endured because it has been viewed by successive U.S. governments as an effective, if at times inelegant, means for containing the postwar Soviet military threat at both the nuclear and conventional force levels. Both superpowers have opted to minimize the extent of their own strategic uncertainty by continuing to designate the other as a major adversary and by controlling, usually unilaterally but at times jointly, the distribution and management of global military capabilities. To Washington and Moscow, war avoidance has been best assured by keeping their allies as clients of extended deterrence, and by preventing states outside their alliances from seriously challenging the superpowers' military predominance.[17]

While U.S. global strategy has remained constant, recent and fundamental shifts have occurred in the United States' economic standing relative to its allies and in Soviet or regionally indigenous threats to U.S. security interests. Nowhere are these changes more evident than in the Asia-Pacific. Many Americans would argue that Japan has now reached equal status with NATO Europe as the most important overseas U.S. security partner, yet the Japanese are simultaneously regarded as the United States' greatest economic competitor, and as a potential threat to American economic well-being. China is now seen less as a Soviet surrogate threatening Western positions and influence throughout East and Southeast Asia than as an independent regional power increasingly willing to stand up to Soviet military power east of the Urals and collaborate with the West economically (a situation unlikely to change, even following China's domestic political turmoil in mid-1989). ASEAN states are now viewed by the U.S. as promising trade partners, but as much less important as security collaborators. New Zealand's recent decision to remove itself from the U.S. extended deterrent in the Southwest Pacific, and the relaxation of U.S. containment strategy in Southeast Asia after 1969, have led some critics to observe that U.S. extended deterrence commitments in the Pacific now can be identified along clear lines of demarcation: i.e. "everything north of Manila is vital; nothing to the south."[18]

COMPARATIVE U.S. DOMINANT PLAYER POSTURES: EUROPE AND THE ASIA-PACIFIC

THE LONG-TERM viability of Washington's Dominant Player deterrence posture is contingent upon its success in meeting the threats which confront its national security interests while retaining the credibility of commitment to its allies. As a global power, the United States continuously faces the problem of reconciling its international security interests with the local security priorities of its regional allies. Extended deterrence has been viewed by postwar U.S. security planners as the most effective means available for fulfilling its overseas strategic commitments without endangering the key objective of central deterrence strategy: preventing nuclear war from reaching U.S. territory. This strategy simultaneously fulfills a positive function by reinforcing commitment to one's allies and a negative function by denying an opponent access to territory, resources, or institutions which are deemed critical to the integrity of an alliance system.

Despite intermittent and mostly unsuccessful refinement efforts by the Reagan administration and its postwar predecessors, the basic elements of U.S. extended deterrence strategy have endured for nearly four decades. While differing over size and budget, U.S. military planners have never questioned the fundamental importance of the nation's defense commitment to Europe. This commitment, moreover, has been largely understood and supported by the U.S. public. In contrast, only a small portion of the U.S. electorate, and few U.S. defense planners, would be able to define specific rationales for an American extended deterrence strategy in the Asia-Pacific. Public appreciation of the strategic importance of the region is mostly limited to: (1) the very general feeling that U.S. access to that theater's sea lanes of communication must be preserved in the interest of trade with the region's increasingly prosperous nations and the transport of oil supplies from the Persian Gulf to Japan and the West; and (2) despite ongoing strains in economic and trade relations between Washington and Tokyo, the imperative of minimizing Soviet economic access to and political influence within Japan.

Washington has nevertheless continued to "globalize" its deterrence strategy, in response to its views of the effects of Soviet military power in Eurasia. This policy approach is incompatible with the desire of many Asians to remove their region from the vortex of global power competition and to seek security guarantees focusing more on their own survival and immediate regional stability. Until the requirements for U.S. extended deterrence in the Asia-Pacific are more clearly distinguished from those still confronting Washington in Western Europe despite the extent of political change now occurring there, American efforts to continue a Dominant Player posture in the Asia-Pacific theater will be misunderstood by the U.S. electorate and, even more importantly, will seem increasingly irrelevant to Washington's Asia-Pacific allies. As a result, U.S. global strategy cannot be effectively applied interregionally until its Asia-Pacific security policies are reconsidered, understood, and accepted by its allies in the region.

Of course, a case can be made that a de facto multi-theater deterrence posture already exists. It could be argued, for example, that the joint U.S.-South Korean military command and the U.S. nuclear tripwire in that country reflect a Northeast Asian parallel to the NATO format of organization and strategy (although on a much smaller scale). Increased U.S.-Japanese defense coordination may eventually lead to bilateral arrangements similar to those which exist between Washington and Seoul (although there is little prospect for a trilateral U.S.-Japanese-South Korean defense consortium). In geographic terms, Japan parallels Britain and the Scandinavian NATO members, by sitting astride the key chokepoints through which a major Soviet fleet would need to break to contest American naval power on the high seas and to interdict U.S. reinforcements during future Asia-Pacific contingencies. A historical parallel between Japan and NATO has also recently become more evident. As Japan's military strength begins to grow, a number of her strategists are asking questions similar to those of French leader Charles de Gaulle in the early 1960s when he challenged the legitimacy of U.S. extended deterrence strategy in Europe: i.e., does nuclear parity, in reality, decouple U.S. survival from that of its Asian allies or, as a key component of U.S. extended deterrence strategy, is Japan destined to become involved in any future superpower military confrontation, even at the nuclear level, arising in Northeast Asia?[19] Questions of allied burden-sharing, relative to the continuing credibility of U.S. deterrence commitments, are now the subject of increased discussion in Japan and South Korea and are similar to those which have been driving a comparable European debate for over two decades.

At more fundamental levels, however, the conditions for realizing deterrence objectives in the Asia-Pacific are asymmetrical to those in Europe, requiring different responses to the differing geographic and political factors.[20] Politically, the European NATO members are concerned about preventing their comparatively small land space and their traditional institutions from becoming engulfed in a superpower global nuclear confrontation. In contrast, numerous sources of political instability exist in the Asia-Pacific which relate only indirectly to the East-West conflict but which are instead generated from indigenous disparities in resources or from uniquely historical or ethnic roots. Many disruptions of regional stability can also be attributed to much of the Asia-Pacific's recent decolonization and to the lack of highly developed national institutions that typifies Third World regions.

East-West military capabilities are much more clearly explicable in Central Europe than the Asia-Pacific. Japan's maritime geography is one factor in U.S. strategy in this region, allowing Americans usage of naval and air capabilities for a much wider array of contingencies from the outset of a regional crisis, in this theater than in Europe. A second, but most uncertain, factor in a potential Asia-Pacific conflict with the Soviet Union is the willingness of China to commit its land forces. The People's Liberation Army (PLA) has the ability to match Soviet land strength quantitatively, releasing the U.S. and Japan to neutralize the USSR's air and naval assets in Northeast Asia and to cut off Soviet access to, and reinforcement of, Cam Ranh Bay in Vietnam, its one distant Southeast Asian outpost. Nothing comparable to Chinese land power exists in Central Europe. The significance of the China factor is further underscored when the steady growth of Chinese nuclear capabilities is considered, both in global and regional contexts. The development of China's nuclear weapons program has sustained a momentum which is indicative of a true Aspiring Player deterrence strategy and which is now clearly matching the nuclear force development programs of the world's other "middle nuclear powers," Britain and France. While China's nuclear buildup was previously directed primarily toward the Soviet threat, U.S. defense planners will increasingly need to weigh the PRC's growing and increasingly diversified nuclear arsenal's effect on other aspects of the Asia-Pacific's regional power balance: i.e., growing Indian maritime power projection into Southeast Asia, various levels of Japanese rearmament, and Beijing's own efforts to promote its naval power in the East China Sea and beyond.

While the maritime element is a common denominator of U.S. extended deterrence strategy in both theaters, Western military strategy differs in each to the point that the prospect of a formal "grand coalition" of NATO European and pro-Western Asia-Pacific states is remote, short of a global war. The geographic expanse of the Asia-Pacific theater makes the nuclear tripwire, and thus escalation control management, more ambiguous than for a land war fought on the geographically compressed NATO front. The Korean Peninsula, where heavily armed forces confront each other within a highly concentrated space, is an exception. The Pacific Ocean's vast distances create challenges in reinforcing and sustaining forward deployed forces in that theater, notwithstanding the presence of U.S. basing operations in the Philippines, Guam, and Hawaii. On the other hand, Soviet naval interdiction efforts would need to be spread over a much wider circumference in this theater than around the entry points into Northern and Central Europe.

U.S. EXTENDED DETERRENCE STRATEGY: THEORY AND PRACTICE

AS DETERRENCE theory in general has recently been examined more closely and challenged by developments in superpower doctrine, so too have the assumptions of extended deterrence. Central or strategic nuclear deterrence is a willingness to run the highest risks of war to protect one's homeland against a designated external threat. By contrast, *extended deterrence* is "an attempt to prevent a military attack against an ally by threatening [some form of] retaliation."[21] Deterrence in this context can be applied at either the nuclear or conventional level. Extended deterrence is most credible when the deterrence guarantor has a clear advantage over a perceived attacker or has a much more vital interest in defending an ally than an aggressor does in attacking it. A number of Western deterrence scholars believe that extended deterrence operates "existentially" by leaving ambiguous the conditions and types of response to an attack on an ally but creating enough uncertainty in a potential attacker about any such response as to minimize the threat of a war actually taking place.[22] The search for specific distinctions between a "tight" nuclear or strategic deterrence and extended deterrence postures, however, has complicated arguments about the effectiveness of extended deterrence.

Another source of confusion is the need to differentiate extended deterrence strategy at the *immediate* and *general* levels of operation. Most historical and behavioral data assessed by the growing body of scholars interested in the extended deterrence question fall into the "immediate deterrence" category: "a confrontation between adversaries in which the threat of armed conflict is a distinct [and imminent] possibility if neither the potential attacker nor the defender retreats."[23] Historical case studies have been widely used as a means of evaluating the success or failure of extended deterrence because they provide sufficient documentation to reach conclusions about national leaders' deterrence decision making.[24] A basic criticism of the case study approach, however, is that it fails to account for the escalation control factor, which has been an integral part of general deterrence strategy in the nuclear era. General deterrence is less "testable," and therefore more intuitive, than its immediate deterrence counterpart. It may, therefore, be less appealing to the social scientist searching for data that fits a particular mode of strategic behavior.

General deterrence is nonetheless a more useful concept to the Dominant Player because, if applied credibly, it transmits a sense of constant risk to his adversaries. Crises and hostilities are better modified than allowed to escalate. In such a context, most crises directly involving the deterrence guarantor are averted, and the probability of those which do materialize ending in nuclear war is remote.

The analysis of general deterrence, which involves superpower nuclear and strategic behavior, is obscured by a lack of consensus regarding the motives and considerations underlying Soviet and U.S. involvement in successive crises. Assuredly, one must rely on intuition regarding an opponents' instincts and behavior in nuclear deterrence politics. Since no actual nuclear conflicts have taken place, however, counterfactual assessments emerge by default. No one can delineate which side is "rational" or "irrational" in cases where nuclear war is deterred, or even with certainty what those cases might be, without access to significantly more declassified data than is currently available. Ivo H. Daalder has aptly summarized this conceptual problem: subjective assumptions about the nature of the threat to be deterred and about how a conflict would escalate if deterrence fails to work lead to varying interpretations about the requirements of extended deterrence, none of which is necessarily absolute.[25]

Important studies on extended deterrence (George and Smoke, Huth and Russett, Betts) have recognized that most Asia-Pacific security problems since World War II have encompassed disputes between the United States and communist powers which have been outside the realm of direct nuclear confrontation, or between communist states vying for influence in Southeast Asia through the use of proxies. What Asia-Pacific case studies are available to the deterrence analyst comprise, to paraphrase Betts, "a motley assortment" which could be "grouped analytically in a number of conceivable ways."[26] Until a firmer consensus is reached about guidelines for effective general extended deterrence, "Dominant Player" policy-makers have little recourse other than to be guided by "worst case" contingency planning. In fact, as R. B. Byers has correctly noted, "there has been a notable disjunction between deterrence as theory to guide national security policy and the reality of security policy."[27]

How much extended deterrence actually facilitates the United States' strategic objectives is being debated by several factions of U.S. defense analysts. A major concern expressed by one group is that, while extended deterrence is recognized as a key component of the United States' national security posture, it remains an underdeveloped strategy relative to the increasingly complex problems of weapons technology, arms control negotiations, and global political change. The interrelationship between nuclear and conventional forces, according to this school of thought, also complicates the application of this strategy, regardless of what geostrategic imperatives may be present.[28]

Others disagree, arguing that U.S. extended deterrence strategy has not only been successful in neutralizing most threats to pro-Western states, but that it has evolved dynamically in response to the changing nature of threats and security environments and will continue to do so given the U.S. ability to modernize nuclear forces while building up conventional force strength. These analysts contend that the operative requirements of Western extended deterrence strategy—flexible response and force survivability—have been met in Europe, Japan, and South Korea, even in an era of superpower nuclear parity. The assertion is that the West, by adopting a doctrine of calculated ambiguity regarding the use of nuclear weapons, reinforces U.S. conventional deterrence strategy in these locales.[29] To a lesser extent, however, this group shares the first group of analysts' lack of confidence in Washington's ability to manage a wide diversity of extra-European conflicts with adequate skill and restraint. They are concerned, as well, about the credibility of non-NATO alliance deterrence and conflict resolution strategies.

A third policy group views the entire strategy of extended deterrence as a "chronic problem." The deterrence guarantor, this group asserts, is caught in an impossible position, because it must commit to its allies that it will use military force on behalf of their security, but simultaneously assure them that their survival will not be jeopardized if deterrence fails and escalation control is lost.[30] The contradictory logic of extended deterrence, according to this group, encourages decoupling by those allies who doubt that their alleged benefactor will really commit nuclear suicide on their behalf as well as by those allies who fear that the U.S. deterrence posture may itself precipitate a war. Thus, de Gaulle's Fifth Republic opted to break away from NATO's "pact of faith" during the 1960s, opting to build its own nuclear deterrent independently of NATO's command structure. New Zealand, not wanting to be dependent upon *any* nuclear deterrence strategy, disassociated itself from all nuclear dimensions of the ANZUS alliance some twenty years later (1984–1986).

Adherents to this school of thought can be further demarcated into two distinct subgroupings. Some who deride the coupling thesis integral to extended deterrence offer no real alternative for overcoming the ambiguities and difficulties of the problem. A second version of the anticoupling faction asserts that the superpowers have tended to rely too much on extended deterrence strategy rather than apply it more sparingly and, therefore, more effectively. This latter view closely coincides with the arguments of the *revisionist-pragmatist* school summarized in this volume's introduction.

BRIDGING EXTENDED DETERRENCE THEORY AND U.S. POLICY

IF EXTENDED deterrence is an important component of war avoidance and conflict management, but one lacking consensus, how can its effectiveness in Western global and regional strategic postures be measured by U.S. and allied defense analysts responsible for its implementation? In the absence of a more comprehensive model, three factors appear to be particularly relevant to bridging extended deterrence theory and practice: escalation control, interalliance transferability, and credibility of strategic commitment. These factors are important to an understanding of American global and Asia-Pacific deterrence strategies in the light of changing U.S. threat perceptions and strategic resources. The applications and factors of the three Dominant Player criteria for extended deterrence are diagrammed in figure 2.

Escalation Control

IN ANY crisis, antagonists look for a set of limits or "saliencies" (a term initially coined by Thomas Schelling) which both sides can observe while establishing the ground rules for their conflict behavior. In defining their expectations about the other's conflict behavior, belligerents often demarcate geographic boundaries, the relative lethality of weapons systems, or traditional conventions of war (i.e., distinctions between combatants and noncombatants) as saliencies to be observed during negotiations conducted in a wartime environment. The bargaining is tacit and is carried out by the combatants' actions, rather than by their words.[31] Escalation control, then, is the process of successfully maintaining the parameters of conflict within mutually recognized limits, until conflict resolution is achieved.[32] Ideally, escalation control should still be available at higher levels of conflict, even if it fails at lower levels. At some point, moreover, conflict within escalation control limits should impose sufficient costs on one's enemy that he will be dissuaded from continuing the conflict in question at a higher (i.e., nuclear or strategic nuclear) level of conflict.[33]

Much like deterrence theory in general, however, the logic of escalation control has come under increased attack. How are successive or intervening stages of escalation between counter-insurgency wars and apocalyptic nuclear exchanges identified, other than through the rather intuitive and ambiguous process of salient delineation? As the immediate deterrence theorists would remind us, what constitutes significant escalation is in the eyes of the beholder, and what leads to prospects for miscommunication and miscalculation across the entire continuum of warfare is untestable.

FIGURE 2. The Dominant Player Posture in the Asia-Pacific:
Factors and Applications

FACTORS	APPLICATIONS		
	Conflict Risk	*Conflict Scope*	*Conflict Termination*
Escalation Control	1951–1960s: Conventional aggression unthinkable due to possible nuclear retaliation		
		Aggressor-Deterror recognize that saliencies exist; little deterrence to insurgency wars	Three Options: Defensive tactics, Offensive-Defensive tactics; and Offensive (war-fighting) tactics
	Post-1960s: Threat of retaliation at a undefined level of conflict, lowers likelihood of aggression		
Interalliance Transferability	Plans to shift forces between theaters on a contingency basis, lower deterrence and increases vulnerability in Asia-Pacific region	Geopolitical incongruities between theaters impede integration of regional with global strategies	Neutrality seen as best protection against "spill over" from other theater conflicts
Commitment Credibility	Effective communi-cation of commitment reduces risk of aggression; intensity of commitment is critical	The extension of U.S. deterrence at nuclear levels in Asia-Pacific region causes allies to fear an entrapment/ abandonment dilemma	The relationship of commitments to re-gional stability vs. conflict must be monitored, and if ineffective adjusted or terminated

In the absence of any real theoretical consensus, U.S. policy-makers have approached the escalation control problem by gauging relative Soviet-U.S. weapons capabilities against U.S. national security objectives with respect to NATO, its Asia-Pacific alliances, and other areas of vital concern. Richard Smoke has traced the evolution of U.S. extended deterrence since Washington first began assuming postwar security commitments, identifying four successive escalation control "endpoint" concepts underlying the strategy: massive nuclear retaliation against the USSR in the event that Soviet forces launch a major attack on Western allies and friends (in the 1950s); defeating a conventional Soviet attack with the use of nuclear weapons in theater (late 1950s/early 1960s); defeating such an attack with an appropriate "flexible response" of conventional and possibly nuclear force use (1967 onward); or alternatively, conducting limited nuclear strikes (limited nuclear options) in a highly selective manner without allowing a conflict to escalate to general nuclear war between the superpowers (since 1973–74). All four of these "endpoint" concepts, however, were and are dependent upon the deterrent guarantor's perceived ability to maintain escalation control and to sustain the credibility of his commitments before his own survival becomes an issue. Smoke concedes that the Soviet Union's achievement of strategic parity with the U.S., along with the proliferation of numbers and types of nuclear delivery systems, threatens to erode the credibility of escalation control.[34] A number of Western strategists have cited what they believe to be "the crisis in American self-confidence" over the extent to which escalation control makes security commitments more problematic.[35]

Specific measures have been proposed to rectify such uncertainty. Samuel Huntington, for example, has outlined three ways that conventional forces can deter through *denial* and *retaliation:* (1) increase the uncertainties and potential costs of aggression, even if the defender has no real hope of prevailing in a conflict; (2) raise the possibility of a successful conventional defense; or (3) retaliate against and punish the aggressor *after* the initial attack.[36] Traditional escalation control strategy conforms to the first option. Recent proposals by Western strategists to incorporate exotic (and more costly) technologies into the West's existing conventional force structures relate to the second posture. Strengthening deterrence through identifying an optimum "mix" of offensive/defensive tactics with which to confront the enemy at the outset of battle comprises the third approach. Huntington believes that a Western deterrence strategy which is based on "offensive retaliation" would circumvent uncertainty regarding escalation control by presenting an adversary with unacceptable levels of defensive firepower from the outset of a conflict and with the correspondingly unpleasant prospect of a protracted war. Critics have refuted Huntington's argument, however, by asserting that strengthened conventional power at lower conflict levels does not translate into "the capacity to deter escalation at a higher level or the capability to terminate the fighting on favorable terms." [37]

The Reagan administration moved during the mid-1980s to adopt yet another variant of offensive retaliation which effectively carried the escalation control debate beyond Europe to the global level. "Maritime Strategy" prescribed offensive retaliation by moving beyond a merely American sea lane defense against Soviet interdiction capabilities during the initial stages of war and toward "seizing the initiative" through the forward movement of carrier and anti-submarine warfare (ASW) forces. The effects would be to compel Moscow to move its nuclear submarines into "bastions" or "sanctuaries" in the Norwegian Sea, the Eastern Mediterranean, and Pacific approaches to the Soviet homeland, and to inhibit Soviet air defenses supporting USSR land forces conducting offensives along the peripheries of Eurasia. [38] Early U.S. forward fleet movements would also involve what John Mearsheimer has labeled "counterforce coercion" carried out against Soviet nuclear ballistic missile submarines (SSBNs) by conventional naval power and air support. [39] Threatening Moscow's second strike nuclear capability, under the reasoning of maritime strategy, would deter the USSR from engaging in conflict escalation by rapidly shifting the nuclear strategic balance against Moscow and by presenting the Soviets at the outset with the risk of underestimating U.S. intentions or resolve to fight a nuclear war. Under such circumstances, it was argued, the Soviets would have the incentive to terminate a conflict rather than escalate it.

Mearsheimer and other scholars have emphatically rejected Maritime Strategy on the basis of comparative force balances and superpower concern for force survivability. Submarine-to-submarine exchange ratios, for example, would initially favor the Soviets in both the NATO and Asia-Pacific theaters, inhibiting the penetration of U.S. carrier groups in the critical bastions adjacent to the Soviet homeland. Under such circumstances, the ability of the United States to establish unquestioned naval supremacy by quickly destroying Soviet force projection assets, blocking Moscow's access to open waters and forcing the USSR to surrender or escalate to global nuclear war becomes highly questionable. Instead of promoting crisis stability, the Maritime Strategy would effectively deprive one's opponent of the opportunity to pause and to deliberate costs and risks, an opportunity which could allow for a restoration of escalation control or even war termination.

U.S. allies in the Asia-Pacific largely dissented from the Reagan administration's original efforts to portray the Maritime Strategy as a means for strengthening alliance coherence. They questioned how protracted U.S. naval offensives conducted in or near the USSR's home waters would relate to, much less enhance, their own security when the major Soviet objective for defeating the strategy would be to evade U.S. barriers, disperse throughout the Pacific, and directly escalate the threat. Writing in mid-1987, Japanese Masashi Nishihara summarized a basic concern widely shared by Japan and Washington's other Asia-Pacific allies: a U.S. coupling of conventional naval defense in the Pacific with nuclear escalation as a *tactical* component of global war must be reconciled with fears of the Japanese, South Koreans and other allies that it would have major *strategic* ramifications for their own theater.[40]

Most Western defense planners would prefer to establish defense-in-depth to survive a protracted conventional war rather than risk all at the outset of a war by committing all their forces to strategic surge and forward defense. For example, without adequate airlift/sealift to sustain military operations in the Asia-Pacific theater, the U.S. cannot hope to deter credibly or fight a conventional war in the theater efficiently, regardless of how impressive the initial American state of military readiness might be. The U.S. currently lacks adequate airlift, sealift, and pre-positioning capacity to sustain a global conventional warfighting posture beyond the first few weeks of a conflict.[41] While subsequent chapters will argue that the relative decline of U.S. military power in the Pacific is not as serious as PACOM officials sometimes have represented it to be since the Vietnam War, U.S. force planners are still left deciding between an offensive retaliatory strategy at the outset of conflict or concession of vital territory and sea lanes of communication (SLOCS) to an opponent in favor of sustaining shorter, but more manageable, supply lines.

Indeed, the fine line between offensive and defensive acts of Maritime Strategy would tend to compromise any nuclear threshold. The sea-launched "Tomahawk" cruise missile currently deployed on many U.S. Pacific Fleet surface units and nuclear attack submarines, for example, carries either nuclear or conventional warheads. It can be used in attacks against Soviet air defenses and airfields in the Soviet Far Eastern command. Its great accuracy, combined with its relatively slow velocity, plays into a "launch-on-warning" strategy and the rationale that U.S. carrier task forces need to be protected against Soviet bombers "before they leave the ground."[42] If the U.S. Pacific Fleet introduced such a weapon in great numbers during a future limited conflict in the Asia-Pacific, the escalation control function of deterrence against war-widening or war-intensification would be all but lost.

The risk of loss of escalation control through the application of Maritime Strategy was eventually deemed too great for that strategy to be permanently incorporated into the Dominant Player posture. It could not be shown likely that a Soviet-American naval confrontation would remain at the conventional level, or that such a confrontation would be terminated on terms favorable to the United States. Nor could it be demonstrated that any real linkage existed between what the Soviets or the West would do in a naval confrontation and whether or not they would escalate the intensity of conflicts on land. The proponents of naval warfighting by the Maritime Strategy had appeared to conclude that Western naval offensives could neutralize Soviet land power so effectively as to preclude the Soviets or the West from escalating a land confrontation to nuclear levels before war termination. This reasoning, as two U.S. strategic analysts have recently written, constituted a "particularly dangerous form of strategic escapism" in the light of traditional U.S. and NATO theater doctrines anticipating that nuclear use could be required almost from the outset of battle.[43]

"Maritime Strategy" was discreetly modified by U.S. strategic planners following the resignation in February 1987 of one of its most forceful advocates, Secretary of the Navy John Lehman. While the Navy still uses the term interchangeably with that of "Competitive Strategy" (taking maximum advantage of U.S. military strengths against the military weaknesses of potential U.S. adversaries), President Bush's Secretary of the Navy was, by early 1989, acknowledging to Congress that Maritime Strategy needed to be widened beyond the imperative of controlling vital Atlantic, Mediterranean, and Asia-Pacific chokepoints during wartime and must embrace the mission of deterring "lower-order" conflicts."[44] In late April 1990, Secretary of Defense Dick Cheney announced plans to scale back the U.S. carrier force from fourteen to twelve ships and to reduce the purchase of A-12 advanced tactical carrier-based aircraft from 858 to 620 over the early 1990s. If implemented, this decision would further reduce U.S. capabilities to sustain a maritime strategy offensive as envisioned by its original proponents.[45]

Another effort to overcome the ambiguities of escalation control was the Reagan Administration's consideration of a "war-widening" or "horizontal escalation" American defense posture in 1981–1982. This concept envisioned that, if NATO defenses proved insufficient to check an invasion, U.S. forces would multiply combat theaters to disperse Soviet forces and prevent them from reinforcing an initial attack against Western Europe. The ambiguity associated with the timing of NATO's resort to nuclear defenses, was to be replaced by a concept of "asymmetrical response," as the defender compensated for his strategic weaknesses in one region by counterattacking in a region where the aggressor was equally vulnerable.[46] The Asia-Pacific was envisioned by most U.S. strategists to be the logical theater of operations from which to initiate a counterattack. U.S. naval superiority in the region, for example, could be used to bottle up the Soviet Pacific Fleet in the Sea of Japan or to neutralize Soviet transport and port facilities east of the Urals, effectively cutting the USSR in half economically and strategically. Alternatively, it was hoped, China would be willing and able to exert military pressure against the Soviet Far Eastern command by conducting low-grade military harassment against Soviet troops stationed along the Sino-Soviet border. In pursuing such a compensatory strategy, it was reasoned, the mutual vulnerabilities of each side would become quickly apparent and an end to the original conflict could be negotiated.

It was soon concluded, however, that retaliatory offensives in separate theaters would further obscure, rather than more precisely define, the United States' overall extended deterrence strategy. Any U.S. effort to defend Europe, the Asia-Pacific, and the Persian Gulf simultaneously would only result in the breakdown of any still effective local deterrence mechanisms. In a war confined to Northeast Asia, for example, the Sea of Japan would provide "deterrence by denial" by substantially increasing the costs of a full-fledged amphibious invasion against Japan's home islands.[47] In a global conflict, however, this geographic "buffer zone" would be less effective because it would become imperative for Soviet forces to outflank Western maritime positions on the Korean and Scandinavian peninsulas. Nor was it certain, because of the USSR's physical proximity and interior lines to key areas of contention (Central Europe, China, Japan, and the Persian Gulf), that U.S. forces could escalate more effectively than their Soviet counterparts in a multifront Eurasian conflict. The Soviet Union's geographic position eases Moscow's traditional fear of waging multifront warfare of the sort that horizontal escalation was originally designed to exploit.[48] By early 1987, Defense Secretary Caspar W. Weinberger, an early advocate of horizontal escalation, confirmed the Reagan Administration's fundamental shift away from that posture and back towards a reliance on traditional escalation control premises.[49]

Escalation control has thus survived a number of recent attempts to revise or discard it, because other policy alternatives, such as "Maritime Strategy" and "horizontal escalation," have failed to promise better prospects than the original concept. These alternatives have also proven to be unacceptably insensitive to the costs/risks side of the deterrence equation, and, consequently, could not be incorporated into a responsible Dominant Player strategic posture. While escalation control is still uncomfortably ambiguous and imprecise in the eyes of many U.S. strategic planners and critics, it remains in place, for the want of a better alternative, as a major theoretical premise of U.S. extended deterrence strategy in both the Asia-Pacific and the other Eurasian theaters.

Interalliance Transferability

A SECOND problem related to the application of the Dominant Player posture must also be addressed: the interaction of theaters of military operation within a global strategic framework. Recently, interalliance transferability has become the most discussed factor in extended deterrence, because of the perceived or real issue of American imperial decline. Critics of American strategic planning argue that Washington still has not adequately defined priorities for determining its global commitments, nor has it been diligent in reviewing what commitments it retains to ensure the realization of fundamental U.S. security interests. As Jeffrey Record has argued, a "worldwide strategy is not a strategy but testimony to an absence of a strategy."[50]

The problem of dealing with multiple theaters has always complicated postwar U.S. deterrence planning, but has become even more difficult within the past decade, as the bipolar world of Soviet-American strategic competition has evolved into a much more complex and diffuse international system. This has become especially true as debate has intensified over how to reconcile still formidable Soviet military capabilities with the difficulties confronted by *both* superpowers in coping with international security challenges beyond their immediate purviews. In early 1978, Senator Sam Nunn, one of the United States' most influential and knowledgeable defense experts, asserted that U.S. military posture in Asia was inconsistent and vaguely defined, suffering from misplaced preoccupations of a unitary global Soviet threat, and resulting in an inadequate American grasp of interregional strategy and resources: "all too often it is assumed that U.S. ground forces can be shifted from Asia to America, and then to Europe, without any loss in effectiveness. This assumption is both false and perilous."[51] The Senator could have added that future Asia-Pacific conflicts may well explode for reasons only remotely connected to superpower global politics.

The 1979 disclosure of the Pentagon's "swing strategy" for shifting naval and air power from PACOM to other regions underscored Nunn's concerns. At that time, the "swing strategy" was presented by the Carter administration as a remedy to the sharp attrition of U.S. naval surface units during the immediate post-Vietnam era and as an alternative to the U.S. Navy's obvious inability to simultaneously establish sea control in all parts of Eurasia. This plan emanated from Consolidated Guidance Study no. 8, a U.S. contingency plan leaked to the public during late 1979, that advocated redeploying American naval power from Asia to Europe in the event of an escalating NATO crisis.[52]

The swing strategy fueled Asian apprehensions that the United States was pursuing a Eurocentric priority in its post-Vietnam deterrence posture. More fundamentally, the Asia-Pacific allies recognized and were frustrated by both the uncertainty of their "fit" into America's global security strategy and the inability of the American public to empathize beyond its dread of involvement in "seemingly endless" Asian ground wars.[53] The Navy itself soon rejected this approach by declaring that it would *not*, in a conventional war, "swing" its forces from the Pacific to the Atlantic or vice versa. In part, this was due to the PACOM's recognition of its responsibility for the northwest Indian

Ocean and most of the West's oil lifelines. Washington also became acutely conscious of Asia-Pacific allied—and especially, Japanese—resistance to any contingency plan which envisioned the siphoning of the Seventh Fleet and supporting air support assets from the Pacific to endorse what appeared to be a replay of the "Europe-first" deterrence strategy that eventually precipitated the Korean War.[54] If the United States had carried through with the swing strategy, the Asia-Pacific allies' apprehensions about coupled security and U.S. escalation control capability would have multiplied.

Toward the end of President Reagan's first term of office, apprehension over U.S. extended deterrence strategy shifted to European allies, as Henry Kissinger, Lawrence Eagleburger (the Under Secretary of State for Political Affairs), and other prominent U.S. policy analysts speculated that long-term changes in the U.S. defense orientation from a European to an Asian emphasis was underway. They noted a widening gap between European regional security concerns and U.S. global strategic interests, leading to "a different set of perspectives and imperatives."[55] Subsequent political damage control efforts by the State Department focused on the argument that European security in the NATO treaty area was directly affected by events in Asia and in other third world regions, and presented NATO European states and pro-Western Asian countries with unique "opportunities to cooperate as allies even though the alliance per se may not be the appropriate instrument for managing that cooperation."[56] Such arguments were only partially successful in meeting European allied concerns, and more relevantly here, in assuaging Asia-Pacific allied concerns about U.S. geopolitical priorities and commitments. The recent joint Chinese-Japanese opposition to an exclusively "European" intermediate nuclear force (INF) treaty which would have left Soviet missiles pointing at Asian targets demonstrates the continuing nature of such concerns. Washington cannot assume that friendly Asia-Pacific states would be willing to support an American deterrence strategy that allowed any European or Persian Gulf conflict to spill over into their own region.[57]

The task of recognizing and dealing with the problem of interalliance transferability is all the more formidable because neither the Persian Gulf nor Asia-Pacific theaters have the geographic or political coherence of the Central European front. Consequently, judgments about their importance to American interests have varied greatly. Most strategic analysts would agree that there is little understanding of how extended deterrence, as applied to NATO, might affect Dominant Player military objectives and power applied to other theaters. For example, does the presence of a carrier task force deployed just outside the Persian Gulf in the northwest Indian Ocean and normally assigned to PACOM act as a deterrence tripwire in ways similar to or different from U.S. ground forces assigned to positions west of the Elbe? Does an "over-the-horizon" U.S. air and naval presence in Southeast Asia contribute to a regional power balance in the Asia-Pacific equivalent to the U.S. Sixth Fleet's stabilizing NATO's southern flank? What proportion of the Soviet military power in East Asia is directed toward China rather than toward nations covered by the U.S. nuclear umbrella? Is that proportion substantial enough to render U.S. deterrence calculations toward Northeast Asia asymmetrical to those applied toward Europe? Each of these questions involved U.S. resource allocation and fundamental U.S. strategic choices between containing Soviet military capabilities within Eurasia or responding to more indigenous sources of regional instability that may directly affect American national security interests.

Credibility of Strategic Commitments

THE THIRD, and perhaps most important factor affecting the relationship between extended deterrence theory and policy is the problem of the intensity of a deterrence guarantor's commitment to the threatened beneficiary and the credibility of that commitment in the judgment of a would-be aggressor. As noted by Mearsheimer, the credibility of commitment concerns the question "whether, given the great risks and costs associated with the use of military force, a nation will use it, especially outside national borders, to defend certain interests."[58] It may well be, as some have contended, that there is no simple way "to translate such explanations of American commitment in any foreign area into strengths of commitment."[59] However, as Thomas Schelling has noted, commitments are usually interdependent with relation to the threats they are designed to deter, i.e., "Essentially, we tell the Soviets that we have to react here because, if we did not, they would not believe us when we say that we will react there."[60] Often, the commitment credibility problem is assessed in terms of how effective the guarantor is in communicating his intolerance of limited attacks or incursions against the beneficiary, or in quickly establishing "escalation dominance" in the event that extended deterrence strategy initially fails.[61]

Commitments, however, are subject to change, if the guarantor finds that the original expectations or interests underlying his initial decision to extend deterrence have not been achieved or served, or if expectations are not reinforced through allied behavior. In Europe, the "Flexible Response" strategy implemented by the Kennedy/Johnson administrations signaled that the United States would be more discriminate than before in using nuclear weapons to defend NATO because it realized that its allies were becoming increasingly skeptical of American willingness to defend them by escalating a conflict against the Warsaw Pact to the nuclear level. Flexible Response was nevertheless still viewed as credible by European NATO members because the threat of a Soviet conventional invasion was regarded as diminishing. The idea of Warsaw Pact armies risking the destruction of Europe's strategic and industrial assets by precipitating either a large-scale conventional or a limited nuclear war against the NATO allies seemed more unlikely-given that the loyalty of Pact allied armies to Soviet commanders was questionable (a factor only further underlined by Eastern Europe's process of political liberalization unfolding throughout 1989–1990) and that prevailing wind patterns in the European theater are from west to east, thus subjecting Pact nations to greater prospects of long-term radiation effects in the aftermath of a nuclear conflict. The credibility of the "revised" U.S. extended deterrence strategy in Europe would thus be compromised only in the unlikely possibility that Moscow could fight and win a conventional war in Europe while intimidating Washington not to respond at the nuclear level.[62]

Defeat in Indochina, however, left Washington disillusioned over the costs of the deterrence commitments it had long maintained in Asia. Escalation control had been achieved by securing a termination of the Korean conflict in 1953 and by preventing Sino-American military confrontations in the Taiwan Straits during 1955 and 1958. Yet extended deterrence proved largely irrelevant to other Asian conflicts involving U.S. interests, as the Vietnam experience graphically illustrated. This called into question the very relevance of extended deterrence in its "tighter" or nuclear context in a postwar timeframe increasingly dominated by limited wars. Should the United States continue to risk conflict escalation to nuclear levels if the indigenous populations of Asian allies were clearly disinclined to fight and die for their pro-Western leaderships at lower levels of conflict? If not, was the coupling of the United States' own security to that of those allies a strategy predicated upon erroneous assumptions that Washington's global security objectives coincided with local or regional security objectives?

The Nixon Doctrine attempted to respond both to the American willingness to underwrite those Asian deterrence commitments still entailing a visible nuclear dimension and to the realities of Asian warfare.[63] Vietnam was a case where the United States assumed a commitment based upon a broader strategy (containment), but a commitment that gradually became untenable. As Patrick M. Morgan has recently observed, "the greatest difficulty with extended deterrence is that a conflict set off by a challenge to a commitment might spread, with costs and consequences larger than the deterror expected or wished."[64]

Given this reality, the question of commitment *intensity* becomes critical. Alliance behavior appears to be a particularly relevant measure of commitment intensity. The nature of the security guarantee underlying an alliance, and the degree of consensus among allies regarding how this guarantee will be honored, is central to the issue of how commitment is perceived by friends, adversaries, and the international system at large. Commitment intensity relates to the *quality* of commitment within a specific alliance, as well as to the *scope* of that commitment.

The quality of commitment is measured by the level of risk the deterror is willing to assume on behalf of its allies and by the type as well as the extent of national security assets it is willing to allocate. On the basis of history, culture, and political-economic ties, U.S. decision-makers still regard NATO as their most critical security commitment. That treaty's language is the most binding of any formal security arrangement Washington maintains. The United States' postwar forward deployment of several hundred thousand troops and the existence of a formal NATO high command adhering to a "possible first-use" nuclear strategy provided graphic evidence of the depth and scope of U.S. extended deterrence strategy in Europe.

The problem of scope in the U.S. deterrence commitments extended toward Asia-Pacific allies relates to the "entrapment-abandonment" issue which has long confronted Washington's NATO allies in Europe and the search for a middle ground for Asians fearful of either becoming overly involved in, or completely irrelevant to, U.S. global strategy.[65] Postwar U.S. alliance systems in both Europe and in the Asia-Pacific have become increasingly strained by allied concern that they are trapped by a U.S. global strategy destined to involve them in future wars neither of their own making nor in their own national security interests. Resolving this dilemma by identifying and managing an acceptable "balance" of commitment is the price which a Dominant Player must pay for its efforts to integrate the various geographic components of a global deterrence posture.

THE DOMINANT PLAYER APPROACH TO ASIA-PACIFIC ALLIES

SINCE THE Nixon Doctrine articulated the United States' strategic disengagement from Indochina in August 1969, Washington's extended deterrence strategy in the Asia-Pacific has been inconsistent. President Nixon sought to retain the credibility of American security commitments by reassuring U.S. friends in Southeast Asia that his administration would respond positively if they were to come under external attack. But when North Vietnam routed U.S.-backed South Vietnamese forces on the battlefields of Laos in March 1971, the Americans sent only evacuation helicopters to extricate what was left of the once-proud South Vietnamese Rangers—a psychological blow from which neither the American-supported Laotian nor South Vietnamese governments ever recovered.[66] As the U.S. moved to extricate itself from the Vietnam War through a diplomatic settlement, most Asians sensed that any treaty advertised to prevent Hanoi's annexation of Vietnam would be unenforceable.

It was in this atmosphere that the U.S. tried to induce Japan into accepting a more visible security posture in Northeast Asia in return for Okinawa's reversion to the Japanese mainland. Tokyo, however, was no more enthusiastic about assuming that role in 1969 than it had been during earlier U.S. campaigns to prod it into rearmament (see chapter 2). From the perspective of the U.S. Asia-Pacific allies, the overall pattern of American extended deterrence strategy as applied to their region throughout this period was one of strategic drift, if not outright neglect. The United States' reconciliation with China only served to increase the strategic uncertainty of Washington's Asia-Pacific allies. President Nixon and his National Security Adviser, Henry Kissinger, moved quickly to implement the Sino-American rapprochement despite the uncertain and complicated implications which the geopolitical maneuvering of Washington and Beijing had for the Asian regional security environment. With the United States' acceptance of the People's Republic of China as a legitimate and important participant in the international system, the need to deter what had previously been represented as a unified communist threat in Southeast Asia was outdated; any sense of permanence in U.S. regional security commitments was outmoded. Recognizing the inevitable, the Thai and Philippines' foreign ministers issued a joint communique in July 1975 announcing the phasing out of the Southeast Asia Treaty Organization (SEATO) organization, but the retention of the Manila Treaty against the unlikely event that Thailand or the Philippines would experience an external invasion.

Having extricated itself from a protracted Asian ground war in which it could claim no tangible strategic success, Washington was accused of exercising benign neglect toward the Asia-Pacific theater during the years of the Carter administration (1977–1980). A growing faction of U.S. military planners was viewing China as a strategic counterweight to a reduced American strategic presence in the theater (see chapter 2), and the same type of U.S. burden-sharing arguments that had given rise to the politics of the Mansfield Amendment were now increasingly directed at the United States' prosperous Japanese and South Korean allies in Northeast Asia. The deteriorating U.S. position in Iran and the Persian Gulf, moreover, focused American attention upon naval competition in the Indian Ocean and eventually prompted the Carter Doctrine's commitment to defend the West's oil lifelines in those locales. Meanwhile, the price of strategic neglect in Europe during the U.S. military involvement in Vietnam manifested itself during 1977–1978, forcing the U.S. and its NATO allies to respond to Soviet theater nuclear force modernization and to embark upon a long-range and highly expensive conventional defense modernization program.

U.S. deterrence postures in the Asia-Pacific suffered commensurately. Throughout the late 1970s, the Commander-in-Chief, Pacific Forces' (CINCPACs') annual Congressional testimony on U.S. force strength and readiness in his theater was increasingly pessimistic. In

February 1979, Admiral Maurice F. Weisner related that the withdrawal of a battalion from the U.S. 2nd Infantry Division in South Korea, combined with an expanding Soviet naval presence in the Pacific, caused Japanese speculation about the credibility of U.S. deterrence commitments in Northeast Asia. A Senate Armed Services Committee "Pacific Study Group" corroborated Weisner's assertion by reporting that, based on its interviews with Asia-Pacific leaders, it had no other choice but to conclude that "U.S. attention to security matters may have shifted too far to NATO."[67] Even Australian-New Zealand confidence in U.S. commitments to the ANZUS alliance was shaken by what Canberra and Wellington regarded as the growing superiority of Soviet naval power in the Indian Ocean. The strength of U.S. Air Force deployments in CINCPAC, Weisner reported, had decreased 50 percent since 1974, ground combat forces by 10 percent, naval strength by 10 percent (although half of the U.S. Navy's major surface combatants remained in the PACOM theater), and American conventional forces were estimated to be between 20 and 30 percent understrength. Two aircraft carrier groups had been removed from the Pacific theater, increasing Soviet ability to interdict critical sea lanes and oil routes, and U.S. theater nuclear forces also experienced significant attrition throughout the latter 1970s. Weisner concluded that "reduction of force levels following the Southeast Asia conflict has diminished overall PACOM capabilities."[68]

Assuming office in 1981, President Reagan was determined to reverse these trends. Incorporating the Asia-Pacific into U.S. global deterrence strategy more explicitly than had his predecessors, the Reagan Administration moved to establish a 600–ship navy, to strengthen both U.S. strategic and theater nuclear forces, and to support forward-deployed forces with enhanced sealift/airlift capabilities and larger stockpiles of military equipment pre-positioned in overseas theaters. However, the Reagan Administration's efforts to strengthen U.S. deterrence capabilities in the Pacific were undercut by its own early attempts to integrate Eurasian theaters into global war planning without adequate deference to the individual security characteristics and requirements of each. The preoccupation of Reagan administration officials with defining and implementing a new American "grand strategy" during 1981–1982 impeded their ability to determine how global planning would fulfill region-specific strategic objectives.

Differences between Weinberger and Secretary of State Shultz over this point emerged in early 1984. Shultz noted the importance of selectively backing counter-insurgency efforts by U.S. allies in the Third World as a U.S. deterrence option, concluding that unless the U.S. was willing to use limited force to restore the status quo in limited contingencies, the credibility of U.S. deterrence commitments would suffer. Weinberger countered by embracing the Nixon Doctrine's thesis that coercive diplomacy would only create more Vietnams and that deterrence was more credible if force was used by the U.S. with the clear intent of winning.[69] Neither U.S. official, however, anticipated the determination of Asia-Pacific states to restructure the parameters of Washington's Dominant Player regional deterrence posture. This oversight left the Reagan administration unprepared for the coordinated Chinese-Japanese diplomacy on the "globalization" of the Soviet-U.S. INF Treaty, for coping with the intensification of South Korean and Filipino nationalism, or for neutralizing New Zealand's campaign to create a "non-nuclear" ANZUS.

Notwithstanding differences between key U.S. policymakers over how to apply the Dominant Player approach to limited wars in developing regions, the majority of U.S. allies in the Asia-Pacific still complied with Washington's prerequisites for extending deterrence to their own territory—what the U.S. State Department has termed "the shared responsibilities of a democratic alliance," including that of accepting the nuclear component of U.S. strategic deterrence. A number of American military strategists have argued that the sheer expanse of the Asia-Pacific theater requires broad U.S. access to all of its parts, if extended deterrence is to remain viable.[70]

Ideally, from the U.S. vantage point, the Dominant Player posture should give potential adversaries serious pause before planning military incursions against U.S. Asia-Pacific allies (Japan, South Korea, and Thailand). Indeed, a mere U.S. military *presence* and its potential stablizing function, may be the most useful and productive aspect of American extended deterrence policies in the Asia-Pacific as opposed to any effort by Washington to fit such policies, somehow, into more global strategic imperatives. A number of U.S. friends in the region confront no immediate external threats at present (Korea excepted); the U.S. economic and geopolitical presence in their immediate environs is designed to buy time for such countries to pursue long-term national development strategies without fear of being diverted by external security issues.

It can be argued that aside from a consistent and relatively benign offshore U.S. military presence, U.S. extended deterrence in the Asia-Pacific has been less than fully relevant to the politics of regional change. Civil wars and ethnic strife, for example, have been prevalent throughout much of the Asia-Pacific landscape over recent decades. The Dominant Player posture has yet to become responsive to what Robert Scalapino has labeled "Asianization," i.e., "the development of ever more complex, integral relations among and between Asian states themselves, and apart from external involvements."[71]

Do Washington's Asia-Pacific security partners really believe that the U.S. will fight on their behalf? Japan and Australia have chosen not to question the U.S. on this issue. They prefer, instead, to assume that extended deterrence is valid under their respective security treaties with Washington—accepting the ambiguous nature of general deterrence. It should be noted that the Japanese and Australians do so, secure in the knowledge that they are by far the most valuable allies in the region to the U.S. for economic and political reasons.

The intensity of U.S. Asia-Pacific security commitments has, however, been questioned no less in Tokyo and Canberra than similar American commitments in Western Europe. The nature of the U.S.-Japan Mutual Security Treaty (MST) was, for example, renegotiated during the late 1950s, when the Japanese complained that the prerogatives of Japan's sovereignty were unrecognized in the original 1952 draft to the extent that U.S. forces stationed in Japan could be used for any purpose without first consulting Tokyo. The revised terms of U.S. extended deterrence preserved the American commitment to defend Japan, but modified Japanese obligations for acquiescence in regard to the *type* and *destination* of U.S. force projection from Japanese facilities. What has evolved has been labeled by one Japanese defense analyst as "a deterrence of uncertainties." Alliance commitment is sustained by the deliberate preservation of uncertainty over the intensity of U.S. military response.[72] Australia has conducted a number of recent defense reviews focusing on the continued relevance and viability of U.S. security guarantees under ANZUS (see chapter 2).

South Korea, New Zealand, the Philippines, and Thailand have also had reason in recent years to question the U.S. deterrence commitment. The U.S. State Department accompanied President Carter's 1977 decision to reduce U.S. ground forces in. South Korea with a statement that U.S. involvement in a future Korean war is "automatic" only in that the President would have to make an immediate decision about the nature of the U.S. military response in the event of a North Korean attack.[73] New Zealand has disassociated itself (for other reasons) from a U.S. extended deterrence posture that included an opportunity to consult and cooperate on only those problems of conventional deterrence perceived by the U.S. as relevant to New Zealand's national security interests.[74] Various Filipino military leaders have predicated their recent shift toward greater skepticism of U.S. deterrence guarantees under the U.S.-Philippines Mutual Defense Treaty on similar grounds. Philippine regional security interests such as internal insurgencies and offshore territorial disputes in the East China Sea seem increasingly remote from the sweeping global purview embodied within the U.S. Dominant Player posture.[75] Thailand evidenced visible feelings of abandonment throughout most of the 1970s, as the U.S. reduced and eventually removed the 50,000-strong U.S. contingent originally stationed there to support the Vietnam War effort. The U.S. defense officials talked about "consulting lawyers" before obligating Washington to defend Thailand from external attack, "publicly undermining what little deterrent value remained in the U.S.-Thai security relationship."[76] In response, Bangkok has sought to reach beyond its Manila Pact security tie with Washington and secure supplementary external defense guarantees for its security from China and, more tacitly, from the Five Power Defense Agreement (FPDA) signatories (Australia, Britain, Malaysia, New Zealand, and Singapore).[77]

CONCLUSION

U.S. EXTENDED deterrence policy in the Asia-Pacific region is now viewed as badly designed by a growing number of Western and Asian critics. They believe it is misapplied to a region which no longer is subject to the types of threats with which that strategy was originally designed to cope. Opponents of the Dominant Player posture, moreover, assert there is no real evidence, as demanded by immediate deterrence theorists, of the "workability" of U.S. strategies. Nor has a nuclear crisis materialized in this theater over the past two decades, creating uncertainty about the applicability of the "general deterrence" assumptions found within traditional U.S. strategy. One could argue that the Korean War, the 1954 Indochina crisis, the Taiwan Straits crisis (1954–1955/1958), and most recently, the February 1979 Sino-Vietnamese war represented the only tangible instances in post-World War II history where deterrence theory was significantly applicable to Asia-Pacific conflict situations. To its detractors, the Dominant Player posture has been relevant primarily to Western Europe, but has been distorted since the Nixon Doctrine to serve American strategic policy ends in the Southwest Asian and Asia-Pacific theaters and to compensate for dwindling U.S. strategic commitments and resources in those theaters. The unsatisfactory result, according to these analysts, has been an intensification of Asia-Pacific allied uncertainty about remaining U.S. deterrence commitments (the "entrapment-abandonment" dilemma) and about a greater risk of compromising escalation control in future conflict management.

Those supporting Washington's continued application of the Dominant Player posture counter that a preponderance of U.S. military power deployed in the region is still decisive as a factor in war avoidance at both the conventional and nuclear force levels. They also believe that while a number of the Washington's early postwar collective defense treaties with Asia-Pacific allies may have changed over time, U.S. security commitments extended to them remain sufficiently credible to deter what external threats they do confront and to safeguard their region's extraordinary economic development. According to this line of reasoning, extended deterrence remains an appropriate Asia-Pacific strategy.

The current U.S. extended deterrence policy was interrupted briefly during the 1980s when U.S. policy planners weighed replacing traditional postwar extended deterrence approaches with a more offensive-oriented global strategy. The experiment was short-lived, however, and, by early 1989, Washington had reverted to the more traditional deterrence-through-denial posture which had been effect since the Nixon Doctrine was introduced two decades before.

If the primary intent of general extended deterrence, as implemented by Washington, is to avoid war and preclude the loss of allies and friends to one's strategic opponents, then the Dominant Player posture has been largely successful up to the present in an Asia-Pacific context. Current geopolitical changes in the region, however, promise to render the old assumptions and strategies underlying that posture less relevant to the security concerns of regional actors. The normalization of Sino-American relations has transformed the area's strategic landscape considerably throughout the past two decades. A qualified Sino-Soviet rapprochement or a more sophisticated Soviet approach to Asian affairs than its past unidimensional reliance on military power could have much the same effect during the 1990s. Further, the United States no longer commands the same level of relative industrial and economic power as when the Dominant Player posture was originally shaped.

The Soviet Union's recent initiatives to Asia-Pacific states imply a move away from traditional, and exclusive, Soviet reliance on military force projection as a means to derive influence in the Asia-Pacific. Mikhail Gorbachev's initiatives (see chapter 3) have compelled Washington to prove the relevance of the Dominant Player posture, with its inherent emphasis on military threats and capabilities. However, President Bush's early 1989 journey to Northeast Asia—during which he attempted to represent the United States as the defender of the status quo through (presumably) continued adherence to the U.S. extended deterrence strategy in place—offered little encouragement about the United States' ability to reconcile this approach with local regional concerns.[78]

Recent developments in China, and their possible effects on Sino-American security relations, present yet another possible challenge to current U.S. extended deterrence strategy. The Chinese still view American offshore power as a useful counterweight to Soviet military capabilities, which clearly still threaten China's peripheries. Nevertheless, the hostility of Beijing's current leadership to American values and its lingering suspicions about U.S. strategic objectives are unmistakable. U.S. treaty allies in Northeast and Southeast Asia regard the United States' growing domestic problems of debt, crime, and narcotics; its serious trade deficit with most other industrial powers; and the American public's fascination with the global decline literature as signs of an impending and sustained U.S. strategic retrenchment.[79] The "entrapment-abandonment" dilemma, long testing the credibility of U.S. extended deterrence strategy, may well become instrumental in finally unraveling it. The United States' Asia-Pacific allies, while fearing each others' intentions and capabilities at least as much as U.S. efforts to lock them into an interdependent global alliance network, may, in this changing geopolitical environment, seek an Asia-Pacific power equilibrium in which the U.S. would play a much less significant role.

American policy in this theater faces a major challenge: to link essential U.S. extended deterrence approaches and strategies to regional policy objectives which will be relevant to the long-term visions of regional peace and stability of America's Asia-Pacific friends and allies. A comparative examination of other—alternative or supplemental—regional security approaches should lead to a better understanding of the adjustments necessary to retain American strategic access and influence in the Asia-Pacific.

CHAPTER 2

The Dominant and Transitional Players in the Asia-Pacific Reconciling Global and Local Deterrence Objectives

TO PREVENT a hostile power from dominating the Eurasian landmass between 1951–1954, the United States structured a number of postwar formal defense treaties with the Asia-Pacific's most important non-communist nations. Most of these were bilateral accords between the United States and friendly states in the region (the exceptions were the ANZUS treaty which involved both Australia and New Zealand and the SEATO accord which included those two countries with Thailand, the Philippines, and several extraregional powers). The Dominant Player posture was incorporated in the Pacific treaty system from its outset.

The U.S.-Japan Mutual Security Treaty (MST) was one product of the American determination to shape the entire context of postwar deterrence strategy for the Asia-Pacific region. Japan's economic and industrial potentials were regarded by the original architects of U.S. global containment politics as critical regional power determinants to which Soviet access or control must be denied. The U.S. Mutual Defense Treaty with the Republic of Korea was another illustration of the Dominant Player approach. The Korean peninsula is the primary access point to both the Japanese archipelago and to China's industrial heartland, a geopolitical reality which drew American and Chinese forces into conflict during the Korean War. South Korea's strategic location continues to be the major reason that the United States deploys a large military ground presence and tactical nuclear capability in that country.

Until its abrogation in 1980, the U.S.-Taiwan Mutual Defense Treaty provided the United States with a critical offshore link in its Pacific defense arc, which stretched from the Aleutians, Japan, and the Ryukyus down into the Philippines and the Southwest Pacific. American air reconnaissance and naval interdiction capabilities based in Taiwan compensated for Japan's lack of strategic resources and its constitutional restraints, guarding its oil lifelines through the east Indian Ocean and the Southeast Asian littorals. While postwar Australia faced no security threats comparable to those encountered by Japan, South Korea, or Taiwan, ANZUS was nevertheless forged as an instrument of Western collective defense to replace the "shattered safety net of the British Empire."[1] Over time, Australia became more important to U.S. global deterrence strategy, hosting critical intelligence and tracking installations, providing transit facilities for U.S. B-52 surveillance missions in the Indian Ocean, and contributing to American deterrence strategy in Southeast Asia with the adoption of an Australian "forward defense posture."

U.S. STRATEGY TOWARD ASIA-PACIFIC ALLIES: CONVENTIONAL FORCES AND NUCLEAR AMBIGUITY

COMPARED TO NATO Europe, U.S. strategy in the Asia-Pacific was less well defined throughout most of the postwar timeframe (although recent events in Eastern Europe may substantially complicate American policy toward NATO as well). For close to four decades, a clear and stable bipolar system of deterrence was sustained in the NATO theater because little doubt existed that the United States and the USSR adhered to their security commitments there at both the nuclear and conventional levels. In contrast, in the Asia-Pacific, the development of global nuclear parity between the superpowers led the United States to assign its conventional forces in that theater a higher level of importance. This resulted in an overall military balance more favorable to the West than that which existed in Europe. U.S. forward projection forces in Northeast Asia, for example, are critical relative to Japanese fears that dependence upon the U.S. nuclear umbrella alone would entail the risk of nuclear devastation. From Washington's perspective, the loss of a conventional force balance and the resort to nuclear weapons in any Asia-Pacific conflict involving Soviet or Chinese nuclear delivery systems could bring possible nuclear retaliation against the U.S. homeland. Given such circumstances, the role of conventional forces becomes important to the United States, both to maintain escalation control during Asia-Pacific crises and to retain the credibility of its allied commitments.[2]

An emphasis on conventional deterrence strategy, particularly in Northeast Asia, underscores U.S. dependence upon flexible response options similar to those which exist in NATO force planning. However, the strategic ambiguity associated with U.S. extended deterrence commitments in the Asia-Pacific is designed to avoid policy conflicts which might otherwise arise between the United States and its allies in the region. This "existential deterrence" is based upon an abiding belief by U.S. allies in the region that the presence of conventional U.S. military forces is sufficient to deter aggression against them and does not require the more provocative step of openly deployed U.S. nuclear weapons on their territory.

An exception to the Dominant Player's application of existential deterrence, of course, is South Korea. The South Koreans have accepted the presence of a U.S. nuclear trip wire and the need for theater nuclear options because of its border with North Korea, an obvious military threat to Seoul and one which has traditionally deployed greater military power on the Korean peninsula. Australia, too, in successive defense reviews, has reaffirmed the importance of its ties with the American global deterrence posture and provides the U.S. access to various facilities for tracking and signaling missions integral to the realization of that posture.

Although no longer a formal ally of the U.S. or playing a direct role in American military strategy, Taiwan continues to rely upon Beijing's uncertainty about Washington's inclinations to defend that offshore island if it were to be invaded by the Chinese forces. Even the PRC, while publicly decrying any nuclear presence in the region other than its own, has depended indirectly upon both Soviet and American nuclear deterrence capabilities to deter the other superpower from launching military operations against China.

ASIA-PACIFIC ALLIED CONCERNS: WHY U.S. ALLIES HAVE BECOME "TRANSITIONAL PLAYERS"

AS THE United States initiated a strategic retrenchment in the Asia-Pacific during the Nixon Administration, its regional allies became worried that Washington would be more inclined to endorse an overly provocative nuclear posture in the theater despite its traditional conventional and nuclear defense strategy there. American strategic ballistic missile submarines (SSBN) deployed in the Pacific, for example, still remained relatively invulnerable to detection by Soviet anti-submarine warfare. An American massing of SSBNs in the Sea of Japan during a future regional crisis, however, could generate pressure for rapid Soviet mobilization of its less formidable SSBN force during such a crisis and precipitate overall strategic escalation in the theater.[3] These concerns intensified during the early 1980s as the Reagan administration introduced the Maritime Strategy and the horizontal escalation concept. Both approaches, along with the "swing strategy" doctrine which preceded it during President Carter's final year in office, were viewed as too Eurocentric. The Asia-Pacific allies, moreover, viewed the U.S. deployment of several thousand sea-launched cruise missiles and modernized offshore nuclear delivery systems throughout PACOM during this time as needlessly accelerating a regional arms race with Moscow. Such deployments were regarded by U.S. force planners as cost effective, particularly as Washington faced intensified fiscal problems that could impair its willingness or ability to sustain conventional force advantages. They also implied that the United States was placing an increased premium on allied defense burden-sharing efforts below the nuclear threshold, despite the fact that the extent to which the Japanese, South Koreans, or Australians were willing to make such efforts was questionable.

U.S. allies and friends in the Asia-Pacific were also concerned about Washington's belief that it could entice China into becoming a strategic surrogate for American security interests in this theater. Beijing's modest but growing nuclear force, combined with the gradual military modernization of its conventional forces, was regarded by U.S. force planners as a potential strategic asset for the West in its global containment scheme. It impelled the USSR to base approximately one-fourth

to one-third of its total military assets east of the Urals. An unexpectedly rapid Chinese achievement of superpower status, however, could
threaten to upset the Asia-Pacific power equilibrium, particularly if
accompanied by a serious erosion of the U.S. strategic position in the
region. A more powerful and aggressive China could precipitate accelerated Japanese rearmament intensify Sino-Soviet regional strategic
competition, and seriously disrupt Southeast Asian countries' economic and political development plans.

All of these developments have caused U.S. security affiliates in the
Asia-Pacific to become "Transitional Players" in regional deterrence
matters. A review of the U.S. Dominant Player posture as it applies to
treaty alliances with Japan and South Korea provides a basis for assessing the continued viability of that posture with respect to these two
postwar allies. Taiwan's pursuit of a more self-reliant deterrence posture since the termination of its security treaty with Washington is also
instructive as to how a Transitional Player can adjust its own strategy
in response to a reduction in security commitments by its former major
guarantor. Indicative, too, is the recent evolution of Australia's strategic outlook away from its traditional "forward defense" posture to
one more concerned with defending its immediate environs in the
Eastern Indian and Southwest Pacific Oceans. Nevertheless, almost all
of the U.S. regional allies still wish to maintain selective fealty to some
facets of the Dominant Player posture as insurance against future
strategic miscalculations.

POLICY CONFLICTS: DOMINANT PLAYER
VERSUS TRANSITIONAL PLAYER

WITH RESPECT to each Transitional Player, there are examples of
inherent conflict between the objectives of the U.S. Dominant Player
posture and the Transitional Players' regional security objectives. U.S.
strategy in Japan has, for example, been directed toward achieving a
major U.S. policy objective despite a major policy constraint. The
objective was deterrence through denial: committing U.S. forces to the
defense of Japan to prevent the USSR from gaining control over
Japan's geostrategically critical maritime straits, and thus denying Soviet access to the formidable Japanese industrial capacity. The con-

straint was the essential reconciliation of American global and Japanese local deterrence objectives.

The Korean peninsula is also an instructive case study of how escalation control and interalliance transferability can impede, rather than reinforce, a Dominant Player posture. From the outset of the postwar period, the military balance on the peninsula favored North Korea over South Korea. It was essential for the United States to compensate by deploying ground forces and high levels of firepower in the South. The geographic vulnerability of Seoul to North Korean blitzkrieg—style ground and air attacks intensified tensions during the cold war. The immediacy of the threat to be deterred caused the United States to sustain its closest operational military ties in the Asia-Pacific with the South Koreans, even though Japan and, more recently, a friendly China were higher priorities for American geostrategic interests. The uncompromising hostility of Pyongyang and the inordinately high levels of military readiness it maintained in the face of a struggling economy caused South Korea's security to become extraordinarily important to the Asia-Pacific balance of power and an exaggerated gauge of U.S. strategic will in a global deterrence context. During the 1970s, Washington's attitudes towards its Korean ally began to shift. While the bilateral alliance with South Korea still represented an important component of American management of the central strategic balance, dwindling U.S. strategic resources imposed defense burden-sharing pressures on a more industrialized South Korean economy and an increasingly self-confident South Korean political system.[4]

It is useful to review the U.S. Dominant Player strategy with respect to Taiwan, because it was a focal point of early American efforts to apply that posture against Soviet and Chinese power in Northeast Asia. The Taiwan Straits crises of 1955 and 1957–58 were instances where the U.S. came very close to transforming nuclear deterrence into the actual combat use of nuclear weapons. As the cold war receded, however, the strategic utility of Taiwan to the Dominant Player posture appeared to decrease relative to the advantages inherent in encouraging a Chinese mainland "tilt" toward the West. From the mid-1970s until the late 1980s, U.S. extended deterrence strategy had the objective of preserving Beijing's security against the threat of Soviet attack. This objective was a component of the U.S. broader strategy to preserve a regional and global military balance of power against the USSR's growing military capabilities. Accordingly, Taiwan's role in U.S. military strategy was diminished, even as its success as an Asian capitalist state and as a nation capable of implementing gradual democratic reform appeared to validate earlier U.S. deterrence commitments.

The Australian government still views U.S. security ties as integral to its own regional deterrence needs, including the acceptance of the U.S. extended deterrent with its nuclear dimensions.[5] Australian defense planners continue to believe that their country's alliance ties with the United States buy Canberra greater influence in the world than if it were to pursue its political-strategic interests independent of U.S. deterrence guarantees. Australia's acceptance of the Dominant Player posture, however, is becoming more conditional. Along with Washington's other Asia-Pacific treaty allies, it has become a Transitional Player, increasingly concerned about how the nuclear dimension of the American deterrent specifically relates to Canberra's own regional security agenda. Australia increasingly has assumed the role of a friendly but not subordinate ally to Washington, advising its senior partner on those areas of its own "primary strategic interest": the South Pacific, Southeast Asia, and the eastern parts of the Indian Ocean. It does so, however, with little illusion about its long-term indispensability to U.S. global strategy. In a government statement to his nation's Senate in December 1989 on Australia's regional security, Foreign Minister Gareth Evans noted that "it would not be wise to assume the United States will continue to maintain its present level of security activity in this part of the world . . . with the decline in ideological competition and other global and regional developments, U.S. attention on the region may well become over time increasingly less geopolitical and more oriented to its major economic interests."[6]

ASIA ENTERS THE COLD WAR: TESTING ESCALATION CONTROL

TO BETTER understand how the Dominant Player posture has evolved and endured as the linchpin of U.S. alliance politics in the Asia-Pacific, a brief review of its initial relationships to Washington's mutual defense treaty partnerships is in order. Assessments will then be made of selected contemporary issues raised by the growing divergence of deterrence and security objectives between the Dominant and Transitional Players.

Korea

PRIOR TO the Democratic Peoples Republic of Korea's (DPRK's) invasion on June 25, 1950, U.S. security planners viewed the Republic of Korea (ROK) as only of peripheral interest to their global containment strategy. The ROK was seen as vulnerable to both Soviet and Chinese penetration, and as a potential drain of American strategic resources better allocated to defend what State Department Policy Planning Director George Kennan specified as the most critical areas for U.S. postwar containment strategy: the Western Hemisphere, the Atlantic Community and the Asian-Pacific "defense perimeters" of Japan, Okinawa, and the Philippines.[7] In early 1949, Secretary of Defense James Forrestal testified before the Senate Foreign Relations Committee that American industrial might and control of the world's sea lanes, along with the United States' preponderance of nuclear striking power, constituted the most fundamental aspects of U.S. deterrence strategy.[8] If so, the United States did not need—nor could it afford—to extend protection to locales situated beyond what were regarded as the "core areas" of American geopolitical interest: Britain, the Rhine Valley, and Japan. Kennan later observed that Japan, as the "sole great potential military-industrial arsenal in the Far East." was far more important to U.S. deterrence strategy than China, despite the "strange fascination that China has seemed to exert at all times on American opinion . . . [Americans] tended to exaggerate China's real importance and to underrate Japan."[9] Secretary of State Dean Acheson's infamous "defense perimeters" speech delivered to the National Press Club in Washington, D.C., on January 12, 1950 confirmed Kennan's worst fears. While contending that "the first and greatest rule in regard to the formulation of American policy toward Asia" is that "anyone who violates the integrity of China is the enemy of China and is acting contrary to our own interest" (presuming the Soviet Union would attempt to dominate the Chinese Communist Party), Acheson defined a U.S. defensive perimeter in Asia which left unaddressed how the Truman Administration proposed to defend Japan in the event the Korean peninsula, always regarded as Japan's strategic jugular, fell into hostile hands.[10] The Secretary of State also remained unconvinced, until the Korean War, of Taiwan's strategic utility to the United States, discounting Army Chief of Staff J. Lawton Collin's argument made in late December 1949 that the island's "diversionary value" would prevent, or at least delay, Chinese infiltration and subversion of pro-Western governments in Indochina, Thailand, and Burma. An American deterrence commitment extended to Taiwan, Acheson responded, could only magnify U.S. policy setbacks already suffered on the Chinese mainland if Beijing launched an all-out invasion against Chiang Kai-shek's remaining forces that would very probably result in Chiang's ultimate defeat.[11]

Following North Korea's invasion of the South, however, the Truman Administration came to regard both South Korea and Taiwan as critical strategic assets which could, with their large armies and intelligence bureaucracies, form a viable defense buffer for Japanese economic reconstruction without compelling the reluctant Japanese postwar leadership to siphon national resources into a massive rearmament program.[12] This policy view was continued into the next administration. The strategic inter-relationship between these two U.S. allies was especially appreciated by the Joint Chiefs of Staff which advocated an American acceptance of Chiang Kai-shek's "standing offer" to send two Nationalist Chinese divisions to South Korea to relieve the United Nations' manpower shortages. U.S. State Department personnel, however, perceived Chiang's offer as a highly dangerous ploy to extract deterrence commitments from Washington at a time when U.S. diplomats were most concerned with inducing the PRC to negotiate a Korean armistice.[13]

After assuming office in early 1953, President Eisenhower's attentions were directed toward the problem of infusing greater credibility into U.S. nuclear deterrence strategy. The American nuclear stockpile was still too small for Washington to deter the Soviets in Europe and to simultaneously fight a limited nuclear war in Asia. Eisenhower was also intent on keeping down the size (and cost) of U.S. general purpose forces.[14] Consequently, South Korean and Taiwanese military power was increasingly viewed as a cost-effective means for implementing containment against communist forces in the Far East.

As the Korean War persisted, Eisenhower and his advisers were forced to weigh the risks of U.S. nuclear escalation. In confronting Chinese and North Korean forces with nuclear weapons, the prospects seemed very real that the Soviets would retaliate by launching military offensives in the NATO theater or against Japan. This complicated the American need to secure British cooperation in carrying out global strategy, particularly in organizing a NATO High Command. Conflict escalation in Korea would seriously affect NATO armament programs by requiring additional ammunition and war materials allocation for the Far East.

The British Labour government was already skeptical about the benefits that would accrue to the Western Alliance by raising the stakes of limited war in a remote East Asian battlefield.[15] British and French opposition to Eisenhower's decision to escalate the Korean War with nuclear attacks against China and North Korea, if Beijing and Pyongyang refused to enter into armistice negotiations, indicated just how far the inter-theater ramifications of U.S. deterrence commitments had developed in the less than three years since the North Korean invasion. In April 1953, a National Security Council memorandum (NSC 147) concluded that, except for South Korea and Taiwan, Washington's "principal allies" and most UN members would "strongly oppose" the unilateral U.S. escalation of the Korean conflict. In early June, the Joint Chiefs of Staff estimated that European "neutralist sentiment" could well intensify from any such American escalation. The limited American political objectives involved—i.e. securing Chinese and North Korean acquiescence to an armistice on the Peninsula—effectively eliminated the *political* option, according to the JCS, of escalating hostilities to a point where the United States could unleash its nuclear arsenal against communist forces.[16] Despite such warnings, Eisenhower communicated his willingness to use nuclear forces in Korea via UN negotiators meeting with North Korean representatives at Panmunjom in May 1953 and, indirectly, to the Chinese via Indian intermediaries the same month. In early June, UN proposals for the exchange of prisoners were accepted by Beijing and Pyongyang, breaking the negotiations deadlock and clearing the way for more extensive armistice negotiations.[17]

As it deliberated the costs and benefits of implementing a high-profile escalation control strategy for Korea, the United States moved to develop the means for carrying out nuclear strikes in Northeast Asia, if necessary. The American nuclear stockpile had increased from just under three hundred atomic bombs in mid-1950 to over a thousand by the end of 1953.[18] American bombers deploying tactical nuclear weapons and atomic munitions were introduced in Okinawa during the spring of 1953 (and a subsequent deployment of the *Honest John* medium-range ballistic missile system was initiated there two years later). Most recent studies of the Eisenhower administration's Korean War strategy have concurred with Marc Tractenberg's conclusion that by early 1952 qualitative improvements in tactical nuclear weapons delivery systems would have allowed Air Force and Navy fighter planes stationed at Japanese bases or on carriers offshore to deliver atomic bombs light enough and small enough for application to battlefield conditions. Accordingly, "(the) result of this buildup was an increasing ([U.S.] willingness . . . to escalate the war in Korea if no armistice agreement could be reached . . . it was clear that nuclear weapons had become an integral part of the overall policy of escalation." [19] By October 1952, the Joint Chiefs of Staff informed President Truman that U.S. nuclear strikes against North Korean and Manchurian targets were technically feasible. [20]

Taiwan

FOLLOWING THE Korean armistice, both Eisenhower and Dulles clearly believed that if U.S. and Communist Chinese forces were ever again to enter into direct conflict, the use of tactical nuclear weapons would be necessary to prevent limited conventional wars in the Asia-Pacific theater from escalating into a global nuclear conflict. This view predominated during the 1955 Taiwan Straits crisis. [21] In this instance, Dulles had concluded by late 1954, in deliberations with the Joint Chiefs of Staff and the National Security Council, that a U.S. defense of the offshore islands would "probably lead to the use of atomic weapons." [22] As in the Korean case, however, Eisenhower was highly concerned about European allied response to the loosing of the American nuclear trip wire in Asia. He was also impressed by intelligence reports that the Chinese were ill-prepared to launch an invasion against either the offshore islands or Taiwan proper. [23] Less clear was to what extent the President feared Soviet intervention on behalf of the PRC, either through the deployment of aircraft stationed on Chinese airfields in the South China Sea or through diversionary military probes of NATO positions in Europe. [24]

The 1955 Taiwan Straits crisis differed from Korea in that Washington was less sure of its ability to manage escalation control and of the risks associated with nuclear use. Central Intelligence Agency estimates prepared in 1954 warned of large-scale civilian casualties resulting from any nuclear defense of the islands, perhaps spilling over into Taiwan itself. Subsequent Soviet diplomacy may also have been decisive in persuading the PRC not to test the American deterrent extended on Chiang Kai-shek's behalf.[25]

Ultimately, Eisenhower's comparatively ambivalent position on nuclear use appeared to be effective in deterring Beijing from invading Taiwan, as compared to his more overt communications (via Indian intermediaries) bringing the Chinese to the conference table in Korea. Admiral Felix Stump, U.S. Commander-in-Chief, Pacific (CINCPAC), however, had envisoned the early use of atomic weapons against Chinese mainland airbases and troop concentrations in operational plans he had drawn up for Eisenhower concerning the defense of Jinmen and Mazu during early 1954. Mao Zedong reacted to such American nuclear posturing by directing his own scientific community to accelerate plans for developing an indigenous Chinese nuclear weapons force. In the absence of a clear escalation control scenario for the East China Sea and because of JCS disagreement over what type of Soviet response would be forthcoming to the U.S. introduction of nuclear forces in a defense of Taiwan, United States political and military leaders agreed that "An alternative to either surrender or nuclear war had to be found."[26]

In an extended deterrence context, the 1958 Taiwan crisis was more similar to the Korean situation in 1950 than to the 1954–1955 Taiwan episode. A Sino-Soviet defense technology agreement had been signed in October 1957, soon after the USSR had successfully tested an intercontinental ballistic missile and had launched Sputnik. Flush with the prospect of Moscow gaining military technology supremacy over the West, Mao regarded another probe against Taiwanese defenses as a logical test of Soviet strategic prowess and of Moscow's willingness to underwrite the advance of international communism, much as the Chinese had viewed their intervention in Korea during December 1950 as a logical outgrowth of the Sino-Soviet Friendship Treaty signed in February of that year. Chinese leaders had grown more skeptical about the Soviet Union's willingness to directly confront American military power over the years; they viewed such a test as of value in defining the Soviet/PRC relationship.

The PRC's leaders believed that they could force Moscow's hand if they opted to challenge the Americans over control of the Taiwan Straits (see chapter 3). Accordingly, Chinese forces intensified their siege against the Chinese Nationalist-controlled offshore islands in

August 1958, forcing 20 percent of Taiwan's entire army to be entrenched in defensive positions in these outposts. Six U.S. aircraft carriers, laden with nuclear-capable aircraft, were subsequently deployed to Taiwan. Nuclear cannon were installed at the Nationalist garrisons on the offshore islands, and *Matador* nuclear-tipped missiles were also installed in key positions around the island. Taiwanese runways were lengthened to accommodate the landing of American B-52 bombers. However, as was the case in 1954–1955, U.S. intelligence reports indicated that millions of Taiwanese residents would die through collateral damage resulting from the United States' use of nuclear weapons in a "defense" of the Taiwan Straits. As for Beijing, expected Soviet backing against the U.S. escalation of weapons deployments in the Taiwan area failed to materialize. While Soviet leader Nikita Khrushchev sent several tough letters to President Eisenhower in early September, warning that Moscow would extend nuclear deterrence to the Chinese mainland if the United States moved against communist positions, he timed their dispatch so that the President would receive them only *after* the real crisis had passed and the Chinese had been forced to back down to superior American military power. Later that month, U.S.-PRC bilateral negotiations aimed at winding down the crisis were resumed at Beijing's initiative.[27]

Escalation Control Lessons: Existential Deterrence

THE MOST compelling lesson of nuclear strategy emanating from the Asia-Pacific region's cold war crises is that existential deterrence was an effective means of maintaining the Dominant Player posture. In both the Korean and Taiwan cases, the United States made clear the American capacity and will to initiate nuclear strikes against an opponent previously unmoved by U.S. and allied conventional military power. American leaders, however, were deliberately ambiguous in signaling when or how much nuclear firepower would be applied to the conflict in question, partly to compound the uncertainties and fears of their adversaries and partly to measure the levels of dissent within the Western Alliance which would have to be overcome if the United States actually did introduce nuclear weapons. The ambiguity was designed to reinforce the U.S. ability to maintain escalation control by offsetting China's ability to reinforce its conventional forces in greater numbers. It was also meant to contain any nuclear combat to tactical levels and to the conflict's immediate locale, taking advantage of Soviet reluctance to support the Chinese by matching the levels of U.S. and allied military commitment.

Conventional Deterrence

WHILE THE United States maintained escalation control in Asia's cold war crises primarily due to its overwhelming nuclear superiority over the USSR, it proved less apt in establishing the credibility of its other regional deterrence commitments or in reconciling the interalliance transferability issue. Acheson's defense perimeters speech reflected a U.S. tendency to react to strategic events in this theater as opposed to implementing policies designed to minimize conflict risk and achieve conflict termination below the level of nuclear risk. The abrupt change in both South Korea's and Taiwan's perceived strategic value to the United States following the outbreak of hostilities in Korea illustrated the paucity of systematic thinking in Washington about how its deterrence posture and capabilities in the Asia-Pacific should fit into its overall global containment strategy. The Eisenhower Administration's approach to conflict termination in Korea and in Taiwan (by threatening to conduct nuclear strikes against China), moreover, appeared to be only remotely connected with Japan's local deterrence requirements. Japan's concerns were shared at the interalliance level by Britain. London was alarmed that a U.S. escalation of the Korean War to nuclear levels would cause Moscow to retaliate against NATO or would complicate Britain's own strategic position in the Malayan Peninsula and elsewhere throughout the Asia-Pacific. France, increasingly dependent upon American military assistance to sustain its interests in Indochina, similarly feared a Soviet reaction to American nuclear escalation.

THE MUTUAL SECURITY TREATIES AND DETERRENCE COMMITMENTS

Japan

THE CREDIBILITY of the U.S. extended deterrence commitment to Japan has been questioned by some who have asked why the United

States would sign a formal defense treaty obligating it to defend the Japanese but requiring no reciprocal obligation. The answer is to be found in Article 9 of Japan's constitution, which renounces war as a sovereign right of that country. This proviso also allowed the United States to station its forces in Japan, providing Washington with forward bases in the Asia-Pacific which it had coveted for most of the century. Article 9 established the United States as the guarantor of a peaceful Japan (by assuring other Asia-Pacific states that Washington would not allow Japan to pose a military threat to them). Most importantly, from the U.S. perspective, Article 9 fulfilled and legitimized aspirations entertained by the U.S. Joint Chiefs of Staff to extend the U.S. "Pacific Barrier" of deterrence from an immediate postwar "blue zone" (stretching from the Aleutians to the Philippines and back to Hawaii) to Japan, directly adjacent to the Eurasian heartland.[28]

Successive Japanese governments have interpreted the language and intent of Article 9 as sufficiently broad to give Japan the right of self-defense against a direct external attack. Nonetheless, as the Mutual Security Treaty came into force in early 1952, U.S. officials outlined what they believed to be a strong case for the United States to deter attacks on Japan by outside forces. They have gradually become comfortable with the interpretive ambiguities of the MST treaty commitment which have given the United States more flexibility in applying deterrence commitments to Japan than is generally appreciated.

Japan controls the East Asian maritime chokepoints through which Soviet naval and air contingents must travel to reach the open sea. Without entry through those chokepoints, Soviet access to its ports in the Kamchatka Peninsula and to the open waters of the Pacific Ocean would be virtually cut in half. Japanese territory intersects the key sea lanes of communication (SLOCs) extending from Vladivostok, the key naval command and supply center for the Soviet Pacific Fleet, to the Sea of Okhotsk where Soviet ballistic missile submarines capable of attacking targets on the U.S. mainland are concentrated. Along with the Barents Sea north of Murmansk, the Sea of Okhotsk represents the major deployment of Soviet second-strike nuclear deterrence capabilities. In any superpower confrontation, both these Soviet SSBN concentrations and American-Japanese efforts to neutralize them from the straits adjacent to Okhotsk would be critical factors of warfare. Accordingly, as two respected Japanese defense analysts have recently asserted, "the increase in the strategic value of the Okhotsk . . .

signifies an increase in the strategic value of the Japanese islands."[29] Japan also occupies a central position along air and sea routes stretching from North America and the important North Pacific trading routes into areas contiguous to the South China Sea and Indian Ocean. It thus sits in the middle of what many strategists regard as the most important Pacific region for projecting U.S. naval power and for deployment of U.S. forces to distant Asian conflicts. The presence of U.S. forces in over six hundred Japanese ports and bases at the outset of the Korean War, for example, constituted one of the two or three most extensive centers of noncommunist military power in the world.

In general, the strategic value of Japan in the context of the U.S. Dominant Player posture rests on the *denial* of Japanese industrial potential and Japan's strategic location to a hostile adversary. A National Intelligence Estimate prepared by the Department of State and the U.S. military services in early 1951 concluded that Japan's ultimate political alignment would be the decisive factor in whether the Soviet Union or the West would control the Asia-Pacific balance of power. The report stressed that, with Japan's logistical support, and access to its bases, the United States could maintain a cost-effective deterrent in Northeast Asia. Without these assets, U.S. defense lines in the Western Pacific would be seriously breached, if not irreparably compromised. The loss of Japanese ports and industries, moreover, would deprive the West of an industrial complex which could eventually rival those existing in the United States and Europe.[30]

From Japan's perspective, the MST was the best deterrence it could secure at a time when the East Asian region appeared to be polarizing rapidly into cold war blocs. The Korean War reinforced those Japanese feelings but also underscored differences in American and Japanese leaders' threat perceptions. The MST was publicly justified in the United States as a response to the Chinese military intervention in Korea (December 1950); Beijing's lack of serious air or naval forward projection capabilities, or the industrial resources to build them, made attack from China of small concern to Japan.[31] Soviet military power was more worrisome.

The outbreak of the Korean War and the subsequent consummation of the MST signaled a change in U.S. attitudes toward Japan—now seeing it as an essential ally, instead of a defeated aggressor. Reflecting this shift in attitude, the United Nations Command Headquarters for

Korea was established in Tokyo. Japan became the training, logistics, and supply center for U.S. forces fighting in Korea and, under the terms of the MST, American troops could also be dispatched from Japan to any Asia-Pacific crisis point, whether or not Washington secured Japanese approval (although "consultation" with the Japanese was mandated within the Treaty). Japanese industrial potential, moreover, was viewed by U.S. officials as a strategic asset that could eventually allow Japan to play an instrumental and active military role in its own right, deploying upwards of ten divisions (350,000 men) and allowing for a substantial withdrawal of American forces following a Korean peace settlement.[32]

Initial U.S. expectations about Japanese willingness and ability to contribute manpower and arms to the West's collective defense were excessively optimistic. Japanese Prime Minister Shigeru Yoshida opted to direct Japanese policy along a course which rejected both complete pacifism and large-scale rearmament. This formula was endorsed by most Japanese politicians and subsequently became known as the "Yoshida Doctrine."

The communist threat to Japanese security during the early postwar years, of course, was undeniable. Yoshida, however, had no intention of rebuilding a Japanese army of some 350,000 as demanded by Ambassador John Foster Dulles and, subsequently (in 1953), by the members of the U.S. House Special Study Mission to Southeast Asia and the Pacific and other U.S. officials. Yoshida rejected the American argument that Japan should upgrade its defense forces, as a quid pro quo for Tokyo benefiting from U.S. deterrence commitments, that could be immediately dispatched to fight in Korea, thus allowing the U.S. to deploy more American troops in Japan as a strategic reserve.[33] Washington had insisted during MST negotiations on the freedom to move U.S. forces from Japan and Okinawa into other parts of the Asia-Pacific at the outset of future regional crises. The Japanese were therefore concerned that their newfound American defense guarantee could involve their country in future conflicts beyond the confines of self-defense. The Yoshida government initially resisted the prospect of a joint headquarters for U.S. and Japanese forces under U.S. command. During the negotiations leading to the signing of the MST, Japanese officials such as Kumao Nishimura, Head of the Treaty Section of the Japanese Foreign Ministry, and Katsuhiko Okazaki argued that under such an arrangement "there cannot be a relationship of equal partners between the United States and Japan as in the case of NATO nations, but only that of subjugation of the latter to the commander." [34]

In April 1952, the MST and its requisite Administrative Agreement went into force, replacing the Far Eastern Commission, the Allied Council, and the Supreme Commander of Allied Powers (SCAP), and marking the return of full sovereignty to the Japanese state. At this time, two somewhat contradictory strands of policy evolved in Japan's security relations with the United States: (1) an attempt by Tokyo to establish more specific American commitments to defend Japan; and (2) a tacit resistance to the nuclear dimensions of U.S. extended deterrence by efforts to downplay, and later remove, American land-based nuclear weapons from Japanese soil. Japan did accept an offshore U.S. strategic presence with both nuclear and conventional dimensions that benefited its security without Japanese involvement in its management or deployment.

The "consultation" feature of the MST, in particular, spurred Yoshida and his successors to push for terms more acceptable to the Japanese public. While promising Japan that the United States would honor the MST's deterrence commitments, U.S. State Department personnel were simultaneously reassuring members of Congress that the terms of the new U.S.-Japan agreement, the U.S.-Philippines Mutual Defense Treaty, and the Tripartite (ANZUS) Treaty—all signed at the San Francisco peace conference during September 1951—"would not automatically draw the United States into a war." Moreover, the State Department argued, the MST would not legally bind the United States to fight in the event that Japan was attacked. Instead, it would "simply make available to the United States, strategic bases and facilities" in the event that the U.S. committed itself to defending Japan. [35]

The qualified nature of U.S. deterrence commitments to Japan is known as the "Monroe Doctrine" approach to collective defense. As has been the case in U.S. security relations with Latin American states since 1823, Washington's postwar strategic involvement with Asia-Pacific nations would be focused on preserving their independence and regional security. The U.S. would stop short, however, of automatically commiting itself to war. Its rationale is that action by the allies in response to an attack on an ally would be determined through consultations and in accordance with each ally's constitutional processes. From the outset, the Monroe Doctrine approach utilized the consultation formula to preclude a dispute between the Truman Administration and Congress over the latter's right to declare war. Without such a formula, the American legislative branch could have blocked ratification of the Pacific treaties by the U.S. Senate.[36] It is in contrast with the NATO approach, in which all the members of that treaty are automatically committed to defend one another when a signatory is attacked.

The Monroe Doctrine formula was more appropriate to the U.S.-Japan MST because of the unique self-defense criterion found in Japan's peace constitution. Not every Asia-Pacific contingency in which U.S. forces might be used could be linked to Japan's survival. To the Japanese, however, this logic could be extended to rationalize U.S. war avoidance in contingencies where *only* Japanese national security interests might be at stake. Thus, for Japanese leaders, the MST's exclusion of an automatic U.S. response to an attack against Japan became a major impediment to the credibility of American deterrence commitments. From Tokyo's vantage point, the ambiguity of U.S. intentions mandated a concentrated Japanese effort to renegotiate a more reciprocal collective defense relationship.

The tumultuous developments leading to the signing and ratification of a revised MST in 1960 are covered extensively elsewhere.[37] Of most concern here is the extent to which the new agreement made U.S. extended deterrence strategy more acceptable to Japan by allowing Tokyo a greater role in its implementation. The Kishi government was successful in attaining a "prior consultation" clause in the new version, whereby Japan would not only be informed, but its formal approval sought, before U.S. forces were redeployed from Japanese soil to Asia-Pacific conflict zones. The 1960 treaty also eased the way for the U.S. removal of nuclear weapons from the Japanese mainland and for the subsequent declaration of Japan's three "Non-Nuclear Principles" (1967).[38] Most importantly to Japan, the revised MST provided U.S. recognition of Japan's full sovereign status. In return, Washington was allowed to retain control of the Ryukyu Islands (including the right to deploy nuclear weapons there), and Japan incurred the obligation to build a Self-Defense Force adequate to successfully resist armed attack. The evolution of the SDF and of the overall U.S.-Japan defense relationship is briefly summarized in table 1.

South Korea and Taiwan

U.S. SECURITY accords reached with South Korea and Taiwan differ in that there initially was less willingness by these U.S. allies to share

TABLE 1. U.S.-Japan Security Relations (1951–1988): Milestones and Highlights

1951	Sept. 8	U.S.-Japan Security Treaty concluded
1952	Feb. 28	Japan-U.S. Administrative Agreement signed
	Apr. 28	Peace Treaty and Japan-U.S. MST Treaty takes effect
	Jul. 26	Japan-U.S. Facilities and Areas Agreement signed
1953	Jan. 1	U.S. Security Advisory Group in Japan inaugurated
	Oct. 30	Ikeda-Robertson talks; Joint Statement for Gradual Increase in Self-Defense Strength issued.
1954	Mar. 8	Mutual Defense Assistance Agreement signed
	May 14	Japan-U.S. Naval Vessel Loan Agreement signed
	Jul. 1	Japan Defense Agency established
1955	Aug. 31	Shigemitsu-Dulles meeting: Joint Statement Concerning Revision of MST issued.
	Nov. 14	Japan-U.S. Atomic Energy Agreement signed
1956	Jan. 30	Japan-U.S. Joint Statement for Reduction of Defense Expenditures issued
	Mar. 22	Japan-U.S. Technical Agreement Based on MDA signed
1957	Jun. 21	Kishi-Eisenhower talks; Joint Statement on the Early Withdrawal of U.S. Forces, Japan, issued
	Aug. 6	Japan-U.S. Security Council inaugurated
1958	Sept. 11	Fujiyama-Dulles Meeting (Washington); agreement reached on need to revise MST
	Oct. 4.	Treaty Revision negotiations commence
1960	Jan 19	Revised MST signed
1969	Apr. 4	U.S.-Japan Agreement on Japanese Domestic Production of F-4EJs signed
	Nov. 21	Nixon-Sato Joint Statement on Continuation of MST and Reversion of Okinawa to Japan
1971	June. 29	Kubo-Curtis Agreement on U.S. Force Presence in Okinawa signed
1972	May 15	Okinawa Returned to Japan
1973	Jan. 23	14th Japan-US Security Consultative Committee agrees on consolidation of U.S. Bases in Japan (Kanto Program)
1976	July. 8	Subcommittee on Japan-U.S. Defense Cooperation established

U.S.-Japan Security Relations (1951–1988): Milestones and
Highlights (continued)

1977	Dec. 28	National Defense Council decides on introduction of F-15s and P-3Cs in Japan
1978	Nov. 27	Japan-U.S. Security Consultative Committee approves "Guidelines for Japan-U.S. Defense Cooperation
1979	Jan. 11	Japanese Cabinet approves introduction of E-2C Early Warning Craft in Self Defense Force
	Sept. 29	U.S. F-15s introduced at Kadena Air Base
1980	Feb. 1	Announced in Diet that Japan would allow the U.S. to use Japanese bases for troop movement to crisis points in Middle East
	Feb. 26	Maritime Self-Defense Force participates in RIMPAC Naval Exercises for first time with U.S. and other Asia-Pacific allies
1981	May 8	Visiting Prime Minister Suzuki formalizes Sea Lane Defense Commitments with President Reagan; allows the term "Alliance" to be used in final communique, causing political upheaval in Japan
	Oct. 1	First U.S.-Japan combined communications training for land forces staged at Higashi-Fuji Maneuver Area
1982	Feb. 15	First U.S.-Japan Combined Command Post for land forces is staged at Takigahara
1983	Jan. 18	Prime Minister Nakasone visits U.S.; pledges upgraded Japanese maritime surveillance/air defense roles in Japanese archipelagoes
	Nov. 8	Exchange of notes on transfer of Japanese Military Arms Technology to U.S.
	Dec. 12	First U.S.-Japan Air Combined Command Post exercise staged at Fuchu
1985	Apr. 2	U.S. deploys F-16 jet fighters at Misawa Air Base
1986	Sept. 9	Chief Cabinet Secretary announces Japanese intent to participate in SDI research
	Oct. 27	First Japan-U.S. integrated military exercise staged
1987	Jan. 30	Agreement on Japanese labor cost for support of U.S. Forces; Japan signed
	Jul. 21	Intergovernmental; agreement on Japan SDI research participation signed

	Oct. 6	First COCOM-related session held in Japan
	Oct. 21	Japanese Government announces intent to purchase F-16 jet aircraft design for development of FS-X Aircraft to succeed indigenous Japanese F-1 jet fighter
1988	Nov. 29	FS-X Development Accord signed

Source: Defense Agency, Japan. *Defense of Japan*. Various annual editions.

in the task of strengthening Western deterrence capabilities in Northeast Asia. The leaderships in Seoul and Taipei were principally concerned that their own national securities were incidental to Washington's ultimate objectives of protecting Japan and coming to terms with the reality of a modern and powerful China under communist rule.

In October 1953, with an armistice reached in Korea, the United States signed a Mutual Defense Treaty with South Korea, formally incorporating the latter into its regional security network. From the outset of this relationship, however, South Korea's *national* imperatives and the U.S. *global* containment objectives embodied in the Dominant Player posture created tension between the signatories. The South Koreans rightfully and unhappily concluded that their country was integral to U.S. vital interests in the Pacific only as a regional buffer zone on behalf of Japan, the real strategic prize of Northeast Asia. It was evident to them that the American policy objectives in Korea were to reinforce U.S. strategic influence in Northeast Asia, as opposed to addressing specific Korean national security objectives, and to preserve a geopolitical buffer west of Japan which would complicate Soviet or Chinese military designs to neutralize Tokyo in any future regional crisis.[39]

The "qualified" character of the U.S. security commitment to Korea was soon manifested in a number of ways. The most important of these concerned Washington's insistence on formal jurisdiction over the mechanisms of escalation control in its Korean deterrence strategy. This included demanding a U.S. commander for the U.S. and South Korean Forces (a similar arrangement ended in Japan with the signing of the 1960 U.S.-Japan MST) and U.S. control over the size, composition, and duration of ground forces stationed in South Korea. Given this leverage, only the United States could determine the conditions for deterrence management and identify the territorial parameters within which both U.S. and South Korean forces could actively engage North Korean troops. Moreover, tactical nuclear weapons deployed on the peninsula would remain firmly under lock and key until such time as U.S.—not South Korean—political and military leaders decided that conditions warranted their use. The United States was determined to retain control of the limited war deterrence mechanisms operating in Korea to ensure that any future conventional conflict would remain limited in terms of intensity (below the nuclear threshold) and objectives (localizing the conflict to alleviate the risk of direct superpower confrontation). Washington was not about to allow a military government which had seized power in Seoul via a coup d' etat in 1961, rather than through more democratic processes, draw the United States into a strategic imbroglio which could present an American president with the same choices regarding escalation control which faced Eisenhower in early 1953. South Korean leader Syngman Rhee's previous insistence (in 1955) that the U.S. support a reunification of Korea "by any means," the departure of Chinese troops from North Korea in 1958, and continued strains between South Korea and Japan had already distanced the United States' global deterrence priorities from what the South Koreans deemed more immediate security imperatives.[40]

Unlike the Korean case, the United States entered into a formal mutual defense treaty with Taiwan *before* the outbreak of hostilities between Chinese Communist and Nationalist forces on the Dachen (Tachen) Islands in December 1954. Washington entered into the agreement, however, only after it obtained assurances that Chiang Kai-shek would undertake no military offensives against the Chinese mainland without U.S. approval, a pledge which the Americans were unable to extract from the South Koreans prior to the 1953 armistice. The Nationalist leader's concession to American military planners was significant, given that approximately 70,000 Nationalist troops habitually used Dachen, Quemoy, and the other offshore garrisons to conduct tactical raids against mainland Chinese targets. Under the Dominant Player posture, Taiwan's conventional military power was better restrained within the parameters of the American existential deterrent and subject to U.S. escalation control. If Taiwanese forces had been left under the absolute control of Chiang, still harboring ambitions for "liberating" the Chinese mainland through force if necessary, Washington could have been pulled into a protracted Asian ground war similar to that which proved so disastrous to the French in Indochina in 1954. The MST negotiated with Taiwan was as much about restraining one's ally as about deterring on its behalf.

As was the case in Korea, the success of U.S. deterrence strategy regarding Taiwan was mixed, with escalation control assured by the tactical superiority of the Nationalist air force over that fielded by the PRC and by the constant deployment of the American Seventh Fleet in the South China Sea throughout the 1950s and 1960s. Unlike in Korea, the U.S. deployed no onshore combat forces on Taiwan, because of their high vulnerability to Chinese air strikes during future crises and because of American concerns that deployment of U.S. ground forces would exacerbate relations between Washington and Beijing and preclude any chance for settlement of the "two Chinas" question. Furthermore, President Eisenhower and most of his military advisors were clearly disturbed over the high numbers of Chiang's forces deployed on the Nationalist-controlled offshore islands (by 1958, exceeding one hundred thousand troops or approximately one-third of the entire Nationalist army).[41] They feared that even a loss of indefensible islands could have a devastating "psychological effect" on the United States' other Asian allies. Accompanying these apprehensions were concerns that U.S. extended deterrence commitments to Chiang could become inextricably linked to the retention of the islands, thus "complicating" the problem of defending Taiwan itself. Eisenhower noted in his memoirs that, while the U.S. was bound to respond militarily to an outright Communist Chinese invasion of the Taiwanese mainland, a "lesser U.S. response" was justifiable if more distant Nationalist outposts were attacked. A minority of the President's military advisors, led by Admiral Arthur W. Radford, Chairman of the Joint Chiefs of Staff, were unsuccessful in convincing Eisenhower and Dulles to "adjust" U.S. national security policy toward allowing American naval and air intervention on Taiwan's behalf if "selected" island garrisons came under siege.[42]

While clearly understanding this U.S. policy dilemma, Chiang Kai-shek and his Nationalist colleagues nevertheless sought opportunities to compel Washington to reaffirm the credibility of U.S. deterrence guarantees. By the mid-1960s, U.S. military authorities considered revising the Dominant Player posture, in response to Chinese nuclear power, by "reducing American personnel and equipment in fixed positions near China and increasing capacity for rapid deployment by improved air-and sea-lift facilities."[43] Interalliance transferability was nonexistent in the South China Sea by this time, as well. Britain and France recognized Beijing, rather than Taipei, as the legitimate Chinese government, and the Europeans dissented from the rationale behind the U.S. military intervention against the Chinese-backed communist forces in Indochina.

ANZUS/Australia

FROM THE outset, some uncertainty has existed over interpretation of U.S./ANZUS security committees. It has been unclear at what point a threat would cause ANZUS guarantees to be applied. For example, Australian Prime Minister Percy Spender was concerned about the prospects of Japan remilitarizing and the security implications of a newly independent and intensely nationalist Indonesia.[44] The Korean War, while not completely removing such doubts, neutralized them to the extent that an American alliance was now regarded by both Antipodeon states as desirable for deterring an emerging communist threat. Remaining less certain was Australia's and/or New Zealand's expected contribution to the ANZUS deterrent.

In the early days of the cold war, American military planners tended to downplay the prospects of *any* Australian/New Zealand deterrence role in the Pacific."[45] Just before the first ANZUS Council meeting in the spring of 1952, the U.S. Joint Chiefs of Staff observed that the ANZUS agreement was designed to get some Australian and New Zealand troops into the Middle East "(t)he whole point of this has been to protect them in the Pacific in order that they could do something in the Middle East."[46] Dean Rusk, one of the key U.S. participants in the ANZUS Treaty negotiations, has since recalled that "in a real sense, the establishment of ANZUS was an effort to allay" Australian and New Zealand fears of a possible Japanese military rearmament.[47]

Throughout the cold war era, Australia structured its defense posture around what Australian Defense Minister Kim Beazley recently characterized as a "single level of threat . . . the overwhelming threat of international communism." In retrospect, Beazley opinioned, Strategic Basis Papers produced by successive Australian governments to justify that posture were "disastrously" misguided because they overrated Soviet and Chinese power projection capabilities and proposed misappropriation of Australian defense resources on arcane strategic commitments far from home.[48] At the outbreak of Malaysia's Confrontation or *Konfrontasi* with Indonesia in 1963, for example, Canberra had few assets to spare for helping to man a joint Commonwealth defense force. The Australians had just completed a twelve-year assistance effort in quashing Malaysia's communist insurgency movement (see chapter 5) and had redeployed force assets from Malaya to Thailand for participation in SEATO maneuvers. After two years of building up Australian force levels in Borneo and Sarawak through a national draft, Canberra nevertheless felt compelled to dispatch yet another battalion from an Australian army strained to its limits to supplement the American war effort in Vietnam. All of these force allocations could be traced to an Australian conviction that "these forward commitments were . . . so involving and ingratiating Australia with its great power ally that were Australia itself ever to come under direct threat, the United States' response would be assured."[49]

Throughout much of the 1950s and early 1960s, both Canberra and Wellington, as the junior ANZUS partners, rationalized their close ties to the U.S. Dominant Player posture as assuring Washington's security commitment to their own survival. This remained the case even though successive Antipodeon governments remained uneasy about the prospects of ANZUS becoming a direct appendage of U.S. global deterrence strategy at the expense of their own regional security priorities in Southeast Asia and in the South Pacific.

REFINING THE DOMINANT PLAYER POSTURE: MAINTAINING ESCALATION CONTROL

THROUGHOUT THE 1960s, with an inordinate proportion of U.S. theater force assets deployed in Vietnam, and into the 1970s with substantial reductions in U.S. military deployments as that conflict drew to a close, adjustments in the escalation control component of American extended deterrence strategy in the Asia-Pacific were inevitable. Foremost in the minds of Washington's allies was the extent to which the United States retained the ability to control future conflicts in either Northeast or Southeast Asia when tested by anti-Western forces. Japan became increasingly concerned over U.S. attempts to define more specifically under what conditions Washington would introduce nuclear weapons into a defense of that country—attempts which might disrupt the heretofore delicate calculus of existential deterrence. Consequently, Tokyo sought regular and comprehensive consultation mechanisms with the United States on questions of strategic doctrine. It sought a U.S. policy for the Asia-Pacific which would emphasize multifaceted approaches to regional stability, instead of those merely encompassing deterrence and defense.[50]

By contrast, the South Koreans continued to support an *overt* U.S. emphasis on military strategy for stabilizing the Korean peninsula. They were shocked when President Carter announced unilateral U.S. troop withdrawals from the ROK in 1977 and felt vindicated when Washington's assessments of a declining North Korean military threat proved to be misplaced and premature.[51] Taiwan was perhaps the most accommodating U.S. ally in the theater throughout the 1950s and 1960s, allowing U.S. forces there extraordinary leeway in what surveillance and interdictions missions they carried out in the East China Sea and providing logistical support for U.S. Air Force operations during the Vietnam War. It thus perceived itself as increasingly victimized when it became more expendable within the American regional deterrence framework as the Sino-Soviet rift intensified. As the U.S. increasingly weighed the advantages of strategically collaborating with Beijing to counter growing Soviet military power throughout the Asia-Pacific, earlier U.S. commitments and institutional support for Taiwan's survival against Chinese amphibious and air incursions became questionable. Speculation about Taiwan opting for an indigenous nuclear weapons capability or for an alliance with the Soviet Union as substitutes for the American deterrent proved unfounded.[52] However, the abrogation of the U.S.-Taiwan Mutual Defense Treaty only a few short years after the American military withdrawal from South Vietnam underscored for other U.S. regional treaty allies their need to review their own standing in U.S. global and regional deterrence strategy. After conducting such a reevaluation under a Labor government in the early 1970s, Australia revised its forward defense posture and moved to distance itself from Washington's global deterrence policies. This move was short-lived, however, as more conservative successor governments reaffirmed Australia's need for close affiliation and consultation with the Americans and allowed greater U.S. access to Australian bases and tracking installations.

Japan

A U.S. decision to deploy nuclear-capable rockets and artillery in Far Eastern positions in mid-1955 forced Japan to come to terms with the escalation control component of U.S. extended deterrence strategy. This issue had already been raised in NATO Europe, where six U.S. battalions of atomic cannon were in place. However, aside from the stockpiling of tactical nuclear weapons which occurred during the Korean War, the dispatch of nuclear-capable units to Okinawa and Japan was the first instance of permanent U.S. nuclear arms deployment to the Asia-Pacific theater (transit of nuclear-armed aircraft had already occurred at Guam). On July 29, the U.S. Army announced it was strengthening its "deterrent power" in the region by transferring the 633rd Field Artillery from Fort Bragg, South Carolina, to Okinawa and equipping it with the 280–millimeter atomic cannon. The Fifth Field Artillery Battery, equipped with the 762–millimeter *Honest John* rocket would be deployed at the U.S. Army facility at Camp Drake (near the Asaka air base) in Japan itself.

Imbued with a "nuclear allergy" resulting from the U.S. atomic attacks against Hiroshima and Nagasaki during World War II, the Japanese Diet, press, and much of the country's public opinion opposed the American deployment of nuclear weapons in the country. Foreign Minister Shigemitsu assured his countrymen that the *Honest Johns* would not be fitted with nuclear warheads except during the most serious regional crisis. It was admitted, however, that the Okinawa-stationed U.S. contingents would indeed be nuclear in composition. Moreover, the outgoing Commander of the U.S. Forces, Japan, interviewed by *Asahi Shimbun* in early August, claimed that in his discussions with Shigemitsu the issue of whether the *Honest John* would be installed with nuclear or conventional warheads "was not brought up" and that the United States therefore assumed that the deployment of nuclear warheads would not be a problem. After additional communications with the U.S. Department of Defense, the Hatoyama government announced that the U.S. would not place atomic warheads on the *Honest Johns* unless Tokyo approved such a move during a specific national or regional crisis.[53] In May 1958, the Joint Chiefs of Staff argued that, "overriding security reasons forbid any reduction" in U.S. control over the Ryukyu Islands, and that without the ability to introduce nuclear weapons into Japan proper, "the importance of Okinawa as a base for the IRBMs increased."[54]

Analysts of Japan's postwar security policy disagree about the extent to which that country has been comfortable with the U.S. extended nuclear deterrent and escalation control strategy for Northeast Asia. The 1960 revisions of the MST explicitly committed Washington to the defense of Japan against external attack. Subsequent U.S. defense posture statements were clear in linking or "coupling" Japan's conventional defense with the threat of a U.S. nuclear retaliatory strike if external aggression against Tokyo could not be neutralized with conventional forces alone. Tokyo has since acknowledged the utility of nuclear deterrence in preserving its own national security.[55] Japan has been comfortable with the American nuclear deterrent's offshore (sea and air based) identity, thus obviating the need to deploy U.S. nuclear weapons on Japanese territory. This gives Japan greater discretion in its deterrence relationship with Washington, as compared to South Korea, where American tactical nuclear weapons comprise the backbone of that security relationship's military strategy.

However, Japan has sought to reinforce its antinuclear diplomatic posture by espousing the so-called three nonnuclear principles (no production of, acquisition by, or introduction of, nuclear weapons into Japan). Japanese conservatives who had argued during the 1970s and early 1980s that their country should consider developing an independent nuclear capability are less influential as present Soviet military cutbacks have brought into greater question the utility of rationalizing "autonomous strategic national defense" as a viable Japanese policy option.[56] One American analyst has recently characterized the Japanese position as "a dual strategy of calling for nuclear disarmament and prohibiting the presence of nuclear weapons inside Japan, while acknowledging the utility of deterrence and security by an extended nuclear deterrent from the United States . . . The Japanese government purposely maintains public ambiguity between formal statements and underlying truth."[57]

To most of the Japanese leadership and electorate any formal revision of the "nonintroduction" clause giving the U.S. explicit rights to transit visits of nuclear capable warships and aircraft would undermine the existential deterrence that allows Japan to enjoy the best of both worlds: benefiting from U.S. extended deterrence in practice, while publicly appearing to align itself with the moral arguments of regional nuclear disarmament. Tokyo views the U.S. offshore nuclear presence in Northeast Asia as backing up the U.S. conventional forces that are deployed as a first line of defense against regional threats involving Japanese security. Successive Japanese governments have demonstrated little inclination to compromise such insurance by demanding greater U.S. accountability than the current American policy of "neither confirming nor denying" the deployment of nuclear weapons aboard its ships and planes docking or transiting in Japan, even as the United States assures Tokyo that it "respects" the Japanese nonnuclear principles. Nor do Japanese policy planners wish to specify how U.S. bases or communications and intelligence facilities directly tie into U.S. nuclear strategy in the Asia-Pacific region, because the ensuing debate could well undermine the delicate consensus on existential deterrence presently supported by the majority of the Japanese public.

This attitude cannot be dismissed, as some have argued, merely as a "puzzling attitude probably . . . caused by a lack of knowledge of the role of the strategic nuclear infrastructures planning for nuclear war."[58] Nor has it been seriously affected by intermittent revelations by retired U.S. Admiral Gene LaRocque, former Ambassador Edwin O. Reischauer, and others that U.S. warships entered Japanese ports with nuclear arms or that U.S. aircraft "lost" hydrogen bombs off the Japanese coast.[59] The contemporary Japanese approach to nuclear weapons instead reflects a sophisticated determination to preserve the *flexibility* and *operational viability* of the U.S. deterrent extended to Japan, within the political constraints generated by that country's nuclear allergy.

Japan's reliance upon U.S. escalation control capabilities as a legitimate and important aspect of its own security creates difficulties for over all alliance deterrence strategy. The strategic benefits which Japan has accrued from the U.S. nuclear umbrella, a growing number of defense observers argue, have not been matched by even a minimal Japanese effort to reciprocate through more visible support of—and participation in—U.S. deterrence strategy. They contend that Japan must openly discuss nuclear contingency planning with Washington. They envision a situation developing similar to that in South Korea, where the continued deployment of U.S. tactical nuclear weapons necessitates at least minimal coordination between U.S. and South Korean military planners. They conclude that Japan can no longer afford to cede nuclear strategy to the Americans by default, in the interest of maintaining a public image as a nation opposed to nuclear arms.[60]

South Korea

ESCALATION CONTROL has also been an issue in U.S.-South Korean defense relations but in different ways than in Japan. Ironclad U.S. control over American nuclear weapons deployed in South Korea has been justified as necessary to preclude miscalculation by either the North *or* South Koreans, which could lead to uncontrolled conflict escalation on the peninsula. Yet U.S. Secretary of Defense James Schlesinger appeared to depart from this cautious American stance in June 1975, speculating about the need for "nuclear first use" in response to what he viewed as overwhelming North Korean conventional force superiority.[61] A U.S. and South Korean consensus on how to respond to the North Korean military threat has been difficult to maintain at times because of the differences between American global and Korean local deterrence objectives. Schlesinger's observation may realistically have evolved, in part, from the fact that, with the withdrawal of Chinese forces, Korea had simply become less integral to the global balance of power from Washington's perspective and U.S. forces had, as a result, been reduced from over 200,000 in 1954 to under 60,000 in 1960. Consequent South Korean entreaties for the United States to strengthen deterrence against North Korea may have necessitated reiteration of the continued viability of the nuclear tripwire in South Korea in lieu of a conventional force buildup.

In early 1977, President Carter announced a decision to withdraw remaining U.S. ground combat forces (the 2d Division) from South Korea, over a four- to five-year period. He thus fulfilled a campaign pledge, which originated from his determination to exercise leverage against what he considered to be excessive South Korean human rights violations. After 1982, according to the withdrawal plan, the United States would retain around 12,000 personnel stationed south of Seoul, to support a modernized U.S. tactical fighter wing, a small naval element and an Army intelligence center. Following a July 26 Security Consultative meeting between Secretary of Defense Harold Brown and

Korean Defense Minister Suh Jyong Chul, Washington also agreed to deployments of additional fighter aircraft in South Korea and to upgrading American military assistance to Seoul.[62] The credibility of the U.S. deterrence commitment would no longer revolve around the land presence of the U.S. Second Division on South Korean territory. The Carter administration was prepared to implement an alternative deterrence structure in Korea which would include:

> (1) continual reaffirmation of the 1954 Mutual Defense Treaty; (2) statements stressing continuation of the U.S. "nuclear umbrella; (3) emphasis on the deterrent nature of the U.S. air wing; (4) statements pledging expanded joint military exercises with the ROK and stressing U.S. reinforcement capability; and (5) pledges to boost ROK military capabilities and thus provide deterrence through a strong ROK defense.[63]

The issue of removing U.S. tactical nuclear weapons deployment from South Korea was "to undergo further study," but those already deployed there would be left in position during the ground forces' withdrawal.[64]

The Carter administration's approach to the Dominant Player posture contrasted with South Korean perspectives, which were driven more by the calculations of regional deterrence. Just as the Nixon Administration believed that an emphasis on mobile reserve forces was the most politically appropriate and cost-effective means of fulfilling U.S. extra-European deterrence commitments in 1971, the Carter administration relegated the Korean trip wire to a secondary geopolitical status six years later. Under Secretary of State Philip C. Habib conferred with South Korean President Park Chung-hi in Seoul (May 1977) and returned to testify before the House Armed Services Committee that the United States required greater flexibility to meet its worldwide deterrence commitments. This was especially true in Europe, Habib contended, where recent improvements in Soviet military capabilities were thought to be the most threatening development to U.S. national security interests.[65] While relations between Japan and Korea were generally marked by tensions and mistrust, they closed ranks on this issue, arguing that the symbolic effect of a U.S. troop pullout from South Korea would be highly detrimental to Asia-Pacific stability.

By mid-1978, Congressional opposition to the withdrawal, along with visible moves by the Carter administration to enhance other aspects of South Korean deterrence, indicated that the initial pullout timetable was under reconsideration. Toward the end of the year, new intelligence data emerged showing that North Korea had more ground divisions and tanks than previously estimated and, by late July 1979, the withdrawal plan was suspended, pending a 1981 review. Soon after his election, President Reagan hosted South Korean President Chun Doo Hwan, taking the occasion to dispel publicly any further U.S. thoughts about withdrawing U.S. ground forces. With Reagan's election, the Dominant Player posture was reasserted on the Korean peninsula.

Recent discussion in the United States about force reductions in South Korea has been prompted by the increased cordiality of both Soviet and Chinese relations with the South (see chapter 4) and by what Washington perceives as Seoul's increased ability to defend South Korean territory with its own conventional forces. By 1987, Combined Forces Command (CFC) Commander-in-Chief General Louis Menetrey contended that, in view of increased South Korean military power, the likelihood of any situation developing in which nuclear weapons employment would be necessary was remote. Other retired American generals who had commanded U.S. forces in South Korea went so far as to advocate the complete withdrawal of nuclear weapons from the peninsula.[66] Most South Korean officials (except for leaders of some political opposition parties) remained largely unconvinced by such arguments and wary about the United States withdrawing *any* component of its force presence in their country.[67] Korean leaders and the majority of the Korean public remained visibly less enthusiastic about prospects for a Northeast Asian nuclear-free zone than various factions promoting this concept within the Japanese Socialist Party and the Japanese electorate-at-large. If South Koreans were to have cause to become even more uncertain over American willingness to preserve a nuclear trip wire on the peninsula, a wholesale reevaluation of Seoul's affiliation with the Dominant Player posture could soon follow.

Washington did make several important changes in its South Korean defense strategy in return for Seoul's understanding of and reluctant compliance with broader American strategic objectives. The Nixon-Sato communique accompanying the Okinawa reversion agreement, for example, contained an explicit and historic Japanese acknowledgment that South Korea's security was "essential to Japan's own security." This declaration strengthened local deterrence in South Korea's estimation by "lessen(ing), if not dissipat(ing), South Korean concern over

Japan's role in the defense of South Korea with respect to the use of American bases in Japan."[68] Escalation control could be managed more effectively in any Korean contingency if the full complement of U.S. military and logistical capabilities in Northeast Asia were available.

An even more important adjustment was made in 1973 when U.S. Forces, Korea, responded to a substantial force buildup of the North Korean Army and shifted from an "active" to a "forward" defense posture. U.S. and South Korean forces had previously relied upon American tactical nuclear weapons deployed in the South to offset superior North Korean conventional military strength. As the South Korean economy and political life increasingly evolved around Seoul, it became critical to prevent that city's takeover by North Korean forces if at all possible. Escalation control would be more difficult for the U.S. to implement, if, as it was now believed, North Korea planned to mount a blitzkrieg-style offensive, preclude the use of tactical nuclear weapons by emphasizing close-in fighting within heavily populated areas, and essentially settle hostilities in Pyongyang's favor prior to the arrival of U.S. reinforcements sent from well south of the capital.

Forward defense emphasized the application of decisive conventional firepower and mobility to stop the enemy's advancing echelons at the outset of war. Anti-tank systems, artillery, and air support—all using the latest weapons technologies to achieve maximum lethality and maneuverability—would be employed in ways designed to eliminate the necessity for escalation to higher levels of combat.[69] The shift to a forward defense posture also signaled that South Korean conventional military strength was becoming sufficiently formidable (with air power and industrial capacity compensating for military manpower deficiencies) that tactical nuclear weapons would only complicate rather than supplement the calculus of deterrence. Between 1975–1985, Korean military spending increased from $US 1.1 billion to $US4.9 billion per annum, a pace which enabled the ROK to become a major weapons manufacturer. By 1985, Seoul was coproducing its own advanced jet fighter aircraft (the F-5) and tactical unguided missiles (the *Honest John*). However, the United States reportedly upgraded its own extended deterrent in South Korea during 1986 by replacing its aging *Honest John* and *Sergeant* medium-range nuclear delivery systems with newer *Lance* missiles.[70]

South Korean force strength was gradually improved during the early 1980s to an extent where a forward defense posture was viewed as more attainable than in 1979, when the Carter administration's reevaluation of North Korean military power forced a halt to the scheduled U.S. pullout of ground forces from the peninsula. Even so, there is little question that the South Koreans still confront a formidable military threat across their border. In the years preceding Kim Il-sung's 1984 conference with Soviet leaders, North Korea built up a surprise attack capability which went beyond any pretense of maintaining a defensive posture. Between 1980–1984, Pyongyang increased its army's manpower strength by almost 100,000, doubled its number of tanks and added over 200 ships and some 200 aircraft to its force inventories.[71] Spending roughly 20 to 25 percent of its national budget on defense, its active army outnumbered South Korea's by close to 200,000 personnel (750,000 to 542,000); its navy dwarfed the South's inventory in numbers of submarines (21 to 3) and surface combatants (369 to 27, although South Korea deploys a number of destroyers and frigates which North Korea lacks); and its air force fields some 800 combat aircraft to 473 for the South (although the latter's planes constitute a more updated inventory).[72]

In the late 1970s and the 1980s, the South Koreans began expanding their own military modernization programs, especially under the Force Improvement Plan II program (1982–1987). The successful completion of such programs, combined with South Korea's growing GNP, was projected to go far in alleviating the conventional military imbalance on the peninsula by the mid-1990s. The North Korean quantitative edge in manpower and in land-based weapons systems density and its ability to launch an attack against the South with only one day warning is at least partially offset by South Korea's highly fortified defenses along narrow passes through which the bulk of any North Korean invasion force would have to pass. Meanwhile, South Korean air power, artillery, and battlefield missile systems are all qualitatively superior to anything in Pyongyang's force inventories. South Korea's two to one edge in population and vastly superior economy would also allow it to sustain a protracted war better than its North Korean rival.

By the mid-1990s, South Korea will deploy its own version of Japan's FS-X jetfighter, side-looking airborne radar, advanced indigenous intelligence-gathering systems and state-of-the art air-to-ground attack systems. The Korean "FX" will not be quite as sophisticated as its Japanese counterpart (because it involves joint manufacturing projects with U.S. firms based on existing aircraft designs rather than codeveloping an entire new generation of aircraft). The F-16 or F-18 offshoots produced, however, should be more than adequate to allow the South Korean air force to retain air superiority over the outmoded MiG-16s, MiG-17s, and SU-7's that still constitute the bulwark of a North Korean air force that only maintains a 30 percent readiness status.[73] Only the South Korean navy will remain inferior to North Korea's in terms of interdiction capabilities (North Korea deploys twenty *Romeo* and *Whiskey* attack submarines). The South Korean navy's ten-year plan, however, calls for the purchase of twelve to eighteen modern destroyers to spearhead an aggressive ASW and coastal patrol national defense mission.

The December 1988 South Korean Defense White Paper's estimate that only 65 percent of its overall deterrence capabilities would remain in the event of a U.S. force departure seems less credible if one evaluates the changing force balance on the peninsula and South Korea's own ability to project forward defense over the ensuing decade.[74] As noted in the Introduction, the U.S. Senate had passed a resolution in August 1989 directing President Bush to draw up a five year plan identifying options for a gradual reduction of U.S. military personnel in that country. Later that month, General Menetrey speculated that if present rates of South Korean economic growth continued, and if neither the USSR nor PRC substantially increased their military assistance to Pyongyang, there would be little need to keep U.S. troops on the peninsula past the mid-1990s. Menetrey qualified his assessments by emphasizing that some type of offshore U.S. deterrent would need to be maintained in the area to avoid a repeat of the miscalculations which fueled the Korean War.[75]

As intimated in the critique of Samuel Huntington's thinking offered in chapter 1, the United States and South Korea could both learn from the history of Asian warfare. A determined North Korean opponent backed by still substantial Soviet and/or Chinese political support and military assistance could disrupt Washington's calculations of forward defense—particularly if U.S. commitments to the survival of the present South Korean government are eroded by differences in trade or by the resentment of a younger Korean generation more intent on national reunification than on retaining American protection. Realizing this, both Moscow and Beijing are carefully calibrating their military assistance to Pyongyang. If U.S. policies were to become so ambiguous that Kim Il-sung or his successors were to question the credibility of the American extended deterrence commitment toward South Korea, both superpowers, China, and Japan would risk an unwanted renewal of hostilities on the peninsula—victims of a balkanized conflict with global ramifications beyond their control.

Despite the implementation of forward defense, differences in U.S. and South Korean threat perceptions and in the levels of their strategic concern could well hinder efforts by Washington and Seoul to sustain common deterrence policies. The United States remains concerned about prospects for North Korean aggression but feels it has to gauge extended deterrence strategy within a broader frame of reference. Medium-range U.S. strike aircraft deployed offshore, combined with precision-guided munition technologies (PGMs), give Washington improved escalation control options. The Reagan administration's replacement of older tactical nuclear-capable missiles with the *Lance* was also a symbolic display of the continued U.S. commitment to preserving its nuclear trip wire in the Korean peninsula. As these forces are presently configured, however, the precise relationship between the U.S. treaty commitment to South Korea and the need to deploy several hundred (estimated) American tactical nuclear weapons on that country's territory as a local component of that commitment remains unclear. Are these weapons to be applied psychologically against the North Koreans in the sense that their use is threatened in a massive retaliation strike against Pyongyang in the event it initiated new hostilities?[76] Or are they still viewed as insurance against the prospect of direct Soviet and/or Chinese military intervention on Pyongyang's behalf in a future Korean conflict?

If the latter calculation drives U.S. policy, then one must ask how the United States intends to maintain escalation control in such a contingency. Weapons more lethal and longer range than *Lance* missiles or atomic demolition munitions would be needed to interdict Soviet and/or Chinese force structures and supply lines.[77] Most importantly, do the South Koreans, becoming more prosperous and more intrigued by possibilities for eventual national unification, still regard the U.S. nuclear umbrella to be a legitimate instrument of support for their own national security interests? A series of editorials appeared in mainstream South Korean newspapers in early 1983 which, for the first time, publicly questioned the value of the U.S. nuclear guarantee: "we are seized with panic and uneasiness because of nuclear damage even if we win [a nuclear war in Korea]."[78]

Taiwan

CHINA'S ENTRY into the Korean War (November 1950) made a formal U.S.-Taiwan defense arrangement inevitable. Indeed, most of the mechanisms and institutions needed to support such an arrangement were already in place. In a highly publicized trip during July-August 1950, General MacArthur, in his capacity as Chief of U.S. Pacific Forces, concluded that such a step was critical to overall U.S. security in the region. By 1952, Congress had earmarked $US 300 million for military and economic assistance to the Chinese Nationalists under the Mutual Security Act. A U.S. Military Assistance Advisory Group (MAAG) was also in place, staffed by more than 700 U.S. military personnel stationed at eleven sites around Taiwan and on selected offshore islands. In December 1954, the Eisenhower administration concluded a Mutual Defense Treaty (MDT) with Taipei, obligating the United States to defend Taiwan and the Pescadores in return for a promise by Chiang Kai-shek not to launch a military invasion against the Chinese mainland except in cases of "emergency self-defense" and in consultation with the United States. The treaty also created a United States Taiwan Defense Command (separate from the MAAG) to assist Taipei in deterring a Communist Chinese attack and to facilitate U.S. Pacific Command operations. President Eisenhower subsequently received Congressional authorization in the form of the "Formosa Resolution" to take whatever further action he felt necessary to protect additional Nationalist-controlled offshore islands not directly covered by the MDT (most notably Jinmen [Quemoy] and Mazu (Matsu) from outside invasion—an authorization retained by successive U.S. presidents until 1970.[79]

While much has been written about how U.S. deterrence commitments to the ROC were tested during the Taiwan Straits crisis, less analysis exists on how U.S. forces used the MDT to link the East China Sea to the United States' overall extended deterrence strategy in the Asia-Pacific. Taiwan provided critical logistical support for both Seventh Fleet operations and American air power, especially during the years of U.S. military involvement in Vietnam. Just under 200 U.S. military personnel were assigned to the Taiwan Defense Command (TDC). They coordinated aerial reconnaissance missions from Taipei Air Station, devised contingency plans for Taiwan's defense, and, in conjunction with CINCPAC, directed the Formosa Straits Patrol in which elements of the Seventh Fleet regularly transited through the area. The 327th Air Division also manned a number of sensitive radar sites in Taiwan which linked that island's military communications systems with systems in the Philippines and other PACOM bases of operation. During the Vietnam War, its strength was increased from 3,700 to near 10,000 U.S. military personnel to support refueling operations for military transport aircraft. The Taiwanese government reportedly lengthened its runways at the Hsinchu and Ching Chuan Kung (CCK) air bases in anticipation of a U.S. request to use them for B-52 bombing operations conducted against targets in North Vietnam; however, Congressional oversight and the precedent of Philippine refusal to allow such operations to originate from its territory precluded any such development. Several U.S. jet fighter squadrons were dispatched to Taiwan, however, to assist in offshore surveillance and air defense operations (one such squadron was deployed in 1962, a second in 1965). Without the TDC infrastructure, U.S. military officials estimated Taiwan could not hold out against a full-fledged PRC invasion for more than two or three weeks.[80]

The Military Assistance Advisory Group operated separately from the TDC and was primarily responsible for the training of Taiwanese military personnel. Throughout the 1950s and 1960s, over $US 2.5 billion in U.S. military assistance to the island nation passed through MAAG hands.[81] As one observer has noted, such aid: "enabled the Nationalist Armed Forces on Taiwan to transform themselves into an efficient fighting force . . . judged to be one of the best trained and equipped forces in Asia."[82] Taiwan's qualitative advantages in military equipment over the PRC later led a number of officials in the Carter administration to conclude that modest levels of continued U.S. military assistance under the Taiwan Relations Act would be sufficient to offset Beijing's huge quantitative edge over the Nationalists in the East China Sea's balance of power.

Australia and ANZUS

BY THE mid-1960s, U.S. defense relations with Australia were becoming more intricately tied with U.S. global deterrence strategy. U.S. naval intelligence and tracking operations began at the Harold E. Holt communications station on Australia's North West Cape in 1968 and were subsequently incorporated into the U.S. National Security Agency's Defense Satellite Communications System (DSCS).[83] Various U.S. intelligence agencies began monitoring Soviet missile testing in the Pacific from Pine Gap near Alice Springs the same year. In 1971, the U.S. Air Force began operating at the Nurrungar base, some 300 miles northeast of Adelaide. U.S. early warning satellite monitoring at Nurrungar, as well as satellite reconnaissance carried out at Pine Gap, were soon to become critical to U.S. strategic planning and operations.[84] Australia and New Zealand became key transit points for American nuclear-capable air and naval units over the years. This was a significant turn of events considering Washington's reluctance to involve its ANZUS partners in *any* form of Pacific defense planning during the early days of the cold war.

With the election in 1972 of the first Australian Labor government in over two decades, the American extended deterrent came under increased Antipodeon scrutiny. Australian Labor Prime Minister Gough Whitlam directed that U.S. intelligence operations carried out at Australian installations be reassessed in terms of how they might compromise Australian sovereignty. At the regional level, the new Prime Minister became an active lobbyist for general disarmament in the Indian Ocean, at a time when the Soviet navy was increasing its deployments there to fill the power vacuum left by the British pullout "East of Suez" (1967–1971).[85] The Whitlam Government also moved toward reversing Australia's long-standing forward defense posture in Southeast Asia. It argued that the liklihood of a resurgent Japanese or expansionist Chinese military threat had receded and that the Nixon Doctrine had all but acknowledged this reality. This position, of course, contradicted growing ASEAN concerns about the growth of Chinese military power and about the implications of greater Japanese defense burden-sharing. Internationally, however, the Australian Strategic Basis Paper released by the Whitlam government in late 1975 chided New Zealand for pressing the South Pacific nuclear free zone (NFZ) concept too far, given the realities of the international security environment, and the Antipodes' continued dependence on Washington for military intelligence, assistance, and related support. The vaguely worded NFZ proposal, sponsored by the members of the South Pacific Forum (including a reluctant Australia), was adopted by the General Assembly 110 to 0, with 20 abstentions (including the U.S., the USSR, Britain, and France.) The initiative died quietly when conservative governments assumed power in Canberra and Wellington during 1975.[86]

With the return of the conservatives, ANZUS relations reverted to more familiar patterns of Antipodeon collaboration with U.S. extended deterrence strategy. Australian Prime Minister Malcolm Fraser and his New Zealand counterpart, Robert Muldoon, called for an "ANZUS Doctrine" to deter the growing Soviet commercial presence in the South Pacific from turning into a politico-strategic presence. The Ford administration moved to strengthen existing ANZUS maritime and surveillance (ANZUS MARSAR) arrangements and to incorporate a more extensive New Zealand naval role into such activities.[87]

Even while pressing for upgraded U.S. security cooperation in the South Pacific, Canberra and Wellington remained wary of becoming too openly affiliated with Washington's global strategic planning. Australia quickly declined an American request to contribute manpower to future rapid deployment force operations in the Persian Gulf. While both Australia and New Zealand continued to assume marginal defense responsibility for those Indian Ocean littorals most contiguous to the Australian west coast and to the Malayan peninsula (American B-52 surveillance aircraft were allowed to refuel at Darwin on their way from Guam to Diego Garcia, for example), both ANZUS allies went to some length to designate the Southwest Pacific as their primary regional defense priority for the 1980s and beyond.[88]

EXTENDED DETERRENCE COMMITMENTS:
PROBLEMS OF DEFINITION
AND MANAGEMENT

U.S. THREAT perceptions and strategic objectives underwent rapid change in the 1970s, significantly affecting the scope and operational aspects of the Dominant Player posture in Northeast Asia. Following the pullout of U.S. forces from Vietnam, the United States was determined to avoid further ground wars in Asia. This translated into a March 1970 National Security Decision Memorandum (NSDM) calling for the reduction of American troop levels in South Korea and envisioning greater overall levels of allied defense burden-sharing below the nuclear threshold. The NSDM concluded that if the U.S. were to extract the anticipated political and economic benefits from the Vietnam withdrawal, Washington's Asian friends would have to endorse, in principle, the Nixon Doctrine's emphasis on greater allied strategic self-reliance.[89]

From the perspective of Washington's Northeast Asia allies, however, such reasoning constituted a potential basis for an erosion of U.S. will to sustain the credibility of its traditional extended deterrence commitments in their region. For Taiwan, the logic of Nixon's strategy was even more portentous. If U.S. military power receded throughout the Asia-Pacific theater while Soviet force strength continued to grow in the region, Washington's incentive for reaching a strategic modus vivendi with Beijing would likely intensify. The abrogation of the U.S.-Taiwan Mutual Defense Treaty by Nixon's successor in 1979 confirmed the Nationalist Chinese regime's worst fears.

Australia also entered the 1980s harboring increased suspicions about its own strategic relevance to the U.S. following a decade of superpower preoccupation with arms control and with regions other than the Southwest Pacific (e.g., the Middle East). Consequently, American extended deterrence strategy was again challenged with the election of another Australian Labor government in March 1983. Foreign Minister Bill Hayden announced that Canberra would conduct a review of Australian policies toward ANZUS. While serving notice that Australia would henceforth consider itself a more mature and independent ally, the defense review produced no real change in the Australian security relationship with Washington. U.S. and allied nuclear-capable/nuclear-powered ships were still allowed access to Australian ports and airfields on an NCND basis.[90] Canberra qualified this endorsement, however, with a stated desire for developing greater self-reliance against potential noncommunist threats to its immediate north, in the South Pacific, and in the Eastern Indian Ocean approaches to its own shores. Robert O'Neill summarized implications of the new Australian orientation: "there will probably not be the same old global security arguments [advanced by Australian governments] to keep the U.S. as actively committed to the region as previously."[91]

Japanese "Angst"

DURING THE Nixon administration, the U.S. finally consented to a reversion of Okinawa to Japanese control. This action, along with the

removal of U.S. nuclear weapons from that island at Japan's request in
the early 1970s, accompanied Tokyo's growing unease about possible
discontinuity of U.S. strategic commitments. The Nixon Doctrine's
shifting of U.S. strategy from a two-and-a-half war to a one-and-a-half
war commitment and the plans for withdrawal of the U.S. 7th Division
from South Korea signified a more qualified American extended deterrent. Questions about the continued credibility of U.S. escalation control options were raised by both Japanese and American defense analysts. Writing in 1973, for example, Masataka Kosaka speculated that
"a real danger will be the possibility of Japan placing too little trust in
the Japan-U.S. Security Treaty, in contrast to the excessive trust she
had before . . . one can logically deduce such a possibility from the
'Nixon Doctrine.' "[92]

A more sanguine view of Japanese attitudes at this time is that
Tokyo believed the credibility of the U.S. nuclear umbrella extended
toward Japan was still intact, despite the removal of U.S. nuclear
weapons from Okinawa. Proponents of the Dominant Player posture
argued that what counted most was the beliefs of those who were to be
deterred (the USSR and China), even if U.S. or Japanese leaders
harbored doubts about extended deterrence strategy. Moscow and
Beijing already had proven themselves unwilling to test the United
States' escalation control strategy and U.S. conventional and nuclear
superiority in the region sustained the Dominant Player strategy's
credibility of commitment. A land-based nuclear trip wire, such as that
in place throughout NATO Europe and in South Korea, was thought
to be unnecessary for deterring an attack on Japan because the U.S.
Pacific Command retained sufficient offshore nuclear retaliatory capability (aircraft carriers, nuclear ballistic missile submarines, etc.) to
make the prospect of even a limited U.S. nuclear response unthinkable
to Soviet and Chinese leaders.[93]

Throughout the late 1970s and early 1980s, however, Japan grew
uneasy about changing U.S. strategic doctrine and behavior. In spite
of the importance of its ambiguity, the nature of the U.S. deterrence
commitment appeared to be compromised. The U.S. "swing strategy,"
publicly revealed in 1979, was a major concern to Japan, because it
threatened to remove significant elements of U.S. offshore nuclear and
conventional power from the Asia-Pacific if conflicts erupted in Europe
or the Middle East. The Maritime Strategy/horizontal escalation variants of the Dominant Player posture were also of concern. The Mari-

FIGURE 3. U.S. Extended Nuclear Deterrence

DIFFERENCES BETWEEN

NATO	Japan
—Relies on the threat of nuclear use for deterrence of all conflict	—Relies on conventional strength first to defend Japan
—Soviet land-based theater nuclear forces met with comparable U.S. theater nuclear forces	—Soviet land-based theater nuclear forces met with no comparable system; continuation of sea and air-based systems
—British. French independent nuclear forces	—No independent Japanese nuclear force
—Land-based systems in Europe invoke a fear of escalation from conventional to nuclear war	—Since conventional balance favors the United States and Japan, no need for theater options inside Japan to threaten nuclear war in response to conventional attack
—NATO members involved in Nuclear Planning Group	—Japan *not* involved in high level planning or operational guidelines planning; passive reliance on U.S. nuclear strategy
—NATO members pick at credibility issue	—Japan does not pick at or question openly the U.S. guarantee

DETERRENCE BASED ON

NATO	Japan
—NATO Treaty, cohesion of alliance	—Bilateral security treaty, closeness of bilateral security relationship
—U.S. central strategic systems, presence of U.S. nuclear forces in Europe	—U.S. central strategic systems, presence of U.S. nuclear forces around Japan
—British and French nuclear forces	
—Existential fear of nuclear war based on flexible response	—Existential fear of nuclear war based on flexible response
—Defense of Europe integral to defense of U.S. forward strategy	—Defense of Japan integral to defense of U.S. forward strategy
—Political-economic-cultural affinity and interdependence	—Political-economic-(cultural?) affinity and interdependence
—Integrated force structure	—Coordinate force structure

James R. Van de Velde, "Japan's Nuclear Umbrella: U.S. Extended Deterrence for Japan," *Journal of Northeast Asian Studies* (1988) 7(4): 32.

time Strategy would require Japanese support of American *offensive* operations against Soviet targets at the outset of war, testing the concept of "self defense" to its very limits. Horizontal escalation could involve Tokyo indirectly in future Middle Eastern or European conflicts by widening the scope of conflicts beyond their points of origin and into Northeast Asia. James Nathan has recently summarized the implications: "In the end, the attempt to implicate allies in a vast maritime coalition may find the allies demurring, arguing that the Maritime Strategy is peripheral to their central interests. The Maritime Strategy is dominated by the logic of global coalition war. The larger interest of the strategy is to 'prevail' over the Soviets in a conventional war. Such a grand purpose, almost of necessity, overrides the immediate interests of regional allies." [94]

Such revisions in the U.S. posture, even if only temporary, threatened to undermine Japan's traditional preference for a U.S. global and regional deterrence posture within which it could maneuver between accepting Washington's nuclear protection and simultaneously exercising a low strategic profile in its own immediate vicinity. Moreover, incorporation of Japan more directly into U.S. global strategy planning would highlight Tokyo's political vulnerability to Washington's adjustments in light of political and strategic change occurring beyond Northeast Asia. Indeed, almost a decade after horizontal escalation had been introduced and quickly retracted as a U.S. strategy and thirty years after the 1960 MST revisions, the Japanese Foreign Ministry was reportedly drawing up a study (in June 1990) of how Japan's security ties would shift in response to the declining Soviet military threat in Europe and the promise of similar modifications of the Asia-Pacific threat environment. [95]

Besides generating tension between Washington and Tokyo over what should be Japan's role in bolstering Western deterrence against Soviet power in Northeast Asia, recent U.S. military planning has created more specific tests of Japanese confidence in the credibility of U.S. deterrence commitments. Japanese press reports have noted, for example, that if American estimates are correct in asserting that Hokkaido currently cannot be defended by Japan's Ground Self Defense Force (GSDF), the conversion of the U.S. Army's 25th Division from an ordinary to light infantry division certainly does not help rectify the situation. Stationed in Hawaii, this unit is intended to reinforce U.S. and GSDF troops in the event of a Japanese "national emergency." A number of U.S. military planners envision a lighter and more flexible U.S. attack force, supported by naval surface units controlling adjacent sea lanes, transporting troops, and supplying tactical air cover for U.S. reinforcement.[96] While the commander of U.S. Army forces stationed in Japan has argued that a light infantry division will speed up the deployment of U.S. reinforcements to Japan (the 25th Division could be airlifted from Hawaii to Hokkaido in two days), heavy equipment such as howitzers and tanks would have to be transported from the U.S. West Coast via some 500 air sorties over 10 days.[97] The 25th's reconfiguration to light division status means that, while the reinforcement process could take place more rapidly, much less U.S. conventional firepower is initially deployable to back up the Japanese in defense of their northern perimeters.

Japanese concerns are valid. Aside from the obvious risks the proposed reinforcement strategy entails in confronting Soviet interdiction capabilities throughout the wider Pacific, U.S. defense officials have admitted in recent (September 1988) Congressional hearings that U.S. forward deployments of U.S. ground forces are far preferable to mobile reinforcements for implementing escalation control strategy. Maximum U.S. and allied force assets, they argue, need to be applied to combat at the outset of a war.[98]

The deployment of U.S. F-16 jet fighter squadrons at Misawa air base in Northern Honshu (one air wing was introduced in 1985 and two additional fighter squadrons composed of 50 additional such aircraft were added in 1987) at least partially compensates for the designation of less U.S. manpower in the first days of a Hokkaido defense. These aircraft have enough range, with midair refueling, to attack Soviet military installations in southern Sakhalin and Siberia.[99]

By 1987, Japanese pessimism about U.S. intentions had become clearly apparent. Only 43.1 percent of those Japanese surveyed in a United States Information Agency poll that year believed that Washington was willing to risk a nuclear war on Japan's behalf. As many as 47 percent expressed little confidence in the American nuclear commitment to Japanese security, and only 13.4 percent believed U.S. extended deterrence guarantees applied if the risk of a retaliatory attack against U.S. territory was high.[100] In releasing its 1988 Defense White Paper, the Japan Defense Agency urged Washington to retain its deterrence commitments to Japan, in spite of perestroika, based upon what it regarded as a continued Soviet military buildup in the Far

Eastern theater (see chapter 3).[101] Clearly the USSR's increased capability to threaten U.S. interests in Northeast Asia had intensified the Japanese public's concern that the U.S. Dominant Player posture could no longer be relied upon to face down the Soviets.

Given both Northeast Asia's changing military balance in the face of greater nuclear parity between the superpowers and declining Japanese confidence in the credibility of the U.S. nuclear umbrella, the issue of greater Japanese defense burden-sharing is seen as an increasingly appealing corrective option by the Dominant Player. From Japan's perspective, however, significant increases in Japanese defense capabilities through the development of a sophisticated conventional weapons inventory within Japan's Self Defense Force (SDF), would primarily exacerbate regional tensions.[102] A major Japanese rearmament, in the absence of a sufficient U.S. force presence to sustain the American deterrent, could intensify the risk which long-term Japanese restraint on defense spending and military deployments had been designed to avoid.

The most extreme Japanese response to a lack of faith in the American extended deterrent would be the deployment of an indigenous nuclear force. However, there has been little doubt about Japan's revulsion to this idea. While not specifically prohibited by Article 9 of its constitution from deploying such a force as a means of self-defense, the political liability of the nuclear image still rules in Japan. This is especially the case given that country's limited land space and high vulnerability to nuclear attack. The declaration of Japan's three non-nuclear principles by the Sato government in 1967 has remained a symbolic cornerstone of Japanese national security policy, despite overwhelming evidence that U.S. naval vessels and aircraft have been allowed to transit nuclear arms through Japanese ports and airspace (see chapter 6).

Strategic Uncertainties for Seoul

A DECADE after the United States' last major withdrawal of forces from the peninsula, Korea's place in U.S. global defense priorities and commitments has again become a source of increased concern to South Korea. Anti-American sentiment has grown within South Korea's younger generation which has little memory or objective frame of reference about the U.S. role in the Korean War. It instead points to the Bush administration's pressure on the government of Roh Tae

Woo (which assumed leadership of the country in February 1988) for substantial concessions in reevaluating the Korean won, for the opening of Korean domestic markets to U.S. goods and for liberalizing other sectors of trade and investment. If there is any one element which binds concerned U.S.analysts and South Korean opposition groups it is the belief that "American attitudes, behavior, and policy have not kept pace with the growth of South Korea's power . . . [or its] . . . new sense of self-importance." [103]

Controversy has been generated as South Korea has agreed to take on a larger share of the alliance defense burden. It expends approximately $US 2 billion annually in total support funds for the maintenance of U.S. forces in South Korea (compared to U.S. expenditures of about $US 3 billion annually). [104] In late October 1989, Seoul announced the purchase of 120 new F-16/F-18s, more than half of these to be produced by Korean companies which would have learned the techniques of assembly. U.S. opponents of the deal, contended that it allowed for an unwarranted transfer of U.S. aerospace technology to an increasingly ungrateful ally that could offer the U.S. little in return. They also disagreed with Washington consenting to import enough South Korean goods to offset 30 percent of the aircraft's total value during a time when the United States maintains a $US 10 billion dollar trade deficit with the ROK. Clyde V. Prestowitz' biting criticism typified the opponents' feelings regarding U.S. policy behavior:

> Imagine, here is a country that owes its existence and current prosperity almost entirely to the United States. In an address to Congress, South Korea's president . . . urged the legislators not to reduce U.S. troop levels in his country under any circumstance, because that would invite attack. Nevertheless the next day his minions told U.S. officials that Korea can always buy planes elsewhere if we don't want to accept Korean terms . . . why can't U.S. officials simply point out that if South Korea can find other places to buy airplanes, the United States can find other places to keep troops? [105]

With the current U.S. force configuration, it is likely that any Northern attack would prompt a massive U.S.-South Korean retaliation with air, sea, and possible nuclear strikes against North Korean positions. If the defense of the ROK had to be entirely based upon conventional forces, and be increasingly reliant on Japanese cooperation, it is doubtful that most Koreans would welcome any Japanese surrogate guarantees for traditional U.S. extended deterrence commitments to their country. Japan's aversion to any form of nuclear escalation, especially any that might involve its own forces, could lead to a very different and qualified form of defense commitment for Seoul.

Thus, South Korea currently has few security alternatives to maintaining close defense relations with the U.S. Although it seems resigned to gradually assuming a larger share of defense burden-sharing costs within that alliance, ongoing political and economic change in the ROK are undoubtedly straining the patience of both sides. Accordingly, recent pressure for Washington to remove South Korean armed forces from U.S. operational control, along with Seoul's obvious resentment of U.S. requests to assume a greater share of the expenses of keeping American forces in the peninsula, could lead to a breakdown of alliance relations over the issue of sovereignty, with obviously detrimental long-term ramifications for South Korean security.

Despite such concerns, U.S. defense officials testified before Congress in May 1988 that the United States had decided to transfer the operational command of Korean forces to Seoul sometime during the early 1990s. The U.S. has also agreed to redeploy its remaining ground forces away from Seoul to establish a "lower American military profile" in South Korea.[106] South Korean President Roh Tae Woo initially resisted both U.S. Congressional efforts to reduce U.S. forces in South Korea by 10,000 troops (out of a remaining total of approximately 43,000 ground forces) between 1989 and 1992 and U.S. Defense Department proposals to transform the U.S.-ROK Combined Forces Command structure. He has argued that "with the persistence of the military threat from North Korea, this is no time to discuss . . . a change."[107] Roh, and officials in the Bush administration resisting such cuts also maintained that North Korea had not modified its bellicosity toward the South to the point where American troop withdrawals were merited. South Korean leaders further insisted that until U.S. force reductions could be linked to meaningful North Korean initiatives toward peaceful reunification, reductions in U.S. force levels would be highly destabilizing. Nor, they argued, were the Soviet Union or China, preoccupied with their own domestic political turmoil, in a position to restrain Kim Il-sung. North Korean acquiescence to the Soviet use of its air space for military overflights, the transfer of late model Soviet jet fighter aircraft (including MiG-29s), and the recent emplacement of SAM-5 antiaircraft missiles that could seriously threaten air operations over most of South Korea were also cited as ongoing evidence of a continued, serious North Korean military threat (see chapter 3).[108]

Supporters of American troop reductions countered that South Korea's economy combined with a reduced North Korean threat justify a more self-sufficient South Korean deterrent. Two key U.S. Senators advocating U.S. force cuts in South Korea, J. Bennett Johnston and Dale Bumpers, argued that maintaining 43,000 American troops in that country amounted to $US 2.6 billion each year, creating "permanent and costly expectations" from Seoul that Washington would be willing to sustain such force levels and costs. With a multibillion dollar annual trade deficit, with a South Korean GNP seven times that of the North, and with increased anti-Americanism among South Korean opposition groups ("our troops are there to defend, not to irritate"), Johnston and Bumpers concluded, the United States had no other rational choice than to ask Seoul to pick up a greater share of the defense burden in Northeast Asia.[109] Other critics point to Seoul's intensified economic ties with Moscow and Beijing (including a June 1989 visit to Moscow by Korean opposition party leader Kim Young Sam). They also cite the need for U.S. Forces Korea (USFK) command to improve its "tooth-to-tail ratio"—the number of front-line personnel to support troops and for South Korea to become more self-sufficient in developing the military competency of its indigenous armed forces to confront external threats as opposed to concentrating on internal policing functions.[110]

A shift in both the American and South Korean positions, was revealed in late January 1990 when U.S. Secretary of Defense Richard Cheney released plans for overseas basing cutbacks as part of the FY 1991 federal budget. He informed the South Korean government that U.S. Air Force operations would be closing down at three installations in the ROK (at the Kwangju, Suwon, and Taegu Air Bases), involving the withdrawal of 18 U.S. RF-4C reconnaissance aircraft and 2,000 noncombatant support personnel. He also intimated that the Bush administration's forthcoming East Asian Strategic Initiative (EASI) would be calling for the withdrawal of an additional 5,000 to 6,000 ground troops, reducing the number of U.S. combat forces in the ROK from 43,000 to 37,000. South Korean diplomats leaked impressions of "uneasiness mixed with shock" to Western press representatives over the U.S. decision. The South Korean government, along with Japan, argued to Cheney and other U.S. defense officials that, despite the monumental political changes developing in Eastern Europe, no commensurate reduction of the Soviet threat in Northeast Asia had yet materialized. They concluded that any U.S. force reductions must not compromise "the basic element of deterrent defense [which] remains in Korea." [111]

What could moderate North Korea's willingness to confront the South, over time, are Pyongyang's continued dependence on the USSR as its major weapons supplier and the growing perception by all parties involved that South Korea's booming economy will be able to produce more technologically impressive and more reliable weapons systems than North Korea can obtain from Moscow or Beijing. The Soviets have been supplying the DPRK with advanced Soviet aircraft and surface-to-air missiles to complement Pyongyang's impressive naval amphibious capabilities (see chapter 3). To counterbalance such transfers, South Korean F-16s (and its planned follow-on procurement of a Korean FS-X aircraft), 155 mm. self-propelled howitzers and Seoul's increasingly impressive military production capabilities (producing three-quarters of its military equipment domestically, including the highly regarded T-88 tank) combine with its manpower, air support, and overall firepower superiority to give the South Koreans a better chance of indigenously defending their territory than at any time in the post-war era. However, before accepting the optimistic premise that the strategic momentum on the peninsula rests completely with the South, the distinction between "sufficient deterrence" and an "indigenous military balance" should be weighed carefully by American and South Korean military planners and electorates: "there is a significant difference between sufficient deterrence and an indigenous military balance between North Korea and South Korea. The former is the sum total of factors that dissuade North Korea from launching an invasion. The latter is a calculation in military terms of the ability of South Korea on its own to defeat an invasion. The indigenous military balance may be a part of the deterrence equation, but it is only a part and probably not the decisive part." [112]

The key considerations in implementing any phased reduction of U.S. forces on the peninsula are timing and perception. A well-tailored public information effort will need to be undertaken by both Washington and Seoul, explicitly designating what components of local deterrence South Korean forces can reasonably assume on their own, and in conjunction with remaining U.S. land support elements and American offshore power (an example of the latter is South Korea's scheduled participation in the 1990 "Rim of the Pacific" or RIMPAC naval exercises with U.S., Japanese, British, Canadian, and Australian naval units). Preferably, U.S. force reductions should be timed to serve as bargaining chips in arms control negotiations with the North, which may be prompted by its Soviet and Chinese backers in the interest of stabilizing the peninsula at a time when their own internal political situations demand greater attention. At a minimum, U.S. force reductions should be implemented only when U.S. and South Korean intelligence are able to confirm that such cutbacks will not adversely effect the peninsula's balance of power or spur Pyongyang to intensify its own arms buildup to create an imbalance. It is not in the interest of either the Korean and U.S. governments to risk the type of strategic miscalculations which could evolve from repeating the Carter administration's experience of underestimating the threat of conflict in this area of the world. Careful joint planning by the American and South Korean political and military leaderships, producing a consensus on the timing and nature of adjustments in the Dominant Player deterrence posture, can significantly decrease the probability of such miscalculations.

U.S. Extended Deterrence and the "China Card"

A CENTRAL premise behind the Nixon Doctrine's replacement of the two-and-a-half conventional war strategy with a one-and-a-half war commitment was, as the President noted in early 1970, that "the prospects for a coordinated two-front attack on our allies by Russia [in NATO Europe] and China [in East Asia] are low because of the risks of nuclear war and the improbability of Sino-Soviet cooperation." [113] By this time, U.S. extended deterrence strategy reflected Washington's growing belief that the Sino-Soviet rift significantly reduced the Chinese threat to pro-Western East Asian and Southeast Asian states. Increasingly, Washington's policymakers had come to believe that China shared a common interest in pinning down Soviet forces on the Eurasian land mass and could eventually become a strategic counterweight to Soviet military power throughout the region—in lieu of greater U.S. force deployments.

The appeal of Sino-American military cooperation intensified in Washington during the mid-1970s and early 1980s as the Soviets continued to strengthen their central strategic forces and to project a greater military presence into Southeast Asia and more distant third world regions. Several government or quasi-official studies prepared by the Department of Defense, the RAND Corporation and other institutions during the late Ford and early Carter administrations argued that closer Sino-American security ties would provide concrete advantages.[114] These advantages were outlined in fairly specific fashion:

1. Increased Chinese military capabilities deployed in defensive positions along the Sino-Soviet border could tie down large percentages of Soviet ground, naval, and air forces, thereby reducing the Soviet threat to NATO, Japan, and South Korea.

2. U.S. military technology transfers and arms sales to the PRC would create a dependency by the Chinese military establishment on Western sources of supply. Consequently, if deterrence failed, resulting in an Asia-Pacific conflict, China's defense establishment would pressure the country's leadership to align itself with the West.

3. Limited intelligence exchanges, military exercises, and other forms of Sino-American military cooperation during peacetime would help deter a Soviet preemptive strike against the PRC, stabilizing the Asia-Pacific theater. Such cooperation represented a "cost-effective" alternative to the U.S. sustaining a two-and-a-half war strategy.

Overall, these studies emphasized, the U.S. needed to strike a delicate balance in order to build up China as a surrogate for U.S. deterrence objectives in the Asia-Pacific. On the one hand, U.S. security assistance to Beijing must be effective to the point of truly enhancing Chinese defensive capabilities. On the other, it must not be so extensive as to unduly alarm Moscow or U.S. Asia-Pacific allies within China's strategic reach. When the United States adjusted its traditional postwar containment policies in favor of moving toward detente with Moscow, the vision of a more pro-Western China gradually became perceived to be an integral part of that reorientation, especially after the death of Mao Zedong and the Gang of Four's political downfall in 1976. Yet, as Lucian Pye warned U.S. policymakers at the time, to play such a China card would constitute "an extraordinary act of

[American] faith . . . that 'modernization' and exposure to the outside world [would] quickly 'mellow' the Chinese regime, strengthen [its] 'democratic' cravings, and generally turn China's heart away from its Marxist-Leninist convictions." [115]

The dilemma of how far to play the China card was essentially left unresolved and become even more intractable following the unfolding of events in Tienanmen Square during June 1989. In strategic terms, Sino-American ties have experienced considerable strain as Soviet military capability in the Asia-Pacific becomes less important, as China's international arms sales grow, and as the U.S. Congress steps up its pressure against the Bush administration to impose additional sanctions against Beijing. Recent efforts by the president to keep Washington's lines of communication open to the PRC (such as dispatching his national security advisor to the Chinese capital during July and December 1989) appeared to many as cynically placing U.S. geopolitical interests above the promotion of democracy and human rights.

Scrapping the Taiwan MST

NOTWITHSTANDING THEIR continued difficulties in identifying and shaping the parameters of Sino-American ties, U.S. policy planners elected to pursue the China card. In December 1978, President Carter announced the decision to end formal U.S. diplomatic and military ties with Taiwan in favor of normalizing relations with the PRC. In renouncing the U.S.-Taiwan Mutual Defense Treaty only four years after allowing an allied government in South Vietnam to suffer military defeat and two years after announcing an ill-timed force reduction in South Korea, the United States further undermined its image of reliability among Asian governments. [116] In the immediate aftermath of the Soviet invasion of Afghanistan, Secretary of Defense Harold Brown undertook a week-long visit to the PRC in January 1980 and announced that the United States was prepared to sell both dual use technology and "nonlethal" military support equipment to Beijing. In March, the U.S. State Department issued *Munitions Control Letter*, no. 81, which authorized the sale of a wide range of dual-use technology and military support equipment to the PRC. The sale included helicopters, transport aircraft, and communications equipment but still excluded the sale of lethal arms such as missiles, tanks, ships, and other types of offensive weapons systems.

While diplomatic expediency may have governed the Carter administration's decision making on the China normalization issue, critics of the new American policy were concerned over what to them appeared to be a serious U.S. miscalculation, one which could only play into the hands of the Soviet Union. As Soviet air and naval power became more evident at Cam Ranh Bay and Danang in Vietnam, and the Soviet Pacific Fleet more able to challenge U.S. forces in the Pacific via enhanced offshore strike capabilities, the relinquishing of an erstwhile reliable ally in the East China Sea area seemed ill-timed from the perspective of at least some American and Asian observers of military affairs. Apart from the obvious political imperatives behind Sino-American normalization, the strategic utility of a continued American basing presence on Taiwan could not be discounted. Such a presence would have provided air cover for a future American defense of allied maritime access to the East China Sea and provide sophisticated maintenancing and servicing for the U.S. Air Force.[117]

Even if Washington declined to pursue the option of residual strategic cooperation with Taipei, the Nationalist government's startling success in achieving a viable local deterrence against China by the late 1980s (see chapter 4) may lead U.S. strategic planners to reconsider the feasibility of Beijing's serving as an effective counterweight to Soviet military power in Asia. By way of illustration, U.S. efforts to assist in the modernization of fifty Chinese F-8 fighter interceptor aircraft have been frustrating. Even before the suppression of the prodemocracy movement led the United States to stop arms sales to the PRC, the Chinese military had decreased its military spending on the modern aircraft and conventional force assets which Washington had originally hoped would facilitate regional deterrence against the Soviet military threat. Taiwan, by contrast, has channeled a significant portion (reportedly more than $US 1 billion) of its prosperous economy toward developing an indigenous jet fighter which will go into full production during 1990 to counter the PRC's *Jian*-8 aircraft. It has modernized its F-5E jet fighter squadrons to maintain qualitative superiority over the PRC's *MiG*-21s, and purchased frigates and submarines in sufficient numbers to strain any Chinese effort to impose a blockade in the East China Sea. While the PRC's superior resource base and determination to strengthen its naval amphibious capabilities may allow Beijing to surpass Taiwan's conventional force capabilities over the long-term, the Taiwanese have demonstrated marked resourcefulness in maintaining their qualitative advantages in weapons development, and in maximizing their geostrategic advantages as an easily defensible island nation.[118]

Despite such considerations, three successive U.S. administrations have opted to eschew a Taiwanese component of extended deterrence strategy other than the very ambiguous stipulations contained in the Taiwan Relations Act. They have instead encouraged Beijing to "tilt" geopolitically toward the West by issuing a series of joint communiques recognizing the principle of "one China" under the rule of Beijing's current leadership. In return, U.S. policy planners have expected China to counterbalance Soviet military power with what could only generously be described as a modest deterrence capability against Soviet military power in the Northeast Asia theater. How successful this approach has been is questionable. This appears especially true as China's domestic political situation has effected greater strains on Sino-American relations and as successful Sino-Soviet border negotiations expand into more comprehensive discussions on confidence-building measures and arms trade between Moscow and Beijing (see chapter 3). Such trends make any prospects of that country entertaining a future strategic policy orientation toward the West highly uncertain.

Australia's Defense Posture: Merging Global and Local Deterrence

THE AUSTRALIAN Labor government was successful during the late 1980s in publicly representing the ANZUS deterrent as one smoothly bridging both Australian local and American global deterrence objectives. As Coral Bell has noted, an explicitly guaranteed U.S. response to a future Australian military contingency arising from an expansionist Indonesian move toward Papua New Guinea or from a confrontation in the South Pacific islands cannot be expected as part of the ANZUS package. However, "even the shadow of United States' power can have a deterrent effect on policymakers balancing the potential costs of such adventures."[119] The credibility of the U.S. ANZUS commitment lay in the power of its ambiguity.

More recently, the Labor government has sought to underwrite the cause of greater Australian defense self-reliance through independent intelligence-gathering. For example, a new defense satellite communications station at Geraldton is scheduled to become active in 1993, and to be manned solely by Australian personnel, although sharing data with both the United States and New Zealand. Australia has opposed the United States' Strategic Defense Initiative and has been integral in fashioning a nuclear free zone for the South Pacific to which the Americans have dissented. Canberra has also initiated indigenous weapons system construction (i.e., the "ANZAC Ship Project," designed to build new frigates for both the Australian and New Zealand navies)[120] While continuing to affiliate with selective aspects of U.S. global deterrence strategy, Australia has moved visibly, as a Transitional Player, to forge its own strategic identity along more regional lines.

On at least three separate occasions during the 1980s, however, Canberra officially stressed the importance of Australia's security posture relative to U.S. ability to maintain a favorable global balance of power between itself and the USSR. In 1981, the Australian Parliament's Joint Committee on Foreign Affairs and Defense observed that while U.S.-Australian defense operations at Pine Gap, Nurrungar, and elsewhere could be targeted by Soviet missiles and bombers during an international confrontation, these facilities strengthened U.S. efforts at deterring global war. In March 1983, the "Hayden Doctrine" evolved from the Foreign Minister's aforementioned defense review, contending that U.S.-Australian military cooperation directly contributes to global and regional stability by providing early warning of Soviet strategic developments and better verification of existing arms control agreements. Although the joint installation arrangements in Australia are not part of the ANZUS obligation per se, Hayden added, they "clearly represent an important reflection and instance of the shared interests which the Treaty embodies . . . the contribution made by the joint defense facilities to the deterrence of nuclear war fully justifies any risk that might be seen as arising from our having those facilities in Australia." [121] The third reaffirmation of Canberra's adherence to U.S. extended deterrence strategy occurred during 1986–1987. In March 1986, an independent review of Australia's defense strategy and capabilities was commissioned by the Australian Defense Department and prepared by a widely respected defense analyst, Paul Dibb. It concluded that while ANZUS consultation procedures offered no explicit guarantee for an automatic American military intervention on Australia's behalf for every defense contingency that might arise, the U.S. defense connection remained indispensable as a deterrent against "higher level" threats. [122]

Dibb was most careful to note that common grounds do not always exist between U.S. global strategy and Australia's national security interests. Adopting a Transitional Player posture on regional deterrence problems, the "Dibb Report" saw no requirement for Canberra to become involved in U.S. contingency planning for global war. Instead, future Australian military contributions in support of "distant diplomatic interests" of the Western Alliance should be regarded by the United States as a gesture of Australian goodwill—not an Australian defense obligation under ANZUS. Australia, the report concluded, should instead concentrate on developing the capacity for a territorial "defense-in-depth," concentrating its air and maritime strike interdiction forces within a 1,000 nautical mile radius of its own shoreline. [123]

A number of Australian defense experts supportive of a strong U.S.-Australian alliance viewed the report as a prescription for strategic isolation. Typifying the concerns arising from Dibb's recommendation that Canberra adopt what he termed a "strategy of denial" was the response of Vice Admiral David W. Leach, former Australian Chief of Naval Staff:

> [Dibb's] recognition . . . that our geography should be a major determinant of our strategy and that this should have a strong maritime element is welcomed . . . . [However,] . . . it must be remembered that countries are becoming increasingly interdependent. A defense force structure must be compatible with a foreign policy that accepts regional responsibilities and we should contribute something more to the ANZUS alliance than hosting U.S. bases in Australia and accepting ship visits. The [Dibb] review identifies a sphere of primary strategic interest extending throughout Southeast Asia, the Eastern Indian Ocean and the South Pacific but this does not seem to have much point if we have no means to influence it. [124]

Consultation between allies is an integral factor in extended deterrence. In this regard, Australia's continued hosting of some of the United States' most important overseas intelligence installations enhances ANZUS military planning and serves Australian *regional* deterrence objectives as well. The Nurrungar satellite ground station, as part of the U.S. Defense Support Program (DSP) which underlies American global command and control operations, serves as an early warning station for strategic missile attacks against the United States. [125]

The Pine Gap facility near Alice Springs hosts a signals intelligence

(SIGINT) satellite system important for verifying arms control agreements. It also collects information on Soviet strategic nuclear weapons programs and testing and serves as a key verification facility for monitoring of superpower arms control agreements through the monitoring of electronic signals intelligence originating from the USSR and through telemetry interception of Soviet test rocket flights.[126]

Predictable opposition by the Australian peace movement has centered around the alleged compromise of Australia's sovereignty by American global deterrence strategy. Critics of U.S.-Australian defense relations argue that past American disregard for Canberra's interests in Indian Ocean negotiations, for the helpful Australian position on the SPNFZ, and for emerging political instabilities in the South Pacific have rendered tenuous the U.S. extended deterrent commitment to Australia. Australia would be better off, they assert, opting for greater strategic self-reliance as opposed to continuing the American security tie. They maintain that tie is nothing more than an illusory policy gamble. A complete transition, these critics assert, must occur in Canberra's defense outlook and behavior.[127]

In reality, however, the broader context of U.S. and Australian security perceptions and behavior is far more compatible than the alliance detractors have acknowledged. Both countries have made visible progress in adjusting global and regional threat perceptions to allow for the value of arms control and of diplomacy over armed confrontation (although the United States has not moved as far in this direction). Both allies understand, however, that neither can afford, in the words of Henry Albinski, to become overly "infatuated by a mindless haste to leap in new directions, including a precipitous standing down of defense preparedness."[128] Canberra and Washington are also in agreement on the importance of assisting and coordinating nation-building and development assistance efforts throughout the South Pacific.

Consultation procedures on American base access and operations in Australia have been revised over the past fifteen years in Canberra's favor. The January 1974 Barnard-Schlesinger Agreement, emanating from the Whitlam government's consternation over what it viewed as the unauthorized American use of the Northwest Cape installation during the Yom Kippur War, guarantees the Australian Embassy's defense attaches, at *Australian* discretion, immediate access to the U.S. command structure at the outset of an international crisis. In 1979, this arrangement was expanded to encompass all U.S.-Australian operations conducted at the Australian joint facilities.[129]

The Australian navy and airforce joins Australia's tracking installations in playing a critical role in the U.S. global deterrence posture. Dibb's defense-in-depth prescriptions for Canberra's defense posture actually call for Australia to strengthen its capabilities in providing regional defense for the littorals spanning the Indian and South Pacific oceans.

Substantial elements of the Australian defense force have been shifted to the remotely populated, but strategically situated north and northwestern sectors of the country to form land, air, and naval barriers from Learmouth in the northwest through Derby, Darwin (headquarters of the new Northern Command land operations center) and Townsville in the northeast (opposite key sea lanes of communication, transversing through the eastern Indian Ocean and the southern straits area of Southeast Asia into Papua New Guinea). An Operational Deployment Force—the 3 Brigade—is deployed at Townsville and can be supplemented by the 1 Brigade paratrooper group located in Sydney. The Australian submarine fleet is to be stationed at Cockburn Sound and half the surface fleet at the *HMAS Stirling* installation near Perth. Australian F-18 fighter aircraft will be deployed increasingly at the new Tindal Air Base complex near Darwin, although two squadrons of these aircraft remain on station at the Royal Australian Air Force (RAAF) base at Williamtown (in New South Wales) for patrolling duty in the South and Southwest Pacific. Some F-111 strike and reconnaissance aircraft remain in service for interdiction missions in either the Indian or Pacific Ocean theaters. While the South Pacific was declared to be an area of equal strategic interest to Canberra, the "shifts north" by the Australian Defense Force (ADF), away from the most densely concentrated urban areas of the southeast, continue to be the predominant trend of force deployment and logistics. For example, by committing Australian forces to an initial defense of the Cocos and Christmas Islands, Australia's Indian Ocean territories, some 1800–2200 miles northwest of Perth but only several hundred miles from Java Head at the entrance of Sunda Strait, Australia can conduct air operations in support of the maritime ASEAN states' defense against external attack or conduct a holding action against air or sea invasions targeted against Australia's western and northwestern approaches.[130]

Throughout much of the 1980s, Australia upgraded its strategic presence in the South Pacific as a response to the ANZUS view of this area's importance in the global deterrence equation. A Soviet basing capability in this region would theoretically provide Soviet naval interdiction units with a 1,500 nautical mile operating radius covering the Hawaiian Islands to the northeast, the Australian east coast in the Southwest, and the tip of New Zealand's North Island to the south and position shipboard command and control systems in the area to relay targeting data to Moscow via relay stations such as Cam Ranh Bay.[131] Early in any global conventional war between the two super-powers, the Soviet Union would desire to cut the American west coast's major sea lines of communication to Hawaii, Guam, the Philippines, Australia, New Zealand, and the other Pacific waystations to which U.S. access would be required for reinforcement of allies in the Asia-Pacific theater. Notwithstanding recent and projected cutbacks in the strength of the Soviet Pacific Fleet (see chapter 3), Australia's efforts to expand naval and air coverage throughout the Southwest Pacific still provide a critical link with U.S. Seventh Fleet projection missions.

Overall, Australia is justified in continuing to value its ties with the Dominant Player while simultaneously pursuing opportunities for greater self-reliance in its regional defense capabilities. In March 1987, the Australian Defense Department issued a Defense White Paper which modified Dibb's effort to detach Australian local deterrence priorities from global deterrence politics. It asserted that during "the remote contingency of a global conflict" Australia "would have regard in the first instance to the situation in our immediate region," but would nevertheless fulfill surveillance and patrolling responsibilities related to the safety of Western shipping in the Pacific as defined by the 1951 Radford-Collins Agreement and work with the U.S. and other Western allies to sustain global intelligence-gathering capabilities.[132] Australian defense officials also argued that what Dibb termed a "strategy of denial" for Australia in the South Pacific could not be realized solely through local deterrence strategy or ANZAC capabilities. Even Dibb noted that Australia could not by itself defend Papua New Guinea against a concentrated enemy attack for at least another five to eight years due to a lack of surveillance, command, and control capabilities and of munitions stocks. Neither could Australia alone protect the "area of direct military interest" which includes the Timor and Arafura Seas, the Coral and Tasman Seas, and Australia's Indian Ocean approaches as well as Papua New Guinea, the Solomons, and Vanuatu to the north and northeast: "The area thus involved measures more than 4,000 nautical miles from the Cocos Islands in the west, to New Zealand in the east, and more than 3,000 nautical miles from the archipelagic chain and Papua New Guinea in the north to the Southern Ocean in the south . . . some 10 percent of the earth's surface . . . a formidable task for a nation of less than 16 million." [133]

In the final analysis, the Australian outlook on alliance politics in a post-ANZUS context is indicative of the posture adopted by other U.S. allies at a time when the Soviet Union is revising its strategy for enhancing its global influence. Australia, along with a growing number of European NATO states, believes that the ground rules of strategic competition are rapidly changing from those emphasizing military power and containment to something quite different: that great- and middle-size powers are intensifying their competition for regional and international influence through means other than military power alone, and particularly through managing economic and resource relations more efficiently. In order for Australia to compete in this changing international environment, it must first address its own regional interests and redirect its security priorities accordingly. If the United States fails to recognize and accommodate these new factors in Australian geopolitics, it could increasingly find itself at odds with Canberra. In such circumstances, Australia's deterrence posture could be transformed from that of a "Transitional Player" to a more clearly nonaligned power. Such a development would clearly undercut U.S. deterrence strategy at both its regional and global levels of application.

THE DOMINANT PLAYER POSTURE: SELECTED REGIONAL ISSUES

THE SHIFT of the U.S. Dominant Player global posture from a two-and-a-half war to a one-and-a-half war strategy followed recognition of a major transformation in the global balance of power. American strategic predominance was no longer so great that the credibility of its numerous deterrence commitments in the Asia-Pacific was unquestionable to its regional allies and friends; indeed, the gap between the number and credibility of those U.S. security commitments widened during the 1970s and 1980s. Yet, as Samuel Huntington has observed, this reality (commitments exceeding power) was not confronted directly by the Nixon administration or its three successors. Instead, he concludes, "no administration has seriously considered a reduction in American commitments in Western Europe, East Asia, or the Western Hemisphere." [134] As U.S. strategic resources become more finite, however, a fundamental contradiction within the Dominant Player posture may evolve. The U.S. may once more be tempted to increase its reliance upon "cost-effective" nuclear deterrence to underwrite its overstretched global strategic commitments at the same time that the technology of warfare demands, and pending arms control breakthroughs necessitate, a restructuring of that deterrent toward more effective but more expensive conventional military forces. If the United States' security commitments throughout the Eurasian littorals are to remain viable, its allies and friends will need to contribute a greater share to the defense burden. Otherwise, U.S. commitments will need to be adjusted or reduced in accord with changing threat perceptions and deterrence requirements.

Japanese Defense Burden-Sharing

PRESIDENT BUSH is the first American postwar leader to confront the prospect of his electorate viewing Japanese economic acumen as a greater threat to its national security than Soviet military power. U.S. leaders remain frustrated by Japan's continued self-appointed insularity from global geopolitics and what they view as Japan's singularly narrow interpretation of global leadership as no more than balancing account ledgers. As the managing editor of *Harvard Business Review* recently observed:

> Honest American observers recognize a discontinuity of historic proportions. Economic power and world leadership have become uncoupled. Japan's dynamic economy has seized the momentum and propelled the nation into the first position of global wealth; but Japan has no view of its role in the world, no mission or purpose for its new found economic power . . . it is clear that Japan needs to change and cannot without *gaiatsu* —external pressure from the United States. So rapid has been Japan's advance from ashes to affluence that virtually every institutional dimension in its way of life desperately needs reform, or risk ending up an anachronistic victim of Japan's economic success. [135]

Two lines of argument now shape the ongoing debate about the U.S.-Japan alliance. The first relates to how the widening trade dispute between the two nations affects the politico-security context of the relationship. The second deals with the question of defense burden-sharing in light of the Japanese economic superpower's reluctance to increase its contribution to overall Western defense efforts.

A chic cottage industry of "Japan bashing" has evolved within the U.S. academe and community of letters. The writings of Daniel Burstein, James Fallows, Chalmers Johnson, Clyde Prestowitz, and Karel van Wolferen have gained international notoriety in their determination to identify and condemn a Japanese "grand strategy" to become the world's economic hegemon while leaving to the United States the task of defending the new world order. Fallows is perhaps most critical, attacking what he labels as Japan's global "money politics" which he defines as Japan "continuing to launch new industrial assaults in America and all over the world . . . suggest(ing) that it does not accept the basic reciprocal logic of free trade."[136] Special interest politics prevail within the domestic Japanese polity, according to Fallows and other critics of Japanese behavior, to the extent that they preclude Tokyo's ability to create and sustain the type of reliable and enduring trade-offs it needs to generate influence with its allies and throughout the international system.

The Bush administration has applied a mixture of policy coercion and inducement to convince Japan of the need to open more of its domestic markets to international competition and to counteract what U.S. officials view as Tokyo's propensity for monopolizing production in key high technology industries. The most notable American pressure tactic to date was the sanctioning of Japan by the Office of the U.S. Trade Representative on May 25, 1989, for violation of the "Super 301" provision of the U.S. Omnibus Trade Act. The violations related to semiconductor research, to telecommunications (commercial satellites) and to import bans against U.S. forest products. The USTR pointedly warned Japan that U.S. trade protectionism against Japanese goods could result unless the two sides moved quickly to remove "structural impediments" to trade and balance-of-payments adjustments within the two countries' bilateral relationship.[137]

A gradual shift in U.S. attitudes toward Japan is also occurring with respect to the defense relationships of the two countries. During the late 1970s and 1980s, American presidents and legislators prodded

Tokyo to do more in terms of building up its military defense capabilities against a perceived Soviet military threat in the key straits and littorals surrounding Japan and to assume some responsibility for defending the sea lanes stretching from the Japanese homeland to the southeast and southwest. Concurrently, gradually losing its technological, industrial, and organizational superiority, the United States ceded commercial and financial power to Japan. This new power permitted a significant Japanese military buildup. By 1989, Japan had become the world's third largest military spender (based on a fluctuating dollar-yen exchange ratio) and could field an array of destroyers, antisubmarine forces, and jet fighters to defend itself below the nuclear level.

The innocuous American catchphrase of "burden-sharing" (meaning different things to different people) no longer seemed adequate to define what Japan could or should do as a defense actor. A note of caution was struck during the Bush presidential campaign in 1988 when two former Secretaries of State (Vance and Kissinger) warned that "any attempt to deal with the [U.S.] deficit by pressing Japan to step up its defense efforts" would backfire.[138] This could certainly be the case in East Asia, where other U.S. treaty allies and the ASEAN states might perceive their "worst case" apprehensions about Japanese remilitarization as having come true.

The policy dilemma confronting Washington is that it will be unable to sustain the $40–50 billion annual outlays it has until recently expended for maintaining its postwar Asia-Pacific security commitments. President Bush has admitted that the U.S. "must enhance the ability of (its) friends to defend themselves."[139] His Acting Assistant Secretary for East Asian and Pacific Affairs went even further in noting that because the United States can no longer dominate economically in the region, it must work in concert with its friends and allies there to find "more subtle and flexible [security] policies."[140]

American and Japanese security analysts who still value the U.S.-Japan Mutual Security Treaty contend that it is worth saving to protect the sea lanes of communication and trade which are the economic lifelines for the Pacific Basin's economic growth. Consequently, they argue, the United States has little choice but to redefine the Treaty context to one that reflects "a new partnership based on equality and true reciprocity in terms of the maintenance of national security of both countries."[141]

Japan, with its increasingly formidable economic base, faced with increased U.S. expectations of defense burden-sharing, has maintained a desire not to generate fears of revived Japanese militarism. Most Japanese remain content to interpret Article 9 literally, as allowing only for Japanese defense capabilities sufficient for self-defense against external aggression. During the latter stages of the Carter administration, however, a growing number of U.S. officials felt an expanded concept of the self-defense mandate was justified, an interpretation which prevailed throughout the Reagan administration. The U.S. Congress was especially prone to tying U.S.-Japan trade and economic issues to U.S. continued willingness to extend deterrence on Japan's behalf. U.S. dissatisfaction over the extent of Japan's defense efforts remains substantial in the 1990s, despite Prime Minister Yasuhiro Nakasone's (1982–1987) adopting a policy of gradual Japanese defense spending increases while developing more cordial relations with its regional neighbors.[142]

Japan has hoped to facilitate an image as a nonthreatening regional security actor, allowing its international economic interests, and particularly its access to global trade and investment venues, to be developed apart from strategic considerations. Nakasone's successors, Noburo Takeshita, Sosuke Uno, and Toshiki Kaifu have all pushed for greater Japanese influence in U.S. strategic decisionmaking as well. It is less certain is to what extent the Japanese Socialist Party would modify its opposition to Japan's continued support for the Dominant Player posture if it gained national power on its own or in coalition with other political opposition groups.

Despite spending only slightly more than 1 percent of its gross national product on defense, Japan ranks anywhere from third to fifth among the world's nations in defense expenditures (1.006 percent of the country's gross national product was designated for Defense Agency spending in Fiscal Year 1989), depending on how economists measure the yen's given strength relative to the value of the U.S. dollar at any given time.[143] Defense spending figures, of course, do not measure how effective Japan's defense efforts have been. Indeed, Japanese journalist Osamu Kaihara has argued persuasively that caution should be employed when using an arbitrary ranking system for comparative defense expenditures. Noting that assertions about Japan becoming the world's third largest defense spender are now "trendy," he questions the basis of the calculations. He notes that pension payments of retired SDF personnel cannot be equated in terms of military power to British or French nuclear capabilities or to West Germany's large standing army and reserve system. In real terms, Kaihara concludes, Japan defense outlays and combat capabilities really only amount to about three-fourths of those expended by NATO's three major European powers. Moreover, he asserts, using the "volatile yardstick" of the dollar-yen exchange ratio is, at best, "a questionable practice" in assessing the real extent of Japanese military prowess.[144]

What concerns American critics is *how* Japan plans to employ its sixty destroyers (more than twice as many as the Seventh Fleet has covering both the Pacific and Indian Oceans), recently modernized ground forces, and Asia's most modern air defenses outside the Soviet Far East. Toward the end of President Reagan's tenure, one Congressional study disappointedly concluded that Japan was still unable to protect the Japanese archipelago from invasion with its own forces, could not protect its sea lanes of communication out to 1,000 nautical miles, and could not block the Japanese straits from Soviet access during wartime. This was true, the study concluded, notwithstanding previous U.S. agreements with the Nakasone government that Japan would assume a key role in defending the straits and littorals of Northeast Asia, while U.S. naval forces protected maritime commerce in the waters of Southeast Asia and Western oil supplies from the Persian Gulf.

Japan has limited its military manpower authorization to 245,000 active duty personnel, has a minuscule weapons research and development base, and pays two to three times as much for indigenously produced military equipment than for American or European versions of the same systems. As James Fallows has facetiously observed, the Japanese Self Defense Force "may be the only military force in the world that regularly makes the Pentagon look like it gets bargains."[145] Despite these costs and recent increases in Japanese military strength, the United States still carries a disproportionate financial responsibility for maintaining deterrence in Northeast Asia. One recent estimate of the annual cost absorbed by the United States in maintaining its Asia-Pacific network of bases, naval and air exercises with allies in the region, sea lane protection and fulfilling general surveillance and deterrence missions was between $36 billion and $50 billion.[146] Congressional proposals have surfaced for Japan to pay an annual "defense tax" equivalent to a set percentage of its gross domestic product, especially if the expense of preserving the Dominant Player posture's commitments within CINCPAC become too prohibitive for Washington to continue.

In rebuttal, the Japanese government has articulated the policy of "comprehensive security" (*sogo anzen hosho*)—a multifaceted approach to national and international security encompassing the notion of balancing defense burden sharing with self-imposed constraints on one's military policies. The comprehensive security outlook envisions Japanese provision of substantial Overseas Development Assistance (ODA) to Asia-Pacific and Third World states and financial support for an international security role. In deference to the peace constitution, it falls short of authorizing the participation of Japanese military personnel in peacekeeping forces in Cambodia and elsewhere.[147] American critics of this policy note the opposition in the Diet to such ventures, based on the position that such financial assistance would violate 1978 legislation prohibiting Japan from supporting military forces in other countries.[148] A number of Southeast Asian countries also remain wary of any upgraded Japanese role in defining and shaping international security issues due to Japan's historical legacy of militarism. By itself, Japan has little international leverage to press for an independent agenda in international security affairs because its diplomatic and strategic identity are still largely intertwined with its choice to stake its ultimate survival on the continued viability of the U.S. extended deterrent.

Is the United States reducing extended deterrence commitments to Japan which, until now, have reinforced the credibility of the MST? Tokyo could be led to ask such a question, especially if continuing American fiscal restraints cause Washington to reduce its overall military presence in the Northeast Asian theater and leave Washington less able to manage escalation control on Japan's behalf than was the case throughout the 1950s and 1960s. George R. Packard has ably summarized Japan's policy quandary:

> If dependence on America hurts [the Japanese] national pride, they are also frustrated by the lack of attractive alternatives. To abandon the security treaty with the United States would require unacceptably high defense costs—and a crippling domestic struggle over whether to possess nuclear weapons. It might also result in a loss of U.S. market share and severe restrictions on future direct and indirect investments in the United States. There is a Soviet card to play but Japanese leaders long ago weighed the advantages of joining in the development of Siberia . . .

and concluded that partnership with the United States was safer, more profitable, and more congenial in general in dealing with the Soviets, who have ever appeared threatening and untrustworthy.[149]

Japan's faith in the commitments and benefits which the U.S. Dominant Player posture allegedly represents may fade in the absence of what the Japanese would consider to be a sensitive U.S. understanding of Tokyo's constraints in undertaking greater defense responsibilities. Under the present circumstances, Japan most likely will continue to pursue Nakasone's approach of finessing its defense relations with the United States. This would ensure Japan's continued place within the U.S. extended deterrent, but allow Japan to assert its own regional and international security interests should opportunities arise. As Susan J. Pharr has pointed out, Japanese proponents of this "internationalist" view "may disagree among themselves over what Japan's security needs are, but they agree over how to approach the issue."[150] They are in favor of repealing the one percent defense spending ceiling mandated by the 1976 National Defense Program Outline (NDPO), and of relating defense budgetary assessments to actual strategic needs. They also advocate additional Japanese foreign aid spending in lieu of increased defense budgets as the most viable measure for Japanese contributions to overall Western security.

Extended Deterrence and U.S.-Japanese Military Technology Relations

U.S. DEFENSE officials have increasingly regarded the transfer of indigenous Japanese military technology to the United States as one of the most promising areas of Tokyo's defense burden-sharing collaboration with the U.S. Both the Reagan and Bush administrations have strongly pressed for the continuation and upgrading of joint U.S.-Japan collaboration in the defense research and production sector. They have done so on the premise that U.S. security interests lie in promoting closer interdependence with Japan as opposed to driving that country to an independent defense position. American critics of this policy warn that the United States could become militarily dependent on Japanese civilian corporations for access to technologies critical to U.S. national security. These analysts fear that Japan could thus provide or deprive Washington of critical high technology components in accordance with its own political will.[151]

Prime Minister Nakasone announced in January 1983 that transfers of military technology to the United States would be exempted from Japan's "three principles of nonarms transfer" and that a Joint Military Technology Commission would be set up to implement a then-pending (November 1983) Exchange of Notes. U.S. defense officials were interested in gaining access to Japanese electronics technology (millimeter-wave, micro-wave, and electro-optics) which could enhance U.S. defense communications systems, navigation and guidance components for weapons delivery systems, and intelligence-gathering operations.[152]

In the years following this agreement, only a few, and largely inconsequential, exchanges of Japanese military technology with the United States actually took place. Discussions have been conducted by the Joint Military Technology Commission, for example, on the so-called Conventional Defense/Balanced Technology Initiatives (CDI/BTI). This program was mandated by the U.S. Congress in 1986 and directed that U.S./allied research be conducted in the areas of smart weapons technology, reconnaissance, surveillance and target acquisition (RSTA), armor/anti-armor technology programs, high power microwave programs, and "special technology opportunities" related to superconductor materials and tactical missile defense.

Little progress has been made in the CDI/BTI area, because U.S. firms are reluctant to share their advanced military technology with a country known for exploiting foreign licenses by assimilating and marketing high technology at the expense of original foreign licensors. While Japan's indigenous surface-to-surface missile (SSM) and sonar technology have been praised as highly advanced, most Western military experts still believe Japanese defense equipment has yet to match state-of-the-art Western counterparts and will not match it until Japanese defense companies such as Mitsubishi Heavy Industries (MHI), Fuji Heavy Industries, and Toshiba are able to develop their weapons systems independently of colicensing agreements with the West.[153]

Only 2.21 percent of the 1988 Japanese defense budget was allocated for use by the Japan Defense Agency's Technical Research and Development Institute (TRDI), and weapons purchases take up well over 60 percent of that budget.[154] Some U.S. observers argue that even with such a spending cap, the TRDI has made remarkable progress in military R&D with Japanese radar, defense electronics, and tactical missile systems now rivaling comparable U.S. systems. In May 1989, the U.S. Defense Department released a study which contended that

Japan led the United States in six of twenty-two key technologies which the Pentagon labeled "crucial to national security and the long term qualitative superiority of American weapons systems." These included micro-electronics circuitry, gallium arsenide and other compounds related to the development of semiconductors, robotics, integrated optics, superconductivity, and biotechnology.[155] The majority of U.S. analysts, however, believe that significant Japanese defense modernization is unlikely to occur as long as Japan must continue to rely upon U.S. defense firms for the manufacture of its most critical equipment, such as the new FS-X jet-fighter.

The FS-X episode stands out as a particularly important yardstick for how integral a role U.S. policymakers want Japan to play in the Western Alliance's deterrence strategy. The procurement and use of Japanese high technology in future U.S. weapons systems is an appealing prospect to the Pentagon. However, the U.S. Department of Commerce, various Congressmen, and U.S. defense industries all share a common perception that if allowed too much access to American state-of-the-art military technology, Japan will inevitably move to produce superior aerospace products and to extricate the United States from one of the few sectors of the Japanese marketplace where American firms can still compete effectively.

In October 1987, Japan announced it would enter into a $7 billion program with General Dynamics to build a follow-on jet fighter (FS-X), modeled along the lines of the F-16, to replace its aging fleet of F-1 aircraft. Subsequent and acrimonious negotiations took place about the nature of U.S. aerospace technology to be transferred and concerning the amount of American production work to be allowed. Over the ensuing eighteen months, the United States continually demanded "clarification" of the original agreement's terms and, in late April 1989, won Japanese concessions to revise the contract by allowing U.S. firms a larger (40 percent) share of production, limiting Japanese access to U.S. software critical to F-16 production, and gaining access to whatever indigenous technology the Japanese brought to the project.

The major lesson of the FS-X incident, from the Japanese perspective, was to demonstrate that the credibility of U.S. security commitments to help strengthen Japan's local deterrence capabilities (in this case, through deploying more advanced air defenses) is susceptible to erosion by American domestic political and business concerns which attempt to link the U.S.-Japan alliance to the broader issues of international trade and finance. In the wake of the FS-X dispute, Ryozo Tsutsui, Director of the Japan Defense Agency's Technical Research and Development Institute, called for greater Japanese self-sufficiency in weapons design and production, noting that "Japan should keep to the highest state of the art in military technology as a [self-reliant] deterrent." [156]

U.S. techno-nationalism has affected U.S.-Japanese coordination of deterrence strategy in other instances. Congressional delays in approving the sale of the *Aegis* air defense system for Japan's guided missile destroyer-type ships, for example, threatened to impede Japanese ability to effectively patrol its adjacent sea lanes and provide early warning on Soviet Pacific Fleet movements. Masaru Kohno has argued, there is little prospect that Japan will be successful in asserting its own defense interests within the context of U.S.-Japanese high technology relations in the near future. Japan's "continuing dependence on foreign markets and resources" compels Tokyo to become a "cosupporter of the global hegemony that the United States cannot sustain alone . . . [and] the FS-X [decision] reflects the growing Japanese perception that it is more important to preserve trans-Pacific harmony than to become preoccupied with specific bilateral conflicts." [157]

Reconciling U.S. Global and Japanese Local Deterrence Objectives: "Forward Development Strategy" in Northeast Asia

PRESIDENT REAGAN's Commission on Integrated Long-Term Strategy report on "Discriminate Deterrence" emphasized the importance of U.S. "forward development strategy" as a part of future overall U.S. deterrence strategy in areas along the Eurasian peripheries. [158] Forward development strategy underscores the need to develop and sustain more powerful U.S. and allied military forces in those areas most likely to be contested by an adversary during the *first* stages of a global conventional war. Unlike the traditional Dominant Player posture, it assumes that maximum conventional firepower will be applied at the outset of battle. While the strategy concedes that "if nonnuclear force proves inadequate, we must be prepared to use nuclear force to stop a conventional invasion," it nevertheless emphasizes that any force used as a deterrent by the West must be "effective and discriminate—kept under control rather than a suicidal bluff." [159]

Greater Japanese ability to wage successful self-defense in a conventional war environment is a key aspect of Japan's contribution to a Western discriminate deterrence posture. Recent Japanese defense doctrine and force procurement behavior has reflected Tokyo's acknowledgment that, while it still has far to go before achieving such force levels, progress has been made. The 1988 *Defense White Paper of Japan* noted that, despite budgetary pressures on U.S. defense spending, Washington would continue extending deterrence to Western Europe and Northeast Asia. Accordingly, the White Paper concluded, Japan should cooperate with the United States in developing joint defense research, interoperability of forces, and better logistical support systems along the lines of the U.S.-NATO Mutual Support System. [160] These measures would be integrated into the three designated missions of sea control, straits blockage, and air defense, through procurement of appropriate weapons systems and military technology. For example, maritime air defense of the sea lanes would be achieved through the deployment of over-the-horizon (OTH) back-scatter radar, with ranges out to 4,000 kilometers at Kikagashima, south of Kyushu, or on Iwo Jima. This system could track much of the Soviet military traffic in eastern Siberia. A number of E-2C early-warning aircraft (AWACs) are also scheduled to enter service. As previously noted, two *Aegis*-type naval vessels will be built for air defense over Japan's western and southern sea-lanes and to escort Japanese maritime commercial traffic during any future Northeast Asian crisis. Japan's 1986–1990 Mid-Term Defense Estimate calculated that, by the early to mid-1990s, Japan would deploy an air defense capability of 100 FX air-to-surface support fighters, 200 F-15 and 100 F-4 *Phantom* interceptors, along with air-refuelling tankers, to deal with Soviet *Backfire* and *Bear* bombers. Many of these aircraft will be outfitted with the *Phoenix* long-range air-to-air missile. If the full 300 interceptors are deployed, Japan will have as many tactical defense aircraft as currently defend the continental United States. Additional P-3C tracking planes will also be built and SH-60 helicopters deployed to strengthen Japanese antisubmarine warfare capabilities and to fulfill related sealane patrol missions. [161]

Enough weaknesses still remain in Japanese force planning and logistics, however, to sustain U.S. doubts about Japan's ability to fulfill its local deterrence objectives. First, Tokyo has no coherent strategy in place for achieving local deterrence and defense. At best, as one Japanese commentator recently noted, "what passes for defense policy [in

Japan] are merely requests for more weapons and equipment." [162] The Japanese have yet to reconcile the need to strengthen the mechanisms of bilateral security cooperation with their characteristic, and comfortable, "business as usual" policy management style. [163] If Japan continues to limit its own contingency planning in such a fashion, relying on U.S. capabilities to deter on Japan's behalf in the event of a major war, this may prove to be a tragic miscalculation. One needs only recall the shock registered in Tokyo when Washington's "swing strategy" was disclosed a decade ago. If the United States is preoccupied in several theaters at once, or if U.S. budgetary constraints lead to a further series of force reductions reminiscent of the "Nixon shocks" in the early 1970s, Japan's failure to project strategic requirements for the 1990s will leave that nation increasingly vulnerable to potential strategic intimidation.

The second weakness of Japan's local deterrence posture evolves from the first: an inability or unwillingness to sustain the combat readiness of the various Self Defense Force components. Ground force strength has usually fallen around 25,000 personnel short of authorized levels, and critical shortages of noncommissioned officers and jet fighter pilots exist. It is not clear that forces-in-place, lacking a nationwide unified command system, are adequately trained to fight in an amphibious warfare environment of the type which would most likely involve the defense of Hokkaido. Simulated defense exercises have indicated that Ground Self Defense Force antiarmor, antiaircraft, and tank systems are inadequate, without U.S. intervention, to stem the tide of a Soviet assault. [164] Certainly, Japanese defense forces would need more ammunition than the estimated thirty-day supply cited by most recent Japanese Defense White Papers. And despite its growing inventory of destroyers, frigates, and mine warfare ships, the Japanese Maritime Self Defense Force still falls short of attaining forward projection capabilities over a 1,000 nautical mile zone to the south because it lacks sufficient air cover and carrier platforms. The JDA has argued that the Japanese constitution does not prohibit Japan's deployment of a "defensive" lightweight carrier with antisubmarine helicopters; however, that attack aircraft carriers such as those found in the U.S. Navy would be disallowed. [165] Domestic political constraints related to Article 9 will need to be addressed, in any case, before further steps can be taken to rectify Japan's military shortcomings. Nor are there imminent prospects that stronger Japanese efforts will be directed toward either rectifying gaps in equipment and training or procuring more credible logistical support capabilities.[166]

Even those defense burden-sharing efforts which are pursued by the Japanese in the interest of merging local deterrence interests with U.S. regional deterrence strategy have often generated controversy among the Japanese electorate. Illustrative are tensions which surfaced during August 1988 over reports that Kadena Air Base in Okinawa would eventually host the U.S. 26th Attack Unit and four *Hercules* C-103 transport planes currently stationed at Clark Air Base in the Philippines. This move was projected because of the uncertainty of continued U.S. military access to Clark following the expiration of the U.S.-Philippines basing treaty in 1991. Kadena has hosted three American airborne warning command (AWAC) aircraft for some years for patrolling air space over Japan, South Korea, Southeast Asia, and Oceanea; three additional AWAC were to be deployed to replace the *Blackbird* surveillance aircraft's operations over North Korea (maintenance costs forcing the *Blackbird* into premature retirement). Plans were also drawn up for the possible transfer of warship repair facilities from Subic Bay to Yokohama, generating similar basing tensions.[167] Japanese residing near the U.S. bases in their country are sensitive to *any* upgrading of U.S. operations, largely for environmental reasons. The noise of U.S. Air Force aircraft maneuvering at the Atsugi Air Base near Yokosuka has generated extensive complaints from the surrounding population. Tensions between U.S. Marine personnel stationed at Okinawa and local residents have also intensified in recent years, presenting U.S. force planners with the serious challenge of how to reconcile U.S. deterrence strategy with local Japanese politics.[168]

Japan's International Security Policy

DESPITE THEIR reluctance to think in global strategic terms, Japanese policymakers understand that the Asia-Pacific theater has always been more fluid geostrategically than Europe because the dividing line between Soviet and Western spheres of influence in the Asia-Pacific has never been as sharply defined. Until recently, the Mutual Security Treaty has allowed Japan to cushion itself from the effects of nonalignment movements and of East-West competition for the allegiance of weak governments. As American strategic resources become increasingly strained, however, it is evident that the scope of traditional U.S.

extended deterrence commitments to Japan and to other Northeast Asian friends and allies may be narrowed. Accordingly, Japan has begun to consider ways in which it can supplement Washington's efforts to sustain Western economic, political and strategic interests by introducing discrete security policy initiatives in its own region and beyond. Barry Buzan is among those who have argued that "as a declining America will have progressively fewer resources to devote to international leadership," Tokyo will increasingly be challenged to not appear "either threatening or weak." Yet it must be acknowledged that "(a)lmost none of Japan's relationships in East Asia can be described as warm." [169] Accordingly, the Japanese cannot appear to be even contemplating an Aspiring Player posture in affairs of strategy and deterrence.

Recent burden-sharing politics between Washington and Tokyo underscore the point. Policy initiatives which might enable Japan to become a more important player in the broader international security arena would be welcomed by U.S. strategic planners who are ever more pressed to apply credible deterrence at the global level with a clearly diminished national resource base. Japanese leaders, of course, must contain any such initiatives within the spirit of their country's "peace constitution" so that their own electorate does not become completely alienated to limited rearmament nor its neighbors become overly concerned that Japan may be returning to a strategy of military expansionism reminiscent of the 1930s. As one Japanese Foreign Ministry official has admitted: "It is a deep-rooted perception in Southeast Asia, in Korea and perhaps China as well, that, as long as the United States maintains a strong military presence, and as long as Japan relies on the United States for its security, Japan is unlikely to break away from the framework of its special relationship with the Americans and so is unlikely to constitute a threat to its neighbors." [170] U.S. officials tacitly hint that efforts to pressure Japan into greater defense spending may yet result in other East Asian nations viewing Japan as a rising threat to local security. They therefore assert that a "sudden increase" in Tokyo's defense budget from 1 percent to 3 percent GNP would be too high. [171] The underlying implications of U.S. burden-sharing initiatives, however, are not lost on Japan's neighbors. The U.S. Dominant Player posture is regarded as less effective than before by most Asia-Pacific states as an adequate control mechanism against Japan's remilitarization. With recent military cutbacks by both superpowers in the

Asia-Pacific, defense officials and analysts in the region believe they may have increased grounds for worrying about an increased Japanese military assertiveness evolving from a resulting power vacuum.[172]

Despite its continued economic differences with Washington, Japan has begun to demonstrate that it is willing to support U.S. global security interests beyond the restricted framework of the MST. For its part, the United States has appeared increasingly amenable to consider Japan's interests within overall Western strategic decision-making. Throughout early to mid-1980s, a number of proposals for more systematic trilateral security consultations and cooperation between the U.S., NATO Europe, and Northeast Asia were advanced by such security analysts as Robert Pranger, Edward Olsen, Hisahiko Okazaki, Seizaburo Sato, and Masashi Nishihara.[173] Most of their proposals were designed to overcome the geographic and political differences between Europe and Asia which still preclude the establishment of a more coordinated Western deterrence and defense posture.[174] At a June 1990 NATO Ministerial Council meeting in Brussels, attended by a Japanese delegation, American officials urged their West European counterparts to "envisage joint armed internations, in conjunction with Japan, to respond to crises outside Europe in the future."[175] Critics of greater Japanese participation in NATO, however, point to what they believe is still a "lack of maturity" in Tokyo's world view. They argue that Japan needs to develop a more pragmatic bilateral relationship with the USSR, a more visible and independent policy on global arms control problems, and regular communications on a range of economic and political issues with the European Community.[176]

When the Iran-Iraq war threatened to sever Western oil traffic in the Persian Gulf during 1987 and early 1988, the Japanese sold a multifaceted package of navigation systems to pro-Western Arab states and made offers of financial assistance and personnel for peacekeeping forces. Both of these actions were designed not only to contribute to the Gulf's stability but to undertake additional defense burden-sharing in compensation for U.S. efforts to protect Japan's oil supplies. A number of Western observers criticized this Japanese package as insufficient, considering the ramifications of an oil supply cutoff to Japan's economy.

Following Iraq's invasion of Kuwait in early August 1990, Japan pledged $2 billion in economic assistance to disadvantaged gulf states and another $2 billion in support of the U.S.-led military operation to deter an Iraqi attack of Saudi Arabia. In November 1990, however, Prime Minister Kaifu's proposed United Nations Peace Cooperation Bill to authorize the deployment of Japanese Self-Defense Force units to the Persian Gulf or to other Third World crisis areas was defeated by the Diet.

Tokyo's efforts to address and respond to a security issue outside the MST purview, however, must be considered a significant first step in Japan's willingness to coordinate "out-of-area" security policy with the U.S. and other NATO states. This effort also compared favorably to South Korea's response when the U.S. solicited compensation for American warships protecting both South Korean oil access and the stability of South Korean investment projects in the Gulf. Seoul refused to provide $20 million worth of free repairs and maintenance to U.S. naval vessels en route to or returning from the Gulf because, it was argued, South Korea could not become involved in an extraregional dispute. Seoul did commit $220 million in late 1990 to help defray U.S. logistical expenses for *Operation Desert Shield*.

The interalliance security cooperation that has occurred is principally strategically predicated economic assistance rather than consultations about specific global deterrence matters. In late September 1988, for example, Japanese, South Korean, and Australian officials were present at a NATO Foreign Ministers meeting convened by President Reagan at the United Nations, the first time that Asia-Pacific representatives had attended a clearly defined NATO function. The basic reason for their attendance was to discuss ways to upgrade and coordinate Overseas Development Assistance (ODA) to developing countries —a form of security burden-sharing where Japan has now surpassed the United States as the world's leading assistance donor by earmarking $9.6 billion worldwide for 1989 compared to $8.9 billion for the United States.[177] Another Japanese delegation attended the aforementioned NATO Ministeral meeting in Belgium. It expressed Tokyo's wish for developing a closer trilateral relationship with the United States and Western Europe on Security cooperation short of formal Japanese membership in major international security institutions (i.e., NATO, the UN Security Council, or the Conference for Security and Cooperation in Europe). Instead, Japanese officials in attendance suggested that the annual summit meetings of the seven leading industrial democracies be expanded to include deliberations on Western security interests.[178] In conjunction with the Persian Gulf crisis, the U.S. and

Japan have also discussed with the Federal Republic of Germany, in particular, and with other NATO members, a $US 10 billion aid package known as the "Philippine Marshall Plan" to promote economic development and political stability in that strategically located country.[179] The South Koreans, by contrast, have rejected an initial American request to absorb additional costs of American fleet operations conducted in Southwest Asia but promised to "study" subsequent U.S. proposals for Seoul to extend economic assistance to the Philippines.[180]

Japan has, furthermore, responded to American and Australian arguments that politically vulnerable and economically destitute South Pacific island regimes would constitute a danger for future Western collective defense interests. In January 1987, Japanese Foreign Minister Tadashi Kuranari toured the South Pacific and advanced the "Kuranari Doctrine" promising more Japanese financial support for the area's microstates. However, Japan's ODA assistance volume to South Pacific Forum member-states remains exceeding modest (less than 2 percent of Tokyo's total bilateral ODA in 1986) because of difficulties in identifying appropriate development projects to fund without the South Pacific islanders accusing Tokyo of ulterior motives: i.e., merely participating to extract short-term profits.[181]

Finally, Japan has become more involved in the shaping of U.S. extended deterrence policies by taking an active stand on arms control matters which are of direct relevance to its own national security, beyond its public anti-nuclear rhetoric. Prime Minister Nakasone, for instance, was successful in pressing Japan's case at the 1983 Seven-Industrial-Nation Summit in Williamsburg for negotiating intermediate nuclear force (INF) reductions in Asia commensurate to those in Europe. He was later instrumental in enlisting Chinese assistance for pressuring the Reagan administration into a final INF agreement which reflected this approach and which facilitated more effective verification of INF systems relevant to those negotiations.[182] The Japanese INF position directly affected U.S. global strategy by increasing Washington's readiness to look upon arms control policy as a preferable alternative, in this case, to the usual ambiguities underlying the U.S. extended deterrent in Northeast Asia. Japanese analysts have also suggested measures for confidence-building or strategic "reassurance" in Northeast Asia: advanced notification of naval maneuvers, and the implementation of common force-level verification procedures. Unlike confidence-building proposals (CBMs) introduced by the Soviet Union, the Japanese CBM formula envisions no prior reductions in regional military strength (i.e., basing pullouts, nuclear free zones, etc.). Instead, the apparent Japanese intention is to directly reduce prospects for unintended war and to increase the predictability of deterrence behavior in the Asia-Pacific region.[183] If progress toward attaining such conditions is realized, the Dominant Player posture could be still viewed as more appropriate to contemporary Japanese security needs than whatever other limited policy alternatives may be available for Japan during the next decade.

Extended Deterrence on the Korean Peninsula: Future Prospects

THE SUCCESS of future U.S. extended deterrence policy on the Korean peninsula will depend on two factors, one internal and one external. Internally, the effects of what Robert Scalapino terms the process of "Asianization" will introduce new elements of nationalism into South Korea's national security outlook.[184] Indeed, ongoing internal political events and economic developments in both Koreas could well fuel already strong reunification sentiments. If so, the U.S. commitment to sustain deterrence on behalf of its South Korean treaty ally will be sharply tested. Specific U.S. gestures of good will, such as working toward the eventual reverting of the Combined Forces Command to a Korean officer during peacetime or shifting the American emphasis even further toward air and naval power, may not be enough to salvage it. A more preferable outcome, from the Dominant Player's vantage-point, would be what one Korean-American defense analyst has labeled a "transition to a reciprocal dependence" from U.S. strategic hegemony within the bilateral American-South Korean military relationship. In essence, what began as a manifestation of American extended deterrence is about to become "an exemplar of interdependence, in which the calculus of interests will dictate what each side gets [from the security relationship] and how."[185]

Externally, the direction of Soviet policies toward the peninsula could either reinforce Pyongyang's long standing animosity against the Americans and South Koreans, or help moderate it, and lead to tangible negotiations to fulfill Korean unification sentiments, following Kim Il-sung's death. This choice, in part, will depend on the extent to which the new North Korean leadership interprets as a strategic bellwether the current unfolding of more extensive Soviet and Chinese trade relations with the prosperous South.

Moscow and Beijing have both modified their animosity toward South Korea in recent years for reasons of economics and trade. If the present Soviet regime continues to be preoccupied with the development of economic and political institutions in its own country, its interest in attracting Seoul to participate in the USSR's development projects should increase. Even though the Soviets sustained only $150 million in trade volume with South Korea during 1987 (only about one-tenth of the South Korean-PRC trade volume), they have set up a trade office in Seoul in the aftermath of Mikhail Gorbachev's September 1988 observation that the time was ripe for expanded economic ties between the USSR and South Korea (the first time a Soviet leader has publicly acknowledged South Korea's existence since the Korean War). Unless unexpected political developments prompt Japan to look toward the Soviet Union as an alternative market for money, technology, and capital goods, South Korea represents the most attractive alternative for the Soviets as a possible conduit to Western markets and technology and as a source of finance for the Gorbachev regime's "free enterprise zones" throughout the Soviet Far East.

This explains the Soviet leader's willingness to meet with South Korean President Roh Tae Woo during the former's visit to San Francisco in early June 1990. Despite the allure of its new-found South Korean commercial ties, Soviet policy analysts remain sensitive to the risk of antagonizing Pyongyang by going too far in developing relations with Seoul. One Soviet expert on Asian affairs recently noted that "We don't like to embarrass the North Koreans and they don't like being embarrassed . . . . the South Koreans [still] expect too much politically of the Soviet Union." [186] The Gorbachev-Roh meeting, however, was a major step toward Moscow and Seoul normalizing diplomatic relations the following September notwithstanding obvious North Korean consternation at such a prospect.

Despite the recent crackdown against political dissidents in the PRC, Beijing's leaders are determined to continue attracting outside investment. They view building trade and investment relations with outside parties as the best way to modernize China and South Korea is increasingly regarded as a primary candidate for assisting in the modernization process. In 1987, unofficial Sino-South Korean trade volume reached $1.4 billion and that total was expected to exceed $2 billion in

1988.[187] Ranking among each other's top ten trading partners (although Hong Kong intermediaries handle most Sino-South Korean commercial transactions), joint ventures are planned in the areas of auto manufacturing, electronics and various quality consumer goods. If this trend continues, the likelihood of Beijing encouraging North Korean bellicosity on the peninsula, with the risk of stifling its burgeoning economic ties with a South Korean regime willing to trade and invest with the PRC, will decrease over time. Barring an unexpected reversal of South Korean President Roh Tai Woo's "Northern Policy," designed to improve relations with the USSR, China and Eastern Europe as a means for eventual improvement of relations and eventual reunification with North Korea, the continued relevance of the Dominant Player posture as the most appropriate means for ensuring stability on the peninsula could become sharply tested in the years ahead.

Soviet and Chinese willingness to use military power on the Korean peninsula should thus decrease relative to the increased levels of trade both countries conduct with the South Koreans. If so, Pyongyang may well be forced to reassess its own confrontational posture toward the South and apply more subtle means to influence the course of political development. The result could be a permanent relaxation of tension in what has been the most volatile frontline of Asia-Pacific geopolitics, and a commensurate decline in the strategic relevance of the Dominant Player posture.

The question of continued U.S. nuclear weapons deployments at Kunsan Air Base in South Korea promises to be especially sensitive. No longer are nuclear weapons regarded, as they were in Eisenhower's time, as merely "additional firepower of a large magnitude," usable if the circumstances require it. A new generation of South Koreans now view nuclear weapons and conventional armaments in entirely different categories. While they remain interested in preserving American extended deterrence guarantees for their homeland, they are, as previously noted, questioning, to a much greater extent than ever thought possible during the height of the cold war, the purpose of a land-based American nuclear trip wire on their soil. Koreans opposed to the American nuclear presence further argue that it only serves Washington's global strategy of deterring Moscow from opening a second front in Northeast Asia in the event war breaks out in another Eurasian theater but otherwise has little relevance to local Korean defense problems. U.S. military experts have counterargued that Korean opponents to U.S. Dominant Player posture no longer appreciate the value of nuclear retaliatory capabilities "in one of the few places in the world where a convincing argument can be made that nuclear weapons have been an instrument of peace." [188]

By contrast, those traditionally extending deterrence to the North Koreans, particularly the Chinese, worry that Seoul might develop and deploy an indigenous South Korean nuclear force if the American force presence were to be removed from the peninsula. [189] Such concerns could well account for why both the USSR and PRC until very recently continued to assist North Korea with building its own nuclear reactors at Yongbyon and Kunson near Pyongyang, despite the obvious risk of Kim Il-sung's regime developing an indigenous nuclear weapons capability and bringing distant South Korean targets (i.e., Kwangju and Pusan) within targeting range of nuclear-armed North Korean SCUD-B missiles. Some independent Western analysts suspect that Moscow has attempted to control the North Korean nuclear energy program in order to preclude North Korean ability to produce weapons-grade plutonium as a byproduct of its nuclear fuel reprocessing. [190] In early 1990, Moscow suspended the sale of four nuclear reactors to the North Koreans and withdrew its nuclear technicians from the Yongbyon complex. The PRC reportedly refused Kim Il-sung's request for substantial military assistance when he visited Beijing in November 1989.

The related challenges for future U.S. security planners are to sustain the Dominant Player posture on the Korean peninsula and to overcome Washington's image of inconsistency and ambiguity in defining its strategic interests there. As South Korea matures and redefines its own national identity, the value of U.S. extended deterrence is increasingly questioned by idealistic Koreans enamored with prospects for eventual reunification with the North. Two respected American analysts have summarized this trend concisely: "the failures of U.S. security policy in Korea have been less inadequacies in efforts to bolster and maintain the deterrent forces than inadequacies in policy conception and articulation . . . instill(ing) doubt in the minds of all Koreans as to the reliability of the U.S. commitment . . . [and] to generate broad public support for the commitment." [191] While it is unlikely that the appeal of the North Korean "one nation, two systems" formula for unification will be compelling enough for the South to give up the economic advantages and progressively democratic political breakthroughs it has obtained through patience and national sacrifice, the possibility of a DPRK military strike cannot be totally discounted. Pyongyang's leadership understands that South Korean economic power could eventually translate into clearcut military superiority. The current domestic strife between South Korea's government and its youth may be the last "window of opportunity" for an invasion before Kim Il-sung's death. While the North is more likely to continue its present tactics of alternating negotiation offers with military buildups, the strengthening of its own forward units, the procurement of more sophisticated weapons systems from the USSR, and the construction of tunnels and underground fortresses near the DMZ are continued sources of anxiety for Washington, Tokyo and Seoul.

After ANZUS: The South Pacific Agenda

FOLLOWING THEIR August 1986 decision to jettison ANZUS in light of the U.S.-New Zealand dispute over nuclear free zone politics, the U.S. and Australia restructured their own defense relations along bilateral lines (see chapter 6). Australian policy planners directed many of their efforts to strengthening Antipodeon (Australian/New Zealand) conventional regional deterrence capabilities. Recently, however, there have been increased strains in defense relations between Canberra and Wellington. New Zealand's growing economic problems have led it to vacillate on an original Defense Ministry commitment to purchase at least two—and preferably four—West German-designed and Australian-built frigates to strengthen its South Pacific patrolling capabilities (see chapter 6). U.S. defense planners cannot take much comfort from the prospect that, as new economic and political nerve centers emerge in the Asia-Pacific region, Australia and New Zealand military forces cannot be effectively coordinated.

The most likely South Pacific threats to Western security interests are disruptions of fragile, indigenous economies, local ethnic strife escalating to civil wars, and continued aid dependency which could be exploited by opportunistic external powers. In March 1989, an Australian Parliamentary Joint Committee on Foreign Affairs, Defense, and Trade released a White Paper on Australia's relations with other South Pacific states. The White Paper underscored and documented the argument that domestic threats to established South Pacific regimes constituted the most serious challenge to the area's overall regional stability. Although not to be completely ignored (see chapter 6), conflicts materializing from external competition over political control or resource access were deemed less likely to occur.[192]

A new generation of emerging Pacific island-state leaders is clearly intent on widening their range of economic and political contacts beyond traditional American, French, or Antipodeon ties. However, most remain comfortable with the regional geopolitical status quo. Pacific islanders believe that, despite what they perceive to be the Western industrial countries' track record of insufficient political deference and economic aid to the region, Australian and Western allied policymakers are still more prone to and more capable of, responding to their concerns than are other outside powers which have recently come to view the South Pacific as strategically important. Yet, prospects for *Western* power intervention in the subregion are still a matter of significant concern to a number of South Pacific island-state elites.[193]

In this context, a key strategic issue is to what extent the South Pacific microstates can identify an acceptable balance between political autonomy and strategic affiliation with the ANZUS powers. As the ANZUS dispute intensified, American and Australian military planners moved to expand coverage of Southwest Pacific and Eastern Indian Ocean zones of commercial and naval activity previously allocated among all three ANZUS allies proportionately under the 1951 Radford-Collins Act. The U.S. expanded its defense and economic assistance programs to South Pacific island-states (such as the U.S. Army's Expanded Relations Program's civic action teams' recent construction projects in the Federated States of Micronesia).[194] Joint U.S.-Australian military exercises such as the annual *Kangaroo* war games were also expanded substantially to demonstrate U.S. and Australian willingness to operate militarily throughout the Southwest and South Pacific.[195] Australia conducts its formal Defense Cooperation Program (DCP), extending a military presence throughout the region through regular consultations between Australian and South Pacific nations' defense officials, through visits by Australian naval vessels and air surveillance missions throughout the area, through the provision of patrol craft to selected South Pacific nations, and through various military training and funding projects. Papua New Guinea (PNG) is singled out for almost half of Australia's military assistance funding ($A 24.9 out of DCP funding total of $A 45.5).[196] In December 1987, Australia and PNG signed a "Joint Declaration of Principles" solidifying Australia's commitment to defend that country against external attack. Since Indonesia remains the PNG's primary external threat due to unresolved border management problems between the two countries and due to Jakarta's suspicions that the PNG is supporting insurgents in Irian Jaya, Canberra has effectively extended the South Pacific trip wire to Southeast Asia's doorstep. Acknowledging this reality, the Australian government announced in February 1987 that it was giving defense cooperation with the South Pacific "the same priority" as that given to Southeast Asia.[197]

CONCLUSION

THE DOMINANT Player posture has thus far remained intact in Northeast Asia because the U.S. and its allies have shared a common interest in preserving a favorable regional balance of power. The Nixon Doctrine, however, called for greater burden-sharing to sustain conventional deterrence in both Europe and Northeast Asia, fueling tensions among the Japanese and South Koreans by implying that their failure to respond would reduce the scope and intensity of subsequent U.S. deterrence commitments to their security. Such a commitment reduction did materialize in the case of Taiwan, as China used its closer alignment with United States to assume a pivotal position between a perceived rising Soviet and declining American hegemon. While Tokyo and Seoul questioned, based on Taiwan, the credibility of U.S. extended deterrence commitments, Beijing applauded Washington's belated acknowledgment of the PRC as an independent—and legitimate—great power in both an Asia-Pacific and international context.[198]

Recent U.S. efforts to adjust the Dominant Player posture in Northeast Asia have created further uncertainty among Washington's allies there because they have accentuated the limits of American power and the U.S. need for defense burden-sharing. As "Transitional Players" in the Asia-Pacific's rapidly changing strategic environment, Japan remains uncertain about the strategic benefits of seeking alternatives to the ambiguities of existential deterrence, Taiwan is skeptical of any U.S. deterrence commitment in the absence of a formal MST, and South Korea is increasingly concerned regarding the appropriate balance between the nuclear and conventional components of its local deterrence requirements. Japan and, to a lesser extent, South Korea have acknowledged the reality of U.S. burden-sharing pressures but have increasingly defined and implemented their own approaches to deterrence and international security.

Further south, future Australian-American security relations will depend on how successful Washington and Canberra are in achieving a balance between the traditional deterrence postures of global strategic denial (still integral to U.S. strategy) and emerging Australian needs to effectively address regional stability and defense in the South and Southwest Pacific. U.S.-Australian defense ties should be coordinated sufficiently to preclude any serious challenge to the South Pacific regional order by any would-be external predator. If such coordination eludes American and Australian defense planners, expansionist outside parties, or indigenous, anti-Western forces could advance their own political and strategic agendas at both Washington's and Canberra's expense.

These illustrative trends point to an Asia-Pacific environment of strategic uncertainty: to potential difficulties with the Dominant Player posture regarding extended deterrence and the effects of that posture on the perceived local and regional security objectives of the Asia-Pacific's Transitional Players. The question remains whether this posture can be revised to serve U.S. and allied interests in the Asia-Pacific, or if it must give way in whole or in part to the alternative strategies adopted by others within the region who are capable and willing to supplant the U.S. brand of deterrence with one less global in scope and more regional in its objectives.

CHAPTER 3

Aspiring Player I: The Soviet Union

THROUGHOUT ITS history, the Soviet Union has viewed the Asia-Pacific with both fascination and fear. Considerations of expanding national power have combined with the USSR's preoccupation with reducing the vulnerability of its distant frontiers to cause a strategic identity crisis in this region for successive generations of Soviet leaders. The result has been ambiguity in Soviet attitudes, both toward its own minority Asian ethnic groups (constituting about 20 percent of the USSR's total population) and toward the Asia-Pacific states that are contiguous to the three-fourths of the Soviet territory east of the Ural Mountains. John Stephan has noted that in both historic and geographic terms, "Asia's special interpenetration with the Soviet Union is symbolized by the vast Eurasian plain which stretches from the Urals to Mongolia . . . An awareness of the plain's historic permeability and ethnic evanescence leaves many Russians with a half-formed sense of territorial insecurity that manifests itself not only in the predilection of strong central authority but in what amounts to a national fixation on frontier defense."[1] Moscow's failure to reconcile its legacy of expanding political authority to its pervasive sense of not belonging to Asia has complicated Soviet defense planning east of the Urals.[2]

The postwar Soviet deterrence problem in the Asia-Pacific has involved intermittent phases of expansionism and defensiveness. The Sino-Soviet alliance, operating effectively throughout much of the 1950s, is the most graphic instance of Moscow's attempt to break American global containment strategy in an extra-European context. As is argued in the following chapter, the Chinese tested the effectiveness of the

Soviet alliance on at least three occasions (Korea in 1953, and Taiwan in 1954/1955, and again in 1958) and found it wanting. China's disillusionment with post-Stalinist Soviet leadership intensified into major ideological and geopolitical differences between 1958 and 1964 as the USSR became more sensitive to the risks of nuclear war and explored peaceful coexistence with the West. Worsening tensions between Moscow and Beijing led to a massive Soviet force buildup along the Sino-Soviet border to deter an increasingly hostile and nuclear-armed China from conducting military strikes against contested border areas. This took place even as the Soviet Union was attempting to work *with* the Chinese in assisting a North Vietnam threatened with conflict escalation by American forces. Another version of Soviet regional extended deterrence strategy unfolded between 1972 and 1985. This strategy embodied Soviet behavior reflecting its fears of strategic encirclement, comparable to that occurring just prior to World War II. It has, therefore, been labeled the "1941 complex." Moscow signed a security treaty with a unified communist Vietnam, intensified an already growing security relationship with India, and courted North Korea more intensively despite Pyongyang's oscillating diplomacy between the Soviets and Chinese, all while simultaneously refining Soviet military capabilities throughout the Asia-Pacific. All this was in response to what the Soviets perceived to be the forming of an American-Chinese-Japanese security coalition.

Yet another strategy has accompanied Mikhail Gorbachev's rise to power in March 1985 and culminated with the Sino-Soviet summit four years later. It has embodied a multidimensional Soviet approach to dividing the United States, PRC, and Japan, enhancing Soviet influence on the Asia-Pacific diplomatic and economic fronts, and adjusting Soviet military posture toward "reasonable sufficiency."[3] To the extent that this approach to Asia-Pacific security issues represents increased Soviet self-confidence about its ability—or at least its right —to exercise greater influence in the Asia-Pacific, Moscow can now be perceived as an "Aspiring Player" in the region. Recent improvements in Sino-Soviet relations, coupled with an at least tacit superpower modus vivendi as evidenced by the recent extension of the intermediate nuclear force or INF agreement into Asian as well as European locales, have given Moscow the opportunity to resurrect a more active and effective Asia-Pacific diplomacy. The challenge to Moscow's policy planners, however, is to infuse this new approach with sufficient credibility to overcome what are suspicions still widely held within the region that underneath its so-called "smile diplomacy," Moscow has nothing more to offer than divisiveness and confrontation. The USSR still projects nuclear and conventional military power into the region, confronts Japan in the Northern Islands, contests China's territorial claim to Bear Island (Heixiazi) to safeguard the strategically critical city of Khabarovsk, and subsidized, until recently, Vietnam's economy to the extent that Hanoi could maintain the world's fourth largest army. As Donald Zagoria has noted, such behavior, more than current Soviet rhetoric, demonstrates that the Soviet Union "has not become a status quo power."[4]

SOVIET DOCTRINAL SHIFTS

MODERN WEAPONS technology, the ongoing political liberalization of East European societies, and the weakness of the Soviet economy have changed the USSR's thinking about deterrence in general and particularly in the Eurasian theaters. The Soviets have traditionally focused on achieving military victory both against the U.S. boundaries and against allied forces adjacent to the Soviet homeland.[5] Moscow, however, overcompensated throughout the 1970s. It brought its strategic nuclear forces and homeland air defenses to levels far beyond what was needed for protecting Soviet territory and structured offensive capabilities (mechanized and armored infantry divisions, formidable aviation support, and an extensive fleet of hunter/killer submarines) to neutralize U.S. forward theater forces. William Odom has summarized Soviet deterrence strategy during the 1970s as seeking a unique "'triad' of capabilities: to defend the rear, to seize the contiguous land theaters, and to project war into noncontiguous theaters that may affect Eurasia."[6]

By the mid 1980s, the Soviet General Staff, under the direction of Marshal Nikolai Ogarkov, initiated "new thinking" in Soviet military strategy, contemplating the feasibility of global war fought with highly sophisticated conventional weapons systems. In part, this may have been a response to U.S. emphasis on intertheater conventional warfare scenarios. A more likely factor, however, was a growing Soviet perception that a protracted conventional conflict against the West could materialize as the decisive stage of modern war. In such a conflict, technology and tactics would count more than brute strength represented by the number and lethality of nuclear warheads.

After assuming power over the Soviet Communist Party in mid-1985, Mikhail Gorbachev dumped Ogarkov and proceeded to incorporate the "new thinking" as his own. Gorbachev's "reasonable sufficiency" policy separates the concept of nuclear warfighting from the traditional Marxist emphasis on the inevitability of conflict between classes and states.[7] In his book, *Perestroika,* Gorbachev argues that the avoidance of nuclear war is a "humankind interest" superseding international strategic competition.[8]

Soviet policymakers, of course, are probably no more capable than their American counterparts at eliminating domestic political infighting within leadership circles or of overcoming economic and physical resource constraints to a degree where they can confidently forge a "master plan" of geopolitics for the Asia-Pacific. Gorbachev's Asia-Pacific politico-diplomatic strategy, however, is clear—to undermine U.S. geopolitical predominance in this theater and establish Moscow's own credentials as a legitimate and powerful regional security actor. Even as the Soviets develop their new policy initiatives, they remain dedicated to military power that is reasonably sufficient at the nuclear level and formidable at the conventional level. Moscow is also sustaining its security ties with North Korea and Vietnam to hedge against a future Asia-Pacific crisis that would compromise the reasonable sufficiency posture beyond repair.

The Soviet Union is attempting to preclude an anti-Soviet strategic coalition from emerging in a region where Moscow's past policies have largely failed. It is currently moving to defuse its conflicts with China, to secure greater access to the Japanese and South Korean economies, to become an active participant in the Pacific Economic Cooperation Council (PECC), to drive a wedge in the U.S.-Japan alliance, to cultivate better ties with South Korea (notwithstanding its continued overtures to Pyongyong) and the ASEAN states, and to exploit antinuclear politics. Gorbachev's new approach, as an Aspiring Player, has been instituted at a time when the U.S. faces some potentially serious problems in the Asia-Pacific in dealing with China's "independent foreign policy," confronting Japan's economic challenge, and in responding to the traumas created by political and economic modernization now taking place in South Korea and the Philippines. This chapter argues that Asia-Pacific leaders have thus far been as skeptical of Gorbachev's regional confidence-building initiatives as they have been critical of American intransigence regarding their views about regional security. Nevertheless, Gorbachev's track record for policy "salesmanship" is impressive, and Moscow has at least some room for optimism that its Aspiring Player challenge to traditional U.S. extended deterrence policies could produce, over time, some tangible benefits for Moscow's regional security agenda.[9]

PHASES OF SOVIET DETERRENCE STRATEGY IN ASIA

FROM A Western perspective, the Soviet Union has clearly been a rising and potentially hostile military power on the East Asian mainland since the defeat of the Japanese Imperial Army in 1945. However, the USSR's strategic objectives in the region were not immediately evident during the initial years of Moscow's strategic competition with the West. More recently, they have been illuminated by an increasing number of memoirs (i.e., by Nikita Khrushchev, Andrei Gromyko, and Soviet defector Arkady N. Shevchenko), and by policy statements and military writings offered during the recent era of glasnost or "openness" in Soviet society. Broad policy trends of the past four decades can now be more readily identified and evaluated to provide a useful, if rudimentary, historical blueprint of Soviet deterrence "phases" in the Asia-Pacific. They have included: (1) establishing strategic buffer zones in East Asia during the 1940s and most of the 1950s (i.e., China and North Korea) without precipitating direct military conflict with the United States; (2) strategically detaching itself from an increasingly hostile China during the late 1950s and 1960s and compensating for the failed Sino-Soviet alliance with increased military deployments in the Far Eastern Theater; (3) deterring China and the West throughout the late 1960s and early 1970s through confronting Chinese military power along the Sino-Soviet border; (4) strengthening its indigenous military power throughout the late 1970s in response to what it perceived as a growing Sino-Japanese-U.S. anti-Soviet coalition; and (5) after July 1986, de-emphasizing the military dimensions of its Asia-Pacific strategy through revival of collective security diplomacy and by seeking an Asia-Pacific balance of power which could facilitate the USSR's quest to become a "legitimate" leading regional actor.

Throughout the first years of Gorbachev's reign, the Bush administration has reacted to the latest Soviet policy trends with what its critics regarded as undue caution. Until late 1989, with political liberalization suddenly enveloping Eastern Europe, U.S. officials publicly contended that "the rhetoric of Soviet 'new thinking' has outpaced the reality" of any changed behavior for the better. They still see no equivalent change in Asia to the collapse of the Warsaw Pact.[10] A more basic consideration, however, is whether the USSR will accrue greater regional influence in the Asia-Pacific by employing a judicious mix of diplomatic, economic, and military policy assets. To the extent that Moscow succeeds in doing so, will U.S. strategic interests in the region be compromised? This chapter will review the salient historical and the contemporary aspects of Soviet policy to answer this question.

Phase 1: Early Patterns of Soviet Extended Deterrence in Asia—1950–1957

THROUGHOUT MOST of the late 1940s, the Asia-Pacific was relegated to a secondary priority in Soviet foreign policy, as Joseph Stalin moved to consolidate Eastern Europe under Moscow's control. Two developments, however, took place which served to elevate the region's importance in the USSR's deterrence strategy: the Chinese Communist Party's ascension to power in Beijing (October 1949) and the outbreak of the Korean War (June 1950).

Mao Zedong's December 1949 journey to the Soviet capital, and his two-month bargaining session with the Soviet leadership leading to the signing of the Treaty of Friendship, Alliance, and Mutual Assistance on February 14, 1950, constituted the first postwar instance of the USSR extending deterrence commitments to an Asian ally.[11] Article I of the Treaty committed the Soviets and the Chinese to defend one another if either were attacked by Japan or states allied with Tokyo. The Chinese later argued, in September 1963, that Moscow violated this commitment as early as mid-1953, when the U.S. Seventh Fleet began conducting regular aerial observations over Chinese territory.

Beijing was especially bitter about Soviet conduct during the second Taiwan Straits crisis of 1958 (see chapter 4) during which, Beijing claimed, Soviet statements of support for Chinese military objectives were forthcoming only when "there was no possibility that a nuclear war would break out and no need for the Soviet Union to support China with its nuclear weapons."[12] The Soviet rejoinder underscored Moscow's belief—and, indeed, its outright expectation—that Soviet deterrence capabilities would ultimately be needed to bail China out of self-imposed crises. As Harvey Nelson later characterized the situation: "It was not that the Soviet deterrent was failing to protect China, rather it was smothering it. [Nikita] Khrushchev kept demanding Soviet basing rights in the PRC, probably with the ultimate goal of achieving command integration with the Red Army."[13] As the United States quickly moved to supply Taiwan with arms and equipment for shelling mainland China's coastline, and deployed its own nuclear forces in the area, Mao was indeed forced to seek maximum Soviet support to prevent conflict escalation. But Mao commenced actual hostilities in late August after notifying the Soviet Ministry of Defense. He thus made clear to exasperated Soviet leaders China's determination to establish its political and strategic independence within the international communist movement.[14]

The Korean War established a precedent of cautious Soviet behavior regarding direct military confrontation with the United States. From Moscow's viewpoint, the Korean situation went from a perceived opportunity for unification of the Korean Peninsula under Marxist rule to a major problem of escalation control. In this case, the Chinese appear to have served in the role of an unwilling geostrategic buffer. After arming and training seven North Korean divisions during the American force withdrawal from Korea, and when Acheson and others were excluding Seoul from Washington's perimeter of defense, the Soviets initially accepted Kim Il-sung's assurances (as recounted in Nikita Khrushchev's memoirs) that the North Korean army could quickly unify the peninsula through force, create a fait accompli, and preclude wholesale American intervention which could lead to the type of direct superpower confrontation Joseph Stalin desperately feared.[15] Recently declassified Chinese documents obtained by Western scholars indicate that both Moscow and Beijing were maneuvered into supporting a North Korean invasion of South Korea during talks between Stalin, Mao, and Kim Il-sung in Moscow during late 1949/early 1950. Both the Soviet and Chinese leaders were reluctant to back Kim's plan for fear of losing influence to the other, although Mao was particularly skeptical that the U.S. would stand aloof from the ensuing conflict.[16]

From the Soviet perspective, a successful North Korean offensive could at least be rationalized as forcing the United States to allocate strategic resources earmarked for Western Europe into Japan. It would also increase the likelihood of Chinese strategic dependence on the Soviets, legitimizing an expanded Soviet military presence in industrial northern China (Manchuria). Indeed, Beijing became convinced that it had no other choice than to rely upon Soviet military and economic aid as a counterbalance to American modern weaponry applied Chinese troops in Korea. As Adam Ulam recalls, "The Korean venture could thus be rationalized as promising great advantages to the Soviet Union with minimal risks." [17]

The unexpected intensity of the American reaction to the North Korean invasion quickly altered such calculations, and converted the Soviet posture in Northeast Asia from that of strategic opportunism to one of almost no extended deterrence. Even while the Chinese were repeatedly warning Washington that a concentrated UN Forces drive north of the 38th parallel would trigger Beijing's military intervention, the Soviets remained largely silent on events in Korea. In interviews conducted with People's Liberation Army (PLA) prisoners of war throughout early 1951, concerns surfaced about the level of Soviet support for China in the event Korea escalated to a nuclear conflict. As Alexander George has since recounted, there was growing concern among Chinese troops fighting in Korea that the United States would eventually use the atomic bomb against them. [18] Soviet small-arms transfers accelerated with the introduction of more Chinese troops into Korea during April-May 1951. Beijing, however, was forced to buy this material and military expenditures represented about half of China's national budget by 1951. [19] The Soviets were, in all probability, exercising extended deterrence by proxy, with a fallback strategy of Manchurian occupation in the event of an American attack against the Chinese mainland. This scenario has been implied by recent Soviet historical treatises which have underscored the Soviet defensive role in Manchuria during the Korean conflict. [20]

While documented evidence is still lacking on what finally prompted the Soviets to approve an armistice following Eisenhower's atomic threats against China in early 1953 (described more fully in chapter 4), it is clear that Stalin's death in early March ushered in a period of internal political crisis which critically affected the USSR's ability to sustain its policies of strategic confrontation abroad. This domestic uncertainty totally changed the opportunistic calculus Moscow had used in approving the North Korean invasion almost three years before. President Eisenhower's massive retaliation strategy was promising to rewrite the rules of the deterrence game. The Soviets were no longer certain that they could continue escalation control in the Korean conflict without discrediting their public commitment to Chinese security. The USSR recognized its inability to defend the Chinese against the growing American nuclear stockpile and U.S. deployments in Okinawa, the East China Sea, and elsewhere in the region. The Korean War had not provided them with the strategic opportunity to capitalize on Western vulnerabilities in Europe as was originally anticipated. Indeed, the U.S. had successfully dealt with the problem of interalliance transferability by strengthening the West's military command structure in NATO Europe even as it was preventing a communist military victory in this Northeast Asian outpost. In this instance, U.S. extended deterrence strategy had proven effective and the Soviets were compelled to back away from testing it.

Phase 2: Deterrence and the Sino-Soviet Rift

GROWING SINO-SOVIET differences over nuclear strategy during the 1960s were instrumental in widening the rift between the Soviet and Chinese which was already in evidence toward the end of the 1950s. The Soviets were gradually moving toward acceptance of many of the premises underlying American deterrence theory, including the use of Soviet nuclear forces as an escalation control mechanism to prevent regional conflicts such as the Taiwan crisis from resulting in attacks against the Soviet homeland.[21] Moreover, Khrushchev (not unlike Mikhail Gorbachev two decades later) was devoting increased attention toward pressing domestic economic problems and an entrenched bureaucracy.[22] By contrast, the Chinese, under Mao, viewed recent Soviet military-technology breakthroughs in intercontinental ballistic missile (ICBM) missile testing and in satellite launches (with their implications for military command and control breakthroughs) as an opportunity to mobilize Socialist forces for a more intense politico-military struggle against the West. Such mobilization, Beijing surmised, could be carried out because U.S. nuclear forces would be less able to contain "the forces of national liberation" (i.e., Chinese or Chinese-supported military actions against pro-Western elements in Asia-Pacific locales) than was previously the case, given enhanced Soviet nuclear power. Moreover, the PRC concluded, the Soviets would be obligated by the 1950 Friendship Treaty, by a subsequent Sino-Soviet New Defense Technical Accord signed in October 1957, and by ideological affinity to support China's quest to advance global Marxist revolution.

The October 1957 Accord was the product of China's new position of strength. It included a Soviet promise to transfer a prototype atomic bomb and related technical data to the PRC, Soviet assistance in building Chinese diesel and nuclear submarines, and Soviet transfer of equipment needed for the production of Chinese nuclear warheads in the newly-built Lanzhou Gaseous Diffusion Plant.[23] Khrushchev had already been attempting (unsuccessfully) to bring the Chinese military under formal Warsaw Pact (and, therefore, the Soviet Military Command's) tutelage.[24] By early 1958, the Soviets once again began to look for quid pro quos they could extract from the PRC while simultaneously beginning to "modify" the quality of industrial technology and equipment being transferred to China under the 1957 Accord. In April, the Soviet Union requested permission to build a long-wave radio station on Chinese territory so that, according to Khrushchev, "we could maintain communications with our submarine fleet operating in the Pacific." The Chinese refused Moscow's request on the grounds that such a station would violate China's national sovereignty, and also rejected a follow-up request that the Soviet Pacific Fleet be given access to Chinese ports for refueling in return for Chinese fleet access to Soviet ports in the Arctic.[25] China had just regained control of Port Arthur in May 1955, the last of the Soviet footholds on mainland China emanating from World War II. The symbolic meaning of that development reinforced what Adam Ulam succinctly described as the bottom-line Chinese limit to the USSR's extended deterrence posture: "the Chinese did not want Russian soldiers on their soil."[26]

A number of Western analysts have concluded that the second Taiwan crisis of September 1958 led to Soviet policy reconsideration. On August 16, 1958—a week before the PRC instituted its blockade against Quemoy and Matsu—the Chinese journal *Hongqi* [Red Flag] contended that any U.S. attempt to impose nuclear blackmail against Beijing in future crises would be met by Soviet nuclear deterrence.[27] The article coincided with a secret meeting taking place between Khrushchev and Mao (July 31–August 3, 1958). In that meeting, Khrushchev may have created the impression that, unlike in 1954, the USSR would support a Communist Chinese takeover of the two off-shore islands and intervene on the PRC's behalf in the event the U.S. responded by using tactical nuclear weapons against the PLA. In his memoirs, Khrushchev asserts that the USSR transferred aircraft, long-range artillery, and air force advisors to China in support of the latter's operation against Chiang Kai-shek. When the Chinese failed to press their advantage gained during the initial skirmishes of the crisis, the Soviets, according to Khrushchev, "were very perplexed."

Khrushchev's own account of the Taiwan Straits crisis, however, accuses Beijing of provocative behavior.[28] In warning messages sent to Washington, Khrushchev only went so far as to pledge Soviet intervention in the event the United States attacked positions on the Chinese mainland. Only after Beijing offered to negotiate with the Washington to lift the blockade in early September did the Soviet leader resort to tougher polemics in his communications with the Americans. Nor did Moscow put its forces on alert or conduct military maneuvers during the height of the crisis. To some degree, this may have been attributable to Mao's earlier reluctance to move against Nationalist positions on the offshore islands. A more likely cause for Soviet restraint was the rapid and highly visible buildup of the U.S. Seventh Fleet's nuclear firepower (six aircraft carriers and the emplacement of atomic cannon on Matsu), shattering Beijing's confidence in its ability to overcome the islands and that of the USSR in the ability of China to effectively manage any crisis with the West. In Mao's own words, "I simply did not calculate that the world would become so disturbed and turbulent."[29] Other Chinese sources later asserted that Mao moved quickly to alleviate Soviet fears of a nuclear confrontation by assuring them that if the Taiwan crisis did erupt into a Sino-American military confrontation, "the Soviet Union would not have to participate."[30]

There is little doubt that by early 1959 the Soviets had concluded that China under Mao had become unpredictable. They moved to effectively sever the New Defense Technical Accord by suspending nuclear assistance to the Chinese in June. As Allen Whiting has since noted, if Mao was as reluctant to discuss and formulate a comprehensive strategy with Khrushchev during the latter's visit to Beijing several weeks prior to the Taiwan crisis as appears to be the case (later claiming that Taiwan wasn't even discussed), "it reveals a betrayal of trust on the Chinese side of the alliance which would seem to strengthen subsequent Soviet accusations." [31]

Khrushchev's proposals for renewed Soviet access to Chinese—and particularly Manchurian—ports signaled the Soviets' return to their earlier, guarded, approach: "seeking to extract specific extraterritorial military rights from the Chinese Communist regime, hoping on the one hand to compensate themselves for the risks they were taking in building Chinese military strength and, and on the other hand to create a mechanism to help control Chinese use of that strength." [32] Without access to the Chinese landmass, the Soviets lacked the geostrategic buffer in the Asia-Pacific which they enjoyed in Eastern Europe, thus rendering vulnerable their Far Eastern ports and territories. Without access to China's long coastline, Soviet naval and air elements operating out of Northeast Asia would, in all likelihood, be deprived of ready access to open waters by superior U.S. offshore power. When China subsequently gave every indication that its sovereign defense interests ranked above those of the Socialist camp as a whole, the Soviets began to slow the military technology flow called for by the October 1957 New Defense Technical Accord and to reconsider their nuclear technology assistance to the Chinese. By August 1960, a year after the Soviets had "postponed" their transfer of a nuclear bomb prototype to China on the pretext of facilitating nuclear test ban negotiations with the West, all Soviet economic and technical advisors had been withdrawn from the PRC.

Soviet-Chinese acrimony became public with Khrushchev's denunciation of Maoism at the Third Congress of the Communist Party of Romania in June 1960, and Zhou Enlai's walking out of the Twenty-second Congress of the Communist Party of the Soviet Union in October 1961. While Khrushchev was intent on reaffirming the USSR's ideological precedence over an increasingly recalcitrant Chinese leadership (Mao always loved an ideological battle) and on imposing the doctrine of peaceful coexistence with the West, the problems of war and deterrence were among those at the heart of the Sino-Soviet dispute. Moscow continued to refer to the risks of nuclear war and the need to prevent "small wars of national liberation" from escalating to superpower confrontation. The Chinese, on the other hand, adhered to a more orthodox interpretation of Leninist dogma, emphasizing the inevitability of war and the need to sustain uncompromising revolutionary class warfare, even in the nuclear age.[33] Ideological dispute over the proper international Marxist strategy was accelerated in the press and culminated in a series of blistering attacks and counterattacks beginning in mid-June 1963.

Even then, however, the Soviets still perceived some advantages in negotiating Chinese territorial grievances along the Sino-Soviet border during mid-1964, and collaborating with Beijing to sustain the North Vietnamese war against South Vietnam and its U.S. backers. Soviet motives for doing so became more apparent in early 1965, with their effort to revive a Chinese component of their Asia-Pacific extended deterrent. Khrushchev had been deposed in October 1964, and the new Brezhnev-Kosygin regime had postponed plans to expel the Chinese Communist Party from the international Marxist fold. Instead, the new Soviet leaders argued that Vietnam could only be saved from an accelerated U.S. bombing offensive and from rapidly increasing deployments of U.S. ground forces in Southeast Asia by a "united front." According to a *White Book* published by Hanoi in 1979, Alexei Kosygin's visit to the North Vietnamese during February 1965 was designed to involve the Chinese in deterring a U.S. escalation of the Indochina conflict.[34] During April 1965, the USSR forwarded letters to Beijing ("on at least two occasions" according to Vietnam's *White Book*) proposing that China open an air corridor to Vietnam and that the USSR be granted access to a base in Yunan, adjacent to Vietnam, to build airfields.[35] China, however, believed that the USSR wanted to control its airspace in the guise of helping Vietnam and it rejected the presence of Soviet military personnel on Chinese soil on the basis of the sovereignty principle.[36]

Phase 3: Moscow Plays a Dual Deterrence Game—1965–1972

BY MID-1965, the USSR, resigned to dealing with what it regarded as China's continued intransigence, began to structure a posture of "dual deterrence." It accelerated a military buildup along the Sino-Soviet border by gradually expanding manpower, units, and military equipment (from approximately 20 divisions in 1965 to around 40 in 1970, 45 in 1979, 50–51 by 1982, and 56 by 1986; see table 2). While a number of these divisions were below "Category 1" or full combat readiness strength, the Soviets determined that given their qualitative advantages, a 400,000 strong deployment would be sufficient to deter the Chinese from using force to resolve outstanding Sino-Soviet territorial disputes by use of force.[37]

At the same time, Moscow also looked toward Vietnam, India, and other nations along China's periphery to contain the Chinese potential for regional power projection by building up strong indigenous military forces and by working with the USSR to create an eventual security order more conducive to its own strategic interests than to those of either Beijing or Washington. Brezhnev's proposal for an Asian collective security pact, advanced in 1969, although unsuccessful, was an expression of the USSR's determination to encircle China politically and militarily.[38] It proposed the convening of Asian negotiations on resolving still-contested postwar boundaries, settling related territorial disputes, and confidence building measures which would effectively blunt the geopolitical influence of American offshore military power and growing Chinese nuclear capabilities in the region. Brezhnev's plan also envisioned the dissolving of postwar U.S. alliances in the Asia-Pacific and liquidation of SEATO. In return for gaining the USSR entree into a region where it previously enjoyed little access or influence, the Brezhnev regime was prepared to conduct normal relations with East and Southeast Asian states previously allied with the West against the Soviet bloc (although it did not renounce the right to sponsor what it regarded as legitimate national liberation movements in the region).

The Brezhnev-Kosygin regime opted to downplay Khrushchev's ideological concerns about China and instead approached "the China problem" from the perspective of a straightforward geopolitical power struggle.[39] Moscow broadened its security agenda to focus on China and Japan, though the "China problem" remained the most significant component. Beijing's nuclear capability required that a greater Soviet concentration of nuclear and conventional forces be directed against China during the late 1960s and early 1970s. Most of the USSR's ground forces deployed in the Asian theater remained China-oriented. Both U.S. and West German press accounts reported that Moscow had deployed over 400 medium-range ballistic missiles (MRBMs) against China out of an estimated total of 750 to 1000 for the entire Soviet force.[40] This concentration of Soviet nuclear assets could be traced, in part, to the initial Chinese deployment of DF-2 medium-range and

DF-3 intermediate-range missiles between 1967 and 1969. During 1967, the USSR shifted approximately 40,000 troops from sites in Eastern Europe to positions facing the Chinese border to support a preventive strike against Chinese nuclear missiles and installations and to coerce Beijing back toward the Soviet bloc. Strengthening Soviet manpower levels became particularly important to Leonid Brezhnev and his colleagues in the Politboro, as their entreaties to the Warsaw Pact allies to join in a military strike against Chinese border positions and nuclear assets proved unsuccessful.[41]

The double deterrence phase culminated in 1969, with a Sino-Soviet border clash which only indirectly involved the West.[42] This dispute was largely self-contained but U.S. diplomatic efforts at escalation control were very much in evidence. American efforts were given impetus by the very real prospect that the USSR would carry out its nuclear threats against China. These threats followed major clashes between Chinese and Soviet forces at Zhenbao (on March 2 and March 14) and another in Xinjiang during mid-August.

Analysts differ as to who deterred whom in the crisis. The Soviets put forth a credible escalation control strategy by positioning artillery, rockets and other military equipment along the Sino-Soviet border. In comprehensive press accounts, they emphasized the success of Soviet offensives into China prior to and during World War II, while simultaneously releasing extensive information about current force buildups. All of this was orchestrated for the benefit of what the Soviets may well have read to be an unpredictable and even irrational adversary, whose leaders had misread and misapplied the Soviet extended deterrent during the 1958 Taiwan crisis, had rejected a logical pooling of the socialist world's strategic assets against the West in 1958 and 1965, and had instigated border clashes in the face of overwhelming Soviet military superiority.

The Chinese proved in this instance, however, to be more "rational" than many Soviet policymakers expected. They gradually moved from a posture which discounted the USSR's will to carry out a nuclear strike against Chinese targets to one in which the risks of *not* returning to the negotiating table outweighed the benefits of standing firm. While continuing civil defense preparations and the deployment of nuclear weapons aboard its fleet of aging and highly vulnerable bombers, China still did not have a credible second-strike nuclear force of its own. Indeed, the few DF-2s and DF-3s deployed by late 1969 were highly unreliable and vulnerable to a Soviet first strike due to their liquid fueling systems.[43]

Soviet efforts to deter further Chinese military incursions following the March 2 confrontation on the Ussuri River were largely successful. The Chinese gained a greater appreciation of Soviet commitments to defend territory under its control. The Soviet leadership, meanwhile, discovered that the West was not inextricably tied to a policy of interference in Asia-Pacific crises at Soviet expense. It is an apparent strategic reality that when a crisis develops between two nuclear powers, outside parties appear to respond by adopting very moderate and nonthreatening postures of their own.

Phase 4: The *"1941 Complex" Revisited*—1972–1986

IN THE aftermath of President Nixon's visit to China in February 1972, and the subsequent normalization of Sino-Japanese relations, Moscow became preoccupied with the prospect that China, Japan and the United States would form into a hostile bloc in Northeast Asia. Of special concern was China's increased readiness to seek military or "dual use" (military/civilian-applicable) technology from the United States and from NATO European states, as well as to enter into low-key military exchange relationships with retired Japanese military personnel and military scholars. An even more serious aspect was growing evidence of U.S. encouragement for Japan's remilitarization as part of the Nixon Doctrine's emphasis on military self-sufficiency. Ivan Kovalenko (also known as I. I. Ivkov), Section Chief of the Communist Party of the Soviet Union's International Department and, until his retirement in 1988, the USSR's reigning expert on Japan, linked these factors together into what he viewed as evidence of an anti-Soviet coalition materializing in the aftermath of the U.S. military withdrawal from Vietnam. His observations reflected the mid-1970s Soviet "worldview" regarding anti-Soviet coalition politics and deserve to be quoted at some length:

> In order to equip its army with all modern types of weapons the PRC more and more often solicits the assistance of Western Powers . . . The imperialists willingly supply the PRC with various types of military equipment and combat weapons in the hope that the Chinese war machine would be turned against the USSR and other socialist countries, and the developing states . . . Hardly a month passes without an emis-

sary from the PRC visiting the capital of a NATO member state or a country with a developed armaments industry . . . Voices are already singing in unison that China is NATO's "16th member," that it is the NATO of the East, and that by helping China with weapons the NATO countries are simultaneously protecting themselves against a "Soviet threat." . . . Beijing responds by welcoming (the) U.S. presence in Asia and also in the Pacific and Indian Oceans, lauds the Japanese-American security treaty as an important factor of "stability" in Asia and is against the dismantling of American military bases in Japan, South Korea, Thailand, Taiwan, and the Philippines.[44]

Moscow's apprehension about its strategic isolation on both the European and Asian fronts had more fundamental roots. It had been in evidence long before Deng's Xiaoping's diplomatic machinations came onto the scene. It was fueled by a long-standing siege mentality dating back to Operation Barbarossa (the German invasion of the USSR in June 1941) and by Moscow's subsequent propensity throughout much of the postwar era to emphasize military power as the best means for neutralizing real or imaginary adversaries. In this sense, Soviet behavior represented a self-fulfilling prophecy in East Asia throughout much of the 1970s. It was regarded by many Asia-Pacific states as going beyond the limits of an understandable deterrence posture and as a misplaced and crude effort to win regional influence through military intimidation.[45]

There was a paradox in Moscow's military buildup in Asia in the late 1970s, a buildup which culminated with an expansion of Soviet basing activities in Vietnam's Cam Ranh Bay and with the USSR's military intervention in Afghanistan (December 1979). The Soviet military-political leadership's quest for absolute security in the theater became counterproductive and produced exactly the opposite effect. It tended to exacerbate rather than defuse regional tensions with the Americans, Chinese, and Japanese. It presented an image of Soviet behavior motivated by the pursuit of geopolitical opportunity, indifferent to the threshold of strategic risk, and uncaring regarding the sensibilities of indigenous Asian governments. As Sheldon Simon has neatly summarized this paradox: "Because of a limited ability to use political persuasion and the general lack of appeal in its economic blandishments, Soviet Asian policies appear disproportionately power oriented."[46] For all of its faith in the use of a strong military to gain regional influence, the USSR remained nothing more than a marginal regional security actor during this timeframe.

In response to what it perceived as the rise of a NATO-Chinese-Japanese coalition against the Soviet Union, Moscow's strategy in the Asia-Pacific was directed toward achieving capabilities to meet three key objectives. The first was to conduct an Asia-Pacific component of any global war successfully against U.S. forces in the theater and against those regional allies of the United States hosting such forces (Japan, South Korea, and the Philippines). The second was to sustain adequate military power for defeating, or at least neutralizing China, in any future Sino-Soviet conflict or as part of a global war. The third was to pursue geopolitical opportunity wherever possible by supporting the revolutionary politics of Vietnam and South Korea in their respective subregions.[47]

Several developments in Soviet military forces were especially important in pursuing this strategy. Moscow, above all, believed that an interregional strategy based upon maintaining theater nuclear superiority in both Europe and Asia provided the best means to avoid a multi-front war with its adversaries. The new, longer-range, and more accurate nuclear missile and aircraft systems deployed in both Europe and Asia during the late 1970s were designed as much for political intimidation as for military purposes, even (or in spite of) past Soviet legacies of overplaying the utility of intimidation, solidifying anti-Soviet coalition movements as a result.[48]

The Soviets also structured what could be termed an "anti-hegemony countercoalition" strategy, initially directed toward drawing the United States away from China by means of detente with Washington during the early 1970s.[49] They strengthened their military presence and power opposite U.S. and Chinese strategic deployments in Northeast Asia and attempted to encircle the PRC geostrategically by intensifying their alliances with Vietnam and Mongolia (North Korea was less central to Soviet strategy until 1984) and their less direct, but still formidable, military ties with India. They also began to explore ways of gaining strategic footholds in more distant outposts previously conceded to be within the West's strategic purview; most notably the Oceania-Southwest Pacific region. By doing so, the Soviets could take greater advantage of interdiction opportunities afforded by a reduced U.S. offshore naval and air presence and the diminished U.S. political commitment to Southeast Asia sensed in the region following the American withdrawal from Vietnam. Moscow could also advertise its strategic surge or "breakout" capabilities more effectively than from the relatively distant and contained Northeast Asian straits.[50]

From a deterrence perspective, Moscow was seeking to rectify its strategic liabilities east of the Urals by adopting the position that the best defense is a good offense. It sought to deflect any U.S. or Chinese efforts to break its tenuous lines of communication in Siberia, the Baikal-Amur Mainline (BAM), and Trans-Siberian railway systems. It significantly increased its ground and air force deployments in the Northern Islands opposite Japan. It implemented, in 1978, a Far East Theater of Operations High Command for the Soviet command structure facing China. It quickened the pace of SS-20 IRBM, *Backfire* bomber, and SU-24 *Fencer* fighter bomber deployments in the Siberian, Tranbaykal, and Far Eastern Military Districts. It modernized over 50 of the 140 airfields in the Far East Military District-airfields which support Soviet aircraft capable of threatening China, Japan, South Korea, and Northeast Asia's most critical sea lanes.[51]

At the same time, from the mid-1970s onward, the Soviets pursued deployment patterns in the Far East specifically as a "China component" of their theater nuclear forces. For example, of 380 SS-11 and SS-18 ICBMs deployed at seven different launching sites throughout the Soviet Far East, one-third have depressed-range configurations clearly for use against Chinese targets.[52] Most of the USSR's ground forces in the Far Eastern theater, armed with a wide array of tactical nuclear, conventional and chemical weapons, could be regarded as China-oriented by the early 1980s, with only three divisions on Sakhalin and Kamchatka, and one division-size unit in the Northern Islands, geared toward contingencies involving U.S. or Japanese forces.

By contrast, Soviet attack/ballistic missile-launching submarines deployed in the Sea of Okhotsk and in deep-water trenches along the eastern coast of the Kamchatka peninsula clearly are primed to strike U.S. and Asia-Pacific allied targets. With the unlikely exception of the USSR instituting a coastal blockade against a still rudimentary Chinese navy, Soviet naval and naval air support assets would be concentrated on interdicting U.S. and allied maritime assets along critical Northeast and Southeast Asian chokepoints and sea lanes. Most Chinese ships or submarines capable of damaging Moscow's Pacific Fleet would be destroyed, along with other military facilities, in an initial Soviet missile attack against China's ports.

Any Soviet effort to apply escalation control in any of the three conflict levels with which its force capabilities were concerned. however, could well have broken down in the face of the multiple threats which Moscow believed it faced during the mid-to-late 1970s. Theoretically, as Banning Garrett and Bonnie Glaser have pointed out, Soviet theater deployments could allow for a nuclear attack against China without the use of ICBMs, which could be held in reserve for deterrence/warfighting purposes against Washington, if it were inclined to intervene on China's behalf in a Sino-Soviet conflict.[53] As already noted, the behavior of "uninvolved superpowers" during times of nuclear crisis tends to be cautious. If Soviet war planners accepted this premise, they could concentrate on the Chinese threat without becoming completely obsessed with the need to attain "absolute security" against the Americans and their Asia-Pacific allies as well as against the PRC.

However, if Western analysts who assert that, throughout the late 1970s and early 1980s, the USSR could not fight a war against China or the West without the other moving to take advantage of Soviet vulnerability are correct, the issue of force component discrimination is reduced to one of only separate targeting missions to be carried out in an expanded, but inevitable global conflict. Faced with insufficient aircover, the vulnerability of Cam Ranh Bay to rapid wartime destruction by Seventh Fleet operations, and Soviet inability to field more than 15 percent of its submarines against Western and Japanese ASW operations at any given time, Soviet military planners, according to this school of thought, concluded they had little choice but to return to a more traditional strategy—defending Northeast Asian approaches to the USSR's homeland waters where second-strike SSBN nuclear missions could be carried out with greater confidence (see below).[54]

As China's own nuclear forces increased in quantity and were strengthened qualitatively, the "theater" versus "global" distinction in Soviet nuclear missions became increasingly blurred. Soviet antiballistic missile (ABM) and ballistic missile defense (BMD) testing facilities at Sary Shagan were sustained, at least in part, by calculations similar to those governing U.S. strategic planners' "sufficiency criteria" for deterrence in the late 1960s and early 1970s: to gain "relative immunity vis-a-vis third [nuclear] powers" such as China by deterring a Chinese attack against "even more vulnerable and adjacent [Soviet] targets."[55] Strategic arms limitation negotiations with the United States, however, have complicated Soviet objectives to continue ABM/BMD research with Soviet protestations against U.S. Strategic Defense Initiative (SDI) research undermining the credibility of any Soviet case to be made for maintaining strategic defenses. As China's camouflage and dispersal efforts and its strategic ballistic missile nuclear submarine program enhance that country's second-strike deterrence capabilities, Soviet aspirations to apply strategic compellance or intimidation against the Chinese in a future regional conflict become less realistic. Accordingly, both the Soviet and Chinese nuclear weapons deployments in the Asia-Pacific "may be seen as insurance against the other; neither [force deployment] is pursued at too forced a pace—because of the awesome technological and financial costs that such a pursuit would entail, because of the destabilizing consequences that would ensue, and because such pursuit might occasion a counter-effort sufficient to nullify any [strategic] achievements [or advantages]. In a low-threat context, both [the USSR and China] find the existing ambiguity satisfactory." [56]

As noted in chapter 4, the Chinese began to reassess the Soviet threat during the later stages of Phase 4 of the USSR's postwar strategy in the Asia-Pacific. By 1984–1985, two key trends had set the stage for Mikhail Gorbachev's modification of Soviet defense policies. First, a convergence of serious social difficulties, economic lethargy, and technological limitations began to undermine Moscow's abilities to sustain its customary postwar levels of military expenditures and force levels. [57] Second, as already intimated above, Soviet military power, far from demoralizing Soviet adversaries, spurred them to embark upon force buildups of their own. China's strategic force modernization programs continued to receive the highest priority despite Chinese leaders' overall inclinations to rank defense as the number four priority in their Four Modernizations program. President Reagan, in the meantime, accelerated U.S. military spending throughout the early 1980s to levels which the USSR could not hope to match in terms of qualitative force improvements.

Phase 5: Gorbachev's "New Thinking" and East Asian Deterrence

FROM 1986 onward, Mikhail Gorbachev initiated a series of diplomatic and political initiatives designed to reverse the "worse-case" orientation of Soviet strategic thinking. The new Soviet leader was determined to press for an Asian security agenda compatible with a strategic doctrine revised to emphasize reasonable sufficiency and diplomatic realpolitik.[58] In May 1985, and again in April 1986, Soviet government spokesmen had proposed an "All-Asian Forum." This proposal resurrected an earlier (1969) "Asian Security" concept which implied a "community of interests" among the USSR and Asian states and explicitly omitted the United States. In July 1986, however, Gorbachev delivered a landmark speech at Vladivostok, which acknowledged that the United States "is a great Pacific power with legitimate and political interests in the region." He instead focused on the illegitimacy of U.S. strategic *behavior* in the region, arguing that the large-scale U.S. buildup of forces in the region is "turning [the Asia-Pacific] into an arena of military and political confrontation . . . This is alarming . . . for us from all points of view, including for considerations of security in the Asian part of our country." The Soviet leader projected what Robert Manning has aptly characterized as "bold sounding proposals that have little effect on the Soviet military posture allow[ing] Gorbachev to project a benign image while making the U.S. posture more vulnerable."[59] These proposals included establishing Korean and Southeast Asian nuclear free zones, imposing ceilings on superpower naval deployments and maneuvers in the Pacific, curbing antisubmarine warfare activities there, and implying a Soviet withdrawal from Cam Ranh Bay if the United States were to leave its basing operations in the Philippines.

Gorbachev's new Asia-Pacific agenda still envisions, as did its predecessor, the U.S. strategic role in the region as competing with Soviet objectives in the region. The Soviets now view American military power there, however, as a rationale for cultivating a more legitimate image for themselves in the region by promoting arms control initiatives and cultivating economic and political ties with prosperous, if still pro-Western, Asian states. Over time, Gorbachev hopes to convince heretofore skeptical regional actors that Soviet strategic intentions are increasingly benign, that the USSR should be taken more seriously in the Asian marketplace, and that Soviet participation in forging a new regional security order should be based on "equality, mutual respect, and mutual advantage."[60]

Since the Vladivostok initiative, the new Soviet diplomacy has been highlighted by frequent Asia-Pacific tours by Foreign Minister Eduard Shevardnadze and his deputy Igor Rogachev, emphasizing Moscow's version of regional disarmament, confidence-building, and peacekeeping. Soviet diplomats have emphasized that improved relations with both China and Japan now have greater priority. Yet they have not hesitated to emphasize "the China threat" in their discussions with ASEAN states, urging acceptance of a Cambodian peace settlement that will guarantee Vietnamese security objectives while maintaining a Soviet military foothold at Vietnam's bases. Their backing of nuclear free-zone movements in Southeast Asia is suspect in light of their own strategic vulnerabilities and U.S. deterrence capabilities in the area.

Gorbachev's 1987 decision to accept a "double-zero" proposal for the elimination of the Soviet Union's key intermediate nuclear forces —specifically, removal of its SS-20 missiles from the Asia-Pacific as well as from the European theater—coincided with the broader Soviet strategy of isolating the United States and those European/Asian security partners adhering to the principle of unrestricted transit and deployment of nuclear weapons within alliance territories. The Soviet leader opted for this broader geopolitical policy approach over the purely military consideration that remaining Soviet short-range nuclear forces (SRNFs) not covered by the treaty would be unable to reach most Japanese targets or less able to threaten China with its strategic depth and the increased hardening or dispersal of its nuclear forces. Soviet measures to upgrade the penetration and strike capabilities of the Soviet Pacific Naval Aviation (SPNA) through increased deployment of the *Backfire* and *Blackjack* long-range bombers were designed to compensate for the force assets sacrificed to the INF accord. The USSR's military planners were, nonetheless, reportedly distraught about losing the SS-20, with its longer-range attack characteristics which assured an intertheater Soviet deterrent below the central strategic or global level of warfare.[61]

Gorbachev pressed the Soviet campaign against the U.S. Dominant Player posture in the Asia-Pacific with another important speech delivered at Krasnoyarsk in Siberia on September 16, 1988.[62] Compared to his Vladivostok address, the Krasnoyarsk presentation was both more ambitious and specific in context. Among the seven "proposals for peace" were an offer to relinquish Soviet access to Cam Ranh Bay in return for the United States withdrawing from Clark Air Base and the Subic Bay naval installation in the Philippines. The latter are far more extensive complexes, largely responsible for U.S. power projection throughout the Pacific and Indian Oceans. The timing of Gorbachev's offer was also suspect, as the Americans were in the midst of sensitive base negotiations with the Philippines while the Aquino government was searching for ways to justify a continued U.S. military presence to an increasingly nationalistic and anti-nuclear Philippines electorate.

The Krasnoyarsk address underscored Gorbachev's determination to link continental and maritime power in future conventional arms negotiations regarding the Asia-Pacific. If Soviet armor and artillery were to be reduced along the Sino-Soviet border, for example, commensurate streamlining should take place in Western naval forces where the United States and its allies retained a decisive advantage. Other possible linkages were also raised by Soviet diplomats and military officials throughout 1988. These included freezing levels of Soviet nuclear aircraft in the Far Eastern military district in return for the U.S. agreeing not to deploy more aircraft capable of striking the Soviet Union and relating U.S. levels of sea-launched cruise missiles in the Pacific to levels of ICBM reductions in superpower talks on the central strategic balance.[63]

The Soviet leader also exploited the anti-nuclear dimension of Moscow's new Asia-Pacific diplomacy by calling upon the U.S. and "other nuclear powers" in the region not to deploy "supplementary nuclear weapons" (a clear reference to the pending U.S. deployment of approximately 750 *Tomahawk* nuclear cruise missiles in the Pacific theater) and promising that the USSR would not expand its own nuclear weapons arsenal in the Asia-Pacific region. Soviet military analysts had already noted that the USSR had taken the most significant regional disarmament step to date with the scheduled dismantling of the 162 SS-20's deployed east of the Urals by the end of 1987, along with SS-12 and SS-23 short-range nuclear missiles scheduled for elimination by the end of 1991. They also suggested that U.S. cruise missile delivery systems could be differentiated in terms of nuclear versus conventional warhead capabilities by newly developed Soviet verification procedures. They proposed that a "compromise" could thus be implemented in which the U.S. Navy could be limited to deploying 400 nuclear sea launched cruise missiles and 600 conventional ones.[64] The United States contested Moscow's claims of sophisticated verification techniques, arguing that until such verification capabilities were really achieved, any efforts to discriminate between Soviet and U.S. nuclear/nonnuclear cruise missile components were superfluous.

The Americans were clearly outmaneuvered by the implementation of Soviet "new thinking" on issues of regional arms control. The flurry of Soviet diplomacy in this policy sector was viewed as in step with the majority of Asia-Pacific peoples who, justifiably or not, have like their European counterparts, become increasingly impatient with the calculus of deterrence as defined in its original cold war terms. During the UN Special Session on Disarmament held in May/June 1988, Shevardnadze announced that the Soviet Union would reveal the presence or absence of nuclear weapons on Soviet ships in naval ports if the U.S. and its Western allies would do the same. This appeal was linked by subsequent Soviet press reports to the need for U.S. cooperation in perfecting technologies for the greater detection and verification of nuclear weapons on naval surface units applicable to future naval arms control agreements.[65] This was a position designed to enhance Moscow's credibility in the eyes of New Zealand's Labour government— which had jettisoned the ANZUS treaty with Washington over precisely this issue—as well as with a number of Southeast Asians, Japanese, and Australians. They were already impressed with Moscow's readiness to ratify the August 1985 Treaty of Roratonga establishing the South Pacific Nuclear Free Zone (SPNFZ), and its support for a similar arrangement in ASEAN (the U.S. opposed both the existing Treaty and any follow-on arrangements for other regional nuclear free zones).

Gorbachev employed the UN setting in December 1988 to add yet another dimension to his diplomatic offensive for enhancing Soviet influence in the Asia-Pacific. He announced a unilateral troop reduction in the Soviet armed forces by 500,000, with some 40 percent of these originating from deployments along the Sino-Soviet border, including a 75 percent cut of the 75,000–strong Soviet force presence in Mongolia and a reduction of 120,000 personnel along the Manchurian border.[66.] A deputy head of the General Staff Foreign Department subsequently told the Western press that "all forces remaining in Europe and Asia will be deployed in a clearly defensive manner." No specific designations were offered, however, as to exactly where within the vast Far Eastern theater any pending force reductions were to occur, and influential components of the USSR's military leadership were reportedly still against them taking place at all.[67]

At the May 1989 Sino-Soviet summit, the Soviet leader proposed initiating negotiations for a "progressive demilitarization" of the Sino-Soviet border and the resumption, after three decades, of military exchanges between the Soviet and Chinese militaries.[68] The Soviets acquiesced to China's interpretation of the Sino-Soviet boundary along the Amur River. A Sino-Soviet working group on border issues was established at the summit to consider the presence observers at such exercises, a cessation of exercises along designated border regions, and no military movement along the border without prior agreement. Sufficient progress on these issues was achieved during early 1990 to allow for the signing of a border demilitarization agreement by Chinese Premier Li Peng during his April 1990 visit to Moscow. The agreement provided for a mutual reduction of Soviet and Chinese troop levels to a "minimum corresponding to normal good neighborly relations." [69]

Since Li's trip additional reports have surfaced of meetings in late May 1990 between Chinese and Soviet military officials, producing Soviet offers to sell high performance jet fighter aircraft (MiG 29s and SU-24s) to the PLA.[70] Western analysts interpret China's interest in discussing this possible transaction as Beijing's way of signaling to the United States that it has alternative options to high technology dependence on the West if the Bush administration persists in freezing military cooperation with the Chinese in response to Tienamen Square.

Moscow's diplomacy has placed U.S. strategic planners on the defensive, compelling them to justify a military posture which is gradually appearing to be isolated from the region's politico-diplomatic mainstream. They nevertheless contend that enough Soviet nuclear-capable fighter aircraft systems remain in place throughout the Soviet Far East to comprise a distinctive and formidable nuclear force. They feel that, because of the still formidable array of nuclear missile delivery systems found in Soviet naval surface and submarine units, the imposing of any significant restrictions on American SLCM capabilities is still unwise. The Soviets, however, have scored public relations gains with regional antinuclear groups and with established governments by their increasingly sophisticated diplomacy.[71]

Gorbachev's efforts to promote *glasnost* and *perestroika* at home have been accompanied by a shift in Soviet foreign policy, away from concentrating on the break up of Western regional alliance systems through the deployment of more military capabilities. Nor does Moscow's new policy cling to the obligatory cultivation of Marxist revolutionary politics in Third World societies. Instead, the Soviet Union now appears to be most concerned about its image as a superpower. It desires to be viewed as legitimate a security actor in the Asia-Pacific as was its longtime American rival throughout most of the postwar period, so as to play a major role in structuring the region's future political development. It seeks to achieve such status by expanding its scope of regional involvement from one primarily characterized by what many Asians view as an obtrusive military presence to a multidimensional economic and diplomatic posture.

The USSR's approach to the Asia-Pacific is increasingly concerned with providing breathing space for Vietnam. Moscow is hoping Hanoi will pursue domestic economic recovery more efficiently and establish its regional political legitimacy in ways that will eventually relieve the Soviets of massive economic and military subsidization. Despite recently announced reductions of Soviet force levels at Cam Ranh Bay (see below), the Gorbachev regime still regards the USSR's military presence at Vietnamese bases as a convenient means of showcasing the strategic reach of the Soviet Pacific Fleet. Regional perceptions of Vietnam, particularly by Indonesia which Moscow deems to be increasingly critical, have become relatively more important to the Soviets. Important also is the Soviets' need to resolve their long-standing differences with China and Japan, who are destined to become the two most critical Asia-Pacific politico-economic actors by the end of this century.

Soviet diplomatic efforts in the region are still constrained by their lack of genuine economic and ideological appeal and by the Soviets' inability to completely discard their Eurocentric bias toward international politics. Nor do the leaders of developing Asian nations fail to realize that Soviet demands for the United States to leave Subic Bay and Clark Air Base in return for their own exit from Cam Ranh Bay, or the USSR's proposals to reduce arms to a level of reasonable sufficiency in the Asia-Pacific, are unlikely to be implemented.[72] Even so, Gorbachev and his colleagues may well anticipate that the anti-nuclear sentiments of Asians offers real prospects for eventually politically decoupling the American extended deterrent in ways not possible by military efforts alone. The Soviets also need arms control in the Asia-Pacific, just as it was needed in Europe, to curb Soviet military spending, and to encourage prosperous Asians (e.g., the South Koreans or, less likely, the Japanese) to invest in the exploitation and distribution of as yet untapped Soviet natural and economic resources in Soviet Asia.

OFFENSE VERSUS DEFENSE: IDENTIFYING A "BALANCED" ASPIRING PLAYER DETERRENCE POSTURE

ONGOING DEVELOPMENTS in the USSR's strategic doctrine and force deployments have intensified disagreements on the role of deterrence in Moscow's global strategy. A number of analysts, described as "essentialists," contend that the USSR aspires to attain *absolute security* through the development of *war-winning* nuclear and conventional force capabilities, because expansionism is integral to the existence of the Soviet state.[73] They also maintain that the Soviets still believe any superpower conflict would inevitably escalate to general nuclear warfare, ultimately resulting in a "socialist" (i.e., Soviet) victory. The essentialists believe that doctrinal writings in the *Soviet Military Encyclopedia* [Sovietskaia voennaia entsiklopedia], military journals, and newspapers reflect Moscow's intention to defeat the United States at any level of conflict.

Another group of Western analysts, the "contextualist" school, argues that expansionism is not necessarily inherent in Soviet foreign and defense policy.[74] Over time, according to this group, the Soviet political leadership has grown to believe that "thresholds," subject to escalation control, exist between strategic nuclear, theater nuclear, and conventional warfare; that this thinking supersedes the earlier theories of Marshal V. D. Sokolovskiy, Admiral S. G. Gorshkov, and others who envisioned the *inevitability* of total nuclear war in any superpower military confrontation.

The Soviet military is reorganizing its air force and air defenses to enhance long-range aircraft strike capabilities and strengthen air support for Soviet ground forces. It is streamlining its operational maneuver groups (OMG's) in Soviet Asia so they can penetrate and disarm enemy defenses prior to the introduction of nuclear weapons. It is still modernizing its tactical nuclear forces against CINCPAC and Chinese positions, both to compensate for the loss of its SS-20s and to match U.S. offshore cruise missile capabilities. It is strengthening its nuclear and conventional frontal aviation capabilities to protect the ability of its SSBNs deployed in North Sea and Pacific sanctuaries adjacent to the Soviet coasts.[75] All of these developments indicate that while Gorbachev's "reasonable sufficiency" may have been designed to broaden

Soviet geopolitical influence beyond purely military lines, it may have only reinforced the already strong suspicions entertained by a number of East and Southeast Asian leaders that the Soviets' Aspiring Player posture still relies, to a significant extent, upon military power and intimidation.

The Soviet Strategic Challenge to the U.S. Dominant Player Strategy in the Asia-Pacific

IN THE Asia-Pacific, the Soviet Union still represents the major threat to U.S. national security interests and the only one capable of escalating a regional confrontation with U.S. or allied forces to global dimensions. The force capabilities aspects of this threat are illustrated in table 2. North Korea and Vietnam constitute intraregional threats to U.S. theater allies but are not really central to U.S. extended deterrence strategy and the global balance of power. Their relevance to U.S. extended deterrence questions are best understood in a regional context (see chapters 2 and 5).

In recent years, the Soviet military presence in the Asia-Pacific region has exceeded the levels anticipated by the Nixon Doctrine. Still, as Allen S. Whiting has argued, the Soviet rate of deployments in its Far Eastern TVD has less to do with either Moscow's willingness to confront the U.S. there or its intent to transform the overall Asia-Pacific power balance than with the complex process of reinforcing its global deterrence posture.[76] Moscow's overall objective is to avoid the escalation of a conflict anywhere in Eurasia to a level where its second strike nuclear capability against U.S. and allied forces' antisubmarine operations and air strikes is jeopardized. Under such circumstances, a Soviet surprise attack against U.S. bases in Japan or the Philippines is a remote contingency. Increasingly, this can also be said about a Soviet nuclear strike directed at China, since Beijing has acquired a rudimentary, but steadily growing, second strike capability . If a Sino-Soviet conflict did materialize, the main Soviet objective would be to eliminate Beijing's nuclear weapons as quickly as possible to minimize nuclear devastation of the eastern Soviet territories' supply lines and industrial assets.[77]

The Soviet ability to operate in the East China Sea's and Southeast Asia's critical sea lanes is still present. So, too, is its ability to project substantial naval power from Vladivostok and its other Far Eastern

TVD ports into Pacific waters and to contest air superiority in the immediate vicinity of the Northern Islands (opposite Japan).[78] As previously noted, Soviet strike assets include *Backfire* and *Blackjack* bombers, armed with cruise missiles. The Soviets also deploy about 250 tactical strike aircraft in the Far Eastern Military District, which could threaten U.S. and allied bases or ships in Northeast Asia. Soviet airborne forces and supporting MiG-23 fighters continue to be deployed in the southern Kuriles. Military overflight rights, as well as occasional port access, have been elicited from North Korea. About 35 percent of the Soviet Union's entire nuclear ballistic submarine inventory and approximately 30 percent of its surface combatants are now assigned to the Pacific Fleet, and prospects are good that Soviet anti-surface warfare and ASW capabilities will improve significantly over the next few years.

During his mid-May 1989 visit to Beijing, Gorbachev proposed mutual reductions of Sino-Soviet force levels along the Soviet-Chinese border and pledged to eliminate twelve Soviet divisions, eleven air force regiments, and sixteen warships from the Asia-Pacific region unilaterally. As noted above, a formal agreement for the demilitarization of the Sino-Soviet border was announced during Chinese Premier Li Peng's April 1990 visit to Moscow, although no specific timetable for such reductions was stipulated.[79] Gorbachev is facing ongoing resistance to these cuts, and to prospects for further negotiated decreases, however, from some elements within his own military.

Soviet Weaknesses and Policy Alternatives in the Asia-Pacific

WHETHER PRESENT Soviet force deployments in the Far Eastern TVD could sustain a conflict for long against a concerted U.S.-Chinese-Japanese coalition or even against U.S. and allied forces fighting without Chinese help is quite uncertain. Soviet forces still deployed along China's border, for example, would primarily adhere to fixed positions, with only occasional diversions to seize or secure critical straits or islands along the Far Eastern TVD peripheries.[80] This reflects Moscow's problems in converting its Far Eastern TVD buildup from one primarily designed to contain the PRC to one more attuned to deterring a de facto United States-Japan-China strategic entente. Unlike Europe, where territorial proximity has always given the Soviets a military option to use massive ground forces to seize wealth and terri-

TABLE 2. Soviet Military Power Projection Capabilities in the Asia-Pacific

Navy (the Pacific Fleet)	1985–86	1986–87	1987–88	1988–89
Submarines	88	77	76	112
	26 SSGN/SSG	25 SSGN/SSG	26 SSGN/SSG	Strategic: 24 SSBN, 6SSB
	62 SSN/SS	52 SSN/SS	50 SSN/SS	Tactical: 22 SSGN, 28 SS
				4 SSG, 6 SSB
Principal	2 Carriers	2 Carriers	2 Carriers	2 Carriers
Surface	14 Cruisers	15 Cruisers	14 Cruisers	12 Cruisers
Ships	17 Destroyers	14 Destroyers	13 Destroyers	12 Destroyers
	22 Frigates	21 Frigates	22 Frigates	47 Frigates
	30 Corvettes	30 Corvettes	31 Corvettes	
Strategic Forces				
SLBM	385	385	385	366
ICBM	380	387	387	440
IRBM	207 (7 fields,	171 (4 fields,	171 (4 fields,	132 (deployed
(SS-20's)	20 sites)	19 sites)	19 sites)	launchers)
Bombers	150	170	170	160
Tactical Aviation				
Combat Aircraft	1460	1350	1390	1100
Ground Forces	53**	53***	56****	56****
(Divisions)	7 Tank	7 Tank	7 Tank	7 Tank
	45 Motor Rifle	45 Motor Rifle	48 Motor Rifle	48 Motor Rifle
	1 Airborne	1 Airborne		
		2 Air Assault Brigades	2 Air Assault Brigades	2 Air Assault Brigades
		4 Artillery	5 Artillery	5 Artillery
		1 Coastal Defense	1 Coastal Defense	
Main Battle Tanks	14,500	14,900	14,900	13,900

*Asia-Pacific Region includes Central Asian, Siberian, Transbaykal, Far Eastern, and Mongolian Military Districts.

**Number indicated does not include Artillery.

***Number indicated does not include Air Assault Brigades, and Artillery.

****Number indicated does not include Air Assault Brigades and Artillery.

Sources: The International Institute for Strategic Studies, *The Military Balance*, 1985–86, 1986–87, 1987–88, 1988–89 (London: The International Institute for Strategic Studies, 1986, 1987, 1988, 1989).

tory, the Soviets can exercise this option in Asia only at China's expense. Moreover, the Sea of Japan and other geographic barriers provide U.S. allies in Northeast Asia with advantages which the NATO European countries lack.[81]

Given the present Northeast Asian military balance, Soviet forces would have a harder time sustaining the protracted air and sea capability necessary to occupy parts of China, Japan, or the Korean Peninsula than would the U.S. and allied counterparts in defending these locales. There is no viable means of transporting war material overland in the Soviet Union from west to east, and the 10,000 mile long southern supply route, from the Mediterranean through the Indian Ocean and Southeast Asia, to the Far East, is highly vulnerable to interdiction by U.S. and allied forces. In reality, Soviet forces are still geared predominantly to fighting in contiguous areas of Eurasia, rather than to operating at great distances from their homeland.

Moscow's ability to protect its naval battle groups, or to conduct airlift and amphibious operations beyond its own ports, still remains inferior to U.S./allied capabilities, particularly outside Europe. This, in turn, seriously effects Soviet capabilities to institute a protracted strategy of escalation control in the Asia-Pacific theater. Its need to achieve "surge mobilization" rapidly by deploying as many submarines, and surface units to sea as it can at the outset of a regional or global crisis is paramount. The Soviets must effectively disperse *Yankee*-class SSBN's in the Eastern Pacific to credibly threaten targets on the American west coast, and must deploy enough *Delta* and *Typhoon* SSBNs in protected "sanctuary" waters around the USSR to stave off U.S. and Japanese ASW operations and to conduct either long-range strikes against American targets or midrange attacks against in-theater targets. This Soviet "bastion doctrine" is at the heart of the USSR's second-strike deterrence strategy: the fanning out of Soviet cruise-missile (SSGN) and hunter-killer (SSN) submarines with naval air support to form an successive layered defenses against U.S. and allied penetration against Soviet SSBNs deployed close to the Soviet coastline. Absent such dispersion and deployment, prospects for naval force survivability are dim against superior U.S. command and control and offshore strike assets.[82]

In a global war, Soviet geographic disadvantages in Northeast Asia are only partially offset by the USSR's geographic proximity to the Persian Gulf and Northeast Asia. These disadvantages are accentuated by the recent loss of its military allies on its western flank, by the vulnerability of Soviet forces to U.S. air and naval power along the south and southeastern perimeters of the USSR, and by the combined deterrent capabilities of Chinese land power and U.S./allied naval and tactical air superiority in the Far East. Thus Moscow would face the problem of escalation control early on in most Eurasian contingencies.

In Southeast Asia, the Soviets until late 1988 maintained a substantial naval and air presence at Cam Ranh Bay, including between twenty-five and thirty warships (ten surface combatants, ten to twelve surface auxiliaries, three to five submarines), an 8,500 ton floating dry-dock, BEAR and BADGER reconnaissance and strike aircraft, a battalion of naval infantry, and sophisticated electronic intelligence facilities. Their presence at Cam Ranh put Soviet air strike assets less than two hours away from U.S. Seventh Fleet positions at Clark Air Base and Subic Bay, in the Philippines. Cam Ranh also gave the Soviet Pacific Fleet some lead transit time (by several days) to the Persian Gulf over the Seventh Fleet, thereby posing a potentially significant naval surface warfare and sea lane interdiction threat to U.S. forces in the region. Indeed, half of Asia's oil supplies and 80 percent of its strategic commodities pass through the Malacca, Sunda, and Lombok Straits, all within easy striking distance of modern Soviet aircraft which have been known to operate from the Vietnamese base.[83] Finally, Cam Ranh provides Moscow with some amphibious assault capabilities in the event of a limited Sino-Soviet war erupting in the East China Sea. *Kiev*-class carriers and *Ivan Rogov*-class troop transport ships have participated in recent amphibious assault exercises off the coast of Vietnam and have been labeled as a serious regional threat by the Chinese press.[84]

In January 1990, the U.S. Department of Defense reported that the Soviets had withdrawn the one squadron of twelve to fourteen MiG-23 jet fighter aircraft it had deployed at Cam Ranh throughout much of the 1980s, along with at least half of the sixteen TU-16 *Badger* long-range bombers also stationed at that base. The TU-16s which remained were reportedly not well maintained and were not considered to be threatening to Western naval or air operations. Four TU-95 *Bear* long-range reconnaissance aircraft were still thought to be stationed at Cam Ranh and the Defense Department reported that, despite obvious Soviet efforts to cut defense expenditures by reducing the number of "high seas" deployments and Pacific naval exercises, up to twenty small fighting and support vessels were still at the Vietnamese base.

One Pentagon official observed that "the [Soviet] ships have not left. The people have not left. Strategically, it's still pretty important to their deployments in the Indian Ocean. There is no sign that they intend to leave."[85] During the ensuing months, however, Western analysts speculated that Moscow's complete pullout from Cam Ranh is only a matter of time.[86] Both Soviet Foreign Minister Shevardnadze and Vietnamese officials have related to American legislators Moscow's plans to withdraw all Soviet forces from Cam Ranh by 1992, to improve the USSR's relations with Asia-Pacific nations heretofore impatient with Moscow's peace proposals failing to correlate with its continued force presence in Vietnam.[87]

Admittedly controversial estimates of Soviet levels have been offered by Western news reports, and analysis by the Rand Corporation. In 1988, the number of Soviet strategic submarine deployments were 75 percent down from their 1986 peak, primary ship deployments down 82 percent from their 1983 peak, and naval combat aircraft down 87 percent from their 1986 levels. Western defense analysts suspect that the USSR's recent economic problems have brought about a shortage of fuel for Soviet ships and aircraft. Gerald Segal concludes that "the old cry of the expanding Soviet military presence in the Pacific is no longer accurate."[88] If one were to seek a middle ground between the Pentagon's and Segal's perceptions, it might be to conclude that Soviet priorities have shifted to applying greater power to where it believes it is most threatened by U.S. and allied forces—in the straits of Northeast Asia close to its own home waters and ultimate second-strike SSBN deterrent. The effects of the USSR's retrenchment on its conventional strategic projection capabilities and on its extended deterrence commitments to traditional allies will be assessed below.

Notwithstanding its past efforts to engage in a force buildup in Indochina, overall Soviet military power in Southeast Asia is still far short of fully compensating for the USSR's inherent geographic and long-term military vulnerabilities in this part of the Asia-Pacific theater. Moreover, the Soviets are dependent on a "reluctant ally" for much of their ability to project meaningful strategic power here as growing political and economic tensions between the Soviet Union and Vietnam have made Hanoi apprehensive about the long-term advantages of its strategic relations with Moscow. Most Vietnamese remain bitter about the Soviet Union's reluctance, only months after the signing of a Soviet-Vietnamese Friendship Treaty (November 1978), to intervene more forcefully on their behalf during the 1979 Sino-Vietnamese conflict. Article Six of that treaty allows for "consultations" between the parties if one or the other is attacked or threatened, but allows the Soviets broad discrimination over when it will or will not become involved.[89] The financial drain caused by Soviet economic and military assistance to Hanoi, combined with both countries' desire to cultivate better and separate relations with China and the ASEAN countries, may indeed cause Soviet basing operations in Southeast Asia to be discontinued.

In interviews conducted by the author during August 1987, PACOM officials expressed confidence that most targets in the South China Sea could be neutralized during the first hours of combat. Early in 1988, the Department of Defense publicly verified this assessment in its annual Soviet threat assessment publication.[90] Such assessments, however, are predicated upon assumptions that the United States will retain access to its current Philippines basing system and that PACOM resources are not diverted to other missions or theaters prior to this neutralization. If the USSR were successful in removing its bombers and fighter aircraft from vulnerable Soviet bases in the Far Eastern TVD prior to attacks by American, Japanese and South Korean aircraft, while *simultaneously* conceding the South China Sea to the West, Moscow would be more able to carry out a strategic defense of the Far Eastern TVD and other homeland theaters in a protracted global war. It would do so, however, by abandoning its goal of effective sea denial missions against U.S. and allied forces in the wider Pacific. At best, it could hope to disrupt Japanese-American sea lanes of communication through limited interdiction campaigns, while simultaneously fulfilling the more critical mission of fending off U.S. nuclear strikes on Soviet Asia and, during a global war, in multiple combat theaters.

A key consideration under such conditions is how effective the USSR would be in neutralizing Japan, short of an all-out nuclear strike against the Japanese homeland and its highly prized industrial-technological base. Limited nuclear strikes against densely populated Japanese land space by Soviet *Backfires* or by *Golf* diesel-powered ballistic missile submarines (SSBs) operating in the Sea of Japan would be tantamount to an all-out strike. They would therefore be highly questionable in achieving the "limited war objectives" of neutralizing Japan's alliance affiliation with the West, occupying Hokkaido, blockading Japanese energy supplies or crippling its shipping terminals. Serious interdiction efforts by the Soviets against Japanese shipping, moreover, would risk levels of bomber and submarine attrition from U.S. and Japanese ASW counterstrikes that could permanently compromise the Soviet Pacific Fleet's capabilities. As noted at the beginning of chapter 2, such efforts and counterstrikes could force the Soviets into "use it or lose it" decisions concerning their strategic nuclear ballistic missile submarines (SSBNs). A move by Soviet forces to launch an amphibious attack against either Hokkaido or along the Nemuro-Kushiro axis, opposite the southern Kurile Islands, would be confronting close to a third of the entire Japanese Ground Self Defense Force's manpower assets and an even higher percentage of Japan's total tank and conventional missile assets. Much of the Soviet air support would be originating from bases in the Soviet Maritime provinces over 700 to 800 kilometers away.[91] There is even less probability of the Soviets attacking the Japanese mainland from a northeastern avenue of advance, across the Yellow Sea or the Sea of Japan, because of the need for access to North Korean bases to carry out such an operation.

In summary, the risks to the USSR of undertaking a military offensive against Japan would seem to outweigh almost any benefits imaginable. Soviet Foreign Minister Shevardnadze's December 1988 journey to Tokyo was indicative of the Soviets' growing dilemma. It is apparent that Tokyo has not been coerced at all in regard to softening its claims against the Soviet-occupied "Northern Territories."[92] Present political and strategic conditions would appear to negate Soviet efforts to counter Tokyo's expanding *politico-strategic* influence in Northeast Asia, given its continued alliance relations with Washington and its generally stable politico-economic ties with Beijing. Regardless of how the politics of deterrence unfolds in the Asia-Pacific, it remains evident that Japan will indefinitely continue to be a complicating factor in Soviet deterrence calculations in the Asia-Pacific.

THE USSR'S FORMAL EXTENDED DETERRENCE COMMITMENTS: NORTH KOREA AND VIETNAM

THE IRONY of recent Soviet efforts to enhance its influence throughout the Asia-Pacific is that while the USSR's military presence in the region is certainly more significant than when Moscow entered into its first pro forma deterrence commitment in the region some four decades ago (China, 1950), Soviet political influence has continued to wane. During the mid-1950s, China and Indonesia could be considered as powers friendly to the USSR, Japan was moving to "balance" its strategic dependency upon the U.S. by seeking normalized diplomatic relations and increased economic ties with the Soviets and John Foster Dulles' SEATO containment policies at times seemed to play into Soviet hands. By the mid-1980s, the Sino-Soviet rift had been ongoing for well over twenty years, the Northern Islands dispute with Japan as well as increased Japanese military spending had engendered what appeared to be a permanent chill in Soviet-Japanese relations, and the Soviet invasion of Afghanistan, its alliance with Vietnam, and its increased military presence throughout Southeast Asia had alienated a number of important Asia-Pacific regional actors.

As one result, the Soviets have joined their American counterparts in becoming guardians of Korean conflict avoidance. For their own reasons, the Soviets share Washington's uncertainty over the ramifications of a "unified" Korean Peninsula, although still backing for public consumption Pyongyang's political line on unification. As the U.S. has prompted Japan to undertake greater defense burden-sharing responsibilities within the framework of the U.S.-Japan Mutual Security Treaty, Soviet policy planners have become, along with their Chinese and Southeast Asian counterparts, more apprehensive about Japan entering the international security arena in any meaningful way. While Moscow cannot be enthusiastic about China's efforts to build up its nuclear force capabilities, it has joined China's current pragmatic leadership in wishing for a respite in Sino-Soviet tensions so that both sides can concentrate on meeting intensified domestic economic challenges. Notwithstanding its expressed anti-nuclear politics, it remains questionable to what extent the Soviets would truly be prepared to subject its own naval and air movements to the veto of Asia-Pacific states intent on linking anti-nuclear politics with neutrality movements and motivated by a single-minded determination to remove external military powers from their region altogether.

Given such considerations, what sustains the Soviet Union's two formal extended deterrence commitments in the region—to North Korea and to Vietnam—is far from self-evident. Both relationships are marked by undercurrents of tension which belie intermittent declarations of Marxist solidarity. Both are now undergoing significant change due to revised security priorities now becoming increasingly apparent in both Pyongyang and Hanoi. Because the Soviet Union is, in actuality, hard pressed to accommodate such transformations in its regional strategic agenda despite Gorbachev's All-Asian security proposals, it is uncertain to what degree either of these bilateral security relationships will endure.

Soviet-North Korean Security Relations

INITIAL POSTWAR Soviet efforts to impose what North Korean leader Kim Il-sung has called "dominationism" for purposes of exploiting his country's physical and economic resources created a legacy of distrust between the Soviet Union and North Korea that has never been totally overcome. Notwithstanding their suspicion of each others' motives, the North Koreans well understand that, despite China's intervention on their behalf against UN troops in 1950, it has been Soviet military power which has been Pyongyang's ultimate deterrence guarantee against American military power in Northeast Asia. The Soviets are encumbered by the geostrategic reality of North Korea's proximity to Vladivostok, headquarters for Soviet Pacific Fleet operations and gateway to the USSR's Far Eastern TVD. In this sense, even if American troops were not deployed in South Korea, Soviet military planners would be required to invent a pretext for guaranteeing North Korea's security.[93] This remains true despite Kim's determination to apply *chuch'e* or self-reliance, which can be translated as balancing relations with the Soviets and the Chinese so as not to become overly dependent on either.

The September 1961 Soviet-North Korean Friendship Treaty, and a similar Chinese-North Korean pact, were signed the same day, emblematic of the logic of *chuch'e*. Although there is no real consensus in the West as to the reasons for Kim eliciting formal security commitments from Moscow and Beijing simultaneously, it appears almost certain that the North Korean leader was motivated by two factors: (1) the military takeover of South Korea that year; and, (2) apprehensions over the Soviets and Chinese becoming so preoccupied in their own evolving dispute that their concerns for North Korean security would become buried in the process. At the same time, Moscow was sensitive to North Korea siding with China on critical ideological aspects fueling the Sino-Soviet dispute and was thus inclined to limit the rupture in the Soviet bloc to Beijing if at all possible. Accordingly, the USSR acquiesced to treaty language which was categorical in its scope, mandating that the Soviets respond automatically to any threat designated by its Korean ally, without deference to sovereign prerogatives such as those found within the United States' security treaties with its Asian allies.[94]

The Friendship Treaty represented what was until 1984 perhaps the most conciliatory Soviet act on North Korea's behalf since the military assistance program conducted during the Korean War, although a noticeable warming of ties occurred during the height of American— and more limited South Korean—military involvement in Vietnam during 1964–65.[95] Yet the Soviets were careful to avoid acknowledging North Korea as a single sovereign Korean entity. They instead tended to focus on the U.S. military threat in the South as the major barrier to reunification, as much to impress Pyongyang with the seriousness of U.S. intentions regarding deterrence as to condemn Washington. To extend to Kim an unconditional extended deterrence guarantee, Moscow feared, would precipitate another Korean conflict by encouraging the volatile North Korean leader to unleash his armies in yet another effort to unify the peninsula militarily. For his part, Kim reciprocated what he considered to be lukewarm Soviet backing by refusing to visit the USSR between 1967 and 1984 (although it could be surmised that Moscow would not have been overly enthusiastic about such a visit given Kim's "tilt" toward Beijing in the Sino-Soviet ideological dispute and North Korea's provocative behavior toward the Americans, represented by its seizure of the *USS Pueblo* at a time when Moscow was exploring detente with Washington). Soviet-North Korean tensions have been fueled by Kim's tendency to compare Moscow's ultimate intentions toward his own country with Mongolia's subservience to the Soviets, by his ability to initiate crisis with the South in ways which inevitably involve the superpowers, and by the Soviets' reluctance to transfer "state-of-the-art" weapons systems to North Korea.

With Kim's May 1984 journey to the Soviet capital, the texture of Soviet-North Korean military relations changed significantly. Both sides found they shared a growing apprehension about the Reagan administration's encouragement of a tacit U.S.-Japanese-South Korean security coalition, and about China's willingness to accept a higher Japanese military profile as long as it was directed toward the Soviets. Whereas the Soviets and North Koreans both advocated the unqualified removal of U.S. troops from South Korea, Beijing supported such a development only if it could be assured that the regional power equilibrium would not be adversely shifted to favor the USSR.[96]

Kim's 1984 discussions with Soviet leaders appeared to strengthen Soviet extended deterrence commitments to North Korea. North Korean opposition to Soviet military policies in Afghanistan and Cambodia was less evident. The Soviets transferred twenty-six MiG-23 fighter jet aircraft to Pyongyong—and later, according to some Western sources, even some MiG-25s *Foxbat* and MiG-29 *Fulcrum* fighters and SU-25 *Frogfoot* ground attack fighter-bombers—to compensate for ongoing deployments or sales of more advanced American jet aircraft in Northeast Asia (F-15s and F-16s to Japan and F-16s to South Korea). Some SA-3 and SA-5 surface-to-air missiles, AA-7 air-to-air missiles, and the "Tin Shield" early warning radar network reportedly have also been transferred.[97] North Korean naval units and fighter aircraft also began visiting the Soviet Union for in 1986. The Soviets, in turn, secured overflight rights for their military aircraft (according to at least one South Korean report, Soviet technicians are jointly manning the Wonson air control center with their North Korean counterparts) and North Korean port access (to Wonson, on the Sea of Japan, and probably Nampo, close to Pyongyang) for their naval units.[98] Kim's visit also led to joint Soviet-North Korean naval exercises taking place near Vladivostok during October 1986, and again in October 1987 in the Sea of Japan, although the extent of such maneuvers failed to impress U.S. or Japanese military planners.

Overall, as Robert Scalapino and Masataka Kosaka have noted, while security relations between Moscow and Pyongyong have never reached the intensity of the USSR's alliances with Mongolia or Vietnam, the intensification of Soviet-North Korean ties has meant that Moscow could strategically counterbalance what it views as the recent development of an American-Japanese-South Korean strategic entente and increase its visibility and status in the region.[99] It would also enjoy the strategic bonus of encircling China strategically from the east, as a large part of North Korea (approximately 640 miles) borders China's industrial region.[100]

Neither the Soviet Union nor the United States has any interest in permitting a Korean conflict to escalate to the nuclear level, as noted by President Reagan and General Secretary Gorbachev at their Moscow summit held in late May 1988.[101] North Korea has achieved an unquestionable surprise attack capability and has increased its ability to wage a protracted war against South Korean and U.S. forces if American military strategy discounts early use of its tactical nuclear weapons inventory against North Korean units. Soviet geographic proximity to North Korea may well operate as a significant inhibiting factor against such nuclear use, if a renewed conflict were to break out between North and South Korean forces. The levels of American conventional military power likely to be deployed to the peninsula during the first few days of combat would be sufficient to slow North Korea's initial offensive in the absence of an initial blitzkrieg-style North Korean victory at the outset of any such conflict.[102] Both Soviet and American extended deterrence postures in Korea appear to be oriented toward preserving at least a rough status quo in the absence of conflict or restoring it in the event of hostilities. Indeed, Soviet extended deterrence strategy in North Korea is intended as much to control the strategic behavior of a difficult ally as to protect that ally from external threats. In this regard, it parallels the American situation in the South and must be regarded as an important component of the USSR's "Aspiring Player" posture.

Soviet-Vietnamese Security Relations

THE TWENTY-FIVE year USSR-SRV Treaty of Friendship and Cooperation was signed November 2, 1978 in Moscow. Unlike the pact Moscow signed with North Korea in 1961, the Soviet-Vietnamese treaty does not commit the USSR to provide "immediate aid" to Hanoi but merely to enter into "immediate mutual consultation" in the case of a threat to or in the event of an attack on Vietnam. Little is known regarding the precise motives for this pro forma solidification of the Soviet-Vietnamese defense relationship. However, it appears that China's cutoff of economic and military assistance earlier that year convinced Vietnam's leadership to drop its heretofore "evenhandedness" in balancing relations between the USSR and PRC. The Soviets were apparently determined to secure guaranteed access to a locale from which they could preempt Chinese and U.S. military power across the South China Sea into the East Indian Ocean. Cam Ranh Bay, for example, is roughly halfway between Vladivostok (ten sailing days north) and the Indian Ocean, presenting a staging area for developing Soviet maritime surge capabilities.[103]

At inception, the treaty was most likely anti-Chinese in thrust. It was meant to check burgeoning Chinese naval activity and to demonstrate the potential of the newly established Soviet basing infrastructure in Vietnam. (Recent Soviet reductions at Cam Ranh may be partly attributed to progress toward a Sino-Soviet rapprochement.) The original Soviet force buildup at Cam Ranh was, additionally, a move to support Vietnam's efforts to consolidate Indochina under its de facto political control. The treaty was designed not only to deter China from launching a major attack on Vietnamese territory but to outflank China strategically by reinforcing a major conventional military power adjacent to Beijing's southern border. As will be discussed more fully in chapter 4, the Chinese *were* deterred from conducting a more extensive military campaign in February 1979, after their initial incursion into Vietnam's northern provinces.

That the Soviets did not enter the 1979 conflict was less a result of Chinese reassurances that the skirmish would remain limited and be over quickly than of the PLA's inability to sustain a logistical lifeline or establish air support during the course of battle. While some new Soviet small arms equipment found its way into the hands of Vietnamese troops defending the Sino-Vietnamese border *after* the Chinese withdrawal, Soviet resources were channeled toward the Vietnamese war effort in Kampuchea.[104] In the context of Soviet strategic interests, Vietnam can be regarded as a consolation prize: Moscow extends deterrence on behalf of Hanoi primarily to bolster Soviet leverage vis-a-vis the Chinese and because Moscow finds itself unable to compete with the West economically in the ASEAN subregion and the Southwest Pacific. It is much less intended to support the nationalist aspirations of the Vietnamese, or to underwrite their competition with the PRC for predominance in Indochina or for greater influence in Southeast Asia.

It is instructive in this regard that, as late as April 1983, Soviet Deputy Foreign Minister Mikhail Kapitsa threatened to supply Hanoi with enough arms to foster Southeast Asian insurgency movements if ASEAN continued its campaign to challenge the Vietnamese military presence in Cambodia.[105] Less than five years later, Vietnam, in its quest to diversify sources of economic assistance, had announced its own timetable for withdrawing its 150,000 troops from Kampuchea (originally by the end of 1990, later shortened to September 1989).[106]

In the meantime, (September 1988) the USSR began negotiating with China on the new government in Phnom Penh after a Vietnamese military withdrawal. This discussion was part of broader Sino-Soviet efforts to resolve the long-standing dispute between the two Marxist giants.[107] The Gorbachev regime was clearly implementing its Aspiring Player deterrence posture in a way which downgraded the original premises of the Sino-Vietnamese Friendship Treaty—at least for the short-term—in favor of increasing Soviet geopolitical influence among the ASEAN states. It attempted to rectify the long-standing ASEAN conception that Moscow is historically and psychologically distant from the region, that their own security and political standing are unimportant to Moscow relative to the more important Northeast Asian states and, consequently Soviet threats or coercion directed toward their subregion could generally be discounted outside the framework of global war.[108] By no later than 1985–86, it appeared that the Soviets were eschewing the politics of deterrence through military intimidation in favor of pursuing trade and investment opportunities through government-to-government relations and downplaying, at least for the time being, the threat of Marxist insurgencies coming to power there.

Even in the aftermath of its partial Cam Ranh pullout, however, it is unlikely that the Soviets will allow themselves to become completely expendable to Hanoi. They will not relinquish their access to intelligence facilities which can monitor U.S. air and naval movements around the Philippines and throughout the Asia-Pacific, the support facilities for Soviet TU-16 maritime reconnaissance aircraft, and modest ASW operations. In peacetime, such operations provide reliable counteroperations to the long-established Five Power Defense Arrangement (FPDA), the U.S.-Philippines surveillance/ASW vectors, and the Integrated Air Defense System covering the Malayan Peninsula, southern Thailand and critical points in the east Indian Ocean (see chapter 5). With at least some residual presence in Cam Ranh, the Soviets can link their Southwest Asian/Indian Ocean naval presence, which has been militarily significant since the late 1970s, with a homeland command and control system (Vladivostok and the Far Eastern TVD). They can thus still function as a quasi-global military power in distant but critical littorals, if not to the same extent as the U.S., at least to the point where Gorbachev's demands that the Soviets have a role in building a new Asia-Pacific regional security order must be afforded credibility.

The Indochina region is valuable to Moscow because it advertises a heightened Soviet ability to "wage a defensive military campaign on the Asian front." It uses a Vietnamese linchpin against burgeoning Chinese and ongoing U.S. maritime power. "Indochina now forms the southern base-perimeter (Mongolia and the Soviet heartland, the northern; and close military ties with India, the southwestern) of Soviet efforts to delimit Beijing's influence within Chinese territorial borders." [109] Cam Ranh, Danang, and the Kampuchean port of Kompong Song can be employed to support selective amphibious support operations in the South China Sea on behalf of Vietnam, less to benefit Hanoi than to check the expansion of Chinese offshore power over contested islands in those waters. [110] Illustratively, the Soviets offered only tepid verbal support to Vietnam during the March 1988 Chinese-Vietnamese naval clash off the Spratly Islands, demonstrating that while Vietnam may be a closer ally to Moscow than is Beijing, it is a less valuable relationship to Moscow than would be the strengthening of Soviet-Chinese strategic and regional cooperation.

During wartime, Soviet military assets still remaining in Indochina would be quickly severed by U.S. and allied forces, but not before the Soviet High Command could use the immediate prewar intelligence and tracking data in ways needed to exercise credible escalation control and inter-theater strategy. Such data would be particularly important in any effort to destroy the formidable U.S. extended basing system in the Asia-Pacific. This system, as the annual official Soviet assessment of "the U.S. threat" recently noted, gives the United States an extraordinary defense-in-depth within the theater and adds to the United States' ability to fight a protracted maritime conflict in a global context. [111]

By contrast, the new defensive orientations, which increasingly characterize Soviet military doctrine and an unquestionable relaxation of Sino-Soviet tensions, have clearly reduced Vietnam's strategic relevance to Moscow. Ideological affinity between the Soviet Union and Vietnam has evolved by developments in Eastern Europe during 1989 and 1990, and by less Soviet propensity to support client states throughout the Third World. As long as Sino-Vietnamese relations remain strained, the Soviet-Vietnamese relationship will be asymmetrical, with Hanoi needing Soviet political support and security guarantees to a greater extent than the USSR is willing to provide. Consequently, the Soviet-Vietnam defense treaty will be observed by Moscow in only a qualified context, with Soviet leaders even more reluctant than before to become pulled into future Vietnamese confrontations with U.S. or Chinese allies in Southeast Asia.

Striking a balance between lower-key commitments to Vietnam without appearing to completely abandon Hanoi in the process constitutes a major regional security challenge for Gorbachev and other Soviet policy planners. While the Soviet-Vietnamese Friendship Treaty may be viewed by some in Moscow as a growing liability, Moscow will find continued value in sustaining extended deterrence commitments to the Vietnamese for as long as the U.S. offshore presence in the Philippines and its reach into the Southeast Asian littorals remains intact. The importance of the USSR-SRV pact to the Soviet Union's deterrence calculations, however, is dependent upon the increasingly uncertain political and strategic trends in the region. The value of the Soviet-Vietnamese alliance could hinge upon the nature of a Cambodian political settlement or upon U.S. dismantling of its basing operations at Clark Air Base and Subic Bay. A continued warming of Sino-Soviet relations could alter the context of Soviet defense relations with Hanoi, giving Moscow much greater flexibility in its relations with what has traditionally been a highly nationalistic Vietnamese nation.

THE WIDER PACIFIC

FOR THE Soviet Navy, the parameters of Asia-Pacific military operations include an area stretching from Siberia and the Bering Sea at their northernmost point to those waters lying just above the Australian archipelago.[112] Soviet naval and air support operations are primarily concerned with containing the expansion of Chinese power, and with providing homeland defense against U.S. naval and air power. Since most Soviet Pacific Fleet operations are directed toward the north end of this theater's north/south axis (i.e., the straits and archipelagoes surrounding Japan and Korea), the extent to which it can operate effectively in distant locales such as the Indian Ocean or the western defense perimeter of the United States (represented by some 2,000 miles of Pacific island chains) is questionable. Yet unless it can do so, the major rationale for the USSR's decision taken in the early 1960s to build up that fleet as a counterdeterrent to the U.S. Navy's *Polaris* (and later *Poseidon*) SSBN strike force becomes invalid. Apart from a wholesale retraction of U.S. maritime power unexpectedly occurring within the Asia-Pacific, the Soviets cannot hope to move beyond a sea interdiction capability against the Seventh Fleet. The Soviets acknowledged this reality by the early 1970s, by redesignating theater priorities and moving significant naval strike assets to southern Europe and the Persian Gulf to counter U.S. SSBNs in the Arabian Sea and the U.S. Sixth Fleet in the Mediterranean.

The Soviet deployments which do exist in the South China Sea must be regarded as reinforcement for efforts by the Soviet Pacific Fleet to break out of Northeast Asian chokepoints during a global war and to conduct limited interdiction missions against superior U.S. maritime power. Soviet air and naval support activities throughout the critical straits and chokepoints transversing the East Indian Ocean into Southeast Asia (e.g., the Straits of Malacca or the Sunda Straits) would be likely during a protracted conventional conflict in the Pacific. The vulnerability of Soviet road and rail infrastructures east of the Urals would cause the Soviet Pacific Fleet to seriously consider undertaking at least limited interdiction operations against U.S. and allied naval elements in these waters. This rationale is behind the construction of a pier at Cam Ranh for nuclear attack submarines (although this project is now on hold unless Soviet-U.S. global and strategic competition were to again intensify) and the USSR's continued interest in outflanking China's modest naval assets in both the northern and southern waters of the South China Sea.

Soviet dry-docking facilities still operating at Cam Ranh, as well as petroleum and ammunition storage facilities throughout Vietnam, Kampuchea and Laos, appear tailored to provide Soviet naval and air units with sufficient sea-borne replenishment services to give them at least a chance of establishing a supply line from the east Indian Ocean to Vladivostok. Remaining Soviet Tu-95 reconnaissance aircraft and TU-16 medium-strike bombers armed with air-to-surface missiles are not nearly enough to prevent the outright destruction of the Indochina bases during nuclear war conditions. They may, however, be sufficient to make a difference during a limited conventional war or in the event Hanoi was eventually confronted with domestic unrest similar to that in the Philippines where American aircraft were used in a show of support for the status quo.[113] By doubling the Soviet Pacific Fleet's patrolling time on station in the Persian Gulf-Indian Ocean-South China Sea region in 1985–1986, as compared to the pre-1979 period, the Soviets demonstrated their willingness and capability to contest and interdict the Americans throughout most of the key straits and archipelagoes of the wider Pacific, even if only from a defensive posture.[114]

The Soviets lack meaningful strategic surge or the power projection capability to fight a protracted conventional war in the Indo-Pacific maritime environment against the United States. Only 10 percent of the Soviet Pacific Fleet is normally deployed outside the northwest Pacific strategic sanctuaries.[115] The Soviet tactical air force is too short-range to sustain a credible deterrent to U.S. carrier groups operating in the region, nor are Soviet amphibious capabilities anywhere near sufficient to establish a substantial ground presence in peninsular Southeast Asia.[116] Any Soviet effort to obstruct the Malacca Straits between the Malayan Peninsula and Indonesia, and the Sunda Straits through Indonesia must take into account that neither of these straits is deep enough for Soviet nuclear attack submarines to hide effectively for any length of time from U.S./allied ASW operations. It is far from certain that enough Soviet surface units would be able to break through their Northeast Asia barriers to provide for comprehensive interdiction operations. The relative strategic value of contesting the West in a Southeast Asian maritime environment, in other than a global conflict, would seem to be low because of the risk of conflict escalation in an area not central to Soviet geographic concerns and distant from the Soviet homeland. In this context, any Soviet effort to interdict Japanese oil supplies or to deny the U.S. access to Singapore or ports in Thailand, even in the aftermath of a U.S. pullout from its bases in the Philippines, would be improbable given the strategic risks such actions would entail.

In accordance with its Aspiring Player posture, therefore, the USSR has become more *politically* active in distant subregions of the Asia-Pacific theater such as the South Pacific. In this area, long-standing Western security systems have become more vulnerable to the forces of nationalism. The national development aspirations held by the small island-states which constitute most of the South Pacific's political entities creates increased opportunities for strategic exploitation by the Soviets, the Chinese and even the Libyans, counterbalancing what many of the island leaders regard as long-standing U.S., French, Australian, or New Zealand quasi-hegemonism in their subregion.[117]

Thus, while according to statements offered by Australia's Defense Minister in 1988, no Soviet surface warship has been sighted in the

South Pacific since World War II (Soviet submarines *have* been sighted in this sub-region), a strengthened Soviet political and economic presence and influence there is capable of turning an area which was at one time an unquestionable adherent to, and beneficiary of, Western extended deterrence postures into a center for international rivalry and conflict.[118] To date, however, initial Soviet efforts to develop commercial ties and maritime access in the South Pacific—specifically, through signing one-year fishing rights agreements with Kiribati and Vanuatu in 1985 and 1987, respectively—have not expanded into more strategic sectors of activity (despite the Vanuatu agreement including landing rights for Soviet aircraft). Neither agreement was renewed, as the U.S. and Australia countered with more extensive assistance programs of their own.

Moscow's persistence in its economic diplomacy may yet produce political dividends among the South Pacific island-states, if only because these countries are so poor and resource-deficient that any development assistance offers are seriously considered without reference to geopolitical considerations. Some strategic factors are still potentially significant, from a Soviet military planner's perspective, to merit further investigation of a fusion of politico-economic and strategic objectives. Greater surveillance capabilities of the U.S. missile testing range and SDI research center in the Marshall Islands are certainly appealing. So, too, would be increased Soviet access to key sea lanes from Australia and New Zealand to Hawaii and the U.S. west coast.

In the unlikely event that the Soviets were able to develop relationships with enough disenchanted South Pacific island-states to establish even a modest basing network in the South Pacific, a second avenue of advance would be opened up for Soviet SSBs. They could establish positions for nuclear strikes which would complement the traditional northwest Pacific target areas. More likely, logistical support could be provided for interdiction operations carried out by Soviet hunter/killer diesel submarines. It remains doubtful, however, that the Soviets will be able to transform modest economic assistance programs to selected South Pacific recipients into an integrated strategic game plan anytime soon.[119] Such operations, in any case, would only be viable during a protracted global conventional war; elements of the U.S. Seventh Fleet and of the French Pacific Naval Squadron in Polynesia could be deployed in a subregional contingency far more quickly and effectively than whatever Soviet reinforcement efforts might be made.

CONCLUSION

SEVERAL VISIBLE shifts in Soviet extended deterrence strategy have been evident since the Korean War. Moscow's initial postwar approach could be viewed as one of relatively high risk, challenging U.S. containment strategy through encouraging its East Asian allies (North Korea and later China) to engage in regional warfare against U.S. forces in Northeast Asia and to perpetuate Marxist or Marxist-Maoist revolutionary politics throughout the region. Even this high-risk strategy had limits, however, as the Soviets could not—or would not—supply allies with the necessary military assistance, or provide them with the all important nuclear guarantee neçessary for them to complete a war of attrition against the West when the Eisenhower administration threatened to escalate the Korean conflict to nuclear levels.

While not the product of a deliberate American policy, the Korea and Taiwan stalemates effectively divided the communist world and forced the USSR to revise its deterrence posture from an extended one toward a preoccupation with defense of the Soviet Far East from an increasingly formidable Chinese nuclear and conventional military threat. Only when a more pragmatic Chinese leadership focused inward toward economic modernization did the Soviets feel free to employ the military power originally developed to confront the Chinese threat toward expanding Soviet influence on a regionwide basis. In doing so, they created an incentive for China to unite with the West in an anti-Soviet coalition that proved effective in checking Soviet geopolitical influence throughout the Asia-Pacific, notwithstanding the establishment of a more formidable Soviet military presence in that region.

Mikhail Gorbachev's embracing of "reasonable sufficiency," due to domestic economic conditions and changing technology, led to its forging of a more sophisticated and multidimensional approach to strengthening Soviet influence. Moscow's new approach seeks to exploit the West's political vulnerabilities, to achieve qualified rapprochement with Beijing, and to obtain economic access to the formidable Japanese and South Korean economies. It balances Soviet military capabilities with politico-diplomatic initiatives tailored to appeal to the antinuclear and nonaligned instincts of Asia-Pacific states. It can be regarded as the USSR's current "Aspiring Player" posture, competing with the United States' traditional Dominant Player approach to extended deterrence and international security in the region.

The current Soviet deterrence posture in the Asia-Pacific is more formidable than its predecessors because of its broadened political but more discriminate strategic agendas. Its roots lie in the USSR's own deepening economic crisis which, unless at least partially resolved, will impede prospects for successful Russian influence and competition in the international system. Gorbachev's policy modifications appear to defer to this reality. Moscow's Aspiring Player Posture could impel American political leaders and military planners to adjust their own Asia-Pacific strategy significantly if the viability of U.S. security objectives is to remain intact.

CHAPTER 4

Aspiring Player II: The People's Republic of China

WHILE THE Soviet Union since 1986 has shifted its deterrence strategy from one primarily composed of military dimensions to an increasingly multifaceted geopolitical approach, the People's Republic of China has revised its strategic orientation from an emphasis on local defense based on Maoist doctrine to one of greater regional and even extra-regional dimensions. Beijing's assumption of the "Aspiring Player" posture is predictable: nations expand the range of their strategic interests when their national power increases. The political suppression of China's prodemocracy movement in June 1989 has prompted the present leaders of the Chinese Communist Party to become obsessed with preserving their domestic political legitimacy and power. As both superpowers become increasingly preoccupied with political changes throughout Europe and with domestic problems of their own, how-ever, a future Chinese leadership successful in restoring a government capable of unifying its populace could seek increased opportunities for the PRC to assert itself in the Asia-Pacific region.

China has always been driven by the legacy of "greatness lost." The PRC's slow pace of economic development has precluded it from achieving complete military parity with the superpowers. However, substantial reductions in American and Soviet military power in the Asia-Pacific have intensified Chinese geopolitical ambitions to establish a heightened strategic presence and influence in the region. China's long-term strategic goal is to successfully establish a national military-industrial base sufficiently formidable to neutralize potentially serious military threats posed to Beijing by the superpowers or by other regional actors (e.g., India or Japan). With the advent of its Four Modernizations program in 1977, economic development has been an assigned priority in China's quest to join the ranks of the world's great powers by the end of this century. Yet while recognizing that a strong economy is a prerequisite for great power status, China has felt that the ability to project a military capacity was also mandatory.[1]

Since China emerged from the Great Proletarian Cultural Revolution (GPCR) in 1966–1969 and from the domestic political intrigues involving the Gang of Four during the mid-1970s, it has demonstrated interest in a wider spectrum of geopolitical issues in locales more distant from its boundaries. This interest has been a logical outgrowth of the PRC's drive to secure its borders and to pursue an expanding politico-strategic agenda. China's February 1979 "lesson" directed toward Vietnam—reminding everyone that the Southeast Asian balance of power could not be restructured without Beijing's acquiescence—typifies the deterrence behavior of an Aspiring Player. So, also, do the pending Chinese annexation of Hong Kong, Beijing's continued pressures for the political subjugation of the Nationalist Chinese regime on Taiwan, and recent tensions with the United States over the PRC's arms sales in the Middle East.[2]

The June 1989 suppression of China's prodemocracy movement by that country's aging leadership has, however, affected the PRC's ability to project its Aspiring Player posture, both regionally and globally. Most fundamentally, Beijing's ability to attract the Western, Japanese, and South Korean investment needed to preclude economic disruption, its status as a contributor to a more stable and peaceful Asian security environment, and its progress toward creating higher levels of political and social well-being for its own people are all now at greater risk.

CHINA'S STRATEGIC INTERESTS AND ITS DETERRENCE POLICIES

HOW HAS China combined its growing set of strategic interests with its outlook on deterrence? First, it has formulated a more comprehensive strategic doctrine than that incorporated in early postwar Maoist security outlooks. Chong-Pin Lin, author of what may be the best recent study of Chinese nuclear strategy, has argued that China's military thinking has evolved through three phases: (1) a "Maoist predetonation period" (1949–1964) before China's first nuclear weapons test; (2) the "Maoist postdetonation period" (1964–1976), ending with Mao's death; and (3) the "post-Mao period" (1976–present).[3]

Maoist strategy, spanning the first two periods demarcated by Chong-Pin Lin, was primarily concerned with preservation of Chinese sovereignty and, secondarily, with territorial denial against invading enemy forces. Mao's notion of People's War, Ellis Joffe has since argued, represented "the final counterweight to the inferiority of the [Chinese] armed forces in weapons and equipment and the ultimate deterrent to a general invasion of China."[4] The post-Mao phase of Chinese strategic development, however, must be divided into at least two periods. From 1976–1981, Chinese leaders regarded the Soviet military threat as the predominant feature of the Asia-Pacific and global power balances and adjusted its own military doctrine and preparations in accordance with such thinking. After an interim period of reassessment between 1981–1984, Chinese military planners lowered their expectations of imminent war with Moscow, and assigned the United States equal billing to the USSR as a declining but still potentially confrontatory superpower to China's own national and regional security aspirations.

Signs of China's reassessment of the Soviet threat appeared as early as 1981, when the Reagan administration embarked on a major arms buildup promising to restore what Beijing previously viewed as an imbalance of global power favoring Moscow. In January 1982, the People's Liberation Army Deputy Chief of Staff, Wu Xiuquan, speculated to Japanese reporters that the USSR might have difficulty conducting a large-scale assault against Chinese positions along the Sino-Soviet border.[5] By November 1984, Deng Xiaoping was speculating to Western visitors that war was not necessarily inevitable—a major revision of orthodox Maoist ideology which emphasized the fundamental irreconcilability of rival class systems. By the middle of the following year (May 1985), Deng concluded that "the forces that can prevent war have developed rather encouragingly."[6] Unencumbered by high-intensity external threats, the Chinese leadership anticipated a long and benign period for the implementation of their national modernization strategies. They failed to anticipate the internal threat of such modernization becoming inevitably linked with the greater liberalization of Chinese society only a few short years later.

Since 1978, Chinese military planners have supplanted Mao's "People's War" with "People's War Under Modern Conditions" (PWUMC). This change in military strategy was prompted by the post-Mao Chinese leadership's growing realization that China risked falling irretrievably behind the superpowers militarily without strengthening its abilities to fight a modern war. In September 1981, a major military exercise was conducted in North China which served over the following four years (1981–1985) as the basis for many definitive Chinese writings on military doctrine. From these works, Western analysts were gradually able to describe the successor Chinese strategic doctrine to Mao's People's War.

The new strategy could be viewed as responding to three different types of external threat confronting China and embodying three levels of response to such threats. These threats were outlined in such definitive sources as *Military Geography of the States Adjacent to China* (a classified text authored by Chen Li and Chen Weile and studied by Chinese military officers, the existence of which is well-known in the West) and the writings of such contemporary Chinese strategic thinkers as Jiang Siyi, Vice Head of the Academy of Military Sciences, and the late Huan Xiang. They were (1) a direct attack on the Chinese homeland; (2) strategic intimidation by one or both of the superpowers; and (3) "potential threats," primarily originating from limited conventional wars in regional settings escalating into confrontations with Soviet or American nuclear power. The Chinese have prepared to deter such threats by enhancing their capability to conduct a limited strategic nuclear response against direct, all-out Soviet or American military aggression, by planning to engage in mobile warfare along China's borders at the outset of a large-scale conventional war prior to introducing tactical nuclear weapons (a form of escalation control), and by resorting to People's War as a residual strategy if all else fails. Chinese military strategists Jiang Siyi and Rong Zhi (an analyst at China's National Military Science Academy) have offered recent assessments, which together, summarize concisely the ongoing evolution of Chinese strategic thought.

Simply speaking, the strategic shift is the change from the earlier orientation of "*zaoda, dada, dahezhanzheng*" (to fight early, to fight big, to fight a nuclear war) to a ready-to-fight posture, to making use of the peaceful [international] environment for achieving a fundamental improvement of national defense modernization, and to enhance the construction of the modernization and familiarization of the revolutionary forces.[7]

We should not give up People's War. It can still scare away invaders. . . .But we should be serious about nuclear war. We should emphasize the importance of protecting our cities and industries. Conventional weapons should be modernized . . . .We should have a limited nuclear force. Our next generation of missiles would be better employed on submarines. Land-based missiles should be small, mobile, and we should experiment with our own cruise missiles.[8]

The updated Chinese strategic doctrinal approach also seems to emphasizes the value of calculated ambiguity in deterrence posturing (as opposed to what Allen Whiting has termed "calculated irrationality," used by Mao and his cohorts to distort superpower calculations of Beijing's views on nuclear war). PWUMC also emphasizes the importance of strategic retaliation as well as strategic denial; of active defenses as opposed to protracted warfare (i.e., "luring an enemy into the deep"); of greater force survivability through more systematic command and control, logistics, and weapons development. Beijing is aware of how vulnerable its nuclear capability still is as compared to that of the superpowers. China therefore relies on the "psychological dimension" of nuclear deterrence with "(D)eception and ambiguity of intentions . . . used . . . to keep its better armed nuclear adversaries off balance."[9] PWUMC emphasizes greater use of quick reaction forces.

Having largely discounted the threat of an imminent war with the superpowers, China has reorganized its land defenses by applying a "rapid response" strategy to attain the same type of mobility and quick strike capabilities already found in U.S. flexible response strategy in NATO Europe and the Persian Gulf, to deal with local or limited regional warfare.[10] China's naval air arm and amphibious capabilities are required to "safeguard 16,000 kilometers of offshore [Chinese] territory through the employment of airborne units and the tactics of modern submarine warfare," effectively coordinating such forces over long distances.[11]

The PRC has not only encompassed war avoidance in its deterrence posture but, on occasion, has sought to deter by fighting—i.e., intra-war deterrence—at a limited, conventional level of conflict.[12] As illustrated by its intervention in the Korean War (1950), its skirmish with India (1962) and its forays against Vietnamese positions (1979), China has orchestrated limited engagements against its adversaries to signal its resolve and to signal in advance, to the greatest extent possible, its definition of allowable geographic parameters of conflict. As a result, as Patrick Morgan has observed, China has practiced extended deterrence "not only to seek protection from an initial attack but to impose constraints on any fighting that occurs." [13]

Chinese Deterrence Perceptions

CHINESE PERCEPTIONS about deterrence have changed considerably since the PRC was established in October 1949. Within the past few years, the Chinese have embarked upon a more systematic effort to reconcile Western concepts of deterrence and extended deterrence with their military heritage. While traditionally they have disclosed very little information on what they believe is the relationship between nuclear war, strategic force planning, overall deterrence problems, and China's national security planning, this situation is now beginning to change. With the recent establishment of institutions modeled after Western defense think-tanks, the scope and quality of both theoretical and policy discourse between Chinese and Western strategic analysts has improved significantly. We now know, for example, that Chinese analysts have selectively utilized classical writings on war and strategy in their country, such as the *Art of War* by Sun Zi (Sun Tze) and the *Three Kingdoms Chronicles*, to develop a theory of deterrence similar to that recognized in the West: to threaten the enemy with an unbearably powerful retaliation so that he will not dare attack. [14] The Chinese, moreover, appear to recognize—and acknowledge the validity of— extended deterrence as a concept of modern strategy: "they [nuclear weapons] may also serve as a nuclear protective umbrella for one's allies." [15] Drawing upon its own experience with the Soviet Union during the Korean and both Taiwan Straits crises (1954–55/1958), Chinese analysts acknowledge that extended deterrence may not be credible if a Soviet-American strategic confrontation occurs. They have concluded, however, that "there is no sign yet that nuclear deterrence [itself] could fail." [16] The PRC, moreover, is reaching a stage in its own nuclear force development where extending deterrence to North Korea, to its own sovereign but contested territories in the South China Sea, or even to selected Southeast Asian states (Thailand or a Cambodia governed by the Khmer Rouge or by other factions amicable to

Beijing) may become a more serious option as an Aspiring Player deterrence posture.

If the Chinese have indeed begun the process of merging Western deterrence concepts into their own strategic thinking, analysts who still insist upon diminishing China's outlooks on modern war and strategy may be too critical. John Wilson Lewis, for example, has speculated that "words other than deterrence probably should be used to label Chinese [nuclear] doctrine" because the PRC's leaders are more concerned with surviving a war than with postulating a state of mutual assured destruction which could prevent one. Yet Lewis also notes that, like Western deterrence planners, PLA military commanders are greatly concerned with how changing military technology affects the adequacy of their forces to either prevent a military attack against China or preclude escalation of an initial conflict.[17] Chong-Pin Lin provides an interesting tour de force of Chinese semantical approaches to "deterrence." It differs from the West's understanding of the term —i.e., *hezu* = "to frighten into inaction"; *weishe* = " to deter"; *weixe* = "to awe and threaten." He concludes, with Lewis, that the Western deterrence concepts of "mutual assured destruction," "deterrence by punishment" versus "deterrence by denial," or "minimum deterrence" versus "warfighting" have only recently entered the Chinese lexicon of strategic reference.[18] The fundamental point is, however, that Western ideas *have* been incorporated into China's strategic debate. This is the case, despite historical and cultural barriers to assimilation. Along with Lewis, Chong-Pin Lin acknowledges this development by observing that "the leaders of contemporary China tended to respond to the [theoretical] challenges by synthesis. The traditional and antitraditional factors would be reconciled in an integration of the two."[19]

Understanding China as an Aspiring Player

EVOLVING CHINESE deterrence doctrine and behavior have been shaped as much by factors beyond China's control as by internal debates over how that nation's military posture should be defined. The changing interational power balance has forced Beijing to confront strategic problems related to escalation control, interalliance transferability, and credibility of commitment. This is the case even while Chinese military planners may correctly regard such problems to be of more concern to those who would adopt a Dominant Player approach to extended deterrence.

As will be seen, China was given a harsh introduction to escalation control problems in the nuclear age during a succession of crises involving brinkmanship with one or the other superpowers in the 1950s and 1960s. Also, China's strategic commitments to North Korea and to parts of Southeast Asia come increasingly into question as postwar bipolarity yields to a more complex process of multipolar power competition in the Asia-Pacific. This, in turn, has forced China to weigh the *global* implications of its regional and intercontinental strategic capabilities with more pragmatism and less ideology than was the case when it originally decided to embark upon an indigenous nuclear weapons program.

A brief review of Chinese military history will help to explain the roots of her contemporary deterrence postures. The chapter will then trace the development of Chinese deterrence during the postwar era. It will also assess the more significant components of the PRC's present deterrence posture and its defense capabilities. A final section will weigh the relationship of China's evolving deterrence posture to its regional security outlooks and policies. The major premise of this chapter is that as China's military capabilities become more sophisticated, the PRC will increasingly seek to realize its ambition to supplant both the U.S. Dominant Player and Soviet Aspiring Player as the predominant strategic influence in the Asia-Pacific. In seeking increased geopolitical clout, however, Beijing will be required to become less ambiguous about its strategic intentions and more sensitive to the interests of other global and regional deterrence players.

CHINA'S MILITARY HISTORY AND CONTEMPORARY DETERRENCE POSTURES

AFTER CENTURIES of neglect, Western historians and security analysts have "rediscovered" the writings of Sun Zi, along with the *Romance of the Three Kingdoms, The Chronicle of Warring States,* and other Chinese military classics. They are turning to these writings in an effort to gain better insights into China's contemporary strategic thinking and behavior.[20] However, trying to identify patterns of Chinese military strategy and deterrence behavior on the basis of historical generalization runs a number of risks. As Gerald Segal has pointed out, despite several thousand years of practice in defending itself, China actually lacks a unified tradition of military history and strategy.[21] Tai Ming Cheung has seconded Segal's argument by noting that, despite Beijing's extraordinary effort to manufacture its own atomic bomb, it had no real strategic legacy with which to apply such a weapon to military ends.[22]

Continuity in Chinese Military Theory and Practice

CHONG-PIN LIN, Edward Dreyer, Stanley Henning, and others have counterargued that the continuities in Chinese military theory and practice override the discontinuities, focusing around several key concepts: the primacy of man over weapons, a preference for defensive strategies over offensive warfare, and a tendency to employ the tactics of deception whenever possible.[23] Lin further argues that four additional "underlying strategic themes" can be identified throughout China's history: (1) combining military and extramilitary (i.e., political, psychological) elements into a "total strategy"; (2) unifying opposing methods and objectives into "integrated dualism" (i.e., rule with consistency; fight using tactics of deception and surprise); (3) employing the principles of "flux" and "fluidity" in terms of their relevance to timing and force strengths in a combat environment; and (4) manipulating "negative" strategic factors into positive strategic results by motivating one's troops through fear and by using a minimum amount of one's own resources when they are inferior to those of an adversary's. Lin summarizes these underlying themes as representing two broad strategic principles: *integration* and *indirection*. Integration is the identification and use of multiple strategic factors to form a unified military strategy. Indirection is the building of strategic consensus from opposites by converting military weaknesses into military strengths and by avoiding the unnecessary proliferation of one's own strategic objectives.[24] Lin's critics argue that such an interpretation of Chinese strategy is based on "logical progression rather than real evidence" and that, in his determination to identify historical linkages in Chinese military thinking, he fails to take into account what they regard as very real external influences on China's strategic doctrinal approach.[25]

A cursory survey of China's military tradition would appear to support at least some of Lin's views. In general, however, Segal is

correct that a military tradition along the lines of those readily identified with Germany's blitzkrieg or the U.S. maritime heritage does not
exist in China. Sun Zi's maxims of stealth and surprise, for example,
went against the orthodox tactics of Chinese warfare practiced in his
time. Even Mao Zedong, generally regarded as championing the importance of military morale over firepower and technology, recognized
the importance of change in the conduct of war, warning the Chinese
Communist Party Central Committee in 1965 that "in modern warfare,
aircraft have to fly high in the sky at supersonic speed. Fighting on
horseback is gone."[26] His earlier adoption of guerrilla tactics during
China's revolutionary period was symptomatic of his recognition that
the PLA's position within China's military power balance was inferior
at the time. Nor did Mao totally embrace the notion of protracted war
(which Sun Zi strongly resisted) or totally reject the tactics of positional
warfare and forward defense. He was aware that they had been successfully implemented by the emperor Shi Huangdi (Shih Huang-t'i) in
the third century B.C., by General Qi Jiguang (Ch'i Chi-Kuang) in the
sixteenth century A.D. as well as by a number of other Chinese
historical military figures. As Segal has concluded, "it seems impossible to identify continuity in military operations if only because of the
vastness of Chinese experience."[27] Mao Zedong would apparently agree.
In a December 1936 lecture at the Red Army College in northern
Shanxi, he concluded that "the different laws for directing different
wars are determined by different circumstances of those wars—differences in their time, place, and nature."[28]

Nevertheless, there is evidence that strands of continuity in China's
military heritage do play a role in shaping contemporary Chinese strategic perceptions. While conclusions about China's classical strategy in
relation to contemporary deterrence problems must be guarded, some
premises advanced by Sun Zi and found within the other classical
writings on Chinese warfare *do* appear to have relevance to modern
Chinese deterrence policy.

This is particularly true if one accepts that Sinocentrism has endured
to become a factor in the formulation of contemporary Chinese foreign
and security policy. Allen S. Whiting, for example, notes that, historically, China will most likely apply deterrence strategy through demonstrative and limited use of force only when it feels highly vulnerable
relative to militarily superior external powers. In such instances, the
Chinese will time their deterrence tactics to maximize their warning ef-

fect and to allow an adversary face-saving opportunities for retreat before going to war.[29] While taking Whiting's observations as appropriate starting points for assessing Chinese deterrence behavior, three additional premises appear important. One such premise is attacking the strategy of the enemy and prevailing without actually engaging in battle. A second reates to strategic deception, with both positive and negative connotations for implementing sound deterrence strategy. A third relates to avoiding an enemy's strengths and exploiting his weaknesses, relying upon understanding one's opponent and the opponent's view of himself.

Linkages Between Chinese Military Tradition and Deterrence

SEVERAL INCIDENTS involving postwar Chinese extended deterrence relate to the first premise. Prior to its intervention in the Korean War (December 1950), China sent a number of strong signals to the United States concerning its displeasure over the UN Command's offensive into North Korea. These signals included protests against alleged U.S. airspace violations into northeast China and the shifting of the Fourth Field Army from Fujian province, opposite Taiwan, to northeast China.[30] China, prior to the 1962 Sino-Indian border crisis, sought—unsuccessfully—to "educate" the Indians on Chinese interests and intentions in an effort to avoid misunderstanding or miscalculation of China's intense opposition to New Delhi's so-called "forward policy" implemented in November 1961.[31] In the Sino-Soviet border dispute (1969) and the Sino-Vietnamese war (February 1979), Beijing also attempted to define its strategy in advance and act deliberately on it rather than to hide China's intentions from a prospective adversary.

With respect to the second premise, China has attempted deception with respect to its strategic nuclear component, similar to Nikita Khrushchev's tactics which created the pseudo "missile gap" between the USSR and the United States during the late 1950s. Such Chinese behavior conforms to the dictums of Sun Zi and the parables found in *The Three Kingdoms*, urging the use of deception when, by doing so, one can reduce costs and control risks vis-a-vis a superior enemy force. Until U.S. and Soviet satellite surveillance became more refined during the early 1970s, China's use of caves and remote mountain valleys for the emplacement of crude, liquid-fueled, mobile nuclear missiles compensated, to some extent, for the inability to launch them either time-effectively or accurately. Recent Taiwanese analysis has revealed that

China's land based missiles were dispersed at some 150 sites through-out Xinjiang, Inner Mongolia, Tibet, and other locations.[32] Both the USSR's move to upgrade its *Galosh* surface-to-air missile system around Moscow during the late 1960s and the Nixon Administration's ratio-nale for deploying an antiballistic missile capability proximate to "na-tional command centers" during this time were predicated, in part, on the *perceived* Chinese threat—a good indication that the superpowers had begun to take Chinese deterrence capabilities and commitments more seriously. Deception, however, became a less useful means of establishing the credibility of China's nuclear missile deterrent when the superpowers' strategic missile forces' lethality (multiple warheads), accuracy, and control simply overwhelmed China's limited capabilities.

The third premise, maximizing one's own strengths and exploiting an adversary's weaknesses implies, for China, emphasizing selective concentration of mass and firepower along with refinement of com-mand and control. Applying military skills effectively, rather than relying exclusively on brute force, usually constitutes the key to achiev-ing victory in modern warfare. China has stressed advanced training in managing the contemporary means of deterrence since the late 1970s. With the fall of the Gang of Four and the institution of the Four Modernizations development program, there has been the renewed emphasis on "professionalism" at the expense of revolutionary ideol-ogy and People's War. While a number of PLA officers are currently under investigation for collaborating with the recently suppressed pro-democracy movement, most are escaping with nothing more than a reprimand from party officials. It is uncertain to what extent Chinese leaders can really afford to emphasize "politics over professionalism" without completing alienating the younger, better educated officer corps of the PLA.[33]

Even during past political crackdowns, China's nuclear weapons program has always been assigned top priority by the country's leader-ship. This was especially true in the aftermath of the Soviet Union's refusal to extend deterrence on China's behalf in the Taiwan Straits during the late 1950s and its ill-fated attempt to incorporate Chinese military forces into the USSR's Eurasian strategic network. China has since "evaded" Soviet domination by exploiting Moscow's fear of a two-front war and by refining its "united front" politics of tacit coali-tion with the West. More recently, the PRC has projected a stance of "independent foreign policy" to avoid strategic overdependence on the

United States and its allies. Ultimately, Beijing has relied upon the fundamental ideological differences of East and West to ensure that no winning coalition will be formed against China.

THE EVOLUTION OF CHINESE POSTWAR DETERRENCE OUTLOOKS

THROUGHOUT THE two decades following Mao's ascension to power, Chinese strategists were hesitant to develop new strategic doctrines because they were reluctant to incur Mao Zedong's displeasure if he perceived them as revising People's War too readily. Nevertheless, two *external* factors were important in shaping Chinese perceptions toward deterrence strategy and its applicability to China's own national and regional security interests. One was coming to terms with the unpredictability of United States' Dominant Player strategy. U.S. deterrence behavior appeared to be intermittent, if not completely inconsistent, to Chinese defense planners. They could not understand why the Americans "amassed an extraordinary array of military power in and around the Korean Peninsula only to constrain its use" due to political and diplomatic constraints.[34] The other factor was the qualified levels of extended deterrence Moscow was willing to provide to the PRC for supporting Beijing's regional security agenda, even after China's credibility as an ally had been verified by its military intervention against the United States in the Korean War. As time passed, Chinese leaders understood more clearly that they could not ultimately rely upon Soviet support if Moscow feared that such assistance could precipitate a conflict escalation with the West in which its own deterrence capabilities would be tested against those of Washington and found wanting.

The Sino-Soviet Alliance

FOLLOWING THE signing of a Sino-Soviet Treaty of Friendship, Alliance, and Mutual Assistance in February 1950, the PRC was content to rely upon the Soviet Union to deter nuclear coercion by the United States or intimidation by a revitalized Japan. In the meantime, Chinese military leaders began to quarrel among themselves over whether to modernize the People's Liberation Army (PLA) through "quick fixes":

i.e., extensive purchase of Soviet weapons systems and a high level of dependence on Soviet military assistance—or through an industrial development program aimed at achieving long-term military self-sufficiency at the expense of immediate weapons procurements. This decade-long conflict between key Chinese political and military figures is extensively assessed elsewhere.[35] It is sufficient to note in passing that Marshall Peng Dehuai and other members of the so-called "professional" faction of the PLA were purged at the Lushan Plenum (August 1959), signaling the Chinese leaderships' ultimate backing of Mao Zedong's position committing the PRC to a long-term strategy for achieving military self-reliance.

Throughout most of the 1950s, Beijing's attitude toward its Soviet guardian oscillated between enthusiasm for Moscow's technological breakthroughs in its nuclear force capabilities and disillusionment over the refusal of the Soviets to make explicit commitments to Chinese regional security interests in Korea and Taiwan. Soviet extended deterrence behavior toward China, as it unfolded through the Korean War (1950–1953), caused Beijing to question the credibility of Soviet extended deterrence commitments in the case of a nuclear fait accompli by Washington.

Mao believed he had elicited binding security guarantees from Joseph Stalin when he visited Moscow the winter prior to the commencement of Korean hostilities. He committed his best troops to North Korea's defense when China intervened in October 1950. China absorbed massive casualties resulting from the overwhelming U.S. advantage in firepower (approximately a half million troops during the first year of fighting). Soviet aid was viewed as too little and too late to preclude a military stalemate or to prevent, at worst, an American military presence on the banks of the Yalu River in the aftermath of a total North Korean capitulation. General MacArthur's dismissal from his command in April 1951 for resisting President Truman's determination to exercise restraint in escalating the conflict against the Chinese homeland was a welcome development in Beijing, and one which encouraged the Chinese to press their Soviet allies for a reaffirmation of earlier deterrence guarantees.

The issue of the Soviet credibility of commitment to China's security objectives intensified for Mao throughout the 1950s. In February 1953, for example, the Eisenhower administration initiated a series of moves threatening to escalate the Korean War in order to end it with noncommunist South Korea intact. On February 2, the President announced the temporary repositioning of the Seventh Fleet away from the Taiwan Straits, creating the prospect that the Chinese Nationalists would be free to conduct limited offensives against the Chinese mainland and intensifying pressure against Beijing to end their military campaign in North Korea. At the same time, Eisenhower was conferring with his National Security Council about the effectiveness of nuclear weapons against Chinese and North Korean positions on the Korean Peninsula and the utility of extending the war to the Yalu River in Chinese territory. On February 24, China dispatched a high level delegation, including Qian Sanqiang (Ch'ien San-ch'iang), the PRC's most eminent nuclear scientist, to Moscow. The Chinese argued that the Soviet Union should intervene on China's and North Korea's behalf in the event the Americans used nuclear weapons in North Korea. Although Soviet pilots and military advisors were stationed in Beijing and in other parts of industrial Manchuria to deter U.S. nuclear strikes against China's heartland, the USSR proved reluctant to extend Soviet defense guarantees to "Chinese People's Volunteers" fighting beyond China's borders.[36]

It remains unclear why the Soviets declined to support the Chinese. Some accounts have downplayed the effects of Eisenhower's implied nuclear threat on Stalin's successors (the Soviet dictator had died in early March). They argue that the USSR's new leadership did not want to enter "a rapidly expanding and unpredictable military conflict—one which would certainly involve atomic weapons . . . the atomic aspect no doubt worsened the Soviet dilemma, it did not itself create the problem."[37] Others cite the impressive growth of the U.S. nuclear weapons stockpile during the Korean War years; by the end of 1953, it outnumbered the Soviet equivalent by approximately 1,000 to 120, a ratio which would allow Washington to deter war in Europe and to escalate the Korean War to nuclear use at the same time.[38] Without the prospect of Soviet intervention in Korea, the Chinese signaled their willingness to negotiate for prisoner exchanges in late March 1953, a key turning point in U.S. efforts to secure an armistice for the conflict. It also represented the first major instance in which the Chinese questioned the credibility of the Soviet extended deterrence commitment.

Marshal Nie Rongzhen later asserted in his memoirs that Mao's geopolitics had been vindicated by China's success in limiting the Korean War to Korea, that China's Soviet ally, because of excessive caution, had little to do with this success.[39] By the end of the war, Mao had clearly established a threefold pattern of strategic behavior, thoroughly compatible with the classical postulates of Sun Zi, if not deliberately modeled on them. First, be sure you are able to control the scope and level of any conflict with an adversary so that it cannot threaten your own regime's survival. Secondly, only use military force if it can be linked unambiguously to a specific strategic objective and can be employed in concert with diplomacy to pressure an adversary into making concessions. Third, utilize escalation control against a militarily superior adversary by retreating if his vital interests become truly threatened. Numerous speeches delivered by Mao during both the Korean War and Taiwan Straits episodes reveal all three patterns of strategy as axiomatic to his views on Sino-American military confrontation and China's place in the global balance of power.

The 1954–55 Taiwan Straits crises (reviewed in chapter 2) further disillusioned China, as the USSR once more demonstrated that it was unwilling to support the PRC in any military actions which would risk a direct Soviet confrontation with the United States. Consequently, as the recent work by John Lewis and Xue Litai has described, a Chinese Politboro decision was reached as early as January 1955 to embark upon an indigenous nuclear weapons program.[40] This decision was based upon "conclusions they [the Chinese] had reached during the Korean War and the era of American nuclear threats." In a definitive speech to the Politboro, Mao Zedong portrayed the atomic bomb quite differently from his earlier characterizations of it as a "paper tiger," now arguing that even though a Chinese nuclear force would not be as large as the superpowers, it would nevertheless "boost our courage and scare others." Nie Rongzhen, Vice-Chairman of the Chinese Communist Party's Central Military Commission and head of China's strategic weapons program from 1958 until the Cultural Revolution, expressed China's determination to ascend to independent nuclear power status even more graphically in his recently published *Memoirs:*

> We had the experience of the Korean War, in which we suffered heavy losses due to the backwardness of our equipment's technology . . . we greatly needed to develop science and technology . . . In order to terminate the bullying and humiliation of our country by the imperialists for more than a century, we [decided we should] develop sophisticated weapons, symbolized by missiles and A-bombs, so that we would have the minimal means to stage a counterattack in case our country suffered

a surprise nuclear attack by the imperialists. At the same time, through the "twelve-year science plan" and the experiences of studying and producing sophisticated weapons, we felt strongly that *liang dan* ["two bombs"—a missile and an A-bomb] are the crystalization of modern science and technology . . . [and that] the development of *liang dan* would promote the development of modern science and technology in our country.[41]

The Chinese thus visibly moved away from their earlier glorification of revolutionary struggle and People's War in favor of developing their own nuclear deterrence capabilities and military-technological know-how—initially depending heavily on the Soviets for providing such knowhow and the strategic support necessary to allow China to exploit it. By 1955, the PRC had accepted Soviet help in building the country's first nuclear reactor and joined other Soviet bloc nations in sending nuclear scientists to the Joint Institute for Nuclear Research at Dubna in the USSR (the Dubna connection was advertised as engaging only in research on the "peaceful" uses of nuclear energy).

The Chinese later accused the Soviets of reneging on an October 1957 agreement to supply China with a "prototype" nuclear weapon and to provide technical assistance for the production of Chinese nuclear weapons. In 1986, Deng Jiaxian, the director of China's nuclear weapons program for almost three decades, revealed that the 1957 agreement was to provide the Chinese with a "teaching model" nuclear device.[42] According to Chinese spokesmen, the agreement was broken in June 1959. While not directly admitting to the nuclear weapons transfer commitment, Nikita Khrushchev later explained in his memoirs that the Sino-Soviet rift had negated the rationale for *any* nuclear weapons technology transfers: "They [the Chinese] had already begun their smear campaign against us and were beginning to make all sorts of incredible territorial claims as well. We didn't want them to get the idea that we were their obedient slaves who would give them whatever they wanted, no matter how much they insulted us. In the end we decided to postpone sending them the prototype."[43]

It is almost certain that the USSR moved to exert greater control over Chinese strategic behavior in the aftermath of the second Taiwan crisis in late 1958. By that time, Mao felt Washington was truly on the defensive, both in Asia and globally; and that escalation control would be guaranteed by Soviet support of Mao's objectives.[44] Beijing's demands on Moscow to confront the Americans were all out of proportion to what the Soviets were actually willing to incur on behalf of their recalcitrant Chinese ally. Based on their recent interviews with senior Soviet specialists in strategic affairs, Lewis and Xue conclude that the Soviet decision to renege on the USSR's initial commitment to supply a prototype atomic bomb was made even prior to the crisis' outbreak in August, perhaps as early as March 1958, when Nikolai Bulganin— a major supporter of the transfer decision—was deposed by Khrushchev during an ongoing political power struggle within the Kremlin. Khrushchev's Deputy Premier, Anastas Mikoyan, and his minister in charge of Soviet nuclear weapons development, Yefim Pavlovich Slavskii, were opposed to the transfer.[45]

The Chinese later reported that during April 1958, and in subsequent meetings between Soviet and Chinese leaders, the Soviets demanded that the PLA, with its impending nuclear component, be placed under a dual command and control system, similar to the Warsaw Pact and under Moscow's strict supervision.[46] The Soviet demands were summarily rejected by Mao, increasingly suspicious of Moscow's unwillingness to defend the Chinese mainland at the nuclear level and fiercely protective of China's sovereign prerogatives. Even the nature of Soviet extended deterrence was apparently at issue. A number of Soviet and Western specialists on postwar Sino-Soviet relations contend that the Chinese were reluctant to ask for Soviet military intervention even if the Americans used tactical nuclear weapons but ready to accept Moscow's help—and strategic predominance—if U.S. strategic weapons were employed against the Chinese mainland.[47]

Without an enduring Soviet commitment, China lacked a credible deterrent against the U.S. and its East Asian allies, and was vulnerable to U.S. nuclear strikes as well to as future conventional attacks against China's peripheries.[48] As Beijing continued to resist Moscow's demands for control, Soviet assistance to China in uranium processing and enrichment equipment construction at key nuclear facilities declined sharply. Chinese sources have since claimed that Moscow delivered only about 5 percent of the nuclear reactor equipment parts it originally promised for transfer to Beijing and only about 60 percent of the nuclear reactor blueprints/design drawings originally agreed to in 1957–58.[49] By August 1960, when all the Soviet scientists and technicians had departed, China's program to develop a nuclear weapons program was in unquestionable disarray.[50]

"People's War" and China's Strategic Independence

CHINA ACCELERATED its development of an indigenous nuclear force under the direction of Marshal Lin Biao (Peng Dehuai's successor as Defense Minister), Nie Rongzhen (head of the Defense Science and Technology Commission which oversaw the PRC's nuclear weapons program), nuclear physicist Qian Sanqiang, Deng Jiaxian, and Liu Jie (head of the Ministry which supervised the PRC's fledgling nuclear industry).[51] The advanced stage of this force was to be a Chinese thermonuclear weapon (H-bomb) and ballistic missile delivery systems. Work on the H-bomb started in 1963, one year before the explosion of China's first atomic weapon; work on a ballistic missile delivery system was undertaken around 1965.[52]

Until such time as the PLA's nuclear capabilities would become formidable enough to deter a superpower attack against the Chinese mainland, however, China continued to embrace People's War as the best means of establishing a national defense-in-depth (luring an invading enemy deep into the Chinese hinterland and then subjecting him to powerful counterattacks). From 1964 to 1971, China moved to create an indigenous strategic and industrial reserve in remote parts of southwestern and western China—the "Third Front" or "Third Line"—to compensate for the dissolution of its Soviet alliance and to minimize prospects that a future superpower attack against China's nuclear weapons production and storage sites could succeed.[53] While Chinese leaders maintained that China's less concentrated population and industries would allow it to emerge from nuclear strikes in relatively better shape than the superpowers or European countries, they remained sensitive to the effects of nuclear radiation and to the prospect of follow-up invasions against Chinese territory following such strikes. Mao and his colleagues in the Chinese Politboro were also aware of Soviet contingency plans in the late 1960s to conduct "surgical strikes" against Chinese nuclear installations and to militarily occupy parts of China north of the Yangtze River through airborne operations. China's subsequent efforts to seek political rapprochement with the West can be better understood in this context.[54]

People's War, as Joffe and other Western analysts have argued, underscored as much as rectified China's strategic vulnerability.[55] The

USSR's geographic proximity to China allows Moscow the option of punishing or deterring what it may deem to be undesirable Chinese behavior at lower levels of conflict. The Soviets could instigate minority unrest among the Muslim inhabitants in Xinjiang and other non-Han populations beyond Manchuria and China's coastal areas, presenting the Chinese government with a potentially serious security problem. The Soviet Pacific Fleet could interdict Chinese maritime traffic and offshore drilling operations (China has no ASW capability). Soviet bombers could conduct surgical strikes against selected Chinese nuclear positions or military concentrations. Combined-arms task forces could carry out punitive raids or invade and occupy border regions without the sustaining of the complex logistical tails required for similar operations against NATO or in the Persian Gulf. In an atmosphere of worsening Sino-Soviet tensions, Moscow's pursuit of low intensity military options against China would incur low risk of direct U.S. military intervention on China's behalf. In short, as Donald Daniel and Harlan Jencks have argued, the People's War approach to deterrence failed to come to terms with the dilemmas presented by modern limited wars.[56]

Although aware of the limited-war problem, Mao and other Chinese leaders remained convinced that strengthening the morale of PLA personnel, otherwise badly outgunned by Soviet and U.S. technology and firepower, was the best strategy for China at that time. Until China's nuclear deterrent was capable of an assured second strike nuclear capability, Beijing's ability to manage escalation control in limited conflicts and to sustain its regional politico-strategic commitments (Pyongyang, Marxist insurgency movements operating throughout Southeast Asia, and North Vietnam) would be predicated upon applying tactics of attrition against an American enemy who could not afford to remain engaged in Asian ground wars. The Chinese counted on the Soviets' keen appreciation of history to restrain Moscow from pursuing even limited military options against the PRC. Certainly, Soviet leaders could not help remembering Japan's "low intensity" military efforts against a fragmented Chinese polity in the 1930s and how completely those campaigns failed. How could the USSR expect to do any better against a unified and nuclear-armed Chinese state several decades later?

In 1965, the PRC faced its first real test of extended deterrence relatively independent of the Soviet factor. The issue involved how to respond to U.S. bombing raids against North Vietnam. Beijing feared that Washington might extend such air strikes to installations in southern China that were providing logistic support to the Vietnamese.[57] Marshal Luo Ruiqing, the PLA's Chief of Staff and Secretary General of the Military Commission, advocated the deployment of Chinese forces and equipment to deter U.S. incursions against Chinese territory, including the emplacement of elaborate air defenses along the Sino-Vietnamese border. This would, however, drain the financing for the PRC's burgeoning nuclear weapons program. Lin Biao, on the other hand, believed that U.S. strikes against the Chinese homeland were improbable. If they occurred, he advocated withdrawing PLA forces from the brunt of U.S. airpower and into China's interior, in conformity with People's War. Chinese leaders had already instituted extensive civil defense measures against possible U.S. air strikes during the Korean War. Now, a decade later (in a January 1962 speech), Lin suggested that new Chinese military and industrial bases could be set up as alternatives to the complexes interspersed throughout the eastern and northeastern parts of the PRC that were highly vulnerable to American or Nationalist Chinese attacks if other East Asian conflicts (i.e., Vietnam) were to spill over into China itself.[58] China was apprehensive that conflict escalation could occur in Vietnam in ways which could force the PRC to once more become dependent on the USSR strategically.

Compromise and Change in the Chinese Strategic Posture

FOLLOWING A decade-long hiatus, the result of domestic political turmoil and economic disruption, Mao Zedong's successors began to reconcile the PRC's legacy of revolutionary ideology and People's War with the need for incorporating state-of-the-art military technology and equipment into China's military strategy. In the meantime, the Chinese had steadily improved the capabilities of their nuclear forces, establishing a strategic missile command known as the "Second Artillery Corps" in July 1966. By the early 1970s, China had deployed some twenty medium-range ballistic missiles (MRBMs) in northeast and northwest China, capable of hitting Soviet urban areas and communications centers throughout much of the USSR's Far Eastern frontier and up to 1,500 kilometers away. A smaller number of intermediate-range ballistic missiles (IRBMs) with 2,800 kilometers range, and limited-range intercontinental ballistic missiles (ICBMs) with 4,800 kilometers range, capable of hitting more distant Soviet targets throughout Eurasia, had also been deployed. Chinese TU-16 medium bombers, capable of delivering nuclear payloads within a 2,000 kilometer radius along with smaller numbers of B-5 light bombers and F-5 fighter planes (capable of carrying tactical nuclear weapons), supplemented the PRC's growing strategic missile force.[59] But Soviet deployment of the extremely powerful SS-12 "Scaleboard" MRBM, and signs that the USSR was about to commence an unprecedented nuclear force buildup in the Far East still threatened the survivability of China's nuclear retaliatory forces, and compelled the PLA to disperse and camouflage a number of its missile sites. Even during the late 1980s, according to some U.S. and Taiwanese analysts, older land-based Chinese missiles remain deployed in caves and in widely dispersed isolated mountain valleys of Tibet, Qinghai, and Sichuan provinces.[60] Cave bases also facilitate missile maneuverability and survivability by providing a network of storage centers from which CSS-3 missiles can be transported to remote launching sites.

At this juncture, the Chinese were faced with a basic decision. Should they opt to strengthen a regional "minimum deterrent" by reinforcing their MRBM-IRBM and medium-range bomber force components, thus leaving few resources for diversifying China's conventional military power? Or should they move toward developing a more flexible and diversified PLA which, over the long-term, could become more competitive with a wider array of Soviet and U.S. weapons systems? Western analysts differ on which approach Beijing chose to pursue during the immediate post-Cultural Revolution period. John Lewis and Xue Litai have argued that the memoirs of Nie Ronzhen, and recently documented statements by Chinese Defense Minister Zhang Aiping and other sources, confirm the Chinese adoption of a minimum deterrence posture, striving to ensure for China "the minimal means to stage a counterattack in case our country suffered a surprise nuclear attack by the imperialists."[61] This "minimal deterrence thesis" argues that Beijing remains preoccupied by the vulnerability of its own nuclear forces to a superpower preemptive strike and employs deception and ambiguity of intentions to compensate for its relative paucity of nuclear force capabilities while publicly renouncing a Chinese first-strike option. It should be noted that the contexts in which the Chinese have weighed strategic doctrine have changed con-

siderably in recent years and thus have prompted those initially supporting the minimal deterrence thesis to modify their arguments in line
with more recent Chinese thinking.

Harlan Jencks, Robert Johnson, and Chong-Pin Lin have countered
the application of minimal deterrence thesis to China's situation in the
1960s by arguing that Mao and his cohorts rejected the deterrent value
of a small nuclear force against an opponent so determined to achieve
his strategic ends as to contemplate nuclear use in the first place.[62] If
their argument is correct, the Chinese approach to deterrence would
differ from that of France—another significant middle nuclear power
—which relied upon "proportional deterrence" to persuade the Soviets
that French nuclear capabilities were sufficient to wreak unacceptable
retaliatory damage on Soviet "soft" (urban/industrial) targets, thereby
making a nuclear strike against French targets irrational. Chong-Pin
Lin has also argued that China's geographic contiguity to the USSR
intensifies the escalation potential for any Sino-Soviet military confrontation compared to the European middle nuclear powers' probability
of fighting a theater nuclear war against the Soviets in Europe. The
Soviet and Chinese homelands would both be damaged in any local
tactical nuclear conflict occurring between the USSR and PRC. Therefore, "deterrence by punishment"—the calculable and finite level of
nuclear damage which British and French nuclear retaliatory forces
believe deter the Soviets from escalating a European conventional or
tactical nuclear conflict to the theater nuclear level—does not apply in
the Sino-Soviet case.[63] Accordingly, Jencks, Johnson, and Chong-Pin
Lin have concluded that Chinese strategists have constantly rejected
such Western concepts as mutual assured destruction in favor of adopting a "strategic nuclear counterattack" posture: the use of nuclear
weapons to confront and defeat an aggressor through retaliatory warfighting rather than to reestablish the previous strategic balance prior
to the outset of conflict.[64]

Both schools of thought reflect the general lack of consensus within
China itself on the best way to shape its overall deterrence posture,
given limited financial, scientific and technological resources. The military resource gap was underscored with the Chinese leadership's 1978
decision to relegate defense to fourth place within the Four Modernizations program in favor of developing the Chinese economy and
technology base. Military development was delayed, even though a
number of influential Chinese factions (including Chinese Communist

Party illuminaries Su Yu, Xu Xiangqian, and Xiao Ke; the National Defense Industry Office or NDIO; and the National Defense Scientific and Technological Commission or NDSTC) advocated crash programs to upgrade the quality of the PLA's conventional defenses throughout 1978 and especially after the PLA's miserable performance against Vietnamese forces in 1979. Other equally powerful elements within Chinese political and military circles, however, continued to insist that Mao's axiom of "people, not guns, decide wars," must not be disrupted if the legitimacy of Maoist ideology was to remain viable.

The compromise formula to quell these factions emerged in the form of People's War Under Modern Conditions. Important articles by members of the Chinese Academy of Military Science, the General Political Department, and by several of China's successive Defense Ministers confirmed that the PRC would revert to traditional People's War tactics in the event of a full-scale invasion of the Chinese mainland.[65] Such a contingency, however, was less likely to occur under "modern conditions" of warfare which, they concluded, "differ from the People's War in our army's history." More importance was assigned to positional warfare, or what the Chinese term "active defense," to defend China's key cities and lines of communication. The development of "combined arms warfare," moreover, would supplant the PLA's traditional reliance on ground forces for national defense, and logistical support would be assigned greater importance. The PLA would be "professionalized" by releasing it from most civil affairs functions and by subordinating "political considerations" to military priorities during future international crises and wars. The major significance of PWUMC to China's deterrence posture was its recognition that conventional war planning should supplement the nation's nuclear deterrence strategy if the benefits of the Four Modernizations campaign were not to be endangered by prospects of an invasion against the central Manchurian basin and/or China's coastal industrial centers. Mountain passes controlling access to the populous centers of the northeast would now be vigorously defended, as would the coastline and offshore islands. Aerial defenses would be upgraded. These measures would change the PRC's traditional reliance on protracted guerrilla war.

During late 1982 and early 1983, Chinese Defense Minister Zhang Aiping authored several definitive articles on the implications of PWUMC. Zhang recognized that the emphasis on self-reliance espoused by People's War might have previously inspired an "esprit de corps" within the PLA. He nevertheless advised Chinese technicians to study foreign technology with the intent of reproducing it domestically. Although not mentioning the episode directly, Zhang's remarks clearly addressed the PLA's dismal performance during the 1979 Sino-Vietnamese war as evidence that China's conventional forces remained badly underequipped and operationally outdated. Zhang, Deng Xiaoping, and other Chinese leaders were convinced that the PRC's military modernization would only be achieved within the broader context of a growing Chinese economy and scientific-industrial base attained through a combination of indigenous effort and outside assistance. Zhang Aiping communicated his strong belief that the West would refrain from supplying China with its most advanced technology, and that Beijing had no other choice over the long-term but to pursue defense self-reliance.[66]

Major shifts in Chinese military doctrine and modernization strategies occurred at a Military Commission session held during late May and early June 1985.[67] "Active defense" (*jiji fangyu*) was identified as the foundation of China's war readiness doctrine and the "professionalization" of the PLA was once more assigned the highest priority—a development vindicating Peng Dehuai and his purged cohorts at the Lushan Plenum over two decades earlier. The PLA was to be restructured by reducing China's military regions from eleven to seven and its manpower by one million personnel. Combined arms operations supplanted the infantry-based axioms of People's War and "group armies" were formed to bring together infantry, artillery, tank and other components of China's ground forces into a unified command structure. China's preoccupation with defense problems in the context of a Sino-Soviet war was acknowledged as insufficiently broad in strategic and doctrinal focus, notwithstanding the reality of the Soviet threat, still the PLA's paramount concern. A "long view" of strategy was instead adopted by the Military Commission on the premise that no major war would be fought for the remainder of this century. China's Aspiring Player deterrence posture needed to incorporate strategies for a limited war along its peripheries and to account for the technological changes increasingly affecting both nuclear and conventional warfighting environments.

By the mid-1980s, the PLA was testing this new "local war strategy" in a series of military exercises regularly conducted near the Sino-

Soviet border (reportedly, 120 defense simulations involving nuclear and chemical warfare were conducted from 1983–1988).[68] These maneuvers involved the deployment of highly mobile units to check a hypothetical Soviet blitzkrieg attack in the Lanzhou military region, situated along China's northwest sector. Vietnam and India are also designated as potential adversaries in future regional warfare scenarios.[69]

AMBIGUITY IN CHINA'S DETERRENCE POSTURE: A STRATEGIC ASSET OR LIABILITY?

CHINA'S CURRENT nuclear posture remains ambiguous to outsiders and perhaps to the Chinese as well. As in the case of the Soviet Union, little hard data are available on Chinese strategic decisionmaking other than occasional inferences drawn from interviews with Chinese officials, from intermittent releases of biographies dealing with key Chinese political officials, and, more recently, from military exchanges and arms control briefings conducted between Chinese and Western government representatives. An occasional "authoritative" document does find its way to the West—e.g., Mao Zedong's major policy address to the Chinese Politboro on the "Ten Major Relationships" dealing with the relationship between defense and economics, and the *Bulletin of Activities of the People's Liberation Army* drawn up by Lin Biao and the Chinese Communist Party's Military Commission in 1961.[70] There is nothing in China, however, comparable to the U.S. Defense Secretary's public annual posture statement, which allows for a systematic tracking of U.S. strategic doctrinal continuity and change from year to year.

"Calculated Irrationality"

IN THE absence of extensive information on Chinese strategic thinking, the manipulative extent of China's nuclear intentions remains unclear. Whiting has argued that Beijing frequently adopts a posture of "calculated irrationality" by confronting one or the other superpower during successive Asia-Pacific crises, accepting the risk that if war were to break out, greater physical damage would be inflicted upon it than it could inflict upon its adversary.[71] While such a posture certainly demonstrates Chinese resolve, it nevertheless also points to an obvious weakness. If China accepts the possibility of conducting strategic counterattacks in a war-fighting mode instead of applying a proportional deterrence strategy against a militarily superior opponent, Chinese belligerency could be interpreted as justification for offensive counteractions—preempting China's existing strategic capabilities, or compensating for uncertainty about China's strategic intentions by intensifying force readiness. If so, calculated irrationality actually *encourages* conflict spirals and *discourages* escalation control. Under such circumstances, the prospects for war increase commensurately.

Faced with situations of strategic inferiority in the past, China has usually backed down (Mao's third "adoption" of Sun Zi's legacy). The Taiwan Straits crises and the 1969 Sino-Soviet border conflict are examples of initial Chinese belligerence later giving way to Chinese concessions. In both of these cases, the Chinese gave way to retain *political* control of the specific conflict at hand—contesting the legitimacy of a rival and isolated Chinese regime (in Taiwan) or pressing their case for sovereign control of disputed territory (on the Sino-Soviet border) without losing unacceptable levels of credibility in their demands. The 1979 Sino-Vietnamese border war is less illustrative because it represented only a tactical Chinese move to signal its displeasure against a weaker regional actor. Soviet interests in this conflict were not as directly involved as when U.S. forces were stationed in the East China Sea or Soviet forces were deployed along the Chinese border in the previous instances. China's use of calculated rationality in the Asia-Pacific region, then, has been a means of circumventing the tactical efforts of Washington and Moscow to contain the Chinese within their own region, while allowing Beijing to signal its continued respect for the superpowers' strategic advantages over the PRC. It has been a useful means for China to exercise political deterrence.

At the level of general nuclear deterrence, the success or failure of any Chinese efforts to apply "calculated irrationality" or other variants of its deterrence posture against the U.S. in the 1950s or against the USSR in the 1960s can only be inferred, since declassified Chinese documents similar to those covering the American decision-making process during the Cuban Missile crisis are unavailable and no nuclear conflicts have occurred to discredit them. An argument has been made, however, that China has been well aware that it has the ability to inflict enough damage on either the USSR or U.S. in a nuclear showdown to render one dangerously vulnerable to the other. This is a source of considerable deterrent leverage and potential strategic influence for Beijing. As time passes, and China's nuclear capabilities grow relative to the total global nuclear stockpile, the expense to Washington and Moscow of technological countermeasures to an "ambiguous" Chinese deterrent could become even more prohibitive.[72]

"Selective Revelation"

THERE IS a second argument supporting the idea that China employs "the artful manipulation of ambiguity" as part of its nuclear weapons strategy. The Chinese use concealment and "selective revelation" to confuse the superpowers' perceptions of how China merges its nuclear intentions (doctrine) with its nuclear force capabilities.[73] Concealment may take the form of complete Chinese silence on nuclear retaliatory scenarios, the physical hiding of weapons systems, or other tactics designed to frustrate a potential adversary's thinking about Beijing's strategic posture. Selective revelation is the intermittent demonstration of various Chinese force capabilities, timed to confuse rather than clarify an opponent's intelligence about how the PRC's force planners plan to deploy or use various nuclear weapons systems.

Throughout the late 1970s, for example, a number of Western observers believed that China was stressing the development of its regional nuclear forces at the expense of longer term programs emphasizing global nuclear strike systems.[74] As noted above, China had begun to develop its ICBM capability no later than the mid-1960s. Beijing chose to "reveal" the true extent of its ICBM research and development program to the outside world, however, only during a national day parade in 1984.[75] Western intelligence circles, of course, were aware of Chinese work on the longer-range missiles. Yet the PRC opted to downplay their actual significance to its nuclear planning until confident enough in their strategic utility to abandon its clear tilt or "united front" politics toward the West and adopt a more independent strategic posture against both superpowers. With more Chinese information regarding sensitive military matters appearing in the West during the 1980s (inevitable, given China's realization that it needed much greater access to Western knowledge and technology to accrue more formidable military capabilities), selective revelation appeared to be less relevant as a Chinese deterrence approach. Increasingly, strains in Sino-American ties resulting from Chinese domestic suppression will very likely reinstitute the importance of accurate knowledge of China's nuclear capabilities.

"Inadvertent Ambivalence"

IT HAS also been argued that whatever ambivalence may be found in Chinese deterrence postures is inadvertent rather than "calculated." For example, one Western study argues that, during a June 1958 Military Affairs Committee meeting, the Chinese concluded that they needed their own "set of [deterrence] codes," thus apparently deciding to break away from the Soviet nuclear umbrella but leaving the question of what specific "codes" the Chinese would adopt unresolved.[76] Other analysts disagree with this interpretation. They counter that Chinese nuclear weapons technology was still relatively crude, and achieving greater sophistication in the formulation of its nuclear doctrine would require much time and many revisions. Instead, they assert, Mao Zedong preferred to avoid "codes and regulations taken in their entirety from the Soviets" and work toward a more autonomous Chinese method of thinking about nuclear strategy and weapons.[77] Over thirty years later, strategic doctrinal development remains problematic and strategic "doctrinal inadvertence" could materialize through default. Chinese strategic ambiguity, Jencks has concluded, is "more likely to be the result of failure to formulate doctrine than of calculated Chinese policy."[78]

Lacking formidable indigenous nuclear capabilities, according to this school of thought, China's doctrine for the operational use of its early MRBM-IRBM force remained underdeveloped and could not be credibly linked to a counterforce or war-fighting role against far more sophisticated American and Soviet nuclear weapons systems. But with the introduction of tactical nuclear weapons into PLA inventories, and the development of mobile delivery platforms ensuring a second-strike capability, the Chinese began to think more systematically about limited nuclear war and battlefield tactics (*zhanshu*).[79] The theories about military science and operations developed by Mao during the 1930s and constituting the fundamental axioms of People's War needed to be updated to better address contemporary battlefield problems of massive firepower and rapid mobility.

Tactical nuclear warfare received increased attention as did problems of nuclear escalation, targeting, maneuver, and command, control, and communications/intelligence (C3I).[80] A number of China's short-range nuclear missiles, for example, could be used in tactical nuclear roles. Such an employment could compensate for the Chinese lack of armor to check advancing Soviet tank divisions, especially in the sparsely populated areas that constitute one of the most logical avenues of advance for an invader through the Mongolian-Chinese border. In 1982, military exercises specifically designed to test the PLA's performance under conditions of tactical nuclear warfare were conducted, with the specific objective of focusing on "break(ing) up concentrations of enemy forces."[81] In December 1984 and in September 1988, the Chinese conducted very-low-yield nuclear test explosions (between one and five kilotons). The second explosion was reported in Western accounts to be an enhanced radiation warhead, indicating that China was diversifying its nuclear weapons development program from one solely emphasizing long-range delivery systems to also developing battlefield nuclear systems designed for local defense of PLA command and control systems. Analysts at the Stockholm International Peace Research Institute (SIPRI) concluded that, if true, it would "belie Chinese assertions that China wants to have only a minimal [deterrence] nuclear force."[82] Chinese military planners have closely followed developments in Sense and Destroy Armor (SADARM) and other types of precision guided munitions (PGMs) as a possible way to neutralize future land armor threats. However, any such modifications in China's battlefield inventories would have to be accompanied by a strengthening of the PLA's communications systems between such national command centers as the Central Military Commission and the General Staff Department and the lower levels of command where field commanders would be faced with time-critical decisions about nuclear use and targeting.[83]

The "doctrinal inadvertence" thesis seems convincing. China's nuclear counterattack posture has yet to be refined into a discernible and functional military deterrence strategy so that the ultimate risk of "calculated irrationality" can be overcome. "People's War Under Modern Conditions" has anticipated China's coming to terms with the characteristics and requirements of the modern battlefield, but it has yet to offer the Chinese commander something more than the unpleasant prospect of a bloody strategic and tactical war of attrition against a stronger adversary. Until doctrine is better integrated with technology, China can only adopt what Thomas Robinson has labeled a "requirements approach" to military modernization: moving toward gradual improvements in the PLA's military capability while simultaneously seeking to increase the costs of aggression against it.[84]

Doctrinal Ambiguity—Benefits and Risks

CHINA SEEMS to regard an ambiguous deterrence posture as a way to preserve doctrinal flexibility. Such a posture allows the PRC to overrepresent the lethality of its nuclear forces by means of propaganda or concealment in the hope of creating greater uncertainty among Soviet and U.S. intelligence analysts about their own estimates of Chinese strategic inferiority. Given the unquestionable sophistication of Soviet and U.S. reconnaissance satellites in discerning and verifying actual weapons deployments, the use of ambiguity in formulating a strategic posture becomes questionable. However, it may still strengthen the morale of the PLA's rank-and-file and enhance the external credibility of Chinese deterrence commitments unless deception is publicly exposed—an unlikely event given China's tightly controlled decision-making and information systems and the superpowers' interest in keeping their intelligence estimates to themselves.

A greater risk is that a prospective attacker will *believe* that Beijing has the ability to retaliate at unacceptable levels and conclude that a preventive or preemptive strike must be conducted during an escalating crisis, and before Chinese strategic retaliatory forces can be unleashed. A superpower might thus prefer to either preempt Chinese military action against itself or to reduce the collateral damage in any future nuclear showdown with Beijing. The USSR came very close to instituting a nuclear preemption strategy during the 1969 border dispute, while the U.S. justified the research and deployment of an antiballistic missile component to its strategic forces based on what Washington believed what was a more formidable Chinese nuclear delivery capability than later proved to be the case.[85] Twenty years later, Chinese strategists are once more speculating about the utility of responding to any Soviet conventional invasion with a quick release of the PRC's growing and increasingly sophisticated tactical nuclear weapons arsenal.[86] In a future crisis, the growing diversity of China's nuclear deterrence force will tend to intensify superpower apprehensions about Chinese predictability. If Soviet military planners believe China is moving toward a launch-on-warning regional nuclear deterrence posture, nuclear pre-emption is the most obvious means of neutralizing it.

Another test case for restraint in Washington's and Moscow's nuclear deterrence postures regarding China is the PRC's strategic submarine development program. For better or worse, the Chinese consider the "09 Project" as a major strategic advance in China's quest to become an international actor accountable to neither superpower. In 1988, the International Institute for Strategic Studies estimated that one *Xia* nuclear-fueled ballistic-missile submarines (SSBN) had become operative.[87] One respected defense analyst from China's National Defense University told this author that, while the *Xia* had experienced major problems in achieving operational status, the Chinese now appear to be overcoming previous impediments in design, testing problems, and cost that rendered the highly publicized October 1982 and September 1985 Chinese *Xia* SSBN tests at least partial failures, notwithstanding initial Chinese intimations to the contrary.[88] More recent tests (most notably, a test missile fired from a submerged *Xia*-class SSBN in September 1988) have been relatively successful. Chinese writings on the PRC's nuclear ballistic missile submarine program are candid in relating this program to China's immediate deterrence objectives and long-term power projection aspirations. To cite one such account:

> The Chinese-developed first generation solid-fuel booster rocket capable of underwater-to-surface launch . . . was yet another major new achievement in the most advanced branches of science and technology, following upon China's successful tests of an atomic bomb, a hydrogen bomb, and a long-range booster rocket, as well as the launch of satellites. It showed a new development for the modernization of the People's Navy, that the real power in national defense had been strengthened, and that with one jump, China had leaped into being the fifth nation in the world to have the capability of launching a strategic missile from underwater.[89]

The same Chinese article ended by citing a respected American journal of naval affairs: "the PRC has become the fifth nuclear nation in the world to have a sea-based nuclear threat . . . That it has that threat complicates not only the strategic force estimates of the Soviet Union but also those of the United States."[90]

Doctrinal ambiguity may enable China's bureaucracy to avoid hard financial or political commitments to aspects of the strategic nuclear weapons program. Such evasion may be necessary to avoid alienating those in the PLA or in the Chinese Communist Party (CCP) who favor greater emphasis on conventional force capabilities, or who support the People's War doctrine for reasons having little to do with military efficiency and much more to do with preserving their own political power bases. Political tradeoffs over military programs can always be justified by arguing that greater attention needs to be given to developing more sophisticated second or third generation weapons. Emphasis on long-term planning is less controversial and postpones struggles over political turf and resource allocation. Ambiguity thus allows for greater doctrinal flexibility, enabling China's decisionmakers to compromise between the contending "minimum deterrence" and "strategic counterattack" deterrence postures by incorporating elements of both.[91]

LINKING STRATEGIC DOCTRINE TO CHINA'S STRATEGIC OUTLOOK AND CAPABILITIES

IF CURRENT developments in China's strategic forces are an accurate gauge of Chinese strategic intentions, deterrence of a nuclear attack against the Chinese mainland continues to be the paramount security objective of Beijing's defense planners. This is true, whether China seeks to deter an adversary through either a minimum deterrence posture, or through one emphasizing nuclear counterattack. At present, China is still highly vulnerable to a massive first strike initiated during either a regional or global war and is thus unable to apply a credible escalation control strategy against either superpower. As Chinese defense analysts have readily acknowledged, an aggressor could not be relied upon to select attack options that would facilitate Beijing's own escalation control options: "when war decisionmakers select weapons, it is generally the weapon's performance with regard to the effect on the target that is given more consideration and not cautiously controlling the level of combat that is in first place."[92] Chinese apprehensions can only be intensified by the offensive postures the superpowers have intermittently incorporated into their own strategic doctrines throughout the past two decades.

Threat Assessments

SINCE THE late 1960s, Soviet military power deployed along China's border has represented the most serious external threat to Chinese security. While, as already noted in chapter 3, the majority of the 56 divisions deployed in the Soviet Far Eastern Strategic Theater are below combat-ready strength (more typically at between 35 and 50 percent of full strength), they could be rapidly augmented during a worsening Sino-Soviet crisis to confront some 100 PLA divisions, only half of which are designated as "Main Force" or highly mobilized elements. Recent Soviet peace overtures to the Chinese, including the scheduled removal of SS-20 missiles from the Far Eastern theater, the withdrawal of Soviet forces from Afghanistan, Gorbachev's troop reductions in Mongolia and in the Far Eastern theater, and direct Sino-Soviet midlevel talks on Cambodia have made some progress in removing what Beijing previously has designated as "obstacles" in improving Sino-Soviet relations. Yet, even with the straining of Sino-American relations after the June 1989 crackdown against China's political dissidents, too overt a Chinese tilt toward rapprochement with the Soviets could signal a sharp change in the East Asian balance of power in Moscow's favor and jeopardize long-term U.S. support for Beijing's economic development. Even the octogenarian Chinese leadership has acknowledged that such a development could seriously compromise China's long-range ambitions to become a strong regional and global power.

More fundamentally, the Soviet Union's geographic proximity, the composition of its strategic force in which approximately one-fourth of its nuclear arsenal is reportedly directed toward Chinese targets (during the early 1980s, two-fifths of all Soviet ICBM fields with were located in Siberia, approximately 250 Soviet IRBM warheads were thought to be targeted against the PRC, and close to 200 long-range nuclear-capable bombers were deployed in the Far Eastern Strategic Theater), and Soviet air defense systems capable of neutralizing large segments of China's own nuclear retaliatory capability comprise the most immediate concerns for Chinese defense planners.[93]

The December 1987 Intermediate Nuclear Forces (INF) agreement between the United States and USSR, effectively removing Soviet SS-20 warheads from Siberia, was welcomed by Beijing. It remains to be seen if this step will be followed by similar reductions in Soviet strike aircraft, bombers, armored units, attack submarines, and amphibious capabilities—all of which still underscore Chinese strategic weaknesses in firepower, mobility, and logistics. One Western analyst has noted that "by redirecting less than 10 percent of their *strategic* nuclear warheads, the Soviets could attack [Chinese] targets that had been [previously] covered by their SS-20s."[94] The attractiveness of any such redeployment is somewhat mitigated by a Soviet realization that future superpower arms control agreements and the survivability of remaining Soviet strategic forces will need to be weighed against retargeting options involving China. Realizing Moscow's need for prudence in this regard, China has continued to move ahead with its own nuclear modernization program, complicating Soviet military planners' estimates of "how much is enough" to deter a Chinese nuclear threat. In cultivating this factor of strategic ambiguity, Beijing is *reinforcing* a Soviet posture of worst-case planning in East Asia and detracting from the Soviet incentive to enter into follow-on strategic arms reduction commitments with Washington. Further, as Gerald Segal has observed: "The Soviet [strategic] posture [against China] is a result of myriad factors, many of which have their roots in Soviet defense culture rather than a strictly unified, rational calculation of 'needs.' "[95]

An "American threat," although latent, nevertheless still exists for Beijing. The Chinese are particularly attentive to two trends: (1) U.S. technological prowess—most specifically related to strategic defenses and cruise missiles—which Chinese defense planners believe could someday render their own modest strategic missile inventories ineffectual; and (2) the buildup of U.S. naval or air attack capabilities in the Pacific and Indian Oceans which could be employed against the PLA in future contingencies involving the Taiwan Straits, the Korean Peninsula, or territorial claims against Japan, the Philippines or other U.S. allies.[96] China is less concerned about the U.S. Strategic Defense Initiative (SDI) than about both Soviet and Western efforts to deploy more effective surface-to-air missile systems. Beijing realizes that the funding and technological barriers embodied within SDI research and development are unlikely to create any early breakthrough in strategic defense technology which could negate the deterrence value of a middle nuclear force such as China's. The PRC's nuclear retaliatory force is designed to destroy cities ("counter-value" targeting-oriented). Soviet or U.S. counter-force or military target-oriented point defense cannot yet provide blanket coverage to large enough an area to escape all damage from incoming Chinese missiles.[97]

On a relative scale, therefore, the threat to China represented by Soviet military capabilities deployed adjacent to China's own territory continues to outweigh concerns about U.S. power projection. U.S. forces are still viewed in Beijing as a necessary counterweight to Soviet power in Northeast Asia, a preferred alternative to full Japanese rearmament, and as a reality forcing Soviet military planners to face the prospect of a two-front war in Europe and the Asia-Pacific.[98]

CHINESE NUCLEAR DETERRENCE CAPABILITIES: SURVIVABILITY/ LETHALITY/CONTROLLABILITY

THROUGHOUT THE 1960s and early 1970s, the Chinese structured their forces around what Paul Godwin has termed the principle of a "deterring balance": reinforcing its largely outmanned divisions along the Sino-Soviet border with an almost unlimited manpower pool from the country's interior, which, along with a limited nuclear weapons arsenal, would be expected to fight a protracted war and to destroy enough Soviet targets to counterbalance the USSR's more lethal and more mobile warfighting potential.[99] When Chinese strategic doctrine began to endorse "active defense" as a prerogative for a developing modern state and as Soviet missile capabilities became more accurate, the problem of sustaining a "deterring balance" evolved into a more complex issue than one merely resolved by traditional Chinese inclinations toward calculated irrationality and strategic ambiguity. Reducing the vulnerability of Beijing's strategic and conventional force assets became a major concern in determining to what extent China's relatively small strategic nuclear force could effectively deter a sophisticated Soviet threat.

The problem was magnified by a growing Chinese realization that the quantity and sophistication of the forces needed to deter the superpowers was beyond their financial and technological means. The Chinese

were faced with improving their missile guidance systems, and perfecting solid-fueled rocket technology, hardening and/or mobilizing an
array of missile delivery systems, accelerating SSBN development,
implementing more reliable command and control mechanisms and
moving toward production of more sophisticated tactical nuclear weapons with lower yield-to-weight ratios, all of which would allow the
PLA's nuclear forces to hit targets more accurately, cause less collateral
damage, and thus exercise at least some increased escalation control
during a nuclear conflict.[100] Implementing all of this at once was out of
the question; however, temporary improvisations for a crude, but
gradually more effective, counterforce nuclear warfighting capability
were not. China's plans for structuring an interim nuclear deterrent
have thus underscored the point of those arguing that its Aspiring
Player posture constitutes more than an exclusive adherence to proportional deterrence. Instead, Chinese nuclear deployment patterns evolve
around the concepts of *survivability*, *lethality*, and *controllability*.

Survivability

CHINA IS greatly concerned about ensuring the survivability of its
nuclear retaliatory capability. As noted previously, China's Second
Artillery (redesignated the "Strategic Rocket Force" in 1984) has deployed its MRBMs and IRBMs (approximately 100 CSS-2s and fewer
than 10 CSS-3s) in widely dispersed areas of northeast and northwest
China (near the Korean border and the Mongolian People's Republic,
respectively) and has sufficiently concealed them so that satellite reconnaissance pinpointing of their locations has become extremely difficult.
Once located, however, China's missile sites come within easy range of
Soviet forces located in the USSR's Far Eastern Theater and of U.S.
offshore Pacific Command locations.

China's ICBMs (approximately 5–6 CSS-4s) are deployed in more
secure sites in central or western China. While they lie beyond the
range of conventional or tactical nuclear strikes initiated from Soviet
territory, these missiles are liquid-fueled, leaving them vulnerable to
Soviet or U.S. intermediate or intercontinental-range missile attacks
because they require several-hour prelaunch notice and cannot be kept
in a readiness status for long. The emplacement of a rudimentary
ballistic missile warning system in the western part of the PRC has
given the Chinese advanced warning time to shield or launch away its

CSS-4's from incoming Soviet missiles. Preserving the CSS-4 with enough range to reach Moscow and other critical Soviet European targets with countervalue strikes, is China's most fundamental deterrence objective because it forces the USSR to confront China at two distinct levels of warfare: coping with Chinese conventional forces and absorbing a likely Chinese nuclear retaliatory strike against at least some of its urban and industrial areas. This dual Chinese threat presents the Soviets with a wider array of problems than if the Chinese would adopt the French "proportional deterrence" strategy, which relies almost exclusively upon second-strike nuclear capabilities to deter an attack by a superior nuclear power.

By developing its current inventory of nuclear weapons systems, Beijing has bought time until it can develop a new generation of such systems. The new generation will encompass solid-fuel technology, and either be encased in hardened silos or deployed in ways which provide greater force mobility. The PLA has already expanded its training exercises for deploying and operating land-based, mid-range, mobile missiles in the Wuzhai area of the Shanxi province.[101] While China's strategic nuclear program may not be as "carefully conceived" as claimed by the Defense Intelligence Agency and other U.S. government sources, due to shortages of funds, technical personnel and, political infighting, its missile deployment patterns have reflected Beijing's determination to ensure survival of its relatively small nuclear force against the superpower's nuclear arsenals.[102]

Lethality

THE LETHALITY of China's strategic deterrent is related to the missile throweight and warhead capabilities of its nuclear force as well as to the levels of accuracy with which those warheads can be targeted and delivered. The liquid-propelled missile boosters used by the Chinese have improved in both range and in power for the transport of higher yield weapons. The CSS-2 intermediate range missile, for example, was first tested in 1969 to carry a one to three megaton single warhead payload against major Soviet cities situated along the Trans-Siberian railroad system or U.S. basing operations in the Philippines. However, both target designations were "soft" or "countervalue"-oriented rather than "hard" targets such as missile silos or fortified weapons systems and command centers. Moreover, the Chinese had already experienced elastic vibration problems in their earlier missile tests. These factors caused Western analysts to question the accuracy of China's burgeoning missile force.

By late 1985 or early 1986, however, China appeared well on its way to overcoming the lethality problem in its nuclear force. Beijing conducted tests of several CSS-2 ICBMs, as well as CSS-NX-4 and JL-1 SLBMs, which—as previously noted—are most likely designed for eventual MIRV configuration.[103] When fully modified, their targeting accuracy and penetration capabilities should go far to overcome the shortcomings of the PRC's "first generation" of strategic ballistic missiles.

China's progress in "second generation missile research" may now be reaching fruition. In late 1987, a solid-fueled tactical ballistic missile deployed on a transporter erector launcher, comparable to the Soviet SS-23 *Spider*, was publicly demonstrated. This was the first indication of greater Chinese nuclear lethality. The introduction of such a weapons system would reduce the vulnerability of Chinese forces to a Soviet combined arms (nuclear/conventional) attack in a limited war situation, and increase China's nuclear response options beyond indiscriminate attacks against urban/industrial targets in the USSR.[104] Moreover, some reports of additional progress in China's development of solid-fuel nuclear propellants have recently surfaced. During late 1989, the Chinese press reported that the PRC had achieved "substantial breakthroughs" in strategic nuclear missile technology (although specific details were not provided).[105] A recent Hong Kong report cited ongoing assertions in the Chinese press that Beijing is now be prepared to deploy a "supersonic, minimum-altitude flying, cruise missile possessing an over-the-horizon attack capability, and an automated and accurate guidance system."[106] In mid-1987, officials of the U.S. Defense Intelligence Agency testified before Congress that China's nuclear delivery forces would double in size and increase substantially in their sophistication within ten years.[107]

Controllability

ESCALATION CONTROL is best achieved when lines of communication and intelligence between national political authorities and the military chain of command are well established and when a variety of offensive delivery/defensive shield capabilities can be employed as part of a deterrence strategy. The 1984 reorganization of the PLA's Second Artillery into a Strategic Rocket Force command and the increased blending of Chinese strategic theory with actual PLA nuclear missions has, according to recent Chinese press reports, become more "in-depth and systematic" throughout the late 1980s. The effort to streamline its nuclear forces' command and control is another indication that China's Aspiring Player posture is moving away from a preponderant reliance on ambiguity in nuclear intent for keeping adversaries off balance and for deterring them from preempting Chinese strategic "irrationality" with nuclear strikes of their own during future regional crises. But Western observers remain skeptical of the Military Commission's ability to control PLA operations in the military regions (MRs), based on a history of political rivalries between the PLA's central offices in Beijing and MR commanders and on the lack of reliable communications technology.[108] China's ability to achieve diversification and redundancy in its nuclear offensive and defensive systems also impedes its ability to exercise escalation control.

More specifically, the Chinese have yet to convert a well-grounded theoretical understanding of satellite and telecommunications equipment into the type of applied systems needed to improve targeting data and real-time imaging from satellites. The lack of advanced radar and electronic countermeasures disallows China's 1950s vintage H-6 medium bombers penetration capability against modern Soviet air defenses (by contrast, advanced Soviet and U.S. aircraft penetration technology promises to reinstate the manned bomber as one of the linchpins of the superpowers' escalation control strategy). Chinese submarine communications also remain problematic as the *Xia* SSBN is reported to have "antiquated" sonars and guidance systems while Chinese diesel/electric powered *Romeo*- and *Whiskey*-class submarines lack range, endurance, and quietness. All of these factors hinder China's ability to implement strategic deterrence through either its naval or air forces, although additional funding has reportedly now been allocated to enhance China's land and space-based early warning and reconnaissance systems.[109]

Summing Up China's Nuclear Deterrent

HOW EFFECTIVELY Beijing rectifies its relative nuclear deterrence shortcomings will be determined, in large part, by factors beyond its control. Much will depend upon what new weapons technologies the Soviet Union and United States deploy that actually *widen* the gap in strategic power between themselves and China. Despite recent efforts to achieve greater doctrinal clarity and to streamline the command and control of its nuclear forces, China's Aspiring Player deterrence posture, as it operates at the nuclear level, is *reactive* and *compensatory*, primarily designed to reinforce China's status as an independent strategic actor to the greatest extent possible within technological and fiscal constraints. Moreover, the reality of China's nuclear inferiority to the superpowers makes it most difficult for the Chinese to develop a cohesive, long-range program for military modernization without selectively assimilating both Soviet and Western weapons technology and compromising the ideal of strategic self-reliance.

PROBLEMS OF CONVENTIONAL DETERRENCE

CHINA'S DEFENSE planners have become increasingly worried about the effect of advanced conventional weapons technologies on their country's ability to deter or to fight in an Asia-Pacific conflict environment. They argue that the adoption of precision guided munitions and advanced explosives is narrowing the gap between the lethality of conventional and nuclear weapons in a counterforce battlefield environment.[110] China has thus attempted to identify conventional war scenarios and the objectives of such contingencies. The previously mentioned Soviet options for limited military confrontation with the PRC are certainly included within such scenarios. So too are border clashes with neighboring states (China shares frontiers with twelve countries), particularly Vietnam and India; amphibious operations against hostile units deployed on contested offshore islands; and Chinese military involvement on the Korean peninsula or in Southeast Asia. In all such contingencies, Chinese military objectives need to be sufficiently limited to contain the parameters of conflict in two ways: (1) to facilitate a shift from an offensive phase to a more easily sustained defensive posture capable of preserving the new status quo ante—what John Mearsheimer has labeled a "limited aims" strategy;[111] and (2) to preclude direct military involvement by the superpowers.

The PLA's Conventional Weapons Needs

AT LEVELS less than matching the quality of advanced Soviet and Western conventional weapons systems, China must still be more successful than it has been to date in modernizing its armed forces. Just to maintain its regional military security at current levels, it must improve the PLA's mobility and firepower, below the nuclear level, by developing greater proficiency in combined arms operations.[112] Presently, significant deficiencies are to be found in the weapons categories utilized by each service of the PLA. While direct comparisons with Soviet or Western systems were less significant when China relied upon the protracted war strategy of People's War, its more recent positional defense strategy envisions unit-for-unit combat between invading and Chinese forces.

China lacks modern antiarmor and antiaircraft systems. The *Sagger* antitank guided missile introduced in 1979 is based on twenty-year-old Soviet technology and PLA armored personnel carriers, self-propelled artillery and most of its tanks are similarly outdated. The PLA's decision to develop its own antitank missile instead of purchasing technology to produce a prototype of the U.S. tube-launched, optically-tracked, wire-guided (TOW) system has backfired. Production of the Chinese system has been delayed by frequent breakages of the guidance wire at ranges of 1,500 meters and by a Chinese inability to modernize the plant equipment needed to streamline its older anti-tank missile designs.[113]

The PLA also deploys woefully insufficient numbers of the trucks and other military transport vehicles needed for timely reinforcement of its front lines. It has yet to field a modern jet interceptor/fighter aircraft which could give the PLA Air Force any hope of achieving air superiority over Soviet, U.S., or modern Asian air forces; and this situation will not change so long as the Chinese are unable to develop or buy the type of navigation and weapons-aiming subsystems needed to compete with the aircraft of other modern military powers.

While the PLA Navy is larger than those of Taiwan, Vietnam, and South Korea (but not as formidable as those deployed by North Korea or Japan), it is extended to its very limit in patrolling Chinese maritime interests throughout the Yellow, East, and South China Seas. Chinese frigates and destroyers cannot compete with Soviet, U.S., and Japanese

ASW and combat surface capabilities nor project real firepower beyond coastal and offshore island defense missions. A major amphibious operation against an opponent the size of Taiwan or South Korea is out of the question. Most naval aviation support is carried out by helicopters deployed either on some of the larger naval vessels (*Luda* and *Jiangnan*-class destroyers and frigates) or on coastal bases.

The gap in relative conventional military capabilities between the superpowers and China may well widen by the end of this century without greater funding allocations than currently earmarked under the Four Modernizations program or significantly increased access to foreign capital, technology and weaponry.[114] Only more extensive U.S. or Western infusions of aircraft technology, for example, could provide the Chinese with the type of advanced air power capabilities needed to reach distant Asia-Pacific targets on land or sea. At present, according to authoritative U.S. reports, China could not support its land or naval forces with effective air cover, nor could its bombers, with their limited armament, reach—much less penetrate—Soviet, Vietnamese, or ASEAN air defenses. Inadequate pilot training, combined with weak logistical support functions (e.g., no in-flight refueling) add to the disparity between China's current capabilities and its aspirations for a state-of-the-art air force. It is also difficult to envision conducting naval air support operations in the East or South China seas and combating either the Vietnamese air force (which it could not do during the 1979 Sino-Vietnamese War) or Taiwan's air defenses anytime soon. Nor is the PLA capable of implementing more than the most basic air defense operations against a Soviet or other regional opponent.[115]

The Technology Gap

SUCH CHINESE force deficiencies lead to a second drawback which Western defense analysts believe China must overcome before it can move from the status of an Aspiring Player to a Dominant Player in its regional deterrence posture. Despite China's recent successes in developing a regional nuclear force and its aspirations to modernize its conventional military strength, much of the West's military technology and equipment is still too complex for the PLA to use effectively. China's track record to date, for example, in assimilating foreign technology into its aircraft design and production processes has been mixed, although Britain, Italy, Sweden, and the United States have all been active in transferring modern aviation components to the PLA's inventories.[116] Other foreign reports on Chinese military preparedness have noted that the quality of training for PLA officers is substandard. Nor are China's "best and brightest" young people joining the PLA's ranks. It is unlikely that this trend will be reversed anytime soon, since the military has earned the contempt of China's students and general population for firing on unarmed civilians at Tienanmen Square in June 1989.[117] Consequently, U.S. efforts to support Chinese defensive capabilities in Northeast Asia appears to risk little at the present time in terms of freeing Beijing's military resources to support insurgency movements or to contest its territorial disputes in the region by force (the March 1988 Sino-Vietnamese naval confrontation off the Spratly Islands is illustrative). This could change as China's capacity for assimilating foreign military technology becomes more formidable. As one U.S. Department of Defense analyst has noted:

> Looking at the [PLA] air force, all of China's neighbors are probably happy with the antiquated state of equipment . . . How could this military balance change by the transfer of U.S. or COCOM [Committee on the Coordination of Export Controls to Communist Countries] controlled technologies? First, by developing advanced radars and electronic countermeasures that improve the survivability of PLAAF aircraft. Second by developing an air-to-air refueling capability, thereby increasing the range of bombers and fighters. Third, by developing the ability to deploy China's ground forces by air . . . Because the PLA has not demonstrated the capability to do these things, regional security is not affected by concerns over force projection by China.[118]

Given China's present military policy and infrastructure, it is now unlikely Beijing will "surprise" Western military observers with its conventional warfare technology as it did with the rapid development of its first generation nuclear force during the late 1960s.

Modernization and Technology Dilemmas

THE NEED for China to engage in military reform and modernization was again highlighted by Zhang Aiping during the PLA's celebration of its 60th anniversary in 1987. The military's share of China's total national budget, according to the U.S. Central Intelligence Agency, had plummeted from 18 percent in 1977 to just over 8.6 percent ten years later (1987).[119] In 1990, the PLA received a 15.2 percent increase in allocations from the national budget as a reward for shifting toward an internal security role during Tienanmen and its aftermath. Most of the increase was offset by China's high inflation rate, however, and the ability—or propensity—of China's current leadership to satisfy the PLA's ongoing demands for new aircraft, tanks, or warships needed for regional power projection against external threats at a time of severe economic crisis is obviously limited. Arms sales operations managed by well connected family members of PLA dignitaries will most probably continue to be a major source of revenue for at least the short-term.[120]

From the Four Modernizations program's outset, Zhang and other Chinese military officials reiterated that a reorganized Chinese military needed to be equipped with inventories of more lethal and efficient conventional weapons developed by incorporating high technology into munitions research and production. The Chinese Defense Minister also challenged the PLA to become better organized and to step up training on how to use the new weaponry that would eventually be added to its inventories. He further asserted that the PLA needed to make greater use of electronic and laser guidance components, as well as automated command systems for achieving more formidable rapid response and more coordinated operational capabilities in an era of "conventional war under the threat of nuclear weapons."[121]

By the mid-1980s, Beijing recognized it had to solve a fundamental contradiction in its national security policy—the need to rely on a very basic, cost-effective, and indigenous defense infrastructure, while simultaneously attempting to develop and procure state-of-the-art armaments and technology to reinforce deterrence. China's leadership realized that it could not expend large amounts of scarce foreign exchange for updated equipment and weapons. Some expenditure was nonetheless necessary to overcome the widening "defense technology time gap" between China and the superpowers, given the latters' rapid development of new, even more exotic, weapons systems and weapons-related technology. Various Western defense experts stationed in Beijing or analyzing the PLA from abroad agreed that China remained ten to fifteen years behind in military high technology such as electronic counter-measures, fifteen years behind in aircraft technology, and ten years behind in armor.[122]

Zhang's emphasis upon a "go-slow" approach to the development of Chinese conventional deterrence capabilities contrasted with the views of China's technocrats and younger military officers, many of whom had become increasingly anxious to develop and procure state-of-the-art weapons systems. They envisioned China entering the ranks of the superpowers as quickly as possible through the judicious application of foreign military thinking and purchases of external weapons systems or military technology. But the country's pragmatic leadership, in an effort to avoid overdependence on foreign military suppliers and thus unnecessary deference to foreign security interests, supported Zhang's policy approach and determined that military technology transfers from the West should constitute only one element of a much broader Chinese plan for overcoming the country's military deficiencies. In carrying out this philosophy, Beijing adopted a multifaceted blueprint: (1) limiting purchases of finished weapons systems from abroad; (2) contracting with foreign defense firms for the co-production of high technology items; (3) purchasing "dual use" (military/civilian applicable) technology production licenses; (4) upgrading training of military personnel; and (5) restructuring production in sectors directly involved with integrating foreign technology into China's defense industries. In 1983, the National Defense Science and Technology Commission (NDSTL) and the National Defense Industries Office (NDIO) were merged into a much more powerful Commission for National Defense Science, Technology, and Industry (COSTIND) to oversee these policy mandates.[123]

New trading corporations, such as the North China Industries Corporation (NORINCO), dealing with weapons ordinance transactions; the China National Aero Technology Import-Export Corporation (CATIC), specializing in military aircraft; and the Polytechnologies Corporation, acting as a purchasing agent for the General Staff of the PLA, were established during the early-to-mid 1980s to handle military weapons or military-related technology purchases with the United States and other Western countries. The military- related trade volume which evolved between the United States and the PRC is traced in table 3.

The newly formed Chinese arms trade units, however, did not necessarily coordinate their efforts in the interest of a cohesive national defense and, in reality, only a small portion of the military technology transfer contracts were fulfilled. In many cases, the Chinese companies undermine one another to ensure their access to valued foreign currencies. This trend has caused foreign policy difficulties for China by causing frustration among potential Western suppliers who viewed the Chinese bureaucracy as indecisive, factionalized, and consumed by the need to supplant the PLA's meager defense budget with arms sales to the point of disregarding how such transactions could destabilize regional security environments. Between 1980 and 1987, for example, the PRC's gross arms exports amounted to approximately $US 11 billion, with much of this total representing Chinese sales to both belligerents in the Iran-Iraq war.[124]

Expedient Rapprochement?

OVER TIME, the Chinese devised a source of leverage for increasing American strategic dependence upon the U.S.-PRC relationship and for enhancing their negotiating leverage on the Taiwan issue: experimenting with limited Sino-Soviet reconciliation. Beginning in 1982, they explored prospects for engaging in bilateral negotiations with the USSR leading toward an improvement in Sino-Soviet trade ties and to resolution of outstanding territorial disputes. Such discussions ultimately led to the Sino-Soviet summit in May 1989. At the same time, Beijing remained sensitive that it could only push the Taiwan issue so far, without risking serious alienation of the United States and an unstable regional environment in which China could suddenly find itself at strategic odds with both superpowers at the same time.[125]

Despite China's manipulation of Washington through its pursuit of qualified rapprochement with Moscow, Sino-U.S. military relations moved forward throughout the mid-1980s in the interest of finding

TABLE 3. U.S. Technology Transfer Licenses Approved for PRC by U.S. Department of Commerce

Date	Number of Licenses	Dollar Value
1982	2020	$500 million
1983	2834	$932 million
1984	4443	$2.0 billion
1985	8637	$5.5 billion
1986	6157	$3.4 billion
1987	5777	$2.3 billion

Source: Department of State Briefing Paper (Unclassified) provided to the author in June 1988.

Note: The dollar value of licenses does not reflect actual exports, which are only a fraction of this amount; but they do measure exporters' interests in the China market.

some grounds for such cooperation beyond an anti-Soviet rationale. The pace of such collaboration, however, has been slowed by Chinese opposition to any formal or binding military relationship with the U.S., and Beijing's gradual opening to the USSR.[126] For China, the major incentive to interact with U.S. defense concerns was to ensure continued access to advanced Western technology which had applications for China's own military development. The PRC proved to be much more interested in accruing technology transfer licenses than in purchasing expensive weapons systems outright from the U.S. or other NATO powers.

The Chinese also encouraged a growing number of military "exchange programs" with U.S. officials in the hope of enhancing their knowledge of military strategy and logistics through the most cost-effective means possible. Between 1980 and 1986, exchange visits of U.S. and Chinese military delegations became routine, with members of the U.S. Army's Training and Doctrine Command interacting with Chinese officers at the PRC's newly established National Defense University in Beijing, and Chinese naval personnel completing training at the U.S. Navy's torpedo school in Florida. The latter arrangement stemmed from the 1985 U.S. agreement to sell four sophisticated Mark 46 anti-submarine torpedoes to China and from a broader set of negotiations for the U.S. Navy to assist in the renovation of China's fleet to hunt Soviet submarines.[127] In early November 1986, three U.S. naval vessels made port calls to Qingdao, the first time that U.S. fleet components had visited China since 1949. Another such American naval visit was taking place in Shanghai at the height of China's prodemocracy movement crisis in late May 1989. American and Chinese naval units also have conducted joint "passing exercises" (PASSEX) in waters off Hong Kong since January 1986. Such programs tapered off during late 1987 and 1988, following the *Silkworm* crisis, and were terminated by President Bush in June 1989. Sino-American intelligence cooperation is still taking place in Xinjiang Province, however, with joint U.S.-PRC electronic intelligence operations tracking Soviet missile testing and related strategic force developments.

Is There a "China Card"?

HOW BEIJING'S desire for strengthening its own position within the global strategic balance coincides with specific U.S. extended deterrence objectives, given the continued disparity of Soviet and Chinese military power, still remains largely unclear. This is the case, even though various U.S. officials have intermittently attempted to identify and defend the strategic rationales of incorporating China into U.S. defense and deterrence postures. In 1984 testimony to the House Foreign Affairs Committee, for example, James Kelly, the U.S. Deputy Assistant Secretary of Defense for East Asia and the Pacific, argued that increased security cooperation with Beijing siphoned significant levels of Soviet military resources away from Europe. He also observed that cordial American relations with the PRC conserved U.S. military resources by precluding the need for Washington to sustain a dual deterrence capability against both the Soviet Union and the PRC. Kelly further contended that quasi-strategic relations between Beijing and Washington encouraged China to pursue selectively Western economic development and marketing models.[128] Even following the disclosures of China's *Silkworm* sales to the Iranians, U.S. Secretary of Defense Frank C. Carlucci asserted that Washington's "developing defense relationship with China was still based on common security interests," presumably in cooperating with the Chinese to check Soviet power in Afghanistan and Indochina.[129] Such reasoning was again sharply tested with disclosures of Chinese ballistic missile sales to Saudi Arabia (July 1988).

The extent to which China agrees with the United States on what a stable Asian environment actually is has never been clearly defined. It appears even less certain at a time when China's domestic political situation is in disarray, the Sino-Soviet summit has eased many of the differences between Moscow and Beijing, and cutbacks on U.S. defense spending and restraints in U.S. force modernization would appear to diminish the United States' appeal to China as a strategic counterweight to Soviet power. Furthermore, China's evident reluctance to adopt more temperate policies in such areas as arms sales and nuclear nonproliferation underscores the fact that no amount of U.S. help in China's modernization programs will necessarily give Washington added leverage or influence over China's foreign and defense policies. China's insistence that it has a sovereign right to sell PRC weapons systems to belligerents in the Persian Gulf or elsewhere is symptomatic of a tendency to place its own geopolitical status and independent foreign policy above the regional security interests of the superpowers. Although the PRC agreed not to sell arms to Iraq after the latter's invasion of Kuwait in August 1990, it is by no means clear that Beijing will continue to exercise similar restraint toward Spain or other prospective arms clients in the Middle East. As Beijing aspires to become an independent global strategic actor, U.S. security calculations and policy behavior cannot rely upon China's military outlook or capabilities to support Washington's global deterrence objectives. On the contrary, the U.S. is now facing the prospect that whether China grows stronger and more self-confident militarily or remains strategically weak because of economic mismanagement and domestic political strife, it could elect to disassociate itself from American global and regional security interests. In that case, any policy embraced by Washington which rests on the hope of Sino-American security collaboration would be a strategic liability rather than a geopolitical expediency.[130]

CHINA AS A REGIONAL DETERRENCE ACTOR

THROUGHOUT POSTWAR history, most Asia-Pacific countries have viewed China's size, population base and ideological orientation as potentially threatening to their own security and as possibly disruptive to the region's overall power balance. Since its military embarrassment suffered during the Sino-Vietnamese war, China has cultivated a regional image of moderation, marked by its apparent determination to build up its economy and to institute scientific, technological, and economic reform.

Recently, to counterbalance Vietnam's military presence in Cambodia, the PRC has cultivated upgraded security relations with Thailand. It has strengthened political ties with the other ASEAN states, while maintaining low key security ties with Japan, especially in the areas of intelligence sharing and selective regional arms control policy coordination. Beijing has given every indication of continuing to support a strong U.S. presence in regions outside of Asia, such as Europe and the Persian Gulf, in an effort to keep Moscow from turning eastward in any future global conflict.

As China develops into a major regional military power, however, it is by no means certain that it will pursue extended deterrence policies which will enhance stability in either Northeast or Southeast Asia. If the Chinese perceive Washington's overall military strength to be declining significantly, commensurate American strategic influence with

China could well decline. Further U.S. disengagement in the Asia-Pacific could lead China to reevaluate its post-1975 objections to growing Soviet military power in Southeast Asia. So, too, could intensified Sino-American tensions over human rights, Chinese arms sales to U.S. adversaries in the Third World, or new concessions offered by the Soviets to minimize or end Beijing's further strategic cooperation with the West.[131]

Indochina

TWO TESTS of Chinese extended deterrence have occurred in Southeast Asia since 1949; both have involved Vietnam. In late 1965, the PLA moved 35,000 air defense troops into the Democratic Republic of Vietnam (DRV) to deter bombing escalations by the U.S. Air Force and to prevent U.S. ground forces from moving into North Vietnam. By the following year, Chinese troop deployments had increased to 60,000. However, as Washington demonstrated only limited military objectives—i.e., cutting North Vietnamese supply lines to the Vietcong through the Ho Chi Minh trail—as opposed to the offensive strategies it adopted during the Korean conflict, China's leadership became divided over the need to deter U.S. power in Vietnam. In fact, by 1966, the "American threat" was replaced in Beijing's estimates by a greater concern over rising Soviet-North Vietnamese strategic collaboration. Once American intentions of preventing the Indochina conflict from reaching China's own borders were clear, China's objective was to discourage closer Soviet-Vietnamese strategic collaboration. The Chinese refused to service Soviet transport aircraft supplying the Vietnamese war effort at airfields in Yunan or at other appropriate staging posts. Soviet supplies directed to Hanoi via Chinese railroads were harassed, if not completely disrupted. Chinese interdiction efforts even included blocking what it believed (erroneously) was the planned deployment of a 20,000 man strong Soviet expeditionary force into North Vietnam during 1966.[132]

The second instance of a regional extended deterrence strategy involving the PRC was the Sino-Vietnamese war in February 1979. Several instances of unsuccessful deterrence behavior were to unfold in this crisis. First, Beijing failed to exploit opportunities for escalation control initially available during the early stages of the crisis which could have contributed to defusing it. The Chinese failed, for example, to establish a basis of communication with Vietnam regarding its support for the Cambodian position in the events leading up to Hanoi's military intervention against Phnom Penh in late 1978. By not doing so, they allowed the Vietnamese to misperceive the intensity of Beijing's initial support for the Khmer Rouge. The PRC subsequently attempted to place the Vietnam-Cambodia problem in the context of global strategic competition, polarizing Vietnam toward closer alliance with the USSR as a result. This Chinese approach proved to be another misapplication of Chinese strategy to the Indochina subregion. China then used its bilateral dispute with Vietnam, stemming from very specific grievances over the latter's treatment of its Chinese population and over territorial disputes along the two countries' borders, to position itself into what it regarded as a winning coalition with the United States for strategic predominance throughout Southeast Asia at Vietnam's and the Soviet Union's expense. Subsequent developments were to prove Chinese policy calculations wrong.[133]

The nominal beneficiary of the limited Chinese invasion of Vietnam was the Khmer Rouge resistance in Cambodia, combining the remnants of what had been the Chinese-backed Pol Pot government. Along with Beijing's concerns about Vietnamese incursions against PLA footholds along the Sino-Vietnamese border, however, the Cambodian connection was, at this juncture, a secondary concern. Deterrence was to be achieved in this instance by demonstrating to Hanoi that the benefits of controlling Cambodia under the rule of a puppet government loyal to Vietnam would be outweighed by the prospect of a protracted conflict of attrition along the Sino-Vietnamese border—a confrontation, the PRC's leaders hoped to demonstrate, that the Vietnamese army eventually could only lose. One Chinese official was quoted at the time as saying: "The important thing . . . was to impress upon the Vietnamese that they have been 'hurt.' "[134] The Soviet Union, according to Beijing's calculations, would be deterred from intervening on Vietnam's behalf by American warnings to the Soviets not to do so, and the American threat, it was thought, would prevail despite the signing of a Soviet-Vietnamese security treaty in October 1978.

Like Chinese deterrence efforts involving Vietnam over a decade before, the results of this strategy were, at best, mixed. In 1965, the PLA's military capabilities proved to be irrelevant to the "American threat" originally perceived; in 1979 Chinese military weaknesses were quickly exposed by some two hundred thousand Vietnamese construction troops. Subsequent waves of Vietnamese army reinforcements arriving from Laos, and from southern parts of Vietnam transported by Soviet aircraft, threatened to route an increasingly enveloped Chinese invasion force. Indeed, China failed to deter Vietnam from consolidating its de facto Indochinese confederation and pressing its military campaign against the Khmer Rouge. China conveyed no sense of threat to the Soviets, who were content to watch the PLA struggle to gain a foothold a mere 50 kilometers inside Vietnam's border, and then retreat ignominiously in the face of superior airpower, less than three weeks after the initial Chinese attack against Hanoi's original positions.

In the aftermath of the Sino-Vietnamese war, China has assigned greater priority to strengthening its relations with various ASEAN states and favorably contrasting its policies relative to those of the Soviet Union and Vietnam. As one Western analyst has perceptively observed: "Beijing's opposition to [the Vietnamese and Soviet] threats has affected its relations with ASEAN countries in two ways, differentiated by the varying emphases that ASEAN member states lay on the relative importance of the Vietnamese and Chinese threats to Southeast Asia's security. At the two ends of the spectrum are Thailand and Indonesia." [135]

China's Aspiring Player Posture and Thailand

AMONG THE ASEAN members, Thailand has assigned the most value to increasing its strategic ties with Beijing as a counterbalance to Soviet and Vietnamese regional military power. Bangkok is even buying inexpensive and easily maintained Chinese armor and artillery to strengthen its border defenses against future Vietnamese/Cambodian incursions. In March 1987, the Thai Army Deputy Chief of Staff announced plans to acquire 50–60 medium T-69 tanks and an unspecified number of 130 mm. artillery pieces from China.[136] Two months later, the Thai Defense Ministry purchased 37 mm. anti-aircraft guns from the PRC to be used in defending four air bases in central and northeastern Thailand. In late May it was announced that China had sold Thailand armored personnel carriers (YW 531/T 63 export version); in early August it was reported that China had offered to sell anti-aircraft missiles and submarines. By early 1990, reports of widespread dissatisfaction among Army officers over the quality and maintenance of the equipment surfaced. In September, Bangkok therefore negotiated the purchase of second-hand American M48A5 and M60A3 tanks, which strained previously strong Chinese-Thai bilateral arms relations.[137]

In July 1988, Thailand ordered four type 053 frigates and two larger "Jianghu" type 25T frigates from the China State Shipbuilding Corporation. These units are scheduled to be deployed by the Royal Thia Navy between February 1991 and 1993 but will most likely be outfitted first with U.S. or British weapons systems.[138]

In return for becoming a tacit beneficiary of Chinese extended deterrence, Thailand has been forced to become more deferential to the PRC's foreign policy interests. On assuming office in August 1988, Prime Minister Chatichai Chunhawan announced his intention to turn Indochina's battlefields into marketplaces for Thai products. As an outgrowth of this policy approach, he sought to create a modus vivendi between China and Vietnam regarding the composition of a new government in Cambodia. Believing that pending Sino-Soviet negotiations would facilitate his objectives, Chatichai invited Cambodian Premier Hun Sen to Bangkok to discuss a Cambodian solution. He did so over the objections of his own Foreign Minister, Siddhi Savetsila, Thailand's ASEAN associates, and, most importantly, Beijing—all of whom had strictly enforced an isolationist policy against the Vietnamese-backed regime in Phnom Penh. Siddhi was particularly embarrassed because he had conveyed Thailand's determination to stand by ASEAN and China in opposing Vietnamese hegemony in Cambodia with the expectation that Beijing would gradually reduce its own support for Khmer Rouge participation in a successor Cambodian government. When Chatichai subsequently visited Beijing in late March 1989, he was sharply warned by Chinese officials "not to complicate things." He subsequently announced that Thailand would end high-level discussions with Hanoi and Phnom Penh on the Cambodian situation and that Bangkok would rely upon the Chinese to negotiate with the Soviet Union and other parties for an effective solution.[139]

Beijing and ASEAN have thus maintained their agreement to oppose any settlement which would retain a Vietnamese—and by extension a Soviet—predominance in Cambodia, a country which has functioned as a buffer zone between Indochina and peninsular Southeast Asia. Against the vast body of world opinion, Beijing has continued to extend covert arms assistance to the Khmer Rouge forces, the strongest military arm of the Cambodian resistance movement. It has done so to deter Soviet strategic presence in Indochina and in an effort to avoid the unpalatable option of direct Chinese military intervention.[140] In December 1988, Chinese Premier Li Peng announced that China would begin reducing its military aid to the Cambodian resistance guerrillas "to let the world be at ease" and to alleviate both Vietnamese and ASEAN fears that the Khmer Rouge would hold exclusive power in Phomn Penh in the aftermath of a formal Cambodian peace settlement.[141]

The Chinese have also used Thailand's front-line status (as the ASEAN country most proximate to Vietnamese troop deployments) to cultivate deepening military and diplomatic links with Bangkok— reconciling itself to the defeat of Thailand's communist insurgency movement which it supported into the late 1970s. From the Thai perspective, China has served as a deterrent to Vietnamese military power throughout the 1980s in at least three ways.[142]

First, Beijing indirectly extends deterrence to Thailand by Chinese leaders' intermittent statements that they will not stand by if Vietnam were to invade Thailand outright.[143] Second, three Chinese Integrated Group Armies, (approximating ten infantry divisions) in the Guangzhou Military Region, another seven infantry divisions in the Yunan area (administered as part of the Chengdu Military Region) and an additional two to three divisions of border guards pinned down some thirty elite Vietnamese divisions (approximately 350,000 to 400,000 personnel), which could otherwise have been used to reinforce the at least five divisions Hanoi had deployed in the general Thai border area, twelve divisions in Cambodia (although these were reportedly withdrawn by September 1989), and three more divisions in Laos.[144] Such force strength, from the Chinese perspective, serve as a "reminder" to Vietnamese leaders that they have become involved in a costly war of attrition and China is determined to prevent formation of a greater Indochinese confederation. Third, China has extended significant levels of military assistance to Cambodian resistance groups. In doing so, it has countered Vietnamese pressure against Thailand and the other ASEAN states to recognize Vietnam's dominant status in Cambodia on a permanent basis.

Aside from supporting Thailand, the PRC spends approximately $US 80 million per year to arm and supply the Khmer Rouge (by contrast, the U.S. expends only $US 5 million annually in overt aid (e.g., medicine, tent shelters) for the other two resistance factions and an additional $US 20–24 million on covert assistance (reimbursing

Thailand and Singapore for their costs incurred in the military training of CGDK personnel, the establishment of covert CGDK radio stations, etc.). Despite Chinese Premier Li Peng's announcement that the PRC would slow military aid to the Khmer Rouge and a subsequent Chinese pledge to that effect contained in the May 18, 1989 Sino-Soviet summit communique, Beijing actually increased such assistance during 1989. Weapons systems comprise most of China's aid to its Cambodian allies; by contrast, the United States does not provide weaponry to the other two resistance factions.[145]

China's Aspiring Player Approach: Other ASEAN States' Reactions

IRRESPECTIVE OF China's efforts to counter Vietnam in Indochina, its "Aspiring Player" posture is still regarded with suspicion by Indonesia and Malaysia. These two ASEAN states, in particular, are still reluctant to accept Chinese disclaimers of aspiration for regional hegemony at face value. They remain concerned about both long-term Chinese political objectives toward the region and about U.S. military technology transfer initiatives to Beijing. Indonesia and Malaysia are both highly suspicious of Chinese military power and deeply concerned over any U.S. efforts to strengthen it. Malaysian Prime Minister Mahathir directly confronted President Reagan about U.S. policy motives for military ties with the Chinese, just after Zhao Ziyang had visited Washington in January 1984.

Jakarta still has strong memories of the unsuccessful Indonesian Communist Party coup attempt in September 1965, for which the present Indonesian leadership still holds Beijing largely responsible and opposes, according to a recent Indonesian press account, "American efforts to create a positive image about the PRC in East and Southeast Asia." The article contended that while "the United States believes it needs the PRC's role and position to counter its sole opponent, the Soviet Union . . . [and] for this purpose the PRC should be strengthened economically, militarily, industrially and technologically . . . the present U.S. move . . . [could turn] East and Southeast Asia into a 'PRC sphere of influence.' "[146]

Most ASEAN governments are also concerned about Washington deferring to China's regional security agenda in the interest of meeting American global security objectives. They note that China has more outstanding territorial claims than any other major power and contests boundaries with many of its Asia-Pacific neighbors. Ultimately, most Asian leaders would concur with the tongue-and-cheek inquiry raised by *The Economist* in late 1986: "How long can China go on being an ambassador of peaceful coexistence, a self-effacing arms dealer, and a would-be military power, all at the same time?" [147]

While by virtue of its history, size, culture, and international standing, Beijing must be viewed as a legitimate regional power, these same factors work against the PRC in its efforts to achieve greater strategic influence among the non-communist Southeast Asian nations. The "China threat" is indirect but nevertheless still a major concern to most of the ASEAN subregion. Michael Yahuda has identified three factors which underline the subregion's threat perceptions: (1) China is a *trespasser* in ASEAN security affairs because of its self-proclaimed role as a power broker in a divided Indochina, its sovereign claims over islands in the South China Sea (which are contested by Indonesia, Malaysia, and the Philippines) and, perhaps most importantly, China's development of military power projection capabilities; (2) the PRC is a *cultural impediment* to the development of ASEAN states' sovereign identities because of its emotional appeal to their substantial Chinese minority populations; (3) Beijing still remains a potential source of *insurgency support* for communist political factions against ASEAN's established governments, despite Chinese claims that it views its "state-to-state" and "party-to-party" relations as separate. Thus, many ASEAN elites believe that the PRC ultimately wishes to replace the United States as the major external power exercising strategic influence in Southeast Asia, a prospect which directly threatens ASEAN's own regional neutrality aspirations. [148]

Other Sources of ASEAN Suspicion and Chinese Restraint

A MORE comprehensive survey of the ASEAN states' reticence to affiliate too closely with China in a security context will be offered in the following chapter. At this juncture, however, a brief consideration of three specific issue-areas should illustrate why China will continue to have difficulty in its efforts to extend deterrence into peninsular Southeast Asia.

On March 14, 1988, Chinese and Vietnamese naval units clashed off the Spratly Islands following several months of escalating tensions and acrimonious propaganda campaigns over rightful ownership of the islands. China claimed that Vietnam "recognized" Chinese sovereignty over the island group as early as 1959 but that China's "subsequent period of weakness" during the Cultural Revolution allowed Vietnam, Taiwan, Malaysia, and the Philippines to press their own respective claims to different portions of the Spratly group. In June 1987, Chinese spokesmen had warned that the PRC would reserve the right to use force, if necessary, to recover the islands and incorporate them into the Chinese province of Hainan at "an appropriate time." China has rejected a number of Vietnamese and ASEAN overtures to enter into negotiations over ownership.[149] Aside from the always sensitive issue of China's sovereign territorial identity, the Spratly's potential oil deposits and their strategic location, intersecting the South China Sea's most important sea lines of communication, make them an extremely attractive prize, for which the Chinese might even be willing to risk alienating the contending ASEAN states if the opportunity to control the islands were to present itself. But China is presently unable to contest the islands militarily due to lack of air support for its "Iron Fist" battalion (a small amphibious unit patterned after U.S. and West European rapid deployment forces).[150] Nor is it clear that either U.S. or Soviet naval elements would sit by while the forces of their Filipino or Vietnamese allies presently deployed on various parts of the island-group were overrun by Chinese forces. More evident is that China's role in the March 1988 Spratly's confrontation reinforced already strong fears in various ASEAN states about China's eventual strategic intentions concerning the region.[151]

A second barrier to China's aspirations for influence with the ASEAN members has been their perceptions and suspicions of China's involvement in the Cambodian resistance movement and the Vietnamese-Cambodian war. That Bangkok, for example, should be concerned is entirely understandable, given its historical affinity for regional power equilibriums as the best means of guaranteeing its own national survival. Too many Chinese arms falling into the hands of the Khmer Rouge would risk a more direct confrontation with the Vietnamese or, alternatively, position the Khmer Rouge to recapture absolute power in Cambodia after a tentative political settlement was negotiated for that country. Insufficient military assistance, however, would allow Hanoi's allies in Phnom Penh to extinguish the ASEAN-backed resistance movement altogether. The U.S. decision to increase its own covert military assistance to the non-Khmer Rouge elements of the CGDK during the latter part of 1988 could be directly attributed to Thai and U.S. concern that China has continued to strongly support the Khmer Rouge as successors to a defeated Vietnamese-backed Cambodian regime. Stepped-up Thai and U.S. support also resulted from concerns that the PRC could use a Khmer Rouge-ruled Cambodia as a launching point for establishing a more direct and uncontested military presence in Cambodia—an opportunity the Chinese might otherwise not have because of the roughly 600 mile distance between China and Cambodia's border.[152]

China's recent willingness to explore prospects for a Cambodian political settlement may well stem from Beijing's growing realization that ASEAN and the United States are interested in sustaining a Southeast Asian balance of power in which neither China nor Vietnam (with its Soviet backers) will be able to establish regional predominance at the expense of pro-Western forces. By early 1989, Vietnam had accelerated its military withdrawal from Cambodia and was negotiating seriously with the ASEAN states on establishing a post-occupation peacekeeping force to ensure a legitimate transition of power to a coalition government in that country. Beijing's traditional skepticism of Vietnamese intentions regarding Cambodia had softened to the point where it felt it could generally support ASEAN's diplomatic efforts, talk about eventually reducing its flow of military assistance to the Khmer Rouge, and discuss a successor government in Phnom Penh with Moscow from a position of strength.[153]

China and Vietnam began conducting official negotiations on Kampuchea at the deputy foreign ministerial level in January 1989 and the PRC signaled its growing willingness to restrain its behavior on the Cambodian issue by reducing its artillery barrages along the Vietnamese border throughout the 1989 "dry season," when most fighting in Indochina takes place. A year later (January 1990), the PRC joined the other permanent members of the UN Security Council (the US, USSR, Britain and France) in agreeing to pursue an Australian proposal for ending the Cambodian conflict by appointing a UN governor to supervise the deployment of a UN international peacekeeping force to guarantee legitimate Cambodian elections.[154] As long as the Vietnamese-backed regime remained ensconced in Phnom Penh, however, Beijing resisted outside pressure to end its long-standing military assistance to the Khmer Rouge, which China deems as still best representing Chinese interests in the Indochinese region.[155]

A third problem for Chinese extended deterrence in Southeast Asia relates to Indonesia's persistent, if repressed, aspirations for subregional hegemony over ASEAN geopolitics. The Cambodian conflict highlighted the growing strategic relationship between China and Thailand which has allowed Bangkok to exercise a degree of de facto control over ASEAN's security agenda. Although Indonesia realizes that its own and ASEAN's long-range aspirations for a regional neutrality zone (the Zone of Peace, Freedom, and Neutrality or ZOPFAN) will be impossible to pursue until a political settlement is reached in Indochina, Indonesia and Malaysia, nevertheless, remain very concerned that Beijing is using its Thai relationship to "divide and rule" the noncommunist Southeast Asian states.[156] The Indonesians responded by withholding diplomatic recognition of the PRC, the most readily available means of leverage against what they perceive as growing Chinese influence along ASEAN's northernmost frontline. They hoped to win more explicit concessions from the Chinese, including a guarantee of noninterference in the internal affairs of other countries and restraint in supporting the indigenous communist movements still plaguing most of the ASEAN members.[157] Jakarta's July 1990 diplomatic normalization of ties with the PRC reflected Indonesia's optimism that such concessions would be forthcoming and that constructive trade links between China and the growing ASEAN economies could be pursued. Events at Tienanmen Square, however, put Chinese hopes for legitimizing its role as an accepted political force in the subregion, at least temporarily, on hold.[158]

The Future of the Chinese Aspiring Player in Southeast Asia

THE RISE of nuclear free zone politics throughout Southeast Asia and the Southwest Pacific provides another opportunity for the PRC to convert a tenuous political status among the ASEAN members to more tangible strategic influence. Along with the Soviet Union, China ratified the South Pacific Forum's Treaty of Rarotonga (signed in August 1985 and covered more extensively in chapter 6). By doing so, Beijing has reinforced its self-appointed image as a "vanguard" for Third World security interests. China finds a regional nuclear-free zone initiative to be strategically advantageous because it would reduce the power gap between itself and the two superpowers in a subregion which it regards as geopolitically critical. It would also align China with Indonesia, offering a convergence of interests between Beijing and Jakarta which is lacking in the Cambodian situation.[159]

Over the near term Beijing's preoccupation with its domestic priorities, combined with its inability to project its ground forces beyond its own frontiers without serious lapses in air support, should preclude any Chinese thrust against ASEAN targets. China's limited objectives in its military incursions conducted against Indian defenses during the 1962 Sino-Indian border skirmish, and its similar short offensive waged against Vietnamese forces in February 1979, can be attributed to more than mere self-proclaimed military restraint. These cases clearly demonstrate that the PRC's leadership is sensitive to prospects of superpower intervention against China if either Washington or Moscow perceives that Southeast Asia's balance of power will be seriously distorted by China's unchecked use of force in the sub-region. More fundamentally, serious logistical and financial difficulties would face any future Chinese leadership's attempt to establish and sustain a military offensive into peninsular Southeast Asia or the Indian subcontinent. Even supplying resurgent Maoist insurgency groups operating in the ASEAN region for any prolonged and systematic fashion is probably unlikely for China, given the costs of Beijing's support effort for Cambodian resistance factions and the currently desperate state of its internal economy.[160]

Northeast Asia

IN THE absence of sustaining a more extensive military presence in Northeast Asia beyond its own borders, the PRC has been relatively less sure of what strategic approaches to apply there and less consistent in effectuating those it has chosen to pursue. In a sense, this is because China must take into account the strategic power of those states most active in the Northeast Asian power balance in a way it need not do when looking toward the southeast. There is no Southeast Asian equivalent, for example, to a post-industrial Japan capable of competing with China in any number of strategic categories if Tokyo were suddenly to opt for a defense posture alternative to that represented by the U.S.-Japan security treaty. By virtue of their new-found economic

prowess, South Korea and Taiwan also are vying with China for influence throughout the Asia-Pacific in ways unthinkable during the
apex of the Cold War. And both superpowers have continued to concentrate their primary regional deterrence efforts in Northeast Asia,
with the Soviet Union particularly earmarking a substantial portion of
its strategic resources there to contain American and Chinese military
power.

The Korean Peninsula

THE DEPLOYMENT of Chinese People's Volunteers (CPV) in North
Korea until October 1958 is the only case in which China has overtly
deployed its troops outside its boundaries in a Northeast Asian setting
(some contend that PLA troops briefly entered Soviet territory during
the Zhenbao incident in March 1969, but the facts are sufficiently
disputed to eliminate this case as an instance of either aggression or
deterrence). The motivation for China sustaining this commitment five
years beyond the Korean War is not totally certain, as the data concerning Chinese-North Korean security relations during 1953–1958 is
sparse. The conventional wisdom advanced by Western analysts is that
the Chinese were competing with the Soviet Union for influence in
Pyongyang even in the early 1950s and that this competition was the
real reason for China's willingness to use its forces to deter the remote
prospect that U.S. or South Korean troops would invade North Korea.
It is probable that the CPV pullout in 1958 was a relief to both the
Chinese and North Koreans. CPV engineering projects and economic
assistance to Kim Il-sung's Korean Workers Party (KWP) failed to
mitigate vicious internecine struggle for political power within North
Korean party circles, and was a drain on China's own limited resources
at a time when Mao Zedong was gearing up to build his country's
economy through national self-reliance. In their classic study on North
Korea, Robert Scalapino and Chong-Sik Lee conclude that: "As a
result of the recent deep internal struggles that had racked the KWP,
Kim was undoubtedly motivated more strongly than ever before toward
the reduction of *both* Chinese and Soviet influence *within* North Korea.
In this sense, the evacuation of all Chinese People's Volunteers during
1958 probably relieved Kim's mind and probably improved the overall
position of Peking, too." [161] In any case, the Chinese military presence
in North Korea, which had dwindled by 1958 to a shadow of the

original twenty-eight divisions that had intervened on that country's behalf in December 1950, could not be compared in any way to the extensive American deterrence forces maintained on the other side of the Korean peninsula or in Japan.

Through a mutual defense treaty signed in 1961, China retains the obligation to support North Korea with military and economic assistance. But events on the Korean Peninsula in recent years, along with a softening of the Sino-Soviet competition which prompted the original commitment (China agreed to the treaty weeks after Moscow signed a similar pact with Kim Il-sung), have obfuscated Beijing's deterrence commitments to Pyongyang. So, too, has North Korea's still favorable (if declining) military balance of power over the South, the PLA's own need for more modern weapons, and growing commercial ties between Chinese and South Korean interests. In late 1987, South Korean President Roh Tae Woo felt confident enough about progress in his country's relations with the PRC to propose bilateral Sino-South Korean talks dealing with "general issues" that could be weighed separately from the problem of Korean unification.[162]

China remains apprehensive about Japan's intentions to play a more visible military role in South Korea, considering Prime Minister Sato's 1969 commitment to President Nixon that Japan would consider Seoul's security to be integral to its own. However, the PRC is also highly aware that lingering Japanese-South Korean political animosities, as well as growing economic competition between Tokyo and Seoul, will preclude any real security collaboration between them outside the auspices of their respective alliance ties with the United States.[163] Meanwhile, prospects for Beijing continuing to extend deterrence to North Korea with any real enthusiasm are becoming more remote as the PRC's own domestic strife preoccupies the Chinese leadership and as the U.S. continues to "evaluate" the nature of its own deterrence commitments to the South. The one uncertain variable remains the question of political succession to the aging Kim Il-sung and how new factions in North Korean politics, if they are more inclined to ally with Moscow than Beijing, could effect China's calculations about its future influence in political developments on the peninsula.

Japan

SINO-JAPANESE STRATEGIC relations highlight China's quandary over an Aspiring Player deterrence posture in Northeast Asia. Japan represents both a threat and an opportunity for the PRC. Beijing certainly entertains lingering fears of "militarism" once more rising in Japan to threaten other Asian states. Western analysts differ over to what extent China has sought to apply a deterrence strategy for seeking political advantage at Japan's expense. Some have argued no such Chinese behavior has taken place.[164] Others have interpreted statements underscoring Chinese resistance against Japanese remilitarization during the late 1960s and early 1970s as "implicitly" warning Tokyo of Beijing's readiness to use its own nuclear forces in future military confrontations which may occur between the two countries.[165] It is certain, however, that China remains wary about the implications of Japan's current defense buildup with respect to the credibility of its own regional deterrence strategy.

In this author's interviews with various Chinese strategic analysts during 1987–1989, two broad themes have emerged concerning China's strategic outlook toward Japan. First, Japan's "strategic center of gravity" is perceived by the Chinese to be shifting from north to south. The USSR is still regarded by Beijing as a military threat which concerns Tokyo, but Japanese energies are directed increasingly toward investing and trading in with ASEAN countries and exploring similar opportunities in the South Pacific. This latter trend worries China, which wishes to attract the investment of Japanese capital into the Chinese economy. Second, China remains acutely sensitive to the prospect of Japan exercising even greater economic predominance over the entire Asia-Pacific region. Japan is thus viewed as an economic threat, gaining through economic power what it has not been able to gain militarily as a result of China's regional deterrence posture and of the U.S. effectively restraining Japan as a military actor. Washington's encouragement of Japan undertaking greater "defense burden-sharing" is clearly opposed in Beijing and will be discussed more extensively below.

Since the normalization of Sino-Japanese relations in 1972 and the signing of the Sino-Japanese Peace and Friendship Treaty in August 1978, Beijing has exploited Japanese war guilt to extract political and economic concessions from Tokyo. Most notably, Beijing orchestrated the "textbook controversy" during June-September 1982 (in which the Japanese Education Ministry allegedly considered changing the wording of its history books from the word "aggression" against China to "advance into" against China). Some analysts have speculated that China sought such an opportunity to put Tokyo on the political defensive as a means of neutralizing Japanese consternation over the unilateral Chinese abrogation of commercial contracts worth about Y300 billion the previous year (1981).[166] Five years later (May 1987), Yuko Kurihara, the first postwar Japan Defense Agency director to pay an official visit to China, was admonished by his hosts over Japan's failure to "correct some signs [pointing to] . . . the revival of militarism in Japan" and to "limit the development of Japan's defense forces" within the framework of the U.S.-Japan Mutual Security Treaty "to avoid anxiety and uneasiness among its neighboring countries."[167] Official visits to the Yasukuni war shrine by members of the Japanese government have also been sharply condemned in China. In his recent and very useful survey of China's strategic thinking about Japan, Allen Whiting has concluded that "Chinese suspicions and criticisms of Japan's growing military capability will increase commensurately with that growth . . . regardless of the future Soviet military presence in Asia."[168] If the United States is unable to constrain or control Tokyo militarily, Chinese policymakers are increasingly apt to adopt a more visible posture of strategic confrontation vis-a-vis Japan.

China has also expressed concern about Japanese naval expansion and about Japan exceeding one percent of its GNP for military expenditures, claiming that "such activities and tendencies cannot but arouse intense dissatisfaction and serious vigilance on the part of international society, particularly on the part of those countries and peoples who suffered from Japanese militarist aggression, and give rise to apprehensions about what kind of 'political power' Japan wants to be and what role it will play in future international affairs."[169] Speculation advanced by some Western analysts during the mid-1980s about prospects that a Sino-Japanese security coalition would emerge appears less valid as negotiations between the USSR and PRC have effectively stated Chinese intentions to remain an independent strategic actor.[170]

Even so, the Chinese and Japanese have found some common grounds for collaborative security behavior in areas related to regional deterrence problems. Throughout 1987, China supported Japanese Prime

Minister Nakasone's efforts to tie Soviet SS-20s deployed in Asia into the superpowers' INF negotiations. Japanese and Chinese leaders had coordinated their strong public opposition to Soviet claims that the USSR had a right to move to Asia those SS-20s eliminated by a European INF agreement. The Soviets retreated from that position six months later, promising to freeze SS-20 deployments in Asia to levels existing at the time any European INF agreement was negotiated with the West.[171] Notwithstanding such reassurances, China and Japan moved to upgrade their intelligence coordination regarding Soviet missile testing and deployment activities east of the Urals.[172] In testimony before the Senate Armed Services Committee during February 1988, Edward L. Rowney, a key figure in the INF negotiations process, credited "strong pressure by Asian governments on the Soviet Union" as being instrumental in achieving the final version of the treaty which called for the global elimination of INF missiles.[173]

Taiwan

TAIWAN, OF course, still has the most to fear. The PRC has never renounced its claim to what has now become one of Asia's most formidable economic success stories. Beijing continues to proclaim the right to incorporate this island, by force if necessary. One Western analyst has correctly noted that the Taiwan problem "remains perhaps the most serious threat to China's image as a peaceful participant in the Pacific Century," because if Taipei continues its current rate of economic growth, and if the Taiwanese indigenous population continues to increase its political power on the island, reunification by means other than force will become less—rather than more—likely.[174] Taipei demonstrated its sensitivity to this problem by its visibly restrained behavior during mainland China's domestic political turmoil in May-June 1989. It avoided extensive official comment on that crisis and refused to be provoked by Beijing's claims that Taiwanese provocators were behind many of the student demonstrations. The Taiwanese still fear that being too loud in their criticisms of the PRC's crackdown could lead the Chinese Communist Party to adopt a more bellicose stance vis-a-vis Taiwan to divert attention from China's own internal problems.[175]

At present, China's modernization program and its desire for access to the finances and technologies of the West has constrained its inclinations to exercise a military option in its enduring campaign to reunify Taiwan with the Chinese mainland. Taiwan's projected qualitative conventional force improvements over the 1990s would confront Beijing with another problem if it attempted to invade the Nationalist-held island. Taipei has plans for allocating a $US 6 billion outlay to modernize its navy, build its own advanced jet aircraft, and produce a variety of short-range missiles for defense against amphibious invasions and air strikes. Reports have also surfaced that the Nationalist regime is embarking upon a covert nuclear weapons program, complete with an intermediate range missile delivery system (1500 kilometer range) which could threaten a number of targets in the eastern part of the PRC.[176] Whether true or not, the perception of Taiwan moving toward such capabilities may be as important as the reality in deterring the PLA.

By the late 1980s, however, some Western strategists were beginning to assert that the industrial technology gap between Taiwan and the Chinese mainland was beginning to narrow. The Taiwanese government was also expressing concern about the increased security threat represented by growing Chinese amphibious capabilities in the East and South China Seas and about the clear Chinese intent to expand the PLA Navy. Recent Chinese press accounts have praised the PLA's strengthening of its airborne forces as an effective means "to defend China's . . . coastline."[177] Current Taiwanese and Western intelligence estimates of the PRC's maritime and amphibious capabilities are less flattering. They estimate the PLA could not field more than three brigades of marines suitable for amphibious operations and would have problems neutralizing Taiwanese fast attack craft equipped with modern antiship missiles.[178] While Taiwan is confident it could field some thirty divisions to defend against a PRC invasion which, it is thought, could initially apply only around fifteen divisions, Taiwan's military analysts are still worried that their current military technology advantages could erode over the next decade.[179]

The U.S. has acted to counter Taiwanese fears by allowing its former treaty ally continued access to quality American weapons systems. Even though the August 1982 Shanghai II communique reached by Secretary of State Shultz and Chinese officials committed the U.S. not to undertake military sales to Taipei beyond FY 1979 levels, the Reagan administration applied a broad interpretation of this commitment by arguing that technology transfers to the Chinese Nationalists

lie outside the framework of this commitment. Consequently, private
U.S. defense firms such as Lear Siegler International, General Dynamics, and Garrett Turbine Engine Company are transferring several
billion dollars worth of "know-how" to Taiwan's military. The transfer
includes Indigenous Defensive Fighter (IDF) technology to provide
the aging F-5E/F and F-104 aircraft now deployed by the Taiwanese
air force with head-up display systems equal in sophistication to that
obtained by Beijing in its F-8II avionics transaction with the United
States (see chapter 2).[180]

There is little reason to believe that, even with its gradual willingness to engage in commercial and cultural exchange with Beijing,
Taipei will reduce its military efforts. Nor will the PRC be happy to
see Taiwan's separatist identity reaffirmed by the continued spectacular growth of that island's economy or by the replacement of Guomindang mainlanders with an indigenous, and even more separatist, Taiwanese leadership. It is unlikely the PLA will develop enough
amphibious offensive capabilities to make an invasion attempt against
Taiwan for the remainder of this century. Ultimately, however, both
China and the United States will be required to reevaluate and perhaps
redefine the extent to which their political and strategic interests require a Chinese commitment not to take the island by force and a
continued, albeit tacit, U.S. deterrence commitment extended toward
Taipei by virtue of the 1979 Taiwan Relations Act.[181]

Coping With the Soviet Threat

CHINA HAS adopted a "carrot and stick" approach for reconciling its
insistence on military self-reliance with its lack of indigenous strategic
assets to meet a Soviet threat. Diplomatically, it has sought increased
channels for dialogue with the USSR in an effort to enhance its image
as a significant and independent political actor rather than as an ideological or geopolitical subordinate to Soviet regional power. Normalization talks between the USSR and the PRC resumed in 1982 after
Soviet leader Leonid Brezhnev's March 1982 speech in Tashkent expressed Moscow's willingness to recognize China as a "socialist country" and to negotiate Sino-Soviet differences. Brezhnev took care,
however, to couch his offer of reconciliation by noting that negotiations
could not be conducted "to the detriment of third countries," namely
Vietnam, India, Afghanistan, Mongolia, and other Soviet allies.[182] In

the spring and summer of that year, the USSR withdrew one motorized rifle division and additional forces from Mongolia, reducing their deployed force strength in that country from 65,000 to 53,000.

With his July 1986 speech at Vladivostok, Mikhail Gorbachev demonstrated his willingness to address regional security problems in ways that could lead to tactical concessions at the expense of Russian allies in the Asia-Pacific and to the benefit of improved relations with China. He also promised tangible progress in resolving the Sino-Soviet border dispute and, indeed, border discussions between the USSR and China resumed in February 1987. The Soviets lost little time in agreeing to the Chinese interpretation of the Amur River boundary. Strong evidence exists that Gorbachev moved ahead with force reductions in Mongolia, despite Mongolian objections and in direct response to fears that Soviet forces there could threaten Beijing as "the spearhead" of any future Soviet attack against China. Of equal significance to China was the USSR's agreement to refrain from transferring SS-20 missiles from Europe to Asia as part of the December 1987 INF accord and its willingness to negotiate *further* cutbacks of Soviet deployments in Mongolia—e.g., airborne units and force units manning conventional and tactical nuclear missile systems—in discussions leading to the May 1989 Sino-Soviet summit.[183] The Chinese stopped contesting the Nineteenth century Czarist treaties by which the Russians annexed territory along the northeast sector of the Sino-Soviet border.

Substantive differences between Moscow and Beijing persisted, however, as Gorbachev and Deng convened the summit in the latter city. The lingering dispute concerning the Soviet refusal to recognize Chinese sovereignty over Heixiazi Dao (Black Bear Island) was not even a major item of negotiation as presummit talks became mired down over what ground rules would apply to the two leaders discussing the issue. Cambodia was also downplayed as Cambodian and other Southeast Asian parties communicated their preferences to negotiate a possible settlement in Jakarta later in the year (see chapter 5).[184] Reductions in both sides' military strength along the Sino-Soviet border were discussed with greater success.

During the summit, the Soviets announced a withdrawal of 75 percent of their military presence in Mongolia and substantial troop reductions (120,000 along the Manchurian border), naval cutbacks (sixteen warships from the Pacific Fleet) and contractions in air power (the regrouping of eleven air force regiments). Both sides pledged to continue talks for further reductions along their common border.[185] During the latter part of 1989, the momentum of Sino-Soviet relations slowed as the USSR acquiesced to political liberalization in Eastern Europe and China viewed such a development with heightened skepticism after repressing its own dissidents immediately after Gorbachev's departure from Beijing. A December 1989 visit to China by a key member of the Soviet Central Committee, Valentin Felin, failed to produce any announcement of further bilateral initiatives in the two countries' arms control policies, but Li Peng's visit to Moscow in April 1990 did culminate in an announcement that the Sino-Soviet border would eventually be demilitarized (see chapter 3).

Qualified Sino-Soviet rapprochement has limited other regional communist states' (especially North Korea's) ability to maneuver between Moscow and Beijing to the detriment of Northeast Asian stability. It has also provided some cushion against future Indian imperialism in the Indian Ocean and peninsular Southeast Asia by allowing the Soviets to apply the counterleverage of a limited "China card" against Indian demands for Moscow's political and strategic backing of New Dehli's aspirations for projecting power beyond South Asia.[186]

In an effort to exert influence with or exact leverage from the West, China has continued to publicize its differences with the Soviets underscoring, at appropriate intervals, its own regional and international policy interests. During the late 1970s, Beijing suggested its willingness to facilitate and participate in an international coalition against "Soviet hegemony." It has, in fact, however, throughout the 1980s preserved its policy independence by continuing to oppose U.S. positions on the "peaceful reunification" of Taiwan and on Third World politics. Strategically, the Chinese have coveted Western financing, trading arrangements, and the infusion of military-related Western technology into the PRC—but without the commensurate obligation to buy Western defense items as a quid pro quo. At the same time, China has been cautious in responding to Gorbachev's entreaties for "balanced force reductions" along the Sino-Soviet border. Beijing is aware that the Soviet proposal covers only ground forces, thus protecting Soviet qualitative superiority in regional air and naval power. Not unlike the West's past experience in negotiating mutual balanced force reductions (MBFR) with the Soviets in Europe, Chinese diplomats retain a healthy skepticism of Soviet-proposed confidence building measures in Asia. As one Western observer has since noted: "Certain aspects of Gorbachev's arms control policy are reminiscent of the early 1960s, when the USSR hoped to use arms control to limit China's nuclear program."[187] Avoiding confrontation with either superpower, of course, buys time to strengthen the Chinese economy and build its technological infrastructure to more competitive levels. In the meantime, China maintains nuclear and conventional forces that it hopes will become formidable enough to deter the USSR from exercising the conflict options described earlier, if its relations with Moscow were to deteriorate once again.

The prospects are, then, for a continued Chinese foreign policy which implicitly downplays the intensity of the Soviet threat to China by assuming that the USSR has become preoccupied with own domestic political and economic reform. This policy may ultimately conflict with U.S. and Western desires that China share in the anti-Soviet military burden to pin down significant portions of Soviet military power in Asia. As noted in chapter 2, Washington's initial liberalization of its high technology transfers to the PRC was linked to these desires. A study of U.S. defense technology relations with China recently prepared by the Arms Control and Disarmament Agency (ACDA), however, has suggested that such thinking is, at best, outdated. The report argues that "China does not appear to be overtly anxious about the [Soviet] threat and does not perceive it to be as imminent as the increased Soviet [military] capabilities would lead one to expect, and has not initiated a crash program of [Chinese] military modernization in response."[188] Instead, the Chinese have accorded more attention than their American counterparts to signs of Soviet weakness and overextension, including Moscow's still ailing economy, the military stalemate from which Moscow in Afghanistan, and the continued lack of success by the Gorbachev regime in establishing economic and political influence throughout Asia. Beijing views these factors as evidence that the Soviets represent, at worst, a long-term threat, as opposed to an immediate challenge, to China's own strategic position in the region.

CONCLUSION

THE RELATIVE propensity for various Asian neighbors to view China as a "threat" or as a regional "stabilizer" is largely determined by factors of proximity, size and history. China is, regardless, a nearby land power which, despite recent cutbacks totaling close to a million personnel, still fields a massive army. By contrast, both superpowers must rely upon regional basing arrangements to project strategic power in the Asia-Pacific. Eventually, these could be reduced or terminated due to reassertive nationalistic forces in Northeast Asia and to growing financial and domestic political pressures within both the United States and Soviet Union to reduce regional and global deterrence commitments. Yet, within the region, China would be unacceptable to indigenous governments as an alternative guarantor of regional order. This remains true even though the Chinese have made it clear that they support conflict resolution on the Korean peninsula, have applied extended deterrence effectively on Thailand's behalf against the Vietnamese occupation armies in Cambodia, and have otherwise taken care to cultivate an image of a would-be regional stabilizer over the past decade.

The real significance of China's attempting to develop a first-rate land and seaborne nuclear deterrent is that, if Beijing eventually becomes a major factor in the overall international balance of power it will be able to assert a posture of global strategic deterrence for the first time in the history of the People's Republic. The PLA's efforts to enhance its strategic force survivability, lethality, and controllability reflect a growing realization in Beijing that true global power status cannot be attained by pursuing a "continentalist" strategy alone, but must be realized through development of a strategic nuclear capability applicable to a wider array of conflict environments.

As has been argued in this chapter, China's current land-based strategic nuclear force could probably still not withstand a truly concentrated Soviet or U.S. nuclear strike utilizing MIRVed delivery systems and advanced targeting capabilities supported by sophisticated command and control. The development of a more modern and comprehensive strategic nuclear force, by contrast, would provide China a credible second-strike capability to launch countervalue strikes against an opponent's cities and industrial centers and, after MIRV technology is introduced, to hit vital military targets as well. Extensive deployments of advanced tactical nuclear weapons would also provide the Chinese with a basis of escalation control in any future war against the Soviet Union. Such capabilities should allow China's nuclear deterrent capabilities to become more flexible and secure as this century draws to a close.

Given the PRC's gradual increase in military power and the ensuing shifts in the superpowers' China strategies, Beijing may not be reluctant to exercise its growing strategic power as an instrument of diplomatic coercion.[189] Alternatively, with greater nuclear capabilities, future Chinese leaderships could well assume a more self-confident and less nationalistic role within the international balance of power, one that could prove conducive to a prolonged era of domestic economic development and regional stability. China's security policy during the 1990s cannot be predicted with high levels of confidence in light of the country's present domestic turmoil.

What is clear, however, is that Beijing has applied a variety of policy tactics since 1949 designed to enhance China's regional and global power status. Chinese manipulation of Japanese emotions and finances is symptomatic of the PRC's tendency to adopt a hard-line diplomatic posture when it believes such a stance is justified by its policy ends. The PRC's public resistance to Japanese defense spending increases within the framework of the U.S.-Japan military treaty, its support of nuclear free zone politics in the ASEAN and South Pacific regions which, if implemented in a literal sense, would seriously impede U.S. Seventh Fleet operations, and its diplomatic accommodation with Moscow have been less than helpful. Its cooperation with Tokyo to help achieve a global-zero formula for the INF treaty is illustrative of Beijing's ability to play a constructive role in facilitating international stability. China's recent politics of restraint concerning the Korean Peninsula and Indochina have also had a positive effect on Asia-Pacific stability. The best regional strategic outcome might well be Chinese constraint of superpower competition in the Asia-Pacific and China's continued willingness to work with established governments within that region to achieve greater political stability and more rapid economic development.

China has a major stake in future superpower arms control negotiations. Over the long term, there is little doubt that the PRC will enhance the survivability and diversification of its strategic forces. Its ability to wage a protracted war with either the United States or USSR, however, will remain limited until and unless significant qualitative and quantitative reductions occur in superpower nuclear inventories.

Until deep cuts *are* realized in the American and Soviet strategic arsenals, China, in the words of one Western analyst, "may feel it has a minimum deterrent but it does not feel it has much deterrence to spare."[190]

Chinese arms control behavior to date has been enigmatic. While traditionally distancing itself from superpower-initiated arms control negotiations on the premise that such talks serve Washington's and Moscow's interests more than its own, Beijing was instrumental in pressuring the Soviets to dismantle their SS-20s east of the Urals as part of the INF accord. Although accused by U.S. officials of transferring atomic weapons technology to Pakistan, China nevertheless has joined the International Atomic Energy Agency, thereby acceding to that agency's policies for inspection of nuclear production facilities and restrictions on weapons-grade transfers.

China's future strategic behavior will inevitably affect the viability of the United States' Dominant Player deterrence posture. Unless the U.S. can reinforce the credibility of its outstanding regional security commitments more persuasively than has been the case since the Nixon Doctrine, an economically more self-confident and militarily more powerful China could eventually widen its scope of military activities in ways which could eventually impinge on those commitments. If so, the United States could be faced with a major policy dilemma: that Washington needs a "stable and secure China" to reinforce the legitimacy of its own Dominant Player posture but that the U.S. lacks the leverage and capacity to influence the pace and direction of China's military modernization efforts. The reality is that American policymakers' image of what constitutes a stable China, friendly to U.S. interests in the Asia-Pacific, may well differ substantially from Beijing's own vision of how deterrence and national power should be applied to the region.

CHAPTER 5

ASEAN as a "Reluctant Player"

THE EVOLUTION of Southeast Asian security politics has demonstrated how tenuous the U.S. extended deterrence posture can become. From 1945 through the end of the 1960s, those states which occupy what has been labeled Southeast Asia's "strategic land-ridge"—Thailand, Malaysia, Singapore, Indonesia, and the Philippines, which intersect the "center of gravity" between the East and South China Sea, adjacent to the Asian mainland and the wider Pacific—were mostly concerned with defining and managing their security relations with the United States and the West European powers. Aside from their geographic emplacements, straddling the critical lines of communication across Southeast Asia into the Indian Ocean and the Persian Gulf, their natural resource, and (in the case of Indonesia and the Philippines) their population bases are significant and they provide, in the words of Leslie H. Brown, "a reasonably secure base of operations for supporting American military interests" in the lower part of the Asia-Pacific theater.[1]

The price that Southeast Asia's governments usually paid for access to Western finances and military assistance was formal affiliation with Washington's global containment strategy. Thailand and the Philippines were members of the Southeast Asia Treaty Organization (SEATO) founded in Manila in September 1954, and the noncommunist regimes in Indochina were "Associates" with that pact. This affiliation required them to support U.S. or West European military interventions in Vietnam and, to a lesser extent, in Indonesia. Unlike Britain's efforts to play an integral role in the political development and strategic defense of postwar Malaya, however, Washington proved reluctant to directly link its global deterrence posture with local Southeast Asian security requirements except as a part of its overall global containment strategy. Southeast Asians were largely constrained from developing their own security identities by the extra-regional powers which controlled the markets and resources needed to cultivate greater independence within the postwar international system. The Southeast Asians also had deep concerns regarding Washington's linking of strategic gains or losses in Indochina to the broader "Soviet and Chinese threats." Throughout the early 1950s, the United States seriously contemplated the escalation of Southeast Asian ground wars into a full-scale American nuclear offensive against the Chinese mainland. Under such circumstances, the Southeast Asians questioned the relevance of the U.S. Dominant Player Posture to their own security needs.

The failure of American containment policy in Vietnam intensified the Southeast Asians' efforts to find alternative regional security formulas. The withdrawal of American military power in Indochina signaled a sharp reduction in American interests and power on the Southeast Asian mainland. Throughout the late 1960s and most of the 1970s, this trend was reinforced by the obscurity of successive U.S. policy statements on Asia (i.e., the Nixon and Pacific "Doctrines"). While professing continued American concern about their subregion, the United States urged its friends and allies throughout East and Southeast Asia to "pursue national resilience and cohesion" by whatever means possible.[2] No advice was given, however, as to what level of "resilience" should be sufficient for those nations to achieve their own deterrence capabilities or to what could compensate for the previously high levels of U.S. counterinsurgency assistance. Moreover, the U.S. extended deterrence guarantee, from the Southeast Asian perspective, had become tainted by too many conditions, resulting from Washington's obsession with global geopolitics and its postwar competition with the Soviet Union. As both Soviet and Chinese military power gradually expanded throughout the Asia-Pacific, the potential for external power miscalculations which could further polarize Indochina and peninsular Southeast Asia became too great to defer to the American interest in expanding its nuclear capabilities and presence—the traditional bulwark of its Dominant Player strategy.

To institutionalize and coordinate their own alternative regional security approach, Indonesia, Malaysia, the Philippines, Singapore, and Thailand formed the Association of Southeast Asian Nations (ASEAN) in 1967. This regional organization soon became noncommunist Southeast Asia's primary indigenous enterprise for promoting a stable regional security order. It did so by gradually facilitating the ASEAN members' adoption of what can be termed as a "Reluctant Player" posture relative to U.S. extended deterrence strategy. While not completely disdaining the credibility of remaining U.S. security commitments to their region (various ASEAN states have continued qualified security affiliations with the United States and other friendly external powers), ASEAN leaders have attempted to forge intraregional consensus regarding nonalignment and to encourage the upgrading of the members' defense capabilities to credible levels of regional self-defense. In this context, the Reluctant Player approach to regional deterrence seeks to balance qualified strategic relations with friendly external powers with intraregional initiatives for achieving greater regional stability through nonalignment politics.

The success of indigenous Southeast Asian diplomatic pressure against Washington in opposition to the United States' plans to escalate its military operations in Cambodia during 1970 encouraged the members of ASEAN to explore alternative collective security approaches for infusing greater policy substance into the Reluctant Player posture. In September 1970, the Malaysian government, then under Tun Razak, at the Nonaligned Summit Conference in Lusaka, Zambia, proposed a Southeast Asian neutralization formula with external power guarantees. The following year (November 27, 1971), the Kuala Lumpur Declaration was issued by the ASEAN member-states. It called for the recognition of Indonesia, Malaysia, the Philippines, Singapore, and Thailand as a "Zone of Peace, Freedom, and Neutrality" (ZOPFAN), free from any form or manner of politico-military interference by outside powers. The concept's four cornerstones are: (1) national stability of the ASEAN member states; (2) peaceful intra-ASEAN relations; (3) diplomatic and political accord with other regional powers; and (4) nonintervention in regional security affairs by external powers.[3] ZOPFAN has been retained as an expedient vision around which all of the ASEAN states can unite. Its actual utility as a blueprint for that organization's collective security diplomacy, however, has been limited.

The intent of the chapter is to show that tensions between U.S. global deterrence strategy and the perceived local deterrence needs of

Washington's friends and allies in Southeast Asia have increasingly undermined the effectiveness of traditional extended deterrence in the SEATO/ASEAN region—that successive U.S. administrations have generally failed to learn from the policy setbacks experienced by the Dominant Player posture as it was applied in a Southeast Asian context. The resulting dilemma for the ASEAN states is underlined by their Reluctant Player posture which represents an effort by the Southeast Asians to create a middle ground between nonalignment politics and strategic affiliation with the United States and its allies.

THE DOMINANT PLAYER POSTURE IN SOUTHEAST ASIA: QUESTIONS OF GLOBAL VERSUS LOCAL DETERRENCE

THE U.S., to date, *has* deferred to ASEAN's equilibrium strategy by retaining a low-key offshore strategic presence in the region. ASEAN, in turn, recognizes that to expect the United States or any other major power to commit resources for their economic development and security without acquiring and retaining some regional political influence or strategic access in return is, at best, unrealistic. Meeting each others' strategic objectives halfway has become critical for the U.S. Dominant Player and its Reluctant Player Southeast Asian collaborators.

Charles Morrison and Astri Suhrke have labeled the convergence of U.S. and Asian security relations into *systemic linkage, moderate linkage,* and *partial linkage* relationships: three different ways in which a small Asian state's relationship with a large external power reflects the state of competition between the large powers within the global balance of power. As an example of systemic linkage behavior, South Korea has been a focal point of cold war competition. The intensity of such relations has until only very recently sustained the credibility of the U.S. deterrence commitment to Seoul but has also constrained the Koreans' ability to exercise independent behavior. By contrast, the ASEAN states have adopted either a "moderate" or "partial" pattern of security linkage behavior with the United States and other outside powers. Thailand and Indonesia have used periods of intense superpower competition (especially the early 1960s) to extract security guarantees or military assistance; Thailand from the United States throughout the postwar era and Indonesia from the USSR during the latter years of the Sukarno regime. When superpower competition was reduced during the era of detente, however, both Bangkok and Jakarta modified the extent of military assistance ties with Washington and Moscow. Neither enjoyed the status of South Korea in the deterrence strategy of their respective benefactor, lowering the value of what strategic commitments were extended to them and simultaneously reducing their bargaining leverage with their would-be extraregional protector. Malaysia/Singapore's security relations with Britain, and the Philippines' alliance with the United States may be characterized as "partial." Traditionally these three Southeast Asian countries' security ties with outside powers have been mostly bilateral, relating less to conditions of global power competition than to historical factors of colonial obligation or cultural affinity. The ASEAN states' independent bargaining leverage was reduced as their security relationships were pursued outside the competitive framework of the global power balance.[4]

ASEAN security politics are presently constrained by internal politico-economic vulnerabilities and by emphasis on the business of nation-building rather than confrontation of external threats. The states occupying Southeast Asia's land ridge and outer archipelagoes are, however, confronted by a broad spectrum of internal threats, ranging from insurgency and separatist movements to intraregional interventionism. Ideological polarizations, ethnic divisions, territorial disputes, and other sources of internal or interstate conflict at the subregional level—all reinforce the primacy of local security concerns over those related to the international power balance. As Muthiah Alagappa has argued, the typical "national security paradigm" found in an ASEAN state is relative to the magnitude of its economic and political development problems.[5] Whereas the shared core values underwriting the creation of the North Atlantic Treaty were fairly self-evident to the industrial democracies which comprised its membership, the Western-supported regimes emerging in Southeast Asia with Western support during the cold war were characterized by weak and underdeveloped national institutions, differing levels of public consensus, and a variety of internal security threats. From the perspective of Southeast Asian elites invested with the tasks of building and safeguarding the identities and institutions of their new nations after the Second World War, the establishment of regime legitimacy and the avoidance of external intervention were paramount.[6] Even so, the residual vestiges of colonialism and the inevitable excesses of burgeoning nationalism still needed to play themselves out.

Questioning the Dominant Player Posture's Applicability

THE LESSON of what Southeast Asian leaders increasingly regarded as inconsistent U.S. strategic behavior in their region was that Washington would apply a viable deterrence posture in Southeast Asia only when it was in U.S. global policy interests to do so. During the 1950s and 1960s, for example, U.S. military planners viewed airstrips in Northeast Thailand as a key to implementing deterrence against a Chinese invasion of noncommunist Indochina and as important post-strike recovery sites in the event U.S. middle-range bombers were required to attack targets in southern China. The Thais were more concerned with keeping Vietnam from dominating the Mekong River deltas and with preserving an independent Cambodia as a buffer state between Vietnam and Thailand.[7] Moreover, while the Americans viewed the Anglo-Malaysian Defense Agreement (AMDA) as an integral part of Britain's postwar defense role "east of Suez," they refused to merge AMDA's counter-insurgency role with what they perceived to be a separate deterrence function for SEATO. In November 1954 testimony to the U.S. Senate, Secretary of State Dulles underscored the lack of American interest in becoming committed to local deterrence planning and operations: "[SEATO would require] no material changes in the military planning of the United States maintaining at all times powerful naval and air forces to strike an aggressor by means and at places of our own choosing."[8] The message found within the Secretary of State's remarks to Southeast Asian leaders was clear: the United States and European allies would limit their deterrent commitments to ambiguously defined threats in the SEATO area. AMDA also was to be regarded in U.S. policy making circles as an instrument of local deterrence which could involve British, Australian and New Zealand land forces in a local counter-insurgency role but not those of the United States. This American-global versus British-local demarcation of deterrence responsibility remained in place throughout the duration of Indonesia's confrontation against Malaysia during the mid-1960s.

Until 1969, U.S. deterrence policy in the Asia-Pacific region was predicated upon the assumption that China, despite all of its disagreements with the USSR, still basically served as a Soviet strategic proxy.

The PRC was perceived by the U.S. as the ultimate "bridge" between local and global war contingencies in the Asia-Pacific theater. The Soviets, Washington believed, would not initiate a general war in the Pacific as long as China was regarded by the USSR as serving its strategic purposes within Southeast Asia. This viewpoint became particularly important as the Americans shifted from a massive retaliation posture in Southeast Asia (during much of the 1950s) to one of direct involvement in local contingencies, with the assignment of large-scale U.S. ground force contingents to Vietnam during the 1960s.[9]

The Southeast Asians, "conditioned" to this revised American approach to extended deterrence in their region, were thus understandably shocked when President Nixon once again changed the rules of the game, at Guam in August 1969. Separating local deterrence from global deterrence, he stated that the U.S. would no longer engage in local deterrence operations. As Robert Tilman subsequently observed, the United States eventually was perceived by ASEAN as a "threat" because of the "unpredictabilities and discontinuities" of U.S. foreign and strategic policies and because, the ASEAN states had concluded, "Southeast Asia is viewed by Washington policymakers as a region of low priority and as an appendage of East Asia."[10] Any U.S.-extended deterrence strategy became regarded by ASEAN as much as a potential source of regional destabilization as one of stability.

U.S. EXTENDED DETERRENCE IN SOUTHEAST ASIA: CASE STUDIES

BY EVALUATING how U.S. extended deterrence has been applied to Southeast Asia, we can better assess why the Dominant Player posture has gradually become less relevant to ASEAN security calculations. Some caveats, however, are in order. The declassification of relevant documents covering U.S. and Western deterrence policy in postwar Southeast Asia has been painfully slow. Southeast Asian sources of official decisionmaking are largely nonexistent. Memoirs of ASEAN government officials, interviews and occasional colloquia, and conferences sponsored by quasi-governmental research institutes with access to deep background information, still constitute the major sources of data. Texts of relevant speeches, newspapers and radio broadcasts along with a few books and journal articles comprise the major foundations for case study evaluation.

This chapter, moreover, does not presume to offer comprehensive theories for how American deterrence has evolved in Southeast Asia during the entire postwar timespan. Its purpose is instead to document how a rising sense of discomfort was felt by both the United States' European allies and by its friends within Southeast Asia over early U.S. efforts to transpose the NATO-type Dominant Player posture to a part of the Asia-Pacific theater where threats, vulnerabilities and national attributes varied greatly from those found in Western Europe. A second objective is the evaluation of the extent to which the U.S. has "learned the lessons" of deterrence relevance or irrelevance provided by the successive cases evaluated and, if such learning failed to take place, why not. By examining briefly the gradual alienation of noncommunist Southeast Asians from U.S. deterrence politics as applied in their region, and by offering some observations on the difficulty Washington has had in coming to terms with such alienation, the contemporary premises which underscore the Reluctant Player posture can be better understood.

The JCS Counterattack Thesis: 1953–1954

THE LOSS of the U.S. nuclear monopoly in 1949 generated debate within U.S. policy making circles over the so-called "preventive war thesis." Succinctly stated, this thesis warned that the United States and the West should move to eliminate the Soviet Union's nuclear weapons capabilities before Moscow's nuclear strength matched or exceeded that of Washington's and could be used to threaten the U.S. and/or its allies into strategic submission.

Although preventive war was never adopted as policy by the Truman or Eisenhower administrations, a variant of this strategy was seriously considered by the JCS from July 1953 through the end of 1954. As discussed in chapter 2, the introduction of the hydrogen bomb and of tactical nuclear weapons into the American strategic arsenal prompted a number of American military planners—but especially Admiral Arthur Radford, Chairman of the Joint Chiefs of Staff —to weigh the option of taking advantage of the United States' new-found and probably short-lived strategic advantages over the Soviet Union. According to the JCS "counterattack thesis," superpower confrontations in Southeast Asia, especially those involving Moscow's perceived Chinese surrogate, could be used as a pretext for attacking the Chinese and even the Soviet homelands. This school of thought was most forcefully represented by a study group of military experts known as "Solarium Task Force C." A report to the National Security Council prepared by this group warned that U.S. conventional military power would be insufficient to deter or defend European or Asian allies by conventional means alone. Nuclear escalation, the Task Force argued, would be a more "cost-effective" response in any case.[11]

In the Asia-Pacific, the JCS was assessing how Eisenhower's success in ending the Korean war by use of threats to escalate that conflict might be used to strengthen the credibility of U.S. security commitments to Thailand and of British and French commitments to the security of the Malayan Peninsula and Indochina. The JCS postulated that overt Chinese aggression undertaken in Southeast Asian locales should be "vigorously opposed" but "without diverting military strength from other areas" (NSC 124/2 disseminated in late June 1952). "Vigorous opposition" would be carried out through defending pro-Western Southeast Asians with air and naval assistance and through interdicting Chinese Communist lines of communication to communist insurgency groups in Vietnam and elsewhere throughout Indochina and Malaya.[12] Reflecting upgraded American threat assessments of Soviet and Chinese surge capabilities for attacking Western shipping in offshore island chains straddling the South China Sea, the U.S. Chief of Naval Operations directed the shifting of the First Marine Division from Korea to Hawaii "so as to better position the force for possible action in Southeast Asia."

United Action

ANTICIPATING CONGRESSIONAL opposition to Washington's unilateral employment of tactical nuclear weapons in Indochina, Eisenhower and Dulles attempted to implement a regional security coalition of Western and Southeast Asian states through a so-called "United Action" initiative during March and early April 1985.[13] On March 29, Dulles addressed the Overseas Press Club in New York. Employing classical "global-realist" reasoning, the Secretary of State warned that Indochina was a "grave threat" to all of noncommunist Southeast Asia, the Southwest Pacific, and American strategic interests in the entire Western Pacific area. [14] Taking into account recent U.S. intelligence reports that some 2000 Chinese military advisors had infiltrated Vietnam to support Viet Minh forces, the Secretary of State advocated meeting the threat of indirect communist aggression with "United Action."

Dulles declined to specify precisely what he meant by "united action." Historians recently examining his personal records have concluded that the maintenance of U.S. global deterrence was paramount in his calculations. By declaring that Washington was willing to incur "severe risks" to deter China and Vietnam from overrunning French forces deployed at Dien Bien Phu, Dulles communicated a preference for the counterattack thesis over relying upon diplomatic negotiations to resolve this Southeast Asian crisis. In reality, the Secretary of State knew better than to assume that the usually cautious President Eisenhower would opt for military intervention on behalf of France. He regarded a hard-line policy only as useful for buying sufficient time to structure a series of Asian alliances, expanding the U.S. global containment network from Europe and Northeast Asia to the Southeast Asian region as well.

As Melanie Billings-Yun has since recounted, however, Dulles' policy bluff backfired. France and pro-Western Southeast Asians alike were led to believe erroneously that the U.S. was actually prepared to support a continued French colonial presence in Indochina. [15] When this proved not to be the case, Paris felt betrayed and Washington's friends in the region became more disinclined to form any viable counterpart to NATO, with its own military command structure, in their own region. Robert Bowie, one of Dulles' chief advisors, later characterized United Action as "merely a grand charade of deterrence."

In strategic terms, George C. Herring and Richard Immerman have observed that United Action proponents desired a means for insuring that Washington could intervene against the Viet Minh on the most favorable terms possible, "reflect(ing) the perceived lessons of the Korean War as well as the (Eisenhower) administration's concept of strategic deterrence and its New Look Defense policy." [16] It envisioned U.S. and British force elements hitting the enemy quickly and decisively with high levels of firepower (including tactical nuclear weapons, if appropriate to the battlefield situation) and forcing the enemy to the negotiating table as the preferred alternative to total military defeat. In a military sense, the key to United Action's success was to convince the British and other allies to commit themselves to intervention with the United States before the Viet Minh forced the French to surrender or to negotiate peace terms from a strategic disadvantage at Geneva.

Allied Response

LONDON AND Paris had no intention of endorsing the transfer of the American escalation tactics employed in the Korean conflict to insurgency crises in their Southeast Asian areas of defense responsibility. The Europeans already viewed the U.S. as overly anxious to use nuclear weapons against the Chinese in Korea.[17] For his part, Dulles expressed concern to Eisenhower that the JCS endorsement of the counterattack thesis was becoming so well-known to the Europeans that it might be undercutting his own attempts to forge a regional security coalition for Southeast Asia.[18]

As the Viet Minh siege of Dien Bien Phu unfolded, revealing the hopeless military position of the French Expeditionary Force in Indochina, the British Chiefs of Staff fell into line with their country's political leadership and rejected any proposals for collective Western military intervention in Vietnam. Britain had a long-standing interest in avoiding confrontation with China (it had dealt with the PRC diplomatically at the charge d' affaires level since 1949; Washington had no official relations with Beijing). Britain had little interest in becoming even indirectly affiliated with U.S. military action involving the use of nuclear weapons against the Chinese homeland. British Foreign Minister Anthony Eden was candid in his representation of his country's interests when he conferred with Dulles in early April, telling the Secretary of State that "a bigger affair than Korea would get us nowhere" and that his "chief concern" was "ensur(ing) an effective barrier as far to the north of [Malaya] as possible." Compared to the situation in Indochina, Eden related to Dulles, the deterrence situation in Malaya was "well in hand." [19]

The French resistance to United Action was even more straightforward. Paris wanted an immediate *unilateral* American military intervention in Indochina to avoid an imminent military defeat at Dien Bien Phu and to force negotiations with the Viet Minh from a position of strength as soon as possible.[20] Failing this, the French wanted ceasefire negotiations with the Viet Minh to be internationalized. While understanding Indochina's long-term importance in the global balance of power, Paris was frustrated by the Anglo-American conduct of what was to Fourth Republic leaders nothing more than a debate over abstract theories of global deterrence at a time when their perspective of the conflict was restricted a rear-guard battle against Ho Chi Minh's military power.[21]

Following the Geneva Conference, however, the British began to shift their position to one supporting the counterstrike thesis. This shift, visibly evident by early June 1954, reflected the new British strategy of strengthening the credibility of British deterrence in Malaya by fusing it with the growing U.S. strategic interest in the region. A Five Power Military Conference, involving American, Australian, British, French, and New Zealand military officials was convened to identify strategy for a Southeast Asian collective defense treaty. A key Conference report dealing with possible responses to Chinese aggression in the region endorsed the concept of quick nuclear retaliation through the air and sea against Chinese targets well enough removed from the USSR to minimize prospects for Soviet intervention. This represented a major British concession and spurred Dulles to find new alternatives for extending Western deterrence to Southeast Asian allies.

In summing up the policy debate which undermined the Dominant Player posture's credibility in the 1954 Indochina crisis, the counterattack advocates within American strategic planning circles believed that the United States and its allies should maintain a powerful offshore deterrent, complete with a nuclear dimension. They argued that Communist China was the major source of aggression in Indochina and that air and naval interdiction strikes against "the source of aggression" were the best means to neutralize the communist threat to noncommunist Indochina, Thailand, Burma, and beyond. A majority of U.S. policymakers urged more restraint. Most of the JCS, and even Dulles, came to believe that the alliance politics predicated on land force commitments which had worked so well in Europe, could also be applied to Southeast Asia. They concluded that an automatic nuclear intervention policy as strongly implied by the united front posture would escalate limited Asian conflicts to levels beyond all strategic reason and they sought to implement escalation control mechanisms, even as U.S. allies and adversaries were concluding that Washington was increasing its propensity to deploy and use tactical nuclear weapons in the Asia-Pacific.

The result was that Washington was unable to offer an alliance to its prospective Southeast Asian security collaborators in which U.S.

extended deterrence objectives were clearly understood by that strategy's intended regional beneficiaries. The American posture proved to be unappealing to the containment of communist insurgency in Thailand and Malaya and, even more indirectly, insurance against successful Soviet military strikes at U.S. offshore power. As 1954 drew to a close, both President Eisenhower and Secretary of State Dulles were gradually coming to terms with the inapplicability of nuclear weapons to the deterrence requirements in Southeast Asia and other theaters outside of central Europe.

SEATO as a Successor to the Counterstrike Thesis

BY LATE 1954, the proposed Southeast Asia Treaty Organization (SEATO) was regarded by Washington as the most promising instrument for translating the counterstrike deterrence posture into a viable regional security approach for Southeast Asia. In testimony before the U.S. Senate Foreign Relations Committee in November 1954, Dulles assured Congress that the pact represented the most cost-effective option for extending deterrence to this part of the Asia-Pacific theater because it relied upon "powerful naval and air forces to strike an aggressor by means and at places of our own choosing" without involving permanent deployments of U.S. ground forces or elaborate intraregional basing systems.[22] In such a manner, the Secretary concluded, the SEATO option conformed nicely with the Administration's adoption of NSC 162/2 (in late October 1953) as the United States' basic national security policy: to defend vital areas of the world, even at the risk of general nuclear war, but to do so in response to communist aggression, rather than attempting to preempt such aggression through instigating preventive war.[23] The United States would broaden the deterrence "trip wire" formula already operative in Northeast Asia to incorporate its Southeast Asian defense commitments as well. The JCS and the allies had concluded in April that Indochina was best defended by counterattacking "the source of aggression" (i.e., China or, less likely, the USSR) as opposed to escalating a conflict against communist forces within Indochina itself.

At the same time, however, the United States was careful to restrict its SEATO obligations in two key ways. First, it insisted that SEATO, unlike NATO, respond to a communist military initiative against one or more of its members by regarding it as a "common danger" rather than as "an attack on all" (the NATO response formula).[24] The Americans further diluted SEATO's response mechanism by insisting that the threat would be met "in accordance with" the individual members' "constitutional processes." Second, Washington announced at the beginning of the Manila Conference, which drew up the pact in September 1954, that it would react only against a communist external threat. Mindful of its sizable ground force commitments to NATO, the U.S. faced a clear policy dilemma in defining the credibility of its SEATO deterrence posture.

Critics of SEATO argued that Dulles misrepresented the accord to Congress by contending that it would broaden the NATO deterrent to cover Southeast Asian threats but would do so without obligating the U.S. to an automatic response if a SEATO party were attacked.[25] Supporters of the Treaty countered that SEATO was never intended to be another NATO, with a formal and elaborate command structure, but a deterrent against overt Chinese military intervention in Southeast Asian conflicts. The major purpose of SEATO, Bernard Gordon has concluded, was symbolism rather than substance (in fact, a modest organizational secretariat was formed only in 1959 and defense contingency plans in 1960).[26] While SEATO's "chief objective" at its founding may have been to warn Beijing against supporting North Vietnamese military attacks across the 17th Parallel, the primary concern by 1955 was internal threats to Thailand and SEATO's "Associated States" (South Vietnam, Cambodia, and Laos).[27]

The formation of SEATO provided the leaders of the emerging Southeast Asian states with their first real opportunity to define alternatives to the Dominant Player posture. Southeast Asian leaders grew more reluctant to closely affiliate with any American extended deterrence strategy, believing the Dominant Player posture to be inappropriate to their own threat environments. Even prior to Indonesia's formal endorsement of nonalignment politics at the Bandung Conference in April 1955, that country, the Philippines, and Thailand were united in their desire to link national development priorities with less global approaches to security relations. This attitude constituted the embryo of what was later to become a more visible and assertive Reluctant Player Posture.

Prospective Southeast Asian deterrence collaborators were wary that cooperation with the U.S. Dominant Player would bring unwanted global power competition to their doorstep. The Malays were preoccupied with the so-called "Emergency" efforts to combat a formidable communist insurgency movement and thus had little interest in establishing a higher profile in East-West politics. The Indonesians were concerned that their politics of nonalignment would be compromised by indefinite deployments of American and British military power in the area. Other Southeast Asians were concerned that their geographic proximity to Indochina would result in incessant cold war confrontations within or adjacent to their own territory (the Thais) or that hosting a great power military presence would actually precipitate selective attacks from external sources (the Philippines).

By virtue of its size and geography, Indonesia's membership in SEATO was initially regarded as highly desirable by Washington. One month before convening that pact's organizational conference in Manila, the National Security Council reaffirmed an earlier (November 1953) assessment of U.S. policy toward Jakarta (NSC 171/1), emphasizing the importance of "continued efforts to influence Indonesian government officials to oppose communist infiltration and subversion."[28] The U.S. State Department had already queried Indonesian officials on prospects for their country joining a Southeast Asian collective defense association. Responses to their queries had been put on hold pending the outcome of scheduled elections in that country in mid-1955. Dulles had been previously warned by the Australians, however, that only inconceivable American economic concessions to Jakarta would entice Sukarno to affiliate Indonesia with the West.[29]

All speculation of any Indonesian interest in joining SEATO ended when Prime Minister Ali Sastroamijoyo rejected a plea made by Anthony Eden for Indonesia's participation in the pact during July 1954. In a speech delivered to the Indonesian Parliament in mid-August and in a similar address to the Indian Parliament given in late September, the Indonesian leader declared that "peace in our part of the world cannot be assured by military pacts such as recently concluded in Manila."[30] In his memoirs, Sastroamijoyo reiterated Indonesia's opposition to the pact: (1) it would effectively transpose cold war alliance politics from Europe to Asia, inherently raising tensions in Southeast Asia; and, (2) the language of SEATO applied to deterring communist forces over a designated geographic area rather than merely applying to sovereign members, thereby violating international law by sanctioning "armed interference by foreign powers in the internal affairs of a nation."[31] Indonesia remained highly sensitive to the proximity of

British military power in Malaya as a possible check on its own ambitions to project greater influence throughout peninsular Southeast Asia and as an aggravate to Jakarta's continuing differences with Holland, one of Britain's closest NATO allies, over the status of West Irian.[32] The prospect of East-West competition spilling over from Indochina into peninsular Southeast Asia was viewed as a greater threat to Jakarta than any fear of international communism.

At the other end of the spectrum was the Philippines. By virtue of the March 1947 U.S.-Philippines Military Bases Agreement, the Philippines hosted the only U.S. military contingents permanently assigned to a Southeast Asian country prior to the SEATO organizational conference. However, in a precursor to Manila's reassertive nationalism of the late 1980s, Philippine Senators Claro Recto and Tomas Confessor, along with other Filipino opinionmakers, argued that U.S. extended deterrence strategy was of questionable strategic benefit to Filipino security interests. The senators demanded that Manila enjoy "the same guarantee of automatic protection against external aggression that is enjoyed by the members of the NATO alliance."[33] A few months prior to his country signing yet another defense-related pact with Washington (the U.S.-Philippines Mutual Security Treaty in August 1951), Foreign Minister Carlos P. Romulo countered Recto's arguments by emphasizing the importance of Manila's continued security affiliation with the United States. He warned that his country's adoption of a nonaligned posture would "bring on the very calamity [communist aggression] which by a strategy of aloofness we sought to avoid."[34]

While Romulo's reasoning prevailed in the Philippine's ongoing security relations with the U.S., Recto's campaign had planted seeds of ambivalence in the Magsaysay government. Notwithstanding substantial U.S. military assistance against the Hukbalahap communist insurgency, there was a growing Filipino inclination to view the U.S. basing presence as something which served U.S. global deterrence objectives more than the Philippines' own national defense.[35]

Manila's anxieties intensified following Dien Bien Phu and Geneva. The Philippines approached the SEATO organizational conference held in its capital as an opportunity to lock the United States into a more explicit commitment. It lobbied for SEATO members to deploy fixed numbers of ground troops at various sites throughout the Asia-Pacific similar to those divisions maintained in central Europe by the

NATO allies. Finally, Magsaysay wanted to use SEATO to upgrade U.S. economic compensation to his country and to solidify political commitments to Filipino security beyond those already incorporated into the 1947 and 1951 bilateral treaties. Filipino delegates to the Manila Conference lobbied for the so-called "NATO formula," an automatic military response commitment in the event their nation was invaded as opposed to the "ANZUS formula" which only committed the Americans to "consult" with Manila in such a contingency.[36] Dulles resisted Manila's pressure by "reinterpreting" the deterrent mechanism of the 1951 Mutual Security Treaty. He acknowledged that U.S. forces stationed on Philippine soil were a de facto trip wire for American military involvement in the event of aggression against the host country. He pledged that "an attack on the Philippines could not but be also an attack on the armed forces of the United States . . . and would be instantly repelled."[37]

By using the 1951 Mutual Security Treaty to establish maximum flexibility in its SEATO commitments, the United States was able to avoid interalliance transferability problems even as it moved to broaden its Dominant Player strategy in Southeast Asia. As importantly, it preserved a credibility of commitment in Filipino and Thai estimates by establishing multiple threat assessments in SEATO defense planning. The alliance could be activated to meet either external aggression by the USSR or China as well as internal communist subversion, even though it was unclear in September 1954 which type of threat would eventually be of greater concern to the new alliance's membership. It was this uncertainty that necessitated a more flexible American approach to Southeast Asian security challenges than to those confronting central Europe or even Northeast Asia. Intermittent Soviet air strikes against the Philippines' bases in a global war, or Chinese land offensives to consolidate territorial control as far south as the Gulf of Thailand, could not be discounted by SEATO planners, but these contingencies remained sufficiently remote compared to pressing insurgency challenges in Thailand, Malaya, and the Philippines. Dulles later characterized the situation as one where U.S. responsibilities "were so vast and so far-flung" that a deterrent of "mobile striking power" would be more appropriate than designated forces for the Southeast Asian theater.[38]

Like the Philippines, Thailand would have preferred the United States to assume greater automacity of "action" in response to either an overt attack or covert subversion, as opposed to "consultation." As Sean Randolph has noted, "the Thais were disappointed by the fact [that] they had exposed themselves to the ire of the communist powers without an airtight guarantee of U.S. support in return . . . Doubts about the reliability of the American security commitment would continue to haunt Thai-American relations in ensuing years." [39] By mid-1954, Ho Chi Minh's forces had begun to occupy large areas of Laos stretching along the Mekong River adjacent to Thailand's own boundaries, and Thailand had hoped to incorporate SEATO as the key instrument in pursuing a "forward strategy" of political leverage against the Vietnamese. Subsequent U.S. reticence to intervene on behalf of the Laotian government in mid-1955 against yet more communist forays further affected Thai confidence in the new American security commitments represented by SEATO. [40]

The Laos Neutrality Crisis

THE DEGREE to which a crisis in confidence over U.S. deterrence strategy in Southeast Asia had evolved became apparent during early 1961. With the intensification of fighting between various Western and communist-backed factions in Laos, the Kennedy administration was faced with reconciling widely diverse interpretations of how this crisis would effect the U.S. extended deterrence posture in Southeast Asia. Was the "source of threat" (to use Dulles' traditional terminology) a Communist China which had clearly been distancing itself from Moscow over the past few years? While increasingly skeptical about the need for military action to resolve the Laos situation, President Kennedy was intensely concerned about Chinese strategic intentions regarding Southeast Asia, and about Beijing's imminent acquisition of nuclear weapons. [41]

Did Moscow or Hanoi represent a greater basis of concern? By late December 1960, the indigenous communist forces in Laos—the Pathet Lao—had, with massive Soviet airlifting of supplies from Hanoi, established military superiority over the Western-backed Royal Lao forces. In January 1961, a U.S. "White Paper" on the Laos crisis blamed Moscow for precipitating it. Other U.S. security analysts had by then concluded that Moscow was acting as a stabilizing force, in an effort to preempt what both superpowers were coming to believe was the danger of an unstable China intervening in Laos with its own troops (the

Korean War scenario revisited). Still others believed that the Soviets were less intent on confronting the West than on intensifying North Vietnam's allegiance to the Soviet camp.[42] Some within Kennedy's inner circle of advisors, including Walt Rostow, designated the North Vietnamese as the major source of trouble. He recommended deploying U.S. and SEATO ground forces in Laotian cities as a trip wire against North Vietnamese military advances into Thailand and South Vietnam.[43] What was most evident was the Kennedy administration's disarray on threat assessments regarding Southeast Asia and on the best means to deter those threats eventually designated as critical to Western security interests.

Washington's policy toward Laos during early 1961 tended to further divide the United States and its European and Asian allies over the perceived effectiveness of the Dominant Player posture in Southeast Asia. Britain was concerned that U.S. diplomatic mismanagement of the crisis would result in communist domination of Laos and Indochina, with the risk that superpower or Sino-American military confrontation would expand into a global war. For example, Kennedy's Press Secretary, Pierre Salinger, speculated during the President's March 23 press conference that British troops stationed in Malaya could well be called upon to supplement U.S. forces. From an American perspective, such a remark was to be interpreted as casual, if logical, geopolitical musing about pursuing one policy option among many. Many British policy planners, however, considered such public speculation to be a U.S. policy bombshell, precipitating an urgent midnight cabinet meeting in London on how to implement damage control.[44]

Britain viewed its SEATO affiliation as an opportunity to influence U.S. strategic behavior and especially to restrain American policy officials who, London felt, were overly prone to involve Western forces in Asia's limited wars. Nonetheless, Britain clearly entertained a strategic agenda in Malaya apart from SEATO. The British determination to sustain an independent deterrence posture in the Asia-Pacific theater was reinforced by earlier (1958) American rejections of London's entreaties for the organization of a joint Anglo-American approach to the problem of Malay-Indonesian animosity. [45] By the time Laos exploded on the international scene three years later, the British were convinced that Washington would hold to its traditional position of "noninvolved cordiality" regarding British efforts to deter an Indonesian attack against

Malaysia. Publicly the United States rationalized its stance as one which recognized Malaysia as primarily a British defense concern and responsibility, and a Malaysian-Indonesian confrontation as a contingency falling outside SEATO's designated threat contingencies of communist external attack or communist-supported insurgency movement. In reality, Washington was wary about taking sides with the British and Malays in any such confrontation, lest the United States antagonize both Indonesia and the Philippines by appearing too open in their support of Kuala Lumpur.

Aside from reservations about the U.S. ability to manage escalation control in a manner which could avoid a replay of China's intervention in the Korean War, the British were concerned that Laos would inevitably complicate—if not eventually rupture—their own regional security ties with Malaya and Singapore (the Anglo-Malaysian Defense Agreement or AMDA, formed when Malaya gained its independence in 1957). The British recognized that, unlike most cold war alliances which tended to solidify their adherents' affiliation with either East or West, AMDA's major purpose was to facilitate stability during Malaya's decolonization with no long-term guarantee of politico-strategic allegiance to British global security interests. If the British were to "reengage" there, after Malaya's twelve-year communist insurgency movement ("the Emergency"), Malayan nationalist sensitivities would have to be taken into account.

Britain felt trapped between the Americans at the global deterrence level and the Malays in a local deterrence context, at a time when its global strategic influence was declining and when opposition to the use of Commonwealth Strategic Reserve units to control a nationalist revolution against neocolonialist Laotian factions would be great. Prime Minister Macmillan eventually felt compelled to promise Kennedy that two Gurkha batallions attached to the Commonwealth Strategic Reserve would be dispatched to Laos if the U.S. requested their assistance in a military intervention.[46] Macmillan may well have concluded that doubts about American management of the Laos situation could not be allowed to jeopardize the postwar "special relationship" between Washington and London at a time when Britain was becoming totally dependent on access to U.S. delivery systems to keep its own nuclear deterrent intact.

France retained a military base in south Laos (at Seno) but was largely indifferent after 1954 to the political fate of Laos and Indochina. Charles de Gaulle, however, resisted American domination of the region, as he planned to form a largely nonaligned group of developed and underdeveloped states as a "third force" in international politics. Consequently, France refused to offer military assistance and, instead, urged Washington to back a coalition government in Laos which would include communist elements.

If reticence was the primary European approach to facing events in Laos, the Thai and Filipino postures were entirely prointervention. Displaying little faith in de Gaulle's "third force" thesis, Thailand and the Philippines had committed themselves to an outright strategic affiliation with the United States and viewed Washington's policy on Laos as a key test case for SEATO's future credibility. On the basis of geography alone, Field Marshal Sarit Thanarat's government in Bangkok believed its security to be the most threatened of any SEATO affiliate. It was less prone than the Garcia government in the Philippines, Ayub Khan's regime in Pakistan and Washington's Australian and New Zealand allies to welcome negotiation over confrontation if the Pathet Lao were to be included in a future "neutralist" Laotian government. However, even Thai leaders realized that Laos had evolved into a crisis of international proportions by early 1961, and one superseding their own preoccupations with local deterrence along the Thai-Laotian border.[47]

The Thais had their own ideas about SEATO and Thai security requirements. In May and again in July 1961, Foreign Minister Thanat Khoman delivered two major policy statements enunciating "Thaiism": continued affiliation with SEATO but expanding relations with other Asian countries, projecting of a more independent image and "looking less to other collectivities, which may prove to be ineffective . . . [and] to reexamine our exposed position as well as our obligations which have become one-sided."[48] While Thailand maintained a high degree of strategic association with, and basing access for, the Americans, Washington's reticence to apply a credible extended deterrence strategy in Laos during 1961 led to a gradual erosion of Thai support for American strategic objectives by the mid-1970s, and an eventual end to military involvement with the Americans.

An interim solution to Bangkok's intensified feelings of vulnerability was reached in March 1962, however, when a joint statement was issued by U.S. Secretary of State Dean Rusk and by Thanat (subsequently known as the "Rusk-Thanat Communique") declaring that the security obligation of the United States to Thailand under the Manila Pact "does not depend upon the prior agreement of all other parties to the Treaty, since this Treaty obligation is *individual as well as collective*."[49] This reaffirmation of a determination to deter and defend on Thailand's behalf temporarily forestalled Bangkok's growing apprehension that its security relationship with Washington was "less than equal" to those of Manila, Islamabad, and the Antipodes. Thailand was nonetheless increasingly suspicious of SEATO, a situation which became especially pronounced after the Nixon Doctrine in August 1969 and the American pullout from Vietnam during the early 1970s. Foreign Minister Thanat Khoman expressed what had become the predominant Thai sentiment: "it is all too apparent that the power equation in Southeast Asia is out of balance . . . This is not because of a lack of [U.S.] intensive strength: it is owing to the United States' lack of interest and determination."[50]

The Philippines was conscious of its geographic distance from the Indochinese battlefields and less than optimistic about SEATO's ability to respond decisively to an international crisis. Manila shifted from readying a military contingent for combat against the Pathet Lao on twenty-four hours notice in mid-December 1960 to a gradual acceptance of the Kennedy administration's cautious posture on intervention in March-April 1961. The price Washington paid for this change was a growing bitterness by Philippine Foreign Secretary Felixberto Serranao against the British and French behavior in SEATO. The British had sent a note to Moscow on March 23 inviting the Soviets to join in an appeal for a cease-fire in Laos and had requested the convening of an international conference in Geneva. French representatives had come to the SEATO meeting in Bangkok (March 27–29) determined to block Thai and Filipino efforts to secure an American commitment for military intervention in the conflict. Consequently, when Serranao visited Malaya in February 1961, the message of Asian regionalism was a common bond between the Philippines and Malaya, a message not lost upon either Washington or London. When Vice President Johnson visited the Philippines in May 1961, Serranao lectured him on "the shadow of gloom that distressing developments have cast across the horizon of Southeast Asia."[51] In no sense was SEATO ever regarded by successive Filipino Presidents from Ramon Magsaysay to Ferdinand E. Marcos as adequate for Philippine defense needs. Although Rusk reiterated Dulles' formula that an external attack on the Philippines is a de facto attack on the U.S. (October 9, 1964), it remained clear, as Morrison and Suhrke have noted, that "Washington viewed the American commitment as a series of options, a certain flexibility of what [its] response would be."[52]

Kennedy's predecessor warned him at a January 19, 1961 meeting that "if Laos is lost to the Free World, in the long run we will lose all of Southeast Asia."[53] Accordingly, Kennedy told his advisors the following May that, while the Bay of Pigs episode in Cuba had taught him the value of exercising caution in the authorization of U.S. military interventions, surrendering Laos to communist control would cause an unbearable setback to the credibility of U.S. global security commitments. He stated that while President Eisenhower could stand the political consequences of Dien Bien Phu in 1954 by shifting the blame to French military incompetence, "I can't take a 1954 defeat today."[54]

Throughout the spring of 1961, the President prepared to implement SEATO Plan 5 which called for the deployment of up to 40,000 American troops in Laos and Thailand. U.S. Marines stationed at Udorn air base in Thailand serviced Royal Lao helicopters and T-6 aircraft to counter Soviet air cover for Laotian communist forces. Long-range troop and cargo transport planes were transferred from stateside bases to the Philippines, and U.S. Marine divisions attached to the Seventh Fleet and to bases in Okinawa were put on standby alert.[55] As Plan 5 was being implemented, Kennedy called a press conference to announce the U.S. resolve to end Pathet Lao attacks against Royal Lao forces and to move toward a negotiated settlement of the crisis.

Kennedy was ambiguous about what Washington and its SEATO allies might do if the communist attacks did not stop, leaving the point of U.S. intervention unclear and trying to balance conciliation and bellicosity. The President wanted to avoid a replay of Korea in December 1950, when Beijing entered the war out of fear that the UN offensive then driving back North Korean forces would extend into China itself. Kennedy was reacting to uncertainty in the U.S. military establishment over how deterrence commitments to both pro-Western Laotian elements and Asian SEATO members were to be honored. Indeed, in key National Security Council meetings held throughout the first four months of 1961, Kennedy was exasperated over the Joint Chiefs' indecision over whether to commit ground forces as a trip wire strategy or to employ tactical nuclear weapons against Vietnamese or

Chinese targets as a cover for the landing and deployment of up to 140,000 U.S. forces. Army Chief of Staff General George H. Decker argued that a conventional war in Southeast Asia was "unwinnable" for the United States and that "if we go in, we should go in to win, and that means bombing Hanoi, China, and maybe even using nuclear bombs."[56] Air Force Chief of Staff Curtis Lemay added that Chinese aircraft "could always be moved in to scare us off" but that if the United States intervened in Laos, "we should go to work on China itself and let Chiang [Kai-shek] take Hainan Island."[57]

It was also obvious, however, that U.S. efforts to deter an expanded conflict through "psychological impact" risked unwanted escalation with potentially tragic ramifications for U.S. strategic interests. The JCS had already admitted to Kennedy that the speed with which Chinese or Vietnamese troops could be introduced into Laos would be far greater than that of the 4000 U.S. personnel dispatched from Okinawa and other Pacific positions.[58] Moreover, all three potential antagonists (the Soviets, Chinese, and Vietnamese) were well aware of U.S. reinforcement problems and of how stretched U.S. force strength around the globe actually was at the time. They could reasonably assume that Kennedy would have at least as much difficulty in swaying the SEATO allies to back the introduction of U.S. tactical nuclear weapons into Laos in 1961 as Eisenhower had in convincing the British to support such an option in Indochina during 1954. Vietnamese and Chinese radio commentary monitored throughout late March 1961 underscored the communist nations' awareness of U.S. strategic limitations and of American efforts to control escalation from a limited to a general war.[59]

The Laos crisis thus diluted the credibility of U.S. extended deterrence strategy in Southeast Asia. Despite Kennedy's efforts to preserve the Dominant Player posture's credibility through the use of carrot and stick tactics against the Soviets and Chinese, the divisions among the European and Asian SEATO members over deterrence strategy were sharp. These divisions were too obvious to the West's adversaries for SEATO to be salvaged as a meaningful security instrument. The effective demise of that security organization thus took place in 1961, not during the subsequent U.S. involvement in Vietnam. The U.S. had temporarily secured peace in Indochina but had effectively buried SEATO's credibility.

In retrospect, this was not necessarily detrimental to the Asia-Pacific security environment. As David Halberstam has since observed, however, the West responded to the Laos crisis by engaging in a patchwork set of negotiations which eventually proved to be unsuccessful and which appeared to stiffen Washington's resolve to draw the line of containment at the Vietnamese demilitarized zone. This resolve turned out to be based upon a fundamental misconception about U.S. ability and the Dominant Player posture to check a formidable adversary in Vietnam.[60]

Kennedy's military advisors drew unfortunate parallels between the Laos and Vietnam situations. Typical was the observation made by Secretary of Defense McNamera during the joint Defense/State Department meeting of April 29, 1961. When the President's brother, Attorney General Robert Kennedy, asked Defense Secretary where would be the best place to stand and fight in Southeast Asia, the response was that the United States should take a stand in Thailand and Vietnam but that "if we gave up Laos we would have to attack the Democratic Republic of Vietnam."[61] McNamera's observation proved to be ironically prophetic as the Kennedy administration was forced to look elsewhere in Southeast Asia to reassure pro-Western states that U.S. deterrence strategy remained credible. South Vietnam became, by default, the final measure of the Dominant Player posture in its original postwar form.

The Nixon Doctrine: Moving Toward Self-Reliance in Local Deterrence

THE JOHNSON administration was confronted with the dilemma of preserving the credibility of U.S. deterrence commitments in SEATO and throughout Southeast Asia while escalating its military involvement in Vietnam. For the next three years, the United States attempted to coordinate a strategy of graduated bombing escalation against targets in North Vietnam with unsuccessful efforts to build what President Johnson termed "a successful and effective government in Saigon."[62] While Richard Nixon and Johnson's other domestic political opponents were calling for a tough U.S. posture throughout early 1965, the scope and intensity of the February 1968 Tet offensive shattered any illusions that either controlled escalation or other forms of U.S. military power would be sufficient to compensate for South Vietnam's lack of political willingness to stand up to a more determined communist adversary.

Implementing the Nixon Doctrine

NIXON HAD written an article in *Foreign Affairs* during late 1967 envisioning U.S. Asian allies joining together as Western European governments had done during NATO's formulative years. The article also foreshadowed the United States' normalization of relations with China. By the time Nixon was elected to the presidency (November 1968), the U.S. was faced with the problem of how to disengage militarily from Southeast Asia while still appearing to support a credible deterrence strategy in the Asia-Pacific as part of its global Dominant Player posture. To forsake that posture completely would have deprived Washington of the leverage needed for detente with the USSR (an imperative for American policy planners, since Moscow had reached strategic parity with the United States) and for the forging of a politico-strategic relationship with the PRC as a counterbalance to rising Soviet military power.[63] It would also have created chaos among U.S. friends and allies in the Asia-Pacific.

Nixon and his National Security Advisor, Henry Kissinger, chose to focus on *threat differentials* to rationalize disengagement of U.S. ground forces from Vietnam. Kissinger later described their efforts to "make a distinction between three types of security dangers: internal subversion, external attack by a neighboring county, and aggression by a nuclear power (in practical terms, the Soviet Union or the People's Republic of China)."[64] While in Guam, at the beginning of his late July 1969 Asia-Pacific regional tour, the President announced that the United States would "encourage and has the right to expect" that internal subversion would be increasingly managed by the Asian allies themselves.[65] This approach, as the President later recalled in his memoirs, was designed "not as a formula for getting America *out* of Asia, but one that provided the only sound basis for America's staying *in* and continuing to play a responsible role in helping the noncommunist nations and neutrals as well as our Asian allies to defend their independence." The United States would thus provide military assistance, but no longer would American forces be directly involved in

Southeast Asian counter insurgency operations, "to ensure that there were no more Vietnams in the future."[66]

Within these threat categories, the differences between a "civil war," (in which no U.S. forces would intervene), and "insurgencies fueled by external hostile forces," (where intervention might be required) were left undefined. Given public disillusionment with the Vietnam intervention, this ambiguity in defining future U.S. commitments was deliberate. Nixon insisted that unless an external military attack was overt, the United States would "draw the line in becoming involved heavily with our own personnel, doing the job for them, rather than helping them do the job themselves." In the event of an overt hostile attack, the U.S., according to the President, would "honor its treaty commitments under SEATO."[67] How such commitments would be "honored," especially given the loophole that SEATO's members would act in response to a threat "in accordance with their constitutional processes" was left open. If a "major nuclear power" initiated hostilities against one of Washington's "allies or friends" the United States would respond by using nuclear weapons.[68] This scenario was deemed improbable by most Southeast Asians. They were well aware that the region lacked appropriate nuclear targets, that Soviet strategic projection capabilities in the Asia-Pacific were concentrated against the American west coast and targets in Northeast Asia, and that China could ill afford to waste components of its finite nuclear deterrent on conducting military offensives against ASEAN governments when insurgency tactics had proven to be so much more effective in Indochina. Nixon was, however, seeking to implement in Southeast Asia a flexible response version of the Dominant Player posture in Southeast Asia in a way which would be regarded as credible to those regional friends and allies with whom Washington still desired to retain access and influence.

Nixon's emphasis on scaling back the scope of the U.S. force posture from a two-and-a-half to a one-and-a-half strategy belied his willingness, from the perspective of Southeast Asian leaders, to sustain remaining U.S. security commitments in their region. Between 1969–1971, 260,000 U.S. troops had been withdrawn from Vietnam, 16,000 from Thailand, and 9,000 from the Philippines. Reductions took place even as the Nixon administration was fighting to prevent equivalent U.S. force reductions in Europe as proposed by the Mansfield Amendment. As Leslie Brown later recalled: "Although the Nixon Doctrine was at first defended as an omni-directional policy without geographic bias, it rapidly came to be associated uniquely with Asia . . . the Doctrine seemed to imply that if the forces that had been inadequate for the earlier, more ambitious, strategy should in the event turn out to be inadequate for the lesser one, then her Asian allies, not the United States itself, would be expected to make up the difference, at least in terms of manpower.'[69]

The Southeast Asian Response

HOW U.S. "friends" in Asia would respond to Nixon and Kissinger's policy shift remained uncertain. Clearly, the new administration hoped to prevent Malaysia and Indonesia from gravitating toward a complete nonalignment posture by extending the nuclear deterrence component to these two states. Neither Kuala Lumpur nor Jakarta, however, were willing to accept such a guarantee on Washington's terms.

Nixon visited Jakarta during his July 1969 Asia-Pacific tour to reinforce Indonesia's "central role" in Southeast Asian security. As a trade-off for Indonesian understanding of American security interests, the President publicly conceded that British withdrawal from the Malayan Peninsula would be accepted by Washington as a positive step toward regional stability. This position represented a sharp break from Nixon's predecessors who viewed the prospects of a British pullout from strategic outposts "east of Suez" as causing a serious regional power vacuum. During his visit, Nixon did not propose a formal collective defense arrangement involving Indonesia or a replacement for SEATO, out of respect for Jakarta's policies of regional nonalignment and national self-defense.[70]

Jakarta's political community, however, remained suspicious of Washington's propensity for policy reversal. On the one hand, Indonesia's new leadership felt the Nixon Doctrine was a U.S. effort to enlist Jakarta's support for the U.S. geopolitical agenda in return for economic assistance. Conversely, Foreign Minister Adam Malik and other Indonesian officials believed the Americans still needed to be "educated" to the need for strategic policy adjustment away from bipolar politics and toward recognizing "New Emerging Forces" in an increasingly multipolar world.[71]

Malaysian leader Tunku Abdul Rahman noted during Nixon's trip that Western-oriented defense arrangements which had dominated noncommunist Southeast Asia for almost two decades were "useless." Malaysia, he concluded, needed to define a "more realistic and friendly policy toward her neighbors."[72] Malaysia regarded independent security interests as more important than its traditional reliance upon British and Australian counter insurgency assistance. Malaysian attention was now to be directed toward resolving the Sabah (North Borneo) territorial dispute with the Philippines, security cooperation with Singapore and Indonesia over maritime access to the Malacca Straits, and curbing residual Indonesian aspirations for subregional hegemony over the Malaysian Peninsula. The Nixon Doctrine appeared inapplicable to any of these priorities.

Thailand had fully embraced the U.S. extended deterrent since the founding of SEATO in 1954. The Nixon Doctrine, followed in short order by divisive U.S. Congressional hearings on American security agreements and commitments abroad (November 1969), proved to be the catalyst for Bangkok's gradual shift from an unqualified alliance with Washington toward a strategic adjustment emphasizing greater defense self-reliance. The key was U.S. strategic disengagement from neighboring Vietnam.

Nixon's visit to Bangkok during July 28–31, 1969, gave the Thai Foreign Minister the pretext needed to "support" the Nixon Doctrine by announcing the withdrawal of the 12,000 Thai troops stationed in South Vietnam. These forces, it was emphasized, would be used to enhance Thailand's "self-reliance" in confronting the communist insurgency in its northeastern parameters. More tellingly, the Thai troop withdrawal from Vietnam was a precursor of Bangkok's decision to propose a gradual withdrawal of the 50,000 American troops and 600 supporting U.S. aircraft from Thailand. Thai leaders increasingly viewed the establishment of a viable "collective political defense" by the ASEAN states as an acceptable replacement for American military power in the region.[73] The Thai press was graphic in reflecting the country's feelings about the credibility of U.S. commitments in the region, notwithstanding Nixon's efforts to reassure the Thai government about the steadfastness of U.S. adherence to SEATO: "Would the United States be able to honor its commitments to Thailand, which President Nixon reaffirmed during the visit, when internal and external pressure of the communists was applied? . . . Can a President faced with significant problems at home, the hope of establishing his party's majority in

Congress, and an excessively dangerous autumn on the campuses and the streets resist the pressures which would have him desert the Asian challenge?"[74]

Thai fears appeared to be confirmed by the U.S. Senate Foreign Relations Committee members' complaining in November 1969 hearings that the SEATO countries had done "so very, very little, have made us (the United States) carry the whole load at the same time we are carrying such a tremendous load in Europe." Thailand was especially singled out as earmarking only 14 percent of its army manpower to Vietnam, while the U.S. was said to be keeping Southeast Asian communism from Thailand by maintaining 40 percent of U.S. land forces in Indochina.[75] Thai reluctance to host a continued U.S. military presence intensified after Washinton failed to sustain South Vietnam against the final North Vietnamese offensive in 1973–1975 and as North Vietnam increased pressure on Bangkok to evict U.S. military forces. Prime Minister Kukrit captured the essence of Thai thinking to *The New York Times* in June 1975: "It's like being caught in a bedroom with a gentleman who can no longer operate. You find yourself compromised for nothing."[76] Withdrawal of American forces, which had begun in 1973, was accelerated the following year and completed during July 1976.

Yet no consensus emerged within ASEAN in the immediate aftermath of the Nixon Doctrine on how regional security could be practically achieved without some form of security affiliation and timely military assistance from the U.S., in the case of Thailand and the Philippines, or from Britain, Australia, and New Zealand in the case of Malaysia and Singapore. U.S. military advisors remained highly visible in Thailand even as American troops and aircraft were withdrawn from that country, and the vast American military basing complex in the Philippines remained completely intact. AMDA was replaced by the so-called Five Power Defense Agreements (FPDA). British, Australian, and New Zealand's land and air force presence in the Malayan Peninsula (now known as ANZUK), while significantly reduced, nevertheless remained large enough to provide a tangible deterrent on Malaysia and Singapore's behalf against most external threats which could emerge in the Straits of Malacca, the South China Sea or, more distantly, from Indochina.

U.S. Extended Deterrence in a post-SEATO Era

WHILE IT was true enough that neither the Southeast Asians nor the Western powers had been inclined to activate SEATO during the most critical junctures of successive regional security crises throughout the 1960s and 1970s, the Thais and Filipinos had grown increasingly comfortable with a less than perfect SEATO deterrent. A semblance of integrated command structure and theater deterrence functions had been established during SEATO's lifespan, with over 45 joint maneuvers conducted between 1960 and 1976 and with regular consultations occurring on troop transport, communications, and related command and control operations. SEATO's Secretary-General, Jesus Vargas, noted in 1970 that the "true worth" of the organization was that it was the only multilateral alliance committed to the defense of the entire Southeast Asian region and that overt aggression had, in fact, been deterred for the duration of the postwar era.[77]

The arrival of North Vietnamese and Viet Cong forces in the Cambodian and South Vietnamese capitals during the spring of 1975 shattered this sense of comfort and left most of the ASEAN states (Indonesia by virtue of its size and its "common revolutionary heritage" with Hanoi was the only real exception) wondering how ZOPFAN could proceed without Washington's interest or participation in underwriting a new set of intraregional security guarantees. The North Vietnamese victory prompted reconsideration of a regional modus vivendi with Hanoi, an option which was intermittently pursued until Vietnam's military intervention in Kampuchea in December 1978.

U.S. skepticism of SEATO was concurrently on the rise. On November 2, 1973, a U.S. Senate Resolution (S. Res. 174) was introduced, proposing a review of that treaty commitment, and was approved unanimously. Assistant Secretary of State Robert S. Ingersoll subsequently argued that the United States' continued support for the Manila Treaty was necessary to the Southeast Asian search for self-reliant security. The U.S., he contended, needed to avoid creating "doubt and uncertainty" about the future regional power balance in an area where a significant and ongoing reduction of American military presence was occurring. A clear American abrogation of its SEATO commitment might tempt either Moscow or Beijing to intensify military activities throughout Southeast Asia, resulting in the very type of external attacks which SEATO had deterred for so long.[78]

No strategy was offered by American officials, however, on how the ASEAN nations could become more self-sufficient. Nor was there any real effort during the SEATO hearings to address the nature or sufficiency of the U.S. deterrent still available to Manila Pact or other ASEAN states. ASEAN had already moved to adopt a more autonomous regional security formula modeled on the short-lived Association of Southeast Asia (ASA) (a grouping comprised of the Philippines, Malaya, and Thailand from 1961 to 1963 and briefly again from 1966 to 1967). This approach downplayed the military approach to regional security problems, embodied in the Manila Pact and SEATO, in favor of "confront(ing) problems of political stability through collective attention to their economic causes."[79] The Nixon Doctrine, moreover, had guaranteed U.S. military intervention only if Washington's Southeast Asian friends or allies were attacked by "nuclear powers"—i.e., the USSR or the PRC (other forms of aggression were subject to response on a "case-by-case" basis). Given the size and proximity of the Vietnamese army, ASEAN leaders were quite concerned about U.S. plans for deterring the most relevant threat to their region.

Even at the nuclear level, major uncertainties about the American deterrent emerged. For the most part, the pattern of U.S. nuclear weapons deployment throughout the Asia-Pacific was not appropriate to a Southeast Asian contingency. The U.S. "offshore" power presence might provide a formidable mix of sea, land, and air-based tactical nuclear weapons but little analysis was offered by the Nixon-Ford administrations on how such a capability would actually be employed to meet U.S. theater deterrence objectives.[80] By 1975, it was doubtful that the ASEAN member-states would embrace American use of nuclear weapons on their own territories as part of *any* regional deterrence strategy.

President Ford's enunciation of a "Pacific Doctrine" in Honolulu on December 7, 1975, was meant to reaffirm the United States' determination to play an "active role" in Asia.[81] The ASEAN nations' skepticism about the American executive branch's ability to sustain defense commitments or to wage war without Congressional restrictions, however, was actually sharpened by the President's failure to closely define remaining U.S. strategic commitments or to specify how

Washington intended to honor them. As Singapore's *Straits Times* subsequently observed, the Pacific Doctrine reflected "a vagueness as to the extent of U.S. interests and perceived obligations" which left Southeast Asians feeling less than reassured, particularly in regard to Japanese and Chinese involvement in future U.S. strategic planning and the precise nature of what the President characterized as potential U.S. "gestures of good will" in return for Indochinese restraint toward their ASEAN neighbors.[82]

Security Reorganization in Southeast Asia

ONCE THE die was cast, Washington lost any real opportunity it may have had to repair the SEATO link between its global deterrence policy and localized deterrence in Southeast Asia. The ASEAN states moved quickly, if not with total unity of purpose, to renounce Dominant Player security politics and to replace it with a formula for qualified nonalignment which they hoped would appear credible to the international order, despite their inability to completely eschew their own residual suspicions and hostilities toward each other. Even while adopting the rhetoric of regional self-reliance, however, most ASEAN states recognized the value of retaining limited deterrence relationships with their traditional guarantors. Consequently, the de jure Manila Treaty commitments were retained, even if their existence was downplayed following the abrogation of SEATO itself in 1976.[83]

Both Thailand and the Philippines reaffirmed the viability of their bilateral security ties with Washington. Malaysia and Singapore, similarly, emphasized the consultative and training benefits of the Five Power Defense Arrangement with Canberra, London and Wellington. Residual ties with outside powers were viewed as important counterbalances against an Indonesia still thought to harbor hegemonic instincts. Only five days after President Ford's Pacific Doctrine speech, for example, the Thai press reported that Jakarta had presented a "position paper" to Bangkok's leadership proposing the conversion of ASEAN to a formal defense alliance and had "twisted the arm" of Malaysia for Kuala Lumpur's approval of the establishment of an ASEAN "counter insurgency center" (an idea subsequently abandoned in ASEAN councils). Expressing openly the sentiments undoubtedly shared by all the other ASEAN members toward Jakarta, *The Nation* concluded that while it entertained an "understandable concern" toward recent events in Indochina, "that is not reason at all for Indonesia [to] act as big brother for the ASEAN nations."[84]

ASEAN moved quickly toward adjusting to the new balance of forces which had emerged in mainland Southeast Asia by mid-1975. Each ASEAN government quickly and pragmatically extended diplomatic relations to the new communist governments in Indochina without submitting to Hanoi's demands that *all* military ties between themselves and the West be immediately terminated. While each ASEAN country managed the pace and scope of its own relations with Vietnam and the other Indochinese states, ASEAN's consultative machinery was greatly refined during 1975–1976. It addressed its members' common effort to find the right balance between diplomatic conciliation and firmness toward Indochina and politico-strategic independence from and continued military ties with the Americans. (Some U.S. policy indiscretions made this process more difficult—i.e., the *Mayaguez* affair in May 1975, and the U.S. flying of South Vietnamese military aircraft from Thailand to the Philippines instead of allowing Thailand to return them to Hanoi.[85])

However imperfect, ASEAN committed itself to a Reluctant Player posture of regional deterrence, relying upon the United States' continued need for access to Southeast Asian littorals as a bargaining chip for establishing a regional equilibrium on Southeast Asian terms.

REASSERTING THE DOMINANT PLAYER POSTURE: REAGAN AND THE SOUTHEAST ASIAN 'PILLAR'

PRESIDENT RONALD Reagan was elected to the Oval Office in November 1980, in part because of his determination to resuscitate what the American electorate perceived as a gradual weakening of American global military power and extended deterrence capabilities. While not wanting to become directly involved in the Kampuchean imbroglio— by then the most important local deterrence issue from ASEAN's perspective—the Americans viewed the region as an unavoidable geopolitical focal point in reasserting U.S. power. U.S. Department of Defense studies leaked to the Western press cited ASEAN "strength and cohesion" as key elements in the United States' ability to project offshore naval and air power to Southwest Asia, to conduct rapid deployment operations throughout the Eurasian theater and to deter the threat of Soviet interdiction against American warfighting assets.[86]

Despite ongoing differences in U.S. and ASEAN threat perception, Secretary of Defense Caspar Weinberger, in an address delivered to the Japan Press Club in Tokyo on March 26, 1982, introduced the Reagan administration's "six pillar" defense strategy for the Asia-Pacific. Emphasizing that being a Pacific power was part of retaining the United States' global deterrent (pillar 1), the Defense Secretary nevertheless reiterated the Nixon Doctrine's premise that U.S. strategic resources were relatively smaller than during the immediate postwar era. Accordingly, a higher Japanese defense profile (pillar 2) and a "friendly China" (pillar 3) were critical to supplementing traditional U.S. deterrence efforts on behalf of South Korea (pillar 4) if Soviet military power was to be successfully checked in Northeast Asia. A cohesive ASEAN (pillar 5) would likewise be a vital element in American plans to shift the weight of its offshore power in the CINCPAC theater from the Northwest and wider Pacific to positions more proximate to the Indian Ocean and the Persian Gulf oil lifelines (pillar 6).[87]

The Asia-Pacific theater could now be viewed as integrally related to the calculus of global deterrence just a little over a decade after Richard Nixon had codified regional disengagement. From ASEAN's vantagepoint, however, nothing could be more unappealing than to be drawn into an American "grand design." ASEAN states were especially concerned that the feasibility of this grand design was dependent upon the materializing of a tacit Sino-Japanese defense consortia which might eventually supplant the Americans and threaten ASEAN aspirations for a more enduring regional order. To most ASEAN members, the six-pillars edifice was a recipe for potential geopolitical disaster.

ASEAN politicians and military figures wasted little time in picking apart the six-pillars' strategy. At a minimum, U.S. determination to remain a Pacific power seemed at odds with the Southwest Asian pillar. This was underscored by Singapore Prime Minister Lee Kuan Yew's request to Weinberger in November 1982 that the United States station an additional aircraft carrier and support group in Southeast Asia, as compensation for the potential loss of U.S. naval assets during a Persian Gulf contingency.[88] The Indonesians noted that the Carter Doctrine enunciated in 1979 had already extended the U.S. strategic umbrella from NATO Europe and Northeast Asia into "the oilfields of Saudi Arabia [and] the far reaches of Pakistan," thus incurring the cost of "reducing carrier strength in the Mediterranean and Pacific."[89] Even Japan's Research Institute for Peace and Security interpreted U.S. strategy directed toward the Asia-Pacific theater in 1982 to be of a "lower priority" than Europe and the Middle East. This factor, the Institute concluded, tended to complicate Weinberger's efforts to re-establish the credibility of American security commitments in the CINCPAC theater.[90] A related consideration was Manila's increasing sensitivity about its role as a Southeast Asian nation rather than its long-standing role as an indispensable basing component of the American global deterrence network

ASEAN resistance to pillars 2 and 3—the Sino-Japanese coalition—was even more significant. To prepare ASEAN leaders for the Weinberger address, President Reagan dispatched former Secretary of State Henry Kissinger and Assistant Secretary for East Asian and Pacific Affairs John Holdridge to Singapore, Indonesia, and Malaysia (November 1981) to assure them that the United States would not pursue new strategic ties with Beijing at ASEAN's expense. Their efforts, however, failed to alleviate their hosts' concerns.

The idea of a rearmed Japan capable of projecting air and naval power into the wider Pacific was even more repugnant. Despite Japanese Prime Minister Takeo Fukuda's efforts in 1977–78 to establish "heart-to-heart" relations with the individual ASEAN nations and to renounce any Japanese military role in their region, there was little evidence that traditional Southeast Asian fears of Japanese militarism had subsided.[91] Aside from their memories of Japanese imperialism toward and domination of Southeast Asia during World War II, two additional factors entered into contemporary ASEAN perceptions of increased Japanese military power. First, concerns remained that Fukuda's initial determination to preserve Japanese global economic power without requisite military capabilities might decrease over time if the retrenchment of U.S. military power in the region were to continue through the loss of the Philippine bases or through other developments. In late 1982, for example, Indonesian parliamentarians were widely quoted as asserting that the Japanese need for access to Southeast Asia's raw materials could be underlying Tokyo's plan to build up its naval patrolling capabilities and that "continued vigilance [against Japanese military behavior] was required."[92] The Malaysians, clearly echoing concerns held in Jakarta, linked the implications of Weinberger's "pillar 6" with those of his "pillar 2": "the United States has strongly pressured the Japanese government to strengthen its armed forces . . . this is what causes some Southeast Asian nations to look at the whole issue [of transferring U.S. offshore power to Southwest Asia] with consternation."[93] A related problem from ASEAN's perspective was how a Japanese rearmament program with even limited power projection aspirations would ultimately be received by the Soviets and the Chinese.

To be effective, the renewed Dominant Player posture had to take into account the *national* security interests of the individual ASEAN members. Weinberger's "fifth pillar" relating to ASEAN cohesion and stability, however, failed to specify what policy mechanisms could be adopted for reconciling U.S. global deterrence strategy with ASEAN's local security concerns. How could the U.S. Seventh Fleet or American aircraft stationed at Clark Air Base, encumbered by additional support duties for Indian Ocean or Persian Gulf operations, help fulfill ASEAN's local deterrence requirements in the South China Sea or along the Thai-Vietnamese border? Would the American Congress and electorate, burdened with a declining economic infrastructure in relative terms, find the political will to underwrite Southeast Asian self-reliance policies?

Typical of the ASEAN states' reactions, during his July 1982 visit to Washington, the Supreme Commander of Thailand's military made it clear that Thailand could no longer afford to rely upon the vagaries of U.S. domestic politics to leave the context of U.S.-Thai security relations unaffected: "We will no longer allow others to think for us. Thailand will formulate its own strategies."[94] Such rhetoric can be partially attributed to Thai dissatisfaction over a reduction in Foreign Military Sales Credits and related military assistance, to Thai efforts to generate leverage in its strategic relations with Washington through the use of its own "China card" in the military sales area, and to growing bilateral trade friction as Thailand assumed its place as Asia's latest newly industrialized country. Nevertheless, a strong argument could be made that Bangkok was genuinely concerned that U.S. leaders were less than willing to extend deterrence to a front line state on the Southeast Asian mainland.[95]

CASE STUDY LESSONS

THE HISTORY of U.S. extended deterrence strategy in Southeast Asia provides several policy "lessons" for strategic analysts. First, a deterrence strategy will be viable only if it is clearly defined and restricted to use in those contingencies which unmistakably fit its original purposes. Various American political and military officials failed to observe this axiom during 1953–1954 and again in early 1961, by their willingness to employ nuclear weapons against Chinese targets in response to two different Southeast Asian limited wars (in Vietnam and Laos, respectively). To their credit, Presidents Eisenhower and Kennedy recognized the inapplicability of existing policy in these instances and moved to defuse the crises.

Secondly, the misapplication of extended deterrence strategy through incorrect timing or on behalf of the wrong ally can permanently dilute the credibility of residual extended deterrence commitments toward the region in question. The Nixon Doctrine, of course, was a product of U.S. policy errors in Vietnam. The long-term significance of President Nixon's damage control effort may have been more detrimental for U.S. security policy in the Asia-Pacific than the original problem, when he deemed an American quasi-strategic tie with China as integral to restoring American prestige within the global balance of power. By pursuing this policy choice, he may well have permanently diluted the credibility of the Dominant Player posture and opened the way for an alternative regional security order much less conducive to long-term U.S. strategic interests.

A final lesson relates to the Reagan administration's belated attempt to salvage the Dominant Player posture with the six-pillars approach to Asian security. Washington apparently failed to realize that ASEAN was not preoccupied with the Soviet military threat. The United States then moved very belatedly and somewhat tentatively, following Soviet leader Gorbachev's Vladivostok speech, to link its own global deterrence prerogatives with Southeast Asian security aspirations. The six-pillars policy was, however, an outdated prescription for an ASEAN which had long been searching for alternatives to bipolar balance of power prescriptions as a means of establishing a more stable regional order. It was also a product of an administration where no fundamental unity existed with regard to foreign policy in Asia or to overall problems of Third World security. Secretary of State George Shultz tended to support the concept of using American military power to intervene on behalf of established noncommunist governments in Third World settings or insurgency movements fighting communist regimes—a literal interpretation of the so-called "Reagan Doctrine." Conversely, Secretary of Defense Caspar Weinberger opposed any such application of U.S. military resources unless it included a "war-winning" posture which would enjoy widespread support of the American Congress and the electorate-at-large.[96] With key U.S. decisionmakers at odds over what should constitute their nation's deterrence and security postures, the credibility of any U.S. policy for the Asia-Pacific region was predictably at risk. The trend continued with Reagan's successor, as the Bush administration's reluctance to alter the Dominant Player posture significantly in the aftermath of Mikhail Gorbachev's shifts in Soviet Asian diplomacy disillusioned those in the ASEAN subregion most concerned about the U.S. retaining geopolitical credibility in the Asia-Pacific.[97]

ALTERNATIVES TO THE DOMINANT PLAYER ROLE IN SOUTHEAST ASIA

THE NIXON Doctrine correctly anticipated that both the sources of ASEAN threats and the approaches ASEAN decisionmakers would incorporate for meeting them would undergo significant change. The real "threat" now confronted by most ASEAN leaderships would be their own inability to define and implement national development priorities and to build more enduring as well as more legitimate social and political institutions. Two successive coups d' etat in Thailand in less than two years (November 1971 and October 1973), the declaring of martial law in the Philippines (September 1972), and the continuation of active communist insurgency movements in each ASEAN state —except Singapore—throughout the early 1970s all exemplified how important the strengthening of regime credibility had become. Unfortunately, the military autocracies which ruled in Thailand, the Philippines, and Indonesia during that time suppressed their democratic political opposition, often through violent means. This called into serious question their ability to establish responsible mechanisms for decision making and governance. By postponing such a development process, the ASEAN governments may have preserved their national security over the short term. However, they did so at the price of increasing their long-term susceptibility to hostile outside powers determined to exploit socio-political dissent to their advantage.

While effective mechanisms for overcoming internal societal vulnerabilities are still lacking, Southeast Asian defense self-reliance at both the national and regional levels will remain no more than an elusive ideal. Outside assistance for deterring both domestic and external sources of threat will therefore still be required.[98] Previously, SEATO and AMDA provided formal avenues for noncommunist Southeast Asian regimes to supplement their defense capabilities with outside support. More recently, the ASEAN states have sought other ways to replace their reliance upon the American Dominant Player posture.

Regional Alternatives to the Dominant Player: Precedents

IF THE Dominant Player approach has become a source of disillusionment throughout noncommunist Southeast Asia, the various indigenous security initiatives advanced in that region have not been any more impressive. While agreeing that they wished to disassociate themselves from the vagaries of global deterrence politics, the ASEAN nations have often experienced sharp differences among themselves on what path to embark for transforming the Reluctant Player posture into an enduring and credible local deterrent.

Collective Political Defense

DURING THE transition of political power from Sukarno to a more moderate leadership led by General Suharto in late 1965 and early 1966, Adam Malik was appointed as Jakarta's new Foreign Minister. Supportive of increased Indonesian participation in Southeast Asian regional security, Malik worked closely with Thai Foreign Minister Thanat Khoman to bring Jakarta back into the region's politico-diplomatic mainstream. At the same time, Indonesia's new leadership had no desire to join the old Association of Southeast Asia (ASA) The Indonesians considered ASA to be too pro-Western, given Malaysia's defense ties with Britain, the Antipodes within the Anglo-Malayan Defense Agreement, and the Thailand and Philippines SEATO affiliation.[99]

Malik and Khoman attempted to define a balance between the local deterrence policies (supplemented by external military assistance) still desired by the AMDA/SEATO affiliates and the regional defense self-reliance favored by the Indonesians. They negotiated a "Joint Draft Declaration" in Bangkok and Jakarta in July-August 1966 which called for the forming of a Southeast Asian Association for Regional Cooperation (SEAARC). The Declaration expressed the two principles which later were to become the hallmark of ASEAN's approach to the security issue: (1) the stability and security of the regional order would primarily be the responsibility of indigenous states; and (2) foreign military bases in the region were to be regarded as temporary in nature, eventually to be replaced by great power guarantees for regional neutrality in East-West conflicts. Khoman forged the key compromise between the Indonesian and Malay positions when he proposed ASEAN as the compromise designation for ASA/SEAARC. The new organization was born in the Thai capital during August 1967.

The Thai Foreign Minister had long entertained an interest in what he termed "collective political defense." He refined this concept in a number of speeches and writings during 1970-1971. He envisioned a regional security order in which Thailand would be insured of not becoming isolated either from the other noncommunist Southeast Asian nations or from the West as it moved to create a more self-reliant "first line of defense" against Vietnam or other potential aggressors. In this context, the Nixon Doctrine was viewed as an opportunity for Thailand to distance itself from the United States on Bangkok's terms. This involved moving away from overdependence on Washington (an error which the Thais believed was fatal for the South Vietnamese regime) but relying on the Americans to honor the spirit as well as the letter of the Rusk-Thanat Communique. Khoman viewed collective political defense as "both a supplement to the American alliance and a replacement for it." [100]

As Khoman further refined his thinking of the problem, he advocated Thailand and Southeast Asia "tilting" toward the West but, whenever possible, steering a middle course between the two great Soviet-Vietnamese and Sino-American security coalitions which he then saw forming in the Asia-Pacific. The Rusk-Thanat Communique would remain in force but, short of an outright invasion of Thailand, would be less important than inducing Hanoi (and, by extension, Moscow) to initially endorse and later participate in the implementing of ASEAN-generated neutrality guarantees for all of Southeast Asia. If Bangkok's security relations with the U.S. were too overt, the Vietnamese could not be expected to accept diplomatic solutions over military power as the preferred means to bring about a regional order with which they, along with the ASEAN nations, could accept. Only by adopting a local deterrence posture of "equidistance," Khoman concluded, could the ASEAN states avoid inevitable counterpressures from the Soviets and Vietnamese.[101]

Regional Resilience

CONTRASTING THE Thai approach were Indonesian efforts to apply Jakarta's long-standing concept of "national resilience" to an ASEAN-wide format. Even though Khoman and Malik had initially worked together to bring ASEAN into fruition, the Indonesians gradually became skeptical of Thailand's collective political defense formula. From the Indonesian perspective, Khoman's notions of regional power equilibrium seemed too dependent upon American and (later) Chinese acquiescence. By mid-1971, Malik was arguing that residual ASEAN state security ties with traditional extra-regional deterrence guarantors undercut Southeast Asia's efforts to develop acceptable levels of regional cohesion and stability.[102] Other Indonesian foreign policy analysts asserted that ASEAN countries were still too occupied with "nation-building" to engage in the type of balance of power politics implied by Khoman's regional security design. Instead, they concluded, the priority of nation-building must be observed as long as the newly sovereign "nations of Southeast Asia . . . find it difficult to differentiate between external and internal matters."[103]

Nor, concluded these Indonesian observers, could Southeast Asians realistically hope to enjoy the same level of American security commitments which the U.S. traditionally had extended to Western Europe. How, then, could ASEAN's security be best pursued? Indonesian analysts argued that the organization must increasingly look inward and develop its own capabilities for regional conflict resolution and for establishing long-term regional stability. Each ASEAN state, it was maintained, should assume responsibility for achieving socio-political and economic stability on as self-reliant a basis as possible before a collective ASEAN effort was made. Indonesia's approach was based on its national philosophy of *pancasila:* belief in One Supreme God, Civilized Humanity, Nationalism, Democracy, and Social Justice. If *pan-casila* could bring together a nation as culturally and ethnically diverse as Indonesia, could it not also serve as a model for providing greater regional order and stability to the entire Southeast Asian subregion? While *pancasila* emphasizes overcoming *national* vulnerabilities caused by internal sources of conflict, Indonesians have argued that the fundamental characteristics of national resilience can be applied to an ASEAN *regional* security agenda. The concepts of strong leadership, efficient institutions working toward economic and social development, and, above all, the preservation of social order are all embodied within the *pancasila* credo. The late Ali Moertopo, one of Indonesia's most respected military leaders and a founder of its Center for Strategic and International Studies (CSIS), described the interrelationship between "national resilience" and "regional resilience" as the key element of his country's approach to regional security.[104]

Regional resilience emerged as the major theme underscoring the Declaration of ASEAN Concord produced at the Bali Conference. The Declaration reflected a growing ASEAN consensus supportive of the Indonesian view. In early 1989, the concept was further refined at "the first ASEAN seminar on regional resilience" convened in Jakarta. "Senior ASEAN officials" who attended the seminar concluded that economic, rather than military, problems constituted the most serious threat to ASEAN but that poverty and misery could be easily manipulated into domestic violence against social institutions if not effectively addressed. "Economic resilience" was defined as preventing or overcoming the formation of trading cartels in the world's industrialized trading areas, moving toward greater economic interaction with Indochina once a Cambodian solution was implemented, and achieving the enlightened dissemination of information so that younger generations of Southeast Asians "will not make mistakes in formulating national and regional resilience concepts in the future."[105]

Regional resilience was viewed by most ASEAN leaders as a constructive step forward in defining a Southeast Asian security agenda. Two problems, both pertaining to the interrelationship between external and internal threats to the ASEAN subregion's nation-states, remained to be overcome. First, the internal ethnic and religious tensions, which often plagued individual ASEAN societies, also tended to cross state boundaries. The persistent Chinese minorities question and the recent Islamic resurgence are cases-in-point. Such threats often cause ASEAN elites to become preoccupied with a very narrow range of internal security issues and detract from the building of region-wide outlooks on common security issues. Second, recently decolonized states remain vulnerable to external manipulation and intervention on various security issues. As Mohammed Ayoob and Chi-Anan Samuda-vanija have recently noted, "such external involvement, whether by great powers or by stronger neighbors, usually exacerbates internal insecurities and might even lead to the fracturing or fragmentation of the state concerned." [106]

Zopfan

THE KUALA Lumpur Declaration (introducing ZOPFAN) was initially and widely regarded as a concession to Indonesia's sensitivity over *any* strategic involvement by external powers in Southeast Asia (i.e., "to secure the recognition of, and respect for, Southeast Asia as a Zone of Peace, Freedom, and Neutrality, free from any form or manner of interference by outside powers"). ZOPFAN, however, quickly took form as a less absolute and more pragmatic effort to reconcile external security ties with gradual progress toward self-reliance. Indeed, ZOP-FAN represented an acknowledgment by ASEAN as a collective organization that what the great powers do at the level of global strategy often affects their own region in ways which they themselves cannot control.

During the February 1976 ASEAN Heads of Government summit at Bali, hopes were expressed that a war-weary Vietnam was ready to concentrate on economic development instead of imperial expansion at its neighbors' expense, that Soviet involvement in a postwar Vietnam would be marginal, and that China's economic modernization programs would displace the PRC's traditional tendencies to use its ideological and manpower resources to influence Southeast Asian politics. These hopes were dashed by the events of 1978–1979: Vietnam's invasion of Kampuchea, the Soviet-Vietnamese Friendship Treaty, Soviet expanded presence at Cam Ranh Bay, and the PLA's incursion into Vietnam. [107] As a result, ZOPFAN appeared, as the 1980s unfolded, to have become largely irrelevant to the achievement of a Southeast Asian regional security order.

Some Western analysts have maintained that the interaction between local and global security dynamics has effectively frustrated all attempts by ASEAN to create the type of politico-security community which the Indonesians originally envisioned. They have advanced this argument recognizing that a de facto polarization between Indochina and the ASEAN states continues; that such polarization has prevented the ASEAN members' from reaching a consensus about what would be an acceptable regional order. Since the Vietnamese military occupation of Cambodia begun in late December 1978, Thailand and, to some extent, Singapore have been less prepared than Malaysia and Indonesia to accept Vietnamese political dominance over Kampuchea, and more willing to accept great power presence in Southeast Asia as a guarantor of ASEAN's neutralization. Jakarta and Kuala Lumpur have contended that major powers should not act as guarantors because such an arrangement would imply their right to military intervention if neutrality politics were to disintegrate during future regional crises.[108]

To compensate, in part, for what some ASEAN strategists viewed as Bangkok's excessive propensity to rely on external deterrence guarantees from Beijing and Washington, ASEAN defense officials convened several conferences in 1989 to discuss how increased levels of defense cooperation could be implemented without converting the group into a formal defense alliance. In March, joint patrolling of the South China Sea was discussed at a meeting in Kuala Lumpur. In July, an ASEAN foreign ministers session convened in Brunei considered the gradual establishment of a loosely associated ASEAN "defense community" against the possibility that U.S. forces were to withdraw from military installations in the Philippines without a commensurate Soviet military pullout from bases in Vietnam.[109] Prospects of a lower American strategic profile in Southeast Asia, combined with prospects for intensified competition between would-be regional hegemonists for access and influence in the area, has prompted increasingly open discussions between ASEAN elites about defense self-reliance at regional levels.

Any indigenous regional movement toward a higher ASEAN security profile, moreover, is taking shape in the absence of extensive Chinese support for regional communist insurgency movements or of any prospects for extensive Japanese rearmament. In the near future, no common ASEAN perception of external threat to the region is likely to materialize. There can be, therefore, no systematic and consistent organizational response to Moscow's and Beijing's ongoing attempts, in the wake of the Nixon Doctrine and American strategic disengagement from Indochina, to expand their diplomatic influence and make their military capabilities felt in the region.

However, in July 1989 discussions with ASEAN Foreign Ministers at Brunei, U.S. Secretary of State James Baker reported that until the USSR demonstrated a more concerted willingness to persuade Vietnam to accept a Cambodian peace plan acceptable to ASEAN and completely discontinue its own military operations at Cam Ranh Bay, Moscow would continue to be distrusted in most ASEAN capitals. The Soviets have visibly succeeded in cultivating better state-to-state bilateral relations within individual ASEAN countries (perhaps culminating with Indonesian President Suharto's cordial visit to Moscow in September 1989). However, continued ideological aversion by ASEAN elites against communism and its past legacy for penetrating their own societies, the USSR's lack of appeal in the trade and investment sectors, and the absence of socio-cultural affinity between the Soviet Union and most Southeast Asians (except possibly between Soviet Islamic factions and their ASEAN counterparts—a less than pleasant prospect from Moscow's vantagepoint) all remain as barriers to Soviet-ASEAN relations progressing beyond the stage of "conditional acceptance." [110]

For the time being at least, the Chinese would continue to be viewed "as a bulwark against the Soviet Union in the region" with ASEAN governments, "reluctant to criticize the Beijing leadership too harshly for its crackdown on prodemocracy demonstrators, mainly out of fear that isolating China now might force that country to seek a new alliance with the Soviet Union." [111] Their cautious response to events in China was even more significant, given Gorbachev's own mild criticisms of the Chinese political suppression when questioned in Paris during July 1989. [112]

IMPLEMENTING THE RELUCTANT PLAYER POSTURE: CURRENT PROBLEMS

IN THE absence of a more specific framework for regional coexistence, prospects for the realization of a genuine ZOPFAN in Southeast Asia either through regional or extra-regional initiatives remain dim. This will remain the case, notwithstanding the scheduled withdrawal of Vietnamese forces from Kampuchea by late 1989 and regardless of what Sino-Soviet understandings about the region may have since emerged. The Jakarta Informal Meetings held between ASEAN and Vietnamese diplomats, along with representatives of the warring Kampuchean political factions in July 1988, for example, demonstrated the wide policy differences between Hanoi and ASEAN over what would constitute an acceptable regional security order as well as what type of Kampuchea should emerge from that nation's civil war.

ASEAN neutrality politics have remained largely unfulfilled because of the region's continued importance to American, Chinese, Japanese, and Soviet global strategic interests and no less because of the ASEAN members' unwillingness to adjust their own national security objectives. Instead, ASEAN states continue to rely upon their traditional security ties with outside powers, whether or not such relations undercut the efforts of its ASEAN partners to support and gradually sever their reliance on external deterrence commitments. For example, continuing access to advanced U.S. military aircraft, and to less complex but less expensive Chinese ground combat armaments, has allowed Thai military planners to pursue a strategy of anti-Vietnamese deterrence throughout most of the 1980s even while Malaysia and Indonesia continue to regard Beijing—not Hanoi—as the major long-term threat to ASEAN security.

If the key to ZOPFAN or any other effective regional deterrence alternative remains the securing of external power commitments to noninvolvement in the Southeast Asian region, events taking place since its promulgation at Kuala Lumpur appear to make the concept permanently elusive. Equally obvious, however, is the singular lack of appeal of the Dominant Player posture, with its emphasis on great power competition shaping regional security environments and compelling regional actors' affiliation with extended deterrence strategy. The challenge which ASEAN must overcome is the need to find a consensus of strategic perception. ASEAN member-states must then impose self-discipline on their national security behavior in the interest of promoting a more unified, and thus more credible, regional deterrence posture.

Disparities in ASEAN Threat Perceptions: The Case of Indochina

CONTINUED DIFFERENCES among ASEAN's member-states have thus far marred their success in facing the outside world on a cohesive basis.

The dilemma of finding a basis for political reconciliation between the Indochinese and ASEAN states, while still taking into account both local security concerns and selective extraregional deterrence ties, is especially painful for ASEAN policy architects.[113] The dilemma can be traced to the ASEAN states' history of diverse interpretations about the significance of security threats to Indochina. For example, Thailand, much to Indonesia's and Malaysia's chagrin, has intensified its strategic ties with China and has extended significant levels of covert assistance to the Khmer Rouge to offset Vietnamese military power in Cambodia. Conversely, Indonesia has pursued unilateral diplomatic initiatives directed toward Hanoi, has conducted exchange visits of high military officials with the Vietnamese, and, on occasion, has openly criticized Chinese behavior toward Indochina (the 1980 "Kuantan Principle," in which the Indonesians and Malays denounced any Chinese politico-strategic involvement in Indochina, much to Thailand's embarrassment, is the best known instance of the latter trend).

Recent intra-ASEAN divisions over how the Cambodian political landscape should be fashioned in the aftermath of a Vietnamese military withdrawal have detracted from that organization's ability to influence the future course of political events in Phomn Penh. They have underscored the Reluctant Player posture's difficulties in establishing deterrence credibility when confronted with formidable military resistance. In early May 1989, the Khmer Rouge, the Khmer People's National Liberation Front's (KPNLF's) most powerful military faction, rejected a Thai-negotiated cease-fire between the Vietnamese-backed Hun Sen government and Prince Sihanouk, representing the other two factions of the KPNLF.[114] In rejecting the legitimacy of the Hun Sen-Sihanouk talks, the Khmer Rouge knew that differences between Indonesia and the "majority" ASEAN position represented by Thailand had almost jettisoned ASEAN diplomacy in 1987. Indonesian Foreign Minister Mochtar Kusumaatmadja had resisted an ASEAN role in a political settlement of the Cambodian conflict as an unjustified encroachment on the rights of Cambodia's warring factions and Vietnam.

The Indonesians eventually fell into line and hosted the Jakarta Informal Meeting (JIM) between Vietnamese, Cambodian government and KPNLF representatives in July 1988. However, eventual, if tacit, Indonesian support for a Vietnamese reoccupation of Cambodia if the Khmer Rouge were again to seize power in that country cannot be discounted.[115] A follow-on session, the Informal Meeting on Cambodia (IMC), also held in Jakarta during late February/early March 1990, stalled over differences between the Phnom Penh government and the Khmer Rouge. Both demanded mutually exclusive amendments to a final document of "common understandings." Both sides remained wide apart on the fundamental issues of how Cambodia would be governed until elections could be held under international supervision and to what extent the United Nations would be involved in daily civil administration of the country during the interim. Prospects for any negotiating breakthrough further worsened with reports that Vietnam had reintroduced military advisors into Cambodia to supervise the Hun Sen regime's building of strategic defenses a mere month after Vietnam's announced military withdrawal from that country had been completed in September 1989.[116]

By early July 1990, reports were surfacing in Washington that the Bush administration was reconsidering the value of continuing its modest levels of aid to the two non-communist elements of the antigovernment insurgency for fear of bringing the Khmer Rouge back to power. On July 17, after meeting with ASEAN diplomats in Washington, U.S. State Department officials announced that the United States would withdraw its support of the Cambodian resistance coalition and initiate talks with Vietnam and the existing government in Pnomh Penh.[117] The failure of ASEAN and its Western supporters to fashion a viable Cambodian coalition government through internationally supervised elections led to what could be viewed as the most far-reaching change of U.S. policy toward Indochina in over a decade. The shift also was an unmistakable setback in ASEAN's continued efforts to fashion a regional environment reflecting that organization's own indispensibility as a subregional security actor.

The Philippines Basing Issue

THE PHILIPPINES basing issue has recently emerged as perhaps the most important test of the conflict between local security priorities and the U.S. Dominant Player posture in Southeast Asia. Basing proponents designate Clark Air Base and Subic Bay as essential for the conduct of U.S. global extended deterrence at the conventional level. By extension, they assert, the Philippines and the other ASEAN states enjoy a "free ride" in coverage against possible external aggression by virtue of the U.S. regional military presence. Critics argue that deterrence in the nuclear age does not require adherence to an outdated forward basing strategy. They feel the U.S. military presence in the Philippines undermines relations between Washington and Manila by perpetuating a de facto colonial relationship, thus impeding the Filipinos' progress toward a self-confident nationalism.

The latest bilateral review of the 1947 Military Bases Agreement produced a hard-fought compromise (October 1988) on increased U.S. compensation for the use of Clark, Subic, and other installations in the Philippines through the Agreement's 1991 termination date. The debate has since intensified. The extent to which the United States can credibly demonstrate that the global deterrence commitments and missions fulfilled by the bases also serve the Philippine's defense interests has become the key aspect of the negotiations process.

If it is accepted that Washington, as a global superpower, must remain capable of rapidly projecting or "surging" naval and air power to distant points, the Philippine bases play a central role. Subic Bay is a major ship repair facility with four floating dry-docks that service all but the largest U.S. aircraft carriers. This installation alone performs 60 percent of all repair work for the U.S. Seventh Fleet, a service which would be prohibitively expensive to duplicate at Guam or at other sites in the Western Pacific. Forward-based aircraft at Clark are deployed to fulfill local or regional deterrence missions, with air-refueling and support facilities directly supporting intertheater force mobility capabilities. This was recently—and graphically—illustrated with demonstrative overflights of rebel positions by U.S. F-4 Phantom jet fighters during the December 1989 coup attempt against the Aquino government.[118] P-3C *Orion* anti-submarine warfare tracking planes often refuel at the Cubi Point naval air station next to Subic Bay, adding another critical dimension to American forward projection in the Asia-Pacific by providing surveillance of and potential interdiction against Soviet naval activity in the Pacific and Indian Ocean. The Philippines base structure, with that in Japan and Guam, thus allows the United States to control sea lanes located within a "center of gravity" focusing upon the South China Sea, and to cut the time and distance for combat reinforcement efforts directed toward either Northeast or Southeast Asian combat zones.[119]

ASEAN is committed to a doctrine of regional neutrality. Yet each ASEAN member, for its own reasons, fears a strategic-political vacuum in Southeast Asia due to a U.S. basing withdrawal.[120] U.S. strategic proximity has been represented as simultaneously fulfilling the *local* deterrence needs of Manila and its ASEAN partners by releasing them to concentrate on politico-economic stabilization and counter-insurgency operations under the protective umbrella of the U.S. Seventh Fleet. One of the major advantages of the U.S. deterrent, from the Filipino perspective, is that it provides the Philippines and ASEAN time to build up national resilience and to work toward eventual defense self-reliance.[121]

A second argument concerning the bilateral security implications of the U.S. basing presence relates to the Philippines' relative geopolitical weight within ASEAN. This line of reasoning contends that the U.S. basing presence and defense treaty has provided Manila with the only real leverage it has on territorial issues, such as the Sabah vis-a-vis Malaysia and its ownership of the Kalayaan Island Group in the Spratlys. Washington has been careful to disassociate itself from Southeast Asian disputes over sovereignty and could well decide not to move on the Philippines' behalf in a territorial conflict on the South China Sea unless international maritime corridors became choked as a result of such fighting.[122] Without the American security tie, however, Manila's claims to the Reed Bank as well as to the Nanshan and Thitu islands in the northeastern Spratlys would be weaker with respect to the stronger Vietnamese military detachments deployed in the central part of the Spratlys:

> As long as present circumstances obtain . . . the situation is defused. The present degree of stability will continue as long as there is a dominant U.S. military presence in the region. Without that presence, the situation would become problematic . . . It remains unclear whether mutual security arrangements . . . would entail a U.S. defense of Philippine interests if an external attack were launched against the islands claimed by Manila in the Spratlys. Whatever the case, it seems evident that the presence of major U.S. naval and air units act as a significant deterrent.[123]

The Anti-Bases Coalition (ABC) and other Filipino critics treat the bases as irrelevant or detrimental to Manila's own national security and local deterrence interests. They point to what they believe is an inherent incompatibility between U.S. global defense requirements and the Philippines immediate security problems which are almost exclusively domestic: guerrilla warfare; the polarization of national political opposition groups into radical and, at times, violent factions; and the politicalization of the Philippine armed forces. The Philippines' desperate economic plight cannot be considered as anything less than a national security crisis. How, the critics ask, do these problems correlate with the extended deterrence functions of keeping sea lanes open, deterring the Soviet nuclear threat, establishing a broader perimeter defense for the Northeast Asian corridors, or reinforcing Western access to the Indian Ocean and Persian Gulf?[124]

Moreover, the basing critics question the very applicability of U.S. extended deterrence strategy to the bases. They argue that Clark and Subic have become increasingly irrelevant in a general nuclear war, as well as unrelated to preventing anti-American regimes from taking power in future Asian conflicts, just as they were during the Vietnam War. Recent Soviet force reductions at Cam Ranh Bay, render incredible, they believe, the Pentagon's view that the Philippine bases continue to be a pivotal strategic asset. The credibility of commitment problem inherent to the American strategy, they conclude, is insurmountable. Washington should instead relinquish its high military profile in the Philippines in favor of extending more economic assistance to Manila and helping the Aquino government reclaim for agricultural or commercial development the land now covered by the bases.[125]

The issues of Dominant Player escalation control and intraalliance transferability have also assumed increased importance in the Philippines basing issue. Critics of general U.S. deterrence strategy maintain that the USSR has targeted nuclear weapons against the Philippines' bases only because of the American forces' presence. A new constitution, approved by national referendum in February 1987, contains a provision (Article II, Section 8) which, if strictly enforced, would prevent the United States from storing nuclear weapons in the Philippines and prohibit their transit through that country.[126] The Philippines Senate passed antinuclear legislation during June 1988 (by a margin of twenty to three) designed to tighten restrictions on nuclear visits by subjecting them to approval by a Philippine commission as well as totally precluding nuclear weapons storage. The Nuclear Free Philippines Coalition (NFPC) has asserted that at least 75 percent of U.S. naval vessels which call upon the Subic naval facility carry nuclear weapons and the October 1988 basing accord still allows port calls by U.S. nuclear-armed ships and landings by nuclear aircraft. NFPC spokesmen contend that such visits occur in the Philippines more than any other host country of U.S. basing operations and tend to negate the newly imposed ban on the storage of nuclear weapons in the Philippines.[127]

Western experts have little doubt that Soviet SS-20 missiles have been targeted at the Philippine bases.[128] Yet, as intimated in chapter I, this reality is far less attributable to Manila's alliance affiliation with the United States than to imperatives in the strategic doctrines of both Moscow and Washington. If the Soviet "defensive strategy," now emerging as predominant in the USSR's military thinking, anticipates the need for graduated response to American military action in the Asia-Pacific, such a strategy would be most credible if Moscow can ensure vital access to global choke points *before* an outbreak of regional or global war. In future Asian regional conflicts involving Moscow, the probable mission of Soviet forces in the South China Sea would be to interdict Asia-Pacific economic lifelines through which pass 50 percent of Japan's, South Korea's, and ASEAN's collective oil supplies and 80 percent of their strategic materials. The Malacca, Sunda, and Lombok Straits are thus essential to U.S. allies in both Northeast and Southeast Asia.[129]

If the United States disengaged from its positions in the Philippines in the absence of regional arms control understandings with the Soviets, Washington could risk ceding its traditional ability to interdict Soviet forces in the ASEAN region, notwithstanding the technological "offsets" available to American ships and aircraft operating from Hawaii, Guam, or the Micronesian islands. This reality still confronts American defense planners, despite their optimistic speculation that the U.S. Navy can deploy underway-replenishment ships that could supplant fixed basing operations sooner than expected.[130] While the Philippine press continues to sharply criticize the financial arrangements negotiated during the 1988 basing renewal agreement (Manila was scheduled to receive $481 million per year compared to the previous rate of $180 million, but the U.S. Congress has experienced difficulties in allocating the full amount), a growing number of U.S. force planners and legislative analysts have begun to accept the idea of alternative basing facilities in the eastern Pacific, even knowing that the concentration of facilities and services offered by Clark and Subic cannot be duplicated in any other single PACOM locale.

As tensions concerning the Philippine basing renegotiations intensify, U.S. force planners have begun weighing Asia-Pacific basing alternatives. In August 1989, Singapore offered to provide increased access to U.S. ships and aircraft as a means of preserving a U.S. offshore military presence in the ASEAN region.[131] In early July 1990, additional information on this proposed arrangement emerged, with the United States agreeing to station four F-16 jet fighters at the aging Peya Lebar air defense base six to seven months a year and to deploy 160–170 American military personnel at barracks formerly used by the since departed New Zealand ANZUK/FPDA battalion (see chapter 6). U.S. warships would also have access to Singapore's deep-water port for stores, repairs, and shore leave.[132] In mid-November, the U.S. and Singapore signed an arrangement for limited American access to Singapore's basing facilities.

While other ASEAN states initially voiced opposition to such an arrangement, they were gradually reassured that the Americans were not planning any major realignment of its forces from the Philippines to Singapore. U.S. military support personnel would be assigned only to assist in maintaining "regular rotations of small numbers of U.S. military aircraft," (the F-16s and American reconnissance planes) to commence by the end of 1990, and the U.S. Navy would slightly increase its current use of Singapore's maintenance and repair facilities.[133] Accordingly, Malaysian Prime Minister Mahathir expressed his confidence that such operations would not be converted into full-scale basing operations; other ASEAN leaders soon followed suit.[134]

After Aquino's narrow escape from the coup attempt in December 1989, the U.S. State and Defense Departments commissioned several studies to review alternative basing arrangements. The Defense Department has been moving quietly to gradually remove some support units from operations at Clark and Subic. In early November 1990, U.S. basing negotiators informed their Filipino counterparts that the United States would withdraw the 3d Tactical Fighter Wing from Clark Air Base, leaving no American jet fighters at that installation by the end of 1991. In deciding to withdraw these aircraft, U.S. force planners were clearly weighing other basing deployment or enhancement options. Anderson Air Force Base at Guam could be expanded to provide greater support for strategic airlift. The same objective could be accomplished by building additional maintenance facilities at Diego Garcia or at Yokota Air Base in Japan. Singapore's Paya Lebar complex, or the Changi international airport, could also be used to support strategic airlift operations from Guam to Diego Garcia, and Thailand's numerous airfields are frequently mentioned in basing relocation stud-ies. The Japanese island of Ishigaki-shima near Taiwan has also been considered as a refueling point for U.S. military airlift command units. The ASEAN countries would be solicited for greater U.S. port access but overall American naval traffic would probably be reduced in the region if Subic Bay were lost. An expanded base structure in Microne-sia (Palau), the Northern Marianas (Saipan or Tinian), and possibly in the East China Sea would offer further prospects for naval redeploy-ment.[135]

While a gradual dispersal and decline of U.S. forward defense assets may be acceptable to U.S. military planners in an era of shrinking defense budgets, the political effect on the ASEAN states—especially on perceptions of Washington's force projection in Southeast Asia's littorals—could be to reinforce those uncertainties which already make them Reluctant Players. A lack of American willingness to project power *within* Southeast Asia could prompt greater strategic risk-taking by the remnants of the Soviet Pacific fleet deployed in the region during future crisis. Or it could provoke accelerated efforts by the Chinese and the Indians to accelerate their own maritime and air projection capabilities toward the ASEAN region, thus affecting the ASEAN states' prospects for security through nonalignment.

Rising nationalism and anti-basing politics in the Philippines are viewed with concern by Manila's ASEAN affiliates. They are painfully aware that their own fiscal resources and military power could not begin to compensate for the permanent loss of the U.S. offshore mili-tary presence at Clark Air Base and Subic Bay. Without a concurrent commitment by the USSR to leave its Indochinese basing facilities and (far less imaginable) Chinese guarantees that the PRC would limit its future activities in the region, current levels of ASEAN maritime and air support would be unquestionably inadequate to defend peninsular Southeast Asia without some form of Western assistance. Even the winning of such Soviet and Chinese assurances would appear to be a poor exchange for the loss of the Seventh Fleet's physical assets, which currently are employed frequently in highly visible naval maneuvers and in other types of local deterrence support situations on the ASEAN states' behalf. Malaysian strategic analysts have recently noted that, without the U.S. military presence at Clark and Subic, ASEAN would lack any leverage to encourage the withdrawal of other big-power military installations in Indochina and the South China Sea.[136]

Considerations of interalliance transferability are also directly affected by the status of Philippine basing. Recent basing negotiations with Spain, Greece, and other European allies have modified U.S. attitudes about the necessity of retaining forward deployments. The development of longer-range aircraft, satellite technology and prepositioning greater force mobility have allowed the United States to reduce its reliance on overseas installations (if not to replace them completely).[137] A simultaneous rise in nationalism occurring in many host nations has intensified perceptions that an American military presence on one's soil is as much a strategic liability as an asset in the absence of iron-clad U.S. defense guarantees. All this has led to Washington increasingly accepting the need to make hard choices on overseas basing retention, weighing increasing costs versus continued benefits to U.S. power projection objectives.[138] The Philippines is increasingly regarded by the United States as a bellicose and difficult ally and one whose political stability may well lead to a preemptive U.S. withdrawal of its force presence to safer ground.

Building Subregional Maritime Deterrence Capabilities

THE ASEAN states' security focus and resources are being gradually redirected toward development of their respective maritime capabilities. There is considerable complimentarity between the strategic composition and identity of the ASEAN maritime states and those of their American and Japanese economic role models. All are essentially maritime powers with market-oriented economies, concerned with preserving the unimpeded flow of international goods and resources through key choke points and littorals in the Asia-Pacific region and beyond (see map 1). None has a history of, or a natural propensity toward, maintaining great land armies.[139] Malaysia and Indonesia, the ASEAN states which, along with Singapore itself, lie along the key Indo-Pacific archipelagoes maintain that the Straits of Malacca and Singapore are not international straits but territorial waters. While Jakarta and Kuala Lumpur "fully recognize" the right of international shipping to use the Malacca Straits for innocent passage they remain opposed, in principle, to their unrestricted use by naval surface shipping as a violation of territorial sovereignty (the so-called "archipelago concept").[140]

"Threat," as it applies to sea lane security, can be defined rather easily: any action that may impede the free flow of maritime commerce and trade or expose sovereign territory to infiltration or subjugation by seaborne aggression. Even more than most contemporary nation-states, the members of ASEAN are highly dependent upon ocean traffic for sustaining the import-export volume needed to fuel their economic development. Domestic upheavals or coup d'etats by radical political elements within an ASEAN country could spill over into conflicts on the Southeast Asian sea lanes in ways reminiscent of revolutionary Iran in the Persian Gulf and eventually force great power intervention to restore a status quo ante. Even less extreme disruptions can deprive the region of the equilibrium it needs: piracy, breakdowns in navigational safety, unresolved territorial claims, or outright interdiction of military/civilian shipping.[141] Maritime aggression is facilitated by long exposed coastlines or unsecured archipelagoes—conditions readily found in the ASEAN subregion.

As the 1980s ended, ASEAN's deterrence preoccupations assumed a broader conceptual framework encompassing the defense of territorial waters. All of the ASEAN states weighing how to meet new defense challenges which go beyond their traditional preoccupations with coastal defense of territorial waters, and air defense missions which do more than merely provide close-in support for counter-insurgency operations. Increasingly, fast-attack naval craft with the capability of deploying multiple weapons systems, and fixed-wing dual fighter/attack aircraft were appearing in the weapons inventories of peninsular Southeast Asia nations (Indonesia, Malaysia, Singapore and Brunei) to deter future threats originating from Indochina or from further abroad, and to strengthen regional air and sea defense networks' surveillance and mobility capabilities across Southeast Asia's straits and archipelagoes.[142]

In March 1989, ASEAN defense officials met to discuss implementing an ASEAN-wide joint patrolling of the South China Sea following the recent discovery of "substantial" oil and natural gas reserves there, and to discuss the ramifications of an American strategic retrenchment from the Philippines on their subregion's maritime balance of power.[143] The South China Sea represents a confluence of territorial and maritime interests for the entire Southeast Asian subregion and is the key to any successful long-term neutralization of ASEAN. Any premature departure of U.S. naval power and air support from the Philippines would render the sea lanes and restricted air space of those waters

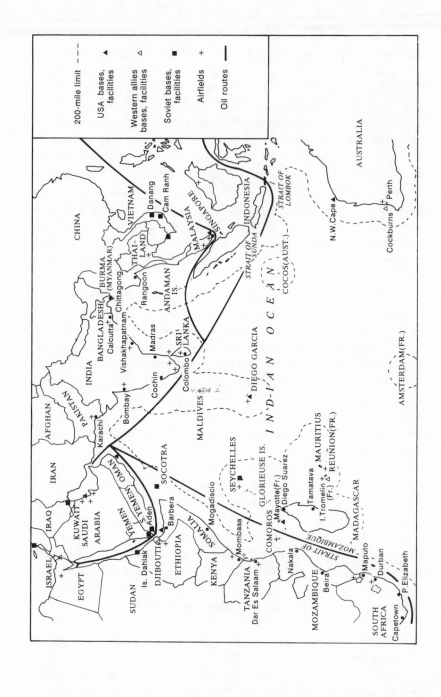

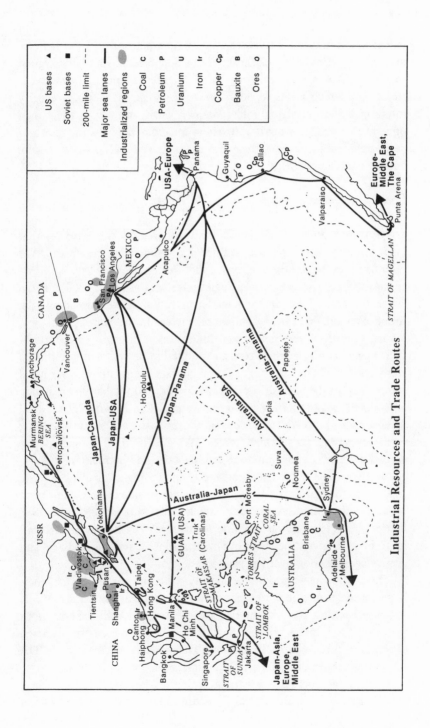

Industrial Resources and Trade Routes

vulnerable to increased levels of strategic competition and conflict (see map 2). A number of Southeast Asian defense analysts have argued that ZOPFAN is a natural component of a subregional maritime security policy which binds together the ASEAN states' national security interests by emphasizing their common desire to secure their own unrestricted access to territorial waters for indigenous commercial and naval traffic and to protect their various straits and archipelagoes against outside encroachment.[144]

Local Deterrence: Emerging ASEAN Approaches

BOTH INDONESIA and Malaysia have adhered to the position that intrusion into their territorial archipelagoes should be minimized. Yet both have, in fact, chosen to regard the Western powers as less threatening compared to the rise of Soviet naval power since 1968 and the lesser threat of Vietnamese naval penetration into areas along the Indonesian and Malaysian continental shelves in the South China Sea. Jakarta, however, has not looked kindly upon intermittent spurts of U.S. naval activity which, from an Indonesian perspective, are threatening strategic behavior that could precipitate future superpower naval competition in the Sunda, Lombok, Makassar, and Ombai-Wetar straits, all claimed as Indonesia's territorial waters. The *Replita III* national defense plan (1979–1984), for example, emphasized a "nation-building role" for Indonesia's armed forces over the need to project power abroad more commensurate to Indonesia's size and population.[145] Presently, Indonesia is far from capable of exercising control over naval and merchant traffic transiting its principal straits. It lacks sufficient small missile-armed escorts, fast attack craft, submarines, and ASW helicopters to enforce the "archipelago concept" with any real credibility, especially given the levels of Soviet, Chinese, and Indian naval and air power projection over the past decade.[146]

The Malays have adopted a slightly different approach than their large southern neighbor to great power presence in the straits. While strongly backing the idea of regional neutralization, Kuala Lumpur has elected to remain active in the loose pro-Western security affiliation afforded to them via the Five Power Defense Arrangement or FPDA (replacing the Anglo-Malayan Defense Agreement in November 1971, the FPDA members are Australia, Britain, Malaysia, New Zealand, and Singapore). Straits patrol is addressed through several FPDA functions: training in the form of low-level air and naval exercises and standard intelligence-sharing procedures.

Malaysia's increased concern over the developments in the South China Sea has also led to intensified efforts to strengthen its indigenous maritime defense capabilities, largely with British external assistance. Following a tense period of British-Malay political and economic strain during the early 1980s, at least partially sparked by Malaysian Prime Minister Mahathir's long-term suspicions of British political and economic motives, London has again reassumed its accustomed position as Malaysia's primary defense supplier. In September 1988, a sale worth between $US 2.5 billion and $US3 billion was completed by British firms for Malaysian receipt of the *Tornado* combat aircraft, two *Oberon* class submarines, medium-range artillery, naval helicopters, *Rapier* air defense missiles, ground-to-air missiles, and other items.[147]

This arms deal signified the culmination of Malaysia's PERISTA Plan adopted in 1979 following Vietnam's invasion of Kampuchea. PERISTA is designed to increase the Malaysian army's manpower base from 70,000 to 100,000 personnel, doubling the strength of the country's navy, and raising its overall military expenditures from under 5 percent GNP to almost 7 percent. Despite its high costs, PERISTA is justified in Kuala Lumpur as contributing to ASEAN's "regional resilience" by: (1) adding to the ASEAN region's conventional force capabilities in ways which preclude the need for an ongoing superpower military presence in the region; (2) countering Chinese, Indian, and possibly Japanese efforts to fill an offshore power vacuum arising from a U.S. naval and air pullout from the Philippines; and (3) protecting key maritime routes and sea-bed resources. Malaysia thus seeks to attain a regional security approach that balances a growing ability to deal with the internal threats and vulnerabilities presented by ethnic divisions and religious extremism and a willingness to maintain qualified security relations with external powers. The latter policy component is demonstrated by the increased bilateral defense ties cultivated with Indonesia and Singapore and the revived FPDA multilateral consultative arrangement. Malaysian defense planners have increasingly viewed regional security arrangements as most effective when they are tacit, unobtrusive, and directed toward local rather than global threats —a process which can be regarded as "growing bilaterialization within ostensibly multilateral (i.e., ASEAN, FPDA) frameworks."[148]

Unlike Jakarta or Kuala Lumpur who both consistently preach the virtues of defense self-reliance, Thailand has not yet demonstrated sufficient confidence in "regional resiliency" to relinquish its close security ties with the United States. Vietnamese troops sporadically attacked "sanctuaries" of Kampuchean resistance groups as well as refugee camps inside Thai boundaries, prompting the Thais to lobby for continued U.S. military assistance and political support in a Kampuchean settlement on Bangkok's terms. The annual *Cobra Gold* Thai-U.S. military exercises, involving upwards of ten thousand troops from Thailand and the United States has shifted its emphasis during the late 1980s from a traditional sea-land joint exercise to one emphasizing land-air coordination in the event of an all-out invasion of Thailand from the northeast (the scope of this exercise, however, is slated to be reduced from 1990 onward, due to budgetary considerations). By more directly addressing what Thai officials regard as their most likely external threat, Washington hopes that the U.S. credibility of commitment for Thailand's local deterrence needs will preserve its strategic influence in Bangkok and throughout ASEAN.[149] The stockpiling of U.S. munitions in Thailand represents another U.S. effort to correlate Thai/ASEAN local deterrence and U.S. global deterrence objectives. There is some concern in Bangkok, however, that prepositioned U.S. arms and equipment would be used for contingencies in the Indian Ocean or the Persian Gulf, despite CINCPAC's assurances that Bangkok "will be consulted in advance" on any use of the stockpile to support military activities outside of Thailand.[150]

As contrast to Bangkok's continued reliance on external defense ties, Indonesia and Singapore have moved toward supporting the gradual formation of a de facto triangular defense community with Malaysia while still underscoring their commitment to deterrence postures predominantly applicable at the national level. In March 1989, the Siabu air weapons testing and practice range, jointly financed by Singapore and Indonesia, opened for use by both countries' air forces. A memorandum of understanding was also signed the same month to allow Singaporean troops access to military training grounds anyplace in Indonesia in exchange for shared military technology with Jakarta. The most important long-term ramification of the triangular defense community, as S. Bilveer has noted, is that "the Island Republic of Singapore has for the first time gained recognition as a military partner in the Malay-dominated world of insular Southeast Asia."[151]

Singapore's "Total Defense" doctrine, however, may best represent

the ultimate ASEAN ideal in implementing regional deterrence politics. The essence of Total Defense is to use every psychological and
social asset found within the nation-state to achieve national unity and
enhance national military power. It is similar to *pancasila* in that it
legitimizes those security policies directed toward engendering a national will to resist internal strife and external aggression. It differs
from the Indonesian concept, however, in its emphasis on meeting any
number of hypothetical threat contingencies which could cut off Singapore from its lifeblood: access to regional and global sea lanes of
communication and, therefore, international trade. By maintaining
what is clearly the most formidable air force in ASEAN, by far the
most sophisticated defense industrial and technology infrastructure in
Southeast Asia, and the most thoroughly trained personnel, Singapore
can—and has—influenced what tangible regional deterrence strategies
are now in place in the ASEAN subregion.[152] While the analogy of
Singapore as "Southeast Asia's Israel" is occasionally raised, there is,
in reality, little similarity in the two states' security environments.
While Israel confronts its regional neighbors, Singapore is the paceset-
ter of ASEAN geostrategic thinking and regional security planning.

Dealing with the Outside Powers

MALAYSIA, INDONESIA, Singapore, and Brunei are increasingly concerned about their vulnerability to external penetration of their respective straits and archipelagoes. Even the Philippines, long preoccupied
by the domestic instability that fostered significant communist and
Muslim insurgency movements, remains concerned about its foothold
in the Spratlys, if challenged by superior Chinese or Vietnamese maritime power. The overall conceptual basis driving the ASEAN member-
states' threat assessments in the years immediately following the United
States' withdrawal from Vietnam has been described succinctly by
Donald Weatherbee: "While they could not militarily influence the
great power balance, they felt an acute need to redress the local balance
of regional military power in order to deter, and, if necessary, repel
any Vietnamese incursions across ASEAN strategic frontiers. These
frontiers include not only the Thai-Kampuchean border, but also the
potential conflict zone in the South China Sea where unresolved conflicts over territorial and maritime jurisdictions pit five of ASEAN's six
members against Vietnam and the PRC."[153] Vietnamese power, how-

ever, was drained throughout the 1980s by the military quagmire in Cambodia and by a sharply deteriorating economic situation at home.

Outside powers have likewise adjusted their threat perceptions regarding the ASEAN maritime environment. Washington is increasingly concerned with the ability of its naval surface units to transverse Southeast Asian straits and archipelagoes as rapidly as possible to reach crisis points in the Persian Gulf and throughout Southwest Asia. This "reactive deployment" aspect of American worldwide mobility requirements has become an integral part of modern U.S. extended deterrence strategy. It may clash with increased Indonesian and Malaysian determination to curb unrestricted passage of great power naval operations through waters they claim as their own.[154] Moscow has an interest in winning greater access to ASEAN port facilities for support of its commercial maritime fleet, thus establishing a *political* legitimacy for a Soviet presence in Southeast Asia. For the reasons already cited, both China and Japan must now be taken into greater account ASEAN maritime power calculations.

Most of the ASEAN states' local maritime strategies command the support of the U.S., but Singapore's regional security objectives are particularly compatible with those held by Washington. These include: maintenance of a regional and external power balance in the subregion, encouragement of a strong Japanese economic orientation toward ASEAN without a requisite military presence, and eventual stabilization of relations between the region's ideologically competitive forces.[155] Singapore's Prime Minister Lee Kuan Yew recently noted that the "key to the whole security and stability of the [ASEAN] region" was the ability of the United States and Japan to define a mutual relationship whereby the U.S. maintains its military presence in Asia while Japan refrains from further militarization while exercising equal partnership with Washington in regional economic affairs.[156] While no longer qualifying as an underdeveloped state, Singapore demanded—and received—stepped-up training exercises with U.S. Seventh Fleet elements in response to increased Soviet use of airfields in southern Vietnam to conduct surveillance missions in the Malacca Straits.[157] Also concerned about possible shifts in peninsular Southeast Asia's balance of power, Indonesia and Malaysia accepted increased levels of U.S. FMS assistance to strengthen their maritime patrol and force mobility capabilities.[158]

The FPDA powers have recently attempted to infuse more life into their multilateral defense umbrella through upgraded maritime defense exercises such as *Lima Bersatu* (conducted in September 1988). However, some fundamental qualifications in the arrangements' deterrence value are readily evident. New Zealand recently decided to withdraw its infantry training battalion from Singapore, underlining the reality that none of the old extra-regional AMDA states (Britain, Australia, and New Zealand) are formally obligated to assist Malaysia and Singapore in quelling internal disturbances or defending them against external threats. In Malaysia's case, such constraints were particularly galling when Britain and Australia responded reluctantly and slowly in providing arms to Kuala Lumpur against rioting in that capital which exploded in 1969, and when all the ANZUK states retained their neutrality in Malaysia's dispute with the Philippines over Sabah.[159]

FPDA channels *have* facilitated a gradual strengthening of Malay-Singaporeon military cooperation that might otherwise not be possible due to traditional ethnic and political tensions between those two countries. While they still do not conduct joint bilateral exercises, both are frequently involved in the FPDA's Exercise *Starfish*. Exchanges of officers for military education programs, Singapore allowing a Malaysian naval installation to remain operational on its territory and Malaysian contracting with Singapore firms for weapons repairs are other indicators that both sides are closer to acknowledging the de facto convergence of their defense environments and postures.[160] Brunei is seriously contemplating joining FPDA as well. It held its first extensive war exercise as a sovereign state (after gaining independence in 1983 and joining ASEAN the following year) with British and Gurkha soldiers still stationed in the country, and has held smaller maneuvers with Malaysia and Singapore.[161] A comprehensive summary of recent military exercises involving the ASEAN states is offered in table 4.

The Southeast Asia Nuclear Free Zone

DURING THE Reagan administration's second term of office (1985–1988), the clearest manifestation of ASEAN's Reluctant Player posture has been the effort to establish a Southeast Asian Nuclear Weapons Free Zone (SEANWFZ). Indonesian and, to a lesser extent, Malaysian support for such an arrangement has been especially worrisome to the U.S. Washington has already been diplomatically isolated by refusing

Table 4. Joint Exercises in the ASEAN Region in 1983–1988

Date	Participating Countries	Types of Exercise	Area	Participating Units	Exercise Name
4-26-83 to 5-11-83	Philippines United States	Maritime	Central Philippines region	15 vessels	Balicatan Tanjunt Flash '83
4-28-83 to 5-1-83	Singapore Malaysia Australia	Air	South China Sea		
5-20-83 to 5-29-83	Indonesia Malaysia Singapore United States	Maritime	Straits of Malacca		
6-3-83 to 6-12-83	5 British Commonwealth Nations	Maritime	South China Sea	18 vessels 16 aircraft	Starfish '83
6-6-83 to 6-27-83	United States Thailand	Maritime/ Air	Gulf of Siam		Cobra Gold '83
8-1-83 to 8-9-83	Malaysia Australia	Land/Air	State of Kedah Malaysia		
8-4-83 to 8-13-83	Malaysia Thailand	Maritime	South China Sea Gulf of Siam		Thaly Sec III
8-20-83 to 8-31-83	Malaysia Indonesia	Land	Kota Kinabalu Malaysia		Tatar Malindo Dua
8-22-83 to 8-31-83	Indonesia Thailand	Maritime	Java Sea Sunda Strait		Sea Garuda IV
11-25-83 to 12-25-83	United States	Air	Thailand		Commando West 6
6-7-84 to 6-11-84	Malaysia Singapore Australia	Air			ADEX '84
6-16-84 to 6-22-84	Thailand United States	Land	Thai-Kampuchean Border		
7-20-84	Thailand United States	Maritime/ Air	Gulf of Thailand		Cobra Gold '84
7-5-85 to 7-16-85	Thailand United States	Maritime/ Air	Gulf of Thailand		Cobra Gold '85

Date	Participating Countries	Types of Exercise	Area	Participating Units	Exercise Name
8-10-86 to 8-31-86	Thailand United States	Maritime/ Air	Rayong Province	33 vessels 100 aircraft incl. 8 F-16	Cobra Gold '86
8-20-86 to 8-30-86	Members of Five-Power Defense Arrangement*	Maritime	South China Sea	26 vessels	Starfish '86
Sept. 1986 (10 days)	Malaysia Indonesia	Land	Penang	Some three battalions	Kekar Malindo 9
2-23-87 to 2-28-87	Thailand United States	Maritime	Thai Eastern Seaboard	20 vessels 43 aircraft	Valiant Usher '87 T/Sea Siam-1
6-22-87 to 7-3-87	Members of Five-Power Defense Arrangement*	Maritime	South China Sea	Appx. 2,000 men from 5 member countries	Starfish '87
8-7-87 to 8-22-87	Thailand United States	Maritime/ Air	Vicinity of Khorat, northern Thailand	More than 5,000 men	Cobra Gold '87
8-10-87 to 8-15-87	Indonesia Malaysia	Land	Blitar, East Java	Indonesia: 2 motorized companies Malaysia: 1 motorized company	Kekar Malindo 10
Aug. 1987	United States Malaysia	Air search and rescue	Butterworth, Malaysia		
9-2-87 to 9-5-87	Australia Thailand	Land	Shoalwater Bay, Queensland, Australia	Thailand: 1 company, Australian Forces	
9-8-87 to 9-11-87	Members of Five-Power Defense Arrangement*	Air			
10-5-87 to 10-16-87	Thailand Singapore	Air	Thailand		Air-Thaising 5/87

Joint Exercises in the ASEAN Region in 1983–1988 (continued)

Date	Participating Countries	Types of Exercise	Area	Participating Units	Exercise Name
10-11-87 to 10-13-87	Members of Five-Power Defense Arrangement*	Land	Malaysia	313 men from 5 countries	Kris Sakti '87-1
3-7-88 to 3-8-88	Thailand Malaysia	Air	Thai-Malaysian Birder	25 aircraft of both RTAF and RMAF	Air Thamal VII
4-18-88 to 5-16-88	Thailand United States	Special Warfare	Don Muang, Thailand	RTAF U.S. Special force unit	Badge Team '88
9-6-88 to 9-9-88	Members of Five-Power Defense Arrangement*	Maritime/ Air and Air	Malaysia Singapore South China Sea	100 aircraft 20 vessels	Lima Bersatu

Source: Research Institute for Peace and Security, *Asian Security, 1984, 1985, 1986, 1987–88* (London: Brassey's Defense Publishers, 1984, 1985, 1986, and 1987).
    *The Five-Power Defense Arrangement consists of Britain, Australia, New Zealand, Malaysia, and Singapore.

to sign and ratify the South Pacific Nuclear Free Zone Treaty, concluded at Rarotonga on August 6, 1985 after the Soviets and Chinese both moved to support that accord. The Americans had similarly refused to continue alliance relations with New Zealand's Labour government because of Wellington's insistence that there be no nuclear dimension to the security relationship. New Zealand moved to bar the entry of nuclear-capable ships and aircraft into its waters or airspace without assurances that such units were nuclear weapons and nuclear-fuel free (see chapter 6).

It appeared increasingly likely by the late 1980s that the U.S. bilateral security tie with Manila could experience a similar fate, as nonnuclear stipulations found their way into the Philippines' new constitution and into the legislation recommended for incorporation into President Aquino's foreign policy. Mikhail Gorbachev's rapid succession of nuclear-free zone proposals for the Korean Peninsula, the South Pacific, and the Indian Ocean clearly put Washington on the defensive diplomatically and geopolitically vis-a-vis the USSR. Such proposals caused the United States to appear as a recalcitrant advocate of a

dangerous and unacceptable status quo, based upon an extended deterrence posture which appeared increasingly rigid, even to those in
Southeast Asia who have traditionally leaned toward the West on
security matters.

The December 1987 Manila Declaration announced that ASEAN
would intensify its efforts to create a nuclear-free zone for Southeast
Asia. The United States responded with the argument that, with the
United States' global and regional security responsibilities, "we believe
a nuclear weapons free zone in Southeast Asia would tend to undermine the policy of deterrence which has served us all well." [162] Several
months later (May 1988), J. Stapleton Roy, the U.S. Deputy Assistant
Secretary of State for East Asian and Pacific Affairs, confronted
SEANWFZ even more directly by arguing that nuclear disarmament
cannot be treated separately from related objectives such as preserving
stability and retaining the credibility of deterrence commitments against
aggression. Instead, Roy concluded, a nuclear-free zone in Southeast
Asia would discard "the remarkable achievement of postwar deterrence" in preventing the recurrence of global war and would undermine the very stability for which the ideal of ZOPFAN stood. [163]

The SEANWFZ idea was initially raised by Malaysian Foreign
Minister Tunku Ahmad Rithaudeen in September 1984. Encouraged
by the obvious momentum of negotiations then leading to a South
Pacific Nuclear Free Zone, Rithaudeen sought to link the SEANWFZ
concept to the more comprehensive premises of ZOPFAN. [164] The
Indonesians viewed nuclear-free-zone politics as a means through which
they could recapture the leadership in defining ASEAN's regional
strategic agenda, a role they had been forced to relinquish to the Thais
in 1980–1981. Jakarta also perceived a ready-made linkage between
SEANWFZ and Indonesia's long-held determination for imposing the
archipelago concept upon superpower naval activity in the Malacca and
Indonesian straits area. Indonesian policy planners reason that the
Chinese and Indian navies of the future will almost certainly have
nuclear strike capabilities and their presence in Southeast Asian waters
might be minimized if SEANWFZ can be instituted prior to that
time. [165] Cost-effective anti-nuclear diplomacy was a considerably more
appealing option to the Indonesians for regional order than a costly
naval arms buildup.

In June 1987, Indonesia and Malaysia introduced a proposal at the
Twenty-First ASEAN Ministerial Session to enact SEANWFZ. The

U.S. expressed its strong opposition on the grounds that any regional effort to enforce a nuclear-free zone would undercut the American maritime presence in the Philippines and throughout Southeast Asia as part of its global deterrence posture. ASEAN's general lack of consensus on issues related to its member-states' strategic relations with outside powers prevailed over any prospects that a groundswell of support would merge for the SEANWFZ. This continued to be the case during the annual ASEAN Foreign Ministerial Meeting held in Bangkok during early July 1988, when Indonesian Foreign Minister Ali Alatas appeared to be the only official in attendance interested in pushing for further discussion of SEANWFZ. Other ASEAN countries' concerns over the ramifications of a U.S. pullout from the Philippines bases, combined with Thailand's determination to press for upgraded defense relations with both the U.S. and China, worked to soften the effect of Indonesian SEANWFZ diplomacy.[166]

Aside from Washington's predictable support for the continuation of nuclear power-based extended deterrence in Southeast Asia, on the basis of its own global interests, a number of other objections to implementing a SEANWFZ have become evident since the notion was originally raised. Southeast Asia's location between Northeast Asia and the Indian Ocean is too critical within the context of overall superpower strategic competition for it to be disassociated from the global balance of power, notwithstanding the individual policy inclinations of the ASEAN states. The South Pacific and Latin America regions, both of which have established nuclear-free zones, are farther removed from the vortex of great power competition. Moreover, leading states within third world regions either with or aspiring to attain nuclear-free-zone status (Brazil and Argentina in Latin America or India in South Asia) have come to terms with the impracticality of the idea relative to their own widening national and international security interests. Experience has thus reversed, rather than sustained, the momentum of the nuclear-free-zone approach to international security and there is no real indication that the superpowers, France, China, India, or other future nuclear-capable states who are strategically active in the Asia-Pacific will accept the SEANWFZ proposal. Finally, verification and control measures for enforcement of a SEANWFZ appear insufficient at present to allow for the type of confidence-building needed to legitimize it at both the regional and international level of operations.[167]

In summing up, the credibility of U.S. formal security commitments to Bangkok and Manila and the continued interests of most ASEAN states in retaining the American strategic deterrent in their region, even with its nuclear trappings, appear sufficiently viable to outweigh the theoretical and emotional appeal of a SEANWFZ. How long and how well the U.S. will be able to sustain a Dominant Player posture in a regional climate becoming more susceptible to "nuclear-free" proposals by Washington's strategic competitors (the USSR and China), however, remains uncertain. If the Southeast Asians perceive the U.S. as incapable of generating constructive proposals for regional disarmament, the logic of nuclear extended deterrence may matter very little to those who yearn for heightened prospects of regional peace and development.

CONCLUSION

THE U.S. Dominant Player role has been difficult for the U.S. to sell to its Southeast Asian allies during the postwar period because of Washington's inability or unwillingness to define how its global deterrence objectives coincide with their evolving national and regional security interests. In each case discussed in this chapter, U.S. policy objectives were fashioned simply to block gains by other powers in the region as opposed to establishing a foundation of mutual strategic interests with regional actors. Early postwar U.S. extended deterrence strategy was intermittently provocative (the counterattack thesis) and ambiguous (the Laos neutrality crisis). Likewise, U.S. security planning incorporated in the Nixon Doctrine and the six-pillars policy had little relevance to ASEAN fundamental security concerns of national sovereignty and politico-economic development.

Even many of Southeast Asia's elites (particularly in Malaysia and Thailand), long the most obvious beneficiaries of Western deterrence commitments, grew wary of remaining too closely tied with all but the most fundamental aspects of the Dominant Player posture. Defense self-reliance became the watchword for the new and more indigenously inclined strategic outlooks held by the ASEAN states. American military intervention would be welcome only in the unlikely event of direct and unprovoked external aggression against one or more of them—a contingency acknowledged by the Nixon Doctrine as remote.

The downplaying of nuclear free zone politics by most of the ASEAN states, as well as their continued inability to defend their maritime approaches on a self-reliant basis, demonstrates that the Dominant Player posture has not become completely irrelevant to the security priorities of pro-Western ASEAN states. Yet, throughout much of the postwar era, and certainly during the past two decades since the Nixon Doctrine became the hallmark of U.S. strategy in the region, the Southeast Asians have become conditioned to expect inconsistency in U.S. policy behavior directed toward them. The Zone of Peace, Freedom, and Neutrality is the most prominent expression of ASEAN's determination to seek alternatives to the "moderate" or "partial" security linkages they have traditionally maintained with the U.S. and other Western powers. Continued U.S. strategic disengagement from peninsular Southeast Asia, an area which has always been less vital to Washington's global extended deterrence posture than the Northeast Asian theater of operations, is regarded by ASEAN as inevitable. To ASEAN policymakers, doubts over American strategic commitments to their region in recent times have focused less on credibility and more on their continued relevance to Southeast Asia's security environment.

The extent to which ASEAN members still choose to collaborate with the United States and other Western nations in a strategic context will largely depend upon how these outside powers can help them to alleviate their own vulnerabilities to both domestic and external threats and contribute to their attainment of independent regional security. The Southeast Asians' future security policies will clearly be multidimensional: avoidance of excessive or permanent strategic dependence on the Dominant Player posture and adoption of "Asianization" whenever possible. Deterring communist takeovers in the Philippines or elsewhere in the region will still be important. ASEAN threat assessments will, however, be less shaped by traditional ideological or geopolitical considerations than by how various internal and external political developments are perceived to effect regime survival and socioeconomic development. Under some circumstances, confidence-building or "reassurance" strategy directed by ASEAN toward the Indochinese states will be preferred to affiliation with any external deterrence or neutrality guarantors. Much will depend on how successful the Southeast Asians prove to be in reaching consensus about the sources of threat to their region and about the best means to overcome such threats on a self-reliant basis.

CHAPTER 6

The Southwest Pacific: "Strategic Denial" versus "The Pacifist Player" Posture

OVER THE years, the ANZUS alliance (composed of Australia, New Zealand, and the United States) seemed immune to the erosion of global containment politics which affected most other U.S. alliances and which, in many cases, ultimately led to their dissolution. ANZUS was created in September 1951 to be simple and small—relatively limited in its purposes and in the obligation which it imposed on the signatory members. Even without a formal military command structure, ANZUS worked smoothly through frequent and cordial consultations between the members on a wide array of issues concerning both global and South Pacific security. Critics of ANZUS have argued that the treaty offered Canberra, and especially Wellington, illusion rather than substance in terms of influence on U.S. foreign and defense policies. However, the unusual commonality of American and Antipodean cultural traditions, political systems, and international outlooks provided for a truly unique strategic relationship under which the emerging island-states of the South Pacific enjoyed unparalleled regional stability for over three decades.[1]

Australia and New Zealand valued ANZUS as the essential deterrent of regional threats to their security. New Zealand's foreign policy was traditionally predicated upon the assumption that "as a small, exclusive, affluent, isolated country, it needed to secure protection in a barbarous world, even when the dangers to be feared cannot be precisely defined."[2] Throughout the first half of the twentieth century, Britain had served this role. By joining the United States and Australia in forming ANZUS, Wellington could be assured that the Americans

would include New Zealand in the structuring of their strategic deterrence and containment postures directed against communist expansionism.

The concept of "strategic denial," utilizing the nuclear umbrella of
U.S. extended deterrence, thus became synonymous with ANZUS.
This alliance substituted for New Zealand's—and to a lesser degree—
Australia's legacy of voluntary strategic dependence on Britain and,
later on, the United States. The strategic denial policies of ANZUS
included a commitment to maintain "friendly Western access to the
[South Pacific] region, and the denial of access to countries regarded as
potentially hostile."[3]

During the Cold War years, evidence of any serious Soviet or Chinese
efforts to project strategic power in the South Pacific or Southwest
Pacific was singularly lacking. As a result, in New Zealand in particular, policymakers began to reflect a growing popular belief that Antipodean involvement in a worldwide nuclear conflict was of greater
concern than the need for regional extended deterrence. Concurrently,
the emerging Pacific island-states, who were presumed to be included
in the ANZUS protective net, sensed that the greatest threat to their
new-found sovereignty was their continued economic and strategic
dependence on traditional external benefactors and the potential exploitation by extraregional commerical interests of what natural resources these island states controlled, not direct takeover by a communist power.

A growing number of Antipodean and South Pacific policymaking
elites and security analysts thus began searching for approaches more
relevant to their own long-term security aspirations than strategic denial or extended deterrence, while not completely disassociating their
own strategic objectives from those entertained by their Western benefactors. The election of New Zealand's Labour government in July
1984 proved to be the catalyst not only for shaping an alternative South
Pacific security agenda but for what was to become one of the most
serious challenges to U.S. extended deterrence strategy by a Western
ally during the entire postwar timeframe.

This chapter will review the evolution of ANZUS as the initial
policy instrument for the U.S. Dominant Player's strategic denial
policy in the Southwest Pacific. It will then document the process by
which ANZUS was eroded by the development of apparently irresolu-
able differences as New Zealand adopted a Pacifist Player posture

(Australia's Transitional Player role in that process is described in chapter 2). The effects of the development and dissolution of ANZUS in the South Pacific island-states are also discussed. In the chapter's conclusion, the implications of the ANZUS dispute with respect to U.S. strategic agendas in other theaters are reviewed.

EVOLUTION OF STRATEGIC DENIAL

AMERICAN STRATEGIC thinking about the South Pacific was largely shaped by the difficulty U.S. forces experienced in pushing back Japanese armies from positions in the Central Pacific seized during the early stages of the Second World War. The Pacific islands constituted the heart of the Joint Chief's of Staff proposed "blue zone" (see chapter 2) in which U.S. military planners projected that a postwar basing system could be established to shield the U.S. homeland and the Western Hemisphere from direct attack. As noted by one U.S. Army general serving on the U.S. Joint Chiefs of Staff Joint Staff Planners group: "our [the U.S.] aims are to exclude from the former Japanese islands in the Pacific any potential enemy and, secondly, to assume United States control over those portions of the area which are vital to our own security and necessary to our strategic base system."[4]

Reconciling Globalism and Regionalism

NEW ZEALAND, still intent on preserving its traditional defense ties with London to the greatest extent possible, joined with Australia in the January 1944 Canberra Agreement, serving notice to Washington that the Antipodes would resist any U.S. drive to forge strategic hegemony in the South Pacific apart from the British Commonwealth. The Agreement transformed the concept of "ANZAC" as a strictly military alliance (the "Australia New Zealand Army Corps") to an instrument of diplomatic unity on regional security issues. Articles Thirteen, Sixteen, Twenty-Six, and Twenty-Seven of the agreement collectively declared an ANZAC "zone of regional defense" "stretching through the arc of islands north and northwest of Australia, to Western Samoa and the Cook Islands.[5] These Articles also stated that wartime American basing operations could not be the basis for "territorial claims or right of sovereignty or control after the conclusion of hostilities" unless resulting from an agreement in which the ANZAC powers were parties "or in the terms of which they have both concurred."[6]

The Canberra Agreement appeared to place New Zealand squarely behind Australia's wartime Labor government in declaring an "ANZAC Monroe Doctrine" as the foundation for strategic denial in the postwar South Pacific.[7] The agreement also intensified U.S. suspicions about the British Commonwealth's future role in the Pacific. The Commonwealth in general was regarded in Washington as a potential instrument which London could use to extract diplomatic leverage as a multiple-vote bloc in future international conferences.

In the case of New Zealand, Washington's fears were at least partially justified. New Zealand officials *were* less certain than their Australian counterparts about the need for an American security presence in the South Pacific and even more apprehensive about Washington's inclinations to exclude the British from a postwar South Pacific defense role.[8] Yet Wellington also realized that the best hope for avoiding a repeat of the Pacific conflict from which it had emerged intact only after observing the British Empire's regional security network wither before the Japanese onslaught of 1941–1942 was continued reliance on American military power. In May 1944, the New Zealand Department of External Affairs submitted a paper to the British Commonwealth Prime Minister's Conference which argued that New Zealand's wartime weakness in defending a critical "inner zone" of Pacific islands, including Norfolk Island, New Caledonia, Fiji, Samoa, New Hebrides (now Vanuatu), and the Cook Islands made an American buffer zone extending across the Marshall, Caroline, and Mariana island groups in the central Pacific absolutely mandatory. In October, the New Zealand Chiefs of Staff released a second study that all but buried the notion of ANZAC predominance in South Pacific regional security in deference to the growing need for ANZAC participation in a global security accord headed up by the United States.[9]

The wartime posturing between the United States and the Antipodes over how strategic denial would be implemented in the South Pacific culminated with the Manus Island dispute between Washington and Canberra in 1945–1946. The locale in question was a coral island located in the Admiralty Islands group (now part of Papua New Guinea) where a substantial American basing complex had been built during the war. Australia attempted to link the continued American use of

Manus to understandings that Australia could use other American bases in the South Pacific.[10]

By mid-1946, however, two factors had surfaced in U.S. postwar strategic planning which rendered retention of Manus less important to U.S. strategy. First, the United States had by that time redesignated a preferred forward line of operations for its "strategic frontier" from the Central Pacific to areas more proximate to Northeast Asia and to the Soviet homeland. The Joint Chiefs of Staff had concluded that bases closer to Japan were needed.[11] By the end of 1945, the JCS recommendation had reached President Truman's desk and was resisted only by the Department of the Navy. "In fact," as later recounted by one historian assessing the Manus episode, "the Admiralty islands were too far south to be of high priority value in United States defense thinking . . . . If pressed hard, the United States could afford to dispense with the base."[12] The second reason for the declining American interest in Manus thus flowed logically from the first: as the President and later the U.S. Congress mandated increasingly sharp cuts in the U.S. defense budget, the U.S. Navy was compelled to concentrate its missions and capabilities north of the equator.[13]

Severing the British Connection

WHILE AMERICAN security planners' changing military thought had at least temporarily undercut the importance of ANZAC's zone of regional defense by the late 1940s, Washington's need to finalize a regional peace treaty with the Japanese restored the South Pacific to a more prominent status at the outset of the new decade. The United States was initially reluctant to enter into any strategic commitments with the Antipodes, as outside its revised strategic frontier or perimeter of defense focusing on Northeast Asia. The Truman Administration nevertheless acquiesced to ANZUS following the outbreak of the Korean War, in view of the increasing need for Antipodean support for the idea that Japan needed to play at least a limited defense role in U.S. global containment strategy.[14]

Britain's role in the Pacific had still been left unresolved by 1951, however. Its inclusion in a Pacific security arrangement as a quid pro quo for Antipodean consent to the proposed Japanese treaty proved to be the most delicate issue in the founding of ANZUS. From Washington's perspective, Britain's inclusion in ANZUS would have obfuscated an otherwise straightforward American extended deterrence commitment to Canberra and Wellington as the other prospective signatories.

U.S. negotiators thus launched a campaign to dissuade Australia, and especially New Zealand, from supporting a British ANZUS membership. The United Kingdom's inclusion, they argued, would involve the other signatories more directly with British responsibilities for the defense of Malaya and Hong Kong even while the Australians and New Zealanders, along with the Americans, dissented from London's recognition of the PRC. More importantly, American diplomats noted, commitment to defend British interests would be undertaken at a time when British capabilities for safeguarding residual Pacific security commitments were declining rapidly. It would also open the way for other Western or pro-Western states such as France, the Netherlands, or the Philippines to demand entry into ANZUS, a development which would inevitably dilute the American commitment to the South Pacific as the major purpose of the proposed treaty.[15]

A British ANZUS affiliation, moreover, would have deepened New Zealand's already intense concern over how it could meet its obligations to the United States in any Pacific security treaty while still designating literally all of its ground forces to a British Commonwealth defense of the Middle East in future global contingencies. A dispatch from the U.S. Embassy in Wellington noted that New Zealand leaders hoped that the United States "would construe its [New Zealand's] contribution to global defense in the Middle Eastern sector as fulfilling obligations under the [ANZUS] Security Treaty."[16] Most importantly, from Canberra and Wellington's perspectives, any British ANZUS component would divert U.S. energies from what both Australia and New Zealand viewed as the most critical security functions to be served by ANZUS: American supervision of a Japanese postwar settlement designed to preclude Tokyo from remilitarizing, and buffering the Antipodes from unforeseen military threats posited by Asian nationalists or communists. This last consideration ultimately proved decisive in convincing Australia and New Zealand to break tradition and ally with a non-Commonwealth power during peacetime for the first time in their history. While Britain retained control over Fiji, the Solomon Islands, and a small number of other dependencies for another twenty to thirty years, it was no longer an integral player in implementing strategic denial in the South Pacific.

ANZUS and Strategic Denial

THE WINNING of U.S. deterrence guarantees via ANZUS secured over a quarter century of stability in the South Pacific. Apart from very brief and highly opportunistic probing by the USSR in Tonga during April 1976, no external power was either willing or capable of seriously contesting American strategic hegemony underwriting the area's security environment.[17]

A critical issue relating to the ANZUS deterrent arose over the geographic scope of the alliance. Article IV of the treaty identifies the "Pacific Area" as the purview of concern. However, a number of analysts have since contended that such a broad designation was used to assure to all three of its signatories maximum flexibility—they could invoke it when they believed their national security was jeopardized or could claim it was inapplicable where an ANZUS ally might request military support.[18] In the years following the signing of the treaty, questions about the relationship between ANZUS and SEATO commitments (all three ANZUS members also became SEATO affiliates in 1954); the security of Indochina; possible Antipodean assistance in the defense of Taiwan (1955) and South Vietnam (1964); and American assistance in the defense of West New Guinea (1958), of Borneo (1964), and the Indian Ocean (1979) all arose. In every case, the treaty was interpreted along restricted lines, with expanded military cooperation between the signatories occurring through informal, and mostly bilateral, channels.[19]

Another fundamental problem was to what extent Washington would acknowledge a "fit" between the regionally-based threats perceived by Australia and New Zealand with the maintenance of its own global deterrence through preserving strategic denial in the region. The weakness of ANZUS strategy in the South Pacific thus lay in the potential incongruity of its member-states' interests there.

By way of illustration, Washington certainly valued Guam and the Marshall Islands as important Pacific components in its global basing network. The berthing of *Polaris* nuclear strike submarines in Guam and the testing of U.S. strategic missile systems at Kwajalein, however, represented part of an American global deterrence strategy which appeared fairly remote to Australians concerned about possible Indonesian irredentist behavior or New Zealanders concerned over the future political stability of New Caledonia. Because of its greater distance from the Asian mainland, moreover, Wellington could not be expected to have as much at stake in Indochinese conflicts, the survival of an independent Malaysia, or the patterns of naval competition in the Indian Ocean as did Australia. However, both ANZUS allies staunchly supported U.S. and British defense efforts in these locales in the belief that, by pursuing "forward defense" postures, they would earn greater consideration in Western defense councils than would otherwise be the case.

ANZUS Alternatives

APART FROM their membership in the South Pacific Commission, formed in 1947 as a consultative forum for those administering trusteeships in the region (the United States, Britain, France, and the Netherlands were also founding members), little precedent for joint Australian-New Zealand security planning for the South Pacific existed prior to Wellington's embarking on its own course of strategic revisionism in 1984. Antipodean defense analysts have particularly cited the inadequacy of the ANZAC "division of labor" during the 1960s. They have presented arguments which ranged from New Zealand retreating from Asia to concentrate on an exclusively South Pacific defense missions to both Australia and New Zealand placing "mutually supporting forward bases" along the previously cited ANZAC "zone of regional defense" to safeguard against future indigenous South Pacific threats originating from social unrest or ideological affinity with procommunist forces.[20] By 1968, delegates to the New Zealand Labour Party annual conference had begun to voice support for their country's renunciation of Commonwealth defense commitments in Southeast Asia and its more active concern for defining a South Pacific security agenda independent from the ANZUS purview.[21]

A more substantial effort to implement an alternative security approach to the Dominant Player posture in this region was to unfold only four years later. From 1972 to 1975, the New Zealand Labour Government moved gradually toward the promotion of a South Pacific Nuclear-Free Zone. Initially led by Prime Minister Norman Kirk, and following his untimely death in office, by Wallace Rowling, the New Zealand Labour Party urged its Australian counterpart to adopt a more independent line concerning Washington's deterrence postures in the Asia-Pacific theater. As Henry Albinski has since recounted, Australian Labor, led by Prime Minister Gough Whitlam, "broadly subscribed to Washington's objection that such an arrangement would deny passage and porting/landing rights to American nuclear armed-forces, which themselves were, for the time being, serving a useful deterrent nuclear-balance function."[22]

Wellington attempted to avoid an alliance showdown with the United States by not directly linking its NFZ politics to the country's ANZUS ties but instead advancing it through the United Nations General Assembly. The Americans, in turn, reciprocated by electing not to ask for naval port visitation rights during New Zealand Labour's tenure in office, thus declining to test New Zealand's traditional observance of Washington's policy of "neither confirm nor deny" (NCND) policy concerning the presence of nuclear armaments on its military ships and aircraft. Washington instead negotiated what it believed was an "understanding" with Rowling that if he were to be reelected nuclear ship visits would indeed be allowed.[23]

With minimal pressure from the United States over NCND, the New Zealand Labour government attempted to win greater international support within the UN for some type of South Pacific NFZ. It was, however, unsuccessful on both the international and domestic fronts, as its proposal failed to win the cosponsorship of Australia (although Papua New Guinea and Fiji did cosponsor the measure). This matter was referred to committee for further study where it met an inconspicuous death. At the same time, widespread labor union resistance and Labour Party rank-and-file opposition to the entry of U.S. nuclear-capable ships indicated that the Kirk-Rowling government's political strategy of separating ANZUS from Wellington's South Pacific nuclear-free zone initiative was too ambiguous for the electorate to accept.[24] It was left to a subsequent Labour government returned to office in the middle of the following decade to project nuclear-free politics into the limelight of both the regional and international arenas and to provide the "Pacifist Player" posture as the first real postwar challenge to U.S. extended deterrence strategy in the South Pacific region.

THE PACIFIST PLAYER EMERGES

IN MID-JULY 1984, the New Zealand Labour Party was elected to power and moved immediately to establish a nuclear-free zone (NFZ) in that country. By doing so, it rejected the extended nuclear deterrence doctrine of the United States to which all of the ANZUS Treaty signatories had subscribed since the signing of the accord in September 1951. The subsequent ANZUS dispute constituted a major challenge to Washington's maintenance of the South Pacific leg of its global extended deterrence network and to the basic intellectual premises underscoring that network. In conjunction with the adoption of the Treaty of Rarotonga, adopted by the South Pacific Forum in August 1985 (also known as the South Pacific Nuclear-Free Zone Treaty or SPNFZT), the thrust of Southwest Pacific geopolitics throughout the late 1980s was the development of an alternative "Pacifist Player" approach to regional security.

The Pacifist Player approach envisions meaningful security cooperation between a nuclear and nonnuclear state without the non-nuclear country accepting or affiliating itself with its nuclear ally's central strategic doctrines and forces. It recognizes the obligation to honor alliance commitments through mutual deployment and maintenance of adequate conventional forces as legitimate self-defense. To maintain those commitments through participation in an integrated nuclear deterrence posture, however, is regarded as morally deficient or strategically unnecessary. New Zealand Labour Prime Minister David Lange, for example, believed that NFZ politics emanated from truly worthy ideals and morality which reflected the nature and history of New Zealand's people since their nation's founding. In his opening remarks delivered in a debate on the "moral defensiveness" of nuclear weapons held at Oxford on March 1, 1985, Lange compared U.S. efforts to compel New Zealand to accept nuclear deterrence strategy as little different from totalitarianism within the Soviet bloc. While expressing an understanding of European adherence to deterrence strategy due to its geography and history, the Prime Minister concluded "There is no moral case for nuclear weapons . . . I would hold that their character is such that they have brought us to the greatest of all perversions, the belief that this evil is necessary when in fact it is not." [25]

A second dimension of the Pacifist Player argument is less concerned with the moral values of nuclear deterrence than with its relevance to its intended beneficiaries' strategic interests and requirements. U.S. extended deterrence guarantees involving a nuclear component are neither wanted nor required by New Zealand to obtain what it views as an acceptable level of national security. In a preelection speech, Lange asserted that New Zealand was not "interlocked" with the United States' front line of defense and, consequently, there was no strategic reason for U.S. nuclear capable ships or aircraft to be deployed in New Zealand.[26]

Washington asserted that exceptions to its "neither confirm nor deny" (NCND) policy regarding the nuclear weapons content of its ships and aircraft would inevitably lead to an ANZUS deterrence posture applicable *exclusively* at the conventional deterrence level. The United States felt it was essential to sustain nuclear and conventional deterrence in both the contemporary international order and the Southwest Pacific. This American outlook has been described by its critics as misleading, erroneously assuming that the credibility of U.S. global deterrence strategy depended on a "seamless web" of compliant allies which "required discipline; the next worst thing to the Soviet threat was failure to demonstrate the will to resist it . . . Allied support for nuclear deterrence became something of a loyalty test, and a determinant of U.S. policy during the ANZUS crisis."[27]

Following Labour's election, however, assessments of possible threats to New Zealand's national security were conducted by the Foreign and Defense Ministries and by a Defense Committee of Inquiry appointed by Lange but independent from the government.[28] Advocates of the antinuclear posture argued to the Committee that no credible military threat to New Zealand currently existed, apart from Wellington's possible involvement in a global war as a member of the Western alliance system. They postulated that, at that time, only the Soviet Union, the United States, and Australia deployed the type of military capabilities appropriate for invading New Zealand and that none of those three powers entertained any motive for doing so. Indeed, the 1986 New Zealand Ministry of Defense Report advocated closer defense cooperation with Australia with "an intention to shape forces for assisting in the Pacific rather than as appendages to wars in distant lands."[29]

The Pacifist Player posture, as defined by New Zealand, emphasizes the danger of U.S. extended deterrence strategy involving Washington's allies in an inadvertent nuclear war. It refutes the notion that allies who develop a "nuclear allergy" or revulsion to the idea of employing nuclear weapons to ensure their security will adversely effect the West's global deterrence posture or encourage Soviet expansionism. Antipodean antinuclear proponents instead point to the 1980s as a time when Soviet expansionism was reversed—not by nuclear deterrence, but by the USSR's own internal political and economic weakness. Andrew Mack has summarized the essence of this argument:

> Deterrence is anything but fragile; indeed, it is extraordinarily robust. It is robust because in the nuclear age there is no conceivable interest which could make aggression waged by either superpower against the other (or the other's allies) a rational act of policy. Moreover, deterrence doctrines which emphasize highly offensive warfighting strategies (like Soviet *blitzkrieg* strategy in Europe or the United States Maritime Strategy) may increase the risks of inadvertent war.[30]

Consequently, Mack and others conclude, nuclear-free zones in New Zealand or throughout the South Pacific cannot possibly relate to—much less erode—American global deterrence postures.

The New Zealand antinuclear movement further argued the irrelevance of nuclear deterrence to their own country's national security requirements to the international level by advancing a "common security" thesis as a variant of the Pacifist Player posture. Common security was introduced by the Palme Report to the Second UN Special Session on Disarmament in 1982. The concept is based on the premise that states can no longer assume that their own security is best attained at each others' expense but can only be attained via cooperative undertakings. Proponents of the thesis also believe the costs of nuclear miscalculation are becoming too great to continue pursuing international security through nuclear deterrence.[31] Accordingly, common security is not merely an alternative security "doctrine" to nuclear deterrence but rather a purported *acknowledgment* of the inability of nuclear weapons to guarantee the attainment of national defense objectives when potential adversaries can assure each others' nuclear destruction.

New Zealand's Labour government has endorsed the common security concept as the basis for regional disarmament measures comprising the first steps in a comprehensive, global, process of nuclear disarmament. While not regarded as a panacea by itself to the nuclear arms race, common security is viewed by the New Zealand peace movement as a constructive foundation for conceptualizing nuclear-free zones, confidence-building measures, and conflict avoidance.[32] New Zealand's common security advocates feel that the Soviets could not hope to prevail in military operations initiated at distant points in Southeast Asia or in the Southwest Pacific against superior U.S./allied maritime power. Reliance on conventional deterrence assets, they argue, makes sense in an age of superpower nuclear parity because Washington is no longer able to establish and maintain escalation control.

The United States has countered New Zealand's "moral" argument as well as its "qualified commitment thesis" by underscoring the importance of reliable alliance values and an evaluation of comparative risk. Lange argued that New Zealand should have a right to exclude American nuclear-armed or nuclear-capable vessels and aircraft from entering its territory as an inherent right "within the pluralistic character of the Western Alliance." U.S. State Department officials responded that "There is no way if you're in an alliance with a nuclear power that you're going to cleanse yourself by banning nuclear ships." [33] In adopting this position, Washington dissented from the Pacifist Player's assertion that if a security treaty fails to explicitly stipulate obligation for nuclear entry, no such obligations exist. Alliance obligations such as ANZUS, the Americans contended, are assumed in the context of a collective good inherent to any viable security relationship. The U.S. position was: "If New Zealand incurred some punitive risks because of its links to a nuclear power, then as the foremost Western power the United States has surely shouldered far more onerous obligations and has run higher risks . . . A functioning ANZUS alliance, mitigated, rather than raised, the risk of global conflict and therefore was in New Zealand's own interest to nurture and sustain." [34]

Opponents to the "nuclear immorality" argument writing in New Zealand and Australia have attacked the Labour government's position on tactical grounds, asserting that considerations related more to factors of domestic political expediency than to morality have shaped New Zealand's nuclear policy. They point, for example, to recent statements attributed to New Zealand Labour government officials praising the U.S. decision to end the Second World War by the use of nuclear weapons against Japan and to continued U.S. military use of the Harewood airfield in Christchurch for Antarctic operations. They also note New Zealand's willingness for its military personnel to exercise with U.S. forces under conditions of NCND beyond New Zealand's territorial jurisdiction, and to Lange's Oxford Union debate where, after stating an uncompromising opposition to both the end and means of nuclear use, he declined to sanction unilateral nuclear disarmament.[35]

Others have criticized the New Zealand government for violating the fundamental axioms of trust and good faith which sustain an alliance. Following his retirement as New Zealand's Chief of Defense Staff in 1987, Air Marshall Sir Ewan Jamieson aired his concerns about his country's policy course. By insisting on an American refutation of NCND, the Air Marshall concluded, Lange paid his domestic political dues, scrapping a tacit compact of good faith "between trusted and trusting friends," and giving up New Zealand's active participation in ANZUS. Consequently, he concluded, New Zealand's isolation was "brought about by an obsessively narrow concentration on the nuclear issue as the primary driving force in shaping our security and foreign relations. What makes this even more foolish, when one considers what harm we have done to our wider relationships, is the fact that there has never been any substance to New Zealand's connection with nuclear weapons and the strategy controlling their improbable use."[36]

If regional force balances are objectively weighed, a global nuclear deterrence posture is not as strategically "inapplicable" to New Zealand's national security as the Labour government has implied. From Cam Ranh Bay, unrefuelled *Backfire* strike bombers could reach as far as the northern tip of New Zealand; such aircraft refueled can hit most New Zealand targets.[37] Combined U.S. and New Zealand intelligence cooperation had become increasingly critical for monitoring the South Pacific oceanic environment as both Soviet maritime projection and the political restiveness of indigenous Pacific populations intensified throughout the early 1980s. From Washington's viewpoint, such cooperation would be hindered by de facto "carte blanche" inventory of U.S. deterrence capabilities every time American units went to sea.[38] Wellington's 200–mile Exclusive Economic Zone and its ongoing security commitments to the Campbell, Chatham, Cooks, and Kermadec island groups and other dependencies encompass a 1.2 million square mile area of important local deterrence responsibility for New Zealand naval and air units which cannot possibly be managed without significant outside assistance.[39] From the American perspective, New Zealand's antinuclear stance thus significantly erodes the West's capability to sustain its traditional strategic denial posture for the South Pacific.

The development by New Zealand of its Pacifist Player posture, and the resulting ANZUS dispute, provides a compelling example of intraalliance misperception and disillusionment. Apart from NATO, ANZUS was considered to be the most stable of Washington's postwar extended deterrence arrangements. By contrast, the U.S. security treaties with Japan, South Korea, and the Philippines all had to overcome intrinsic differences in history, political values, and geographic circumstance between their signatories, but have survived. Unquestionably the most important concern for U.S. defense planners regarding the ANZUS crisis is its potential effect on the framework of global extended deterrence and on Washington's relations with other European and Asian allies.[40] Indeed, the antinuclear stance adopted by New Zealand and other South Pacific Forum members has prompted other U.S. allies in the Asia-Pacific theater to weigh the continued relevance of the Dominant Player approach, in light of both alternative approaches to regional conflict avoidance and growing regional sentiments for arms control and disarmament.

THE ANZUS DISPUTE: 1984–1986

THE BREAKDOWN of negotiations between the United States and New Zealand over the coexistence of antinuclear politics and security obligations under ANZUS provides an instructive case study of how fragile the Dominant Player posture can become when allied threat assessments and strategic thinking change over time. Some of the key terms and concepts pertinent to the ANZUS crisis and this case study are briefly summarized in Table 5. As long-term defense collaborators, the U.S. and New Zealand entertained comfortable illusions about each other's willingness and ability to make fundamental concessions with regard to their national security agendas. In the early 1980s, when such proved not to be the case, the trust and good will between the two affiliates throughout the postwar era, gradually deteriorated into acrimony and feelings of betrayal.

Testing the NCND Criterion

"NEITHER CONFIRM nor deny" has been an operational component of U.S. extended deterrence strategy since 1958. It is predicated on the assumption that the release of information on the location of U.S. nuclear weapons can seriously compromise U.S. national security ob-

TABLE 5. Key ANZUS Dispute Terms/Acronyms

ANZAC: Originally applying to the Australian-New Zealand Army Corps which fought during World War II, the term has since taken on the connotation of any form of joint Australian-New Zealand defense cooperation apart from U.S. involvement.

ANZUS: The Australian-New Zealand-United States Tripartite Security Treaty signed in September 1951 at San Francisco.

ASROC: Antisubmarine Rocket. It was believed that the *USS Buchanan* was capable of carrying and concealing this nuclear weapons system, and the *Buchanan* was rejected by the New Zealand Labour government for a port visit during early 1985.

"Chinese Formula"/"Trust Me"/Trust Us" Formula: "Case-by-case" approach to allowing the entry of U.S. military vessels and aircraft based on the host nation's evaluation of those units' nuclear capabilities. The host nation's leadership does not ask the United States to provide information about the nuclear or nonnuclear capability of the entering unit but makes its own sovereign judgment about such a capability. Entry is allowed if national means of verification determines the vessel is not carrying nuclear explosives, weapons, or delivery systems and is not nuclear-powered. The formula allows the United States to avoid directly violating its "neither confirm nor deny" policy (see below) but relinquishes U.S. sovereign authority over the content of its ships and aircraft to the host nation during the visit. The People's Republic of China insisted on these conditions prior to the first visit of U.S. naval units since the 1949 communist takeover of that country. The U.S., however, rejected its application in the ANZUS case because it could not, it argued, conduct normal alliance operations under the restriction of "trusting" New Zealand's Prime Minister and/or his advisors to make an arbitrary determinations of U.S. ships' nuclear capabilities without adequate intelligence, and could not risk media disclosures.

Extended Deterrence/The ANZUS Context: The U.S. application of strategic power—including nuclear capable forces—to protect its Southwest Pacific allies from external attack or the outbreak of regional war. With the Labour government's election in July 1984, New Zealand rejected the logic of *nuclear* extended deterrence as a component of its national security policy.

"Japanese Formula": Developed tacitly by U.S. and Japanese defense planners since the advent of the U.S.-Japan Mutual Security Treaty

(1952), it allows U.S. naval vessels and military aircraft to operate in Japanese territory under the "neither confirm nor deny" criterion while simultaneously recognizing Japan's three "nonnuclear principles" (Japan will not possess, introduce, or manufacture nuclear weapons on its soil." The U.S. is not questioned about the nuclear capabilities of its military units in Japan as long as it publicly "respects" the nonnuclear principles and Japan's peace constitution.

Ministerial Talks: Held annually by Australia and the United States from July 1985 in lieu of the tripartite ANZUS Council talks. The United States insisted it could not consult regularly with New Zealand on common defense problems as long as that country rejected the "neither confirm nor deny" criterion as a basis for alliance cooperation.

NCND: "Neither confirm nor deny" the presence of nuclear weapons or power on a military ship or aircraft. The United States, Britain, and the world's other declared nuclear powers have adhered to this practice throughout the postwar era in the interest of maintaining confidentiality about the deployment patterns of their nuclear forces at all times. After July 1984, New Zealand argued that it could not accept the NCND criterion and guarantee the enforcement of a nuclear-free zone on its own sovereign territory.

"Nordic Solution": Norway and Denmark retain NATO affiliation but do not allow the deployment of nuclear weapons on their territory during peacetime. In April 1988, the Danish Parliament adopted a resolution requiring the government to notify visiting warships of Copenhagen's ban on nuclear weapons. No enforcement mechanism has been implemented, however (setting Denmark apart from New Zealand in this sense), and the "informed" allied warships are still free to transit Danish waters on an NCND basis. Unlike the "Japanese Formula," there is no expectation that the "informed" ally will acknowledge the Danish government's message. Unlike the "Chinese Formula," no denial of ship entry is based on the host country's evaluation of a particular vessel's nuclear capability.

NFZ: Nuclear Free Zone, the avowed national security objective of the New Zealand Labour government elected to office in July 1984. A nuclear-free zone is usually comprised of one or more political units which bind themselves by national legislation or international treaty to eradicate the presence of nuclear weapons and power from a specific geographic area and enforce it through a system of verification and compliance. The concept was embodied in the Nuclear-free Zone, Disarmament and Arms Control Act introduced into the New Zealand Parliament during December 1985 and in the South Pacific Nuclear-free Zone Treaty signed by most of the South Pacific Forum members at Roratonga, Cook Islands, in August 1985.

SIGINT: Signals Intelligence areas of cooperation and exchange governed by the 1947 USUKA Agreement which brought together the communications networks of intelligence organizations for the United States, the United Kingdom (Britain), Canada, Australia, and New Zealand. Under the current division of responsibility, Australia is responsible for covering the Indian Ocean and parts of Southeast Asia and the Southwest Pacific while New Zealand is responsible for covering that part of the Southwest Pacific not covered by Australia. Since the ANZUS dispute, New Zealand still conveys intelligence collected from its area of responsibility to its USUKA partners but the U.S. and Britain severely restrict New Zealand's access to USUKA data collected by their own agencies. SIGINT originally committed that the five powers standardize their communications intelligence activities.

SPNFZT: The South Pacific Nuclear-free Zone Treaty or Treaty of Rarotonga drawn up by the South Pacific Forum (SPF) regional organization in August 1985. The Treaty reflects a moderate "case-by-case" approach in which each signatory has the right to enforce the treaty in accordance with its own sovereign judgment relative to extraregional military units which may carry nuclear arms. Australia and most of the signatories do allow the docking of U.S. ships on the basis of NCND while New Zealand, Kiribati, the Solomon Islands, and Papua New Guinea do not. Vanuatu also bars U.S. nuclear ship visits but is not a SPNFZT signatory. Tonga, also a SPF nonsignatory, allows such visits. The United States, Britain, and France have refused to ratify the SPNFZT, or "spinfizz" as it is referred to in diplomatic circles; the USSR and China have signed the treaty.

jectives and missions.[41] Critics of NCND, testifying before Congressional hearings on American nuclear strategy conducted in 1974, argued that the policy added little to extended deterrence but was designed to neutralize allied public opposition to the deployment of U.S. nuclear weapons on allied soil by avoiding disclosure of their presence. U.S. security planners have countered that NCND serves as a valid means to achieve deterrence by enhancing the element of surprise. A recent statement issued by the U.S. Navy's Political Military Policy and Current Plans Division contends that "to ensure the maximum effectiveness of [nuclear] weapons and the platforms upon which they are deployed . . . every effort must be made to safeguard information as to the location, distribution, type, number, and deployment patterns . . . . Such secrecy enhances the deterrent value of ships and aircraft and significantly complicates a potential enemy's tactical planning."[42] In specific reference to ANZUS, a 1985 exchange between Paul Wolfowitz, the U.S. Department of States' Secretary for East Asian and Pacific Affairs, James Kelly, Deputy Assistant Secretary of Defense for East Asian and Pacific Affairs, and Representative Stephen J. Solarz, Chairman of the House Foreign Relations Committee's Asian and Pacific Affairs Subcommittee is instructive:

Solarz: Do they [the New Zealanders] have any hopes that we will change Our policy? In effect agree to ships that they can accept by indicating in advance whether the ships don't have nuclear weapons?

Wolfowitz: I can't speculate on what hopes they may have, but we have made it very clear that we simply can't do that.

Solarz: Why can't we? Why can't we simply say privately to the Prime Minister, "We can't say anything publicly, but privately there are no weapons on this ship, so it is not incompatible with your policy"?

Wolfowitz: It is the kind of information that, in this world, we have simply got to keep very strictly to ourselves. It is a matter essentially of deterrence. We can't be telling the Russians which ships have nuclear weapons on board or when they do and when they don't, nor can we be saying it implicitly by letting potential adversaries say whichever ships visit those ports must be OK.

Solarz: How does it contribute to deterrence by not letting other countries know which ships have nuclear weapons and which ones don't? Presumably the Soviets know which of our ships are nuclear capable, they have satellites that must enable them to follow the progress of these ships around the seas. Can you elaborate on why it is that you think the divulging of the information New Zealand is seeking would in fact diminish deterrence?

Kelly: Our ships go on deployments which can last for many months . . . it is not possible for them to tailor their deterrence to the desires of a particular ally and I think it would be unreasonable for us to ease our adversaries' tracking and targeting problem by identifying which of our ships have the greatest capability.[43]

A few days after his election, Lange met with U.S. Secretary of State George Shultz, who was attending the annual ANZUS Council meeting hosted by the outgoing Muldoon government. Shultz emphasized to the Prime Minister-elect that (1) a high proportion of U.S. naval vessels were nuclear-powered and that New Zealand's rejection of their entry into its territory would be tantamount to rejection of overall Western deterrence strategy; and (2) the NCND criteria which had traditionally underscored U.S. operations with its ANZUS allies was, therefore, nonnegotiable. Shultz balanced this hard line, however, by assuring that Washington would not employ economic sanctions against New Zealand to pressure Labour into changing its policies. The Secretary of State was determined to allow the new government "breathing space" to resolve New Zealand's domestic political debate. He also cited the Australian Labor government's recent review of its ANZUS obligations and Canberra's reaffirmation of support for existing alliance arrangements. Shultz said he hoped the election of a New Zealand Labour government would make no greater difference to U.S.-New Zealand defense relations than had the Australian election, thereby indirectly reinforcing a long-standing American tendency to integrate New Zealand defense issues with U.S.-Australian security ties.

For his part, Lange reassured Shultz that despite obvious differences over the extent to which NCND constituted an actual alliance obligation, the incoming Labour government would be willing to negotiate with the United States in an effort to find a compromise which both governments could accept.[44] Lange's determination to negotiate a compromise was reinforced by a series of cabinet papers prepared through the office of New Zealand's Secretary of Defense, Denis McLean. These studies warned New Zealand's new government that the country's military services and their ability to operate in the South Pacific—the most likely area of future operations for New Zealand forces—would be seriously impeded if they were unable to interact with other ANZUS forces or denied access to military equipment and intelligence data provided by the U.S. and Australia. They emphasized that New Zealand's ANZUS ties allowed Wellington to *reinforce* its independence and sovereign influence rather than slip into strategic isolation.[45]

Throughout late 1984, Washington was led to believe that New Zealand's Chief of Defense Staff, Air Marshall Ewan Jamieson, was laying the groundwork for a "nuclear-capable but not nuclear-armed" formula designed to resolve ANZUS tensions. Specifically, the requirement for the United States to make an explicit statement about the capabilities or armaments of any of its ships or aircraft visiting New Zealand would be sidestepped or shelved. In return, the U.S. would announce that it "respected" New Zealand's sovereign concerns about nuclear armaments in their territory. This formula could be interpreted as New Zealand inviting Washington to make a request for a ship entry and hoping that Washington would select a vessel which was clearly nonnuclear. The ship would be acknowledged as such (by the Lange government) and be invited into New Zealand's harbors. It could be perceived as a tacit approval by Wellington for the U.S. to send an "unprovocative" and aging destroyer capable of deploying a standard antisubmarine nuclear weapons system but unlikely to be so equipped due to the "conventional deterrence" nature of most ANZUS-related military exercises. The content of many key discussions conducted between July 1984 and August 1986—when the dispute culminated without reconciliation—remains classified. Subsequent interviews by this author with both American and New Zealand officials involved in the negotiations, however, revealed the U.S. belief in at least *tacit* assurances about forthcoming modifications in the Labour government's hard line against U.S. nuclear extended deterrence policies.[46]

Several other negotiating variants for preserving an American extended deterrence guarantee toward New Zealand were introduced and weighed. While still an Opposition leader in early 1983, Lange had floated the idea of "nuclear-powered" but not "nuclear-armed" ship visits. After Labour Party regional conferences in May, he shifted to a harder line position in an effort to gain party unification prior to the July 1984 election. As prime minister, he again sought a compromise by suggesting that New Zealand rely upon its own intelligence resources to designate "acceptable U.S. ships" without directly challenging Washington's NCND policy—the so-called "trust us" formula. This proposal was not accepted by the New Zealand peace movement, however, which believed that it compromised NFZ by giving the prime minister too much discretion in ascertaining the nuclear composition of foreign vessels.[47]

Other options for salvaging the ANZUS extended deterrence posture were discussed when Shultz and Lange met again in New York during September 1984, prior to the New Zealand leader's maiden speech to the UN General Assembly. Lange asked the Secretary of State for more time to sway other Labour Party leaders and the New Zealand peace movement toward a compromise on U.S. naval ship visits. He hinted at a possible compromise: (1) adopting "nuclear-capable" rather than "nuclear-armed" or "nuclear-powered" criteria as the minimum basis for U.S. military access to New Zealand ports and airfields; or (2) sidestepping NCND by moving toward what later became known as the "Japanese" (preferred by the U.S.) or "Chinese" (New Zealand's backup position) formulas. In interviews conducted by the author with U.S., Australian, and New Zealand officials throughout 1985–1987, it became clear that Washington and Canberra believed an ANZUS solution would incorporate a precedental set of procedures similar to the Japanese formula lines. Wellington believed a case-by-case application of either the Chinese formula or on Lange's earlier "trust me" proposal could be applied. Several key New Zealand negotiators were prepared accept the Japanese formula, notwithstanding government resistance to this approach.

As background information, brief descriptions of the Japanese and Chinese formulas may be useful. Since the signing of the U.S.-Japan Mutual Security Treaty (MST) in September 1951, Japan has been deliberately ambiguous in reconciling its peace constitution and three "nonnuclear principles" (established in December 1967) with its desire to be covered by U.S. extended deterrence guarantees in Northeast

Asia. Accordingly, successive Japanese governments allowed U.S. naval units to dock without inquiring about their specific armament as long as Washington promised to "respect" Japanese sensitivity to nuclear weapons and took all necessary measures to "avoid" nuclear deployments on Japanese territory. Consequently, U.S. Fleet movements and related military operations have been allowed to function without interruption.

A number of Japanese and Western observers have argued, however, that the third of the nonnuclear principles—not to introduce nuclear weapons into Japan—had, in reality, been overridden on numerous occasions by the United States via "confidential arrangements" incorporated into the revised Mutual Security Treaty (1960). They also argued that an additional set of lesser known "nuclear principles" were observed by the Eisaku Sato administration and successor Japanese governments. These principles, it has been argued, effectively force Japanese dependence on the American deterrent, including its nuclear components, and take precedence in Tokyo over to the original three nonnuclear principles.[48]

Japanese researchers have uncovered what they claim to be cable traffic between Washington and the U.S. Embassy in Tokyo referring to a secret 1960 agreement affording Washington the right to seek Japan's consent for the transit and deployment of nuclear weapons on Japanese territory. Prime Minister Suzuki subsequently denied in the strongest terms possible (May 1981) the existence of any covert arrangements or consultations. The U.S. State Department, while acknowledging the authenticity of the documents, indicated that the Japanese researchers had "misinterpreted" their intent, which was primarily to reiterate the latitude of U.S. deployment options within the revised 1960 U.S.-Japan Mutual Security Treaty. The terms "confidential" or "secret" were characterized by the State Department as "imprecise wording."

For Japan, the "arrangement of mutual avoidance" concerning NCND resolved the dilemma between necessary support for the nonintroduction of nuclear weapons into Japan "on principle" and the equally critical imperative of honoring American insistence that nondisclosure of its naval and air force units' weapons systems remain in effect.[49] For the New Zealand peace activists and the country's electorate-at-large to accept such an ambiguous formula would have been totally uncharacteristic. Nevertheless, the approach merited Lange's consideration insofar as it had successfully bridged originally substantial differences in the Japanese-American outlook.

By contrast, the Chinese formula had no such precedents. By mid-1984, Beijing appeared to be caught between its affinity for nuclear-free zone politics as a self-proclaimed "vanguard" of Third World politics and a more pragmatic recognition that it could not expect the U.S. to sustain its extended deterrence policies in Northeast Asia without a nuclear dimension. China's small nuclear force was still highly vulnerable, with the survival of its bombers questionable and that of its liquid-fueled missile force equally tenuous (see chapter 4). Until China's indigenous deterrence capacity was more fully developed, an American nuclear presence capable of checking Soviet nuclear firepower adjacent to Chinese territory was viewed as a tactical necessity by the Chinese, although not usually acknowledged as such in their polemics.[50] Moreover, Beijing had already hosted French naval contingents as early as 1978 and British vessels since 1980 without contesting the NCND policy of either.[51]

The Chinese formula was developed more fully—and perhaps inadvertently—by then CCP Secretary General Hu Yaobang at an April 1985 press conference just before his visit to New Guinea, Australia, New Zealand, Fiji, and Western Samoa. Hu related that the United States had issued assurances that a forthcoming visit by U.S. naval units scheduled to take place in Shanghai would involve nonnuclear vessels. In fact, the visit was to involve a nuclear-capable *Spruance*-class destroyer, but Hu's remark prompted a denial by the U.S. State Department that NCND had been at issue or that any American guarantees had been forwarded to Beijing which would have contradicted NCND. Subsequent negotiations between Chinese and U.S. diplomats to resolve this diplomatic *faux pas* produced only a murky agreement to disagree. Beijing would allow intermittent U.S. ship visits on a symbolic, case-by-case basis, while insisting upon the right to veto which American naval units would be allowed to enter China's territorial waters based on an estimate of their nuclear capabilities but not requiring the U.S. to reveal actual weapons composition. Beijing thus implemented a derivative of Lange's "trust me" formula which the Americans eventually accepted when a guided missile cruiser, a frigate, and a destroyer visited Qingdao in November 1986.[52]

The Sino-American and American-New Zealand strategic relationships were viewed as sufficiently different, however, to make the Chinese formula seem inappropriate to the ANZUS case from Washington's perspective. Until June 1989, China was regarded by U.S. policymakers as a "friend" in a guarded fashion but hardly was in New Zealand's accustomed category of "trusted ally." One New Zealander noted that the U.S. naval visit to China was "an exquisite little irony," as Wellington and Washington remained at loggerheads over prospective warship calls.[53]

Compromise Lost

DESPITE THEIR difficulties in reconciling NCND, both sides became increasingly confident by the end of 1984 that a solution to the impasse between Dominant Player and Pacifist Player approaches to deterrence strategy was in sight. The United States was prepared to "recognize" New Zealand's "concern" about nuclear armaments and to reluctantly assent to Lange, declaring *unilaterally* to the New Zealand public that any U.S. destroyer scheduled to visit his country would be nuclear-free—a "Chinese formula" approach. In return, Lange was expected to acquiesce in allowing NCND to remain operative in a de facto sense by not demanding a public disclosure of any visiting ship's contents— a derivative of the Japanese formula tailored to avoid what one U.S. Defense Department official described as "the awful outcome of offering our potential opponents a 'carte blanche' inventory every time we go out to sea" on an ANZUS-related mission.[54] A December 1984 New Zealand government background paper noted that Wellington was indeed anxious to put the ANZUS dispute to bed.

Believing an understanding had been reached on how to accommodate both sides' respective positions, Washington chose to test New Zealand's NFZ policy by requesting that the destroyer, USS *Buchanan*, clearly capable of deploying nuclear antisubmarine rockets, be received into Auckland harbor during the forthcoming "Sea Eagle" ANZUS naval maneuvers. New Zealand responded with its own request that a different ship, preferably of the clearly nonnuclear FFG-7 "Oliver Hazard Perry" class, be sent instead and reasserted the right of exercising veto power over the ship class involved. The U.S. demurred, interpreting Wellington's response as an unacceptable challenge to NCND. On February 4, New Zealand formally declined to accept the *Buchanan,* precipitating a sharp erosion in U.S.-New Zealand alliance relations.

In the aftermath of the *Buchanan* incident, U.S. officials accused Lange of reneging on a commitment to adopt a variant of the "Japanese formula" which they believed had been reached in the aftermath of Lange's discussions with Shultz the previous September. One U.S. negotiator bitterly observed that "Lange has wanted it both ways—an antinuclear policy and full status in ANZUS. Now he will have to choose."[55] To drive home the point, the U.S. successfully prompted Australian Prime Minister Bob Hawke to cancel the "Sea Eagle" exercise. Several days later (February 7), the U.S. canceled a visit of New Zealand parliamentarians to CINCPAC headquarters in Hawaii and notified Wellington that the New Zealand defense attache traditionally stationed at Pearl Harbor would be asked to leave. The U.S. quickly moved to eliminate additional aspects of its defense relationship with New Zealand. By the end of February, Washington had canceled most of its scheduled defense exercises with New Zealand forces, had placed an indefinite moratorium on future maneuvers, had stopped reciprocal visits and cross-training of senior military officers, and had severed Wellington's receipt of most U.S. intelligence.[56]

Following the *Buchanan* decision, ANZUS was transformed into what one analyst correctly described as "a de facto grouping of two parallel alliances . . . a dual alliance between the U.S. and Australia and between Australia and New Zealand."[57] While Australian Defense Minister Kim Beazley visited Wellington at the end of March to explore ways Australia and New Zealand could upgrade their bilateral defense cooperation, Australian officials denied that Canberra was positioning itself as a broker in the dispute and underscored the Australian commitment to resolve the NCND issue on U.S. terms. Australian intelligence also began "sanitizing" information passed to New Zealand from U.S. sources; reportedly over 80 percent of U.S. intelligence data to Wellington was severed. This was the case even though New Zealand opted to continue relaying intelligence data on the South Pacific to the U.S. through the SIGINT network set up under the 1947 USUKA agreement.

While not directly related to the ANZUS dispute, two other developments occurring during mid-1985 should be mentioned. On July 10, French saboteurs sank the Greenpeace ship *Rainbow Warrior* in Auckland harbor. One crew member was killed and the vessel was unable to complete its planned trip to the Mururoa Atoll to monitor French nuclear testing there. The incident tended to harden the New Zealand public's already significant antipathy toward nuclear weapons in the Pacific. The second important event was the signing of the South Pacific Nuclear-Free Zone Treaty at Rarotonga, Cook Islands, by most of the South Pacific Forum member-states on August 6. An "Australian version" of the treaty text was adopted rather than the more restrictive version sponsored by Wellington. Each signatory remained free to determine enforcement on a "case-by-case" basis and in accordance with its own prerogatives. The majority of Forum states opted to allow transit of American nuclear-capable ships and planes through their territories. In defense of Australia's own policy of continuing to permit all U.S. naval vessels into Australian ports, Hawke asserted that even if visiting American ships were "nuclear capable," their armaments could be adjusted to comply with Australian standards of nuclear safety while berthed in Australian harbors.[58]

Salvaging Efforts

NFZ SUPPORTERS within New Zealand's Labour Party and peace groups pushed to have the New Zealand Nuclear-Free Zone and Arms Control Bill introduced into Parliament immediately following the *Buchanan* episode. The government originally promised to introduce such legislation by May 1985 but subsequently chose to delay it on several grounds: (1) Lange wanted to dispatch a New Zealand representative to Washington for consultations on a preliminary draft of the legislation in the hope that an ANZUS compromise could yet be salvaged; (2) a delay of its passage would allow the United States to assess the effect of a South Pacific Nuclear-Free Zone Treaty scheduled to be signed by Australia and other South Pacific Forum members in August; and (3) a "breathing space" would be created in the aftermath of the heightened tensions. Deputy Prime Minister Geoffrey Palmer was selected to carry a draft of the pending legislation to Washington, D.C., during September 20–22.

Notwithstanding New Zealand's signaling that it would be willing to explore a number of avenues leading to an ANZUS reconciliation, the Reagan Administration made it clear that in the event New Zealand's own antinuclear legislation was enacted into law, Washington would review all aspects of the ANZUS Treaty and react accordingly. It may never be known if various British and New Zealand press assertions are true that Shultz and Weinberger never looked at the preliminary draft of New Zealand's antinuclear legislation before meeting briefly with Palmer on September 18. What is clear, however, is that those U.S. officials who *did* read the document felt that New Zealand retained too much discretionary power in the consultative process regarding nuclear ships for Washington ever to accept it as a basis for continuing alliance relations. The key concept found within the Nuclear-Free Zone Legislation: "The Prime Minister may grant approval for the entry of foreign warships into the internal waters of New Zealand by foreign warships if the Prime Minister is satisfied that the warships will not be carrying any nuclear explosive device when it lands in New Zealand (Article 9:2)" directly contradicts the NCND formula's intent of not disclosing the weapons configuration of any U.S. military unit.[59] Article Ten of the legislation extended the same conditions to incoming aircraft, although certain classes of aircraft (such as air transport units) could be granted exemptions upon the Prime Minister's discretion without being subject to Parliamentary inquiry and review. In a perceptive and candid assessment of the legislation's implications, one New Zealand journalist observed that "(t)he very idea that reports on U.S. warship armaments might be scrutinized by Parliamentary committees and be subject to release under the [New Zealand] Official Information Act has obviously been unnerving to Washington as has its opposition in principle to an AN-ZUS ally legislating ground rules for visits by allied warships and aircraft."[60] Any limitation on how the U.S. should arm its naval vessels—much less the codification of such limitations and possible testing in a New Zealand court of law—was clearly unacceptable to the United States.

Shultz, Weinberger, and their advisors believed that NCND could not be salvaged other than through proposed legislation reflecting more of a Japanese formula approach to the ship entry problem. The New Zealanders, on the other hand, thought their legislation represented a compromise in good faith, based on what they understood to be a literal interpretation of the Chinese formula (i.e., the ship really wouldn't be nuclear because the Americans would promise to abide by the law), enforced by the Prime Minister on a case-by-case basis. In interviews conducted by the author with officials in Wellington, it became very clear that New Zealand's key policymakers were truly puzzled by the Americans' reluctance to accept the moral and policy logic behind their antinuclear legislation.[61]

As it became apparent that Palmer's trip would not end in compromise, Lange moved to rewrite key parts of the antinuclear legislation. Specifically, the requirement for Lange to receive reports from the Chief of Staff or other New Zealand defense officials on the nature of a proposed visiting ship's armaments was dropped, with the Prime Minister now able to exercise judgment on a ship's nuclear capability without Parliamentary review. Lange indicated that rewriting the legislation would "make it abundantly clear that we accept the ship visit because we have made the judgment that the ship is nuclear-free and not because we have been given inside information."[62] The U.S., however, saw no difference between these modifications and earlier, unsuccessful efforts by Lange to sell the "trust us" formula to his own Labour Party and to U.S. defense planners who viewed it as an unacceptable replacement for NCND. As Lange introduced the revised legislation into Parliament on December 10, the U.S. State Department warned that its enactment would lead to a "probable termination" of ANZUS. By contrast, Palmer represented the antinuclear bill as having been "carefully crafted" to avoid compromising U.S. and British NCND policies noting that "if they try to seek interpretation of it otherwise, then that is their business." Lange, however, appeared to encourage Washington and London to do just that by proclaiming in the Parliamentary debate that followed the legislation's introduction that it "was the only means of assuring the public the country had disengaged itself from any nuclear strategy."[63]

By early 1986, the realization that the ANZUS dispute was probably nonnegotiable hit both sides unexpectedly hard. The Prime Minister began referring to ANZUS itself—rather than just the ships visit issue —as "an impediment" in pursuing New Zealand's traditionally friendly ties with Washington. U.S. officials characterized the dispute as one where "we have lost an ally and losing an ally diminishes the impact of our Pacific-wide deterrent structure."[64]

The Final Break

THE FINAL stage of the ANZUS dispute unfolded at the second U.S.-Australian Ministerial Talks on Defense held in San Francisco on

August 12–13 1986, in lieu of the by now moribund ANZUS annual trilateral talks. Shultz had already set the process of U.S. alliance termination into motion by meeting briefly with Lange during the Association of Southeast Asian Nations' (ASEAN's) Foreign Minister meeting in Manila during late June. The Secretary of State felt that no compromise proposed by Wellington, no matter how intricate, could reconcile the fundamental American desire to send nuclear-armed vessels to the South Pacific and to New Zealand itself or change the Lange government's unbending resistance to such a prospect. The Reagan administration had no desire to ride New Zealand out of the ANZUS Treaty. It could, nevertheless, live with what Henry Albinski has termed a "New Zealand chair within ANZUS remain(ing) indefinitely vacant" until such time as future American and New Zealand governments could resolve outstanding differences.[65]

Lange made a last effort to sway Shultz toward a more accommodating position during their discussions at Manila. He proposed that the United States make "exceptions" to NCND in New Zealand in the same way he believed that Washington did with Denmark and Norway. In a subsequent press conference at Bangkok, Lange again conducted "public diplomacy" by presenting his version of a "Nordic solution" and other aspects of his conversation with Shultz:

> In fact I put to him the example of Denmark. The Secretary acknowledged that the Danes banned the presence of nuclear weapons including visits by nuclear-armed warships . . . the Secretary also said no nuclear powered vessels were sent there because of the protest movement and safety concerns. I then asked him why he could not substitute the words "New Zealand" for "Denmark." That question was not answered directly. It was not something he proposed to address.[66]

Shultz rejected Lange's proposal on the basis that the confidentiality of such an arrangement could not be ensured, thus inherently compromising NCND. The U.S. Embassy in New Zealand, moreover, disavowed Lange's version of his conversation with Shultz, suggesting that Lange's assertion that Shultz had stonewalled him "was at variance with the facts." The Embassy maintained that the Secretary had merely held firm to the American position established at the outset of the ANZUS dispute: i.e., Article Five of the ANZUS Treaty commits *all the signatories* to act *fully* to meet a threat to any of them; that New

Zealand's acceptance of nuclear ships constituted an integral element of full participation in ANZUS.

The Embassy also denied that the United States operated under procedures similar to those called for by New Zealand's antinuclear legislation with Denmark or any other NATO ally. It was stated that any number of nuclear-capable warships were allowed to transit through NATO's northern flank in a given year without the NCND principle coming under challenge from Copenhagen or Oslo because, while successive Danish governments have opposed nuclear ships as a matter of policy, there is no law to enforce that policy, a deliberate state of affairs tailored to avoid challenging the U.S. policy of NCND. This was confirmed in June 1983 when the Danish Foreign Minister, asked in the Folketing about enforcement of Copenhagen's nonnuclear policies, responded that Denmark would assume that allied awareness of, and compliance with, those policies would be achieved without Denmark explicitly expressing mistrust of her allies.[67] Consequently, the "Nordic solution" is only another variant under which NCND is observed.

Meanwhile, officials in both Washington and Canberra were kept busy trying to construct a new bilateral defense communique which would supersede the trilateral ANZUS mechanisms. While eager to avoid appearing as a broker in the ANZUS dispute, Australia was interested in softening the proposed communique's language. The Australian Labor government desired to sustain, if not necessarily broaden, strong bilateral defense ties with New Zealand. The final Ministerial Talks communique achieved the intended balance of Canberra supporting the United States on the ANZUS dispute, while retaining its own security ties with New Zealand for a continuation of a strategic denial posture in the South Pacific.[68] The San Francisco Ministerial Talks produced what Lange claimed throughout most of the ANZUS dispute would never happen: the systematic exclusion of New Zealand from almost all operative defense relations with the United States.

Another practical effect of the Ministerial Talks communique was to provide Washington a carte blanche for isolating Wellington from the rest of the Western defense network. The Reagan administration elected to manage this process discriminately. New Zealand was excluded from the USUKA/SIGINT network. U.S. State Department spokesmen continued to label the relationship between the two countries as "friendly, practical, and workmanlike," but Wellington nevertheless was excluded from regular defense consultations with other U.S. allies. New Zealand's diplomats stationed in Washington, moreover, were given less general access to other U.S. government agencies such as the Departments of State and Commerce.[69] Issues of weapons access and high technology transfer to New Zealand, however, were conducted on a "case-by-case" basis in accordance with the importance delegated any transactions involving American security interests in the South Pacific. For example, there was no reduction of American support for the New Zealand "Orion" surveillance aircraft, which continued to supply the U.S. Defense Department with information on Soviet fleet movements in South Pacific waters.

With such activities in mind, Lange insisted—even during the Ministerial Talks—that New Zealand had fulfilled its ANZUS obligations and was still willing to come to the military assistance of Australia and the U.S. on a nonnuclear basis.[70] Indeed, Lange *had* displayed some flexibility in his government's antinuclear policy during April 1987, when he agreed to allow U.S. military transport aircraft to continue landing at Christchurch on an NCND basis for the resupplying of the U.S. Navy's Antarctic supply depot. Cynics argued that the Prime Minister made this policy adjustment for fear that the U.S. would move the economically lucrative transport operation from the Harewood/Christchurch airfield to Hobart, Australia, had he refused to compromise. In particular, they noted the pressure applied by a U.S. Congressional delegation led by Representative Samuel Stratton visiting Wellington in January 1986. The delegation linked the ANZUS dispute to the future willingness of the United States to operate from the existing site. While both U.S. officials in Wellington and the New Zealand Minister of Trade David Caygill subsequently downplayed the Stratton visit's significance, it is noteworthy that the Harewood/Christchurch episode developed as the one exception to the Lange government's otherwise uniform insistence that NCND would apply to all U.S. military units entering New Zealand territory.[71]

The U.S. Congress, in the meantime, also continued to assert itself in ANZUS politics. In late 1987, the U.S. House of Representatives weighed legislation proposed by Congressman William Broomfield (the New Zealand Military Preference Exclusion Act) which formally downgraded Wellington's status from "ally" to "friend" in U.S. national security policy. Subsequent efforts to convert this bill into actual U.S. law have failed. The Reagan Administration, however, was successful in changing New Zealand's standing within the U.S. Foreign Assistance Act (which governs a foreign nation's access to U.S. military technology and weapons systems). The Export Control Act (which extended the probation period for acquiring U.S. armaments once any such sales have been approved) was also imposed.

In late April 1989, Lange delivered a foreign policy address at Yale University in which he acknowledged that neither the United States nor New Zealand were likely to change their respective positions on the ANZUS dispute and proposed that New Zealand should formally withdraw from the alliance. This speech was to be one of his last definitive statements on deterrence politics as Prime Minister. Several months later (on August 7), he resigned for health reasons and due to his inability to heal growing political factionalism within the ranks of the Labour Party. The new prime minister, Geoffrey Palmer, related his willingness to conduct further talks with Washington about ANZUS but not at the expense of New Zealand's Pacifist Player posture. An opinion poll taken just prior to Lange's departure reinforced Palmer's stance: 84 percent of the New Zealand electorate approved of their country's nuclear ban. Moreover, antinuclear crusader Helen Clarke's appointment to deputy prime minister was indicative of the antinuclear movement's growing legitimacy within New Zealand politics and of the Labour Party's success in downplaying the criticisms raised by the aforementioned independent Defense Committee of Inquiry in its final report.[72]

During late 1989 and early 1990, some signs of a thaw in U.S.-New Zealand relations emerged as the Bush administration moved to end a four-year ban of contacts between high-level U.S. officials and their New Zealand Labour government counterparts. In early March 1990, U.S. Secretary of State James Baker met with New Zealand's Minister of External Relations and Trade Mike Moore four months after a team of New Zealand officials had consulted with State Department officials on joint approaches to Pacific economic issues (December 1989). However, relations are still far from being restored to their pre-1985 levels. Except for a partial lifting of the ban (in early October 1987) prohibiting New Zealand personnel from attending U.S. military training schools, defense relations between Washington and Wellington have remained dormant.[73] New Zealand's opposition Nationalist Party was reportedly softening its former opposition to its country's existing antinuclear laws in the interest of consolidating its lead in polls leading to an October 1990 election. Secretary of State Baker and U.S. Secretary of Defense Cheney nevertheless rebuffed a plea—made by Australian Foreign Minister Gareth Evans at the U.S.-Australian Ministerial Talks held in early November 1989—to resume military ties with Wellington. The rebuff was made on the grounds that the Palmer government rejects the fundamental postulates of extended deterrence to no lesser a degree than its predecessor.[74] On March 8, 1990, opposition leader Jim Bolger announced the National Party would support the Labour government's nuclear-free zone policy. He cited national opinion polls still showing overwhelming electoral backing of this position. Before resigning his position as National's deputy leader and defense spokesman to protest Bolger's decision, Don McKinnon, concluded that the ANZUS treaty was, from that point onward, "a dead letter."[75]

ANZUS, EXTENDED DETERRENCE, AND THE "RIPPLE FACTOR"

A MAJOR question raised by the ANZUS dispute was whether or not the effects of New Zealand's permanent departure from an established instrument of Western strategic policy would encourage other U.S. allies to dissent from U.S. deterrence postures.

From the U.S. perspective, the timing of New Zealand's challenge to American extended deterrence strategy in late 1984 and early 1985 could not have been worse. Washington was simultaneously lobbying with Belgian and Dutch political leaders to withstand the domestic political pressures generated by those countries' formidable peace movements and to honor their NATO-related commitment to deploy 48 ground-launched cruise missiles in response to increased Soviet SS-20 missile deployments.

In late December 1984, the Belgians and Dutch both deferred their deployment commitments in the hope that an early breakthrough in Soviet-American INF negotiations could be achieved the following March. To U.S. defense planners, the central European states' reticence to move ahead with deployment signaled a clear emergence of a "ripple" or "spill-over" factor originating with ANZUS and now carrying over into the United States' security ties with the smaller NATO allies.[76]

From New Zealand's vantage point, there was no such interrelationship because growing multipolarity in the international system renders any Soviet threat toward New Zealand improbable, relative to whatever indivisibility the Americans assume extended nuclear deterrence strategy may have within overall Western strategic planning. The U.S. perception of global strategy, on the other hand, requires unquestioned American access to Pacific air and naval bases at *all* levels of operation to reinforce key Eurasian conflict points during wartime. In this sense, as one American press report assessing interalliance ramifications of New Zealand's Pacifist posture concluded, "U.S. naval activity in the South Pacific region is just as fundamental to military alliance relations as the deployment of U.S. forces in West Germany."[77]

As for an ANZUS "ripple" affecting NATO allies, Belgium and the Netherlands finally honored their cruise missile deployment commitments (a move which a number of NATO analysts contend was decisive in Moscow's subsequent willingness to reach an INF accord benefiting both Europe and Asia). Denmark elected to keep its U.S. alliance intact by observing the NCND formula for American units transgressing its boundaries. The British Labor Party's electoral misfortunes during the 1980s were at least partly attributable to its entertaining a defense posture similar to Wellington's and totally inappropriate for the influential, middle-sized global power which Britain still aspires to be.

New Zealand's argument that America's Dominant Player posture was too demanding of U.S. allies in terms of nuclear collaboration proved no more convincing and, therefore, created no more "ripples" in the Asia-Pacific than in NATO. The Japanese government was visibly disturbed by New Zealand's NFZ posture, fearing that it could enhance the influence of Japan's own antinuclear movement, with long-term consequences for the Mutual Security Treaty and for the overall regional military balance. The ASEAN states expressed apprehension that New Zealand's nuclear politics could influence political developments in the Philippines in ways which could hasten the departure of the United States' "over the horizon" presence which nearly every ASEAN leader still valued highly.[78] Supporters of Wellington's nuclear-free approach to global disarmament have reconciled themselves to the fact that "there has not been a rush to follow New

Zealand's lead, unfortunately vindicat(ing) the United States punishment of New Zealand." They nevertheless conclude that small states
can still "generate pressures" on nuclear powers to move toward minimal deterrence and eventual disarmament.[79]

THREAT PERCEPTIONS AND THE COSTS
OF DISSENT

IF THE ANZUS crisis were an isolated development within an otherwise benign South Pacific politico-strategic environment, U.S. and
Australian defense planners could abide Wellington's sharp dissent
from the Dominant Player posture as an unfortunate divergence of
values and policy interests between formally close allies. The timing of
the U.S.-New Zealand rift, however, coincided with a simultaneous
increase in tensions in other parts of the Pacific islands area emanating
from factors of sovereign identity, ethnic strife, resource management,
and potentially higher geopolitical profiles by external actors heretofore
mostly uninvolved in the South Pacific.[80]

As U.S. extended deterrence strategy comes under increased scrutiny in both Japan and the Philippines—two of the most critical
postwar staging posts for the American strategic frontier in the Pacific
—the United States' incentive to explore South Pacific basing options
will increase commensurately. The Dominant Player posture converges
with South Pacific geostrategic considerations in the areas of controlling regional sea lanes of communication (SLOCs), projecting adequate
maritime and air power to maintain such control, and denying strategic
or political access to potential U.S. adversaries.[81] U.S. force planning
currently lacks access to enough advanced bases to effectively circumvent the vast distances and long transit times involved in the projection
of U.S. offshore power on behalf of its Asia-Pacific security commitments. The loss of New Zealand as a forward peacetime staging post is
inimical to U.S. interests in this regard. Washington's investigation of
alternative Pacific basing sites which could serve the global deterrence
framework as supply points, fuel depots, and replenishment centers
for U.S. naval and air components has thus become more important,
at least until technological breakthroughs preclude the need for any
advanced staging posts. The Palau Islands in Micronesia, the Northern

Marianas, Manus, Guam, and Pago Pago in American Samoa are all, for example, candidates for relocation of various U.S. force assets in the event the Philippines basing agreement terminates in the 1990s.[82]

In the context of present alliance strategy, the denial to U.S. ships of access to New Zealand ports and the cancellation of ANZUS exercises previously held off New Zealand waters erodes U.S. and allied force readiness and standardization. Not long before the *Buchanan* incident, for example, New Zealand naval personnel were convinced that ANZUS surface units were close to achieving maximum operational efficiency in joint exercises, particularly so because of the ANZAC navies' opportunity to work with U.S. nuclear-capable attack submarines in an ASW-simulated conflict environment. This was the case even though New Zealand naval doctrine envisions ASW in the South Pacific to involve only conventional munitions. Without further access to training with U.S. units, New Zealand's ability to patrol credibly those South Pacific littorals designated by the government's 1987 Defense White Paper as most critical to its own security becomes increasingly questionable.[83]

Regional Threat Assessments and the U.S. Response

THE QUESTION of "deterrence against what" remains central to any discussion about the effect of New Zealand's departure from ANZUS. The Soviet Pacific Fleet remains too far away and logistically too weak to pose much of a threat to New Zealand's territory or to threaten South Pacific sea lanes of communication vital to U.S. or allied naval or commercial traffic. Moscow's commercial maritime/intelligence tracking ships transiting the South Pacific have thus far been unable to obtain a permanent foothold on any of the region's island-states. Under such circumstances, as Robert O'Neill has observed, there seems little temptation for Moscow to target New Zealand with nuclear weapons. However, he concludes, "the real danger . . . is not confined to that which would follow a direct impact of nuclear weapons on its soil, but extend to the wide array of disastrous consequences for the whole planet which seem likely to flow from major nuclear conflict between the superpowers elsewhere in the world."[84] More immediate Western concerns relate to Soviet *capabilities* (as opposed to intentions) to project military power into the South Pacific for *interdiction* of U.S. naval and air operations in the area during wartime, and to otherwise erode traditional widespread American strategic influence within the region. Unconfirmed reports of Soviet submarine incursions into Kwajalein Atoll in the Marshall Islands in July 1987 reinforced U.S. concerns about potential Soviet interdiction capabilities in the South Pacific.[85]

Until recently disclosed Soviet force reductions went into effect there, Soviet air strike capabilities which could be stationed and activated from Cam Ranh Bay were taken very seriously by defense planners in the U.S. Pacific Command. If the USSR was successful in eliminating Pine Gap, Nurrungar, and other Australian potential listening posts integral to early warning of a future military confrontation against U.S. and allied targets in the Pacific theater, the chances of the USSR's *Bear*, *Backfire*, and *Blackjack* bombers evading Western air and naval interceptors and striking U.S. South Pacific bases would improve substantially. A number of Western security analysts have noted that in future Pacific war scenarios involving the USSR, U.S. lines of communication must shift south to minimize Soviet bomber and hunter-killer submarine interdiction efforts and to reinforce Australia as Washington's most important ally south of the equator. While most of these analysts believe New Zealand would feel committed to assist its traditional ANZUS allies under such conditions, the U.S. would need to insist on unconditional rights of nuclear transit even *prior* to hostilities as a best chance to avoid them:

> American nuclear deterrence depends upon freedom of navigation for its ballistic missile submarines . . . [and] forward defense naval strategy, which also places nuclear-armed surface warships in the southern and western Pacific, as well as the Indian Ocean. Restrictions on the legality of passage of these ships would certainly be a major blow to the U.S. Navy . . . Overflight of nuclear-armed aircraft . . . is important . . . . Whether these aircraft are part of the strategic deterrent or play a tactical nuclear role in specific theaters, the necessity to bypass the South Pacific would create major problems for the defense support of individual allies such as Australia.[86]

Mikhail Gorbachev's strategy of establishing a legitimate role for the USSR in Asia-Pacific via confidence-building on regional security issues was not translated into greater Soviet influence in the South Pacific. While Moscow has been successful in establishing diplomatic ties with Papua New Guinea, Western Samoa, Tonga, Fiji, Kiribati, Nauru, Tuvalu, and Vanuatu over the past sixteen years, its legitimacy as a positive political force in the region remains suspect. It negotiated unsuccessful short-term fishing agreements with Kiribati (1985) and Vanuatu (1987), allowing them to lapse after one year because of their failure to provide Soviet personnel access to onshore facilities and Soviet resistance to the financial terms for renewal offered by those two island-states. The Soviets also campaigned diligently for a similar agreement with Fiji but were eventually turned down. Soviet diplomacy directed toward the South Pacific region is more sophisticated than was the case until the mid-1980s. Nevertheless, the levels of diplomatic and economic investment needed to convert a number of island-states into full-fledged antiWestern outposts are still prohibitive, relative to Moscow's more critical geopolitical interests elsewhere in the Asia-Pacific theater.[87]

Domestic internal threats to individual state regimes are presently a more tangible security risk to South Pacific island-states than long-range Soviet opportunism. Throughout the 1980s, *coup* attempts became endemic throughout the Melanesian subregion (see chapter 2). On occasion, nationalist leaderships in Vanuatu, Fiji, the Solomon Islands, and Papua New Guinea have played Soviet or Libyan "cards" to underscore their independence from traditional Western powers or to attract more funding from the ANZUS powers, Japan, and the European Community.[88] The report issued by the Australian Parliament's Joint Committee on Foreign Affairs, Defense, and Trade (see chapter 2) correctly noted that while domestic affairs still played a predominant role in the island-states' post-independence concerns about economic viability and nation-building, evidence is nevertheless surfacing that island-state governments are now giving a wider berth to their place in the world. Accordingly, this report concluded, New Zealand, "with a range of trade, defense aid, and cultural contacts" engendered much concern in the region when it drove Washington ultimately to suspend normal ANZUS operations.[89]

Several issues in U.S.-South Pacific relations are emerging which have aggravated the South Pacific islanders' feelings that Washington is neglecting their development aspirations in favor of a globally oriented Dominant Player strategic denial strategy that has little contemporary relevance to their local security concerns. The U.S. was perceived as callously disregarding the South Pacific island-states' claims of 200 nautical-mile economic enterprise zone (EEZ) jurisdiction over migratory fish species, especially tuna, until it signed a Fisheries Treaty in early 1987 to provide $10 million in licensing fees and to regulate access by American tuna fisherman to South Pacific fisheries over a five-year period. While the U.S. regarded the matter primarily in commercial terms, the South Pacific islanders accused the United States of allowing the wholesale compromise of their means for economic survival.

Insensitivity to the South Pacific island-states' concerns was illustrated, in their view, by U.S. refusal to oppose continued French nuclear weapons testing at the Mururoa Atoll. Nor was U.S. neutrality concerning the French colonial dispute in New Caledonia appreciated. U.S. opposition to the South Pacific Forum's nuclear-free-zone initiative will be discussed below.

To a significant number of South Pacific states, Washington's allegedly initial indifference to these problems, combined with its preoccupation with the extended deterrence implications of the ANZUS dispute, was visibly offensive. As one respected observer of South Pacific politics has concluded: "Washington's reaction to change in the region . . . has been pitched at the level of a superpower protecting global interests rather than a traditional friend involved with the region since the early days of Western contact in the 18th century." [90] The Bush administration has proven more sensitive than its predecessor to these issues, but the need for more visits by high-level U.S. officials to the region, greater American sensitivity to differing Melanesian and Polynesian development agendas, and the provision of adequate development assistance funding—all supplementing Australia's and New Zealand's necessarily primary roles in the South Pacific—would enhance prospects for a benign South Pacific regional order continuing for the remainder of this century and beyond, despite the loss of ANZUS. [91]

Nuclear-Free Zone Politics in the South Pacific

TWO MAJOR aspects of the South Pacific Nuclear-Free Zone (SPNFZ) issue could directly affect U.S. alliance relations with Australia and its future influence with the member-states of the South Pacific Forum. One is the extent to which the United States continues its acquiescence to the French testing of nuclear weapons in the South Pacific. Another is continued U.S. opposition to ratifying the August 1985 Treaty of Rarotonga which established the SPNFZ, a stance announced in February 1987 after the USSR and China had already signed the protocols of the treaty (in late 1986 and early 1987, respectively).

French nuclear testing is opposed by literally every South Pacific country, including Australia. It unmistakably complicates Washington's argument that global deterrence is indivisible, rather than differentiated from region to region. From the perspective of a Southwest Pacific inhabitant, French national interests in maintaining an indigenous nuclear deterrent in central Europe have little meaning compared to the potential environmental risks imposed by its testing program in the South Pacific or to the enduring French disregard for the political and economic sensitivities of the region. Continued American softpedaling of French behavior in the Pacific may well erode what reservoir of good will and strategic influence Washington retains with South Pacific nations.

Three French arguments (all contested) have been offered as the basis for continued testing. Paris claims the testing is safe because of the site's relative isolation from populated centers and because of measures which France has taken to "reinforce" the Mururoa Atoll from shocks and fracturing which testing opponents believe could break up the atoll. (Indeed, in March 1988, the French announced they would soon be shifting all their testing from Mururoa to nearby Fangataufa Island.) The Auckland Geothermal Institute has conducted independent studies on water conditions in and around the atoll and has concluded that a danger indeed exists for nuclear contamination.[92] Secondly, the French argue, the testing site, and for that matter, most of the area which comprises the SPNFZ, is actually in international waters. Consequently, the original statement of Charles de Gaulle in explaining the French decision to test at Mururoa—i.e., "We have a bomb, it is nobody else's problem but ours to decide where to test it" —remains the operative French outlook to this day.[93]

The third French rationale—national sovereignty and its defense— is the most important from this study's perspective of inter-alliance transferability. The attack on the *Rainbow Warrior* surveillance ship in Auckland harbor, in July 1985, by French agents, for example, is seen from the French perspective as a justifiable defense of national sovereignty and of the right to develop nuclear deterrence capabilities on any part of French territory. Paris has actively sought support for this position from the United States, maintaining that the very ability to sustain the independent but pro-Western French nuclear deterrent in Europe is dependent upon the retaining of the Mururoa complex.[94]

The United States has adopted the position that an ally who is also a mid-size nuclear power such as France cannot be expected to surrender sovereign control over what will or will not occur on its overseas departments and territories. The U.S. view was spelled out by Secretary of State Shultz over two years after the *Warrior* incident (June 1987): "If you are going to have operative nuclear weapons, you have to have a place to test them."[95] Reports have recently surfaced that the United States had even offered Paris the opportunity to test its nuclear devices in Nevada (as Britain has done for years).[96] Other reports allegedly discussed the feasibility of testing in the Massif area of metropolitan France without jeopardizing the health of the French population (as of mid-September 1986, however, the U.S. government was unaware of any feasibility studies undertaken by the French government to determine the safety of testing in metropolitan France). Shultz accepted the French argument that the established South Pacific site was environmentally safe and, as part of sovereign French territory, a legitimate site for nuclear testing. That sovereignty factor, and the role that French nuclear weapons played in the overall Western deterrence framework against the Soviet bloc, were predominant in determining the U.S. policy stance on the South Pacific nuclear testing issue.[97]

In response to the South Pacific environmental and political development concerns which eventually led to the Treaty of Rarotonga, the United States responded by employing the jargon of East-West strategic competition: the prospect for greater progress in the arms control arena will allow for significant future cuts in the superpowers' nuclear arsenals and those of the nuclear allies, making the world inherently safer for all its inhabitants. In more candid statements offered to the House Foreign Affairs Committee, U.S. officials argued that there was a difference between the Treaty of Rarotonga and the Treaty of Tlatelolco that governs nuclear weapons free-zone criteria for Latin American and which Washington did ratify in 1969. These included Tlatelolco's more liberal provisions on what types of nuclear devices were to be regulated (only those nuclear devises which were clearly "warlike" in nature, as opposed to a blanket regulation on nuclear devices contained in Roratonga) and Roratonga's broader prohibitions on nuclear stationing and transit which could compromise the United States' application of NCND.

The SPNFZ also prohibits the establishment of U.S. nuclear-capable bases in the Treaty area, a prospect not entertained by Washington at the time of SPNFZ's founding but a disturbing restriction, nevertheless, given Rarotonga's signatories "invitation" to other South Pacific states to accede to SPNFZ and expand its coverage. This was a particularly sensitive issue in Washington, considering its possible future desire to establish a major base at Palau in the event U.S. forces leave the Philippines after 1991, and that Palau's brief (1981–1987) constitutional prohibition of nuclear weapons on its territory (a U.S.-Palauean compact ratified in August 1987 allowed—by majority vote of Palau's legislature—the transit and storage of American nuclear weapons on an emergency basis). While the Treaty of Rarotonga did provide for each signatory to develop a "case-by-case" interpretation of how to apply the treaty stipulations to the naval and air units of outside powers, the U.S. remained concerned that its access to critical sea lanes of communication through the South Pacific into the Asia-Pacific and eastern Indian Ocean littorals would be disrupted by the SPNFZ.[98]

A critique of such reasoning can be postulated. Washington would have accrued long-term advantages in signing the Treaty of Rarotonga. The good will of Australia—the United States' most important ally in the Southwest Pacific and the author of an SPNFZT which left its signatories free to still honor Washington's neither-confirm-nor-deny policy—would have been retained. Moreover, the clauses found in the Treaty were acceptable precedents, which could later be applied to a Southeast Asian nuclear-free zone or in similar arrangements in deference to U.S. strategic interests. As it was, the Dominant Player posture once more was perceived as a reactionary impediment to the forces of constructive regional change.

Australia remains more sympathetic to the Dominant Player extended deterrence posture than most of its South Pacific Forum counterparts. However, Foreign Minister Bill Hayden's observations, shortly following the signing of the Rarotonga Treaty, drew a sharp contrast between global and local deterrence issues regarding French nuclear testing: "It is mainly for the benefit of its metropolitan territory in Europe that France deploys its deterrent force, but the cost of this deployment, in the form of nuclear testing, is inflicted on the nations of the South Pacific."[99] As the United States has allowed out-of-area security and political considerations to override Australia's representations of its interests within the South Pacific Forum's deliberations on SPNFZ, Canberra may well be less inclined to represent Washington's future strategic interests in the region. The U.S., one analyst has observed, initially relied upon Australia to represent a Western collective defense approach, only to later "override regional political imperatives . . . thereby undermining itself and its allies in the process."[100]

ANZAC Deterrence and Power Projection Capabilities in a Post-ANZUS Era

IT APPEARS that the clearest danger for middle and small powers who dissent from the Dominant Player posture is strategic isolation and Washington's indifference to their local defense interests. Despite recent growth in U.S.-New Zealand trade relations, neither American or British policymakers are any longer inclined to argue New Zealand's case in Western military planning circles. This change has resulted in what one respected Australian defense official has characterized as a state where "New Zealand's influence on important matters of United States and allied policy is, in fact, probably now the lowest it has been since the Second World War."[101]

Costs incurred by the New Zealand military establishment due to its isolation from other Western defense establishments have already been substantial and are likely to grow. Hard choices now confront any New Zealand government which opts to pursue defense self-reliance with a paucity of resources. Compensatory measures including weapons purchases, upgrading of indigenous intelligence-collection capabilities, and force training cycles are already exceeding $100 million per annum. In March 1989, the "Quigley Review," a report prepared by private consultants but commissioned by the New Zealand Defense Ministry, concluded that up to fourteen of the country's twenty-two military bases and 75 percent of the defense headquarters staff would need to be cut if a 10 percent overall reduction in defense spending were to be realized in response to growing financial exigencies. It also envisioned New Zealand's intensified dependence on Australian defense industry for frigate replacement and for the provision of other critical weapons systems.[102] New Zealand also has recently withdrawn its 700–troop strong contingent from Singapore, deployed under FPDA auspices, to bring its newly formed Ready Reaction Force up to its allocated strength level of 1,500 personnel for duties in the South Pacific.[103]

Some New Zealand-based security observers still remain optimistic that New Zealand, as "Pacifist of the Pacific," can retain and even increase its defense capabilities in the face of a struggling domestic economy and a national peace movement now intent on monitoring Australian-New Zealand defense ties for any evidence of Australian intimidation. They argue that, while New Zealand armed forces now have less capability to operate with those of Wellington's traditional Western allies, this matters less at a time when New Zealand's objectives are removed from contributing to U.S. and Western extended deterrence strategy in favor of strengthening its local strategic capabilities in the South Pacific.[104]

Critics respond, however, that any foreseeable ANZAC defense collaboration cannot make up for New Zealand's loss of access to high-quality U.S. intelligence, equipment, and logistical supply arrangements. Defense communications at the Government Communications Security Bureau in Tangimoana, are reported to be linked with the U.S. Naval Operational Intelligence Center in Suitland, Maryland. The effectiveness of such facilities, however, are inevitably impaired by the "sanitization" of U.S. intelligence through Australian channels to New Zealand intelligence posts. The Defense Technical Cooperation Program and related U.S.-New Zealand bilateral data-exchange agreements with Australia, Britain, Canada and the United States—the ABCA agreements—have been, for the most part, discontinued. With increased budgetary constraints, New Zealand's air and naval strike elements are arguably years behind those of which can be deployed by most ASEAN countries.[105] Nor can such collaboration merely gloss over the reality of Australia supporting and New Zealand dissenting from Western nuclear deterrence strategy. Australian defense planners have recently opined that strategic denial cannot be differentiated from "defensive deterrence" involving sufficient defense expenditures and capabilities to deter *any* attack contingency on one's homeland short of nuclear conflict.[106] If such a homeland defense is to be of first priority, New Zealand may have no resources left to provide for a credible South Pacific regional defense.

The ANZUS crisis and its ramification for New Zealand's homeland defense capabilities have, in fact, significantly restricted that country's future ability to cope with potential challenges to its own local defense interests in the Southwest Pacific.[107] Structuring New Zealand's forces to conduct forward defense in the South Pacific was defined by the Labour government's 1987 Defense White Paper as the country's priority defense commitment, predicated upon the rationale that "New Zealand will respond to any serious threat to our Pacific Island neighbors."[108] New Zealand's more immediate defense commitments include the Cook Islands, Niue, and Tokelau, but Wellington also extends an informal defense commitment to Western Samoa and the Solomons. While these islands have not experienced the political radicalization or socioeconomic growing pains of Fiji or Vanuatu, New Zealand's ability to sustain a concentrated defense against a determined military opponent is, at best, uncertain.

Of most significance over the long-term, however, is New Zealand's apparent loss of influence and good will among both U.S. and allied policy elites. By 1986, naval exercises with other Western powers were reduced to one-quarter of their 1984 level before increasing again in 1987–1988 with Australia and various ASEAN militaries.[109] Without powerful allies other than Australia, Wellington is incapable of implementing credible local deterrence throughout the South Pacific region, no matter how well intentioned or motivated the central government and the armed forces may be. In what is perhaps the most exhaustive study yet to appear on New Zealand defense policy in the aftermath of ANZUS, Peter Jennings, a highly respected Australian defense authority, has concluded that:

> The ANZAC defense relationship is a necessary, but not sufficient, means of maintaining AFNZ [Armed Forces, New Zealand] capabilities outside of ANZUS . . . . Far from being more self-reliant, the AFNZ have suffered a loss of military capability and have become *more* reliant on the good will of another country—Australia. From from developing a closer ANZAC alliance of equal partners, New Zealand has been accorded a very much more junior role in its defense association with Australia.[110]

Indeed, a growing number of New Zealand analysts suspect that Australia, irritated by the ANZUS rift, will be tempted to use Wellington's increased strategic reliance on its ANZAC partner to establish a more dominant Australian geopolitical role in the South Pacific. Following the August 1986 Ministerial Talks with the United States, the Australians moved carefully to distance themselves from the recommendations of a document prepared by the New Zealand Committee of Inquiry. Best known as the "Corner Report," it called for an enhancement of Australian-New Zealand defense cooperation.[111] Australian defense officials noted that since the early 1970s Canberra's defense priorities had been the defense of Australia itself rather than a "forward defense" posture that might more readily accommodate intervention on behalf of New Zealand defense interests in the South Pacific. In fact, Australia was increasingly focusing more on security threats emanating from points north and northwest of Australia (Southeast Asia and the Indian Ocean) than toward the more traditional ANZAC commitments to the Southwest Pacific.

Canberra *was* interested in exploring joint Australian-New Zealand weapons procurement ventures (most notably, naval frigates) and participated in its own defense exercise series with New Zealand forces. It was, however, concerned that Wellington be willing to finance its own defense capabilities to compensate for the lost U.S. surveillance, intelligence, and force projection assets. Australian critics pointed to the joint exercises conducted with New Zealand forces as superfluous operations inasmuch as they were based upon contingencies relevant to Australia's strategic priorities but that the exclusion of the United States in any such circumstances as would actually develop was unrealistic.[112] The Lange government's subsequent difficulties in funding its prescribed share of a proposed ANZAC project to procure and deploy *Leander*-class frigates engendered visible tension across the Tasman. In late 1988, Lange responded to critics of his government's decision to commit New Zealand to this joint project (which called for the procurement of eight boats for Australia and up to four boats for New Zealand). He argued that Wellington had "no practical or logical alternative to working with Australia to face a regional environment that promised to be "much more complex" over the next ten to fifteen years.[113] Lange adhered to this position despite a successful left-wing resolution at the Labour Party's annual conference to withdraw from the project. One delegate proclaimed the whole *Leander* affair to be a plot by "strongly pro-American Australians who are trying to charm us back into ANZUS."[114] In late 1989, New Zealand became formally committed to purchasing at least two of the *Leanders*. By that time, however, it had become increasingly evident that the ANZAC regional strategic doctrines were significantly diverging. More effective coordination between the ANZAC powers in forging a common strategic outlook and approach to South Pacific security threats and requirements will be required if the local deterrence interests of both are to be realized in a time of potentially volatile change throughout the region.

CONCLUSION

IN JUNE 1987, the New Zealand Nuclear-Free Zone, Disarmament, and Arms Control Bill became New Zealand law. The United States has responded by pursuing a policy course of detachment from its former commitments to extended deterrence on Wellington's behalf at either the nuclear or the conventional levels. As New Zealand political scientist Jacob Bercovitch has observed:

> In the United States . . . the ANZUS crisis was perceived, rightly or wrongly, as a threat to the very fabric of deterrence on which Western security rests. The United States . . . simply accepts as axiomatic the role of nuclear weapons in its system of security. The relevance of nuclear weapons is just not a matter that is open to question. Within this conception, ANZUS, as an American-dominated alliance, would either remain as a link in the overall strategy of extended deterrence, or it would not be maintained at all. The chasm between the United States' position and New Zealand's position could not be wider.[115]

The wounds incurred by the dispute were particularly deep. Both countries assumed the other's national security values and reverence for a long tradition of mutual security cooperation would allow the other side to give enough to preclude a final alliance dissolution. Hard-line posturing is now the norm for justifying their respective positions on nuclear-free zone politics, alliance management, and related questions of international security. In this context, the Dominant and Pacifist Players have not achieved an amicable divorce.

Distancing itself from the United States, a nuclear superpower which, from Wellington's perspective, insisted upon conducting international alliance politics by its own set of rules, New Zealand has been relegated to managing a difficult and perhaps less effective security relationship with Australia.[116] New Zealand simply lacks the physical resources, and hence the strategic leverage, to ensure itself equal status in a bilateral relationship with Australia. However, Australian defense planners have every expectation of New Zealand's sharing reasonably in a Southwest Pacific defense burden made all the more formidable by the removal of American power from areas where ANZUS was formerly operative. They expect that Wellington will accept Australian threat perceptions as its own and will embrace joint approaches to command and control and to defense organization, together striving for greater interoperability of defense equipment. Former Secretary of Defense Denis McLean concisely summarizes the Pacifist Player's current quandary: "There is no more important question for New Zealanders than . . . where is the convergence of interests with Australia leading . . . . Already drawn into the Australian sphere of interest by the inexorable logic of geopolitics, history, and economics, New Zealand is now confronting the implications of its rejection of a balancing relationship with the United States."[117]

There are no winners in an alliance dispute as acrimonious as the ANZUS case. The long-term effects of this dispute for U.S. extended deterrence strategy are still to be determined. It is the United States which has insisted on the inviolability of extended deterrence at all levels of nuclear and conventional conflict management and within each component of America's global alliance network . In doing so, the U.S. has sent a hard, even callous, message to its strategic affiliates, that independence from the Dominant Player posture's rationales or instrumentalities will come at a high price. Such an approach displays little tolerance for democratic pluralism or deference to reasonable variants of national security interests, demanding uncompromising alliance cohesion.[118] In this sense, Washington has left itself open to the criticism that it has learned little from history.

If future political developments produce a new set of leaders within the Western Alliance more sympathetic to the New Zealand Labour government's reasoning, the U.S. will be less able to take the same hard-line approach that it employed in the ANZUS dispute. The implied challenge of the Pacifist Player posture is for U.S. defense planners to adopt international security outlooks more flexible than the East-West, zero-sum calculations which have predominated their strategic calculations for over forty years. Otherwise, the United States' strategic role in the Southwest Pacific may increasingly become that of merely responding to the strategic agendas defined and implemented by others more attuned than are Washington's policy planners to the changing security needs and aspirations of the region.

CHAPTER 7

Conclusion

THE RISE of competing deterrence approaches to the U.S. Dominant Player strategy in the Asia-Pacific has ensued from the United States' failure to effectively relate its global strategy more effectively to regionally indigenous security concerns. Throughout much of the postwar era the rationale and scope of U.S. extended deterrence strategy in the region have not been clearly defined, even though the nature and extent of the threats to be deterred have changed. Equally responsible for the diminishing status of U.S. policy in this theater has been recent Soviet policy behavior. Moscow largely has transformed its image from that of a region-wide threat, justifying a broad defense coalition of Asia-Pacific states to deter Soviet power, to that of an aspiring participant in a highly prosperous and more benign regional security order.

As the politics of strategic bipolarity, which shaped international relations throughout most of the postwar era, begin to recede into history, Washington's Asia-Pacific treaty allies increasingly have become independent in defining national and regional security concerns. They have done so, in large part, because the "global-realists" who orchestrate U.S. deterrence strategy have remained unwilling to tailor the Dominant Player posture to regional security priorities. Until very recently, American leaders have been accustomed to offering only bland assessments concerning the place of Asian friends and allies in the West's global defense burden. The "revisionist-idealists" have offered no better policy course. Their prescriptions for wholesale U.S. strategic withdrawal from the region have generated little enthusiasm among pro-Western regimes in the Asia-Pacific, apprehensive about the uncertain ramifications of the power vacuum sure to follow. "Revisionist-pragmatists" appear largely indifferent to the still compelling need for the United States to participate in regional efforts to modify conflict risks and to underwrite mechanisms for regional confidence-building. American policymakers need to offer more effective prescriptions for a stable regional security environment than those advanced by these three policy schools.

As noted in this volume's introduction, the Bush administration appears to have shifted its approach to Asian security toward the revisionist-pragmatist outlook. Increasingly, the United States is viewing the relative worth of deterrence commitments in terms of expense to the national treasury. Washington has not specifically addressed the security problems of most concern to Asia-Pacific nations—conflict risk, scope, and prevention. Nor has the U.S. adjusted its deterrence strategy by linking recent and planned U.S. defense spending reductions to alternative political designs more conducive to resolving those problems. Neutrality politics and antinuclear movements are symptomatic of a growing frustration in the Asia-Pacific with the United States' inability to approach that part of the world as strategically distinct from other American deterrence interests and commitments. With its formidable maritime power and clear interest in retaining access to vitally important regional markets, the United States can and should contribute significantly to the preservation of Asia-Pacific stability and the implementation of confidence-building measures which could gradually supplant deterrence as the primary means of regional conflict avoidance.

The next sections will summarize the most important aspects of regional strategic change derived from this book's assessments of the competing deterrence postures in the Asia-Pacific. Following, policy recommendations will be offered as to how the United States can assimilate such change more effectively and adjust its extended deterrence strategy to retain greater regional influence.

THE OUTMODED DOMINANT PLAYER

AMERICAN DETERRENCE approaches to the Asia-Pacific need to be reexamined and updated, because the factors which shape that region's balance of power are rapidly changing. There is less prospect for direct engagement between the superpowers than when the Americans and Soviets initially carved out their respective spheres of influence at the outset of their postwar competition. Lawrence Freedman's characterization of this situation is apropos: "General deterrence is altogether more relaxed, requiring merely the conveyance of a sense of risk to a potential adversary to ensure that active hostilities are never seriously considered."[1] There also appears to be less urgency to potential situations of immediate deterrence. Prospects for the outbreak of hostilities between Asia-Pacific actors that could force the United States into military intervention have all but vanished. Policy miscalculations leading to North Korea again invading the South or to efforts by Asian maritime powers to settle offshore territorial disputes in the South China Sea by seizing control of key regional littorals and chokepoints are possible, albeit unlikely, exceptions. This relatively peaceful regional atmosphere is markedly different from that predominating in the early 1950s, when the Dominant Player approach was forged to minimize the risks of regional crisis escalating into global conflict, or during the late 1960s and early 1970s, when massive U.S. force levels were sustained for the Vietnam War.

U.S. extended deterrence strategy and its underlying rationales are perceived as increasingly outmoded by those allies and friends that, hypothetically, should continue to derive the most benefit from this posture. Indeed, current allied discomfort with extended deterrence reflects one of the ironies associated with that posture—the longer general war is avoided in a region, the more remote such a contingency appears to become. Unlike NATO Europe, where U.S. ground forces have comprised an indispensable part of that theater's front line of defense, American naval and air power in the Asia-Pacific theater are primarily assigned to underwrite a regional security balance by applying flexible response from primarily offshore positions. A strong argument can be made by those contesting the Dominant Player's legitimacy in the Asia-Pacific that, when the United States has opted to assert its military power there, it has either risked escalating limited war situations into episodes of intense nuclear brinkmanship or, despite its predominantly maritime strategy, has become mired in protracted ground wars that it could not win.

The Sino-Soviet rift, which emerged in the late 1950s/early 1960s, and the Sino-American rapprochement, which began to take shape in the early 1970s, were two marked turning points in allied perceptions about the utility of U.S. escalatory tactics as an appropriate means of resolving regional conflicts. Regional confidence-building measures and national development programs now are clearly gaining appeal as alternative approaches to the politics of nuclear risk. The Dominant Player posture remains operative, but rests upon a questionable proposition: that the legitimacy of escalation control endures because the United States is willing to commit nuclear suicide and take its allies down with it, if an adversary can be prevented from collecting the spoils of victory. As David Abshire notes, U.S. defense planners still tend to be "nuclear true believers" who "act as if nuclear deterrence in its present form is an article of religious faith and that to question it is heretical."[2]

The problem of interalliance transferability also has become increasingly difficult for contemporary American policy planners. Even the original American architects of postwar deterrence strategy faced major hurdles in convincing Asia-Pacific allies that Washington's global strategy was as applicable to their region as it was to Europe. The Joint Chief of Staff's "counterattack thesis" was regarded as inappropriate to the Asia-Pacific environment. It was firmly opposed by both the European and Asian SEATO members. After the U.S. military withdrawal from Vietnam, Asia-Pacific states further insulated their own strategic interests from those of the United States outside the region. Japan's resistance to the Carter administration's "swing strategy," South Korea's and Australia's rejection of President Reagan's appeals to participate in Persian Gulf peacekeeping, and China's retrenchment during the 1980s from Western European and NATO security affairs are all cases in point. New Zealand's complete disassociation from the American nuclear deterrent symbolizes the most extreme rejection of Washington's long-standing premise that regional and global aspects of U.S. nuclear deterrence strategy are indivisible. Little agreement has been reached over the years, moreover, on the optimum "mix" of U.S. force capabilities for responding to what are often disparate U.S. and allied threat assessments. U.S. allies in the Asia-Pacific, for example, find it hard to comprehend that a U.S. Maritime Strategy calling for the fighting of a protracted conventional war against the USSR's naval and air assets, on or near Soviet territory, could enhance their own local deterrence and security.

The credibility of U.S. extended deterrence in the Asia-Pacific has also been marred by fluctuations in the intensity of U.S. strategic commitment to the region. Charles de Gaulle argued during the 1960s that the United States cannot rationally extend unconditional guarantees for the survival of its NATO allies in the nuclear age. Likewise, the Asia-Pacific allies have questioned the readiness of Washington to fight a general nuclear or even conventional war in support of their survival. During the formative stages of the cold war, Japan, and South Korea both experienced substantial uncertainty over U.S. intentions to extend deterrence on their behalf. When SEATO was proven irrelevant to the defense of Indochina, Thailand and the Philippines criticized the ambiguities inherent in U.S. deterrence policies. China has long argued that both superpowers extend deterrence only to preclude others from developing self-reliant deterrence capabilities.

The true measure of the opposing arguments forwarded by the extended deterrence schools described in this volume's introduction lies in how closely the policy behavior of both friends and foes has conformed to their expectations. As successive chapters have shown, there often has been a credibility gap between U.S. defense planners' expectations about the salience of extended deterrence to regional security needs and the relevance of that strategy to those allies it is designed to protect. The burden-sharing debate, as well as growing allied preoccupation with problems of "local" deterrence and defense, are symptomatic of this issue. Moreover, American adversaries such as the USSR and PRC who *were* deterred by U.S. defense postures and capabilities during the cold war now perceive Washington's strategy to be increasingly ineffectual as a barrier to the establishment of their own Asia-Pacific spheres of influence, rivaling—if not exceeding—that enjoyed by the United States in the region since 1945.

That these Aspiring Players should arrive at such a conclusion is less indicative of a decline in U.S. military capabilities than of Washington's inability to convey its determination to apply such capabilities in a timely and appropriate fashion. The United States, after all, continues to possess a very formidable array of *nonnuclear* force assets with which to exercise deterrence in a regional context. It alone deploys carrier task forces which can respond to a wide spectrum of limited war contingencies at sea, on land, or in the air. Its forward basing system in the Asia-Pacific allows it to exercise a powerful military capability, potentially carrying the offense to any attacker and simultaneously securing access to critical regional sea lanes of communication. Consequently, the United States retains escalation control options which no one else, including the USSR, can even begin to match at the conventional deterrence level.[3]

These force options allow U.S. defense planners the opportunity to employ a wide range of response to regional crises on a case-by-case basis. In contrast, the Dominant Player posture has become relatively static and outmoded in three critical ways. First, the security commitments that the United States extends to its formal Asia-Pacific treaty allies are not equally credible in each case. Extended deterrence guarantees involving possible conflict escalation to Japan, South Korea, and Australia—the Transitional Players—are still in effect. Those guarantees which may still apply to the ASEAN states, New Zealand, or the two Chinas are much more conditional. Second, the American Dominant Player posture is either at odds with or irrelevant to the Aspiring, Reluctant, and Passive Players because of rival geopolitical aspirations or widening gaps between U.S. global strategy and local deterrence needs. Third, even local deterrence needs against external threats are becoming less important to Asia-Pacific elites intent on establishing regime legitimacy and on achieving a more secure and enduring regional order by pursuing nation-building and economic objectives. Given such conditions, the Dominant Player posture will need to revise substantially its traditional assumptions about the linkages between global and regional security politics.

THE ALTERNATIVE POSTURES

MUCH OF the discomfort with which Asia-Pacific nations now regard U.S. extended deterrence strategy can be attributed to their various electorates' growing conviction that security starts at home. Contemporary strategic issues in the region are increasingly driven by social and economic considerations which bear little relationship to the Dominant Player posture's traditional emphasis on external threat assessments, force capabilities, and nuclear politics. More pressing questions are how the dynamic economies of East and Southeast Asia can best interact regionally to maximize their national strengths and resources, where the Asia-Pacific's new lines of political and commercial decision making authority will lie, and how far regional cooperation will take Asians in a post-industrial world.[4] Markets and capital have largely replaced guns and bombs as the primary determinants of international power in the late twentieth century. Consequently, greater energy will be spent by Europeans and Asians on deciding whether to form and join customs unions, free trade pacts, or region-wide economic communities than on sustaining mutual defense treaties or formal alliances, with their connotations of nuclear involvement and geopolitical polarization.

Certainly the case for the decline of extended deterrence politics can be—and has been by others—overstated. The potential for conflicts and their escalation will remain as long as resource competition is a fact of international life. China, Japan, India, and other aspirants to regional influence, anticipating a superpower retreat from the Asia-Pacific's geostrategic landscape, are now clearly engaged in building up their capacities to project maritime power. This is a trend which, if not effectively addressed and mitigated by multilateral confidence-building and arms control measures, could yet lead to regional confrontations and destabilization.[5] For the remainder of this century, however, security in the Asia-Pacific will be concerned with the designation of internal mechanisms for political legitimacy and with the establishment of regional coalitions of sufficient scope and purpose to serve the development aspirations of their members. The flurry of regional diplomacy caused by Australia's recent (April 1989) proposal for a wider Asia-Pacific trading cartel—modeled along the lines of the Organization for Economic Cooperation and Development—grew largely from Indonesian and Malaysian concerns that any region-wide association would overwhelm their own national economies and weaken ASEAN's hard-won influence in shaping Southeast Asia's regional political setting.[6] Japan's campaign for strengthening the Pacific Economic Cooperation Conference (PECC), an informal grouping of Asia-Pacific businessmen, scholars, and government officials established in 1980, is perceived as even more threatening to ASEAN economic security because of Southeast Asian fears that Japan would attempt to use this forum to transform the entire region into a high yen trading bloc.

If the relevance of the Dominant Player extended deterrence posture in its present form is declining in the current Asia-Pacific environment, how relevant or practical are the contending approaches now emerging for achieving more promising avenues of regional defense cooperation? The Transitional, Aspiring, Reluctant, and Pacifist Player postures all represent efforts by their proponents to replace or transcend the disturbingly ambiguous and unimaginative premises of American deterrence strategy. They could, however, intensify the risks of regional and global conflict by encouraging errant political opportunism and strategic miscalculation. The following sections will briefly summarize each of these unpromising postures, in turn, and then examine more advantageous U.S. regional policy options.

The Transitional Player Posture

SECURITY OUTLOOKS among the Asia-Pacific's industrial democracies are increasingly becoming fashioned by developments which hardly could be anticipated when the United States formalized its extended deterrence commitments to Japan, South Korea, Taiwan, and Australia in the early 1950s. Most notably, economic forces are now primarily responsible for shaping of strategic perceptions held by many U.S. Asia-Pacific allies. Such perceptions, moreover, are often independent from the political-strategic interests pursued by Washington.

The emergence of American-Japanese competition over the development and marketing of "dual technology" which can be applied to both commercial ventures and the development of advanced weapons systems, for example, has precipitated tensions between Washington and Tokyo. These stresses could have far-reaching effects on Japan's willingness to collaborate on deterrence problems. If U.S. defense firms are successful in current quests to secure widespread protectionist legislation to block Japanese access to key state-of-the-art technologies needed for the enhancement of Japanese air and naval defenses (i.e., FSX jet aircraft engine components or the *Aegis* naval tracking and missile system), the United States could hardly expect Japan to be forthcoming with the transfer of advanced fiber optics, missile guidance systems, and semiconductor capabilities applicable to more rapid command and control requirements on the modern battlefield. In the face of increased suspicions and acrimony generated by commercial disputes, the defense burden-sharing concept—originally designed to fuse American global and Japanese regional deterrence efforts into a more cohesive and unified strategy—would fail.

Japan's perception of itself as a future international security actor presents an even more fundamental challenge to the Dominant Player posture. Yasuhiro Nakasone's demonstrated interest in linking defense problems to Japan's overall foreign policy interests was extraordinary for a postwar Japanese Prime Minister and invoked two different, but equally disturbing, scenarios for the future of the Mutual Security Treaty. One is an increasing American resistance (and that of almost every other Asia-Pacific nation) to the prospect of an increasingly armed, self-confident, and strategically independent Japan asserting its own will throughout the region by military strength precisely because it feels increasingly isolated from the United States and its other regional allies. Another is the demise of the Liberal Democratic Party and the coming to power in Japan of a political coalition intent on developing a foreign policy of eventual nonalignment, on shifting that country toward a Pacifist Player posture, and on excluding U.S. nuclear warships and aircraft from transiting its waters or airspace. While opposition parties characteristically tend to modify their foreign policy and defense platforms once they acquire national power, U.S. policy planners would still be well advised to prepare contingency plans on deterrence-related issues for a non-LDP or coalition Japanese government.

South Korea has only begun to contemplate the implications of its spectacular economic growth, allowing it to keep pace with or exceed North Korean military power with a smaller proportionate outlay of its national wealth. Indeed, Western analysts have estimated that during the 1990s, North Korea will need to spend close to 40 percent of its GNP to keep pace with the South's military capacity, if Seoul were to spend no more than the present 6 to 7 percent GNP it allocates to defense.[7] This factor, combined with increasing South Korean trade and political ties with China, the Soviet Union, and Eastern European nations, works to infuse South Korea with a sense of national pride and strategic independence, particularly among members of the younger generation whose memories are not long enough to recall the U.S. risking nuclear confrontation with Moscow so that their parents could develop their nation's current prosperity without fear of military invasion or occupation. While the military threat from North Korea remains real and significant (supplemented by a continued Soviet geostrategic interest in, and visits by its naval and military aircraft to, North Korean ports and airfields), U.S. military officials are becoming harder pressed to justify the continued deployment of the 2nd Infantry Division and its combat support elements. Even more difficult is explaining U.S. battlefield tactical nuclear weapons still deployed in a country whose military has developed conventional forces sufficiently strong, and indigenous weapons systems adequately sophisticated, to embrace a credible derivative of NATO's Air-Land Battle strategy for the defense of their own country below the nuclear level. Such weapons could be removed as part of an eventual nuclear-free zone arrangement for the Korean peninsula and as a basis for guarantees by North Korea not to develop or deploy nuclear weapons of its own.

Taiwan and Australia, as the two other Transitional Players in the region, also relate to Washington's deterrence strategy much differently than when they originally affiliated themselves with the U.S. collective defense system. To the Taiwanese, the major issue in their security relations with the United States, under the Taiwan Relations Act, is the credibility of American support in the event China resorts to military force to annex their island. On the other hand, Australian defense policy is increasingly regional in context, and thus far more sensitive than in the past to Canberra's need to avoid involvement in distant conflicts for the primary purpose of demonstrating its loyalty as a U.S. ally.

Both Taiwan's and Australia's frame of reference on conflict escalation and intensity have also shifted over the years. Taiwan supported the deployment of U.S. tactical nuclear weapons by the Seventh Fleet in the 1950s. However, it now measures the credibility of U.S. deterrence commitments in terms of the pace and quantity of conventional arms sales Washington allows U.S. defense firms to sustain with a highly proficient indigenous Taiwanese arms industry. Canberra is selective about which elements of the United States' strategic deterrence policy it will support. Australia has accepted the hosting of highly sensitive U.S. intelligence collection and tracking operations on its native soil as a contribution to the stability of global deterrence. At almost the same time, the Australians rejected participation in the Reagan administration's Strategic Defense Initiative, on the grounds that SDI added little to the credibility of the Dominant Player posture.

The Transitional Player approach to Asia-Pacific security is an ad hoc posture. It lacks a consistent or enduring agenda to set it apart from U.S. extended deterrence strategy, other than intermittent desires for greater national security autonomy within a Dominant Player strategic framework. Unlike Washington's NATO partners, who can help shape and revise Western collective defense strategy for Europe via well-established multilateral alliance instrumentalities in Brussels and elsewhere, the Asia-Pacific treaty allies must bargain with the

Americans separately, and they have little in common with each other strategically, apart from U.S. deterrence guarantees. Their individual ability to influence U.S. region-wide deterrence strategy, apart from opting not to be associated with it, is limited by a continuing inability or unwillingness to meet their own local deterrence requirements beyond very low levels of conflict escalation. Their dependency on U.S. deterrence guarantees still tends to exceed their quest for more American deference to their individual sovereign dispositions on security and defense issues.

The Soviet Aspiring Player Posture

BOTH HISTORICAL and socioeconomic factors preclude the Soviet Union from ever potentially supplanting the United States as the Asia-Pacific's Dominant Player. Nevertheless, Moscow hopes to gradually isolate the United States from the region's political-strategic mainstream. The Soviets are replacing their traditional "essentialist" or "war-winning" approach toward the region with a "contextualist" diplomacy. This shift, Moscow hopes, will ultimately lead to more comprehensive Soviet economic involvement and strategic influence in the region. The USSR's diplomacy has, accordingly, become more innovative and less confrontational. As the Soviets identify policies for resolving their disputes with China, for relating more effectively to an economically and militarily formidable Japan, and for pursuing nuclear-free zone politics with ASEAN and in the Southwest Pacific, their new leadership is determined that they will become a major economic and political force shaping what has become an increasingly multipolar world.[8] The key issue is the extent to which the new Soviet posture can succeed, and this depends, in part, on how enlightened U.S. strategy proves to be.

To date, some Soviet policy inroads appear to have been made. Most notably, less contentious Sino-Soviet relations afford Moscow an opportunity to reduce its military force deployments along the Chinese border. As Donald Zagoria has observed, "the deep freeze" in Sino-Soviet relations has ended, channels of communication are reopening, and a "slow but substantial improvement in the relationship" is occurring.[9] Yet the USSR still has not overcome completely its past image as a bellicose actor in the region, and the Soviets still are not trusted in many regional quarters. The Chinese, with at least some historical justification, remain highly vigilant in their relations with Moscow, and such caution will remain operative in China's foreign policy, regardless of the type of leadership which finally materializes in Beijing following the May-June, 1989 power struggle. The reality of Soviet power encircling China tempers Beijing's enthusiasm for a full-fledged rapprochement with the Kremlin. Under these conditions, China will not distance itself too far from the West and risk losing its strategic leverage with the Soviets. The USSR, in turn, will pursue any accommodation of Beijing with guarded enthusiasm. The legacy of past Chinese threats to Soviet territorial and ideological interests is still too fresh for Gorbachev to ignore. More importantly, Moscow has little real interest in relinquishing progress already made toward defusing the American threat with *perestroika* by introducing too overt a Soviet variant of the China card.

For the time being, Japan remains the most difficult component of the Soviets' Aspiring Player posture. The USSR has yet to offer Tokyo the one inducement which could begin the process of pulling Tokyo away from its security affiliation with Washington: reversion of the Northern islands to Japanese political control. Until that issue is resolved, territorial, historical, and cultural barriers between the Soviet Union and Japan will remain largely intractable, impeding prospects for a meaningful, positive breakthrough in relations between them. Japan's sophisticated technology infrastructure is also a problem from the vantagepoint of Soviet military planners. The Soviet military newspaper *Krasnaya Zvesda* [Red Star] concluded in late 1987, for example, that "Washington, using various channels, will strive to involve Japan, having in mind especially her scientific and technological capability, in its militaristic programs. And, judging by everything, there are those on the Japanese islands, who for the sake of possible profits, are not against allowing the country to be dragged into a costly arms race . . . and one which, most importantly, is fraught with serious consequences."[10] Japan is thus seen by Moscow as a vital contributor to the U.S. Dominant Player deterrence posture and as the Americans' best hope to compensate for any loss of U.S. strategic influence incurred as a result of the ANZUS crisis or from pending U.S. force withdrawals from the Philippines.[11]

Elsewhere in Northeast Asia the Soviets have carefully qualified their extended deterrence commitments to North Korea. They have done so in the interest of facilitating their growing commercial ties with Seoul and the eventual political stabilization of the peninsula. Moscow is encouraging the North and South Koreans to move forward, however uneasily, toward dialogue on unification. The Soviet Aspiring Player posture could also make some inroads into Southeast Asia and into the Southwest Pacific, where antinuclear sentiments and robust apprehensions of potential U.S. and/or Japanese economic hegemony are susceptible to diplomatic manipulation by the USSR. Yet even here, limitations on Soviet influence are readily evident. The Soviet Union's military infrastructure in Vietnam is regarded with suspicion by ASEAN states. Nor does Moscow have any tangible economic appeal for an ASEAN subregion experiencing one of the highest economic growth rates in the world. The Soviets can, however, "sell" their Asian collective security campaign to some Southeast Asian or South Pacific regimes that are subject to sudden and unpredictable power transitions. A number of them lack democratic traditions and institutions, and may resent either American efforts to involve the Japanese too heavily in the security of the region or intensified efforts by the Chinese to involve themselves.

Despite Gorbachev's policy innovations, the Soviet Union has yet to overcome its fundamental security dilemma in the Asia-Pacific. When Moscow has sought to strengthen its influence through military power in the region, it has encouraged opposing coalitions capable of deterring the Soviet threat at both the nuclear and conventional levels of conflict. When the military factor is downplayed in favor of cultivating closer diplomatic and economic ties, the Soviets have traditionally had little to offer. While the Soviet and Chinese barter economies facilitate trade between the USSR and PRC, neither communist power is a major factor in international commerce and finance. Until the Soviets are prepared to seriously negotiate the Northern Islands territorial dispute with Japan (perhaps removing their sizable military garrisons there as a tangible first step), reduce their still significant levels of military support to North Korea, accelerate their initial reduction of military operations at Cam Ranh Bay and at other Indochinese bases, and substantially reduce other Pacific Fleet and air support missions, Gorbachev's confidence-building proposals will be unsuccessful in modifying the Japanese, South Korean, and ASEAN threat assessments which justify the U.S. Pacific Command's missions. Sustaining alliance relations with North Korea and Vietnam and cultivating closer ties with a ruling gerontocracy in Beijing, whose mandate over the

Chinese population appears to be increasingly tenuous, are weak policy alternatives if the USSR is to compete successfully with the U.S. for regional influence.

It remains unclear how Gorbachev's ongoing campaign for internal economic and political reform, underscored by *glasnost* and *perestroika*, will ultimately affect Soviet military planning and behavior. It is, nevertheless, certain that the USSR is becoming more preoccupied with its own identity and destiny and less intent upon expending national resources in global strategic competition with the United States. The prospect of a failure of the the Soviet reform movement is disturbing to American and allied policy planners alike, but there is little they can—or should—do to influence its fate in a deterrence context. Paul Kennedy captures the essence of the problem:

> One could wish the reformers well without the naive enthusiasm that has characterized some Western portrayals of Gorbachev; and one can also dismiss those purblind conservatives who assert that *perestroika* is merely another device in the Soviet armory of deceptive measures. At the moment, Gorbachev seems in charge, and the internal reforms (and external diplomatic gestures) continue. But it is worth recalling that if he is unseated by some internal coup, this will cause all of Russia's neighbors, from the Germans to the Chinese, to be more suspicious of Moscow. The "correlation of forces" is still heavily tilted against the Soviet Union internationally.[12]

The Chinese Aspiring Player Posture

FOR MORE than a decade, Chinese leaders have assigned precedence to economic development over military spending. However, the development of China's independent nuclear deterrent has been a major exception to this policy. Beijing is obsessed with preventing either superpower from ever again exercising coercive diplomacy against the PRC. Chinese leaders, nevertheless, have tacitly and begrudgingly acknowledged extended deterrence as a reality of international life which allows China to "tilt" toward the West or the USSR at different intervals until it is powerful enough to permanently distance itself from what it views as excessive strategic collaboration with either superpower.

Although China has undergone radical domestic political change on several occasions since the Communist Party assumed power in 1949, its approach to the problems of war and deterrence has been remarkably consistent. Over the short term, Beijing has been careful to keep its perceived adversaries off balance. It does so by adopting tactics of calculated ambiguity in conveying its strategic interests and intentions and by applying its military power to regional crises which are perceived as threatening the survival of its own government or its territorial integrity (intrawar deterrence). China seeks to modernize its economy and technological infrastructure, and to prepare its armed forces for all possible levels of combat in the most cost-effective way possible. The relative progress of China's economic modernization program in transforming the country into a major global power has thus become what Robert Sutter has termed "the linchpin" determining the success or failure of the PRC's ultimate quest to become strategically independent.[13]

The Aspiring Player posture has been China's course since Mao Zedong approved the PRC's nuclear weapons development program in the mid-1950s. The Chinese want their country to become one of the world's great economic and military powers and to eventually achieve predominant political and strategic influence throughout East and Southeast Asia. Before realizing such objectives, however, the PRC must overcome several fundamental limitations. First and most significantly, Beijing's strategic influence within the region is restricted by the Marxist-Leninist revolutionary dogma of its government. The national student uprisings in May 1989 indicated that China's internal political system may well be on the verge of a legitimacy crisis. Such a crisis could significantly affect Beijing's drive for economic modernization and independent strategic power. Second, the Chinese will need to reconcile their strategic interests *within* the Asia-Pacific region with a clearer sense of what strategic objectives they entertain *beyond* it. The vague connotations of the "three worlds thesis," initially developed by Mao Zedong and later refined by Deng Xiaoping during the 1970s, have proven to be an inadequate justification for China's self-acclaimed status as the strategic "vanguard" of the Third World. Neither do they adequately rationalize the PRC's development of missile nuclear delivery systems capable of hitting targets not only in India and throughout the Asia-Pacific, but in Soviet Europe and North America as well. Chinese political leaders and military planners will need to advance more compelling reasons for these actions, if they are to overcome regional suspicions about their long-term strategic objectives. Stripped of self-righteous jargon, China's future strategic vision may well, in fact, be no more than an updated version of the Dominant Player posture, complete with prescriptions for escalation control, the forging of coalitions, and the expansion of strategic commitments.

Before the PRC can assume the status of a legitimate world power, it needs to sort out its existing regional security commitments on less xenophobic and more pragmatic grounds. Is the security of the Chinese state, for example, well served by continued alliance with a North Korea that remains politically and economically isolated from the rest of the region? Will compromise with Moscow on long-standing territorial questions yield greater strategic dividends for Beijing than has a rigid insistence that border disputes be completely resolved before full demilitarization of the Sino-Soviet border occurs? Can Chinese claims in the South China Sea be pressed without precipitating anti-Chinese maritime coalitions? Will the continuation of Chinese extended deterrence to Thailand be continued and supported by the United States and ASEAN, with all Vietnamese troops now removed from Cambodia and if a new government is installed in that country which may not enjoy the support of all the external parties concerned? No matter which domestic faction governs China in the aftermath of currently evolving political developments, it will be confronted with these and other difficult regional security policy questions.

A major imponderable in the region is what Sino-American strategic relations will be in the aftermath of the government's suppression of the prodemocracy movement in mid-1989. Over time, both Washington and Beijing may well consider resumption of such relations if they believe that payoffs for their individual national security interests will follow. For the United States, such payoffs should be assessed on the basis of how future Chinese regional security behavior will enhance, rather than detract from, American global and regional deterrence strategies. The extent to which China opts for a more active role in arms control, weapons nonproliferation efforts, and in the politics of conflict resolution will also be an important factor. For the short term, however, Sino-American military ties and related transfers of high technology will remain frozen as part of Washington's response to the Chinese government's crackdown against internal dissent. One can also speculate reasonably that decreased Sino-Soviet tensions along their lengthy mutual border entered into the U.S. decision to stem the flow of American arms technology and defensive weapons systems to China. Certainly, the Bush administration's decision was a source of visible relief to South Korea and to those ASEAN states worried about how

China would adapt naval weapons and communications systems procured from U.S. sources to its heightened maritime projection role in the South China Sea.

Until now, Beijing has provided only limited evidence that its interests coincide with those embodied in present American security policies, although the potential for this to occur cannot be discounted totally. While the PRC's aging leaders have expressed their outrage over what they characterized as disruptive Western influences emerging in post-Mao China, a complete Chinese strategic tilt toward the USSR and away from the United States and its regional allies would appear to be unlikely. This can be argued, particularly in view of both China's historical superiority complex toward what the Chinese regard as a culturally inferior Russian history and more recent, unresolved, territorial and ideological differences with Moscow.[14] Such factors typically are subtle, but pervasive and generally enduring.

It is more likely that China will choose to reaffirm its independent foreign policy from both superpowers, employing divide and rule tactics against both the United States and USSR. From China's perspective, the Americans need to desist from pressing the Chinese leadership on democratic reform and to exercise greater restraint from interfering in China's internal political affairs. The Chinese also want further assurances from Washington that the United States will not threaten to cut back or freeze high technology transfer relations whenever Beijing opts to conduct arms sales to a Third World client unfriendly to the United States. Additionally, Beijing would prefer a more consistent American interpretation of the "one China" principle as a means of facilitating an eventual unification of Taiwan with the mainland. Finally, further reductions in U.S. strategic forces (in conjunction with similar reductions in Soviet nuclear weapons inventories) is a desire of the PRC. Only with these conditions met would Beijing be more likely to participate in future superpower arms control initiatives or seriously weigh other "concessions" to various superpower interests and initiatives for establishing what they would regard as a more stable international balance of power. All of these issues, however, are subordinate in importance to the question of how Sino-Soviet relations will evolve over the next decade. Many Western analysts believe that it is this factor which will prove most important in determining the extent to which China is willing to collaborate, albeit guardedly, with American deterrence objectives, both regionally and globally.

ASEAN's Reluctant Player Posture

QUALIFIED ALIGNMENT with extra-regional powers will continue to be the necessary foundation of ASEAN's security approach, barring the unlikely development of a guaranteed neutrality zone for Southeast Asia. ASEAN, perhaps unrealistically, envisions the Soviet Union, China, and Japan eventually joining the United States as "over-the-horizon" military actors guaranteeing Southeast Asian neutrality.

While such a development could work to forestall proxy wars and to strengthen mechanisms for conflict limitation within ASEAN itself, lingering Southeast Asian apprehensions, particularly about Chinese and Japanese policy intentions in their subregion, remain strong. Moreover, there are conditions required if an authentic Zone of Peace, Freedom, and Neutrality is ever to emerge in the region. Vietnam would need to gradually reduce its reliance upon Soviet economic and military assistance. Similarly, Thailand must forego dependence upon Chinese and American support (the PRC-Thai and U.S.-Thai weapons stockpiles would have to be dismantled, and the pro forma Manila Pact/Rusk-Thanat communique commitments dissolved). Military basing/military exercise relationships with external powers (the U.S.-Philippines basing/Mutual Security Treaty, the Five Power Defense Arrangement) would have to be redefined in terms more acceptable to Southeast Asian nationalist movements. Such redefinition would perhaps have to emphasize training ASEAN forces to defend their offshore and historically contested territories, economic enterprise zones, and coastlines from insurgency or piracy, or would need to integrate military and civilian efforts in the coordination of public works projects.

Alternatively, acceptable levels of ASEAN-external power military interaction could be negotiated in multilateral conferences involving the ASEAN states and their existing "dialogue" partners (the United States, Canada, the European Community, Japan, Australia, and New Zealand). The Soviet Union and China might eventually be invited to at least some of these meetings, in observer roles and as part of broader regional confidence-building efforts. All measures would be designed to realize threat neutralization in a subregion that has known far too much conflict throughout the postwar period.

The reduction and ultimate elimination of great power basing operations is particularly important for the ASEAN states if they are to escape at all from the extended deterrence politics that have traditionally impeded their quest for strategic non-alignment. However, the price these states must pay for realizing strategic disengagement includes greater ASEAN responsibility for establishing and maintaining credible local deterrence. The Philippines has already learned firsthand the ramifications of inflated expectations about U.S. deterrence commitments, while simultaneously insisting on greater leverage in its bilateral security relations with Washington. During the 1988 basing review, U.S. lawmakers accused the Philippines of engaging in alliance blackmail and approved only $94 million, from an original $1.3 billion budget request, for maintenance and improvement of the bases' land utilization and support infrastructures.

The least acrimonious solution to the basing issue would be for the Americans to withdraw while maintaining the confidence of other ASEAN leaders that U.S. offshore power would remain more than adequate to deter any likely external threats. This could well be made possible by the introduction of U.S. offshore naval and air systems less dependent on fixed basing (fuel-efficient warships that can be repaired at sea and maintained for the same or lower costs at alternative ports, and longer-range transport aircraft are two examples). Such deployments would enable a smoother departure of U.S. forces from Clark and Subic and permit Washington to take the lead in forming economic development and financing consortia with Japan and, to a lesser extent, with the world's other industrial powers as the primary means for sustaining political-security ties with the Philippines.

The Pacifist Player

THE PACIFIST Player posture rejects the Dominant Player premises on escalation control and interalliance transferability at the nuclear level. It regards the question of credibility of nuclear commitment to be irrelevant, both on moral grounds and on the basis of changing strategic realities. As adopted by New Zealand, however, moral arguments tend to become entwined with the sentiments of isolationism. New Zealanders pursued the self-assigned mission of teaching others about the virtues of global nuclear disarmament and common security. At the policy level, the Lange government rejected U.S. ships and most aircraft from access to its territory by defending its sovereign prerogatives to unilaterally declare nuclear deterrence irrelevant to New Zealand's national security. The United States, accordingly, was confronted with a problem of alliance management: how to reconcile an ally's changing positions with practical defense relations.

The American response was to conclude that the Lange government was unilaterally and irresponsibly redefining traditional alliance commitments and that moral considerations were beside the point. Washington's decision to terminate most of its formal security relations with New Zealand was not so much a question of superpower "bullying," as one of American insensitivity to Wellington's apprehensions. From the Lange government's perspective, New Zealand was left little choice but to conclude that U.S. national security interests dictated the priority of Dominant Player extended deterrence strategy over continued alliance affiliation with New Zealand. The United States subsequently argued that most of its other allies believed in preserving the Dominant Player posture as the mainstay of Western deterrence politics.

The American premise of nuclear/conventional deterrence indivisibility, however, may be misplaced. To a large extent, alliances *are* about the preservation of common values and about implementing what a growing number of international security analysts view as a common security agenda (see chapter 6). There is increased skepticism among a number of Western electorates about using nuclear weapons to defend or advance the West's shared ideals. Those who question the continued relevance of nuclear deterrence strategy have postulated that Soviet strategic reach has never been so great that Western technology and allied geographic advantages could not be applied effectively with conventional forces. They claim that the original postwar collective defense strategy was misconstrued, lacking both the situations that would justify its existence and the imperative for extended deterrence.

Other allied governments have so far rejected the Pacifist Player approach. They have done so, not necessarily on the basis of conceptual disagreement, but because they value U.S. extended deterrence commitments to their own security more than they believe that some form of nonnuclear "common security" grounded in the values espoused by Lange or other Pacifist Players can credibly replace those commitments. Increasingly, though, American strategists and policy planners are beginning to question total rejection of Pacifist Player arguments. They are evaluating the Dominant Player's capacity to counter intraalliance misperceptions about U.S. defense commitments in an era of changing threat perceptions, increasingly finite U.S. resources, and growing antinuclear sentiments in both Europe and the Asia-Pacific.

REVISING THE DOMINANT PLAYER STRATEGY

THE UNITED States lacks a clear definition of its strategic interests and commitments in the Asia-Pacific theater. This condition has spawned indigenous approaches to regional security. Past U.S. attempts to articulate and underwrite its objectives in the region have often been unsuccessful. They have been either been too encompassing geopolitically (i.e., "horizontal escalation" and the unsuccessful "six-pillars" approach of formally declaring U.S. global and regional deterrence strategy to be integrated), rendering the Asia-Pacific a mere adjunct component of U.S. global strategy, or so ambiguous (e.g., the Nixon Doctrine) as to leave Washington's Asia-Pacific allies as uncertain as its adversaries about what U.S. strategic interests and commitments in the region actually were. This book's major premise is that a far better American policy course involves tailoring U.S. deterrence postures and commitments to fit those security objectives of Asia-Pacific states which coincide specifically with the *regional* interests of the United States. In the process of adjusting its deterrence outlooks to meet this criteria, Washington will be forced to clearly identify what U.S. national security interests are in the region and to formulate more realistic expectations about the willingness and abilities of its regional friends and allies in the region to facilitate those interests.

U.S. Vital Interests

OVER FORTY years ago, George Kennan identified what still remains the most fundamental American national security interest in the Asia-Pacific: to incorporate this region into an international order as an independent center of power and stability, while preserving reasonable U.S. access to its resources and markets and precluding its geopolitical subjugation to a power (or powers) hostile to the United States.[15] Extended deterrence was employed by successive U.S. administrations as a cost-effective way to realize this objective and to allow Asia-Pacific friends and allies the cushion necessary to pursue unimpeded economic and political development. Such development, Washington believed, would confirm to recently liberated Asia-Pacific populaces the innate superiority of democratic over authoritarian institutions of governance and would facilitate the region's pursuit of reasonably free, market-based, trade which could only work to Washington's long-term advantage.

Over time, this broader objective led to the defining of intermediate strategic tasks necessary to achieving an acceptable regional power equilibrium. For example, the United States must retain strategic control of its Pacific sea lanes of communication and must maintain its status as a major political influence throughout the Asia-Pacific region. To do so, it has every interest in countering the Soviet Union's forward projection strategy into distant points of the Pacific (as a means to interdict U.S. maritime power) by exploiting the USSR's lack of a strategic logistical capability in the region and by exploiting its own geographic and historical legacy as a legitimate Pacific power. The United States also must preclude distortion of Asia's military power balance by the blue water ambitions of regional maritime powers such as China, India, and Japan. Their rate of naval development can be controlled to some extent within the context of alliance and/or coalition strategy (e.g., Washington "balancing" Japanese maritime strength in Northeast Asia through remaining the senior partner in the U.S.-Japan Mutual Defense Treaty, or by assisting in the building up of Chinese "defensive capabilities" on land and sea) and through encouraging the development of subregional "defense communities" to counterbalance the growing power of a would-be regional hegemonist (i.e., encouraging ASEAN defense maritime cooperation in response to India's naval buildup and forward defense posture).

Several related U.S. strategic interests can be readily identified. The Japanese and, by extension, South Korean, industrial complexes must remain a part of the Western Alliance. Western influence should be restored and sustained with China, if and when progressive forces are able to govern in that country. If a more repressive Chinese leadership retains power, Washington needs to differentiate between legitimate opportunities for collaborating strategically with Beijing and occasions where such collaboration would be an unwarranted capitulation to Chinese mandated priorities in the vain hope that Beijing would later exercise reciprocity in its relations with the West. Washington has every interest in preserving sufficient U.S. and allied strategic capabilities in the region to meet both a Soviet and a renewed Chinese regional threat. The flow of commercial and military traffic through the Southeast Asia straits must continue unimpaired. Excessive strategic presence and political influence in the Southwest Pacific's burgeoning island-states by anti-Western powers must be limited, if not denied.

The Dominant Player extended deterrence posture can no longer address many of these interests effectively, because the USSR has achieved nuclear parity and because (as the critics of the imperial overstretch thesis readily point out) the Asia-Pacific allies are less prepared to cooperate than they were when the United States enjoyed nuclear superiority. Their increased preoccupation with local deterrence imperatives can be attributed in part to their economic prosperity, giving them the resources needed to defend themselves in situations of immediate deterrence against local or subregional opponents. With its primarily global dimensions, U.S. extended deterrence strategy can be usefully applied only if it is adjusted to meet policy criteria which relate more closely to these types of contingencies. Employment of selective ambiguity in the tactical application of deterrence strategy is merited; ignoring the task of integrating U.S. security interests and doctrine with those held by that strategy's intended beneficiaries is strategically irresponsible.

Initially, the United States can ascertain which security interests of its Asia-Pacific friends and allies it shares and is willing to assimilate into its own deterrence posture in the region. This reassessment of interests and commitments must be more rigorous than, for example, the six-pillars concept. The U.S. must take into account under what circumstances and at what levels it would employ strategic, theater, and tactical nuclear and nonnuclear forces, or a combination of such force assets, in various forms of possible regional conflict in which its allies require defense against external aggression. The continued utility of land-based tactical nuclear weapons in South Korea, for example, should be justified in regard to the primacy of the conventional deterrence and defense strategies in effect there since the early 1970s. If unjustified, they should be removed. South Korean politicians and military planners may well need to become more involved in the joint planning of what U.S. nuclear strategy (if any) is still relevant to the defense of their country. Japanese officials should also be consulted constantly with, and apprised of any U.S. decision making about South

Korean extended deterrence. The Korean Peninsula remains a vital geostrategic buffer for possible aggression against the Japanese mainland.

Washington should also review its positions on the proper balance between offensive and defensive aspects of deterrence as they apply to other CINCPAC contingencies. The feasibility and desirability of missile defenses in Northeast Asia against Soviet, and possibly Chinese, nuclear strike systems is applicable in this regard. Any such defenses should be weighed in terms of how they would effect the credibility of existential deterrence, a policy which has traditionally facilitated the credibility of tacit U.S. nuclear guarantees for a largely antinuclear Japanese electorate. The entire question of conventional deterrence in the theater should be evaluated more systematically by U.S. force planners. As U.S. Secretary of Defense Frank C. Carlucci observed in early 1989, the USSR's increased emphasis on its own conventional force modernization, as part of its "reasonable sufficiency" doctrine, in lieu of theater nuclear systems, requires continued U.S. efforts to maintain and strengthen its own subnuclear forces until reasonable conventional arms reductions are negotiated with Moscow.[16] By signing the treaty limiting Conventional Forces in Europe in November 1990, the USSR has demonstrated its willingness to make asymmetrical conventional force reductions in Europe. The U.S. will need to adjust its traditional deterrence postures in the Asia-Pacific accordingly. How it can do so should be discussed extensively with regional allies to seek theater-wide consensus and to avoid the credibility of commitment problems engendered by the failed expectations of SEATO and the Nixon Doctrine.

Alliance obligations will need to be reassessed and clearly understood by the United States and its Asia-Pacific allies, before future intraalliance disputes threaten to undermine defense relations. Better alliance communications and burden-sharing would enhance the United States' twin objectives of sea lane control and strengthened regional political influence. Robert Scalapino has described this imperative succinctly:

> Since the United States wants to see collective responsibility advanced, it must accept collective decision making, moving away from its past proclivity for unilateralism. Patron-client relationships are giving way almost everywhere to diverse forms of partnership . . . . With military technology and the nature of the security threat rapidly changing, U.S.

strategic policies in the Pacific-Asian region should be thoroughly reexamined in concert with allied and aligned states. The United States must
also prepare for the greater integration of security issues with those now
being negotiated in the West, despite important regional differences.[17]

It is important that the United States become more comfortable,
accordingly, with the notion of *policy* burden-sharing as opposed to
merely requesting increased *defense* burden-sharing from its allies and
friends in the Asia-Pacific theater. In this context, both Congress and
the Bush administration should broaden the mandate of the East Asian
Strategic Initiative beyond its current preoccupation with linking U.S.
force levels to a host allied nation's willingness to pay for a continued
U.S. military presence on its soil. One step toward more integrated
joint strategic planning, although politically controversial, would be
the strengthening of joint U.S.-Japanese-South Korean cooperation on
air interception missions over the Sea of Japan. While fusing the
separate U.S.-Japanese and U.S.-South Korean command structures
into a single entity is out of the question (Korean-Japanese historical
animosities are still too strong), Washington can point to the development of Malay-Singaporean-Indonesian triangular defense cooperation
as a precedental "role model" for upgraded South Korean-Japanese
intelligence exchanges about Soviet and North Korean force movements. The United States should also encourage follow-up collaboration to the Missile Defense Architecture Study, and more systematic
sharing of data on air space violations between Japanese and South
Korean military officials.

Another measure for defining alliance responsibilities more effectively would be implementing more systematic coordination of intelligence data-sharing between joint tracking installations currently manned
by U.S. personnel in Australia, the Philippines, and even in China,
provided they are allowed to remain. Joint naval and air exercises—
such as the biennial RIMPAC maneuvers—between the United States,
its Northeast Asian allies (Japan and South Korea), Australia, and
selected Western allies (i.e., Britain, Canada), should be continued,
both with the intent of demonstrating U.S. concern for overcoming
problems of command and control inherent to interalliance transferability and the objective of upgrading the local maritime deterrence
capabilities of U.S. allies through more extensive training.

Until arms reductions and other confidence-building measures can
be instituted, however, Washington must take care not to employ such

maneuvers in ways which appear overly provocative for the sake of integrating global and local deterrence. CINCPAC, for example, was scheduled to conduct what was widely advertised to be the "largest-scale" military exercise in Asia-Pacific history during September-October, 1989—an exercise designed to simulate an attack on the Kamchatka Peninsula, a PACOM occupation of the southern Kuriles, Western control of the Seas of Okhotsk and Japan, and counterattack operations by Japanese and South Korean forces. The maneuvers turned out to be further away from Kamchatka and the Sea of Okhotsk (they were conducted near the Aleutian islands) and less "offensive-oriented" than originally advertised.[18] However, any image of U.S. and allied forces engaging in war games which appear to endorse "maritime strategy revisited" contrast poorly with Soviet proposals to establish Northeast Asian nuclear-free zones and to impose caps on superpower naval deployments in the region. Such an image is threatening to the credibility and appeal of U.S. extended deterrence efforts in the region. It also does little to induce the USSR to follow through on confidence-building initiatives which could eventually replace deterrence strategy as a preferred means for realizing regional peace and stability.

The Soviets, of course, still express routinely their strong concern that, as Europe moves towards regional disarmament, the Asia-Pacific is becoming more militarized at nuclear and conventional levels. The United States, according to one Soviet analyst, retains "a dangerous chain" of nuclear stockpiles in South Korea, Guam, the Philippines, and on the American West Coast. U.S. officials, he observes, continue to endorse a strategic approach for the region that reinforces its alliances and emphasizes reliance on its extended deterrence posture.[19] Such pronouncements should be regarded, at least in part, as little more than the latest in a long line of propaganda designed to create friends within Asia-Pacific nuclear-free zone movements. A more valid question is the extent to which U.S. extended deterrence strategy may still be overrelying on nuclear weapons systems in this theater, at the expense of America's own and its allies' best strategic interests. Prospects for improving U.S. and allied security by nuclear arms control measures, which could take full advantage of existing or imminent American superiority in conventional weapons forces and technology, while still attracting Soviet participation in arms control negotiations, should be seriously explored.

The real issue is not whether U.S. maritime power should be deployed at full readiness on the Soviet Union's doorstep, but how quickly and how convincingly it could be applied against Soviet offensive forces deployed in the Far Eastern Command and elsewhere at the outset of a regional or global crisis. While the specific number of units required to maintain deterrence credibility may be debatable, "the quantitative strength of U.S. forces in the region is less important than the *perception* that the United States remains truly committed to regional deterrence." [20] The criteria for judging appropriate force levels is the ability to fulfill specific missions which protect vital American interests.

For this reason, the erosion of allied support for an American strategic presence in the Asia-Pacific must be avoided, even as Washington moves to establish more cost-efficient defense burden-sharing with our allies in the region and to establish confidence-building precedents with traditional adversaries there. The Philippines basing situation is instructive. The ASEAN states view Clark Air Base and Subic Bay largely as elements of U.S. global strategy, rather than as serving regional security needs. They nevertheless recognize that, until more cost-effective offshore replenishment facilities are ready for deployment, Washington's withdrawal from those sites would deprive them of a supportive backup resource in the event they are unable to control internal sources of political instability and subversion.

The Philippines bases are not the only situation where U.S. access to regional way stations critical for control of the region's sea and air lanes is becoming more tenuous. Japanese public opinion is increasingly sensitive to the political and economic burdens entailed in Tokyo's logistical support of U.S. military operations in Japan. Sovereign management of basing property rights, environmental considerations, and antinuclearism fueled by recent "disclosures" about past U.S. "violations" of Japan's three non-nuclear principles are all potential flashpoints.

U.S. forces are scheduled to be removed from Seoul, largely because of the symbolic connotations such deployments have in the capital city of an increasingly prosperous country still divided decades after the Korean War. Australian labor unions have long resisted the docking of U.S. and British naval units on a neither-confirm-nor-deny basis. New Zealand's ports, of course, are no longer available. It is unlikely that China would allow regular and systematic American use of its ports in peacetime conditions. Washington's Asia-Pacific base retention problem is that while regional leaders encourage the United States not to relinquish basing rights in the Philippines or in Northeast Asia, their support is qualified because they have offered no concrete measures to accommodate Washington if U.S. access to the Philippines were lost.[21]

Implementing Strategic Reassurance

AMERICAN POLICY planners, accordingly, are challenged to adjust old deterrence assumptions in response to rapidly changing strategic conditions in the Asia-Pacific region. The U.S. must still deploy adequate military power in the theater to preclude miscalculation by rival states about its will and capacity to defend its security interests. Washington must simultaneously, however, work with its strategic competitors to reduce regional tensions and conflicts, or it eventually risks a serious loss of influence in the region because it is perceived by an increasing number of regional actors to be unjustifiably bellicose. This risk is intensified by the Soviet Union and China who, as Aspiring Players, employ both opportunistic diplomacy and military intimidation to offset U.S. extended deterrence strategy. Indeed, in the absence of more equitable allied burden-sharing arrangements, even many Americans would argue that the only policy avenue open is a reduction in U.S. Asia-Pacific security commitments.

While extended deterrence strategy still has a legitimate role to play in the Asia-Pacific, the U.S. should simultaneously explore new opportunities for working with intraregional actors to identify common approaches to achieving and maintaining Asia-Pacific regional stability. The Dominant Player posture is best complemented by a policy of *selective reassurance:* the removal of suspicions and the establishment of mutually acceptable norms for conflict resolution and regional development. As Richard Ned Lebow and Janice Gross Stein have noted, both deterrence and reassurance presume that hostility and conflict will be present in most strategic environments, but reassurance assumes that conflicts between adversaries commence or escalate out of a sense of acute vulnerability, rather than from an aggressor's pursuit of strategic opportunity.[22] Hence, the United States' initiatives for implementing strategies of reassurance must be selective, not pervasive. Selective reassurance, however, is not an end in and of itself. It must be tempered by a realization that some threats are best met and some goals best attained by a demonstrated capacity to use military power when the need arises. U.S. policy must be flexible enough to maintain worthwhile security relationships with allies and friends with whom Washington occasionally disagrees or who prioritize their local deterrence objectives relative to U.S. global priorities.

The operative premise underlying U.S. selective reassurance strategy in the Asia-Pacific should be that Washington is in a greater position of geopolitical strength globally and in this region than at any time since Kennan first introduced containment as the operative postwar U.S. strategy over four decades ago. As leaderships in both the USSR and the PRC struggle to reconcile internal crises of legitimacy and to control worsening domestic economic situations, they are increasingly constrained in projecting military power abroad. Tellingly, each has recently instituted substantial manpower reductions of their military forces. The Soviets' willingness to include Asian-based systems in the first comprehensive theater nuclear arms control agreement negotiated by the superpowers in December 1987, bodes well for future prospects to implement regional confidence-building measures under a more stable Asia-Pacific security regime.[23] As Transitional Players, Japan, South Korea, Taiwan, and Australia understand the manner in which this evolving U.S. power advantage gives each of them more flexibility to assume regional defense burdens that would have been unthinkable only a few short years before. Simultaneously, they are freed to explore ways to diminish regional confrontation. The ASEAN states still desire an American offshore military buffer to safeguard their cautious yet progressive development efforts. Even New Zealand desires some form of continued security affiliation with Washington, if the nuclear deterrence impasse can be resolved. In general, the United States finds itself in a position to define and to largely implement a regional security agenda for the Asia-Pacific, if it moves quickly and forcefully to seize the policy initiative.

As this region's Dominant Player, the United States can enter into confidence-building negotiations with the Soviet Union or China with economic and military advantages which could be used to win major concessions. In return for a freeze and gradual reduction of U.S. and allied conventional forces in Northeast Asia, for example, the Soviets could be pressed to scrap a number of their long-range bombers, dismantle recently built bases in the Far Eastern theater, reduce ballistic missile submarine activity in the Sea of Okhotsk, or support measured and equitable arms control on the Korean Peninsula. The United States and Japan could reduce their antisubmarine warfare capabilities in the Straits of Japan if Moscow agrees to demilitarize the southern Kurile islands and substantially reduce unauthorized overflights over Japanese territory. Further Soviet initiatives to reduce its conventional force strength in the Far East, and inducements to facilitate greater Chinese trade with, and investment, in the PRC by the West and Japan, could add to Beijing's incentive to assume a more meaningful role in future regional arms control bargaining.[24]

At least two additional confidence-building measures could be seriously considered as steps for building a more stable regional security order. One is to encourage greater dialogue between the two Koreas, potentially leading to nuclear-free zone guarantees for the Korean Peninsula. This issue-specific agenda would override more comprehensive problems of how unification negotiations would be structured (a source of dispute between Seoul, Pyongyang, and their respective sponsors for years). The focus would instead be on nuclear risk-reduction by linking the dismantling of North Korean facilities capable of producing weapons grade material with a calibrated withdrawal of American land-based nuclear systems from the peninsula. Monitoring and verification initially could be carried out by the International Atomic Energy Agency (IAEA) with American, Soviet, and Chinese support (all of these powers are IAEA members). U.S. offshore nuclear and conventional forces are more than adequate to achieve escalation control in any foreseeable Korean contingency in the unlikely event South Korea's own growing military power proves insufficient to deter an attack by the North.[25]

A second approach to confidence-building in Northeast Asia is less palatable to U.S. military planners but one which nevertheless may need to be weighed if serious progress in selective reassurance is to be made. With the tempering of Maritime Strategy, the constriction of U.S. naval budgets, and the retirement of over 1,100 aging nuclear weapons systems previously deployed on U.S. naval surface ships in early 1989, the time may be propitious to consider reductions of tactical nuclear weapons for ocean combat as part of a broader Northeast Asian disarmament package. Both the Soviet political leadership and retired U.S. naval officials have advanced related proposals. Mikhail Gorbachev's initiatives advanced at Vladivostok and Krasnoyarsk have already been covered in chapter 3. More recently (January 1990), former U.S. Joint Chiefs of Staff Admiral William J. Crowe testified before Congress that tactical naval nuclear weapons talks should be included in future superpower arms control negotiations if, by doing so, the United States can extract significant arms control concessions from the Soviets in return and preserve the survivability of its own aircraft carriers, otherwise vulnerable to nuclear cruise missile attacks at sea.[26]

The Bush administration continues to argue that such weapons constitute an integral part of the American capability for deterring Soviet attacks against Eurasian allies, attacks using nuclear systems not presently covered by any arms control agreement. It also contends that agreements currently envisioning U.S. reductions of its tactical naval deterrent would give the Soviets too large a concession for what Moscow could give in return, citing the geopolitical rationale that the United States projects power predominantly at sea, while the Soviet Union does not.[27] Proponents of regional naval arms control reply that the United States is more vulnerable to nuclear-armed sea launch cruise missiles in naval warfare involving countervalue or urban/industrial targets than are the Soviets, due to higher U.S. and allied population densities. They also note that cruise missiles are destabilizing in an offshore regional nuclear war-fighting situation, because they can be used to saturate and destroy second-strike systems in rear echelon or "bastion" areas, thus removing any prospects for escalation control against global war.[28] Striking a proper balance between removing outdated or overly provocative nuclear systems at sea and preserving enough offshore nuclear capabilities to sustain legitimate deterrence objectives will not be easy for U.S. force planners. However, the potential benefits to regional stability of lowering the regional nuclear threshold in the Asia-Pacific seems worth the comparatively low risk of talking with Moscow about reducing both land and sea-based theater nuclear systems.

Negotiations between the ASEAN member-states and the regional powers about ways to expedite realization of ZOPFAN could be moved to an expanded and institutionalized setting, modeled after the European Security Conference. Related measures might include establishment of a "cooperative international regime" to exercise control over the Spratly Islands and other contested areas; joint verification arrangements to monitor weapons deployments; and peacekeeping arrangements to be employed in the event conflict resolution cannot be quickly achieved for regional disputes. Data could be exchanged among all Asia-Pacific states on defense spending and threat assessments.[29]

Prospects for strengthening and legitimizing nuclear-free zones in Southeast Asia and in the South Pacific should be taken more seriously. It is not enough for Washington to merely insist that their existence inherently undermines U.S. extended deterrence strategy. While most signatories of the Treaty of Rarotonga and most ASEAN states supporting nuclear-free politics understand that superpower military access to their respective regions cannot entirely foreclose the option to deploy or transit nuclear-capable systems, the aspirations driving the antinuclear movements in these subregions are very genuine. A good number of South Pacific islanders have lived, or now live, on the front lines of American and French nuclear testing, with sometimes horrible environmental and physiological consequences. Not long after their decolonization, most of the ASEAN countries found themselves in the vortex of cold war confrontation between East and West, with American and British nuclear systems deployed in various locales throughout Southeast Asia. The United States has argued that its acceptance of regionally sponsored nuclear-free zones would set precedents which may erode its global deterrence posture. Nevertheless, it appears likely that the momentum of popular grass roots sentiment for nuclear-free zones, combined with the changing global power balance, are too compelling for the policy logic of NCND to prevail in U.S. alliance relations much longer. The Bush administration might do well to again review Australia's formula for reconciling the imperatives of deterrence strategy with the ideals of future nuclear disarmament.

Convergent Deterrence: Accommodating Reassurance to U.S. Strategic Interests

IF STRATEGIC reassurance negotiations produced mutually acceptable results, the United States and its allies could then begin to weigh the advantages and feasibility of modifying the Dominant Player extended deterrence posture in order to preserve it. Several steps can be taken by Washington to ensure the legitimacy of its deterrence policy and commitments in the Asia-Pacific while it moves concurrently to achieve selective reassurance. To implement these measures successfully, however, Washington must become a "Revised Dominant Player," intent on balancing policy means with policy ends by integrating extended deterrence strategy more effectively into regional security priorities.

U.S. policy planners need to determine in advance which American security objectives should be clearly delineated for *each* Eurasian theater and, conversely, which interests are better left undeclared. Such a policy blueprint will allow Washington to appear as less reactionary when regional crisis do emerge and more consistent on other occasions. Traditional communiques, fashioned from backdoor compromises at NATO Ministerial Council sessions or written in advance of intermittent visits by highly placed U.S. officials to Asian allied capitals, are usually too bland in their content and setting to allow much insight into how U.S. deterrence strategy intersects with U.S. regional security interests and commitments. So, too, are annual defense posture statements, which too often simply reflect a presidential administration's effort to justify military spending budgets or to quell interservice rivalries.

A more appropriate means of establishing the relationship of extended deterrence strategy to current U.S. strategic interests is the conduct of a careful, systematic, thoughtful general review of U.S. Pacific strategy. This process would go beyond the East Asia Strategic Initiative which primarily emerged from the acrimony of Congressional burden-sharing debates and the politics of U.S. budget deficits. One deliberative tool for accomplishing such a review is an independently appointed presidential commission. While its views and conclusions generated much controversy in Europe, President Reagan's Commission On Integrated Long-Term Strategy was a constructive first step in meeting the need for strategic reassessment.[30] So, too, were special Congressional hearings on national strategy held during 1987. Other deliberatory bodies, such as a presidentially appointed task force from within existing U.S. executive bodies, vested with the charge of generating input for national policy, or, alternatively, a special National Security Council commission could also operate with a combined executive-legislative mandate and undertake the task of conducting a hard and thorough review of how extended deterrence can remain viable in the separate regions where the United States has retained formal security commitments.

Once the guidelines are set, Washington can then seek to forge a consistent global strategy. Most of the Asia-Pacific allies are distinctly uncomfortable with the revised "world view" and seemingly inevitable changes in strategic doctrine which accompany each new U.S. presidential administration, as well as with the year-long policy paralysis which seems to occur prior to its election. Whatever the merits of democratic accountability may be at home, such fits and starts are viewed from abroad as a critical weakness in American decision making. U.S. officials should work to minimize the effects of our political system on policy consistency toward American allies and friends in the Asia-Pacific and elsewhere, to the maximum extent possible.

Terry Deibal has succinctly described the policymaking challenge:

> The problems decisionmakers face in creating deterrence in an era when the tools of commitment are in short supply are likely to multiply, as are the problems of projecting American military power . . . the tendency will be to extend commitment to more and more marginal countries in order to secure the capability to defend areas that really count . . . perhaps the solution can be found in recalling the concept of alliance used in earlier days, in seeing commitments as part of a sophisticated national security strategy.[31]

The "sophisticated" national security strategy to which Deibel alludes is predicated upon rewarding potential adversaries for restraining from action against a regional or international security system, or, alternatively, deterring them with a preponderance of strength. The immediate postwar balance of power required from the United States, as the Dominant Player, less sophisticated policies of reassurance and deterrence than those historically devised by previous hegemons. Tight bipolarity and, by extension, containment were ingrained as the primary bases of international competition. The challenge now facing the policy architects of U.S. strategy is how reassurance can be reasonably pursued, or deterrence credibly applied in a more complex period involving wholesale international systemic change.

U.S. policy planners should avoid attempting to integrate their distinctly regional security priorities into a "globalist" posture, either on the grounds of satisfying short-term requirements for "cost-effectiveness," or in the interest of addressing alleged or unnecessary, strategic asymmetries. They should instead strive for policy consistency by devising long-term policy guidelines which will allow the United States to realize what this book's introduction labeled as "convergent deterrence": the effective assimilation of contending regional and extraregional strategies into a cooperative security effort. In employing this strategy, Washington would acknowledge openly and frankly, as a power committed to realizing a global security agenda, its shared security interests and differences with allies and potential adversaries in the region. In doing so, the United States would more effectively convey its rationale for extended deterrence and allow it to be examined and evaluated within the region. Such a policy could also establish belief by opponents that the United States will initiate and sustain action only if its national interests justify it and could reassure allies that the United States will use its power and influence in their interest when American global and allied regional interests coincide. In the absence of mutual strategic interests, the United States and each Asia-Pacific ally should explore the ramifications of such policy incompatibilities and ways to achieve stratetic policy compromise.

Although convergent deterrence has not been a predominant concept in U.S. regional security planning for the Asia-Pacific, precedents do exist. The Eisenhower administration's acceptance of the Yoshida Doctrine reflected a gradual U.S. understanding that both Washington and its Japanese ally would benefit more from an existential nuclear deterrent than from Japan's remilitarization to levels where it would inevitably assume a premature and provocative central role in regional deterrence politics. U.S. security relations with Indonesia and Malaysia have long taken into account and minimized policy differences, because the early postwar policies of these two countries "conditioned" the Americans to accept their independence on various security issues. The ANZUS dispute between the United States and New Zealand in the mid-1980s, in contrast, is instructive on how *not* to approach the challenge of strategic policy divergences between allies. New Zealand abruptly shifted from its long-term posture of general strategic acquiescence to Washington's global deterrence requirements to a complete rejection of the premises underlying those imperatives. The Reagan administration, in turn, overreacted to revisions in an ally's regionally grounded security agenda by its unfounded apprehensions that global implications were involved in the dispute.

At the heart of convergent deterrence, then, is the requirement that Washington explore every opportunity to work with its Asia-Pacific allies in forging defense policies which meet both U.S. global and allied regional security objectives. In doing so, U.S. policy planners will be more successful in reinforcing allied confidence in American strategic intentions and policies. With increased alliance consensus, the

United States can relate to the Asia-Pacific with correspondingly greater confidence and will be free to explore selective reassurance initiatives more actively. If adjustments are made to convert the Dominant Player posture into one combining selective reassurance and convergent deterrence, U.S. policy planners can be relatively optimistic about future trends in Asia-Pacific politics and development.

Long-term trends in the Asia-Pacific are running greatly in the West's favor, perhaps even more than we would have dared hoped until recently. Most of the region's nation-states have adopted capitalist, pro-Western, economic systems and are gradually moving toward more democratic forms of governance. Recent events in Eastern Europe and the USSR suggest that the original sources of threat against which U.S. extended deterrence strategy was initially applied are undergoing significant historical change. It is critical that the United States be viewed as a continued force for positive and dynamic evolution in the world order and as a dependable agent for conflict resolution, helping to shape the Asia-Pacific's political and economic destiny. Extended-deterrence strategy still has a role to play in the region's future, but it must be translated into a clear expression of multilateral security cooperation if it is to be effective.

Notes

INTRODUCTION

1. In this volume, the "Asia-Pacific" is defined as stretching from the United States west coast northwest through the Aleutian island chain and into the Far East, Transbaikal and Siberian Military Districts of the USSR, the Seas of Japan and Okhotsk, the Korean peninsula and Japanese archipelagoes, southwest into mainland China, the South China Sea, Indochina, the Southeast Asian straits, and directly southward into the Southwest Pacific and Oceania. The westernmost boundaries of the Asia-Pacific region for purposes of this study are the Andaman Island chain to the north (located in the Bay of Bengal roughly halfway between Thailand and India) and the Cocos island group situated southwest of the Sunda Strait in the eastern Indian Ocean.

2. This definition is a rough composite of those found in Dick Cheney, Secretary of Defense, *Annual Report to the President and the Congress* (Washington D.C.: USGPO, January 1990), pp. 2–3; Anthony H. Cordesman, *Deterrence in the 1980s: Part I—American Strategic Forces and Extended Deterrence*, p. 2; and Richard Smoke, "Extended Deterrence: Some Observations," p. 37.

3. Frank C. Carlucci, Secretary of Defense, *Annual Report to the Congress: Fiscal Year 1990* (Washington D.C.: USGPO, January 9, 1989), pp. 45, 49.

4. A text of NSC 68 is reprinted as "A Report to the President Pursuant to the President's Directive of January 31, 1950 [Washington] April 7, 1950," in *Foreign Relations of the United States 1950* vol. 1: *National Security Affairs; Foreign Economic Policy* (Washington, D.C.: USGPO, 1977), pp. 235–292. The seminal work on the origins of early postwar U.S. strategies of containment and defense remains John Lewis Gaddis, *Strategies of Containment*.

5. See "Note by the Executive Secretary to the National Security Council on Basic National Policy [Washington] October 30, 1953," *Foreign Relations of the United States 1952–1954*, vol. 2: *National Security Affairs, Part 1* (Washington D.C.: USGPO, 1984), pp. 577–597. Two of the best sources covering the transition of U.S. deterrence strategy occurring during the Truman and Eisen-

hower administrations are Samuel P. Huntington, *The Common Defense*, especially pp. 47–88; and Marc Trachtenberg, "A 'Wasting Asset': American Strategy and the Shifting Nuclear Balance, 1949–1954," *International Security* (Winter 1988/89), 13 (3): 5–49.

6. The premises for flexible response were initially posited by General Maxwell Taylor in his classic text, *The Uncertain Trumpet*.

7. The most succinct explanation of the Nixon Doctrine offered at the time was by Secretary of Defense Melvin R. Laird in testimony before the House Subcommittee on Department of Defense Appropriations. See *FY 1971 Defense Program and Budget* (Washington D.C.: USGPO, February 25, 1971). The so-called "Nixon Doctrine" was further developed in successive annual foreign policy statements submitted by the President to the Congress between 1970–1973. See chapter 5, note 66.

8. See, for example, Carter's speech on national security delivered at Wake Forest University, March 17, 1978. Noting that the U.S. entertained longstanding security concerns beyond American and European shores, the President linked the Asia-Pacific and Middle East regions to U.S. global deterrence strategy. The President noted, however, that: "In all these situations, the primary responsibility for preserving peace and military stability rests with the countries of the region." He pledged that the United States would "work with our friends and allies to strengthen their ability to prevent threats to their interests and to ours." Reprinted in *President Carter 1978* (Washington D.C.: Congressional Quarterly, April 1979), p. 141–A.

9. For a concise summary of this strategy, see President Ronald Reagan, *National Security Strategy of the United States*, p. 1.

10. Cheney, *Annual Report to the President and the Congress*, pp. 1–2.

11. According to recent figures provided by the International Institute for Strategic Studies, the USSR deploys just over 5.096 million active duty forces; the PRC, 3.030 million; the U.S., 2.163 million; India, 1.362 million; Vietnam, 1.249 million; and North Korea, 842,000. Iraq deploys approximately 1 million active duty personnel. IISS, *The Military Balance 1989–1990* (London: IISS, Autumn, 1989), pp. 150, 208–211. Force levels for both the U.S. and USSR inevitably will decline over the next few years as budgetary imperatives become more pressing for both superpowers. China and Vietnam have also instituted force level cutbacks.

12. Senators Sam Nunn and John McCain, "U.S. Allies: No More Free Rides," *Washington Post*, August 13, 1989, p. B-7.

13. U.S. Department of Defense, *A Strategic Framework for the Asian Pacific Rim: Looking Toward the 21st Century*, Washington, D.C.: USGPO, April 19, 1990, pp. 16, 18, and 20. See also John M. Broder, "U.S. Plans 10% Troop Cut in 3 Asian Nations," *Los Angeles Times*, February 14, 1990, pp. 1, 10; John M. Broder, "U.S. to Cut Troops 10% in Japan, S. Korea," ibid., April 3, 1990, p. 11.

14. Broder, "U.S. Plans 10% Troop Cut" p. 10.

15. James R. Kurth, "The Pacific Basin versus the Atlantic Alliance: Two Paradigms of International Relations," pp. 37–44.

16. A well-developed version of this argument is found in Norman D. Palmer, *Westward Watch: The United States and the Changing Western Pacific*, pp. 8–9.

17. A recent summary rationalizing this approach is by David Anderson, "Asia Needs the Pax Americana," *The Asian Wall Street Journal Weekly*, March 26, 1990, p. 16.

18. This point is forcefully made by Christopher H. Achen and Duncan Snidal, "Rational Deterrence Theory and Comparative Case Studies," especially pp. 160–163.

19. Bruce M. Russett, "The Calculus of Deterrence," *The Journal of Conflict Resolution* (June 1963), 7 (2): 98.

20. Robert Manning, *Asian Policy: The New Soviet Challenge in the Pacific*, p. 22.

21. "Nuclear Policy Sparks Debate," *New Zealand Foreign Affairs Review* (January-March 1985) 35 (1): 8.

22. This group is assessed in an incisive study by Abraham Ben-Zvi, *The Illusion of Deterrence: The Roosevelt Presidency and the Origins of the Pacific War*, especially pp. 52–57, 110–113. Also see Richard Betts, *Surprise Attack: Lessons for Defense Planning*, p. 134.

23. [George F. Kennan] " X," "The Sources of Soviet Conduct," pp. 566–582 is the definitive source. Also see a sophisticated evaluation of Kennan's approach by John Lewis Gaddis, *Strategies of Containment*, pp. 54–65 and an assessment of how Kennan related global strategy to the problem of organizing NATO in Douglas Stuart and William Tow, *The Limits of Alliance: NATO Out-of-Area Problems Since 1949*, pp. 31–34.

24. Gaddis, *Strategies of Containment*, p. 56.

25. One of the early—and best—works representing this group's regional outlook is a Council of Foreign Relations Study authored by Fred Greene, *U.S. Policy and the Security of Asia*. More recent examples include Richard A. Solomon, ed., *Asian Security in the 1980s: Problems and Policies in a Time of Transition*, produced from a definitive RAND Corporation conference; Solomon, ed., *The Soviet Far East Military Buildup;* Masashi Nishihara, *East Asian Security and the Trilateral Countries*, written under the direction of the Trilateral Commission; and a series of papers authored by Kissinger and other representatives of the global-realist perspective in the International Institute for Strategic Studies, *East Asia, the West, and International Security: Prospects for Peace.*

26. The representative works include William Arkin and David Chappell, "Forward Offensive Strategy: Raising the Stakes in the Pacific," pp. 481–500; Richard J. Barnet, *The Alliance: America, Europe, and Japan—Makers of the Postwar World;* Walden Bello, Lyuba Zarsky, and Peter Hayes, *American Lake: Nuclear Peril in the Pacific;* Noam Chomsky, *At War With Asia;* Bruce Cumings, "Power and Plenty in Northeast Asia: The Evolution of U.S. Policy," pp. 79–106; and George McT. Kahin, *Intervention: How America Became Involved in Vietnam.*

27. Arkin and Chappell, "Forward Offensive Strategy," p. 496.

28. Hayes, Zarsky, and Bello, *American Lake*, p. 10.

29. Cumings, "Power and Plenty in Northeast Asia," p. 103.

30. See especially his "Beyond 1972: The Political-Military Gap," in Earl C. Ravenal, ed., *Peace With China? U.S. Decisions for Asia;* and Ravenal, "The Nixon Doctrine and Our Asian Commitments," pp. 201–217.

31. Donald C. Hellman, *Japan and East Asia: The New International Order*, pp. 125–127; 191–193.

32. Christopher Layne, "The Real Conservative Agenda," pp. 73–93.

33. Edward Olsen, *U.S.-Japan Strategic Reciprocity*, pp. 137–141.

34. Donald E. Nuechterlein, *America Overcommitted: United States National Interests in the 1980s*, pp. 154–155.

35. Stephen M. Walt, "The Case for Finite Containment: Analyzing U.S. Grand Strategy," pp. 5–49 and especially pp. 42–43, 47–48.

36. Olsen, *U.S.-Japan Strategic Reciprocity*, p. 150.

I. EXTENDED DETERRENCE STRATEGY AND THE DOMINANT PLAYER POSTURE

1. See Alexander George and Richard Smoke, *Deterrence in American Foreign Policy*, p. 11; Glenn H. Snyder, *Deterrence and Defense: Toward A Theory of National Security*, p. 3; and William W. Kaufmann, *The Requirements of Deterrence* (Princeton: Princeton University, Center for International Studies, 1954).

2. A number of theorists have argued that deterrence can only become more effective by supplementing it with other conflict management approaches. See, for example, George and Smoke, *Deterrence in American Foreign Policy*, who advocate an "inducement" strategy; Richard Ned Lebow and Janice Gross Stein, "Beyond Deterrence," pp. 5–71, who propose replacing deterrence with a strategy of "reassurance" and Edward J. Rhodes, *Nuclear Weapons, Irrational Behavior, and Extended Deterrence* unpublished PhD dissertation, Princeton University, June 1985, who advocates a deterrence strategy of "commitment through irrationality." Other recent and useful analysis of the deterrence problem includes Philip Bobbit, *Democracy and Deterrence;* Paul Huth, *Extended Deterrence and the Prevention of War* (New Haven: Yale University Press, 1988); Huth and Bruce Russett, "Deterrence Failure and Crisis Escalation," *International Studies Quarterly* (March 1988), 32 (1): 29–45; Robert Jervis, "Deterrence Theory Revisited," pp. 289–324; Jervis, Lebow Stein, et al, *Psychology and Deterrence;* Richard Ned Lebow, "Conventional vs. Nuclear Deterrence: Are the Lessons Transferable?" *Journal of Social Issues* (1987), 43 (4): 171–191; Lebow, "Deterrence Reconsidered: The Challenge of Recent Research," in Catherine M. Kelleher, Francis J. Kerr and George H. Quester, eds., *Nuclear Deterrence: New Risks, New Opportunities* (Washington, D.C.: Pergamon Brassey's, 1986); Patrick Morgan, *Deterrence: A Conceptual Analysis* (Beverly Hills: Sage, 1983); Rhodes, "The Second Wave Revisited: Ahistorical Approaches to Theory," *International Studies Notes* (Winter 1987),

13 (1); Richard Smoke, "Extended Deterrence: Some Observations"; and Stein, "Extended Deterrence in the Middle East," *World Politics* (April 1987), 39 (3): 326–352.

3. One of the better known critiques of deterrence logic is Robert Jervis's *The Illogic of American Nuclear Strategy.*

4. Recent theoretical treatments of deterrence which argue that it is a fundamentally sound strategy for crisis management include Richard Betts, *Nuclear Blackmail and Nuclear Balance;* John Orme, "Deterrence Failures: A Second Look," pp. 69–129; George H. Quester, *The Future of Nuclear Deterrence;* and Erich Weede, "Extended Deterrence by Superpower Alliances," pp. 231–254.

5. Richard Betts argues that "some interests are great enough to justify their continued protection by nuclear threats even at significant risks." Betts, *Nuclear Blackmail and Nuclear Balance,* p. 228. Also see Orme, "Deterrence Failures: A Second Look," and Quester, *The Future of Nuclear Deterrence,* pp. 73–82 for variants of the same argument.

6. The Joint Staff of the JCS, *United States Military Posture For FY 1989* (Washington D.C.: USGPO, 1988), p. 1.

7. Ibid., p. 2.

8. Caspar W. Weinberger, Secretary of Defense, *Annual Report to the Congress Fiscal Year 1987,* pp. 33–37.

9. Testimony of Richard Armitage, Assistant Secretary of Defense for International Security Affairs and Karl D. Jackson, Deputy Assistant Secretary of Defense for East Asia and Pacific Affairs before the House Armed Services Committee, March 18 and March 26, 1987, and reprinted as "U.S. Strategic Interests in East Asia and the Pacific," *Defense '87* (May/June 1987), pp. 14–25.

10. Richard Solomon, Assistant Secretary of State for East Asian and Pacific Affairs, "Sustaining the Dynamic Balance: An Overview of U.S. Policy for East Asia and the Pacific." Testimony before the House Subcommittee on Asia and the Pacific, February 22, 1990 (unpublished draft copy). Solomon's speech, "Asian Security in the 1990s: Integration in Economics; Diversity in Defense" was delivered to The University of California, San Diego's Graduate School of International Relations and Pacific Studies on October 30, 1990. Copy in author's possession. Also see Tokasi Oka, "U.S. Aims to Fulfill . . ."

11. See the subsection on "Global War Perspective" as applied to the Asia-Pacific theater in U.S. Department of Defense, *Soviet Military Power: Prospects for Change 1989* (Washington, D.C.: USGPO, 1989), pp. 113, 117–118.

12. Statement by Rear Admiral T. W. Wright, Acting Deputy Assistant Secretary of Defense (East Asia and Pacific Affairs) before the Asia-Pacific Subcommittee of the House Foreign Affairs Committee, February 22, 1990, pp. 3, 20–21.

13. *U.S. Military Posture FY 1989,* pp. 17, 23–24 and Armitage/Jackson testimony, p. 19. The most comprehensive account of U.S. force structures and strengths in the Asia-Pacific is Ronald D. McLaurin, and Chung-in Moon, *The United States and the Defense of the Pacific,* pp. 55–114. Useful accounts of

the U.S. Army's linking of rapid movement and mobility to forward defense include U.S. Department of the Army, *Trained and Ready in an Era of Change: The United States Army Posture Statement FY 1991* (Washington, D.C.: USGPO, February 1990), p. II-2, and J. R. Wilson, " U.S. Tropic Alert Force: On Standby in Pacific," *Jane's Defense Weekly* (January 13, 1990), 13 (2): 67–68.

14. USDOD, *Soviet Military Power 1989*, p. 113.

15. Paul Kennedy, *The Rise and Fall of the Great Powers*, especially pp. 514–535.

16. A representative assessment is offered by Assistant Secretary of Defense Richard L. Armitage in remarks to the National Defense University's Pacific Symposium at Washington, D.C. in February 1988 and reprinted as "Our Security Role in Asia & the Pacific," *Asia-Pacific Defense Forum* (Spring 1989), 13 (4): 7–15.

17. Kenneth N. Waltz provides a supporting argument for this point in his *The Spread of Nuclear Weapons: More May Be Better*, Adelphi Papers no. 171 (London: International Institute of Strategic Studies, 1981).

18. See, for example, David Williams, "America Pulls Back, Packs Bags, Loses Place in the Pacific Century," *Los Angeles Times*, November 20, 1988, part 5, p. 6.

19. How the Japanese have recently viewed these questions is assessed by Mike Mochizuki, in "Japan's Search for Strategy," pp. 152–179.

20. The following comparisons are derived from Joshua Epstein, *Strategy and Force Planning* (Washington D.C.: The Brookings Institution, 1987), pp. 11–29; J. J. Martin, "Thinking About the Nuclear Balance in Asia," in Solomon and Kosaka, eds., *The Soviet Far East Military Buildup*, pp. 68–69; and Seizaburo Sato, "Convergence and Divergence in East Asian and Western Security Interests: Part I," in *East Asia, the West and International Security: Prospects for Peace—Part I*, Adelphi Papers no. 216 (London: The International Institute for Strategic Studies, 1987), pp. 22–27.

21. Stein, "Extended Deterrence in the Middle East," p. 326.

22. The classical source on "existential deterrence" is McGeorge Bundy, "The Bishops and the Bomb," *New York Review of Books* (June 16, 1983), pp. 3–6. See also Robert Jervis, *The Illogic of American Nuclear Strategy*, pp. 44, 46; Rhodes, *Nuclear Weapons, Irrational Behavior, and Extended Deterrence*, p. 79; and Lawrence Freedman, "I Exist; Therefore I Deter," *International Security* (Summer 1988), 13 (1): 177–195.

23. Huth, *Extended Deterrence and the Prevention of War*, p. 25.

24. Lebow and Stein, "Beyond Deterrence," p. 8.

25. Ivo H. Daalder, *NATO Strategy and Ballistic Missile Defense*, p. 17. The title is a partial misnomer. The first part of the study comprises one of the most thoughtful essays to yet appear in literature dealing with general extended deterrence.

26. Betts, *Nuclear Blackmail and Nuclear Deterrence*, p. 17.

27. R. B. Byers, "Deterrence Under Attack: Crisis and Dilemma," in Byers, ed., *Deterrence in the 1980s: Crisis and Dilemma*, p. 16.

28. See, for example, the remarks of William R. Van Cleave in a debate between Van Cleave and Earl C. Ravenal, " U.S. Defense Strategy: A Debate," in George E. Hudson and Joseph Kruzel, *American Defense Annual 1985–1986* (Lexington, Mass/Toronto: D. C. Heath/Mershon Center, The Ohio State University, 1985), p. 22. Also see Walter B. Slocombe, "Extended Deterrence," pp. 93–103; and Byers, "Deterrence Under Attack," pp. 21–23.

29. For representative arguments, see Jeffrey Record, *Revising U.S. Military Strategy* (Washington, D.C.: Pergamon Brassey's, 1984), pp. 51–52; and Anthony H. Cordesman, *Deterrence in the 1980's: Part I—American Strategic Forces and Extended Deterrence*, Adelphi Papers no. 175 (London: International Institute for Strategic Studies, Summer 1982).

30. Earl C. Ravenal, "Extended Deterrence and Alliance Cohesion" in Alan Ned Sabrosky, ed., *Alliances in U.S. Foreign Policy: Issues in the Quest for Collective Defense*, pp. 29–35, and Robert E. Osgood, *The Nuclear Dilemma in American Strategic Thought* (Boulder, Colo., and London: Westview Press, 1988), especially pp. 41–45.

31. Thomas Schelling, *Arms and Influence*, pp. 137–138.

32. This definition is derived, in large part, from Richard Smoke's concept of "escalation": "a step of any size that crosses a saliency" in circumstances of less than all out war. See his *War: Controlling Escalation*, p. 32.

33. Rhodes, *Nuclear Weapons, Irrational Behavior and Extended Deterrence*, p. 17.

34. Smoke, "Extended Deterrence: Some Observations," pp. 37–40.

35. See, for example, Lawrence Freedman, *The Evolution of Nuclear Strategy*, pp. 200–201, 219–223, 392. Also see Patrick Morgan, "Saving Face for the Sake of Deterrence," in Jervis, Lebow, Stein, et al, *Psychology and Deterrence*, p. 141.

36. Samuel P. Huntington, "The Renewal of Strategy," in Huntington, ed., *The Strategic Imperative*, pp. 21–32.

37. Janice Gross Stein, "Deterrence in the 1980s," in Byers, *Deterrence in the 1980's: Crisis and Dilemma*, p. 43.

38. Three of the most comprehensive statements outlining the stages and parameters of the maritime strategy as it unfolded throughout 1984–1986 are Hearings before the Armed Services Committee, United States Senate, *Department of Defense Authorization for FY 1985, Part 8: Sea Power and Force Projection*, 98th Cong., 2d Sess., March 14, 1984, pp. 3852–3900; Linton F. Brooks, "Naval Power and National Security: The Case for the Maritime Strategy," *International Security* (Fall 1986), 11 (2): 55–88; and the definitive article by then Chief of Naval Operations, Admiral James D. Watkins, "The Maritime Strategy," Supplement to U.S. Naval Institute *Proceedings* 112/1/995 (January 1986), pp. 2–17.

39. Mearsheimer, "A Strategic Misstep: The Maritime Strategy and Deterrence in Europe," *International Security* (Fall 1986), 11 (2): 14–15.

40. Masashi Nishihara, "Maritime Cooperation in the Pacific: The United States and Its Partners," *Naval War College Review* (Summer 1987), 40 (3):

40. Background is also provided by James A. Nathan, "How's the Strategy Playing with the Allies?" *U.S. Naval Institute Proceedings* 114/8/1026 (August 1988), pp. 57–62.

41. Testimony by Commander-in-Chief U.S. PACOM, Admiral Ronald J. Hayes, in Hearings before the Defense Policy Panel of the Committee On Armed Services, House of Representatives, *National Security Policy*, 100th Cong., 1st Sess., March 18, 1987, p. 385.

42. Hearings before the Committee on Armed Services, United States Senate, *Department of Defense Authorization for Appropriations for Fiscal Year 1985 Part 8* 98th Cong., 2d Sess. 1984, p. 3874, and Zarsky, and Hayes, *American Lake: Nuclear Peril in the Pacific*, pp. 261–262.

43. Ivo H. Daalder and Tim Zimmerman, "Banning Nuclear Weapons at Sea: A Neglected Strategy," *Arms Control Today* (November 1988), 18 (9): 21. In early 1990, NATO planners revised this doctrine to one of emphasizing "nuclear use as a last resort."

44. A Report by the Honorable William l. Ball III, Secretary of the Navy, on the Posture and Fiscal Years 1990–1991 Budget of the U.S. Navy and Marine Corps," in Hearings before a Subcommittee of the Committee On Appropriations, House of Representatives, *Department Of Defense Appropriations For 1990—Part 1*, 101st Cong., 1st Sess., March 1, 1989, p. 531–532.

45. A report on Cheney's Announcement is by Molly Moore, "Cheney Offers to Cut B-12 Stealth Force," *International Herald Tribune*, April 27, 1990, pp. 1, 6.

46. See Caspar W. Weinberger, Secretary of Defense, *Annual Report To Congress Fiscal Year 1983*, I-4.

47. This point is discussed by George Quester, "Some Thoughts on Deterrence Failures," in Paul C. Stern, Robert Axelrod, Robert Jervis and Roy Radner, eds., *Perspectives on Deterrence* (Oxford and New York: Oxford University Press, 1989), p. 63.

48. See the arguments of Robert Komer, *Maritime Strategy or Coalition Defense?*, pp. 70–73 and Joshua Epstein, " Horizontal Escalation: Sour Notes of a Recurrent Theme," pp. 19–31. Using somewhat different antecedents, Zbigniew Brzezinski nevertheless derives the same conclusion in *Game Plan: A Geostrategic Framework for the Conduct of the U.S.-Soviet Contest*, p. 170.

49. Hearings on *National Security Strategy*, 100th Congress, First Session, January 12, 1987, p. 27.

50. Testimony in Hearings on *National Security Strategy*, p. 708. Also see pp. 711–712.

51. Sam Nunn, "What Forces for Asia? What Forces for Europe?", p. 11.

52. While Consolidated Guidance no. 8 still remains classified, it was leaked to the American press corps during late 1979. See Rowland Evans and Robert Novak, "The Secret 'Swing Strategy,'" *Washington Post*, October 8, 1979, p. A-21.

53. Richard Solomon, "American Defense Planning and Asian Security: Policy Choices For A Time Of Transition," in Solomon, ed., *Asian Security in*

the 1980s: Problems and Policies for a Time of Transition, (Cambridge, Mass.: Oelgeschlager, Gunn and Hain, 1980), pp. 20–21.

54. For first-hand accounts of the Japanese resistance to this posture, see "Concern About Swing Strategy," *Tokyo Shimbun,* October 22, 1979, p. 5, translated and reprinted in *Daily Summary of the Japanese Press (DSJP),* Office of Translation Services, Political Office, U.S. Embassy, Tokyo, October 26, 1979, pp. 2–3 and Takuya Kubo, "Swing Strategy," *Sankei,* October 19, 1979, as translated and reprinted in *DSJP,* October 31, 1979, p. 4.

55. A compilation of Kissinger's views on "Asia versus Europe" was delivered to the annual conference of The International Institute of Strategic Studies in Kyoto, Japan, September 9, 1986, and reprinted as "East Asia, the Pacific and the West: Strategic Trends and Implications: Part I," in *East Asia, the West and International Security: Prospects for Peace,* pp. 3–10. Also see Eagleburger's address, "The Transatlantic Relationship: A Long-Term Perspective," *Current Policy* (March 7, 1984), no. 556.

56. Under Secretary of State for Political Affairs Michael H. Armacost, "NATO and the Challenges Ahead," *Current Policy* (October 10, 1984), no. 620, p. 3. Also see Deputy Secretary of State Kenneth Dam, "Europe vs. Asia: Is Diplomacy a Zero-Sum Game?" *Current Policy* (August 6, 1984), no. 603.

57. For a contrasting argument, see K. G. Weiss, "The War Will Not Subside: The Pacific Theater in a NATO-Warsaw Pact War," *Comparative Strategy* (1988), 7 (4): 399–410.

58. John J. Mearsheimer, *Conventional Deterrence,* p. 8.

59. Quester, *The Future of Nuclear Deterrence,* p. 96.

60. Schelling, *Arms and Influence,* p. 55.

61. For additional background, see Herman Kahn, *On Escalation: Metaphors and Scenarios,* esp. pp. 57–59 and Smoke, *War: Controlling Escalation,* pp. 36–45.

62. Daalder, *NATO Strategy,* pp. 17–18, 23–26.

63. A good comparison of how the credibility of commitment problem evolved in Europe and in the Asia-Pacific is offered by Patrick Morgan, "American Extended Deterrence in Northeast Asia," paper prepared for The Ilhae Institute, Seoul, Korea, November 1988, unpublished version, pp. 62–63.

64. Morgan, "American Extended Deterrence," p. 10.

65. The "entrapment-abandonment" concept is assessed by Michael Nacht in *The Age of Vulnerability,* pp. 149–166.

66. Robert S. Litwak, *Detente and the Nixon Doctrine: American Foreign Policy and the Pursuit of Stability, 1969–1976,* pp. 132–133.

67. Hearings before the Committee On Armed Services, United States Senate, *Department Of Defense Authorization for Appropriations For Fiscal Year 1980—Part 2,* 96th Cong., 1st Sess., February 20, 1979, p. 713.

68. Ibid., pp. 704–773.

69. The Shultz-Weinberger debate is covered by Sheldon Simon, *The Future of Asia-Pacific Collaboration,* p. 7.

70. See, for example, the arguments of Admiral S. R. Foley, Jr., "Strategic Factors in the Pacific," U.S. Naval Institute *Proceedings* 111/8/989 (August 1985), p. 36, and an address by Gaston Sigur, Jr., Secretary for East Asian and Pacific Affairs, "The U.S. and East Asia: Meeting the Challenge of Change," *Current Policy* (April 18, 1986), no. 821.

71. Robert Scalapino, "Asia's Future," p. 104.

72. Terumasa Nakanishi, "U.S. Nuclear Policy and Japan," *The Washington Quarterly* (Winter 1987), 10 (1): 83.

73. As cited in Franklin Weinstein and Fuji Kamiya, eds., *The Security of Korea: U.S. and Japanese Perspectives on the 1980s*, p. 92.

74. The problem of alliance consultation and commitment in the ANZUS dispute is well treated by Dora Alves, "The Changing New Zealand Defense Posture," *Asian Survey* (April 1989), 29 (4): 371.

75. See, for example, "Enrile Seeks to Abrogate Mutual Defense Treaty," *Philippine Daily Globe*, February 2, 1989, pp 1–8 reprinted in FBIS, *East Asia*, February 2, 1989, p. 56.

76. Karl Jackson, "Thai-U.S. Security Relations," in Jackson and Wiwat Mungkandi, eds., *United States-Thailand Relations*, pp. 164–165.

77. FPDA will be addressed more fully in chapter 5.

78. R. W. Apple, "In Asia, Taking a Long View of U.S. Power," *The New York Times*, February 26, 1989, p. E-1.

79. The most obvious recent example is the highly publicized book written by conservative Japanese parliamentarian Shintaro Ishihara and Akio Morita, chairman of the Sony Corporation, *The Japan That Can Say No*. An accurate English language version is an anonymous posting to the unmoderated news group "Soc.Culture.Japan" on USENET, accessed on computer via Defense Advanced Research Project's Agency's (DARPA) Defense Research Internet. While Ishihara has been characterized as a right-wing extremist and Morita's association with him as a miscalculation for his own image in the international business community, this book reflects the Japanese public's overall concern with U.S. leadership of the democratic world and with the general state of U.S.-Japanese relations.

2. THE DOMINANT AND TRANSITIONAL PLAYERS IN THE ASIA-PACIFIC

1. Edward A. Olsen, "Changing ANZUS: The Impact on Northeast Asia," unpublished paper presented at the Annual Meeting of International Studies Association, International Security Studies Section, Whittier, Cal., November 10, 1989, p. 2.

2. See Richard Betts, "Washington, Tokyo, and Northeast Asian Security," pp. 15–16; and Seizaburo Sato, "Convergence and Divergence in East Asian and Western Security Interests—Part I," *East Asia, the West and International Security: Prospects for Peace—Part I*, Adelphi Papers no. 216 (London: International Institute for Strategic Studies, Spring 1987), pp. 25–26.

3. Edward Rhodes, "Naval Arms Control for the Bush Era," *SAIS Review* (Summer-Fall 1990), 10 (2): 213–215.

4. Joo Hong Nam, "US-ROK Security Relations towards the 1990s: The Role of U.S. Forces in Korea," *The Korean Journal Of International Studies* (Spring 1987), 18 (2): 175–190 and Shin Jung-Hyun, "The Role of the United States in Establishing Peace on the Korean Peninsula," *The Journal of East Asian Affairs* (Winter-Spring 1990), 4 (1), esp. pp. 78–82.

5. William T. Tow, "The ANZUS Dispute: Testing U.S. Extended Deterrence in Alliance Politics," p. 135; and Desmond Ball, *Australia and the Global Strategic Balance*, pp. 58–81.

6. The Minister of Foreign Affairs and Trade, Senator Gareth Evans, "Australia's Regional Security," *Australia Background* (Canberra: Australia Overseas Information Service, December 6, 1989), p. 2.

7. George F. Kennan, *Memoirs 1925–1950*, p. 359; and John Lewis Gaddis, *Strategies of Containment*, pp. 30–41.

8. Robert Jervis, "The Impact of the Korean War on the Cold War," p. 576.

9. Kennan, *Memoirs*, p. 379.

10. Remarks by Secretary Acheson, "Crisis in Asia—An Examination of U.S. Policy," *The Department of State Bulletin* (January 23, 1950), 22 (551): 115–116.

11. "Memorandum of Conversation by the Secretary of State (Washington, December 29, 1949)," *Foreign Relations of the United States* [hereafter cited as *FRUS*] 1949, vol. 9: *The Far East: China* (Washington, D.C.: USGPO, 1974), p. 464.

12. Bruce Cumings, "Power and Plenty in Northeast Asia." p. 91.

13. Central Intelligence Agency, Summary of Department of State, Army Navy and Air Force National Intelligence Estimate (NIE-12), "Consequences of the Early Employment of Chinese Nationalist Forces in Korea, [Washington] December 27, 1950)," *FRUS 1950*, vol. 7: *Korea* (Washington, D.C.: USGPO, 1976), pp. 1605–1610.

14. "Note by the Executive Secretary to the National Security Council on United States Objectives and Programs for National Security (NSC 68) [Washington] April 14, 1950," *FRUS 1950*, vol 1: *National Security Affairs; Foreign Economic Policy* (Washington, D.C.: USGPO, 1977), pp. 265–266; and Daniel Calingaert, "Nuclear Weapons and the Korean War," p. 182.

15. "Memorandum of Discussion at a Special Meeting of the National Security Council, March 31, 1953," *FRUS 1952–1954*, vol. 15: *Korea—Part I* (Washington, D.C. USGPO, 1984, p. 826; and "Memorandum of Discussion at the 174th Meeting of the National Security Council, December 10, 1953," ibid., Part 2, pp. 1654–1655. Also see Rosemary Foot, *The Wrong War: American Policy and the Dimensions of the Korean Conflict, 1950–1953*, p. 209.

16. Foot provides the most comprehensive background of NSC 147 and its implications. See *The Wrong War*, pp. 204–231. Also consult McGeorge Bundy, *Danger and Survival*, pp. 242–243.

17. Alexander George and Richard Smoke, *Deterrence in American Foreign*

Policy, pp. 239–240. Roger Dingman has offered an alternative interpretation, insisting that Eisenhower's concern about Soviet retaliatory nuclear strikes against Japan precluded the United States from applying coercive atomic diplomacy, and arguing that Dulles' talks with the Indians contained no overt or even strongly implied nuclear threat to Beijing. See Dingman's "Atomic Diplomacy During the Korean War," pp. 85–86.

18. David Alan Rosenberg, " U.S. Nuclear Stockpile, 1945–1950," p. 26; Rosenberg, "The Origins of Overkill," in Steven E. Miller, ed., *Strategy and Nuclear Deterrence* (Princeton: Princeton University Press, 1984), pp. 124–126; and Calingaert, " Nuclear Weapons and the Korean War," p. 184.

19. Marc Trachtenberg, "A 'Wasting Asset,' " p. 30. Also see James F. Schneibel and Robert J. Watson, *The History of the Joint Chiefs of Staff and National Policy* vol. 3: *The Korean War—Part II,* pp. 933–934; and Bundy, *Danger and Survival,* p. 239.

20. Schneibel and Watson, *The Korean War,* p. 934.

21. Two comprehensive studies on the 1955 Taiwan Straits crisis using recently declassified data are Gordon H. Chang, "To the Nuclear Brink: Eisenhower, Dulles, and the Quemoy-Matsu Crisis," pp. 96–123; and H. W. Brands, Jr., "Testing Massive Retaliation: Credibility and Crisis Management in the Taiwan Strait," pp. 124–151. Also see John Wilson Lewis and Xue Litai, *China Builds the Bomb,* pp. 22–40.

22. "Memorandum Prepared by the Secretary of State, September 12, 1954," in *FRUS 1952–1954* vol. 14: *China and Japan—Part 1* (Washington, D.C.: USGPO, 1985), Part 1, pp. 610–611. Also see Betts, *Nuclear Blackmail and Nuclear Balance,* pp. 54–57.

23. Chang, "To the Nuclear Brink," p. 100; Brands, "Testing Massive Retaliation," pp. 127–128; and Lewis and Xue, *China Builds the Bomb,* p. 34.

24. Chang, for example, argues that Eisenhower did believe Moscow may have come to the assistance of its Chinese ally while Brands contends such was not the case. See Chang, "To the Nuclear Brink," p. 110; and Brands, "Testing Massive Retaliation," p. 129.

25. Chang, "To the Nuclear Brink," p. 117; and Lewis and Xue, *China Builds the Bomb,* pp. 26, 33–34.

26. Marc S. Gallicchio, "The Best Defense is a Good Offense: The Evolution of American Strategy in East Asia, 1953–1960," in Warren I. Cohen and Akira Iriye, eds., *The Great Powers in East Asia, 1953–1960* (New York: Columbia University Press, 1990), pp 74–75. On the Chinese inclination to step up its own nuclear weapons program in response to U.S.. nuclear strategy in Taiwan, see He Di, "The Evolution of the People's Republic of China's Policy Toward the Offshore Islands," in ibid., p. 228.

27. For background on the 1958 Taiwan crisis, the classical source remains Allen Whiting's "Quemoy in 1958; Mao's Miscalculations," pp. 263–270. Also see Betts, *Nuclear Blackmail and Nuclear Balance,* pp. 71–75; Bundy, *Danger and Survival,* pp. 281–282; He Di, "The Evolution of the People's Republic of China Policy . . . ," pp. 231–241; Morton H. Halperin, *The 1958 Taiwan Straits Crisis: A Documented History,* RM-4900–ISA (Santa Monica: RAND

Corporation, 1975); and John R. Thomas, "Soviet Behavior in the Quemoy Crisis of 1958," *Orbis* (Summer 1962), 6 (2), pp. 38–64.

28. Lester J. Foltos, "The New Pacific Barrier: America's Search for Security in the Pacific, 1945–1947," p. 327. Also see comments by Nathaniel Thayer, "Beyond Security: U.S.-Japanese Relations in the 1990s," *Journal of International Affairs* (Summer/Fall 1989), 43 (1), esp. pp. 57, 63. Also see H. W. Brands, "The United States and the Reemergence of Independent Japan," pp. 389–390.

29. Seizaburo Sato and Yuji Suzuki, "A New Stage of the United States-Japan Alliance," in John H. Makin and Donald C. Hellman, eds., *Sharing World Leadership: A New Era for America and Japan*, p. 159.

30. Central Intelligence Agency, *Feasibility Of Japanese Rearmament in Association with the United States*, National Intelligence Estimate (NIE)-19, April 20, 1951. Reprinted in *Declassified Documents System* [hereafter cited as *DDS*] 001533, 1984. Declassified October 24, 1983. Also see a later assessment prepared by the National Security Council, *U.S. Policy Toward Japan* NSC 6008/1, June 11, 1960. Reprinted in *DDS* 000608, 1982 (declassified on November 8, 1982).

31. Chae-Jin Lee and Hideo Sato, *U.S. Policy Toward Japan and Korea*, p. 18.

32. "Waring to McClurkin, March 18, 1952," *FRUS 1952–1954, vol. 14: China and Japan—Part II*, pp. 1214–1216; Brands, "The United States and the Reemergence of an Independent Japan," p. 388; and Frederick L. Shiels, *Tokyo and Washington* (Lexington, Mass. and Toronto: D. C. Heath, 1980), p. 74.

33. Chihiro Hosoya, "From the Yoshida Letter to the Nixon Shock," in Akira Iriye and Warren I Cohen, eds., *The United States and Japan in the Postwar World*, pp. 24–26. Also see Walter S. Robertson, "The Need for a Strong Japan," in U.S. Department of State, *American Foreign Policy 1950– 55, Basic Documents II*, (Washington D.C.: USGPO, 1957), pp. 2430–2435. Robertson was Assistant Secretary for Far Eastern Affairs during the Eisenhower Administration.

34. "Re: New Proposition of the U.S. Government on Article XII, (February 18, 1952)" *Documents Concerning U.S.-Japan Mutual Security Negotiations* (Tokyo: Diplomatic Records Office, Microfilm Section, released for public use in December 1987), p. 0137. For a provocative but in-depth assessment of Yoshida's policy motives, see Tetsuya Kataoka, " Japan's Defense Nonbuildup: What Went Wrong?" *International Journal on World Peace* (April-June 1985), 2 (2). esp. pp. 14–15.

35. "The Assistant Secretary of State for Far Eastern Affairs (Allison) to Senator H. Alexander Smith of New Jersey (Washington D.C., April 1, 1952)," *FRUS 1952–1954. Volume 14: China and Japan—Part 2*, pp. 1223–1224.

36. See the testimonies of John Foster Dulles, and Dean Rusk, Consultant, in Selected Executive Hearings of the House Foreign Relations Committee 1951–1956, *U.S. Policy in the Far East, Part I: U.S. Policy and Japan; the Korean War and Peace Negotiations; South Asian and Related Problems (Histori-*

cal Series) vol. 17, 81st Cong., 2d Sess., July 11, 1951, and January 21, 1952, pp. 23–59; 97–106. Also see Albert Norman, *The Monroe Doctrine Extended* (Northfield: self-published, 1968), esp. pp. 4–12.

37. George Packard, *Protest in Tokyo: The Security Treaty Crisis of 1960;* I. M. Destler, Hideo Sato, Priscilla Clapp, and Haruhiro Fukui, *Managing An Alliance* (Washington D.C.: The Brookings Institution, 1976), pp. 12–23; Frank C. Langdon *Japan's Foreign Policy* (Vancouver: University of British Columbia Press, 1975), pp. 7–21; and Tadashi Aruga, " The Security Treaty Revision of 1960," in Akira Iriye and Warren I. Cohen, eds., *The United States and Japan in the Postwar World*, pp. 61–79.

38. For background on U.S. policy interests leading to the treaty revision, see Secretary of State Christian Herter's testimony in *Executive Sessions of (The Senate) Foreign Relations Committee (Historical Series)*, vol. 12, 86th Cong., 2d Sess., June 7, 1960, pp. 406–414.

39. Joo-Hong Nam, *America's Commitment to South Korea*, p. 45; and Byung-joon Ahn, "South Korea and Taiwan: Local Deterrence," in James W. Morley, ed., *Security Interdependence in the Asia Pacific Region*, p. 93.

40. Fred Greene, *U.S. Policy and the Security of Asia*, pp. 93–95, 160–161; and Franklin B. Weinstein and Fuji Kamiya, eds., *The Security of Korea: U.S. and Japanese Perspectives on the 1980s* (Boulder, Colo: Westview Press, 1980), pp. 74–75.

41. Dwight D. Eisenhower, *Waging Peace, 1956–1961*, p. 293; and Melvin Gurtov and Byong Moo Hwang, *China Under Threat: The Politics of Strategy and Diplomacy*, p. 76.

42. Eisenhower, *Waging Peace*, pp. 293–294 and "The Acting Secretary of Defense (Anderson) to the President [Washington] September 3, 1954," in *FRUS 1952–1954*, volume 14: *China and Japan* (Washington, D.C.: USGPO, 1985), pp. 556–557.

43. Fred Greene, *U.S. Policy and the Security of Asia*, p. 35.

44. See Spender's memoirs, *Percy Spender, Exercises in Diplomacy* (Sydney: Sydney University Press/New York University Press, 1967) pp. 191–197.

45. T. B. Millar notes that ANZUS was not originally sought by the United States, "which acquiesced [to the pact] only with reluctance." Millar, *Australia in Peace and War* (New York: St. Martin's Press, 1978), pp. 207, 209–210. Also consult Thomas-Durell Young, " U.S. Policy and the South and Southwest Pacific," *Asian Survey* (July 1988), 28 (7): 775.

46. Army Chief Of Staff General J. Lawton Collins as quoted in "Memorandum on the Substance of Discussions at a Department of State-Joint Chiefs of Staff Meeting, [Washington, April 23, 1982]," *Foreign Relations of the United States (FRUS) 1952–1954*, volume 12: *East Asia and the Pacific—Part 1* (Washington, D.C.: USGPO, 1984), p. 84.

47. Personal correspondence with this author, May 15, 1989.

48. The Hon. Kim Beazley, "Thinking Defense: Key Concepts in Australian Defense Planning," *Australia Outlook* (April 1989), 42 (2): 62–63.

49. Ross Babbage, "Australian Foreign Policy: The Security Objectives," in Fedor Mediansky and A. C. Palfreeman, eds., *In Pursuit of National Inter-*

ests: Australian Foreign Policy in the 1990s (Sydney: Pergamon Press, 1988), p. 109.

50. A typical argument reflecting Japanese fears and rationales concerning U.S. strategic doctrine becoming too explicit is presented by Terumasa Nakanishi, in "Japan's Security Policy: Challenges and Opportunities for the 1990s," *Japan Review of International Affairs* (Spring/Summer 1989), 3 (1): 54–85.

51. See Tae-Hwan Kwak, "Korea-U.S. Security Relations in the 1990s: A Creative Adjustment," *The Korean Journal of Defense Analysis* (Winter 1989), 1 (2): 150–154.

52. These options were weighed in detail by Paris H. Chang in testimony at Hearings before the Committee on Foreign Relations, United States Senate, *Taiwan*, 96th Cong., 1st Sess., February 6, 1980, pp. 435–436.

53. *Boei Nenkan Showa 31 nen ban* [The Annual Survey of Defense, 1956] (Tokyo: Boei Nenkan Kanko Kai, 1956), p. 177; Frederick L. Shiels, *Tokyo and Washington*, (Lexington, Mass. and Toronto: Lexington Press, 1980), p. 80; "Atomic Artillery Sent to Far East," *The New York Times* July 29, 1955, p. 3; and Foster Hailey, "Atom Gun Idea Disturbs Japan," *The New York Times*, July 30, 1955, p. 2.

54. Joint Chiefs of Staff, *The Strategic Importance of Okinawa*, J.C.S. 2180/116, May 1, 1958. Reprinted in *DDS* 000053, 1979 (Declassified on June 28, 1979).

55. See the remarks of Isutoma Kowara, then Director General of the Japan Defense Agency, *Defense of Japan 1988 Nihon no boei*, English version, (Tokyo: The Japan Times Ltd., 1988), pp. v, 82.

56. "Bankrupt Deterrence Theory Forces Defensive Shift," and "Japan's Defense Policy Challenged," *The Japan Times*, May 23, 1990, p. 22 and Mike M. Mochizuki, "Japan After the Cold War," *SAIS Review*, (Summer-Fall 1990), 10 (2): 131.

57. James R. Van de Velde, "Japan's Nuclear Umbrella: U.S. Extended Nuclear Deterrence for Japan," pp. 16–23. Background on the Three Non-Nuclear Principles is offered by Shinichi Ogawa et al., *Problems of U.S. Extended Nuclear Deterrence for Japan*, pp. 7–10.

58. Ogawa, *Problems of U.S.. Extended Nuclear Deterrence*, p 16.

59. A pertinent interview with LaRocque by *Kyodo* is reprinted as "La-Rocque Interview" in FBIS, *Asia & Pacific (Daily Report)*, May 21,1981,pp. C-2 through C-3.Reischauer's equally controversial telephone interview with Kyodo is reprinted as "Former U.S.. Envoy Cites Verbal Defense Agreement," FBIS, *Asia & Pacific (Daily Report)*, May 18, 1981, p. C-13. The Foreign Ministry immediately denied Reishauer's assertions. Revelations of a nuclear-armed U.S. A-4E *Skyhawk* rolling off the deck of the aircraft carrier *USS Ticonderoga* in December 1965 and sinking in the ocean 70 miles from Okinawa are covered by John M. Broder, " H-Bomb Lost at Sea in '65 Off Okinawa, U.S. Admits," *Los Angeles Times* May 9, 1989, pp. 1, 16.

60. "U.S. Officials Back Larger Japanese Role," *The Daily Yomiuri*, June 22, 1990, p. 3. For additional background see Seizaburo Sato and Uiji Suzuki,

"A New Stage of the United States-Japan Alliance," in John H. Makin and Donald C. Hellman, eds., *Sharing World Leadership: A New Era for America and Japan*, pp. 153–174 and Tetsuya Kataoka and Ramon H. Myers, *Defending an Economic Superpower: Reassessing the U.S.-Japan Security Alliance*, pp. 86–87.

61. Report by Korean Broadcasting System Correspondent Kim Lo-Chin, " Schlesinger's 20 June Remarks on Defense of Korea Cited," FBIS, *Asia and Pacific (Daily Report)*, June 23, 1975, p. E-1.

62. A Report to the Committee on Foreign Relations, United States Senate, *U.S. Troop Withdrawal From The Republic Of Korea* 95th Cong., 2nd Sess., January 9, 1978, p. 21.

63. Ibid., p. 40.

64. Ibid.; Chae-Jin Lee and Hideo Sato, *U.S. Policy Toward Japan and Korea*, p. 112; and observations of both Allen S. Whiting and Franklin B. Weinstein in Weinstein, ed., *The Security of Korea* (Boulder, Colo.: Westview, 1980), pp. 89–96.

65. Statement by Philip C. Habib made before the Subcommittees on International Security and Scientific Affairs of the Committee on International Relations, U.S. House of Representatives, *Withdrawal of U.S. Ground Forces from Korea*, 95th Cong., 1st Sess. June 19, 1977 (testimony released by U.S. Department of State).

66. "U.S.: No First Use of A-Arms Envisioned in S. Korea," *The Washington Post* December 3, 1987, p. A-54; and Larry A. Niksch, *Visit To South Korea And Taiwan, September 11–24, 1988 Trip Report*, CRS Report 88–740 F (Washington D.C.: Congressional Research Service, Library of Congress, December 6, 1988), pp. 3–4.

67. The Republic of Korea's *1989 Defense White Paper* argued that "it is necessary that U.S.. forces continue to stay in Korea for a considerable period of time. . . . Before the U.S.. Forces can be withdrawn . . . North Korea should first completely renounce its scheme of communizing the South by force." The Ministry of National Defense, The Republic of Korea, *Defense White Paper 1989*, p 131. Also see John McBeth, "Withdrawal Symptoms," *Far Eastern Economic Review* (September 29, 1988), 141 (39): 35; and Steven R. Weisman, " Korean Rejects Demands for a Cut in U.S. Troops," *The New York Times*, June 29, 1989, p. 7.

68. Bae-Ho Hahn, "Korean-American Security Relations in the 1970s: Opportunities and Dilemmas," in Martin E. Weinstein, ed., *Northeast Asian Security After Vietnam* (Urbana: University of Illinois Press, 1982), pp. 159–160.

69. Chung Min Lee, "Holding the 'Hollingsworth Line': Conventional Deterrence in the Korean Peninsula," in Institute For Foreign Policy Analysis, Inc., *The U.S.-Korean Security Relationship: Prospects and Challenges for the 1990s* (Washington D.C.: Pergamon Brassey's, 1988), pp. 69–72.

70. Doug Bandow, "Leaving Korea," p. 83.

71. Sang-Woo Rhee, *Security and Unification of Korea* (Seoul: Sogang University Press, 1984), p. 206.

72. Force strength assessments are taken from The International Institute for Strategic Studies, *The Military Balance 1988–1989*, pp. 167–169, and the Republic of Korea, *Defense White Paper 1989*, pp. 70–82.

73. On the FX project, see Damon Darlin, "Korea Seeks Aerospace Expertise from U.S.," *The Asian Wall Street Journal*, June 15, 1989, pp. 1, 9 and Andy Pasztor, "South Korea Will Use U.S. Design for Jet Fighters, Minister Pledges," *The Asian Wall Street Journal*, July 20, 1989. More general force assessments are offered by General Louis C. Menetrey, USA, Commander, U.S. Forces, Korea before the Committee on Armed Services, United States Senate, February 9, 1990 (unpublished manuscript version in author's possession); Brian Bridges, "East Asia in Transition: South Korea in the Limelight," *International Affairs* [London] (Summer 1988), 64 (3): 388; John McBeth, "Safety in Numbers," *Far Eastern Economic Review* (January 26, 1989), 143 (4): 34; and Young-Sun Ha, "The Korean Military Balance: Myth and Reality," in William J. Taylor, Jr., Young Koo Cha, John Q. Blodgett, and Michael Mazaar, *The Future of South Korean-U.S. Security Relations* (Boulder, Colo.: Westview, 1989), pp. 89–101.

74. Robert Karniol, "South Korea: Preparing to Fill the Arms Gap?" *Jane's Defense Weekly* (February 18, 1989), 11 (7): 270–271. Also see Stephen Goose, "The Military Situation on the Korean Peninsula," in John Sullivan and Roberta Foss, *Two Koreas—One Future?* (Lanham, Md.: University Press of America, 1987), pp. 55–85 for a corroborating argument about growing South Korean military strength. A useful and perhaps more balanced assessment is offered by Young Wahn Kihl, "The Two Koreas: Security, Diplomacy and Peace," in Kihl and Lawrence E. Grinter, eds., *Asia-Pacific Security: Emerging Challenges and Responses*, pp. 157–158.

75. Senators Sam Nunn and John McCain, "U.S. Allies: No More Free Rides," *Washington Post*, August 13, 1989, p. B-7; and Richard Halloran, "South Korea: A U.S. Pullout?" *International Herald Tribune*, August 14, 1989, pp. 1, 5.

76. This deterrence function is cited by Makoto Momoi, "The Nuclear Dimension," in Weinstein and Kamiya, *The Security of Korea*, p. 111.

77. This point is raised by Ralph N. Clough, *Deterrence and Defense in Korea: The Role of U.S. Forces* (Washington, D.C.: The Brookings Institution, 1976), p. 56.

78. *Chosun Ilbo*, January 25, 1983, as cited in Edward Olsen, "Contemporary U.S.-Korean Security Relations," paper prepared for presentation at a forum on Regional Security of Asia and the Pacific, The Washington Institute for Values and Public Policy, October 20, 1988, p. 21.

79. The most comprehensive account of U.S. military operations in Taiwan remains "Statement on United States-Republic Of China Security Relations, Presented by Ambassador Walter P. McConaughy," in Hearings before the Subcommittee on United States Security Agreements and Commitments Abroad of the Committee on Foreign Relations, United States Senate, *United States Security Agreements and Commitments Abroad: Part 4—Republic of China*, 91st Cong., 2d Sess., November 24, 1970, pp. 1113–1141. For general back-

ground, consult Harvey Feldman, "Development of U.S.-Taiwan Relations 1948–1987," in Feldman, Michael Y. M. Kau, and Ilpyong J. Kim, eds., *Taiwan in a Time of Transition* (New York: Paragon, 1989), esp. p. 136.

80. For in-depth assessments, see Edwin K. Snyder, A. James Gregor, and Maria Hsia Chang, *The Taiwan Relations Act and the Defense of the Republic of China* (Berkeley, Cal.: Institute of International Studies, University of California-Berkeley, 1980), pp. 24–45.

81. Michael Ying-mao Kau, "Security and Defense Capabilities," in James C. Hsiung et al., eds., *The Taiwan Experience 1950–1980* (New York: Praeger, 1981), p. 456.

82. Ibid. Also see "Statement by Major General Richard G. Ciccolella, Chief of Staff, U.S.. 1st Army and former chief, MAAG Taiwan," in *United States Security Agreements and Commitments Abroad—Republic of China*, esp. pp. 1062–1073.

83. Jeffrey T. Richelson and Desmond Ball, *The Ties That Bind*, p. 206; Desmond Ball, *Australia and the Global Strategic Balance*, p. 59, and "Aussie To Link Up With U.S. System," *The Straits Times* (Singapore), March 24, 1987, p. 3. For recent information that the importance of the North West Cape installation has decreased with a reduction in signaling strength and a dispersion of very low frequency (VLF) American transmitters for communications to nuclear submarines at other sites outside Australia, see Michael Richardson, "North West Cape's Surprising Secret," *Pacific Defense Reporter* (October 1986), 13 (4): 10, 34.

84. For background on Nurrungar and Pine Gap, consult Richelson and Ball, *The Ties That Bind*, pp. 158, 162, 190–194, 260–267; Ball, *A Suitable Piece of Real Estate* (Sydney: Hale & Iremonger, 1980); Ball, *Australia and the Global Strategic Balance*, p. 59; Defense Science and Technology Division, Australian Department of Defense, *Summary of Official Statements on the Joint Defense Research Facility Pine Gap Near Alice Springs and the Joint Defense Communications Station at Nurrungar Near Woomera* (Canberra: Australian Department of Defense, May 1, 1978); Andrew Mack, *Arms Control And The U.S./Australian Joint Defense Facilities: The Case Of Nurrungar* Peace Research Center Working Paper no. 7 (Canberra: Australian National University, May 1986); and Andrew Mack, "U.S. 'Bases' in Australia: The Debate Continues," *Australian Outlook* (August 1988), 42 (2): 77–85.

85. Whitlam initiated representations to both the U.S. and the Soviet Union in early 1974, urging them to enter into negotiations or "step-by-step reductions" on naval force deployments in the Indian Ocean. He opposed the expansion of the American basing operations in Diego Garcia even while continuing to defend such U.S. operations in his own country. See Henry Albinski, *Australian External Policy Under Labor*, p. 253; and G. St. J. Barclay, "Problems in Australian Foreign Policy," *Australian Outlook* (April 1975), 21 (1): 6–7.

86. A text of the explanatory memorandum and resolution are reprinted as "A Nuclear-Weapon-Free Zone in the South Pacific," in *New Zealand Foreign Affairs Review* (September 1975), 25 (9): 55–57. Also see Helen Clark, "Estab-

lishing a Nuclear-Free Zone in the South Pacific," in Hyam Gold, ed., *New Directions in New Zealand Foreign Policy* (Auckland: Benton Ross, 1985), p. 123; and Greg Fry, "Toward a South Pacific Nuclear Free Zone," *Bulletin of the Atomic Scientists*, pp. 16–20.

87. A fairly sensationalist account of ANZUS MARSAR is offered by Keith Burgess, " A Secret ANZUS Pact," *The Evening Post* (Wellington), May 11, 1985, p. 4. A more balanced review is by Dagger Dirk, " Comments and Discussion," *Pacific Defense Reporter* (September 1986), 13 (3): 3–4.

88. New Zealand's 1983 *Defense Review* argued, for example, that a "wider Pacific horizon" should be demarcated and increasingly patrolled as the best means to check Soviet maritime penetration in this area. New Zealand Ministry of Defense, *Defense Review 1983* (Wellington: P. D. Hasselberg, Government Printer, 1983), p. 17. For a dissenting view on Antipodeon reluctance to overplay their ties to American global strategy, see Coral Bell, "ANZUS in Australia's Foreign and Security Policies," in Jacob Bercovitch, ed., *ANZUS in Crisis*, pp. 146–148.

89. See the testimony of Marshall Green, former Assistant Secretary of State for Asia and the Pacific in Hearings before the Committee on International Relations, U.S. House of Representatives, *Investigation of Korean-American Relations*, 95th Cong., 2d Sess., March 15, 1978, pp. 20–32; and "Pentagon Moving to Reduce Forces," *The New York Times*, June 7, 1970, p. 9.

90. The defense review conclusions are found in Hayden's statement to the Australian Parliament, reprinted in the *Australian Foreign Affairs Record* (September 1983), 54 (9): 513–517. Additional background is provided by F. B. Mediansky, "Nuclear Weapons and Security in the South Pacific," *The Washington Quarterly* (Winter 1986), 9 (1): 31–43; and Mediansky, "ANZUS in Crisis," *The Australian Quarterly* (Autumn-Winter 1985), 57 (1–2): 13–14.

91. Robert O'Neill, "ANZUS and Future Australian-American Relations," *The Round Table* (April 1989), no. 310, pp. 177–178.

92. Kosaka, *Options for Japan's Foreign Policy*, Adelphi Papers no. 97 (London: The International Institute for Strategic Studies, Summer 1973), p. 10. Also see Fuji Kamiya and Kenichi Nagata, "Nixon Doctrine to Nichibei Kankei," ["Nixon Doctrine and U.S.-Japan Relations"], *The Kokusai Mondai* (November 1971), no. 140, pp. 2–13; and Tuji Ramija and Kenichi Nagata, "America No Sokai Senriyaka to Tainichi Seisakuy" ["U.S. Strategy in the World and U.S. Policy Toward Japan"], *The Kokusai Mondai* (October 1973), no. 163, pp. 2–14. *The Kokusai Mondai* is a monthly publication by the Japan Institute of International Affairs. An American assessment which supported this Japanese line of argumentation was offered by Albert Wohlstetter, "Japan's Security: Balancing After the Shocks," in Morton Kaplan (ed.), *International Politics* (Chicago: Aldine, 1974), pp. 424–425.

93. For an assessment of this reasoning at the time, see Morton H. Halperin, "The U.S. Nuclear Umbrella and Japanese Security," in Franklin B. Weinstein, ed., *U.S.-Japan Relations and the Security of East Asia* (Boulder, Colo.: Westview Press, 1978), p. 97.

94. James Nathan, "The Future of the U.S. Maritime Strategy," *The*

Journal of Strategic Studies (December 1988), 11 (4): 469. For a dissenting view supporting the linkage of Maritime Strategy to Japanese conventional defense interests, see Hiroshi Kawaguchi, *The Maritime Strategy*, The Wilson Center, International Security Studies Program, Number 89 (Washington, D.C.: The Smithsonian Institution, 1988), pp. 55–57.

95. Patrick L. Smith, "U.S.-Japan Security Pact: Time of Doubt," *International Herald Tribune*, June 21, 1990, pp. 1, 4.

96. Japanese concerns are outlined in "Will Review Plan for Japan-U.S. Joint Operations in Emergency; Due to Decline of Combat Power of U.S. Reinforcements; Defense Plan General Outline Becomes Unrealistic; Security-Connected Source States," *Sankei*, March 2, 1987, p. 1, translated and reprinted by *Daily Summary of the Japanese Press* [hereafter cited as *DSJP*], Office of Translation Services, Political Section, U.S. Embassy, Tokyo, March 6, 1987, pp. 3–4.

97. Robert Y. Horiguchi, "Ringing the Changes," *Pacific Defense Reporter* (December 1987–January 1988), 14 (6–7): 32.

98. See, for example, Assistant Secretary of Defense for East Asia and Pacific Affairs, Karl Jackson, before the Defense Burden Sharing Subcommittee, Armed Services Committee, U.S. House of Representatives on September 27, as cited in "U.S. Wants Japan to Pay Base Expenses," *The Japan Times* (Weekly Overseas Edition), October 15, 1988, p. 4.

99. Horiguchi, "Ringing the Changes," p. 32.

100. Cited in Muthiah Alagappa, "Japan's Political and Security Role in the Asia-Pacific Region," *Contemporary Southeast Asia* (June 1988), 10 (1): 24.

101. Japanese Defense Agency, *The Defense of Japan 1988* (Tokyo: The Japan Times, 1988), pp. 33–38.

102. Ian Rodger, "Japan Takes a Long Look at Its Burden of Defense," *Financial Times*, December 6, 1988, p. 5.

103. William H. Gleysteen, Jr., and Alan Romberg, "Korea: Asian Paradox," *Foreign Affairs* (Summer 1987), 65 (5): 1038. Also see Bernard Trainor, "U.S. Policy and Northeast Asia," in Taylor et al., *The Future of South-Korean-U.S. Security Relations*, pp. 42–44; and Duk-Choong Kim, "Korean National Security and External Threat in the 1990s: Focusing on the ROK-U.S. Relationship," in Taylor et al., pp. 106–107, 110–111.

104. Research Institute for Peace and Security, *Asian Security 1988–1989* (Tokyo: Research Institute for Peace and Security, 1988), pp. 87–88; and "Seoul to Pay More for U.S. Military Cost," *The New York Times*, June 10, 1988, p. 6.

105. Prestowitz, "Uncle Sam Gets Snookered Again," *Los Angeles Times*, November 14, 1989, Part II, p. 7. Also see Barbara Starr, "Offsets Key to F/A-18 Deal," *Jane's Defense Weekly* 13, no. 2 (January 13, 1990), p. 47.

106. "U.S. to Transfer Control of South Korean Forces," *The Korea Herald*, May 15, 1988, p. 1, as reprinted in FBIS *East Asia (Daily Report)*, May 16, 1988, p. 16; "South Korea: Selected Articles on Military Organization Changes," FBIS *East Asia (Daily Report—Supplement)* January 12, 1990, pp. 1–15; Tim Carrington, "U.S. Military Weighs New Role in Korea," *The Asian*

Wall Street Journal, August 6, 1987, pp. 1, 7; and Sam Jameson, "Roh Asks 'Lower U.S. Military Profile' in South," *Los Angeles Times* November 1, 1988, pp. 1, 14–15

107. Jameson, "Roh Asks 'Lower U.S. Military Profile'; Andy Pasztor, "U.S. Set To Discuss Korean Troop Cuts," *The Asian Wall Street Journal*, July 11, 1989, pp. 1, 28; Melissa Healey, "Senate Bill Proposes U.S. Troops in South Korea Be Cut by 10,000 Over Next Three Years," *Los Angeles Times*, June 24, 1989, p. 10.

108. The Ministry of National Defense, The Republic of Korea, *Defense White Paper 1989*, pp.39–40.

109. J. Bennett Johnston and Dale Bumpers, "An Overly Costly 'Trip wire' in Korea," *The New York Times*, July 21, 1989, p. 29.

110. Doug Bandow, "Leaving Korea," pp. 78–79; "Don't Worry For Now," *The Economist* (February 3, 1990), 314 (7640): 33; McLaurin and Moon, *The United States and the Defense of the Pacific*, pp. 139–141; and Young Koo Cha, "U.S. Forces in Korea: Their Roles and Future," in Taylor et al., *The Future of U.S.-South Korean Security Relations*, pp. 149–150.

111. David E. Sanger, "Seoul Officials Expect Accord on U.S. Troop Cut," *The New York Times*, February 1, 1990, p. 11. Also see Sam Jameson, "U.S. Plan to Cut Troops Worries Allies in Asia," *Los Angeles Times*, January 31, 1990, p. 15; Mark Clifford, "Cut And Share," *Far Eastern Economic Review* (February 15, 1990), 147 (7): 32; and Research Institute for Peace and Security, Tokyo, *Asian Security 1989–1990* (London: Brassey's 1989), pp. 138–140.

112. Larry A. Niksch, "Future Issues in U.S.-ROK Security Cooperation," *The Korean Journal of Defense Analysis* (Summer 1989), 1 (1): 76–77.

113. Richard M. Nixon, *U.S. Foreign Policy for the 1970s, A New Strategy for Peace* (Washington D.C.: USGPO, 1970), p. 129.

114. The most comprehensive public analysis of these studies remains the testimony of Banning Garrett in Hearings before the Subcommittee on Asian and Pacific Affairs of the Committee on Foreign Affairs, House of Representatives, *The United States and The People's Republic of China: Issues For The 1980s*, 96th Cong., 2d Sess. August 26, 1980, pp. 96–108. According to Garrett, a sanitized version of "L-32," the first such study produced by the RAND Corporation, is Michael Pillsbury's "U.S.-Chinese Military Ties?" *Foreign Policy* (Fall 1975), no. 20, pp. 50–64.

115. Lucian W. Pye, "Dilemmas for America in China's Modernization," *International Security* (Summer 1979), 4 (1): 19.

116. Background is provided by Stephen Gibert, "The Isolation of Island China," in Gibert, ed., *Security in Northeast Asia*, pp. 118–123.

117. A. James Gregor, *The China Connection* (Stanford: Hoover Institution Press, 1986), p. 145.

118. Dennis Van Vranken Hickey, "America's Military Relations with the People's Republic of China: The Need for Reassessment," *Journal of Northeast Asian Studies* (Fall 1988), 7 (3): 37–38; Clare Hollingworth, " More Talk of 'One Country: Two Systems,' " *Pacific Defense Reporter* (December 1988–

January 1989), 15 (6–7): 60; Peter Kien-hong Yu, " No 1—Island Still Has Vital Role," *Pacific Defense Reporter* (May 1989), 15 (11): 51; and Tai Ming Cheung, "The Balance Tilts," *Far Eastern Economic Review* (September 29, 1988), 141 (39): 40–41.

119. Coral Bell, "ANZUS in Australia's Foreign and Security Policies," in Bercovitch, ed., *ANZUS in Crisis*, p. 150.

120. On the Geraldton installation, see Paul Kelley, "Paper Views Role of U.S. Commo Bases," *The Australian*, November 25, 1988, p. 69. On ANZAC, consult Robert Lowe, "Continuing Debate on Defense Policy Examined," *Agence France Presse* report, translated and reprinted in FBIS, *East Asia*, November 3, 1988, p. 44.

121. "Review of ANZUS" in Weekly Hansards, *Australian Parliamentary Debate*, House of Representatives, 33rd Parliament, 1st Session—2nd Period (September 15, 1983), pp. 899–901.

122. Report to the Minister for Defense by Mr. Paul Dibb, *Review of Australia's Defense Capabilities* (Canberra: Australian Government Publishing Service, March 1986), p. 46.

123. Dibb, *Review of Australia's Defense Capabilities*, p. 67.

124. "Who-What-Why," *Pacific Defense Reporter* (August 1986), 13 (2): 17–20. Also see Admiral Sir Anthony Synnot, "No. 1—Basic Strategy Is Wrong," and A. W. Grazebrook, "No. 2—Errors of Major Significance," in *Pacific Defense Reporter* (August 1986), 13 (2): 17–20.

125. The most comprehensive study of the possible war-fighting, deterrence, and verification functions carried out at Nurrungar available in the open literature is by Desmond Ball, *A Base for Debate: The US Satellite Station at Nurrungar* (Sydney: Allen & Unwin, 1987).

126. Desmond Ball, *Pine Gap* Sydney: Allen & Unwin, 1988); Graham Barrett, " Pine Gap Crucial to Arms Control," *The Age* [Melbourne], March 14, 1988, p. 13; Paul Kelley, "Paper Views Role of U.S. Commo Bases," November 25, 1988, p. 13, as reprinted in FBIS, *East Asia*, December 23, 1988, p. 68; and Pauline Kerr and Andrew McClean "INF and the U.S. Facilities in Australia," *Pacific Research* (August 1988), 1 (1): 19–20.

127. See, for example, Dennis Phillips, *Ambivalent Allies: Myth and Reality in the Australian-American Relationship* (New York: Penguin, 1988), pp. 146–151 and Joseph A. Camilleri, *The Australian-New Zealand-U.S. Alliance: Regional Security in the Nuclear Age*, esp. pp. 31–51, 100–101, and 168–221.

128. Henry Albinski, "Australian-American Security Alliance in the External Environment of the 1990s," paper published at the Inaugural Meeting on "Australia-U.S.. Defense Relations: An Agenda for the Future," Sydney, December 4–7, 1989.p. 4.

129. For additional background, see Thomas Durrell-Young, "The Australian-United States Strategic Relationship: Merely an Issue of Suitable Real Estate?" *Comparative Strategy* (1989), 8 (1): 129–132.

130. Ross Babbage, *Should Australia Plan to Defend Christmas and Cocos Islands?* Canberra Papers on Defense and Strategy, no. 45 (Canberra: The

Australian National University, 1988) provides extensive background. Data on Australian military forces' "shift north" is extracted from Australian Department of Defense, *The Defense of Australia 1987* (Canberra: Australian Government Publishing Service, 1987), pp. 44–45, 49–50, 54; Statement to Parliament by Senator Robert Ray, representing the Minister of Defense, Mr. Kim Beazley, on March 22, 1988, "Government Defense Policy—A Progress Report," *Australian Foreign Affairs Record* (March 1988), 59 (3): 95–99; Michael McKinley, "Australia and the Indian Ocean," in Mediansky and Palfreeman, eds., *In Pursuit of National Interests*, p. 254; and Thomas-Durell Young, "Problems in Australia's Defense Revolution," *Contemporary Southeast Asia* (December 1989), 11 (3): 256.

131. Testimony of Rear Admiral Edward B. Baker, Jr., Director, East Asian and Pacific Region, Department of Defense, in U.S.. House of Representatives, Hearing before the Subcommittee on Asian-Pacific Affairs, *Developments in the South Pacific Region*, 99th Cong., 2nd Sess., September 10, 1986,pp. 91–94, 138–139; Marc Liebman, "Soviet Naval Initiatives in the Pacific: 1942 Revisited?" *Armed Forces Journal* (April 1987), 124 (9): 58–64; and David Clark Scott, "'Star Wars' in the South Pacific," *The Christian Science Monitor*, June 8, 1989, p. 6.

132. Australian Department of Defense, *The Defense of Australia* (Canberra: Australian Government Publishing Service, March 1987), pp. 3–4.

133. *Review of Australia's Defense Capabilities*, pp. 50–51.

134. Samuel Huntington, "Coping with the Lippman Gap," *Foreign Affairs* (1988), 66 (3): 457.

135. Alan M. Webber, "Our Cold Peace With Japan," *Los Angeles Times*, June 19, 1989, Part II, p. 5.

136. James Fallows, "Containing Japan," *The Atlantic* (May 1989), 263 (5): 48.

137. For background on designation of Japan, India, and Brazil as "unfair traders," see Nayan Chanda, "Bark Worse Than Bite," *Far Eastern Economic Review* (June 8, 1989), 144 (23): 99–100 and Nigel Halloway, "Japan's Price Fixers," ibid., p. 101.

138. John W. Dower, "Japan's New Military Edge," *The Nation* (July 3, 1989), 249 (1): 18.

139. President Bush, "Security Strategy for the 1990s" *Current Policy* (May 24, 1989), no. 1178, p. 2.

140. William Clark, Jr., "FY 1990 Foreign Assistance Requests for East Asia and the Pacific," *Current Policy* (February 27, 1989), no. 1150, p. 1.

141. Tetsuya Kataoka and Ramon H. Myers, *Defending an Economic Superpower*, p. 108.

142. One of the best surveys of Nakasone's policy approach is by Chalmers Johnson, "Reflections on the Dilemma of Japanese Defense," *Asian Survey* (May 1986), 26 (5): 557–572. Also see Muthiah Alagappa, "Japan's Political and Security Role"; and Sheldon Simon, *The Future of Asia-Pacific Security Collaboration*, pp. 45–64.

143. In January 1988, the annual "Wealth of Japan Data Book," using

data provided by the Stockholm International Peace Research Institute, concluded that Japanese defense spending ranked second in the non-communist world. "Nihon no Yutakasa Data Book [Wealth of Japan Data Book]," in *Sekai*, (special edition), (January 1988), no. 510, p. 93. The 1989 defense spending figure is cited in "Yen 60.41 Trillion Budget For Next Fiscal Year Approved," *The Japan Times*, February 4, 1989, p. 1.

144. Osamura Kaihara, "Realism in Defense," *The Japan Times* March 19, 1989, p. 18 and Kaihara, "Comparing Defense Costs," *The Japan Times*, March 20, 1989, p. 18.

145. Quoted in David E. Sanger, "For Japan, Military Challenge Is Balancing Might and Image," *The New York Times*, March 6, 1989, pp. 1, 6. Also see *Report of the Defense Burdensharing Panel* of the Committee on Armed Services, U.S. House Of Representatives, 100th Cong., 2nd Sess., August 1988, pp. 62–65.

146. Tetsuya Kataoka and Ramon H. Myers, *Defending An Economic Superpower*, pp. 99–100.

147. Umemoto Tetsuya, "Comprehensive Security and the Evolution of the Japanese Security Posture," in Robert A. Scalapino, Seizaburo Sato, Jusuf Wanandi, and Sung-joo Han, eds., *Asian Security Issues: Regional and Global*, Research Papers and Policy Studies no. 26 (Berkeley: Institute of East Asian Studies, University of California, 1988), p. 28; J. W. M. Chapman, R. Drifte, and I. T. M. Gow, *Japan's Quest for Comprehensive National Security: Defense, Diplomacy, Dependence* (London: Francis Pinter, 1983), p. xvi; and Roy A. Werner, "America and Japan in a World of Multipolar Tensions," in The Atlantic Council of the United States, *The United States and Japan* (Lanham: University Press of America, 1989), pp. 65–66.

148. Chapman et al., *Japan's Quest*. Also see Paul Kreisberg, "Japan: A Superpower Minus Military Power," *Los Angeles Times*, December 11, 1988, Part II, p. 5 .

149. George Packard, "The Coming U.S.-Japan Crisis," *Foreign Affairs* (Winter 1987–88), 66 (2): 359.

150. Susan J. Pharr, "Japan and the World: The Debate in Japan," *Harvard International Review* (April-May 1988), 10 (4): 36–37.

151. Steven K. Vogel, *Japanese High Technology, Politics, and Power* Research Paper no. 2, Berkeley, Cal.: Berkeley Roundtable on the International Economy, March 1989, and Dower, "Japan's New Military Edge . . . ."

152. For background, see Gregg A. Rubinstein, "Emerging Bonds Of U.S.-Japanese Defense Technology Cooperation," *Strategic Review* (Winter 1987), 15 (1): 43–51; and William T. Tow "U.S.-Japan Military Technology Transfers: Collaboration or Conflict?" *Journal of Northeast Asian Studies* (December 1983), 2 (4): 3–23. Key U.S. Government documents concerning the U.S.-Japan Technology Transfer issue include the Report of Defense Science Board Task Force, *Industry-to-Industry International Armaments Cooperation: Phase II—Japan* (Washington, D.C.: Office of the Under Secretary of Defense for Research & Engineering, June 1984); and Report of the DOD

Technology Team, *Electro-Optics Millimeter/Microwave Technology In Japan* (Washington D.C.: Department of Defense, 1985).

153. For a dissenting viewpoint, see John O'Connell, "Strategic Implications of the Japanese SSM-1 Cruise Missile," *Journal of Northeast Asian Studies* (Summer 1987), 6 (2): 53–66.

154. Bob Johnstone, "Spending Up in the Land of the Rising Gun," *Far Eastern Economic Review* (October 13, 1988), 142 (41): 64–68; and Duane C. Dick, *Japan: Arms Exporter for The 21st Century*, paper presented to the California Seminar on International Security and Foreign Policy, University of California Institute on Global Conflict and Cooperation, February 26–27, 1988, p. 12.

155. Martin Tolchin, "Technology Report Finds U.S. Lagging," *The New York Times*, May 16, 1989, Part IV, p. 7.

156. David E. Sanger, "Tokyo, Unsure of U.S., Talks of Developing Its Own Arms," *The New York Times*, June 28, 1989, p. 7. Also see Gregory P. Corning, " U.S.-Japan Security Cooperation in the 1990s," *Asian Survey* (March 1989), 29 (3): 281; and Masaru Kohno, "Japanese Defense Policy Making: The FS-X Selection, 1985–1987," *Asian Survey* (May 1989), 29 (5): 457–479.

157. Kohno, "Japanese Defense Policy Making," p. 479.

158. Report of The Commission on Integrated Long-Term Strategy, *Discriminate Deterrence*, pp. 23, 31, and 66.

159. *Discriminate Deterrence*, p. 68.

160. Japan Defense Agency, *The Defense of Japan 1988*, pp. 190–192. Also see *Tokyo Shimbun*, August 24, 1988, as translated and reprinted in *DSJP* September 1, 1988, p. 1.

161. *The Defense of Japan 1988*, esp. pp. 92–118. Also see Research Institute for Peace and Security, Tokyo, *Asian Security 1987–88* (London: Brassey's Defense Publishers, 1987), pp. 161–162; and James E. Auer, "Japan's Defense Policy," *Current History* (April 1988), 87 (528): 147–148.

162. Osamu Kaihara, "Strategy for Japan's Defense," *The Japan Times* (Weekly Overseas Edition), February 20, 1988, p. 8.

163. See "Magarikado ni kita Nichi-Bei domei [Burden Sharing for a Military Balance]," *Bungei Shunju*, July 1988, pp. 94–111, as translated and reprinted in *Japan Echo* (Autumn 1988), 15 (3): 45. The Japanese tendency to defer to the U.S. in areas of "high strategy" was also conveyed to the author in discussions with U.S. Embassy, Tokyo, personnel on August 31, 1987.

164. "Soviet Forces Defeat Japanese in 17 Minutes," *Jane's Defense Weekly* (January 12, 1985), 3 (2): 52; and Sarah M. Taylor, "Military Balances in Northeast Asia," in Stephen P. Gibert, "Security In Northeast Asia," p. 146.

165. See Defense Agency Director General Kawara's remarks to the Diet as reported by *Kyodo*, and reprinted in FBIS, *East Asia (Daily Report)*, March 17, 1988, p. 6.

166. Ensign Thomas B. Modly, U.S. Navy, "The Rhetoric and Realities of Japan's 1,000–Mile Sea-Lane Defense Policy," *Naval War College Review*

38/1/307 (January-February 1985), pp. 33–34; and Simon, *The Future of Asia-Pacific Security Collaboration*, p. 53.

167. *Ryukyu Shimpo*, August 5, 1988, p. 5, as translated and reprinted in FBIS *East Asia* (August 16, 1988), pp. 1–2; and "Japan" section of *Pacific Defense Reporter* monthly Intelligence Digest, (May 1989), 15 (11): 35.

168. "Japan" section of *Pacific Defense Reporter* Intelligence Digest (April 1989), 15 (10): 27–28.

169. Barry Buzan, "Japan's Future: Old History Versus New Roles," *International Affairs* [London] (Autumn 1988), 64 (4): 559. 561, and 573.

170. Atsushi Tokinoya, *The Japan-U.S. Alliance: The Japanese Perspective*, Adelphi Papers no. 212 (London: International Institute for Strategic Studies, Autumn 1986), p. 23.

171. See the remarks of Deputy Secretary of Defense Karl Jackson made in Tokyo and summarized as "Increasing of Japan's Defense Expenditures (Will Cause) Uneasiness for Asian Nations; U.S. Deputy Assistant Secretary of Defense Expresses Concern," *Nihon Keizai Shimbun*, September 1, 1988, as translated and reprinted in *DSJP*, September 10–12, 1988, p. 13.

172. Michael Richardson, "Asia Fears New Tokyo Militarism," *International Herald Tribune*, February 20, 1990, pp. 1, 4.

173. Prepared statement of Robert J. Pranger, Director of International Programs, American Enterprise Institute for Public Policy Research before the Subcommittee on Asian and Pacific Affairs, House Committee on Foreign Affairs, *Hearings on U.S. Japan Relations*, 97th Cong., 2d Sess., March 24, 1982, pp. 493–505; Edward Olsen, *U.S.-Japan Strategic Reciprocity*, pp. 120–128; Hisahiko Okazaki, *A Grand Strategy for Japanese Defense* (Lanham, Md., New York and London: Abt Books, 1983), pp. 138–140. Sato's address before Japan's National Foreign Affairs Foundation, January 12, 1981 is covered in "Constitutional Controversy on War-Renouncing Clause Develops," a *Kyodo* report in English and reprinted in FBIS, *Asia & Pacific (Daily Report)*, April 24, 1981, pp. C-1 through C-2. Also see Masashi Nishihara, *East Asian Security and the Trilateral Countries*.

174. This point is underscored by Masashi Nishihara, *East Asian Security*, p. 74. For additional background, see U.A. Johnson and George R. Packard, eds., *The Common Security Interests of Japan, the United States, and its NATO Allies* (Cambridge, Mass.: Ballinger Publishing Company, 1981) pp. 1–25; 198–203; and Wolf Mendl, *Western Europe and Japan Between the Superpowers* (London: Croom Helm, 1984).

175. Fitchett, "At NATO Meeting, Japan Seeks Wider Security Link," *International Herald Tribune*, June 20, 1990, pp. 1, 2.

176. See, for example, Gerald Segal, "Not Ready for NATO's Top Table," *Los Angeles Times*, July 19, 1990, Part II, p. B-7.

177. Sam Jameson, "Japan Reaps New Clout in Aid to Asia," *Los Angeles Times*, June 22, 1989, pp. 1, 12–14; Urban C. Lehner, "First in Foreign Aid, Japan Still Isn't Sure What Purpose It Serves," *The Wall Street Journal*, July 3, 1989, pp. 1, 4; Werner, "America and Japan in a World of Multipolar Tensions," in The Atlantic Council of the United States, *The United States and*

Japan, pp. 69–73; Philip H. Trezise, "U.S.-Japan Economic Issues," in *The United States and Japan*, p. 35; and Makato Sakurai, "Japan-U.S. Economic Cooperation for the Developing Countries," in *The United States and Japan*, pp. 38–51.

178. Fitchett, "At NATO Meeting, Japan," p. 23.

179. Lee May, "Reagan, Allies Discuss NATO's Gains, Costs," *Los Angeles Times*, September 28, 1988, p. 10; Don Oberdorfer, "U.S. Allies Join Plan to Aid Manila," *International Herald Tribune*, May 9, 1988, p. 1; and Sam Jameson and Norman Kempster, " U.S., Japan Lead 19–Nation Plan to Aid Manila," *Los Angeles Times*, July 5, 1989, pp. 1, 12.

180. Yi Chae-sung, "U.S. Asks $20 Million for Gulf Defense," *The Korea Times*, April 30, 1988, p. 1, and "Foreign Ministry Comments," *The Korea Times*, May 1, 1988, p. 1, reprinted in FBIS, *East Asia*, May 3, 1988, p. 18; "Defense Ministry Official Comments," *Yonhap* (Seoul) May 9, 1988, translated and printed in FBIS, *East Asia*, May 9, 1988, p. 11; and "Further on Comments," *The Korea Herald*, May 8, 1988, p. 1, reprinted in FBIS, *East Asia*, May 9, 1988, p. 11.

181. On the Kunahari trip, see Hamish McDonald, "Tokyo Bearing Gifts," *Far Eastern Economic Review* (January 29, 1987), 135 (5): 30–31. Accounts of ongoing Japanese aid programs to the South Pacific include Akio Watanabe, "The Pacific Islands and Japan: Perspectives and Policies," in *Strategic Cooperation and Competition in the Pacific Islands*, vol. 2 (Washington, D.C.: National Defense University, May 17–19, 1989), pp. 241–274; William Nester, "The Third World in Japanese Foreign Policy," *Millennium: Journal of International Studies* (Winter 1989), 18 (3): 392; and "Aid for the 'Home Town,' " *Pacific Islands Monthly* (September 1988), 59 (9): 28–29.

182. For background, see Harry Gelman, "The Soviet Union, East Asia, and the West: the Kremlin's Calculus of Opportunities and Risks," *East Asia, the West, and International Security: Prospects for Peace—Part II* Adelphi Papers no. 217 (London: International Institute for Strategic Studies, Spring 1987), pp. 19–21 and "Noh Kidding," *Asiaweek* (October 19, 1986), 12(42): 36. For an excellent overview of Japan's effort to use the INF episode as a means to underscoring its increased diplomatic weight within the Western Alliance, see Reinhold Drifte, "Japan and Arms Control in East Asia," *The Journal of East Asian Affairs* (Winter/Spring 1990), 4 (1): 233–235.

183. Masahiko Asada, "Confidence-Building Measures in East Asia: A Japanese Perspective," *Asian Survey* (May 1988), 28 (5): 489–508.

184. Robert A. Scalapino, " Asia's Future," *Foreign Affairs* (Fall 1987), 66 (1): 104–105.

185. Tong Whan Park, "Alliance, Extended Deterrence, and Interdependence: Trends and Determinants of the Military Relationship Between Korea and the U.S.A.," *The Korean Journal of Defense Analysis* (Summer 1989), 1 (1): 186.

186. Peter Gumbel and Joseph P. Manguno, "Soviets and Koreans Keen to Do Business," *The Asian Wall Street Journal*, May 30, 1989, p. 10. Also see Sam Jameson, "Communist World Quickly Warms to South Korea," *Los*

Angeles Times, October 16, 1988, p. 5; and Sophia Quinn-Judge, "Walking a Tightrope Between North and South," *Far Eastern Economic Review* (December 8, 1988), 142 (49): 22–23.

187. Jameson, "Communist World Quickly Warms"; "China Prefers the Capitalist Korea," *The Economist* (August 20, 1988), 308 (7564): 30; and Robert Delfs, "Seoul's High Tech Lure Across the Yellow Sea," *Far Eastern Economic Review* (December 8, 1988), 142 (49): 20–21.

188. Harry G. Summers Jr., "Koreans Are Trying to Tell Us Something About the Concept of Nuclear Deterrence," *Los Angeles Times,* December 1, 1988, Part II, p. 7. A good description of the antinuclear position is offered by Shin Jung-Hyun, "The Role of the United States in Establishing Peace on the Korean Peninsula," pp. 87–88.

189. Author interviews, Beijing, August 1987.

190. John J. Fialka, "U.S. Suspects Nuclear Plants in North Korea," *The Asian Wall Street Journal,* July 20, 1989, p. 1; "Japan Scientists Report North Korea Is Building a Nuclear Arms Facility," *International Herald Tribune* (February 10/11, 1990), p. 5; Andrew Mack, "Is Pyongyang the Next Proliferator?" *Pacific Research* (February 1990), 3 (1): 6–7; John McBeth, Nayan Chanda, and Sada Islam, "Nuclear Jitters," *Far Eastern Economic Review* (February 2, 1989), 143 (5): 15; Myung-O Bae, "Prospects of Inter-Korean Military Relations," *Korean Observer* (Spring 1989), 20 (1): 32; and Joseph A. Yager, *Nuclear Nonproliferation Strategy in Asia,* CNSN Paper (McLean, Va.: Center for National Security Negotiations, July 1989), 1 (3): 15–17. Background on the North Korean SCUD-B is provided by G. Jacobs, "North Korea's Arms Industry: Development and Progress," *Asian Defense Journal* March 1989, pp. 32–35.

191. Norman Levin and Richard L. Sneider, "Korea in Postwar U.S. Security Policy," in Gerald L. Curtis and Sung-jo Han, eds., *The U.S.-South Korean Alliance* (Lexington, Mass./Toronto: D.C. Heath, 1983), p. 55.

192. Joint Committee on Foreign Affairs, Defense, and Trade, The Parliament of the Commonwealth of Australia, *Australia's Relations with the South Pacific* (Canberra: Australian Government Publishing Service, Marcy 1989), pp. 149–150.

193. See the comments of Denis McLean, " The Interests of Extra-Regional Powers," in *Strategic Cooperation and Competition in the Pacific Islands,* vol. 2, pp. 317–318.

194. William Maddox, "The U.S. Army in the Pacific," *Asia-Pacific Defense Forum* (Summer 1989), 14 (1): 38.

195. See an Agence France Presse report by Ian Pedley, August 1, 1989, as translated and reprinted in Foreign Broadcast Information Service, *East Asia,* August 1, 1989, p. 2; and Brigadier P. J. Greville (RL), "Kangaroo '89 Rich in Lessons," *Pacific Defense Reporter* (October 1989), 16 (4): 5–6, 8–9. *Kangaroo '89* was the biggest joint exercise between Australia and the United States since World War II, involving some 25,000 personnel.

196. Joint Committee of Foreign Affairs, Defense, and Trade, *Australia's Relations With the South Pacific,* p. 156.

197. Ibid. On the Australian-PNG "trip wire," see David Hegarty, "South Pacific Security Issues: An Australian Prospective," *Conflict* (1988), 8 (4), esp. p. 320.

198. These points are assessed in-depth by Richard Betts, "The United States: Global Deterrence," in James W. Morley, ed., *Security Interdependence in the Asia Pacific Region*.

3. ASPIRING PLAYER I: THE SOVIET UNION

1. John J. Stephan, "Asia in the Soviet Conception," in Donald S. Zagoria, ed., *Soviet Policy in East Asia*, p. 31.

2. Both Hiroshi Kimura and Gerald Segal have noted this dilemma in slightly different ways. Kimura has observed that "the Soviet Union is a power in Asia but is not an Asian power yet." Kimura, "Soviet Focus on the Pacific," *Problems of Communism* (May-June 1987), p. 3. Segal has stated the problem only slightly differently: "The Soviet Union is not an East Asian power, but it is a power in East Asia." Gerald Segal, "Introduction," in Segal, ed., *The Soviet Union in East Asia: Predicaments of Power* (London/Boulder, Colo.: Heinemann/Westview, 1983), p. 1.

3. The basic characteristics of this approach are well summarized by Robert A. Manning, *Asian Policy: The New Soviet Challenge in the Pacific* (New York: Priority Press Publications, 1988), especially pp. 21–40, 80–89 and by Donald Zagoria, "Soviet Policy in East Asia: A New Beginning?" *Foreign Affairs (America and the World 1988–89)*, 68 (1): 120–138.

4. Zagoria, "Soviet Policy in East Asia," p. 121.

5. The classic statement of such Soviet thinking was Marshal V. D. Sokolovskiy's *Soviet Military Strategy*. See a translated edition published by MacDonald and Jane's (London: 1975), especially pp. 201–202.

6. William Odom, "Soviet Military Doctrine," *Foreign Affairs* (Winter 1988–1989), 67 (2): 124.

7. A definitive Soviet treatment of the "reasonable sufficiency concept" is by Col. P. Skonodenko, "Military Parity and the Principle of Reasonable Sufficiency," *Kommunist Vooruzhennykh Sil* (May 1987), no. 10, pp. 14–21, as translated and reprinted in Joint Publications and Research Service (JPRS)-UMA-88-006, March 28, 1988, pp. 19–24.

8. Gorbachev, *Perestroika: New Thinking for Our Country and the World* (New York: Harper & Row, 1987), pp. 144–148. Western analysis is provided by Odom, "Soviet Military Doctrine," p. 129.

9. An early but almost prophetic assessment of superpower competition under the Asia-Pacific's changing conditions of regional security is Donald Zagoria's "Soviet Policy and Prospects in East Asia," *International Security* (Fall 1980), 5 (2): 66–78. Recent and useful assessments of the USSR's posture include Coit D. Blacker, "The USSR and Asia in 1989: Recasting Relationships," *Asian Survey* (January 1990), 30 (1): 1–12; Sophie Quinn-Judge, "Glasnost's Asian Frontier," *Far Eastern Economic Review* 141, (August 4, 1988), no. 31, pp. 24–27; Rajan Menon, "New Thinking and Northeast Asian

Security," *Problems of Communism* (March-June 1989), 38 (2): 1–32; and Gerald Segal, "Soviet Options in the Pacific," in Susan L. Clark, ed., *Gorbachev's Agenda: Changes in Soviet Foreign and Domestic Policy*, pp. 313–353.

10. Testimony of Richard H. Solomon, Assistant Secretary of State for East Asian and Pacific Affairs before the House Subcommittee on Asia and the Pacific, "Sustaining the Dynamic Balance: An Overview of U.S. Policy for East Asia and the Pacific," February 22, 1990, p. 5, of unpublished testimony manuscript in author's possession. Also see a report on Secretary of Defense Dick Cheney's Speech in Tokyo on February 28, 1990, by Fred Hiatt, "Cheney's Message in Asia: U.S. Troops Are Here to Stay," *International Herald Tribune*, February 24/25, 1990, p. 1.

11. A text of the Treaty of Friendship, Alliance and Mutual Assistance is found in *Disarmament and Security: A Collection of Documents, 1919–1955* (Washington, D.C.: Government Printing Office, 1956), pp. 594–595. Additional background on the treaty is found in Raymond L. Garthoff, "Sino-Soviet Military Relations," in Garthoff, ed., *Sino-Soviet Military Relations*, pp. 84–85; and Walter C. Clemens, Jr., *The Arms Race And Sino-Soviet Relations*, pp. 68–71.

12. "Statement by the Spokesman of the Chinese Government," pp. 7–16.

13. Harvey Nelson, "Continuity and Change in Chinese Strategic Deterrence," in June T. Dreyer, ed., *Chinese Defense and Foreign Policy* (New York: Paragon House, 1989), p. 252. Also see excerpts cited from the Soviet military newspaper *Krasnaya Zvezda* [Red Star] August 25, 1963; and the Official Statement of the Soviet Government, September 21, 1963, published in both *Pravda* and *Izvestia*, and reprinted in William E. Griffith, *The Sino-Soviet Rift*, pp. 434, 440, 460.

14. Liu Xiao, the PRC's ambassador to the Soviet Union between 1955 and 1962, recalled in his memoirs that the PLA's General Staff notified its Soviet counterpart before the artillery bombardment commenced. See his *Chu shi sulian ba nian* [Eight Years as Ambassador to the Soviet Union], p. 72. Harvey Nelson, *Power and Insecurity: Beijing, Moscow, and Washington 1949–1988*, pp. 41–42 has previously argued that Mao neglected to inform the Soviets before shelling the offshore islands.

15. *Nikita Khrushchev Remembers*, with an introduction, commentary and notes by Edward Crankshaw. Translated and edited by Strobe Talbott (Boston and Toronto: Little Brown, 1970), p. 368. It should be noted that this edition was later renounced by Khrushchev as lacking authenticity, in Strobe Talbott, trans. and ed., *Khrushchev Remembers: The Last Testament* (Boston and Toronto: Little, Brown, 1974), p. 4, note 2.

16. Jonathan D. Pollack, *Into the Vortex: China, the Sino-Soviet Alliance, and the Korean War* (Santa Monica: The RAND Corporation, forthcoming in late 1990 or early 1991) and Hu Yufan and Zhai Zhihai, "China's Decision to Enter the Korean War: History Revisited," pp. 99–103.

17. Adam Ulam, *Expansion and Coexistence*, p. 520. Also see Alexander George and Richard Smoke, *Deterrence in American Foreign Policy*, pp. 161–162, citing this interpretation as being supported by the first edition of Khru-

shchev's memoirs. For an account of China's strategic calculations in 1951–1952, consult Gordon H. Chang, *Friends and Enemies: The United States, China, and the Soviet Union, 1948–1972*, pp. 79–80.

18. Alexander George, *The Chinese Communist Army in Action* (New York and London: Columbia University Press, 1967), p. 185.

19. Raymond L. Garthoff, "Sino-Soviet Military Relations, 1945–1966," in Garthoff, ed., *Sino-Soviet Military Relations*, p. 85.

20. V. I. Glunin, A. M. Grigoriev et al., *The Recent History of China, 1917–1970* (Moscow: 1972), p. 259, cites "special Soviet air units sent to Manchuria to protect industrial centers of northeastern China against American air raids." "'Alekseyev's Talk: The First Batch of Documents on USSR-PRC Relations'—15th in series entitled 'Fragments of the History of Soviet-Chinese Friendship,' " Radio Moscow in Mandarin to China, November 4, 1982, as translated and reprinted in Foreign Broadcast Information Service (FBIS) *USSR* (Daily Report), November 5, 1982, p. B-2, refers to Soviet pilots shooting down "several dozen enemy aircraft," although the location of such operations is not mentioned.

21. *Khrushchev Remembers: The Last Testament*, pp. 256–257, wherein the Soviet leader reports that his discussions with Mao Zedong in Moscow during November 1957 left the Soviets with the impression that Mao had little appreciation for the logic of mutual assured destruction.

22. Interesting comparisons between Khrushchev's and Gorbachev's situations are offered by Martin McCauley, " Introduction," in McCauley, ed., *Khrushchev and Khruschevism* (Bloomington and Indianapolis: Indiana University Press, 1987), pp. 1–8.

23. *Nie Rongzhen Huiyilu* [Memoirs of Nie Rongzhen] (Beijing: People's Liberation Army Press, 1984), pp. xx. The best Western source on the New Defense Technical Accord is John Wilson Lewis and Xue Litai, *China Builds the Bomb*, pp. 62–64.

24. Chang, *Friends and Enemies*, p. 204.

25. *Khrushchev Remembers*, pp. 259–260. Also see Walter C. Clemens, "China Card Still Doesn't Play," *The Asian Wall Street Journal*, June 9–10, 1989, p. 10, and Liu Xiao, *Chu shi sulian ba nian*.

26. *Adam Ulam, Expansion and Coexistence*, p. 555.

27. Yu Chao-li, "The Forces of Decay," *Hongqi*, August 16, 1958, as translated and reprinted in *Survey of the Chinese Mainland Press*, August 21, 1958, pp. 42–47. Also see J. H. Kalicki, *The Pattern of Sino-American Crises: Political-Military Interactions in the 1950s* (London and New York: Cambridge University Press, 1975), p. 187.

28. *Khrushchev Remembers*, pp. 262–263.

29. A September 5, 1958, address to the Chinese Politboro, as reproduced in *Long Live Mao Tse-tung's Thought* (Beijing: 1974), and cited by Allen S. Whiting, "Quemoy 1958: Mao's Miscalculations," p. 265.

30. He Xiaolu, "A Marshal and a Diplomat," *Kunlun* (1984), no. 4, as cited by Lewis and Xue, *China Builds the Bomb*, p. 64,

31. Allen Whiting, "Quemoy 1958," p. 270.

32. Harry Gelman, *The Soviet Far East Buildup and Soviet Risk-Taking Against China*, R-2943–AF (Santa Monica, Cal.: The RAND Corporation, August 1982), p. 6.

33. On the Bucharest conference, see Herbert Ellison, "Introduction" in Ellison, ed., *The Sino-Soviet Conflict: A Global Perspective* (Seattle and London: University of Washington Press, 1982), pp. xv-xvi.

34. "SRV Foreign Ministry's White Book On SRV-PRC Relations," in FBIS, *Asia and Pacific* (Supplement 031), October 19, 1979. Also see Douglas Pike, *Vietnam and the Soviet Union*, pp. 62–63, 77–78.

35. Gelman, *The Soviet Far East Buildup*, p. 10; "SRV's Foreign Ministry White Book," p. 18; and Pike, *Vietnam and the Soviet Union*, p. 63.

36. Banning N. Garrett and Bonnie S. Glaser, *War and Peace: The Views from Moscow and Beijing*, p. 79.

37. Gelman, *The Soviet Far East Buildup*, pp. 64–68; and Paul F. Langer, "Soviet Military Power in Asia," in Zagoria, ed., *Soviet Policy in East Asia*, p. 267.

38. An early Soviet account of Soviet collective security policies in Asia is by V. Kudryavtsev, "Problems of Collective Security in Asia," *International Affairs* (Moscow), (December 1973), 19 (12): 94–98. Western chronologies tracing the evolution of the concept include Avigdor Haselkorn, "The Soviet Collective Security System," *Orbis* (Spring 1975), 19 (2): 231–254; Arnold Horelick, "Soviet Policy Dilemmas in Asia," *Asian Survey* (June 1977), 17 (6): 499–512; Horelick, "The Soviet Union's Asian Collective Security Proposal: A Club in Search of Members," *Pacific Affairs* (Fall 1974), no. 47, pp. 269–285; Nobuhisa Izawa, "Conditions for Peace in Southeast Asia—An Evaluation of the Soviet Union's Collective Security Concept," *Oriental Economist* (December 1974), 42 (770): 17–24; Malcolm Mackintosh, "Soviet Interests and Policies in the Asia-Pacific Region," *Orbis* (Fall 1975), 19 (3): 763–774; and Langer, "Soviet Military Power in Asia," pp. 259–260.

39. This point is well developed by William Hyland, "The Sino-Soviet Conflict: A Search for New Security Strategies," *Strategic Review* (Fall 1979), 7 (4): 52.

40. "Freikorps Fur Sinkiang (Volunteers for Sinkiang)," *Der Spiegal* (February 16, 1970), 24 (8): 126 and Harrison Salisbury, "Soviet-Chinese Animosity Found Along the Frontier, "*The New York Times*, August 17, 1966, pp. 1, 4.

41. Data on the shift of Soviet troops is found in "Soviet Said to Shift Troops," *The New York Times*, February 3, 1967, p. 3. Further useful background on Soviet strategy and posturing against China during this time period is provided by Gelman, *The Soviet Far East Buildup* pp. 16–48; Michael MccGwire, *Military Objectives in Soviet Foreign Policy* (Washington, D.C.: Brookings Institution, 1985), pp. 164–165; Thomas W. Robinson, "The Sino-Soviet Border Dispute: Background, Development and the March 1969 Clashes," *American Political Science Review* 66, no. 4, (December 1972), pp. 1175–1202; Thomas W. Wolfe, *Soviet Power in Europe 1945–1970* (Baltimore: The Johns Hopkins University Press, 1970), pp. 395–396; and the Testimony of Dr.

Stefan T. Possony in Hearing before the Subcommittee to investigate the Administration of the Internal Security Laws of the Committee on the Judiciary, United States Senate, *Threat to U.S. Security Posed By Stepped-Up Sino-Soviet Hostilities* 91st Cong., in the 2d Sess., March 17, 1970, pp. 60–63.

42. Excellent accounts of the 1969 Sino-Soviet border crisis are given by Gelman, *The Soviet Far East Buildup,* pp. 31–48; Melvin Gurtov and Byoong-Moo Hwang, *China Under Threat: The Politics of Strategy and Diplomacy* (Baltimore: Johns Hopkins Press, 1980); Harold Hinton, *The Bear at the Gate* (Washington, D.C.: American Enterprise Institute, 1972; Robinson, "The Sino-Soviet Border Dispute," *passim;* Gerald Segal, *Defending China,* pp. 176–196; and Richard Wich, *Sino-Soviet Crisis Politics,* esp. pp. 97–112.

43. Lewis and Xue, *China Builds the Bomb,* p. 216, quote officers serving with China's Second Artillery nuclear missile unit during the late 1960s as expressing doubt about the PLA's ability to launch a credible retaliatory missile attack against a Soviet missile attack. For corroborating data, see the International Institute for Strategic Studies, *Strategic Survey 1968* (London: IISS, 1969), p. 41.

44. Ivan Kovalenko, *Soviet Policy for Asian Peace and Security,* pp. 246–248. Also see his "Japanese Militarism Rears Its Head," *Problemy Dal'nego Vostoka* [The Problems of the Far East] (July-September 1978), no. 3, translated and reprinted in Joint Publications Research Service (JPRS) 72621 *The Far East* (January 15, 1979), pp. 52–69, and an interview of Premier Kosygin with Japanese political leader Yohei Kono, as reported by *Kyodo* and reprinted as "Japanese USSR Relations at 'Turning Point,' " FBIS *Soviet Union* (Daily Report), November 27, 1978, pp. M-1, M-2.

45. Report Prepared for the Committee on Foreign Affairs, U.S. House of Representatives, *The Soviet Union in the Third World, 1980–1985: An Imperial Burden or Political Asset?* 99th Cong., 1st Sess., September 23, 1985, pp. 68–69; Paul Dibb, "The Soviet Union as a Pacific Power," *International Journal* (Spring 1983), 38 (1): 238; and Thomas Robinson, "The Soviet Union and Asia in 1981," *Asian Survey* (January 1982), 22 (1): 14; all underscore this point.

46. Simon, *The Future of Asian-Pacific Security Collaboration,* p. 22.

47. Malcom MacKintosh, "Soviet Military Strategy and Operational Capabilities in the 1990s," in Ross Babbage, ed., *The Soviets in the Pacific in the 1990s,* pp. 34–39.

48. Richard Solomon has argued this point especially well. See his "Coalition Building or Condominium? The Soviet Presence in Asia and American Policy Alternatives," in Zagoria, *Soviet Policy in East Asia,* especially pp. 291–294, and his article coauthored with Masataka Kosaka, "Nuclear Dilemmas and Asian Security: Problems of Coalition Defense in the Nuclear Era," in Richard Solomon and Masataka Kosaka, eds., *The Soviet Far East Military Buildup* (Dover, Mass.: Auburn House Publishing Company, 1986), especially pp. 7, 12.

49. The term is Solomon's in "Coalition Building or Condominium," p. 288.

50. Robert Scalapino, "Asia in a Global Context: Strategic Issues for the Soviet Union," in Solomon and Kosaka, *The Soviet Far East Military Buildup*, p. 33.

51. Gelman, *The Soviet Far East Buildup*, pp. 75–78; C. G. Jacobson, *Sino-Soviet Relations Since Mao* (New York: Praeger, 1981), pp. 30–31; and Sarah M. Taylor, "Military Balances in Northeast Asia," in Stephen P. Gibert, ed., *Security in Northeast Asia: Approaching the Pacific Century*, p. 138.

52. The International Institute for Strategic Studies, *The Military Balance 1988–1989* (London: International Institute for Strategic Studies, Autumn 1988), p. 43; and Amitav Acharya, "The United States versus the USSR in the Pacific: Trends in the Military Balance," *Contemporary Southeast Asia* (March 1988), 9 (4): 283. For a useful map outlining the ICBM deployment patterns in the Far East, see Paul Dibb, "Soviet Capabilities, Interests, and Strategies in East Asia in the 1980s," *Survival* (July-August 1982), 14 (4): 155–162.

53. Garrett and Glaser, *War and Peace: The Views From Moscow and Beijing*, p. 109.

54. Particularly cogent analysis of Soviet problems in carrying out a "wider Pacific" interdiction missions is offered by Myles L. C. Robertson, *Soviet Policy Towards Japan: An Analysis of Trends in the 1970s and 1980s*, pp. 119–123.

55. Carl G. Jacobsen, "Sino-Soviet Relations: New Perspectives," in Jacobsen, ed., *Soviet Foreign Policy, New Dynamics, New Themes* (New York: St. Martin's Press, 1989), p. 157.

56. Ibid., pp. 157–158.

57. U.S. Department of Defense, *Soviet Military Power: Prospects for Change 1989* (Washington, D.C. : USDOD, 1989), p. 9.

58. For background, consult Leszek Buszynski, "International Linkages and Regional Interests in Soviet Asia-Pacific Policy," *Pacific Affairs* (Summer 1988), 61 (2): 213–234; Carolyn McGiffert Ekedahl and Melvin A. Goodman, "Gorbachev's 'New Directions' in Asia," *Journal of Northeast Asian Studies* (Fall 1989), 8 (3): 3–24; Graeme Gill, "The Soviet Union and Southeast Asia: A New Beginning?" *Contemporary Southeast Asia* (June 1988), 10 (1): 69–81; Robert A. Manning, "Moscow's Pacific Future: Gorbachev Rediscovers Asia," *World Policy Journal* (Winter 1987–88), 5 (1): 59–61; Manning, *Asian Policy*, pp. 21–40; Richard Nations, "Moscow's New Tack " *Far Eastern Economic Review* (August 14, 1986), 133 (33): 30–34; Sophie Quinn-Judge, "Glasnost's Asian Frontier," *Far Eastern Economic Review* (August 4, 1988), 14 (31): 24–25; Quinn-Judge, "Warm Words from a Frozen Frontier," ibid. (September 29, 1988), 141 (39): 28–30; "A Siberian Serenade," *Asiaweek* (September 30, 1988), 14 (40 19–22; and various chapters in Ramesh Thakur and Carlyle A. Thayer, eds., *The Soviet Union as an Asian Pacific Power*.

59. Manning, *Asian Policy*, p. 35. Also see *Speech by Mikhail Gorbachev in Vladivostok, 28 July 1986* (Moscow: Novosti Press, 1986), pp. 28, 31; and Paul Keal, "Implications for Northeast Asia," in Thakur and Thayer, *The Soviet Union as an Asian-Pacific Power*, p. 65.

60. Coit D. Blacker, "The USSR and Asia in 1989," p. 4; and Gerald Segal, "Soviet Options in the Pacific," pp. 319–320.

61. Dennis M. Gormley, *Double Zero and Soviet Military Strategy: Implications for Western Security* (London: Jane's, 1988), pp. 142–143; and Derek da Cunha, "Soviet Naval Capabilities in the Pacific in the 1990s," in Babbage, ed., *The Soviets in the Pacific in the 1990s*, pp. 57–59.

62. The Krasnoyarsk speech is reprinted verbatim in "*Vremia deistrii, vremia prakticheskoi raboti* [Time for Actions, Time for Practical Work]," *Pravda*, September 18, 1988, pp. 1–3. The author is grateful to Ruth Wallach for translation assistance. An English-language version is reprinted in Manning, *Asian Policy*, pp. 128–129. Also see Ekedahl and Goodman, "Gorbachev's 'New Directions' in Asia," p. 6; Quinn-Judge, "Warm Words from a Frozen Frontier," pp. 28–30; "A Siberian Serenade," pp. 19–22; Michael Parks, "Soviets Propose Mutual Pullout from Asia Bases," *Los Angeles Times*, September 17, 1988) pp. 1, 12.

63. Rajan Menon, "New Thinking and Northeast Asian Security Problems," p. 28.

64. For a typical Soviet argument along such lines, see A. Sergeyev, "Nuclear Disarmament and Security in the Far East," *Far Eastern Affairs* (1988), no. 1, pp. 37–46.

65. See, for example, A. Anichkin, "Scientists Need Politicians," *Izvestia*, January 7, 1990, p. 5, translated and reprinted in FBIS, *Soviet Union*, January 10, 1990, p. 22.

66. Blacker, "The USSR and Asia in 1989," p. 5; and Menon, "New Thinking and Northeast Asian Security Problems," pp. 11–12.

67. Sophie Quinn-Judge, "Reduction Resistance," *Far Eastern Economic Review* (March 16, 1989), 143 (11): 22.

68. Michael Parks, Demilitarized Border Urged By Gorbachev," *Los Angeles Times*, May 17, 1989, pp. 1, 15; David Holley and Michael Parks, "4,500–Mile Border Peaceful—But Tough Questions Remain," *Los Angeles Times*, May 15, 1989, p. 10; and Bill Keller, "Beijing Welcomes the Soviet Leader for Summit Talks," *The New York Times*, May 15, 1989, pp. 1, 4.

69. Michael Dobbs, "Soviets, Chinese Sign Troop Cutback Pact," *The Washington Post*, April 25, 1990, pp. 29, 32–33, and James L. Tyson, "Soviets, Chinese Take Steps to Scale Back Border Forces," *The Christian Science Monitor*, February 27, 1990, p 4. Also see Francis X. Clines, "Soviets and Chinese Sign Broad Pact," *The New York Times*, April 25, 1990, p. 3; Michael Parks, "China, Soviets OK Troop Cuts Along Border," *Los Angeles Times*, April 25, 1990, pp. 1, 11; and Tai Ming Chenng, "Pragmatic Partners," *Far Eastern Economic Review* (April 26, 1990), 148 (17): 12–13.

70. Tai Ming Cheung, "Comrades in Arms," *Far Eastern Economic Reivew* (July 19, 1990) 149 (29): 30.

71. A good comparative background of the respective superpower positions on nuclear-free-zone arrangements and on overall regional disarmament is provided by the Research Institute for Peace and Security, Tokyo, *Asian*

Security 1988–1989 (London: Brassey's Defense Publishers, 1988), pp. 44–47, 151–155.

72. Keal, *Implications for Northeast Asia*, pp. 66– 67 offers excellent analysis on this point.

73. The term "essentialist" is used by Tsuyoshi Hasegawa, "The Military Factor in Soviet Foreign Policy," in Kinya Niiseki, ed., *The Soviet Union in Transition*, p. 148. The Soviet notion of "absolute security" is addressed by John Van Oudenaren, *Deterrence, Warfighting, and Soviet Military Doctrine*.

74. The term "contextualist" is again taken from Hasegawa, "The Military Factor in Soviet Foreign Policy," p. 148. Recent writings reflecting this point of view include Matthew Evangelista, "The New Soviet Approach to Security," *World Policy Journal* (Fall 1986), 3 (4): 561–599; Raymond L. Garthoff, "Mutual Deterrence and Strategic Arms Limitation in Soviet Policy," *International Security* (Summer 1978), 3 (1): 112–147; David Halloway, "Military Power and Political Purpose in Soviet Policy," *Daedalus* (Fall 1980), 109 (4): 13–30; James M. McConnell, "Shifts in Soviet Views on the Proper Focus of Military Development," *World Politics* (April 1985), 37 (3): 317–343; and MccGwire, *Military Objectives in Soviet Foreign Policy*, esp. pp. 59–66.

75. For more details on the recent Soviet measures to "restructure" its land and naval force capabilities in ways necessary to multiply its force use options, see Donald C. F. Daniel, "The Soviet Navy and Tactical Nuclear War At Sea," *Survival* (July-August 1987), 29 (4): 318–335 and Dennis M. Gormley and Douglas M. Hart, "Soviet Views on Escalation," *The Washington Quarterly* (Fall 1984), 7 (4): 76–80.

76. Allen S. Whiting, "Major Power Threats to Security in East Asia," in Scalapino, Sato, and Wanadi, *Internal and External Security Issues in Asia*, pp. 33–34.

77. MccGwire, *Military Objectives in Soviet Foreign Policy*, p. 165.

78. Useful background on recent Soviet force deployments in this theater and their effect on the overall military balance there are John T. Berbich, "Growth of Soviet Military Power in Asia," in Ray S. Cline, James Arnold Miller, and Roger Kanet, eds., *Asia in Soviet Global Strategy* (Boulder, Colo. and London: Westview Press, 1987), pp. 33–40; Kenichi Kitamura, "Soviet Military Strategy in East Asia," in Cline, Miller, and Kanet, *Asia in Soviet Global Strategy*, pp. 51–60; Robertson, *Soviet Policy Towards Japan*, pp. 88–136; U.S. Department of Defense, *Soviet Military Power: Prospects for Change 1989* (Washington, DC: USGPO, 1989), pp. 112–120; Georges Tan Eng Bok, *The USSR in East Asia*, The Atlantic Papers nos. 59/60 (Paris: The Atlantic Institute For International Affairs, March 1986), especially pp. 40–60; and Sarah M. Taylor, "Military Balances in Northeast Asia," in Gibert, ed., *Security in Northeast Asia*, pp. 137–160.

79. Chinese military officials estimated the demilitarization process could take five years or more.

80. U.S. Department of Defense, *Soviet Military Power*, p. 123.

81. This point is raised by Francis Fukuyama, "Asia in a Global War,"

Comparative Strategy (1987), 6 (4): 391. Also see Manning, "Moscow's Pacific Future," pp. 57–59.

82. Paul Dibb, *The Soviet Union: The Incomplete Superpower*, p. 197; Joris Janssen Lok, "Soviet Strategy: Reaffirming the Bastion Doctrine," *Jane's Defense Weekly* (January 27, 1990), 13 (4): 147; and J. J. Tritten, *Soviet Naval Forces and Nuclear Warfare*, pp. 139–150.

83. Simon, *The Future of Asian-Pacific Security Collaboration*, pp. 36–37; Tan Eng Bok, *The USSR in East Asia*, pp. 52–53; Commander David M. Fitzgerald, "The Soviets in Southeast Asia," U.S. Naval Institute *Proceedings* 112/2/96 (February 1986), pp. 50–51; and Yang Razali Kassim, "Uncertainty Over U.S. Bases in Philippines," *The Straits Times* [Singapore], January 1, 1988, p. 20.

84. See Charles McGregor, *The Sino-Vietnamese Relationship and the Soviet Union*, Adelphi Papers no. 232, pp. 59, 66.

85. Michael R. Gordon, "Soviets Said to Withdraw Fighters and Bombers From Vietnam Base," *The New York Times* January 19, 1990, p. 8. Also see Lok, "Soviet Strategy," p. 147; Susumu Awanohara, "Withdrawal Symptoms," *Far East Economic Review* (February 1, 1990), 147 (5): 8–9; and Michael Richardson, "Major Changes in Power Balance as Soviets Withdraw from Cam Ranh Bay," *Pacific Defense Reporter* (March 1990), 16 (9): 13–14. A Soviet account of current and projected withdrawals was offered by Anatoliy Aleksandrov on Radiz Moscow (broadcast in Tagalog to the Philippines), March 13, 1990, as translated and reprinted in FBIS, *Soviet Union*, march 16, 1990, pp. 13–14.

86. Recent reports that the U.S. would seek to use Cam Ranh if and when the USSR completed a total withdrawal of its forces there have been denied by Vietnamese spokesmen. See "Report of Cam Ranh Bay Offer Called 'Unfounded,' " Agence France Presse, April 10, 1990, as reprinted in FBIS, *East Asian* (Daily Report), April 11, 1990, p. 41.

87. Muthiah Alagappa, "Soviet Policy in Southeast Asia: Towards Constructive Engagement," *Pacific Affairs* (Fall 1990), 63 (3), forthcoming.

88. Segal, "Soviet Options in the Pacific," pp. 319–320.

89. F. A. Mediansky and Dianne Court, *The Soviet Union and Southeast Asia*, Canberra Papers on Strategy and Defense no. 29 (Canberra: Australian National University, 1984), p. 32.

90. *Soviet Military Power 1988*, p. 124. The author's interviews were conducted at CINCPAC Headquarters, Honolulu, Hawaii, September 1, 1987.

91. Robertson, *Soviet Policy Towards Japan*, pp. 125–126.

92. Karl Schoenberger, "Soviets, Japanese Report No Progress on Old Territorial Dispute," *Los Angeles Times*, December 20, 1988, p. 11; and Schoenberger, "Japan, Soviets Turn Back Clock on Islands Dispute," *Los Angeles Times*, December 21, 1988, p. 8.

93. See the observations of Donald Zagoria, "Russian Policy Toward Korea: A Historical and Geopolitical Analysis," in Scalapino and Han Sung-joo, *United States-Korea Relations*, pp. 210–211.

94. Chae-Jin Lee and Hideo Sato, *U.S. Policy Toward Japan and Korea*, p. 42; and Ralph Clough, "The Soviet Union and the Two Koreas," in Zagoria, ed., *Soviet Policy in East Asia*, pp. 178–179.

95. Seung-Hwan Kim, *The Soviet Union and North Korea: Soviet Asian Strategy and Its Implications for the Korean Peninsula 1964–1968]* (Seoul: Research Center for Peace and Unification of Korea, 1988), pp. 15–16, 27–28.

96. Peter Polomka, *The Two Koreas: Catalyst for Conflict in East Asia?* Adelphi Papers no. 208 (London: The International Institute for Strategic Studies, Summer 1986), pp. 25–26. The PRC's position was confirmed to the author during his discussions with Chinese analysts at the Institute for Contemporary International Relations, Beijing, August 5, 1987.

97. Zagoria, "Soviet Policy in East Asia: A New Beginning?," p. 128; Li Ki-taek, "Soviet Military Policy in the Far East and Its Impact on North Korea," *Vantage Point* (April 1989), 12 (4): 6 and Jim Mann, "N. Korea Puts New Missiles Along Border," *Los Angeles Times*, June 8, 1988, p. 4.

98. Li Ki-taek, "Soviet Military Policy," pp. 6–7.

99. Scalapino and Kosaka, "Introduction," in Scalapino and Kosaka, eds., *Peace, Politics, and Economics in Asia*, p. 4. Also see Masashi Nishihara, "The Security of North-East Asia—Part I," in the International Institute for Strategic Studies, ed., *East Asia, the West, and International Security: Prospects for Peace*, Adelphi Papers no. 218 (London: IISS, Spring 1987), pp. 4–5.

100. Young C. Kim, "Soviet Policies Toward Korea" in Niiseki, ed., *The Soviet Union in Transition*, p. 199.

101. Also see International Strategic Institute at Stanford, Stanford University, and Institute of Far Eastern Studies, Academy of Sciences of the USSR, *On Strengthening Security and Developing Cooperation on the Korean Peninsula* (Palo Alto: Center for International Security and Arms Control, September 1988), pp. 4–7.

102. Morgan, "American Extended Deterrence in Northeast Asia," pp. 56–57 of unpublished manuscript.

103. Pike, *Vietnam and the Soviet Union*, pp. 184–185,191–192; and Osamu Miyoshi, "Soviet Collective Security Pacts," in Cline, Miller, and Kanet, ed., *Asia in Soviet Global Strategy*, pp. 25–27.

104. McGregor, *The Sino-Soviet Relationship*, pp. 68–70; 76–77.

105. FBIS, *Soviet Union* (Daily Report), April 8, 1983, pp. E-1, E-2. Also see Sheldon Simon, "ASEAN's Strategic Situation in the 1980s," *Pacific Affairs* (Spring 1987), 60 (1): 82.

106. An excellent discussion on the intermeshing of Vietnamese foreign policy and domestic political agendas is by William J. Duiker, "Vietnam Moves Toward Pragmatism," *Current History* (April 1987), 86 (519): 148–151, 179–180.

107. Pasal Sricharatchanya, "On The Offensive Again," *Far Eastern Economic Review* (September 22, 1988), 141 (38): 23; "China Offers Cambodia Plan," *International Herald Tribune*, September 13, 1988, p. 4; and Norman Kempster, "UN Combat Force Urged for Cambodia," *Los Angeles Times*, October 4, 1988, p. 6.

108. Sheldon Simon, "ASEAN's Strategic Situation in the 1980s," *Pacific Affairs* (Spring 1987), 60 (1): 83.

109. Derek Martin de Cunha, "A Moscow Naval Cordon Around the 'Yellow Peril,' " *Far Eastern Economic Review* (September 4, 1986), 133 (36): 28.

110. See Donald Weatherbee, "The South China Sea: From Zone of Conflict to Zone of Peace?" in Grinter and Kihl, *East Asia Conflict Zones*, p. 141.

111. *Whence The Threat To Peace*, 4th ed. (Moscow: Military Publishing House, Progress Publishers, and Novosti Press Agency Publishing House, 1987), p. 31.

112. The best geographic description of the Asia-Pacific's maritime theater of operations remains Michael MccGwire, "The Geopolitical Importance of Strategic Waterways In the Asia-Pacific Region," *Orbis* (Fall 1975), 19 (3): 1058–1076. Much of the discussion in the following paragraph is extracted from his analysis.

113. Some of these points are considered by A. James Gregor, "Soviet Maritime Strategy in the Pacific," *Geopolitics of Security in the Greater Pacific Basin* (Honolulu: International Security Council, December 1987), pp. 58–60.

114. Elucidation on this point is provided by Sheldon W. Simon, "ASEAN and the Indian Ocean: Maritime Issues and Regional Security," in William L. Dowdy and Russel B. Trood, eds., *The Indian Ocean: Perspectives on a Strategic Arena* (Durham: Duke University Press, 1985), p. 387.

115. Dibb, *The Soviet Union as a Pacific Military Power*, p. 10.

116. Andrew Mack, "The Soviet-American Conflict," in Muthiah Alagappa, *In Search of Peace: Confidence Building and Conflict Reduction in the Pacific* (Kuala Lumpur: ISIS Malaysia, 1988), p. 23.

117. Dirk Anthony Ballendorf, "Russian Interests in the Western Pacific: Do They Pose a Threat?" *Asia-Pacific Defense Forum* (Spring 1989), 13 (4): 40–43; Robert F. Miller, "Hidden Text in Soviet Policy," *Pacific Defense Reporter* (December 1988–January 1989), 15 (6–7): 14–17; Theo Roy, "China Adds a String to Its Bow," *Pacific Defense Reporter*, 15 (6–7): 34–35; and Fedor Mediansky, "New Turbulence in South Pacific Waters," *International Herald Tribune*, May 15, 1987, p. 4.

118. See the Statement of Peter S. Watson in Hearing before the Subcommittee on Asian and Pacific Affairs of the Committee on Foreign Affairs, House of Representatives, *Developments in the South Pacific Region*, 99th Cong., 2d Sess., September 10, 1986, pp. 29–30; "Statement of Rear Admiral Edward Baker," *ibid.*, pp. 85–98; Robert Kiste and Richard Herr, *The Potential for Soviet Penetration of the South Pacific Islands: An Assessment*, a paper prepared for the U.S. Department of State, December 1984, and Henry S. Albinski, "The United States and the Pacific Islands: Regional Political Trends." The Australian Defense Minister's statements are reported in "Pacifica Sovietica?," *Pacific Research* (August 1988), 1 (1): 9–10. Also see his answer to a question reprinted in Commonwealth of Australia, Parliamentary Debates, *House Of Representatives, Weekly Hansard* (May 17, 1988), no. 8, p. 2502.

119. An influential Atlantic Council study on global naval power conducted at the apex of the Soviet Pacific Fleet's expansionist period arrived at a similar

conclusion. "In the Southwest Pacific, the potential threat from Soviet submarines is greatly diminished." Paul H. Nitze, Leonard Sullivan, Jr., and the Atlantic Council Working Group on Securing the Seas, *Securing the Seas: The Soviet Naval Challenge and Western Alliance Options* (Boulder, Colo.: Westview, 1979), p. 212.

4. ASPIRING PLAYER II: THE PEOPLE'S REPUBLIC OF CHINA

1. Many observers of international politics would argue that Japan is the present-day exception to this pattern of "war and change" in world politics. As Paul Kennedy has noted, however, none "would find it unsurprising if, one day, a different political leadership in Tokyo decided to turn its economic strength into a larger degree of military strength." Kennedy, *The Rise and Fall of the Great Powers: Economic Change and Military Conflict from 1500–2000* (New York: Random House, 1987), p. 538. For additional background on the commensurate expansion of hegemonic power and strategic interests, see Robert Gilpin, *War and Change in International Politics* (Cambridge: Cambridge University Press, 1981).

2. China's conformity to balance of power political behavior is discussed by Thomas W. Robinson, "China as an Asia-Pacific Power," in Yu-ming Shaw, ed., *Changes and Continuities in Chinese Communism* (Boulder, Colo.: Westview Press, 1988), 1: 292–293.

3. Chong-Pin Lin, *China's Nuclear Weapons Strategy: Tradition Within Evolution* (Lexington, Mass./Toronto: Lexington Books, 1988), pp. 37–40.

4. Joffe, *The Chinese Army After Mao* (Cambridge: Harvard University Press, 1987), p. 70.

5. Cited in David Armstrong, "The Soviet Union," in Gerald Segal and William T. Tow, eds., *Chinese Defense Policy*, pp. 186–187.

6. "Deng Sees Hope for Global Peace," *Beijing Review* (November 19, 1984), 27 (47): 10–11; and "Deng Xiaoping Talks About Two Major Issues in the World Situation," *Zhongguo Xinwen She* [Beijing], May 5, 1985, as translated and reprinted in FBIS, *China (Daily Report)*, May 6, 1985, p. 1.

7. Jiang Siyi, *Zhanlue Xingde Da Zhuanbian—Goufang Xiandaihua Lun Gang* (The Big Strategic Change—Fundamentals on the Modernization of National Defense), (Beijing: PLA Publishing House, 1987), pp. 1–2. Text translated from Chinese text.

8. Rong zhi, "Major Powers Military Strategy and Our Response at the End of this Century, "in the Military Science Academy Military Planning and Analysis Group, *Guo jixing yu Guo Fang Zhan Lue* [The International Situation and Strategies of National Defense] (Beijing: Military Science Press, 1987), p. 73. Translated from the Chinese text.

9. Tai Ming Cheung, "New Bomb-Makers," *Far Eastern Economic Review* (March 16, 1989), 143 (11): 27.

10. Jean Dubois, "New Directions in Chinese Strategy," *International Defense Review* (1989), 22 (11): 1484.

11. See New China News Agency Reports summarized by David Chen, "Media Stress Modernization," *South China Morning Post*, September 21, 1989, p. 12, reprinted in Foreign Broadcast Information Service, *China*, September 25, 1989, pp. 40–41. Also consult Gary Klintworth, *China's Modernization*, p. 41.

12. The author is indebted to Patrick Morgan for developing this concept. See his "American Extended Deterrence in Northeast Asia," pp. 5–6.

13. Ibid., p. 5.

14. For example, see Wu Zhan, "Nuclear Deterrence," in *Meiguo Yanjiu* [American Studies] (February 15, 1988), no. 1, pp. 35–49, as translated and reprinted in Joint Publications Research Service (JPRS) CAR 88–28 *China*, June 8, 1988, p. 1. Also see Zhao Zongjiu and Gao Yinkun, "Theory of 'Grand Strategy,' " in *Guoji Zhanwang* (World Outlook), (1988), no. 18, pp. 12–13, as translated and reprinted in JPRS CAR 88–081, December 22, 1988, pp. 5–7, as an example of Chinese military thought integration with more recent Western strategic thinking.

15. Wu Zhan, "Nuclear Deterrence," *China*, p. 1.

16. Ibid.

17. Lewis, "China's Military Doctrines and Force Posture," in Thomas Fingar, ed., *China's Quest for Independence: Policy Evolution in the 1970s* (Boulder, Colo.: Westview Press, 1980), pp. 154–155.

18. Chong-Pin Lin, *China's Nuclear Weapons Strategy*, pp. 111–112.

19. Ibid., p. 6.

20. Among the most relevant sources are Scott Boorman, *The Protracted Game* (London: Oxford University Press, 1969); Edward Boylan, "The Chinese Cultural Style of Warfare," *Comparative Strategy* (1982) 3 (4): pp. 341–364; Edward Dreyer, "Military Continuities: The PLA and Imperial China," in William Whitson, ed., *The Military and Political Power in China in the 1970s* (New York: Praeger, 1972), pp. 3–24; Frank Kierman Jr. and John K. Fairbank, eds., *Chinese Ways in Warfare* (Cambridge: Harvard University Press, 1974); Stanley Henning, "Chinese Defense Strategy: A Historical Appraisal," *Military Review* (May 1979), 59 (5): 60–67; the "History" chapter in Gerald Segal's *Defending China* (Oxford and New York: Oxford University Press, 1985), pp. 27–45; and Douglas T. Stuart and William T. Tow, "The Theory and Practice of Chinese Military Deception," in Donald C. Daniel and Katherine L. Herbig, eds., *Strategic Military Deception* (New York: Pergamon Press, 1982), pp. 292–316. The most widely cited version of Sun Zi's *Art of War* is by Samuel B. Griffith, ed., *Sun Tzu, The Art of War* (London: Oxford University Press, 1963). A more concise and updated translation is by James Clavell, trans., *The Art of War* (New York: Delacorte Press, 1983). The Three Kingdoms literature is compiled and translated by Moss Roberts, *Three Kingdoms: China's Epic Drama* (New York: Pantheon, 1976).

21. Segal, *Defending China*, pp. 38–40.

22. Tai Ming Cheung, "China's Own Paper Tigers," *Far Eastern Economic Review* (February 2, 1989), 143 (5): 38.

23. Chong-Pin Lin, *China's Nuclear Weapons Strategy*, pp. 17–36; Dreyer, "Military Continuities," p. 3; and Henning, "Chinese Defense Strategy," pp. 60–61.

24. Chong-Pin Lin, *China's Nuclear Weapons Strategy*, pp. 22–35.

25. Tai Ming Cheung, "China's Own Paper Tigers," p. 38; and Georges Tan Eng Bok, "Book Review of *China Builds the Bomb* and *China's Nuclear Weapons Strategy—Tradition Within Evolution*," *Survival* (September/October 1989), 31 (5): 477.

26. "Mao Tse-tung's 'Speech at the Conference on the Question of Intellectuals Covered by the CCP Central Committee,'(January 20, 1965)" *Issues and Studies* (May 1974), 10 (8): 98–99.

27. Segal, *Defending China*, p. 40.

28. Mao Zedong, "Problems of Strategy in China's Revolutionary War," *Selected Military Writings* (Beijing: Foreign Languages Press, 1967), p. 79.

29. Allen S. Whiting, *The Chinese Calculus of Deterrence: India and Indochina*, pp. 202–203.

30. Melvin Gurtov and Byong-Moo Hwang, *China Under Threat: The Politics of Strategy and Diplomacy*, pp. 49–50; and Stuart and Tow, "The Theory and Practice of Chinese Military Deception," p. 299.

31. Allen S. Whiting, *The Chinese Calculus of Deterrence* pp. 11–12; and Stuart and Tow, *Theory and Practice*, pp. 301–302.

32. Xiang Yuchan (Cheng Yuchan), "Zhonggong de hezi zhengee" "Chung kuo de ho tsu cheng yi"] ("Communist China's Nuclear Policy.") Unpublished master's degree thesis at Chinese Culture Institute, Taipei, 1979. In citing Xiang's work, Chong-Pin Lin notes that it has used declassified but nevertheless "deep background" information supplied by Taiwan's Intelligence Bureau. Chong-Pin Lin, *China's Nuclear Weapons Strategy*, pp. 52, 185, n. 63.

33. Tai Ming Cheung, "Rank Insubordination," *Far Eastern Economic Review* (February 1, 1990), 147 (5): 22.

34. Jonathan Pollack, "The Korean War and Sino-American Relations," in Harry Harding and Yuan Ming, eds., *Sino-American Relations 1945–1955: A Joint Reassessment of a Critical Decade* (Wilmington Del.: Scholarly Resources, Inc., 1989), p. 232.

35. See, for example, Alice Langley Hsieh's classic work, *Communist China's Strategy in the Nuclear Era* (Englewood Cliffs, N. J.: Prentice-Hall, 1962) and Harlan Jencks, *From Muskets to Missiles: Politics and Professionalism in the Chinese Army, 1945–1981* (Boulder, Colo.: Westview Press, 1982).

36. Betts, *Nuclear Blackmail and Nuclear Balance*, p. 44. Dissenting views are offered by Edward Friedman, "Nuclear Blackmail and the End of the Korean War," *Modern China* (January 1975), 1 (1): 75–91; and by Harold Hinton, *Communist China in World Politics* (Boston: Houghton Mifflin, 1966), pp. 228, 277. On the Soviet pilot presence in China during the Korean conflict, see Calingaert, "Nuclear Weapons and the Korean War," p. 196; and K. M.

Panikkar, *In Two Chinas: Memoirs of a Diplomat* (London: George Allen & Unwin, 1955), p. 116.

37. Barry Blechman and Robert Powell, "What in the Name of God Is Strategic Superiority?" *Political Science Quarterly* (Winter 1982–1983), 97 (4): 596.

38. Calingaert, "Nuclear Weapons and the Korean War," pp. 183–184.

39. See Pollack, "The Korean War and Sino-American Relations," p. 229.

40. Lewis and Xue, *China Builds the Bomb*, pp. 35–72.

41. Nie Rongzhen, *Nie Rongzhen Huiyilu* [Memoirs of Nie Rongzhen], pp. 769, 814. Translated from the Chinese text by Ms. Xin Gong.

42. The classical citation for this incident remains the editorial, "The Origin and Development of Differences Between the CPSU and Ourselves—Comment on the Open Letter of the Central Committee of the CPSU," in *Hongqi* [Red Flag], September 6, 1963, as reproduced in William E. Griffith, *The Sino-Soviet Rift*, pp. 388–420. Deng Jiaxian's account is in "China's Father of A-Bomb," *Beijing Review* (August 11, 1986), pp. 20–22.

43. Strobe Talbott, trans. and ed., *Khrushchev Remembers: The Last Testament* (Boston/Toronto: Little, Brown, 1974), p. 269.

44. Mao's outlook is discussed elegantly by He Di (with Richard Baum), "The Evolution of the People's Republic of China's Policy toward the Offshore Islands (Quemoy, Matsu)," unpublished paper, July 1987. (In this author's possession).

45. Lewis and Xue, *China Builds the Bomb*, p. 61.

46. Paul H. B. Godwin, *Development of the Chinese Armed Forces* (Maxwell Air Force Base, Alabama: Air University Press, June 1988), p. 19; and Walter Clemens, *The Arms Race and Sino-Soviet Relations*, pp. 32–33. A Chinese account is in "The Origin and Development of Differences," p. 399.

47. Author discussions with Soviet and U.S. specialists at the International Strategic Institute at Stanford, Stanford University, April 1990.

48. Godwin, *Development of the Chinese Armed Forces*, p. 19.

49. John Lewis and Xue Litai, "Chinese Strategic Weapons and the Plutonium Option," *Critical Technologies Newsletter* (April-May 1988), p. 6.

50. Lewis and Xue, "Strategic Weapons and Chinese Power," pp. 541–542.

51. According to U.S. Central Intelligence Agency estimates, the nuclear weapons program used two-thirds of all Chinese military research and development funds between 1965 and 1979. This has since been strongly denied by Chinese defense experts interviewed by the author. See the Central Intelligence Agency, *Chinese Defense Spending, 1965–1979* National Foreign Assessment Center Paper (July 1980), p. 5. Background on the principal individuals and organizations involved with the production of the Chinese nuclear weapons program is provided by Lewis and Xue, *China Builds the Bomb*, pp. 35–59; and by Alice Langley Hsieh, *Communist China's Strategy in the Nuclear Era*.

52. Lewis and Xue, *China Builds the Bomb*, pp. 190–218. Also see their "Strategic Weapons and Chinese Power: The Formative Years," *The China Quarterly* (December 1987), no. 112, pp. 547–548, 554.

53. Lewis and Xue, "Chinese Strategic Weapons and the Plutonium Option," pp. 13–14; Barry Naughton, "The Third Front: Defense Industrialization in the Chinese Interior," *The China Quarterly* (September 1988), no. 115, pp. 351–386; and Gordon H. Chang, "JFK, China, and the Bomb," *Journal of American History* (March 1988), 74 (4): 1287–1310, argues that President Kennedy weighed the prospect of a joint Soviet-American strike against Chinese nuclear installations. However, McGeorge Bundy, Kennedy's national security advisor, denies that any such policy course was considered seriously. See his *Danger and Survival*, p. 532.

54. Chinese intelligence became informed of the Soviet contingency plans during the summer of 1969. See Gu Weiqun, "China's 'Open Door' Policy and the Korean Peninsula," unpublished paper prepared for The International Symposium on Peace and Cooperation in Northeast Asia sponsored by the Institute of East-West Studies, Yonsei University, November 22–23, 1989, pp. 3–4. Gu's sources are former Chinese government personnel who fled to the West following the suppression of China's prodemocracy movement in June 1989. For additional insights on Chinese deterrence perspectives during the late 1960s, see Xiaochuang Zhang, "Chinese Nuclear Strategy," in Yufan Hao and Guocang Huan, eds., *The Chinese View of the World* (New York: Pantheon, 1989), esp. p. 81. The author was formerly a research fellow at the Institute of Contemporary International Relations in Beijing.

55. Joffe, *The Chinese Army After Mao*, p. 74; Jonathan D. Pollack, "The Logic of Chinese Military Strategy," *Bulletin of the Atomic Scientists* (January 1979), 35 (1): 22–33; Robert C. Dabling, "Sino-Soviet Tensions and China's Military Modernization," in Larry M. Wortzel, ed., *China's Military Modernization* (Westport, Conn.: Greenwood Press, 1988), pp. 123–127; Donald C. Daniel and Harlan W. Jencks, "Soviet Military Confrontation with China: Options for the USSR, the PRC and the United States," *Conflict* (1983), 5 (1): 57–87; William C. Green and David S. Yost, "Soviet Military Options Regarding China," in Douglas T. Stuart and William T. Tow, eds., *China, the Soviet Union and the West* (Boulder, Colo.: Westview Press, 1982), pp. 135, 141–142.

56. For further argumentation on this point, see Donald C. Daniel and Harlan W. Jencks, "Soviet Military Confrontation with China," pp. 84–85.

57. Godwin, *Development of the Chinese Armed Forces*, pp. 28–29; Harry Harding and Melvin Gurtov, *The Purge of Lo Jui-ch'ing: The Politics of Chinese Strategic Planning*, R-548–PR (Santa Monica: The RAND Corporation, February 1971); Warren I. Cohen, *America's Response to China*, 3d, ed., (New York: Columbia University Press, 1990), p. 193.

58. Naughton, "The Third Front," pp. 352, 369. On Chinese civil defense efforts during the Korean War, see Mark A. Ryan, "Early Chinese Attitudes Toward Civil Defense Against Nuclear Attack," *The Australian Journal of Chinese Affairs* (January 1989), no. 21, pp. 81–109.

59. "The Expansion of Communist China's Nuclear Weapons Strength," *Kuang Chiao Ching* [Wide Angles], (Hong Kong) (November 16, 1989), no. 206, as translated and reprinted in Joint Publications Research Service *China*, 90-005 (January 22, 1990), p. 21.; Lewis and Xue, "Strategic Weapons and

Chinese Power," pp. 549–550; and Godwin, *Development of the Chinese Armed Forces*, p. 31.

60. Robert E. Johnson, "China's Nuclear Forces and Policies," in Wortzel, ed., *China's Military Modernization*, p. 83; Jack Anderson, "China Shows Confidence in Its Missiles," *The Washington Post*, December 19, 1984, p. F-11; and Arthur S. Ding, "PLA in the Year 2000: Nuclear Force and Space Program," in Richard H. Yang, ed., *SCPS Yearbook on PLA Affairs, 1988*, p. 127.

61. Lewis and Xue, "Strategic Weapons and Chinese Power," p. 554.

62. Jencks, "PRC Nuclear and Space Programs," in Richard H. Yang, ed., *SCPS Yearbook on PLA Affairs* (Kaohsiung, Taiwan: National Sun Yat-sen University, 1988), pp. 107–108; and Johnson, "China's Nuclear Forces," pp. 75–77.

63. Chong-Pin Lin, *China's Nuclear Weapons Strategy*, pp. 116–117.

64. In directly criticizing this school of thought, however, Tai Minh Cheung notes that Chong-Pin Lin and others neglect the fact that China has not exploited its military advantages in its postwar border disputes and security crises. See Tai Ming Cheung, "China's Own Paper Tiger,s" *Far Eastern Economic Review* (February 2, 1989), 143 (5): 38.

65. Definitive Chinese sources describing People's War Under Modern Conditions include an article by Song Shilun, Commandant of the Academy of Military Sciences, "Mao's Military Thinking Is the Guide to Our Army's Victories," *Hongqi* (August 16, 1981), no. 16, pp. 5–15, and reprinted in FBIS *China (Daily Report)*, September 17, 1981, pp. K-10 through K-23; and Chinese Defense Minister Xu Xiangqian's earlier, but still forceful, arguments in "Striving to Achieve Modernization in National Defense," *Hongqi* (October 2, 1979), no. 10, pp. 28–33, as translated and reprinted in FBIS *China (Daily Report)*, October 18, 1979, pp. L-12 through L-19. Western analysis includes Joffe, *The Chinese Army After Mao*, pp. 70–93; his "'People's War Under Modern Conditions': A Doctrine for Modern War," *China Quarterly* (December 1987), no. 112, pp. 555–571; Godwin, "Mao Zedong Revised: Deterrence and Defense in the 1980s," in Godwin, ed., *The Chinese Defense Establishment: Continuity and Change in the 1980s* (Boulder, Colo.: Westview Press, 1983), pp. 21–40; and William T. Tow, "Science and Technology in China's Defense," *Problems of Communism* (July-August 1985), 34 (4): 15–31.

66. Zhang Aiping, "On Questions Regarding Our Country," *Hongqi* April 16, 1982, no. 8, pp. 2–10, as translated and reprinted in FBIS *China (Daily Report)*, May 11, 1982, pp. K-4 through K-11 and "Zhang Aiping on National Defense Modernization," in a *Zhongguo Xinwen She* (New China News Agency) report, February 28, 1983, as translated and reprinted in FBIS *China (Daily Report)*, March 1, 1983, pp. K-8, K-9.

67. An account of the Military Commission proceedings is by Liu Huinan in *Xinhua*, June 11, 1985; translated and reprinted as "Hu, Deng Speak at Military Commission Meeting," in FBIS, *China Daily Report)*, June 12, 1985, pp. K-1 through K-3. Also see the remarks of Zhang Zhen, president of China's newly established National Defense University, in "Shift in China's Strategy for Building Armed Forces Shows New Evaluation of World Situa-

tion," *Ta Kung Pao* (Hong Kong), February 16, 1986, p. 1, as translated and reprinted in FBIS *China (Daily Report)*, February 18, 1986, pp. W-11 through W-12. One of the best Western assessments is by Godwin, "Changing Concepts of Doctrine, Strategy and Operations in the Chinese People's Liberation Army 1978–1987," *The China Quarterly* (December 1987), no. 112, pp. 580–583.

68. Tai Ming Cheung, "New Bomb-makers," p. 28.

69. Tai Ming Cheung, "Goodbye People's War," *Far Eastern Economic Review* (December 1, 1988), 142 (48): 21. For a Chinese assessment, see Jia Wenxian, Zheng Shouqi, Guo Weimin and Long Zhuoqun, "Tentative Discussion of Special Principles of a Future Chinese Limited War," *Guofang Daxue Xuebao* (National Defense University Journal) (November 1, 1987), no. 11, pp. 8–9, as translated and reprinted in JPRS CAR 88–037, *China*, July 12, 1988, pp. 47–48.

70. Mao Zedong, "On the Ten Major Relationships," (April 25, 1976) in *Peking Review* (January 1, 1977), 20 (1): 10–25; and J. Chester Cheng, ed., *The Politics of the Chinese Red Army: A Translation of the Bulletin of Activities of the People's Liberation Army* (Stanford, Cal.: Hoover Institution Publications, 1966).

71. Whiting, *The Chinese Calculus of Deterrence*, pp. 204–208, 218.

72. See William T. Tow, "China's Modernization and the Big Powers: Strategic Implications," in David M. Lampton and Catherine H. Keyser, *China's Global Presence* (Washington, D.C.: American Enterprise Institute, 1988), p. 173; and Alastair Johnston, "Chinese Nuclear Force Modernization: Implications for Arms Control," *Journal of Northeast Asian Studies* (June 1983), 2 (2): 17.

73. Chong-Pin Lin, *China's Nuclear Weapons Strategy*, pp. 68–69, 124.

74. Gerald Segal, "China's Nuclear Posture for the 1980s," *Survival* (January-February 1981), 23 (1): 11–18; and Gregory Treverton, "China's Nuclear Posture for the 1980s," *The Future of Strategic Deterrence: Part I*, Adelphi Papers no. 160 (London: IISS, Autumn, 1980), pp. 38–44.

75. Chong-Pin Lin, *China's Nuclear Weapons Strategy*, p. 69.

76. Jonathan Pollack, *Perception and Action in Chinese Foreign Policy*, Ph.D dissertation, University of Michigan, 1976, p. 310. Pollack interpreted excerpts from "Chairman Mao's Criticism and Repudiation of the P'eng (Thehuai), Huang (K'e-ch'eng), Chang (Wen-t'ien) and Chou (Hsiao-chou) Anti-Party Clique," in *Selections From China Mainland Magazine* (no date and no pages cited).

77. John W. Lewis, Co-Director, Center for International Security and Arms Control, Stanford University in personal correspondence with this author.

78. Jencks, "PRC Nuclear and Space Programs," p. 119.

79. A graphic illustration of China's "new thinking" concerning problems of modern warfare and tactical nuclear warfare is the remarkable Occasional Paper written by Liu Huaqiu, a senior specialist in the PRC's Commission of Science, Technology, and Industry for National Defense while on sabbatical

with Stanford University's International Strategic Institute. See his *China and the Neutron Bomb* (Stanford: Center for International Security and Arms Control, June 1988).

80. In particular, see Liu Huaqiu, *China and the Neutron Bomb*, pp. 33–37; Xu Baoshan, "We Must Be Prepared to Fight Nuclear War in the First Stages of Any Future War," *Jiefangjun bao*, September 16, 1979, as translated and reprinted in JPRS 75825, *China Report*, June 4, 1980, pp. 97–99; and Zong He, "Tentative Discussion on the Characteristics of Modern Warfare," in *Shijie Zhishi* (World Knowledge), (August 1, 1983), no. 15, as translated and reprinted in JPRS *China*, September 29, 1983, pp. 78–88.

81. Paul H. B. Godwin, "Changing Concepts of Doctrine, Strategy and Operations," p. 580. Also see Tai Ming Cheung, "New Bomb-makers," p. 28.

82. William Arkin et al., "Nuclear Weapons," in Stockholm International Peace Research Institute, *SIPRI Yearbook: World Armaments and Disarmament* (Oxford: Oxford University Press, 1989), p. 34.

83. Tai Ming Cheung, "Who's in Charge," *Far Eastern Economic Review* (March 16, 1989), 143 (11): 27. For an in-depth Chinese treatment of emerging conventional warfare technologies, see An Fohua, "Heavy Weapon Trends Prior to Year 2000," *Xiandai Bingdi* [Modern Weaponry], (April 1988), no. 4, pp. 1–6, as translated and reprinted in JPRS, *China*, October 27, 1988, pp. 38–42.

84. Robinson, "Chinese Military Modernization in the 1980s," *China Quarterly* (June 1982), no. 90, p. 234.

85. The most often cited Western source of U.S. intelligence estimates concerning possible Soviet intentions to preempt the Chinese is Richard Nixon's Chief of Staff H. R. Haldeman's memoirs, *The Ends Of Power*, with Joseph Dimona (New York: New York Times Books, 1978), pp. 88–94. During his first year in office, President Nixon and the U.S. Defense Department justified the development and deployment of the *Safeguard* antiballistic missile system largely in terms of the U.S. need for responding to the burgeoning Chinese nuclear threat. See a Statement by Secretary of Defense Melvin R. Laird, *Defense Program and Budget FY 1971* (Washington, D.C.: USGPO, 1970), pp. 5, 42–48.

86. Jiao Wu and Xiao Hue, "Modern Limited War Calls for Reform of Traditional Military Principles," *Guofang Daxue Xuebao* [National Defense University Journal], (November 1, 1987), no. 11, pp. 10–11, 58, as translated and reprinted by JPRS, *China*, July 12, 1988, pp. 49–51; and Jia Wenxian et al., "Tentative Discussion of a Future Chinese Limited War," p. 48, who argue that a Chinese "punitive counterattack" would check "partial hostile intrusions" by waging a "short fight with a quick decisive ending." For a Western assessment, see Tai Ming Cheung, "New Bomb-makers," *Far Eastern Economic Review* (March 16, 1989), 143 (11): 27–28.

87. IISS, *The Military Balance 1988–1989* (London: IISS, Autumn 1988), p. 146.

88. For information on initial Chinese SSBN testing problems, see June Dreyer, "The Reorganization and Streamlining of the PLA," *Issues & Studies*

(May 1987), 23 (5): 40; and Tai Ming Cheung, "Counting the Costs," *Far Eastern Economic Review* (March 16, 1989), 143 (11): 29. A colorful, and overly dramatic Chinese account of the October 1982 test is the recently translated book *Dangdai Zhonguo Haijun* [China Today: The People's Navy] (Beijing: Social Services Publishing House, October 1987), pp. 635–648, as translated and reprinted in JPRS, *China Report*, 90–014 (February 23, 1990), pp. 24–30.

89. *China Today: The People's Navy*, p. 34. Other comprehensive Chinese accounts of the PLA's SSBN program are by Zheng He, "Submerged-to-Land Carrier Rockets," *Bingqi Zhishi* (Ordinance Knowledge), (May 15, 1989), no. 3, pp. 18–19, as translated and reprinted in JPRS, *China*, 89–094 (September 6, 1989), p. 53; and Hu Chunhua, "The Dragon of the Bright Blue Sea—An Interview With Ship's Captain Xu Zuoren 1776 0155 088, First Officer in Charge of a Chinese Nuclear Guided Submarine," ibid., as translated and reprinted in JPRS, *China* 89–094, September 6, 1989, pp. 54–55. An independent assessment of the September 1988 test is by Arkin et al., *SIPRI Yearbook 1989*, p. 34.

90. *China Today: The People's Navy*, p. 34.

91. Johnson, "China's Nuclear Forces and Policies," pp. 78–79.

92. Wang Zhidong, "Some Reflections on the Probability of Using Nuclear Weapons in Actual Combat," *Guofang Daxue Xuebao*, translated and reprinted in JPRS *China* July 22, 1988, p. 51.

93. Johnson, *China's Nuclear Forces and Policies*, p. 81; Paul Dibb, "Soviet Capabilities: Interests and Strategies in East Asia During the 1980s," *Survival* (July-August 1982), 24 (4): 155; and *Soviet Military Power 1988*, p. 125, which asserts that "any enhancements to China's strategic forces over the next five years will likely be counterbalanced by Soviet improvements in their missile defense systems."

94. Rajan Menon, "New Thinking and Northeast Asian Security," p. 12. Emphasis is this author's.

95. Segal, "Defense Culture and Sino-Soviet Relations," *The Journal of Strategic Studies* (June 1985), 8 (2): 182–184.

96. On the SDI problem, see Banning Garrett and Bonnie Glaser, "Chinese Perspectives on the Strategic Defense Initiative," *Problems of Communism* (March-April 1986), 35 (2): 28–44; and John Garver, "China's Response to the Strategic Defense Initiative," in Wortzel, ed., *China's Military Modernization*, pp. 133–157. An analysis of U.S. cruise missile technology's implications for Asia-Pacific warfare is contained in Hayes, Zarsky, and Bello, *American Lake*, pp. 253–263. Compare this assessment with the recent Chinese regional limited war threat assessment authored by Jia Wenxian et al., "Tentative Discussion of Special Principles of a Future Chinese Limited War."

97. Paul Godwin, "The Role of Strategic Nuclear Policy in China's Military Strategy," in Linda L. Lum, ed., *Developments in China* (Washington, D.C.: Center for the Study of Foreign Affairs, September 1988), p. 82.

98. This point was emphasized by analysts with the Institute for Contem-

porary International Relations in discussions with the author, Beijing, August 3–4, 1987. Also see Banning N. Garrett and Bonnie S. Glaser, *War and Peace: The Views from Moscow and Beijing*, pp. 80–85.

99. Godwin, *Development of the Chinese Armed Forces*, pp. 30–31.

100. Godwin, *Development*, pp. 134–136; Jencks, "PRC Nuclear And Space Programs," p. 111; Johnson, "China's Nuclear Forces and Policies," pp. 87–91; Johnston, "Chinese Nuclear Force Modernization," pp. 16–18; and Robert Sutter, "Developments in China's Nuclear Weapons and Attitudes Toward Arms Control," in Lovejoy and Watson, eds., *China's Military Reforms*, pp. 105–106.

101. Ding, "PLA in the Year 2,000," p. 127.

102. The best and most concise explanation of China's nuclear survivability problem is Jencks, *From Muskets to Missiles*, p. 159. Also see Richard W. Fieldhouse, "Chinese Nuclear Weapons: An Overview," *SIPRI Yearbook 1986* (Oxford and New York: Oxford University Press, 1986), pp. 106–107, who cites successive annual posture statements of the U.S. Joint Chiefs of Staff; Godwin, *Development of the Chinese Armed Forces*, pp. 131, 135; Bradley Hahn, "Beijing's Growing Global Missile Reach," *Pacific Defense Reporter* (February 1987), 13 (8): 12–13; Hahn, "Quick Nuclear Leap Leads to Credible Nuclear Deterrent," *Pacific Defense Reporter* (May 1987), 13 (11): 29–30; and Jonathan Pollack, "China as a Nuclear Power," in William H. Overholt, ed., *Asia's Nuclear Future* (Boulder, Colo.: Westview Press, 1977), p. 55, 342, n. 67.

103. "The Expansion of Communist China's Nuclear Weapons Strength," p. 21 notes that "according to Western analysis, MIRV's using solid propellants will be used to arm the Second Artillery [Strategic Rocket Force] in the mid-1990s." Also see Tai Ming Cheung, "Counting the Costs," *Far Eastern Economic Review*, March 16, 1989, p. 29; William M. Arkin et al., "Nuclear Weapons," *SIPRI Yearbook 1987* (Oxford and New York: Oxford University Press, 1987), p. 35; "Missile Range Increases," *Jane's Defense Weekly* (February 15, 1986), 5 (6): 233; and "Chinese Flight Test New Missile Version," *Aviation Week and Space Technology* (June 30, 1986), 124 (26): 16.

104. Tai Ming Cheung, "Counting the Costs," and Sutter, "Developments in China's Nuclear Weapons," p. 105.

105. Li Hong, "Nuclear Weapons Breakthrough," *China Daily*, September 9, 1989, p. 1; and "New Advanced Weaponry for Chinese Armed Forces," *Xinhua*, September 20, 1989, as reprinted in Foreign Broadcast Information Service, *China*, September 20, 1989, p. 42.

106. "The Expansion of Communist China's Nuclear Weapons Strength," p. 21.

107. *Allocation of Resources in the Soviet Union and China*, pp. 182, 215.

108. See, for example, "Conference on Nuclear Strategy," *Jiefangjun Bao*, November 21, 1987, p. 1, as translated and reprinted in JPRS CAR 88–002, February 5, 1988, p. 63, reporting on "major [nuclear strategy] breakthroughs" reached at a national conference on nuclear strategy. In-depth U.S.

assessments of these problems are found in Office of Technology Assessment, U.S. Congress, *Technology Transfer to China* (Washington, D.C.: USGPO, July 1987), pp. 87–93.

109. Tai Ming Cheung, "Counting the Costs," p. 29.

110. See Wang Zhidong, "Some Reflections on the Probability of Using Nuclear Weapons in Combat," p. 51. Zhang Jianzhi, "Views on Medium Powers' Nuclear Strategy," *Jienfanjun Bao*, March 20, 1987, p. 3, as translated and reprinted in FBIS *China (Daily Report)*, April 1, 1987, pp. K-29 through K-33; and Zhang Qinsheng, Liang Hunan and Lee Yong Yen, "A Study of Local War Theory," *Liaowang* (Overseas Edition), (September 15, 1986), no. 37, pp. 15–16, translated and reprinted in FBIS *China (Daily Report)*, September 23, 1986, pp. K-3 through K-7.

111. Mearsheimer, *Conventional Deterrence*, p. 53.

112. The following discussion is extracted partly from Godwin, *Development of the Chinese Armed Forces*, pp. 88–89, 91–92, 107–108, 118–120; and from the Statement of John J. Sloan, Defense Intelligence Agency, before a Workshop Sponsored by the Committee on Foreign Relations, United States Senate and the Congressional Research Service, *The Implications of U.S.-China Military Cooperation*, 98th Cong., 1st Sess., January 1982, pp. 26–36.

113. Dreyer, "The Reorganization and Streamlining of the PLA," p. 40; and the testimony of William Perry, Former Under Secretary of Defense For Research and Engineering, in Hearings before the Subcommittee On Asian And Pacific Affairs of the Committee On Foreign Affairs, U.S. House of Representatives, *The New Era in East Asia*, 97th Cong., 1st Sess., June 10, 1981, p. 271.

114. Hearings before the Subcommittee On National Security Economics of the Joint Economic Committee, Congress of the United States, *Allocation of Resources in the Soviet Union and China—1986, Part 12*, 100th Cong., 1st Sess., August 3, 1987, p. 194. Sloan, *The Implications of U.S.-China Military Cooperation*, p. 35; and *Technology Transfer to China*, p. 172.

115. Clare Hollingworth, "PLA Modernizing Slowly," *Pacific Defense Reporter* (December 1986–January 1987), 14 (1): 43–45, 67.

116. John Frankenstein, "Chinese Weapons Development: Process, Progress, Program?" in Lovejoy and Watson, *China's Military Reforms*, pp. 76–77; Paul Jackson, "The Chinese Puzzle . . . A Solution Emerges," *Armed Forces* (January 1987), 6 (1): 33–37; and Bill Sweetman, "Air Forces," in Segal and Tow, *Chinese Defense Policy*, pp. 71–84.

117. For an account of the PLA's recruiting problems even prior to the student movement's suppression, see Tai Ming Cheung, "Goodbye People's War," p. 21. For assessments of the PLA following the Tienanmen incident, consult June Teufel Dreyer, "The Role Of The Military," *World Policy Journal* (Fall 1989), 6 (4): 647–655.

118. Larry W. Wortzel, "U.S. Technology Transfer Policies and the Modernization Of China's Armed Forces," *Asian Survey* (June 1987), 23 (6): 629.

119. CIA figures on Chinese defense spending trends are taken from *Allocation of Resources in the Soviet Union and China—1986*, p. 194. Also see

Research Institute for Peace and Security, Tokyo, *Asian Security 1989–90* (London: Brassey's September 1989), p. 90.

120. Nicholas Kristof, "China Repays Army for Quelling Protest," *International Herald Tribune*, March 2, 1990, p. 2; and Tai Ming Cheung, "Political Payoff," *Far Eastern Economic Review* (April 5, 1990), 148 (14): 28–29.

121. "Zhang Aiping Views PLA's Successes, Deficiencies," *Xinhua*, June 23, 1987, as translated and reprinted in FBIS *China (Daily Report)*, June 24, 1987, p. K-18.

122. The "technological time gap" concept is defined and developed more precisely by Wendy Friedman, "Foreign Technology and Chinese Modernization," in Charles D. Lovejoy, Jr., and Bruce W. Watson, eds., *China's Military Reforms* (Boulder, Colo.: Westview Press, 1986), p. 65. For other assessments of China's comparative pace in its military modernization programs, see Guy Dinmore, "China Holding to People's Warfare," and "Western Foes Turn Allies as Army Thinks Modern," *Sunday Standard* (Hong Kong), August 7, 1987, p. 5; Lt. Colonel Andrew W. Finlayson, "U.S. Arms for China—a New Look," *Naval War College Review* (January-February 1986), 39 (1): 71–72; and Tow, "Science and Technology in China's Defense, *"passim.*

123. Background on the COSTIND is provided by Wendy Frieman, "China's Military R&D System: Reform and Reorientation," in Denis Fred Simon and Merle Godman, eds., *Science and Technology in Post-Mao China* (Cambridge, Mass.: Harvard University Press, 1989), pp. 280–282.

124. Evan A. Feigenbaum, "Selling Arms For Influence," *China Business Review* (September/October 1989), 16 (5): 29.

125. Robert Sutter, "Realities of International Power and China's 'Independence' in Foreign Affairs, 1981–1984," *Journal of Northeast Asian Studies* (Winter 1984), 3 (4): 6–7; and Douglas T. Stuart, "Quest for Security," in Harish Kapur, *The End of an Isolation: China After Mao* (Dordrecht: Martinus Nijhoff Publishers, 1985), pp. 181–182.

126. Excellent analysis on this point is provided by Tai Ming Cheung, "Looking Outwards: Expanding Sino-Foreign Military Relations," *Pacific Defense Reporter* (February 1988), 15 (8): 33.

127. "U.S. Confirms Sale to China of Top-Line Anti-Sub Torpedoes," *Los Angeles Times*, January 4, 1989, p. 8.

128. Testimony before the Committee of Foreign Affairs, House of Representatives and its Subcommittees on Asian/Pacific Affairs and International Economic Policy and Trade, *United States and China Relations*, 98th Cong., 2d Sess., June 5, 1984.

129. Report of the Secretary of Defense Frank C. Carlucci to the Congress on the *Amended FY 1988/FY 1989 Biennial Budget as of February 11, 1988* (Washington, D.C.: USGPO, February 18, 1988) p. 84.

130. This argument is further developed by Eden Y. Woon, "Chinese Arms Sales and U.S. China Military Relations," *Asian Survey* (June 1989), 29 (6): 601–618.

131. China's Southeast Asian policies are well discussed by Robert S. Ross, "China's Strategic Role in Asia," in James Morley, ed., *The Pacific Basin:*

New Challenges for the United States (New York: The Academy of Political Science, 1986), pp. 116–128.

132. See Douglas Pike, *Vietnam and the Soviet Union: Anatomy of an Alliance*, pp. 86, 103. Other accounts credit the Chinese with pursuing more forthright objectives of "limited deterrence" against an American escalation of the war into North Vietnam. See, for example, Whiting, *The Chinese Calculus of Deterrence*, pp. 170–195, 219; and Segal, *Defending China*, pp. 158–172.

133. Background on the "escalation phases" of Sino-Vietnamese tensions leading to the February/March 1979 conflict is provided by David W. P. Elliot, *The Third Indochina Conflict* (Boulder, Colo.: Westview Press, 1981), pp.11–12; 14–16; Chang Pao-Min, *Kampuchea Between China and Vietnam* (Singapore: Singapore University Press, 1985), pp. 51–90; King C. Chen, *China's War with Vietnam* (Stanford: Hoover Institution Press, 1987); C. G. Jacobson, *Sino-Soviet Relations Since Mao*, pp. 92–107; Harlan Jencks, "China's 'Punitive War' on Vietnam: A Military Assessment," *Asian Survey* (August 1979), 19 (8): 801–815; Daniel Tretiak, "China's Vietnam War and Its Consequences," *The China Quarterly* (December 1979), no. 80, pp. 740–767; Segal, *Defending China*, pp. 211–230; Herbert S. Yee, "The Sino-Vietnamese Border War: China's Motives, Calculations, and Strategies," *China Report* (January-February 1980), no. 1, pp. 15–32. A text of the Soviet-Vietnamese Friendship Treaty is found in *Survival* (January-February 1979), 21 (1): 40–41.

134. A *Kyodo* News Dispatch, "SRV Battlefront Shifting Eastward," in FBIS *China (Daily Report)*, February 23, 1979, p. A-14, as cited in Jencks, "Lessons of a 'Lesson': China-Vietnam, 1979," p. 158.

135. McGregor, *The Sino-Vietnamese Relationship and the Soviet Union*, pp. 33–34.

136. *Bangkok Post*, March 7, 1987, reprinted in FBIS *Asia and Pacific (Daily Report)*, March 9, 1987, p. J-2; Paisal Sricharatchanya, "'Friendship' Arms Sales," *Far Eastern Economic Review* (March 19, 1987), 135 (12): 15–16; and Tai Ming Cheung, "Expanding Sino-Foreign Military Relations," *Armed Forces* (October 1987), 6 (10): 451.

137. Institute of Security and International Studies, Chulalongkorn University, Bangkok, "Chronology of Events," *ISIS Bulletin* (May-August 1987), 6 (2): 16, 18, 26. For a report on the Thai disillusionment with Chinese military hardware, see Gwen Robinson, "Thailand Looking West," *Asia-Pacific Defense Reporter* (November 1990), 17(5), p. 32.

138. "First Thai 'Jianghu' Launched," *Jane's Defense Weekly* (July 21, 1990) 14(3):81.

139. Toemsak C. Phalanuphap, "First of a 2–Part Assessment of Premier Chatichai Chunhawan's Official Visit to Beijing," *The Nation* (Bangkok) in English, March 20, 1989, reprinted in FBIS, *East Asia* March 21, 1989, pp. 49–50; Phalanuphap, "Second of a 2–Part Assessment of Premier Chatichai Chunhawan's Official Visit to Beijing," *The Nation*, March 21, 1989, p. 8, reprinted in FBIS, *East Asia*, March 21, 1989, pp. 50–51; Kawi Chongkitthawon, "China and Thailand Differ on the Khmer Rouge Issue," *The Nation* (Bangkok), October 18, 1988, p. 6, reprinted in FBIS, *East Asia*, October 18,

1988, p. 53; Paisal Sricharatchanya, "Unofficially Speaking," *Far Eastern Economic Review* (February 2, 1989), 143 (5): 13; Sricharatchanya, "Turning Turtle," *Far Eastern Economic Review* (February 9, 1989), 143 (6): 11–12; and "Back to the Battlefield," *Asiaweek* (March 31, 1989), 15 (13): 13 pp. 22, 29.

140. McGregor, *The Sino-Vietnamese Relationship*, pp. 36–38.

141. Nick B. Williams, Jr., "China May Cut Aid to Cambodian Rebels," *Los Angeles Times*, December 22, 1988, p. 9.

142. The analytical framework for China's extended deterrent to Thailand adopted here is from Ansil Ramsay's, "Thailand: Surviving the 1980s," *Current History* (April 1987), 86 (519): 187.

143. See, for example, the statements of Chinese Foreign Minister Wu Xueqian, "Chinese Foreign Minister on China's Reaction to Possible Vietnamese Invasion of Thailand," *Xinhua* (English version), December 25, 1985, reprinted in FBIS *China* (Daily Report), December 27, 1985, p. E-1 through E-2.

144. Figures derived from *The Military Balance 1988–1989*, pp. 149, 181–182; and Denis Warner, "The Region's Bankrupt Bully," *Pacific Defense Reporter* (February 1987), 13 (8): 9–10.

145. Michael Field, Rodney Tasker, and Murray Hiebert, "No End In Sight," *Far Eastern Economic Review* (September 7, 1989), 145 (36): 16; Tasker and Hiebert, "A Test of Arms," *Far Eastern Economic Review* (September 28, 1989), 145 (39): 20; Nayan Chanda, "*Cambodia 1989: The Search for an Exit* (New York: The Asia Society, June 1989), p. 15; Chanda, "Civil War in Cambodia?" *Foreign Policy* (Fall 1989), no. 77, pp. 33, 38; and Steven Erlansen, "Aid to Cambodia Non-Communists Is Detailed," *The New York Times*, November 16, 1989, p. 16.

146. "The United States Is Pampering the PRC," *Merdeka* (Jakarta), May 3, 1985, p. 5, as translated and reprinted in FBIS *Asia & Pacific* (Daily Report), May 16, 1985, pp. N-1, N-2.

147. "Deng-ho," *The Economist* (November 8, 1986), 301 (7471): 46. One of the best recent accounts of Southeast Asian opposition to close Sino-American military/high technology ties is by Robert C. Horn, "U.S.-ASEAN Relations in the 1980s," *Contemporary Southeast Asia* (September 1984), 6 (2): 125–126. Also see Gerald Segal, "As China Grows Strong," *International Affairs (London)* (Spring 1988), 64 (2): 217–231.

148. Michael Yahuda, *The China Threat*, ISIS Seminar Paper (Kuala Lumpur: Institute Of Strategic and International Studies, 1986).

149. For analysis weighing the implications of the Chinese-Vietnamese naval confrontation, see Jerry Cushing, "The Dragon's Long Reach," *Far Eastern Economic Review* (May 5, 1988), 140 (18): 23; Rodney Tasker, "Calculating the Risk Factor," ibid., pp. 24–25. A Chinese view of confrontation is in *Jiefangjun Shenghuo* (PLA Life), (August 13, 1988), no. 8, as translated and reprinted in JPRS CAR 88–067, *China*, October 27, 1988, p. 37. For general background on the Spratly dispute's security ramifications, consult Donald E. Weatherbee, "The South China Sea: From Zone of Conflict to Zone of Peace?" in Grinter and Kihl, *East Asian Conflict Zones*, pp. 123–148; Simon,

The Future of Asian-Pacific Security Collaboration, pp.105–110; and Robert Thomson, "Lure of the Spratly's Empty Atolls," *Financial Times,* March 23, 1988, p. 3.

150. Chinese military thinkers have reportedly reached a consensus that to improve the PLA's rapid reaction capability in a limited war situation, a Chinese rapid reaction force should be developed more extensively, "that is well equipped and that has a fairly high degree of combined arms . . . in the limited war and sudden incidents of the future it should be able to play the role of a 'fist.' " See Li Lun, "Developing Logistic Support for Limited War," *Jiefangjun Bao,* July 1, 1988, p. 3, as translated and reprinted in JPRS CAR 88–064, *China,* October 12, 1988, p. 54. A Western account of the "Fist Battalion" is by Lynne Curry, "Farewell to the Doctrine of People's War," *Financial Times* February 2, 1989, p. 16.

151. For Southeast Asian analysis of the Spratlys crisis, see "Chinese Warships Attack Viet Vessels," *New Straits Times,* March 18, 1988, p. 14; "Indonesians Fear Spillover of Spratlys Conflict," *New Straits Times* April 13, 1988, p. 3 and Bunn Nagara, "Spratlys: A Need to Pacify the Pacific," *New Straits Times,* April 16, 1988, pp. 1, 7.

152. Chang Pao-min, "The Sino-Vietnamese Conflict and Its Implications for ASEAN," *Pacific Affairs* (Winter 1987–1988), 60 (4): 644. Also see his "Kampuchean Conflict: The Continuing Stalemate," *Asian Survey* (July 1987), 27 (7): 748–763, esp. p. 756.

153. "China Offers Cambodia Plan," *International Herald Tribune,* September 13, 1988, p. 4. Also see "Vice Minister Views Cambodia Problem," FBIS *China,* September 14, 1988, pp. 15–16, where the PRC envoy announced on Austrian radio that China will "distance itself" from the Khmer Rouge and support a UN peacekeeping force in Cambodia.

154. Jonathan Power, "United Nations Moving Toward a New Age," *Los Angeles Times,* January 19, 1990, Part II, p. 7.

155. See the comments of Harry Harding in Timothy M. McCully (rapporteur), *The Future of U.S.-Indochina Relations: An International Symposium* (Los Angeles: The Asia Society, October 1989), p. 38. Also see Simon Long, "China and Kampuchea: Political Football on the Killing Fields," *The Pacific Review* (1989), 2 (2): 151–157; and Tim Luard, "China 'Unchanged' in Its Support for Khmer Rouge," *The Daily Telegraph* (London), June 24, 1989, p. 12.

156. "Suharto: I Want Pledge From China," *New Straits Times,* March 2, 1988, p. 4.

157. Author interviews with analysts as the Center for Strategy and International Studies, Jakarta, February 1986.

158. Justus M. van der Kroef, "Indonesia's Slow Boat to China," *Asian Affairs: An American Review* (Spring 1989), 16 (1): 23–44; and John Murray Brown, "China and Indonesia End 20-Year Rift," *Financial Times,* March 1, 1989, p. 4.

159. Muthiah Alagappa, "A Nuclear-Weapons Free Zone in Southeast

Asia: Problems and Prospects," *Australian Outlook* (December 1987), 41 (3): 175, 179.

160. For a corroborating view, see John H. Holdridge, "Threat to ASEAN Remote," *Pacific Defense Reporter* (March 1988), 16 (9: 25, 30–32.

161. Robert A. Scalapino and Chong-Sik Lee, *Communism In Korea, Part I: The Movement* (Berkeley, Los Angeles and London: University of California Press, 1972), p. 558. Emphasis in the original text.

162. Coverage of Roh's offer and of Chinese-South Korean trade is offered by John McBeth, "A Bridge to China," *Far Eastern Economic Review* (January 7, 1988), 139 (1): 15–16. Assessments of China's waning inclination to prop up the 1961 treaty are contained in Ralph N. Clough, *Deterrence and Defense in Korea* (Washington, D.C.: The Brookings Institution, 1976), pp. 15–16.

163. Author discussions with Chinese security analysts in Beijing, August 5, 1987.

164. Jonathan D. Pollack, "China as a Military Power," in Onkar Marwah and Jonathan D. Pollack, eds., *Military Power and Policy in Asian States: China, India, Japan* (Boulder, Colo./Folkestone: Westview/Dawson, 1980), p. 72.

165. See the comments of A. Doak Barnett, *China and the Major Powers in East Asia* (Washington, D.C.: Brookings Institution 1977), pp. 170–172; and Tai Ming Cheung, "Seeking New Scenario," *Far Eastern Economic Review* (December 21, 1989), 146 (51): 29.

166. Background on Chinese tactics to play upon Japan's historical "guilt complex" for diverting attention from its own domestic shortcomings is assessed by Chalmers Johnson, "The Patterns of Japanese Relations with China, 1952–1982," *Pacific Affairs* (Fall 1986), 59 (3): 416–425. A more general discussion on this issue is provided by Allen S. Whiting, *China Eyes Japan* (Berkeley and Los Angeles: University of California Press, 1989), pp. 41–65.

167. See a *Xinhua* dispatch, May 29, 1987, and a *Kyodo* report of the same day, reprinted in FBIS *China (Daily Report)*, June 1, 1987, pp. D-1 through D-2.

168. Whiting, *China Eyes Japan*, p. 199.

169. Xi Louren, "An Exploration of the Issue of Japan's March From an 'Economic Power' to a 'Political Power'," *Guoji Wenti Yanjiu (International Studies)* (October 1987), no. 4, pp. 34–37, as translated and reprinted in JPRS CAR 88–002, February 5, 1988, p. 4.

170. Examples are Robert Taylor, *The Sino-Japanese Axis: A New Force in Asia?* (New York: St. Martin's Press, 1985); and William T. Tow, "Sino-Japanese Security Cooperation: Evolution and Prospects," *Pacific Affairs* (Spring 1983), 56 (1): 51–83. Two analysts more skeptical of long-term Sino-Japanese military ties are Robert E. Bedeski, *The Fragile Entente: The 1978 Japan-China Peace Treaty in a Global Context* (Boulder, Colo.: Westview Press, 1983), pp. 97–102; and Walter Arnold, "Sino-Japanese Relations," *Problems of Communism* (May-June 1987), 36 (3): 72–76.

171. Harry Gelman, "The Soviet Union, East Asia and the West," p. 20.

172. Keiichiro Kubonuma, "Soviet Moves in Asia-Pacific Region May Forge Japan-China Military Link," *The Japan Economic Journal* (October 18, 1986), 24 (1232): 6.; Arnold, "Sino-Japanese Relations"; and Tai Ming Cheung, "Expanding Sino-Foreign Military Relations," p. 459.

173. Edward Rowney, "The INF Treaty: Global Scope, Global Support," *Current Policy* (February 16, 1988), no. 1046, p. 1.

174. Segal, "As China Grows Strong," p. 228.

175. Clayton Jones, "China's Killings Spark Muted Outcry," *The Christian Science Monitor*, June 19, 1989, p. 4.

176. Shim Jae Hoon, "Chinese Missile Sales Shake Taiwan's Diplomatic Ties," *Far Eastern Economic Review* (June 2, 1988), 140 (22): 28.

177. Guo Zhiyuan, "Navy Develops Airborne Unites Capability," *Zhongguo Xinwen She*, September 20, 1989, as translated and reprinted in Foreign Broadcast Information Service, *China*, September 20, 1989, p. 40.

178. Siegfried Thielbeer, "An Invasion of Taiwan Is Hardly Possible," *Frankfurter Allgemeine*, July 31, 1989, p. 8, as translated and reprinted in JPRS, *China*, 89–097, September 20, 1989, pp. 62–63.

179. Tai Ming Cheung, "The Balance Tilts," *Far Eastern Economic Review* (September 29, 1988), 141 (39): 40–41.

180. Robert Karniol, "New Arms for Old," *Far Eastern Economic Review* (July 30, 1987), 137 (31): 15–17; and Karniol, "Using the Loophole," ibid., p. 17. A less favorable assessment of Taiwan's current defense technology and its future development is Claire Hollingworth's "Defense Industries Suffer from Lack of High Tech," *Pacific Defense Reporter* (July 1987), 14 (1): 49. See also "Dynamics Linked to Taiwan," *The New York Times*, June 25, 1988, p. 45.

181. The ambiguous but still viable U.S. security commitment to Taiwan is well treated by Stephen P. Gibert, "The Isolation of Island China," in Gibert, ed., *Security in Northeast Asia*, esp. pp. 121–123.

182. "Brezhnev Speech at Ceremony," carried on Moscow Domestic Television, March 24, 1982, translated and reprinted in FBIS, *Soviet Union (Daily Report)*, March 25, 1982, p. R-7.

183. Rajan Menon, "New Thinking and Northeast Asian Security," pp. 11–12. Also see Harry Harding, *China and Northeast Asia: The Political Dimension* (Lanham and New York: University Press of America/The Asia Society, 1988), p. 25. For general background on the evolution of Sino-Soviet rapprochement from the mid-1980s to the Gorbachev-Deng summit, see Steven M. Goldstein, "Diplomacy and Protest: The Sino-Soviet Summit," *Problems of Communism* (September-October 1989), 38 (5): 49–75; Carl G. Jacobson, "Sino-Soviet Relations: New Perspectives," in Jacobson, ed., *Soviet Foreign Policy: New Dynamics, New Themes* (New York: St. Martin's Press, 1989), pp. 148–162; and Wenguang Shao, "China's Relations with the Superpowers," *Survival* (March/April 1990), 22 (2): 157–172.

184. Goldstein, "Diplomacy and Protest," p. 58.

185. Wenguang Shao, "China's Relations With the Superpowers," p. 161; and Blacker, "The USSR and Asia," p. 5.

186. General background on the changing texture of the Sino-Soviet relationship is provided by Gerald Segal, *Sino-Soviet Relations After Mao,* Adelphi Papers no. 202 (London: International Institute For Strategic Studies, Autumn 1985); Segal, "Taking Sino-Soviet Detente Seriously," *The Washington Quarterly* (Summer 1989), 12 (1): 53–63; and by Dan L. Strode, "Soviet China Policy In Flux," *Survival* (July/August 1988), 30 (4): 332–350.

187. Strode, *Soviet China Policy in Flux,* p. 343. Also see Jonathan Pollack, "Gorbachev in Peking," *Far Eastern Economic Review* (June 1, 1989), 144 (22): 22–23.

188. Henry J. Kenny, "Underlying Patterns of American Arms Sales to China," in U.S. Arms Control and Disarmament Agency, *World Military Expenditures and Arms Transfers 1986* (Washington, D.C.: USGPO, 1987), p. 46.

189. For corroborative analysis, see Joffe, "People's War Under Modern Conditions," pp. 564–565, 568–569; Godwin, "Changing Concepts of Doctrine, Strategy and Operations in the Chinese People's Liberation Army," pp. 581–590; and Segal, "As China Grows Strong," pp. 224, 226–227.

190. Gerald Segal, "China and Arms Control," *The World Today* (August-September 1985), 41 (8–9): 163.

5. ASEAN AS A "RELUCTANT PLAYER"

1. Brown, *American Security Policy in Asia,* p. 21.

2. See, for example, Secretary of Defense Donald Rumsfield, *Annual Defense Department Report FY 1978* (Washington, D.C.: USGPO, January 17, 1977), p. 38.

3. For background on the Southeast Asian neutrality movement throughout 1967–1974, see Dick Wilson, *The Neutralization of Southeast Asia.* A good updated account of ASEAN's nonalignment politics is by Kusuma Snitwongse, "Meeting the Challenges of Changing Southeast Asia," in Scalapino et al., *Asian Security Issues: Regional and Global,* pp. 323–343.

4. Charles E. Morrison and Astri Suhrke, *Strategies of Survival: The Foreign Policy Dilemmas of Small States,* pp. 289–299.

5. Muthiah Alagappa, *The National Security of Developing States: Lessons from Thailand* (Dover, Mass. Auburn House Publishing Company, 1987), pp. 13–14.

6. The threat levels concomitant to the ASEAN states' postwar development experience are discussed by Donald Weatherbee, "ASEAN Military Capacities and Security Concerns," Paper Prepared for the Twenty-Sixth Annual Meeting of the International Studies Association and cited by Sheldon Simon, *The Future of Asia-Pacific Security Collaboration,* pp. 67–68.

7. The early postwar U.S. strategy for Thai bases is covered in R. Sean Randolph, *The United States and Thailand: Alliance Dynamics, 1950–1985,* pp. 23–24. The Thai outlook is discussed by Michael Leifer, *Conflict and Regional Order in South-east Asia,* p. 28.

8. U.S. Senate, Hearing, *The Southeast Asia Collective Defense Treaty: Part*

I, p. 4. Also see W. MacMahon Ball, "A Political Reexamination of SEATO," *International Organization* (Winter 1958), 12 (1): 18–19.

9. Brown, *American Security Policy in Asia*, pp. 5–6.

10. Robert O. Tilman, *Southeast Asia and the Enemy Beyond: ASEAN Perceptions of External Threats*, p. 151.

11. The definitive study of the JCS position is by Trachtenberg, "A 'Wasting Asset': American Strategy and the Shifting Nuclear Balance," pp. 5–49.

12. Marc C. Gallicchio, "The Best Offense is a Good Defense," in Cohen and Iriye, eds., *The Great Powers in East Asia*, pp. 67–68. Also see "United States Objectives and Courses of Action with Respect to Southeast Asia," (NSC 124/2), June 24, 1952," in *Foreign Relations of the United States 1952–1954* (hereafter cited as *FRUS 1952–1954*), vol. 12: *East Asia and the Pacific* (Washington, D.C.: USGPO, 1984), p. 131.

13. "The Attempt To Organize 'United Action,' " Office of the Secretary of Defense, Vietnam Task Force *United States-Vietnam Relations 1945–1967* (hereafter cited as *The Pentagon Papers*) (Washington, DC: USGPO, 1970), part II-B-2, 17–31; "Memorandum of Conversation, by the Officer in Charge of Thai and Malayan Affairs (Landen), April 5, 1954," *FRUS 1952–1954*, pp. 402–404; "Memorandum of Conversation, by the Director of the Office of Philippine and Southeast Asian Affairs (Bonsal)," April 8, 1954, ibid., pp. 405–406; and "Memorandum of Conversation, by the Director of the Office of Philippine and Southeast Asian Affairs (Landen), April 15, 1954," ibid., April 15, 1989, pp. 422–423. Also see Leszek Buszynski, *SEATO: The Failure of an Alliance Strategy*, p. 7.

14. Dulles, "The Threat of a Red Asia," *Department of State Bulletin* (April 2, 1954) 30 (772):539–542.

15. Melanie Billings-Yun, *Decision Against War: Eisenhower and Dien Bien Phu, 1954*, pp. 64–65.

16. George C. Herring and Richard H. Immerman, "'The Day We Didn't Go to War' Revisited," *Journal of American History* (September 1984), 71 (2): 350.

17. Evelyn Colbert, *Southeast Asia in International Politics 1941–1956*, pp. 161–162; and Andrew J. Rotter, *Origins of the American Commitment to Southeast Asia*, p. 214

18. "Memorandum of Conversation with the President by the Secretary of State [Washington, D.C.: 25 May 1954]," in *FRUS 1952–1954*, vol. 12: *East Asia and the Pacific* (Washington, D. C.: USGPO, 1984), pp. 512–513.

19. "The Attempt To Organize United Action," p. B-26; and Rotter, *Origins Of The American Commitment To Southeast Asia.*, p. 216, citing Eden's memoirs, *Full Circle* (Boston: Houghton-Mifflin, 1960). Also see Secretary of State Dulles' reiteration of the British position in "Memorandum of Conversation With the President by the Secretary of State [Washington, May 25, 1954]," *FRUS 1952–1954*, pp. 512–513.

20. "The Attempt To Organize 'United Action,' " pp. B-26 through B-27.

21. Colbert, *Southeast Asia in International Politics*, pp. 241–243.

22. U.S. Senate, *The Southeast Asia Collective Defense Treaty: Part I*, pp.

13–14. Also see "Southeast Asia Collective Defense Treaty Transmitted to Senate," *The Department of State Bulletin* (November 29, 1954), 31 (805): 819–823; and W. MacMahon Ball, "A Political ReExamination of SEATO," *International Organization* (Winter 1958), 12 (1): 19.

23. Trachtenberg, "A Wasting Asset," pp. 42–45.

24. "NATO And SEATO: A Comparison," *The Pentagon Papers*, B1, p. A-14.

25. Critical analysis of Dulles' representations to the Senate is found in the Prepared Statement of Dr. George McT. Kahin in U.S. Senate, Hearing before the Committee on Foreign Relations, *U.S. Commitment to SEATO*, 93rd Cong., 2d Sess., March 6, 1974, p. 36.

26. Testimony of Gordon, ibid., pp. 45–46.

27. J. L. S. Girling, "Regional Security in Southeast Asia," *Journal of Southeast Asian Studies* (March 1971), 2 (1): 61–62.

28. "Statement of Policy by the National Security Council on Review of U.S. Policy in the Far East, (NSC 5429/2)," August 20, 1954, in *The Pentagon Papers*, Bk. 10, p. 731. NSC 171/1 remains classified.

29. "United States Minutes of Informal ANZUS Meeting, Washington, June 30, 1954," in *FRUS 1952–1954*, p. 598; and "Editorial Note," ibid., p. 479.

30. Chatham House Study Group, *Collective Defense in Southeast Asia: The Manila Treaty and Its Implications* (London and New York: Royal Institute Of International Affairs, 1956), p. 99; and Russell Fifield, *The Diplomacy of Southeast Asia 1945–1958* (New York: Harper, 1958), p. 166

31. C. L. M. Penders, ed., *Milestones on My Journey: The Memoirs of Ali Sastroamijoyo, Indonesia Patriot and Political Leaders* (St. Lucia, Queensland: University of Queensland Press, 1979), pp. 281–282.

32. Michael Leifer, *Indonesia's Foreign Policy* (London: George Allen & Unwin, 1983), pp. 32–33.

33. Quoted in Salvador P. Lopez, "The Foreign Policy of the Republic of the Philippines," in Raul P. Guzman and Mila A. Reforma, *Government and Politics of the Philippines* (Singapore, Oxford, and New York: Oxford University Press, 1988), p. 245. Also see William E. Berry, Jr., "The Military Bases and Postwar-U.S. Philippine Relations," in Fred Greene, ed., *The Philippine Bases: Negotiating for the Future*, p. 131.

34. Romulo's commencement address before the University of the East, April 28, 1951, cited in Lopez, "Foreign Policy," p. 246.

35. Charles E. Morrison and Astri Suhrke have noted that "there was a Philippine inclination to view the bases as a Philippine contribution which benefited the United States more than the island republic, or at least more directly." Morrison and Suhrke, *Strategies of Survival*, p. 240. On U.S. military assistance programs directed toward the Philippines during the early 1950s, consult David Wurfel, "Government Responses To Armed Communism and Secessionist Rebellion in the Philippines," in Chandran Jeshurun, *Governments and Rebellions in Southeast Asia* (Singapore: Institute of Southeast Asian Studies, 1985), pp. 233–236.

36. "Memorandum by the Counselor of the Department of State (Mac-Arthur) to the Secretary of State [Manila, September 3, 1954]," *FRUS 1952–1954*, p. 836; "Memorandum for the Secretary Of Defense: Report on the Manila Conference [Washington, September 14, 1954]," in *Pentagon Papers*, Bk. 10, pp. 746–750; Berry, "The Military Bases," pp. 137–138; Leszyk Buszynski, *SEATO: The Failure of an Alliance Strategy*, p. 38; and Wolfgang Pollak, "What Were SEATO's Aims Twenty Years Ago?" *Aussenpolitik* [English Edition], (1975), 26 (1): 110–111.

37. Testimony of McT. Kahin in *U.S. Commitment to SEATO*, p. 39; and Coral Bell, *Survey of International Affairs, 1954* (London: Oxford University Press, 1957), p. 77.

38. George Modelski, *SEATO: Six Studies* (Melbourne: F. W. Chesire, 1962), p. 96.

39. Randolph, *The United States and Thailand*, p. 31.

40. Randolph, *The United States and Thailand*, p. 33; and Pollak, "What Were SEATO's Aims," pp. 117–118.

41. Gordon H. Chang, "JFK, China and the Bomb," *The Journal of American History* (March 1988) 24 (4): 1290, relates the President's prediction to a journalist in October 1961 that when China acquired an atomic bomb, "all of Southeast Asia would fall to the Chinese Communists."

42. David K. Hall, "The Laos Crisis, 1960–1961," in Alexander George, David K. Hall, and William Simons, *The Limits of Coercive Diplomacy*, p. 44.

43. Roger Hilsman, *To Move a Nation: The Politics of Foreign Policy in the Administration of John F. Kennedy*, p. 147; and Charles A. Stevenson, *The End of Nowhere: American Policy Toward Laos Since 1954*, p. 176.

44. "Mr. Kennedy Calls for Peace in Laos," *The Times* (London), March 24, 1961, p. 14.

45. See, for example, a U.S. State Department memo reporting on a talk between Dulles and British Prime Minister Macmillan, NCT MC/19, June 11, 1958, in the *Declassified Documents Reference System*, 02779, 1987, where Macmillan's pleas that "we need to make some very important decisions regarding Indonesia," fail to elicit a specific U.S. response.

46. D. C. Watt, *Survey of International Affairs, 1961* (London: Oxford University Press, 1961), p. 334.

47. Leszyk Buszynski, *SEATO: The Failure of an Alliance Strategy*, pp. 77, 82. Also see "Department of State Memorandum of Conversation [Washington], April 29, 1961," p. 64; P.H.M. Jones, "Laos on the Brink," *Far Eastern Economic Review* (April 13, 1961), 29 (11): 89; and R. Sean Randolph, *The United States and Thailand*, p. 40.

48. Randolph, *The United States and Thailand;* and Watt, *Survey of International Affairs, 1961*, p. 324.

49. "Secretary Rusk, Thai Foreign Minister Discuss Matters of Mutual Concern" *U.S. Department of State Bulletin* (March 26, 1962, 46 (1187): 499. Author's emphasis.

50. Thanat Khoman, "The New Equation Of World Power and Its Impact

on Southeast Asia," *Orbis* (Fall 1976), 20 (3): 618. Also see Justus M. van der Kroef, *The Lives of SEATO* (Singapore: Institute of Southeast Asian Studies, December 1976), p. 24.

51. "Johnson Barnstorms into Philippines," *The Christian Science Monitor*, May 13, 1961, p. 4; and "Manila Is Reported Cooling on SEATO," *The New York Times*, February 8, 1961, p. 2.

52. Morrison and Suhrke, *Strategies of Survival*, p. 241.

53. "Memorandum to the President on January 19, 1961 Meeting [by Secretary of Defense McNamera, January 24, 1961]," in *Declassified Documents System* 001563 (1985).

54. Arthur M. Schlesinger, Jr., *A Thousand Days: John F. Kennedy in the White House*, (Boston: Houghton Mifflin, 1965), p. 339.

55. Hall, "The Laos Crisis," pp. 58–59, citing Stevenson, *The End of Nowhere*, p. 146; and "Department of State Outgoing Telegram to the Vientiane and Bangkok Embassies and CINCPAC [December 14, 1960]," *Declassified Documents System* 02792 (1987).

56. "State Department Memorandum of Conversation [Washington, April 29, 1961]," *The Pentagon Papers*, Bk. 11, pp. 62–66.

57. Ibid., p. 65. For additional background, see Hall, "The Laos Crisis," p. 49; and Schlesinger, *A Thousand Days*, p. 338.

58. "Memorandum of Joint Chief of Staff Conference with the President [January 25, 1961]," *Declassified Documents System* 002864 (1987).

59. "Let Us Stop the Aggressive Hands of SEATO," [Hanoi Radio, in Vietnamese to Vietnam, March 27, 1961, 0461, 1961 GMT—S] as translated and reprinted in Foreign Broadcast Information Service (FBIS), *North Vietnam*, March 28, 1961, p. EEE-1; and "What Is the U.S. Kennedy administration's Policy of War Preparations? [Beijing New China News Agency, Dictation in Mandarin to Rural Press, March 27, 1961, 1500 GMT—W] translated and reprinted in FBIS, *Communist China, International Affairs*, March 28, 1961, pp. AAA-3 through AAA-4.

60. See Halberstam, *The Best and the Brightest* (New York: Random House, 1972), pp. 92–93.

61. "State Department Memorandum of Conversation (Washington, April 29, 1961]," *The Pentagon Papers*, Bk. 11, p. 63.

62. The comprehensive assessment how this U.S. strategy was formulated during late 1964 through early 1965 is in George McT. Kahin, *Intervention: How American Became Involved in Vietnam* (New York: Knopf, 1986), pp. 236–285.

63. Richard M. Nixon, "Asia After Vietnam," *Foreign Affairs* (October 1967), 46 (1): 111–125. Assessments of Nixon's articles are provided by Robert S. Litwak, *Detente and the Nixon Doctrine*, pp. 118–119; and by Richard Butwell, "Asian Security—U.S. Style," *Far Eastern Economic Review* (July 24, 1969), 65 (30): 248–249.

64. Henry Kissinger, *White House Years* (Boston and Toronto: Little, Brown, 1979), p. 223.

65. Richard Nixon, "Informal Remarks with Newsmen in Guam, July 25, 1969," *Public Papers of the Presidents of the United States: Richard Nixon, 1969* (Washington, D.C.: USGPO, 1971), p. 549.

66. Richard Nixon, *The Memoirs of Richard Nixon* (New York: Grosset & Dunlap, 1978), p. 395. The "Nixon Doctrine" was spelled out in greater detail and with various degrees of clarity by a series of annual presidential foreign policy reports to Congress. See "A Report to the Congress by Richard M. Nixon," *U.S. Foreign Policy for the 1970s: A New Strategy for Peace*, February 18, 1970 (Washington, D.C.: USGPO, 1970); Nixon, *US Foreign Policy for the 1970s: Building for Peace*, February 25, 1971 (Washington, D.C.: USGPO, 1971); Nixon, *U.S. Foreign Policy for the 1970s: The Emerging Structure for Peace*, February 9, 1972 (Washington, D.C.: USGOP, 1972), and Nixon, *U.S. Foreign Policy for the 1970s: Shaping A Durable Peace*, May 3, 1973 (Washington, D.C.: USGPO, 1973).

67. Nixon, "Informal Remarks," pp. 549, 554.

68. *Memoirs of Richard Nixon*, p. 395.

69. Brown, *American Security Policy in Asia*, p. 6.

70. For a press survey, see "Press Comments," *FBIS* July 29, 1969, p. N-4; and ibid., July 30, 1969, p. N-1.

71. Peter Polomka, *Indonesia's Future and South-east Asia*, Adelphi Papers no. 104 (London: International Institute for Strategic Studies, 1974), p. 18.

72. Rahman, "Hello—and Goodbye!" *Far Eastern Economic Review* (August 7, 1969), 65 (32): 307. Also see Chin Kin Wah, *The Defense of Malaysia and Singapore*, pp. 121–122, for additional background on Malay suspicions of British-Singaporean collaboration within the AMDA framework.

73. Buszynski, *SEATO: The Failure of an Alliance Strategy*, p. 160.

74. Editorial in *Bangkok World*, July 31, 1969, as translated and reprinted as "Press Questions U.S. Defense commitments," FBIS, *Asia and Pacific (Daily Report)*, July 31, 1969, p. J-1.

75. See especially the remarks of Senator Stuart Symington to U.S. Ambassador to Thailand, Leonard Unger, in Committee on Foreign Relations, *United States Security Agreements and Commitments Abroad*, vol. 1, Part 3: *Kingdom of Thailand*, 91st Cong., 1st Sess., November 10, 1969, p. 706.

76. Cited in Morrison and Suhrke, *Strategies of Survival*, p. 130.

77. "Asia's Balance of Power," *SEATO Record* (April 1969), 8 (2): 13.

78. Robert Ingersoll, *U.S. Commitment to SEATO*, pp. 4–7.

79. Michael Leifer, *ASEAN and the Security of Southeast Asia*, p. 29.

80. These problems are addressed more fully by William R. Van Cleave and S. T. Cohen, "Nuclear Aspects of Future U.S. Security Policy in Asia," *Orbis* (Fall 1975), 19 (3): 1176–1179.

81. See "Address at the University of Hawaii, December 7, 1975," in *Public Papers of the Presidents of the United States, Gerald R. Ford, 1975* (Washington, D.C.: USGPO, 1977), Bk. 2, pp. 1950–1955.

82. "Ford's Doctrine," *Straits Times*, December 10, 1975, p. 14; and Harvey Stockwin, "Ford's Diplomatic Afterthoughts," *Far Eastern Economic Review* (December 26, 1975), 90 (52): 20–21.

83. Leifer, *ASEAN and the Security of Southeast Asia*, pp. 28–30, provides in-depth background on this transition process.

84. "Indonesia Wants Wrong Turn in ASEAN's Future," *The Nation*, December 12, 1975, p. 2 as reprinted in FBIS *Asia & Pacific (Daily Report)*, December 12, 1975, p. J-3.

85. For excellent background on the ASEAN states' efforts to establish an acceptable security environment following the defeat of South Vietnam, see K. K. Nair, *ASEAN-Indochina Relations Since 1975: The Politics of Accommodation*, Canberra Papers on Strategy and Defense no. 30, especially pp. 25–59.

86. Richard Nations, "Calling All Allies," *Far Eastern Economic Review* (June 18, 1982), 116 (25): 11; Gareth Porter, "The United States and Southeast Asia," *Current History* (December 1984), 83 (497): 401–402; and Robert C. Horn, "U.S.-ASEAN Relations in the 1980s," *Contemporary Southeast Asia* (September, 1984), 6 (2): 119–134.

87. "Weinberger Urges Faster Japanese Defense Buildup," *The Japan Times*, March 27, 1982, pp. 1, 2. For additional background, see "U.S. Policy in Asia Based on '6 Pillars,' " *The Straits Times*, March 27, 1982, pp. 1, 4; an interview with Weinberger in *Defense* (July 1984), pp. 2–7; Norman D. Palmer, *Westward Watch: The United States and the Changing Western Pacific*, p. 20; and Nayan Chanda, "American Big Stick," *Far Eastern Economic Review* (June 20, 1985), 128 (24): 45–48.

88. Hong Kong Agence France Presse report reprinted in Foreign Broadcast Information Service, *Asia & Pacific (Daily Report)*, November 2, 1982, p. O-2.

89. Kirdi Dipoyudo, "Important Developments in the Indian Ocean Area," *The Indonesian Quarterly* (April 1982), 10 (2): 9, 11.

90. Research Institute for Peace and Security, *Asian Security 1982* (Tokyo: Nikkei Business Publishing Company, 1982), pp. 23–24.

91. Successive Japanese leaders' efforts to disassociate Japan from assuming any military role in an ASEAN context are discussed by Charles E. Morrison, *Japan, the United States and a Changing Southeast Asia*, pp. 36, 43, 58–59; and Sueo Sudo, "The Road to Becoming a Regional Leader: Japanese Attempts in Southeast Asia, 1975–1980," *Pacific Affairs* (Spring 1988), 61 (1): 34.

92. "MP's Call for ASEAN Vigilance Toward Japan—"Pool Item," Antara/OANU dispatch in English, November 27, 1982, as reprinted in JPRS 82428, *South and East Asia Report* December 9, 1982, no. 1226, p. 9.

93. Kuala Lumpur International Service Broadcast in English, November 3, 1982 reprinted in Foreign Broadcast Information Service *Asia & Pacific (Daily Report)*, November 4, 1982, p. O-2.

94. "Supreme Commander Tells the United States That Thailand Will Defend Itself," *Patinya* (Bangkok), September 6, 1982, pp. 6–8, as translated and reprinted in JPRS 82201, *South and East Asia Report* (November 9, 1982), no. 1212, p. 107.

95. "Thanat Casts Doubt on U.S. Commitment," *Bangkok Post*, August

25, 1987, p. 5; and Kenneth Conboy, "Cracks Appear in the U.S.-Thai Relationship," *Backgrounder* (March 8, 1988), no. 75, pp. 1–11.

96. Simon, *The Future of Asian-Pacific Security Collaboration*, p. 7.

97. See "In Asia, His Cold War's Over [editorial]," *The New York Times*, March 27, 1990, p. 18; and Jim Hoagland, "New Roles in Asia: Washington Looks Confused," *International Herald Tribune*, March 20, 1990, p. 4.

98. Muthiah Alagappa evaluates the relationship between state vulnerability and interregional security guarantees in a Southeast Asian context. See his *The National Security of Developing States: Lessons From Thailand*, pp. 1–31. Also consult Jusuf Wanadi, "Political Development and Regional Order," in Linda G. Martin, ed., *The ASEAN Success Story* (Honolulu: University of Hawaii Press, 1987), pp. 144–145.

99. The Indonesian outlook is well summarized by Arnfinn Jorgensen-Dahl, *Regional Organization and Order in Southeast Asia* (London and Basingstoke: Macmillan, 1982), pp. 35–36; and by Bernard Gordon, "Regionalism in Southeast Asia," in Robert O. Tilman, ed., *Man, State, and Society in Contemporary Southeast Asia* (New York, Washington, and London: Praeger, 1969), pp. 514–515.

100. Morrison and Suhrke, *Strategies of Survival*, p. 133.

101. See Khoman, "The New Equation of World Power and Its Impact on Southeast Asia," pp. 620–621.

102. See Malik's address before the Press Foundation of Asia Assembly, reprinted as "Towards An Asian Asia," *Far Eastern Economic Review* (September 25, 1971), 73 (39): 32. Also see Leifer, *Indonesia's Foreign Policy*, p. 148.

103. Juwono Sudarsono, "ASEAN: The Uncertain Commitment," *The Indonesian Quarterly* (January 1973), 1 (2): 63.

104. Moertopo, "Political and Economic Development in Indonesia in the Context of Regionalism in Southeast Asia," *The Indonesian Quarterly* (April 1978), 6 (2): 31–32.

105. The ASEAN seminar is covered by *Berita Buana* (Jakarta) in Indonesian, March 2, 1989, pp. 1, 9, translated and reprinted as "ASEAN Formulates 'Regional Resilience' Concept," FBIS, *East Asia*, March 10, 1989, p. 2. For an assessment on the role of the Bali Conference in advancing regional resilience, see Michael Leifer, "Indonesia's Foreign Policy," p. 162. An earlier seminar (December 1987) on "Leadership and Regional Strategic Studies in Southeast Asia," concluded that while "order and national security" are necessary preconditions for national—and by extension regional—security, "a dynamic search for economic and social progress" must be simultaneously undertaken if ASEAN development aspirations are to be realized. See T. B. Simatupang, "Indonesia: Leadership and National Security Perceptions," in Mohammed Ayoob and Chi-Anan Sumudavanija, eds., *Leadership Perceptions and National Security*, p. 114.

106. Ayoob and Samudavanija, "Leadership and Security in Southeast Asia: Exploring General Propositions," in Ayoob and Samudavanija, eds., *Leadership Perceptions and National Security*, p. 263.

107. Karl Jackson, "U.S. Policy, ASEAN, and the Kampuchean Crisis," in Robert A. Scalapino and Jusuf Wanadi, eds., *Economic, Political and Security Issues in Southeast Asia in the 1980s*, esp. pp. 128–131.

108. Sheldon Simon, *Asian Neutralism and U.S. Policy*, pp. 51–52.

109. John Doraisamy, "Comment on ASEAN's Future Defense Stance," Kuala Lumpur International Service in English, March 28, 1989, reprinted in FBIS, *East Asia*, March 28, 1989, p. 4; Raphael Pura, "ASEAN Fears Regional Role Is Shrinking," *The Asian Wall Street Journal* July 3, 1989, p. 8; and Zap Dian, "ASEAN Military Cooperation," *Asian Defense Journal* (May 1989), pp. 4–5.

110. Muthiah Alagappa, "Soviet Policy in Southeast Asia," *Pacific Affairs* (Fall 1990), 63 (3), forthcoming.

111. Michael Richardson, "For ASEAN, It's Still the Russian Bear," *International Herald Tribune*, July 8/9, 1989, pp. 1, 5.

112. Agence France Presse report translated and reprinted in FBIS, *Soviet Union (Daily Report)* July 6, 1989, p. 31. The Soviet leader referred to the "terrible effects" which could ensue from the Chinese leaders' use of force against their own people.

113. This view is developed particularly well by Barry Buzan, "The Southeast Asian Security Complex," *Contemporary Southeast Asia* (June 1988), 10 (1): 11. Also see Hans H. Indorf, *Impediments to Regionalism in Southeast Asia: Bilateral Constraints Among ASEAN Member States*, esp. pp. 89–91; and Donald Weatherbee, "The Diplomacy of Stalemate," in Donald Weatherbee, ed., *Southeast Asia Divided: The ASEAN-Indochina Crisis*, pp. 12–13.

114. "Khmer Rouge Reject Plan Backed by Sihanouk for Cambodia Truce," *Los Angeles Times*, May 9, 1989, p. 9; and Charles P. Wallace, "Khmer Rouge Poised to Rule Again, a Decade After the 'Killing Fields,' " ibid., pp. 8–9. An excellent background on events leading to the Cambodian peace negotiations is provided by Elizabeth Becker, "The Progress of Peace in Cambodia," *Current History* (April 1989), 88 (537): 169–172, 200–202.

115. "ASEAN FMs To Discuss 'Cocktail Party' in New York," *The Nation*, August 25, 1987, p. 6; and Nick B. Williams, "Asian Alliance Agrees to Join Cambodia Peace Talks," *Los Angeles Times*, July 6, 1988, p. 4.

116. The breakdown of IMC negotiations is covered by Bryan McManus, "Talks Fail To Reach Accord," Agence France Presse report in English, reprinted in FBIS, *East Asia (Daily Report)*, March 2, 1990, pp. 1–2; and by Steven Erlanger, "Peace Talks on Cambodia Break Down" *The New York Times*, March 1, 1990, p. 3. The definitive report on the return of Vietnamese military advisors to Cambodia remains Erlanger's "Vietnamese Forces Helping Cambodia, Diplomats Assert," *The New York Times*, February 23, 1990, pp. 1, 6. A text of a Vietnamese denial that such assistance had occurred, by the Vietnamese Foreign Ministry, is contained in "News Conference on Davos, Troops in Cambodia," Hanoi Domestic Service in Vietnamese, translated and reprinted in FBIS, *East Asia (Daily Report)*, March 2, 1990, p. 68. The Foreign Ministry labelled the reports as "totally groundless."

117. Clifford Krauss, "A Shift in Policy on Cambodia," *International Herald Tribune*, July 9, 1990, p. 3; and Jim Mann, "U.S. to Shift on Cambodia, Hold Vietnam Talks," *Los Angeles Times*, July 18, 1990, pp. 1, 6.

118. Mark Fineman, "U.S. Planes Turned the Tide," *Los Angeles Times*, December 3, 1989, pp. 1, 20; and "A Close Call for Aquino," *The Economist*, (December 9, 1989), 313 (7632): 29–30. The Phantoms reportedly pinned down aircraft controlled by the rebels at two different air bases.

119. These points are assessed in-depth by Capt. Alva M. Bowen, a National Defense Specialist with the Congressional Research Service. Bowen presented what has since become the seminal unclassified assessment on the Philippines basing situation as it relates to U.S. "grand strategy." See Report of a Workshop Organized by the Subcommittee on Asian and Pacific Affairs of the Committee on Pacific Affairs, The Widrow Wilson International Center For Scholars of The Smithsonian Institution And The Congressional Research Service of The Library of Congress, *Assessing America's Options in the Philippines*, 99th Cong., 2d Sess., February 3, 1986, pp. 67–99. Also see "Prepared Statement of Lt. Col. William E. Berry, Jr.," in Hearings before the Subcommittee on Asian and Pacific Affairs of the Committee on Foreign Affairs, House of Representatives, *United States-Philippines Relations and the New Base and Aid Agreement*, 98th Cong., 1st Sess., June 28, 1983, p. 198; Gregory P. Corning, "The Philippines Bases and U.S. Pacific Strategy," *Pacific Affairs* (Spring 1990), 63 (1): 6–23; Alagappa, "The Major Powers and Southeast Asia," pp. 547–548, 551–552; Simon, *The Future of Asian-Pacific Security Collaboration*, pp. 86–87; and Robert Harkavy, *Bases Abroad: The Global Foreign Military Presence* (New York: Oxford University Press, 1989), pp. 32, 291–292; and James R. Baker, *United States Overseas Basing* (New York: Praeger, 1990), p. 130.

120. Fred Greene, ed., *The Philippine Bases: Negotiating for the Future: American and Philippine Perspectives*, p. 61.

121. See the remarks of Philippine Defense Secretary General Fidel V. Ramos, acknowledging the perceived value of the American presence at the outset of the basing review in early 1988, in an article by Max Sangil, "Ramos Cites U.S. Bases Roles in Defense," *Philippine Daily Inquirer*, February 19, 1988, p. 22, as reprinted in FBIS *Asia & Pacific (Daily Report)*, February 19, 1988, pp. 46–47. The same theme was reiterated in an address by delivered by Admiral Ronald Hays, Commander-in-Chief, U.S. Pacific Command (CINCPAC), before the American Chamber of Commerce of the Philippines, November 28, 1987, and reprinted as "U.S.-Philippine Security Relations: A US-CINCPAC Perspective," *Asia-Pacific Defense Forum* (Spring 1988), 12 (4): 15–16. Also see James Clad, "Subic and Clark Play Pivotal Roles," *Far Eastern Economic Review* (April 21, 1988), 140 (16): 25; and S. Bilveer, "The Future of American Bases in the Philippines," *The Korean Journal of International Studies* (Spring 1987), 18 (2): 203.

122. Marko Milivojevic, "The Spratly and Paracel Islands Conflict," *Survival* (January-February 1989), 31 (1): 76; and Bunn Nagara, "Spratly:

A Need To Pacify the Pacific," *New Straits Times*, April 16, 1988, pp. 6–7.

123. A. James Gregor, *Crisis in the Philippines: A Threat to U.S. Interests* (Washington, D.C.: Ethics and Public Policy Center, 1984), p. 20.

124. See, for example, Ed Garcia and Francisco Nemenzo, *The Sovereign Quest: Freedom From Foreign Military Bases*, especially pp. 8–17. Other useful reviews of the criticisms directed toward the bases are by Lt. Col. William E. Berry, Jr., *U.S. Bases in the Philippines: The Evolution of the Special Relationship*, esp. pp. 282–285; and Ron May, "The Base Issue in Philippines Domestic Politics," in Desmond Ball, ed., *U.S. Bases in the Philippines: Issues and Implications*, Canberra Papers on Strategy and Defense no. 46 (Canberra: Australian National University, 1988).

125. For representative analysis, see James Fallows, "The Philippines: The Bases Dilemma," *The Atlantic* (February 1988), 261 (2): 18–30; the testimony of Rear Adm. Gene R. LaRocque (ret.), Director, Center For Defense Information in *United States-Philippines Relations*, pp. 170–188; and May, "The Base Issue," pp. 34–36.

126. The specific issues related to constitutional interpretation of a nuclear-free zone in the Philippines are covered by Berry, *U.S. Bases in the Philippines*, pp. 286–288.

127. Glenda Gloria, "'Expert' Views Nuclear Issue," in *Philippine Daily Inquirer*, October 20, 1988, pp. 1, 8, as reprinted in FBIS, *Asia and Pacific (Daily Report)*, October 20, 1988, p. 41; and May, "The Base Issue," p. 35. Also see Corning, "The Philippine Bases and U.S. Strategy," p. 19.

128. Simon, *The Future of Asian-Pacific Security Collaboration*, p. 88.

129. Captain R. A. Bowling, "Keeping Open the Sea-Lanes," U.S. Naval Institute *Proceedings* 111/12/994 (December 1985), pp. 93–98; Yang Razali Kassim, "Uncertainty Over U.S. Bases in Philippines," *New Straits Times*, January 1, 1988, p. 20; and Kenneth G. Weiss, "The War Will Not Subside: The Pacific Theater in a NATO-Warsaw Pact War," *Comparative Strategy* (1988), 7 (4): 398–410.

130. Nayan Chanda, "Biting the Bullet," *Far Eastern Economic Review* (September 29, 1988), 141 (39): 24–26; Hans H. Indorf, "The 1988 Philippine Base Review," *Asian Affairs, An American Review* (Spring 1988), 15 (1): 24; John J. Carroll, "U.S. Philippine Bases: Which Side Blackmails?" *Los Angeles Times*, August 21, 1988, part 5, p. 2; Harry G. Summers Jr., "Philippines Shouldn't Bank on Being a 'Vital Interest,'" *Los Angeles Times*, June 1, 1987, part 2, p. 5; and "U.S. Senator Rules Out More Aid for Philippines," *The Japan Times*, August 31, 1987, p. 6.

131. A. Karim Shuker, "Government Proposes to Host U.S. Facilities," *Bernama* (Kuala Lumpur) in English, reprinted in Foreign Broadcast Information Service, *East Asia (Daily Report)* (August 4, 1989), pp. 45–46.

132. Mike Fonte, "A Shot Across the Bow," *Far Eastern Economic Review* (July 19, 1990), 149 (29): 10–11; Jim Mann, "Singapore to Allow U.S. Use of Military Facilities," *Los Angeles Times*, July 6, 1990, pp. 1, 9; and Patrick E.

Tyler, "U.S. Close to Singapore Deal on Access for Pacific Forces," *International Herald Tribune*, July 7 and 8, 1990, pp. 1, 5.

133. Wright testimony to Asia-Pacific Subcommittee, House Foreign Affairs Committee, February 22, 1990, p. 15 of manuscript in author's possession.

134. Michael Richardson, "From Malaysian Leader, Tough Talk on Vietnam Refugees," *International Herald Tribune*, October 30, 1989, p. 2.

135. Donald Putnam Henry, Keith Crane, and Katherine Watkins Webb, *The Philippine Bases: Background for Negotiations* R-3764/1–USDP/DOS (Santa Monica: The RAND Corporation, August 1989); Molly Moore, "Amid Rising Doubts About Aquino, U.S. Speeds Base-Pullout Study," *International Herald Tribune*, February 22, 1990, p. 1; and David Hegarty, "U.S. Bases in the Philippines: Redeployment Options," in Ball, ed., *U.S. Bases in the Philippines*, pp. 57–70. On the U.S. withdrawal of jets, see "All U.S. Fighters to Quit Clark," *International Herald Tribune* November 8, 1990, p. 2.

136. Muthiah Alagappa, "U.S. Military in Asia Should Leave Gradually," *Far Eastern Economic Review* (August 18, 1988), 141 (33): 32–33; David Humphries, "Malaysia Backs U.S. Bases," *The Times* (London), April 18, 1988, p. 7; Noordin Soipee, "ASEAN: In Favor of U.S. Bases in the Philippines," *International Herald Tribune*, March 12, 1988, p. 4. An American assessment is by Bernard K. Gordon, *An ASEAN Perspective on the Philippines and the U.S. Bases*, A USIA Research Report (Washington, D.C.: United States Information Agency, December 1985). Also see his "Asian Angst and American Foreign Policy," *Foreign Policy* (Summer, 1982), no. 47, pp. 48–49.

137. Floating air bases known as Mobile Operational Large Island Airbases are now envisioned as provided the U.S. with autonomous and transportable strategic lift capabilities in the near future. See Donald Henry, et al., *The Philippine Bases*, p. 28; and Cpt. Peter Swartz, "Floating Bases: Moving Out to Sea?" *NATO's Sixteen Nations* (April 1989), 34 (2): 65–71.

138. Thomas E. Crocker, "Challenges and Opportunities in Base Negotiations," *Washington Quarterly* (Spring 1989), 12 (2): 55–67. Also see Jim Mann, "U.S. Facing a Crisis Over Global Bases," *Los Angeles Times*, March 15, 1988, pp. 1, 6, 7.

139. These points are developed more thoroughly by Sheldon Simon, "Toward a U.S. Security Policy in Southeast Asia: A Maritime Emphasis," in Ramon H. Myers, ed., *A U.S. Foreign Policy for Asia* (Stanford, Cal.: Hoover Institution Press, 1982), esp. pp. 70–71.

140. The key passages of a November 1971 Indonesian-Malaysian joint statement are cited in Michael Leifer, *Malacca, Singapore, and Indonesia*, p. 48. Singapore has dissented from the Indonesian-Malaysian stand on straits sovereignty but endorsed the forming of a tripartite navigation safety commission in 1977.

141. Michael Leifer, "The Security of Sea Lanes in Southeast Asia," *Survival* (January-February 1983), 25 (1): 16–24; Lim Joo Jock, "The Security of the Sea Lanes in the Asia-Pacific Region: A Broad Strategic Perspective from Singapore," in Lau Teik Soon and Lee Lai To, eds., *The Security of the Sea*

Lanes, pp. 126–139; and S. Bilveer, "Internal Instability as a SLOC Problem," *Asian Defense Journal*, November 1986, pp. 16–26.

142. Amitav Acharya, "Arms Proliferation Issues in ASEAN: Towards a More 'Conventional' Defense Posture?" *Contemporary Southeast Asia* (December 1988), 10 (3): 257–258.

143. John Doraisamy, "Commentary on ASEAN's Future Defense Stance," (Kuala Lumpur International Service)," FBIS, *East Asia (Daily Report)*, March 28, 1989, p. 4.

144. Dhawon Sukhakanya, "The Security of the Sea Lanes in Southeast Asia," in Lau Teik Soon and Lee Lai To, eds., *The Security of the Sea Lanes in the Asia-Pacific Region* (Singapore: Center for Advanced Studies, Singapore Institute of International Affairs/Heinemann Asia, 1988), pp. 41–42.

145. Tim Huxley, "Internal Security, Defense, and Development in Southeast Asia," *Arms Control* (September 1987), 8 (2): 184–185.

146. Michael O'Conner, "The Naval Capabilities and Strategies of Australia and ASEAN," *Asian Defense Journal* (December 1987), pp. 6, 10.

147. Steve Hoadley, "Malaysia's Military Build-Up: A Political Assessment," *New Zealand International Review* (November-December 1988), 13 (6): 2–5; Nick Seaward, "Buying British Again," *Far Eastern Economic Review* (October 6, 1988), 142 (40): 20; Tai Ming Cheung, "Enemy Spotting," *Far Eastern Economic Review* (November 24, 1988), 142 (47): 23–24; and Denis Warner, "Britain's Big Malaysian Deal," *Pacific Defense Reporter* (October 1988), 15 (4): 30.

148. Chin Kin Wah, "Prospects for Wider Co-operation in the Pacific," in Douglas T. Stuart, ed., *Security within the Pacific Rim* (Aldershot, Hants, England: Gower, 1987), p. 137. Also see S. Bilveer, "Singapore, Malaysia and Indonesia: Growing Defense Cooperation," *Asian Defense Journal* (May 1989), pp. 68–71; Hoadley, "Malaysia's Military Buildup," p. 4; and Alagappa, "Comprehensive Security," pp. 69–70.

149. Kavi Chongkittavorn, "More Than Just an Exercise," *The Nation* (Bangkok), August 25, 1987, p. 6.

150. Michael Richardson, "The U.S. Steps Up Its Power Projection Capability," *Pacific Defense Reporter* (February 1987), 13 (8): 7.

151. S. Bilveer, "Singapore, Malaysia, and Indonesia: Growing Defense Cooperation," p. 71.

152. R. S. Sassheen, "The Singapore Armed Forces," *Asian Defense Journal* (April 1989), pp. 4–26; and Alagappa, "Comprehensive Security," pp. 73–76.

153. Weatherbee, "ASEAN Defense Programs: Military Patterns of National and Regional Resilience," in Young Whan Kihl and Lawrence Grinter, eds., *Security, Strategy and Policy Responses in the Pacific Rim* (Boulder, Colo. and London: Lynne Rienner, 1989), p. 190.

154. The best source on Southeast Asian maritime and international sea law politics remains Michael Leifer's *Malacca, Singapore, and Indonesia*. Useful, if somewhat dated, analysis is also provided by Barry Buzan, *A Sea of Troubles? Sources of Dispute in the New Ocean Regime*, Adelphi Papers no. 143

(London: International Institute For Strategic Studies, Spring 1978), pp. 39–41.

155. Comparisons between the security objectives of the U.S. and Singapore are found in S. Bilveer, "The United States in Southeast Asia," *Asian Defense Journal* (April 1989), pp. 52–58.

156. Karen Elliot House, "Singapore's Lee Urges U.S.-Japan Links," *The Asian Wall Street Journal*, May 18, 1989, pp. 1, 6.

157. Paul Wedel, "Singapore, Asia's Unsinkable Aircraft Carrier," *The Japan Times*, September 15, 1982, p. 14.

158. Research Institute for Peace and Security, *Asian Security 1982* (Tokyo: 1982), p. 27.

159. Amitav Acharya, "Arms Proliferation Issues in ASEAN," p. 245; and K. U. Menon, "A Six Power Defense Arrangement in Southeast Asia?" *Contemporary Southeast Asia* (December 1988), 10 (3): 306–307, 316–319. For background on the British involvement in FPDA, see William T. Tow, "Asia-Pacific Security Alliances: Reevaluating Britain's Transregional Role," *Brassey's Defence Yearbook 1983* (Oxford: Brassey, 1983), pp. 127–128. On recent FPDA maritime air defense exercises and doctrine, see R. S. Sassheen, "Exercise *Lima Bersatu*," *Asian Defense Journal* (October 1988), pp. 13–19; and Brig. General (Reserve) Lee Hsien Loong, "The FPDA and Regional Stability," *Asian Defense Journal* (February 1990), pp. 28–32.

160. Tai Ming Cheung, "The Mouse That Roared," *Far Eastern Economic Review* (September 22, 1988), 141 (38): 28–29; and Steve Hoadley, "Singapore's Security Policies," *New Zealand International Review* (September-October 1988), 13 (5): 22.

161. Tai Ming Cheung, "The Mouse That Roared," pp. 28–29.

162. Cited in Michael Vatikiotis, "Zone of Discord," *Far Eastern Economic Review* (January 14, 1988), 139 (2): 12–13.

163. Roy, "When Banning Nukes Can Increase the Risk of War," *Far Eastern Economic Review* (May 12, 1988), 140 (19): 32–33.

164. J. Soedjati Djiwandono, *Southeast Asia as a Nuclear-Weapons-Free Zone*, p. 2; and S. Bilveer, "Nuclear-Weapons-Free Zone in Southeast Asia: The Initial Idea," *Asian Defense Journal* (December 1989), pp. 38–41.

165. Author interviews with analysts at the Center for Strategic and International Studies, Jakarta, February 1986. Also see the citations of Indonesian studies on SEANWFZ in Robyn Lim, "Nuclear Weapon Free Zones," Paper Prepared for a Conference on Security and Arms Control in the North Pacific, The Australian National University Research School of Pacific Studies, Peace Research Center, Strategic and Defense Studies Center and International Relations Department, August 12–14, 1987, pp. 6–7.

166. 'When Will ASEAN Look After Its Own Affairs?" *The Nation* (Bangkok), July 7, 1988, p. 8, as reprinted in FBIS *East Asia*, July 7, 1988, pp. 48–49.

167. These points are surveyed in-depth by Muthiah Alagappa, "A Nuclear-Weapons-Free Zone in Southeast Asia: Problems and Prospects," pp. 173–180. Alagappa's analysis constitutes the most thorough assessment of

SEANWFZ to date. Also see J. Soedjati Djiwandono, *Southeast Asia as a Nuclear-Weapons-Free Zone*, pp. 4–7; Snitwongse, "Meeting the Challenges," pp. 334–335; and S. Bilveer, "Nuclear Weapons-Free Zone in Southeast Asia: Concepts, Problems, and Prospects," *Asian Defense Journal* (November 1988), pp. 20–30.

6. THE SOUTHWEST PACIFIC

1. These observations are developed further by Henry Albinski in his Prepared Statement for the Hearing before the Subcommittee on Asian and Pacific Affairs of the Committee on Foreign Affairs, U.S. House of Representatives, *Security Treaty Between Australia, New Zealand, and the United States*, 99th Cong., 1st Sess., March 18, 1985, esp. p. 111.

2. F. L. W. Wood, "Political and Strategic Background," in Wood et al., *Defense Perspectives*, p. 24.

3. Richard A. Herr, "Regionalism, Strategic Denial and South Pacific Security," *The Journal of Pacific History* (October 1986), 21 (4): p. 174. Also see Herr, "Diplomacy and History in the South Pacific: Coping With Sovereignty," *Current Affairs Bulletin* (January 1987), 63 (8): 16–22, esp. pp. 20–22; John Ravenhill, "Political Turbulence in the South Pacific," in Ravenhill, ed., *No Longer An American Lake? Alliance Problems in the South Pacific*, pp. 23, 25; and J. H. A. Hoyle, "The Security of Small Island States," in Desmond Ball, ed., *The ANZAC Connection* (Sydney: George Allen & Unwin, 1985), pp. 70, 77.

4. Comment of Brigadier General F. F. Everest, USA, on "Minutes of the Meetings of the Joint Staff Planners, 1946–1947, # 243," in *Records of the Joint Chiefs of Staff*, Part 2 *1946–1953* Reel 7 (Frederick, Md.: University Publications of America, 1980), p. 0427. Also see Lester J. Foltos, "The New Pacific Barrier," pp. 319–320.

5. From Article Thirteen of the Canberra Agreement text found in "The Minister in Australia (Johnson) to the Secretary of State [Canberra], January 22, 1944," *Foreign Relations of the United States 1944*, vol. 3: *The British Commonwealth and Europe* (Washington, D.C.: USGPO, 1965), p. 170.

6. Articles Sixteen and Twenty-Seven of the Canberra Agreement text, ibid., pp. 170–171. The best coverage of Australian and New Zealand diplomacy leading up to the Canberra Agreement remains Coral Bell's *Unequal Allies: Australia-American Relations and the Pacific War* (Melbourne: Melbourne University Press, 1977), esp. pp. 146–159.

7. Michael C. Pugh, *The ANZUS Crisis Nuclear Visiting and Deterrence*, p. 4; and Trevor Reese, *Australia, New Zealand, and the United States: A Survey of International Relations 1941–1968*, pp. 41–42.

8. See, for example, an account of New Zealand's postwar European strategic preoccupations in Roderic Alley, "The Evolution of ANZUS," in Jacob Bercovitch, ed., *ANZUS in Crisis: Alliance Management in International Affairs*, p. 32.

9. Both documents are covered in depth by Bernard K. Gordon, *New Zealand Becomes a Pacific Power*, pp. 219–224.

10. John J. Dedman, "Encounter Over Manus," *Australian Outlook* (August 1966), 20 (2): 142–143.

11. Foltos, "The New Pacific Barrier," p. 326.

12. Reese, *Australia, New Zealand, and the United States*, p. 53.

13. Ibid., p. 55; and Dedman, "Encounter Over Manus," pp. 150–151.

14. T. B. Millar, *Australia in Peace and War*, pp. 204–208, provides excellent background on American calculations leading to ANZUS negotiations.

15. These rationales are assessed in greater depth by Dean E. McHenry and Richard N. Rosecrance, "The Exclusion of the United Kingdom from the ANZUS Pact," pp. 324–325.

16. "Department of State Policy Statement for New Zealand [Washington] July 30, 1951," in *Foreign Relations of the United States 1951*, vol. 6: *Asia and the Pacific* (Washington, D.C.: USGPO, 1977), p. 1483. Also see Ritchie Ovendale, *The English-Speaking Alliance: Britain, the United States, the Dominions and the Cold War, 1945–1951*, pp. 232–233.

17. A good summary of the Tonga episode is offered by Irene Webley, "Tonga and the Soviet Union," *New Zealand International Review* (September/October 1976), 1 (5): 11–13.

18. J. G. Starke, *The ANZUS Treaty Alliance;* and T. B. Millar, *Australia's Foreign Policy*, p. 119.

19. Alley, "The Evolution of ANZUS," in Bercovitch, ed., *ANZUS in Crisis*, pp. 34–38; Henry Albinski, *The Australian-American Security Relationship* (New York: St. Martin's Press, 1981). Michael Stenson, "The Origins and Significance of 'Forward Defense' in Asia," The New Zealand Institute of International Affairs, *New Zealand in World Affairs*, (Wellington: Price Milburn, 1977), vol. 1. pp. 177–196 is more critical of what he argues was the ANZUS powers' inability to discriminate between ANZUS and extra-ANZUS commitments during the Cold War.

20. T. B. Millar, "The Mutual and Shared Commitments of Australia and New Zealand," *Australia Outlook* (April 1968), 22 (1): 18. Also see F. H. Corner, "New Zealand and the South Pacific," in T. C. Larkin, ed., *New Zealand's External Relations* (Wellington/London: New Zealand Institute of Public Administration/Oxford University Press, 1962), pp. 130–152 and W. E. H. Stanner, "British Pacific Island Territories and Papua New Guinea," in T. B. Millar, ed., *Britain's Withdrawal From Asia: Its Implications For Australia* (Canberra: Australian National University Press, 1967), pp. 62–77.

21. Reese, *Australia, New Zealand, and the United States*, p. 301.

22. Henry Albinski, *Australian External Policy Under Labor*, p. 253.

23. In 1985, former National Party Leader Jim McClay contended that the Rowling government had extended "private assurances" to the Americans that such visits would be considered positively in December 1975—a month after the November general election of that year. See J. K. McClay, "New Zealand's Approach—Another Perspective," in Roderic Alley, ed., *Disarmament and*

Security (Wellington: New Zealand Institute of International Affairs, 1985), p. 49.

24. Keith Jackson and Jim Lamare, "Politics, Public Opinion, and International Crisis: The ANZUS Issue in New Zealand Politics," in Berkovitch, *ANZUS in Crisis*, pp. 168–169.

25. David Lange, "The Oxford Union Debate," pp. 7–12. For American and New Zealand assessments respectively on the morality issue contained within Lange's opening remarks, see Henry Albinski, "The ANZUS Crisis: U.S. Policy Implications and Responses," in Berkovitch *ANZUS in Crisis*, p. 85; and Kevin P. Clements, "New Zealand's Role in Promoting a Nuclear-Free Pacific," *Journal of Peace Research* (December 1988), 25 (4): 401–402. To better understand the strength of moral imperatives as formulative elements in New Zealand's history and foreign policy, see Andre Siegfried, *Democracy in New Zealand*.

26. Lange's address is reprinted as "Trade and Foreign Policy: A Labour Perspective," *New Zealand International Review* (September 1984), 9 (5): 2–4.

27. Pugh, *The ANZUS Crisis, Nuclear Visiting, and Deterrence*, p. 36.

28. Kevin Clements, *Back From the Brink: The Creation of a Nuclear-Free New Zealand* (Wellington: Allen & Unwin, 1988), pp. 146–180; Clements, "The Defense Committee of Inquiry: A Unique Opportunity for Public Participation," in Jonathan Boston and Martin Holland, eds., *The Fourth Labour Government: Radical Politics in New Zealand*, pp. 214–241; and Pugh, *The ANZUS Crisis, Nuclear Visiting, and Deterrence*, p. 155.

29. Pugh, *The ANZUS Crisis*. Also see McLaurin and Moon, *The United States and the Defense of the Pacific*, pp. 226–227.

30. Andrew Mack, " 'Nuclear Allergy' in the South Pacific," *The Pacific Review* (1989), 2 (4): 331.

31. *Common Security: A Program for Disarmament: A Report of the Independent Commission on Disarmament and Security,* under the chairmanship of Olaf Palme (London: Pan Books, 1982), pp. ix, 139.

32. These points have been assessed by William T. Tow, "Geostrategy in the Asia-Pacific Region," in Steven L. Lamy, ed., *Contemporary International Issues: Contending Perspectives* (Boulder, Colo., and London: Lynne Rienner, 1988), p. 296. They are a summary of common security-related arguments which have developed in New Zealand over the past decade. Representative accounts of the common security argument from a New Zealand perspective are Kennedy Graham, *National Security Concepts of States: New Zealand*, pp. 155–160; Graham, "Common Security—A Link to the Global Age," *New Zealand International Review* (July-August 1986), 11 (4): 12–16, and the arguments contained in the Report of the Defense Committee of Inquiry, *Defense and Security: What New Zealanders Want,* (Wellington: Private Bag, July 1986), pp. 32–37 and 45–50.

33. Robert Manning, "An Uneasy Alliance," *Far Eastern Economic Review* (August 22, 1985), 129 (33): 40. The remark was in response to comments found in Lange's "New Zealand's Security Policy," *Foreign Affairs* (Summer 1985), 63 (5): 1017.

34. Albinski, "The ANZUS Crisis," in Bercovitch, *ANZUS in Crisis*, p. 88.

35. Ramesh Thaker, "Creation of the Nuclear-Free New Zealand Myth," *Asian Survey* (October 1989), 29 (10): 921–922. Also see Michael McKinley, *ANZUS, New Zealand and the Meaning of Life: An Assessment of the Labour Government's Non-Nuclear Policy and Its Implications*, Legislative Research Service Discussion Papers no. 6, 1985–86 (Canberra: Department of the Parliamentary Library, February 1986), esp. pp. 47–49. McKinley is a New Zealander affiliated with the University of Western Australia.

36. Ewan Jamieson, "Folly of Irrational Nuclear Policy," *Pacific Defense Reporter* (October 1988), 15 (4): 35. Also see his "The Wider Implications of New Zealand's Security Policies," *Asia-Pacific Defense Forum* (Winter 1988–1989), 13 (3): 14–21.

37. John Stackhouse, "Britain Sides with U.S. Over Visits to NZ," *The Bulletin* (November 19, 1985), 108 (5494): 114.

38. Author interviews with U.S. Defense Department officials, March 7, 1985, Washington, D.C.

39. Steve Hoadley, "New Zealand's National Defense Interests, Defense Capabilities, and ANZUS," in Berkovitch, *ANZUS in Crisis*, p. 195.

40. See the telegram sent by U.S. Secretary of Defense Caspar Weinberger to CINCPAC Commander Admiral William Crowe, January 9, 1985, which acknowledges that "a number of other countries with nuclear sensitivities, notably Japan, Australia, and our NATO allies, are watching closely how we handle this situation." The text of the telegram was obtained by Peter Hayes under the United States Freedom of Information Act and is cited in Clements, "New Zealand's Role," p. 402.

41. Background is provided by Pugh, *The ANZUS Crisis, Nuclear Visiting, and Deterrence*, pp. 64–68; by William M. Arkin, "Confirm Or Deny," *Bulletin of Atomic Scientists* (December 1985), 41 (11): 4–5; and by Lt. Commander Nicholas L. Flacco, "Whether to Confirm or Deny?" U.S. Naval Institute, *Proceedings* (January 1990), 116 (1043): 52–56.

42. U.S. Government affidavit submitted as part of the *Hudson River Sloop versus U.S. Navy* lawsuit and cited by Arkin, ibid., p. 4.

43. Hearing before the Subcommittee on Asian and Pacific Affairs of the Committee on Foreign Affairs, House of Representatives, *Security Treaty Between Australia, New Zealand, and the United States*, p. 169.

44. Background to the Shultz-Lange discussions is provided by "Secretary Visits Asia, Attends ASEAN and ANZUS Meetings," *Department of State Bulletin* (September 1984), 84 (2090): 7–22; Roderic Alley, "ANZUS and the Nuclear Issue," in Boston and Holland, eds., *The Fourth Labour Government*, pp. 202–203; and John Beaglehole, "ANZUS No 1—New Zealand: The End of an Era," *Pacific Defense Reporter* (April 1985), 11 (10): 8–11.

45. Background paper on "ANZUS and the New Zealand Defense Forces," authored by the New Zealand Defense Ministry and provided to the author (unclassified version), October 19, 1984, pp. 2–6.

46. Some in-depth accounts of the key negotiations conducted during late

1984 and early 1985, however, are beginning to emerge. See, for example, Ewan Jamieson's remarks in an address delivered to Christchurch on July 20, 1987 following his retirement from active service (unpublished draft in author's possession); Alley, "ANZUS and the Nuclear Issue," in Boston and Holland, *The Fourth Labour Government*, pp. 131–136; and Clements, *Back From The Brink*, pp. 131–136. Also see Jamieson's testimony to the public expenditure committee of the New Zealand Parliament while he was still on active duty in March 1985, testimony covered by Roger Foley, "Policy Admits Nuclear Ships: Defense Chief," *The New Zealand Times*, March 24, 1985, p. 2. The basic expectations driving both sides during this stage of negotiations to resolve the ANZUS dispute are well summarized by Stuart McMillan, *Neither Confirm Nor Deny*, pp. 83–84.

47. McMillan, *Neither Confirm Nor Deny*, p. 85. Also see "Lange Warned On 'Trust Me' Policy," *The Dominion* (Wellington), September 5, 1985, p. 1; and Roger Foley, "'Trust Us' Policy Doomed To Failure," *New Zealand Times*, September 8, 1985, p. 2. For background on Lange's relations with the various Labour Party wings, see Michael Pugh, "New Zealand: The Battle for the Middle Ground," *The World Today* (July 1984), 40 (7): 313–314.

48. Koichiro Ueda, "Sato-Nixon Mitsuyaku to Kaku Gunji Domei" ["Sato-Nixon Secret Agreement and Secret Nuclear Military Alliance"], *Zen Eei* (January 1980), no. 446, p. 3. *Zen Eei* is a publication of the Central Committee of the Japanese Communist Party.

49. Niihara Shoji, *Aabakareta Nichibei Kaku Mitsuyaku* [Exposure of the U.S.-Japan Secret Nuclear Agreement] (Tokyo: Shin Nihon Shuppan Sha, 1987) includes a full English and Japanese text of a February 24, 1966, telegram from Secretary of State Dean Rusk to the American Embassy in Tokyo uncovered by Japanese Communist Researchers in the U.S. Library of Congress during 1987. Also see Tsuneo Akaha, "Japan's Three Nonnuclear Principles: A Coming Demise?" *Peace and Change* (1985), 11 (1): 75–89; and Glenn D. Hook, "The Erosion of Anti-Militaristic Principles in Contemporary Japan," *Journal of Peace Research* (December 1988), 25 (4): 387. Suzuki's counterargument is reviewed by Robert F. Reed, *The U.S.-Japan Alliance: Sharing the Burden of Defense* (Washington, D.C.: The National Defense University, 1983), pp. 26–27. The U.S. State Department response is reported in *Time* (April 20, 1987), 129 (16): 47.

50. This point is developed by John Baylis, "Chinese Defense Policy," in Baylis, John Garnett, Ken Booth, and Phil Williams, *Contemporary Strategy*, vol. 2: *The Nuclear Powers* (New York and London: Holmes and Meier, 1987), p. 136.

51. See "French Navy Destroyer in Shanghai," *Bangkok Post*, April 3, 1978, p. 3, reporting on the destroyer *Duguay-Trouin* docking at Shanghai; and a New China News Agency English language report "Royal Navy Ships' Visit to Shanghai," *Xinhua*, September 5, 1980, and reprinted in British Broadcast Corporation, *Summary Of World Broadcasts* FE/6519/A1/1, September 10, 1980. Also see Peter Van Ness, *China and the Question of Nuclear Ship Visits*, p. 4,

which notes that the British Minister of State for Foreign and Commonwealth Affairs, Baroness Young, reported in mid-1986 that China had not asked about the presence of nuclear weapons aboard ships scheduled to visit Chinese ports during July of that year.

52. "Historic U.S. Navy Visit to Qingdao," *Asia-Pacific Defense Forum* (Summer 1987), 12 (2): 2–10.

53. "Not-So-Slow Boat to China," *The New Zealand Herald*, January 14, 1985, p. 6.

54. In an interview with the author, March 7, 1985, Washington, D.C. Author interviews with New Zealand military officials involved in the negotiations confirmed that the combined Chinese/Japanese formula was the operative basis of the bargaining conducted in mid-August 1987 in Wellington. Also see Robert Manning, "Non-Collision Course," *Far Eastern Economic Review* (January 31, 1985), 127 (4): 26–27.

55. Cited in Robert Manning and Colin James, "ANZUS All At Sea," *Far Eastern Economic Review* (February 14, 1985), 127 (6): 12.

56. Specific accounts of the ANZUS functions canceled or downgraded by the U.S.include Dora Alves, "New Zealand and ANZUS: An American View," *The Round Table* (1987), no. 302, pp. 210–211; John Beaglehole, "Labour's Dangerous New Course," *Pacific Defense Reporter* (December 1985–January 1986), 12 (6–7): 14–16; Paul Malone, "NZ To Lose Joint-Source Intelligence," *The Canberra Times*, March 1, 1985, p. 1; and Michael Weiskopf, "U.S. Will Weaken Its New Zealand Links," *The Age* (Melbourne), December 24, 1985, p. 1.

57. Robert Manning, "An Uneasy Alliance," *Far Eastern Economic Review* (August 22, 1985), 129 (33): 40.

58. A comprehensive assessment of the South Pacific Forum's successful efforts to derive a nuclear-free zone treaty and of its specific provisions is by Paul F. Power, "The South Pacific Nuclear-Weapon-Free Zone," p. 455–475. An objective account of New Zealand's interests and behavior leading up to the treaty is found in Ramesh Thakur, *In Defense of New Zealand*, pp. 161–179. The American government's position is assessed and critiqued in U.S. House of Representatives, Hearings and Markup before the Committee on Foreign Affairs and its Subcommittee on Asian and Pacific Affairs, *The South Pacific Nuclear-Free Zone*, 100th Cong., 1st Sess., June 9 and July 15, 1987.

59. Key excerpts of the New Zealand Nuclear-Free Zone, Disarmament, and Arms Control Act are found in McMillan, *Neither Confirm Nor Deny*, pp. 165–168.

60. Tony Garnier, "Security Alarm Prompts Change," *The Evening Post* (Wellington), December 10, 1985, p. 7.

61. In these interviews, it became apparent that New Zealand was prepared to implement its understanding of the Chinese formula as a solution to the ANZUS impasse even beyond the final U.S.-Australian break from ANZUS at San Francisco a year earlier (August 1986).

62. "Lange Plans To Moderate A-Ship Ban," *The International Herald*

Tribune, January 13, 1986, pp. 1, 6; and Richard Long, "Palmer Signals Ship Ban Rebound," *The Dominion* (Wellington), December 7, 1985, p. 1.

63. "Bill To Ban Nuclear Arms and Ships Introduced," *The Press* (Wellington), December 11, 1985, pp. 1, 3.

64. Testimony of Deputy Secretary of Defense Karl Jackson in U.S. House of Representatives, a Hearing before the Subcommittee on Asian and Pacific Affairs of the Committee on Foreign Affairs, *United States Policy Toward New Zealand and Australia*, 99th Cong., 2d Sess., September 25, 1986, pp. 20–21.

65. Albinski, *ANZUS, the United States and Pacific Security*, pp. 50–51.

66. David Porter, "U.S. Rejects NZ Ship Ban Secrecy Offer," *The Dominion*, June 30, 1986, p. 1.

67. Cited in Pugh, *The ANZUS Crisis, Nuclear Visiting, and Deterrence*, p. 177.

68. "Australia-U.S. Relations: Ministerial Talks: Joint Communique," *Australian Foreign Affairs Record* (August 1986), 57 (8): 645–649.

69. "Military Stance Won't Be Changed," *The Evening Post*, August 18, 1987, p. 3.

70. Elisabeth Sexton, "NZ Still Fulfilling Its ANZUS Obligations," *Financial Review*, August 12, 1986, p. 2.

71. "U.S. Will Review Base's Future," *The Evening Post*, January 11, 1986, p. 1. A sympathetic interpretation of the Labour government's policy regarding Harewood/Christchurch is offered by Kevin P. Clements, "New Zealand Paying For Nuclear Ban," *Bulletin of the Atomic Scientists* (July-August 1987), 43 (6): 43–44. A more balanced account is by Michael Richardson, "Not Nuclear Shy When There's Antarctic Business," *Pacific Defense Reporter* (October 1988), 15 (4): 37.

72. David Clark Scott, "New Zealand to Keep Nuclear Ban," *The Christian Science Monitor*, August 9, 1989, p. 3.

73. On the 1987 U.S. move to liberalize New Zealand's participation in training programs, see Colin James, "Nuclear Ice-Breaker," *Far Eastern Economic Review* (October 1, 1987), 138 (40): 40–41.

74. Colin James, "On Speaking Terms," *Far Eastern Economic Review* (March 15, 1990), 147 (11): 20–21; and Norman Kempster, "U.S. Rejects Pleas to Mend Its Ties With New Zealand," *Los Angeles Times*, November 3, 1989 (P.M. final edition), p. 1.

75. Colin James, "Confirm and Deny," *Far Eastern Economic Review* (March 22, 1990), 147 (12): 27.

76. Author interviews with U.S. Department of Defense officials, March 18, 1985, Washington, D.C. Also see Gary Yerky, "Dutch, Belgians Delay Decision Yet Again on New NATO Missiles," *Christian Science Monitor*, December 6, 1984, p. 22.

77. Brad Knickerbocker, "Unwelcome Mats for U.S. Nukes," *Christian Science Monitor*, February 7, 1985, p. 36; and William T. Tow, "The ANZUS Alliance and United States Security Interests," in Bercovitch, *ANZUS in*

Crisis, p. 66. The New Zealand position is discussed by Pugh, *The ANZUS Crisis, Nuclear Visiting, and Deterrence*, pp. 13–14.

78. Albinski, The ANZUS Crisis," p. 93.

79. Clements, "New Zealand's Role in Promoting a Nuclear-Free Pacific," p. 408.

80. For an overview of such trends, see "A Roar from the South Pacific," *Asiaweek* (April 7, 1989), 15 (14): 28–34. Also see Colin L. Rubinstein, "Troublemakers in the Turbulent South Pacific," *Pacific Defense Reporter* (October 1986), 13 (4): 8–9, 19.

81. John C. Dorrance, "The Pacific Islands and U.S. Security Interests," *Asian Survey* (July 1989), 29 (7): 705; and Commander William J. Stewart, U.S. Naval Reserve, "Oceania: Once More Into the Breach," U.S. Naval Institute *Proceedings*, 111/8/989 (July-August 1985), pp. 46–47.

82. Stewart, "Oceania: Once More Into the Breach," pp. 46–49. Also see testimony of Rear Adm. Edward B. Baker, Jr., Director, East Asian and the Pacific Region, Office of the Secretary of Defense, International Security Affairs in *The South Pacific Nuclear-Free Zone*, pp. 91–93.

83. Author interviews in Wellington, August 1987 and related personal correspondence. Australian Defense expert Peter Jennings has written the most thorough assessment of New Zealand force capabilities yet produced in a post-ANZUS context. In his *The Armed Forces of New Zealand and the ANZUS Split: Costs and Consequences*, p. 13, he concludes that the present level of overseas training contact for the Royal New Zealand Navy is simply "far below that required to maintain adequate operational standards."

84. O'Neill, "Foreword," in Bercovitch, *ANZUS in Crisis*, p. xiii.

85. Ed Rampell, "Kwajalein: Furore in Perspective," *Pacific Islands Monthly* (February 1989), 59 (14): 31–32.

86. McLaurin and Moon, *The United States and the Defense of the Pacific*, p. 248. Also see John C. Dorrance, "The Pacific Islands and U.S. Security Interests," *Asian Survey* (July 1989), 29 (7): 711; "If War Came to the Islands," *Pacific Islands Monthly* (May 1986), 57 (5): 11–14; and David Hegarty, "The Soviet Union in the South Pacific in the 1990s," in Babbage, ed., *The Soviets in the Pacific in the 1990s*, p. 118.

87. For general background, consult Richard Herr, "Soviet and Chinese Interests in the Pacific Islands," in National Defense University, *Strategic Cooperation and Competition in the Pacific Islands*, vol. 1: (Washington, DC: NDU, May 17–19, 1989), pp. 319–345; George K. Tanham, *The Soviet Union in the South Pacific*, RAND P-7431 (Santa Monica: The RAND Corporation, April 1988); and Fedor Mediansky, "New Turbulence in South Pacific Waters," *International Herald Tribune*, May 15, 1987, p. 6. On Fiji see "Tatu Mara Plays the Russian Card," *Pacific Islands Monthly* (August 1986), 57 (8): 20–22; and Ed Rampell, "Soviet Objectives 'To Be Disruptive,' " ibid., p. 22.

88. Denis McLean, "The Interests of Extra-Regional Powers," in *Strategic Cooperation and Competition in the Pacific Islands*, esp. pp. 379–380.

89. Joint Committee on Foreign Affairs, Defense, and Trade, The Parlia-

ment of the Commonwealth of Australia, *Australia's Relations with the South Pacific*, p. xlix.

90. Richard Herr, "South Pacific Islanders Question U.S. Friendship," *Far Eastern Economic Review* (January 16, 1986), 131 (3): 26–27.

91. For additional background on U.S. security perspectives and policies concerning these issues, see Henry Albinski, "South Pacific Trends and United States Security Implications: An Introductory Overview," in R. L. Pfaltzgraff and L. R. Vasey, eds., *Strategic Issues in the Southwest Pacific* (Honolulu: Pacific Forum, forthcoming); Albinski, "Security Issues Within the Pacific Islands Community," in *Strategic Cooperation and Competition in the Pacific Islands*, pp. 161–191; and Ambassador Paul Gardner, "United States Policy in the South Pacific: Reconciling Global, Regional, and Local Interests," *Strategic Cooperation and Competition in the Pacific Islands*, pp. 346–375.

92. Research Institue for Peace and Security, Tokyo, *Asian Security, 1989–90.* (London: Brassey's, 1989), p. 197. Jean Chesneaux, *France in the Pacific: A Tentative Analysis*, p. 3; and Trevor Findlay, "New French Nuclear Test Site," *Pacific Research* (August 1988), 1 (1): 16.

93. Cited in Chesneaux, *France in the Pacific.*, p. 3. Also see Robert Aldrich, "France in the South Pacific," in Ravenhill, ed., *No Longer An American Lake?*, p. 92.

94. Mogami, "The South Pacific Nuclear-Free Zone," pp. 421, 428; and "U.S. Rebuffs Treaty for Pacific Nuclear-Free Zone," *The Washington Post*, February 6, 1987, p. A-17.

95. "Secretary's Visit to Asia and the Pacific: New Conference, Singapore, June 19, 1987," *Department of State Bulletin* (August 1987), 87 (2125): 35.

96. Richard H. Ullman, "The Covert French Connection," *Foreign Policy* (Summer 1989), p. 14.

97. Testimony of James Lilley, Deputy Assistant Secretary of State for East Asian and Pacific Region, *Developments in the South Pacific Region*, 99th Cong., 2d Sess., 10 September 1986, pp. 131–132; testimony of Rear Adm. Edward B. Baker, Jr., *The South Pacific Nuclear-Free Zone*, pp. 88–89; and Norman Kempster, "Shultz Defends Nuclear Testing in S. Pacific," *The Washington Post*, June 24, 1987, p. 22. Also see Thomas-Durell Young, "U.S. Policy and the South and Southwest Pacific," *Asian Survey* (July 1988), 28 (7): 785.

98. See Baker and Lilley testimony in *Developments in the South Pacific Region*, pp. 88–97, 128–132; and Robert G. Sutter, "Trade-Offs in U.S. Policy Toward the South Pacific Region," *Journal of Northeast Asian Studies* (Fall 1988), 7 (4): 4, 8–9. For a more critical assessment of the U.S. opposition to antinuclear diplomacy in the South Pacific, consult Paul M. Kattenberg, "New Strategies for U.S. Security Interests in Southeast Asia, the Indian Ocean, and the South Pacific Region," in Ted Galen Carpenter, ed., *Collective Defense or Strategic Independence?* (Lexington, Mass./Toronto: Lexington Books, 1989), pp. 139–141.

99. Statement in Canberra, November 25, 1985, cited in Chesneaux, *France*

in the Pacific, p. 10. Also see his remarks in Graeme Dobell, "Superpower Fallout May Hit Pacific Mini-States," *New Straits Times*, April 21, 1987, p. 8

100. Thomas-Durell Young, "U.S. Policy and the South and Southwest Pacific," *Asian Survey* (July 1988) 28 (7): 787.

101. Ross Babbage, *The Prospects For Security Cooperation Between The ANZUS Allies Till the Turn of the Century*, The Strategic and Defense Studies Center, Reference Paper no. 145 (Canberra: The Australian National University, February 1987), p. 13. Also see Lewis M. Simons, "New Zealand Military Fears Isolation," *San Jose Mercury News*, April 24, 1988, pp. 15–16; and Knickerbocker, "Unwelcome Mats for U.S. Nukes," pp. 1, 36.

102. "Defense Force Review Calls for Sweeping Cuts [Hong Kong Agence France Presse Report] March 2, 1989, translated and reprinted in FBIS, *East Asia*, March 2, 1989, pp. 58–59. Also see John Beaglehole, "New Zealand Deeply Divided and Deeply Confused," *Pacific Defense Reporter 1987 Annual Reference Edition* (December 1986–January 1987), 13 (6–7): 19–20; and David Clark Scott, "Jilted by US, Antinuke New Zealand Finds Own Way in Military Buildup," *The Christian Science Monitor*, April 13, 1988, p. 7.

103. David Barber, "Phasing Out the Force," *Far Eastern Economic Review* (January 8, 1987), 135 (2): 15.

104. Steve Hoadley, "New Zealand's South Pacific Strategy," in *Strategic Cooperation and Conflict in the Pacific Islands*, pp. 276–313 and David Clark Scott, "Jilted by U.S., Antinuke New Zealand Finds Own Way in Military Buildup," *The Christian Science Monitor*, April 3, 1988, pp. 7, 9.

105. Michael McKinley, "The New Zealand Perspective on ANZUS and Nuclear Weapons," in Ravenhill, ed., *No Longer An American Lake?*, pp. 69, 66–70.

106. Malcolm Templeton, *Defense and Security: What New Zealand Needs*, pp. 28, 34–35.

107. For general background on South Pacific threat perceptions and political change, see William T. Tow, "The ANZUS Dispute: Testing U.S. Extended Deterrence in Alliance Politics," *Political Science Quarterly* (Spring 1089), 104 (1): esp. 141–147.

108. New Zealand Ministry of Defense, *Review of Defense Policy, 1987* (Wellington: V.R. Ward, Government Printer, 1987), p. 6 ; David Barber, "Self-Reliant Security," *Far Eastern Economic Review* (March 12, 1987), 135 (11): 25; and J. H. Beaglehole, "Domestic Constraints and Regional Commitments," *Pacific Defense Reporter* (December 1988–January 1989), 15 (6–7): 19–20.

109. Babbage, *The Prospects for Security Co-operation*, p. 12.

110. Jennings, *The Armed Forces of New Zealand*, pp. 86–87. Emphasis is his. Also see the testimony of Rear Adm. Edward B. Baker, Jr., Director, East Asia and Pacific Region, U.S. Department of Defense, International Security Affairs, in U.S. House of Representatives, Hearing, *Developments in the South Pacific Region*.

111. Report of the Defense Committee of Inquiry, *Defense and Security: What New Zealanders Want*, pp. 66–67.

112. Peter Jennings, "Who Can Put Humpty Dumpty Together Again?" *Pacific Defense Reporter* (August 1987), 14 (2): 24; Simon Kilroy, "Government Acts To Downplay Comments on ANZUS," *The Star* (Auckland), December 13, 1986, p. 1; and Frank Cranston, "Australia To Go It Alone with Kangaroo '86: No U.S. Role in Big Defense Exercise," *The Canberra Times*, June 19, 1986, p. 11.

113. Melbourne Overseas Service broadcast, reprinted as "Lange Defends Alliance with Australia," FBIS, *East Asia*, November 7, 1988, p. 71.

114. Cited in P. Lewis Young, "Australia and New Zealand—Strains in Relations Despite the Camaraderie," *Asian Defense Journal* (May 1989), p. 12; and "Questions Over Frigate Deal," *Pacific Islands Monthly* (October 1989), 59 (21): 16.

115. Bercovitch, "Conclusion," in Bercovitch, ed., *ANZUS in Crisis*, pp. 241–242.

116. This theme is developed by Alan Burnett, *The A-NZ-US Triangle*, pp. 152–154, 164–166; and by a review of Burnett's book by Denis McLean in *New Zealand International Review* (January-February 1989), 14 (1): 28–29.

117. McLean, ibid. Also see Young, "Australia and New Zealand," pp. 15–17.

118. Pugh, *The ANZUS Crisis, Nuclear Visiting, and Deterrence*, pp. 9–10.

7. CONCLUSION

1. Lawrence Freedman, "General Deterrence and the Balance of Power," *Review of International Studies* (April 1989), 15 (2): 203.

2. Freedman, "General Deterrence," p. 91. Also see Nayan Chanda, "A Dispersion Of Power," *Far Eastern Economic Review* (March 30, 1989), 143 (13): 30–32 for a corroborative analysis.

3. For in-depth assessment of this point, see McLaurin and Moon, *The United States and the Defense of the Pacific*, pp. 44–45.

4. These are weighed in some detail by a highly useful survey authored in "The Yen Block," *The Economist* (July 15, 1989), special supplement, 312 (7611): 1–20.

5. Tai Ming Cheng, "Command of the Seas," *Far Eastern Economic Review* (July 27, 1989), 145 (30): 16–20.

6. S. Karene Witcher and Raphael Pura, "Hawke's Asia-Pacific Plan Faces Pitfalls," *The Asian Wall Street Journal*, July 4, 1989, pp. 1, 8; and Raphael Pura, "ASEAN Reacts Coolly to Calls for New Forum," *The Asian Wall Street Journal*, July 5, 1989, pp. 1, 6.

7. The figures are extracted from a 1985 RAND Corporation study and are cited in Doug Bandow, "A Stronger South Korea Can Now Stand on Its Own, So Bring U.S. Troops Home," *Los Angeles Times*, May 9, 1989), part 2, p. 7.

8. Robert A. Manning, *Asian Policy*, p. 34.

9. Zagoria, "The Sino-Soviet Conflict," in Alagappa, ed., *In Search Of Peace*, pp. 14–15.

10. V. Vinogradov, "They Entrap," *Krasnaya Zvesda* [Red Star], December 24, 1987, p. 3, as translated in reprinted in JPRS-UMA-88-006, March 28, 1986, pp. 89–90.

11. For example, see Konstantin Deribas, "New Leaders In Tokyo," *International Affairs* [Moscow] (1988), No. 3, pp. 81–85. Deribas speculated that the Takeshita government and its successors would continue what had been a "visible rightward drift in [Japanese] foreign policy" under Yasahiro Nakasone and that Japanese defense potential would be built up in collaboration with U.S. nuclear strategy.

12. Paul Kennedy, "Can the U.S. Remain Number One?," p. 42.

13. Robert Sutter, "China: Coping with the Evolving Strategic Environment," in Young Whan Kihl and Lawrence E. Grinter, eds., *Security, Strategy, and Policy Responses in the Pacific Rim*, p. 110.

14. Vernon Aspaturian brilliantly characterizes the Soviet legacy of identity crisis vis-a-vis China as it had evolved by the mid-1950s with the following passage: "It was bad enough that the Soviet leaders felt inferior when they compared themselves to the capitalist West. Imagine their shock and surprise to be treated with disdain and almost contempt by their junior Chinese partners, after Mao installed himself in Beijing. Instead of finding leaders whose department and behavior befittingly reflected a country much more backward and poverty-striken than Russia, whom the Soviet leaders could measure themselves against with confidence and self-assurance, they found a group of elegant, highly cultured, aesthetically sensitive, and educated Mandarins, whose contempt and disdain for the manners of their Soviet counterparts were barely concealed."

Vernon V. Aspaturian, "The Domestic Sources of Soviet Policy Toward China," in Douglas T. Stuart and William T. Tow, eds., *China, the Soviet Union, and the West* (Boulder, Colo.: Westview Press, 1982), p. 55. Still outstanding differences impeding Sino-Soviet relations are covered by Steven M. Goldstein, "Diplomacy and Protest: The Sino-Soviet Summit," especially pp. 58–59.

15. Gaddis summarizes Kennan's thesis, advanced piecemeal in a number of documents. See John L. Gaddis, *Strategies of Containment*, esp. p. 56.

16. Frank C. Carlucci, *Annual Report to the Congress FY 1990*, p. 41.

17. Robert A. Scalapino, "Asia and the United States: The Challenges Ahead," *Foreign Affairs* (1990), 69 (1): 114.

18. "The Biggest Military Exercise in History?" *Pacific Research* (February 1989), 2 (1): 13–14. A report on the "modification" of the exercise's simulated offensive mission and a change of its locale is in *Pacific Research* (February 1990), 3 (1): 11.

19. A. Sergeyev, "Nuclear Disarmament and Security in the Far East," *International Affairs* [Moscow] (1988), no. 1, p. 40.

20. Edwin C. Meyer and Paul H. Kreisberg, "Overhaul U.S. Security

Policy in Asia," *The New York Times*, May 19, 1989, p. 15. This author's emphasis.

21. See Grinter and Kihl, "The Prospect for Strategic Rivalry and Security Cooperation in Pacific Asia," in Grinter and Kihl, eds., *Security, Strategy, and Policy Responses*, p. 245.

22. Lebow and Stein, "Beyond Deterrence," p. 40.

23. John W. Lewis, "Defining the Strategic Context of Asia," in International Strategic Institute at Stanford, Stanford University and Institute of Far East Studies, Soviet Academy of Sciences, *Peace, Security, and Cooperation in the Asian-Pacific Region* (Stanford: Center for International Security and Arms Control, January 1989), pp. 3–4; and James E. Goodby, "Stability, Security, and Cooperation in Northeast Asia," also in *Peace, Security, and Cooperation*, p. 91.

24. Some of these measures are suggested by Zagoria, "Soviet Policy In East Asia," pp. 136–138.

25. For a corroborating view, see Andrew Mack, "Is Pyongyang the Next Proliferator?" *Pacific Research* (February 1990), 3 (1): 7.

26. Jeffrey Smith, "Crowe Suggests New Approach on Naval Nuclear Arms Cuts, "*The Washington Post*, January 8, 1990, pp. 1, 4. Also see "Crowe: Time to Control Navies," *Arms Control Today* (February 1990), 20 (1): 33; and "The Navy Way," *Pacific Research* (February 1990), 3 (1): 12.

27. See an interview with Ronald F. Lehman, Director of the U.S. Arms Control and Disarmament Agency, in "Asia-Pacific Arms Control: U.S. Leaves Initiative to Allies," *International Herald Tribune*, April 2, 1990, p. 2. A representative argument is also offered by James R. Blaker, "Naval Arms Control: The Opposition," *Arms Control Today* (February 1990), 20 (1): 16–20. Blacker is a former Assistant Secretary of Defense (1978–1980), and is now with the Hudson Institute.

28. Recent articles supporting this argument include Michael L. Ross, "Disarmament at Sea," *Foreign Policy* (Winter 1989–1990), no. 77, pp. 94–112; and Richard Fieldhouse, "The Case for Naval Arms Control," *Arms Control Today* (February 1990), 20 (1): 9–15.

29. The cooperative international regime proposal for the Spratlys has been suggested by Mark Valencia, "All-for-Everyone Solution," *Far Eastern Economic Review* (March 30, 1989), 143 (13): 20–21.

30. *Report of The Commission On Long-Term Strategy* (Washington, D.C.: USGPO, January 1988).

31. Terry L. Deibel, "Changing Patterns of Collective Defense: U.S. Security Commitments in the Third World," in Alan Ned Sabrosky, ed., *Alliances in U.S. Foreign Policy: Issues in the Quest for Collective Defense* (Boulder, Colo. and London: Westview Press, 1988), p. 128.

Selected Bibliography

INTRODUCTION

Achen, Christopher H. and Duncan Snidal, "Rational Deterrence Theory and Comparative Case Studies." *World Politics* (January 1989), 41 (2): 143–169.

Arkin, William and David Chappell. "Forward Offensive Strategy: Raising the Stakes in the Pacific." *World Policy Journal* (Summer 1985), 2 (3): 481–500.

Barnett, Richard J. *The Alliance: America, Europe, and Japan—Makers of the Postwar World.* New York: Simon & Schuster, 1985.

Bello, Walden, Lyuba Zarsky, and Peter Hayes. *American Lake: Nuclear Peril in the Pacific.* New York: Penguin, 1987.

Ben-Zvi, Abraham. *The Illusion of Deterrence: The Roosevelt Presidency and the Origins of the Pacific War.* Boulder, Colo. and London: Westview, 1987.

Betts, Richard. *Surprise Attack: Lessons For Defense Planning.* Washington D.C.: Brookings Institution, 1982.

Chomsky, Noam. *At War with Asia.* New York: Pantheon, 1970.

Cordesman, Anthony H. *Deterrence in the 1980s: Part I—American Strategic Forces and Extended Deterrence.* Adelphi Papers no. 175. London: International Institute for Strategic Studies, 1982.

Cumings, Bruce. "Power and Plenty in Northeast Asia: The Evolution of U.S. Policy." *World Policy Journal* (Winter 1987–1988), 5 (1): 79–106.

Gaddis, John L. *Strategies of Containment.* New York: Oxford University Press, 1982.

Greene, Fred. *U.S. Policy and the Security of Asia.* New York: McGraw-Hill, 1968.

Hellman, Donald C. *Japan and East Asia: The New International Order.* New York: Praeger, 1972.

Huntington, Samuel. *The Common Defense.* New York: Columbia University Press, 1961.

International Institute for Strategic Studies. *East Asia, the West, and Interna-*

tional Security: Prospects for Peace. Adelphi Papers nos. 216–218. London: IISS, 1987.

Kahin, George McT. *Intervention: How America Became Involved in Vietnam.* New York: Knopf, 1986.

Kennan, George. "X," "The Sources of Soviet Conduct." *Foreign Affairs* (July 1947), 25 (4): 562–582.

Kurth, James R. "The Pacific Basin versus the Atlantic Alliance: Two Paradigms of International Relations." The American Academy of Political and Social Science, Annals, *The Pacific Region: Challenges to Policy and Theory* (September 1989), No. 505. pp. 34–45.

Layne, Christopher. "The Real Conservative Agenda." *Foreign Policy* (Winter 1985–1986), no. 61, pp. 73–93.

Manning, Robert. *Asia Policy: The New Soviet Challenge in the Pacific.* New York: Priority Press, 1988.

Nishihara, Masashi. *East Asia Security and the Trilateral Countries.* New York and London: New York University Press, 1985.

Nuechterlein, Donald E. *America Overcommitted: United States National Interests in the 1980s.* Lexington: University Press of Kentucky, 1985.

Olsen, Edward. *U.S.-Japan Strategic Reciprocity.* Stanford: Hoover Institution Press, 1985.

Palmer, Norman D. *Westward Watch: The United States and the Changing Western Pacific.* Washington D.C.: Pergamon Brassey's, 1987.

Ravenal, Earl C. "The Nixon Doctrine and Our Asian Commitments." *Foreign Affairs* (January 1971), 49 (2): 201–217.

Ravenal, Earl C., ed. *Peace With China? U.S. Decisions for Asia.* New York: Liveright, 1971.

Reagan, Ronald. *National Security Strategy of the United States.* Washington D.C.: USGPO, January 1988.

Smoke, Richard. "Extended Deterrence: Some Observations." *U.S. Naval War College Review* (September-October 1983), 36 (5): 37–48.

Solomon, Richard A., ed. *Asian Security in the 1980s: Problems and Policies in a Time of Transition* Cambridge, Mass.: Oelgeschlager, Gunns & Hain, 1980.

Solomon, Richard A., ed. *The Soviet Far East Military Buildup.* Dover, Mass.: Auburn House, 1986.

Stuart, Douglas T. and William T. Tow. *The Limits of Alliance: NATO Out-of-Area Problems Since 1949.* Baltimore and London: Johns Hopkins University Press, 1990.

Taylor, Maxwell. *The Uncertain Trumpet.* New York: Harper, 1959.

U.S. Department of Defense, *A Strategic Framework for the Asian Pacific Rim: Looking Toward the 21st Century.* Washington, D.C.: USGPO, April 19, 1990.

Walt, Stephen M. "The Case of Finite Containment: Analyzing U.S. Grand Strategy." *International Security* (Summer 1989), 14 (1): 5–49.

I. EXTENDED DETERRENCE STRATEGY AND THE DOMINANT PLAYER POSTURE

Betts, Richard. *Nuclear Blackmail and Nuclear Balance*. Washington D.C.: The Brookings Institution, 1987.

Bobbit, Philip. *Democracy and Deterrence*. London and Basingstoke: Macmillan, 1988.

Brzezinski, Zbigniew. *Game Plan: A Geostrategic Framework of the U.S.-Soviet Contest*. Boston: Atlantic Monthly Press, 1986.

Byers, R. B. *Deterrence in the 1980s: Crisis and Dilemma*. London: Croom Helm, 1985.

Commission on Integrated Long-Term Strategy. *Discriminate Deterrence*. Washington, D.C.: USGPO, January 1988.

Daalder, Ivo. *NATO Strategy and Ballistic Missile Defense*. Adelphi Papers no. 233. London: International Institute for Strategic Studies, Winter 1988.

Epstein, Joshua. "Horizontal Escalation: Sour Notes of a Recurrent Theme." *International Security* (Winter 1983–1984), 8 (3): 19–31.

Freedman, Lawrence. *The Evolution of Nuclear Strategy*. New York: St. Martin's Press, 1981.

George, Alexander and Richard Smoke. *Deterrence in American Foreign Policy*. New York and London: Columbia University Press, 1981.

Huth, Paul. *Extended Deterrence and the Prevention of War*. New Haven: Yale University Press, 1988.

Huth, Paul and Bruce Russett, "Deterrence Failure and Crisis Escalation." *International Studies Quarterly* (March 1988), 32 (1): 29–45.

Hearings before the Committee on Armed Services, United States Senate. *National Security Strategy*, 100th Cong., 1st Sess., 1987.

Huntington, Samuel P., ed. *The Strategic Imperative*. Cambridge, Mass.: Ballinger, 1982.

Jackson, Karl and Wiwat Mungkandi, eds. *United States-Thailand Relations*. Berkeley: University of California, Institute of East Asian Studies, 1986.

Jervis, Robert. "Deterrence Theory Revisited." *World Politics* (January 1979), 30 (2): 289–324.

Jervis, Robert. *The Illogic of American Nuclear Strategy*. Ithaca and London: Cornell University Press, 1984.

Jervis, Robert, Richard Ned Lebow, Janice Gross Stein et al. *Psychology and Deterrence*. Baltimore and London: Johns Hopkins University Press, 1985.

Kahn, Herman. *On Escalation: Metaphors and Scenarios*. New York: Praeger, 1965.

Kennedy, Paul M. *The Rise and Fall of the Great Powers: Economic Change and Military Conflict from 1500 to 2000.]* New York: Random House, 1987.

Komer, Robert. *Maritime Strategy or Coalition Warfare?* Cambridge, Mass.: Abt Books, 1984.

Lebow, Richard Ned and Janice Gross Stein. " Beyond Deterrence." *Journal of Social Issues* (1987) 43 (4): 5–71.

Litwak, Robert S. *Detente and the Nixon Doctrine: American Foreign Policy and the Pursuit of Stability, 1969–1976.]* Cambridge: Cambridge University Press, 1984.

McLaurin, Ronald D. and Chung-in Moon. *The United States and the Defense of the Pacific.* Boulder, Colo./Seoul: Westview Press/Kyungnam University Press, 1989.

Mearsheimer, John. "A Strategic Misstep: The Maritime Strategy and Deterrence in Europe." *International Security* (Fall 1986) 11 (2): 3–57.

Mearsheimer, John. *Conventional Deterrence.* Ithaca and London: Cornell University Press, 1983.

Mochizuki, Mike. "Japan's Search for Strategy." *International Security* (Winter 1983–84), 8 (3): 152–179.

Nacht, Michael. *The Age of Vulnerability.* Washington D.C.: The Brookings Institution, 1985.

Nunn, Sam. "What Forces Europe, What Forces Asia?" *The Washington Review of Strategic and International Studies* (January 1978), 1 (1): 10–18.

Orme, John. "Deterrence Failures: A Second Look." *International Security* (Spring 1987), 11 (3): 69–129.

Quester, George H. *The Future of Nuclear Deterrence* Lexington: D.C. Heath, 1986.

Sabrosky, Alan Ned, ed. *Alliances in U.S. Foreign Policy: Issues in the Quest of Collective Defense.* Boulder: Westview, 1988.

Scalapino, Robert. "Asia's Future." *Foreign Affairs* (Fall 1987), 66 (1): 77–108.

Schelling, Thomas. *Arms and Influence.* New Haven: Yale University Press, 1966.

Simon, Sheldon. *The Future of Asia-Pacific Collaboration.* Lexington, Mass./Toronto: Lexington Books, 1988.

Slocombe, Walter B. "Extended Deterrence." *Washington Quarterly* (Fall 1984), 7 (4): 93–103.

Smoke, Richard. "Extended Deterrence: Some Observations." *Naval War College Review.* (September/October 1983), 36 (5): 37–48.

Smoke, Richard. *War: Controlling Escalation.* Cambridge, Mass.: Harvard University Press, 1977.

Snyder, Glenn H. *Deterrence and Defense: Toward a Theory of National Security.* Princeton: Princeton University Press, 1961.

Weede, Erich. "Extended Deterrence by Superpower Alliance." *Journal of Conflict Resolution* (June 1983), 27 (2): 231–254.

Weinberger, Caspar W., Secretary of Defense. *Annual Report to Congress Fiscal Year 1983* Washington, D.C.: USGPO, February 1982.

Weinstein, Franklin and Fuji Kamiya, eds. *The Security of Korea: U.S. and Japanese Perspectives in the 1980s.* Boulder, Colo.: Westview Press, 1980.

2. DOMINANT AND TRANSITIONAL PLAYERS IN THE ASIA-PACIFIC

Albinski, Henry. *Australian External Policy Under Labor.* Vancouver: University of British Columbia Press, 1977.

Ball, Desmond. *Australia and the Global Strategic Balance.* Canberra Papers on Strategy and Defense no. 49. Canberra: The Australia National University, 1989.

Bandow, Doug. "Leaving Korea." *Foreign Policy* (Winter 1989–1990), 77, pp. 77–93.

Betts, Richard. "Washington, Tokyo, and Northeast Asia Security." *Journal of Northeast Asian Studies* (December 1983) 6 (4): 5–30.

Brands, H. W. "Testing Massive Retaliation: Credibility and Crisis Management in the Taiwan Strait." *International Security* (Spring 1988), 12 (4): 124–151.

Brands, H.W. "The United States and the Reemergence of Independent Japan." *Pacific Affairs* (Fall 1986), 59 (3): 387–401.

Bundy, McGeorge. *Danger and Survival: Choices About the Bomb in the First Fifty Years.* New York: Random House, 1988.

Calingaert, Daniel. "Nuclear Weapons and the Korean War." *Journal of Strategic Studies* (June 1988), 11 (2): 177–202.

Camilleri, Joseph A. *The Australian-New Zealand-U.S. Alliance: Regional Security in the Nuclear Age.]* Boulder: Westview, 1987.

Chang, Gordon H. "To the Nuclear Brink: Eisenhower, Dulles, and the Quemoy-Matsu Crisis." *International Security* (Spring 1988), 12 (4): 96–123.

Cohen, Warren I. and Akira Iriye, eds. *The Great Powers in East Asia; 1953–1960.* New York: Columbia University Press, 1990.

Cumings, Bruce. "Power and Plenty in Northeast Asia: The Evolution of U.S. Policy." *World Policy Journal* (Winter 1987–1988) 5(3): 79–106.

Dibb, Paul. *Review of Australia's Defense Capabilities.* Canberra: Australian Government Publishing Service, 1986.

Dingman, Roger. "Atomic Diplomacy During the Korean War." *International Security* (Winter 1988–1989), 13 (3): 50–91.

Documents Concerning U.S.-Japan Mutual Security Negotiations. Tokyo: Diplomatic Records Office, Microfilm Section, December 1987.

Eisenhower, Dwight D. *Waging Peace, 1956–1961.* Garden City, New York: Doubleday, 1965.

Fallows, James. "Containing Japan." *The Atlantic* 263, no. 5 (February 1988): 40–54.

Foltos, Lester J. "The New Pacific Barrier: America's Search for Security in the Pacific, 1945–1947." *Diplomatic History* (Summer 1989), 13 (3): 317–342.

Foot, Rosemary. *The Wrong War: American Policy and the Dimensions of the Korean Conflict, 1950–1953.* Ithaca and London: Cornell University Press, 1985.

Fry, Greg. "Toward a South Pacific Nuclear Free Zone." *Bulletin of the Atomic Scientists* (June-July 1985), 41 (6): 16–20.

Gaddis, John Lewis. *Strategies of Containment*. New York: Oxford, 1982.

Greene, Fred. *U.S. Policy and the Security of Asia*. New York: McGraw-Hill, 1968.

Gurtov, Melvin and Byong Moo Hwang. *China Under Threat: The Politics of Strategy and Diplomacy*. Baltimore: Johns Hopkins University Press, 1980.

Institute for Foreign Policy Analysis, Inc. *The U.S.-Korean Security Relationship: Prospects and Challenges for the 1990s*. Washington, D.C.: Pergamon-Brassey's, 1988.

Iriye, Akira and Warren I. Cohen, eds. *The United States and Japan in the Postwar World*. Lexington, Kentucky: The University Press of Kentucky, 1989.

Jervis, Robert. "The Impact of the Korean War on the Cold War." *The Journal of Conflict Resolution* (December 1980), 24 (4): 563–592.

Kataoka, Tetsuya and Ramon H. Myers. *Defending an Economic Superpower*. Boulder: Westview, 1989.

Kennan, George F. *Memoirs, 1925–1950*. Boston: Little, Brown, 1967.

Kihl, Young Wahn and Lawrence E. Grinter, eds. *Asia-Pacific Security: Emerging Challenges and Responses*. Boulder: Westview Press, 1986.

Lee, Chae-jin and Hideo Sato. *U.S. Policy Toward Japan and Korea*. New York: Praeger, 1982.

Lewis, John Wilson and Xue Litai. *China Builds the Bomb*. Stanford: Stanford University Press, 1988.

Makin, John H. and Donald C. Hellman, eds. *Sharing World Leadership: A New Era for America and Japan* Washington, D.C.: American Enterprise Institute for Public Policy Research, 1989.

Ministry of National Defense, The Republic of Korea, *Defense White Paper 1989* Seoul: Korean Institute of Defense Analysis, 1989.

Morley, James W., ed. *Security Interdependence in the Asia-Pacific Region*. Lexington, Mass. and Toronto: D.C. Heath, 1986.

Nam, Joo-Hong. *America's Commitment to South Korea*. Cambridge: Cambridge University Press, 1986.

Nixon, Richard M. *U.S. Foreign Policy in the 1970s, A New Strategy for Peace*. Washington, D.C.: USGPO, 1970.

Ogawa, Shinichi. *Problems of U.S. Extended Deterrence for Japan*. USJP Occasional Paper 88–13. Cambridge, Mass.: Harvard University, 1988, Program on U.S.-Japan Relations.

Packard, George. *Protest in Tokyo: The Security Treaty Crisis of 1960*. Princeton: Princeton University Press, 1966.

Pollack, Jonathan D. *Into the Vortex: China, the Sino-Soviet Alliance, and the Korean War*. Santa Monica: The RAND Corporation, forthcoming.

Pye, Lucien W. "Dilemmas for America in China's Modernization." *International Security* (Summer 1979), 4 (1): 3–19.

Richelson, Jeffrey T. and Desmond Ball. *The Ties That Bind*. Boston: Allen & Unwin, 1985.

Rosenberg, David Alan. "U.S. Nuclear Stockpile, 1945–1950." *Bulletin of the Atomic Scientists* (May 1982), 38 (5): 25–30.

Schneibel, James F. and Robert J. Watson. *The History of the Joint Chiefs of Staff and National Policy.* Vol. 3: *The Korean War—Part II.* Washington, D.C.: Historical Division, Joint Secretariat, Joint Chiefs of Staff, March 1979.

Strategic Cooperation and Competition in the Pacific Islands. 2 volumes. Washington, D.C.: National Defense University, May 17–19, 1989.

Tow, William T. "The ANZUS Dispute: Testing U.S. Extended Deterrence in Alliance Politics." *Political Science Quarterly* (Spring 1989), 104 (1): 117–149.

Trachtenberg, Marc. "A 'Wasting Asset': American Strategy and the Shifting Nuclear Balance." *International Security* (Winter 1988–89), 13 (3): 5–49.

United States Senate. Hearings before the Subcommittee on United States Security Agreements and Commitments Abroad of the Committee on Foreign Relations. *United States Security Agreements and Commitments Abroad: Part 4—Republic of China].* 91st Cong., 2d Sess., 1970.

Van de Velde, James R. "Japan's Nuclear Umbrella: U.S. Extended Deterrence for Japan." *Journal of Northeast Asian Studies* (1988), 7 (4): 16–51.

Vogel, Steven K. *Japanese High Technology Politics, Politics, and Power.* Berkeley: Berkeley Roundtable on the International Economy, March 1989.

Whiting, Allen S. "Quemoy in 1958; Mao's Miscalculations." *The China Quarterly* (June 1975), no. 62, pp. 263–270.

3. ASPIRING PLAYER I: THE SOVIET UNION

Alagappa, Muthiah, ed. *In Search of Peace: Confidence Building and Conflict Reduction in the Pacific.* Kuala Lumpur: ISIS, Malaysia, 1988.

Babbage, Ross, ed. *The Soviets in the Pacific in the 1990s.* Rushcutter's Bay, Australia: Brassey's, 1989.

Blacker, Coit D. "The USSR and Asia in 1989: Recasting Relationships." *Asian Survey* (January 1990): 30 (1): 1–12.

Chang, Gordon H. *Friends and Enemies: the United States, China, and the Soviet Union.* Stanford: Stanford University Press, 1990.

Clark, Susan L., ed. *Gorbachev's Agenda: Changes in Soviet Foreign and Domestic Policy.* Boulder, Colo.: Westview, 1989.

Clemens, Walter C. *The Arms Race and Sino-Soviet Relations.* Stanford: Hoover Institution Publications, 1968.

Dibb, Paul. *The Soviet Union: The Incomplete Superpower.* London and Basingstoke: Macmillan, 1986.

Ekedahl, Carolyn McGiffert and Elvin A. Goodman, "Gorbachev's 'New Directions' in Asia," *Journal of Northeast Asian Studies* (Fall 1989), 8 (3): 3–24.

Ellison, Herbert, ed. *The Sino-Soviet Conflict: A Global Perspective.* Seattle: University of Washington Press, 1982.

Garrett, Banning and Bonnie Glaser. *War and Peace: The Views from Moscow and Beijing*. Papers in International Affairs no. 20. Berkeley: University of California, Institute of International Studies, 1984.

Garthoff, Raymond L., ed. *Sino-Soviet Military Relations*. New York: Praeger, 1966.

Gelman, Harry. *The Soviet Far East Buildup and Soviet Risk-Taking Against China*. R-2943–AF. Santa Monica: The RAND Corporation, August 1982.

Gibert, Stephen P., ed. *Security in Northeast Asia: Approaching the Pacific Century*. Boulder, Colo.: Westview, 1988.

Griffith, William E. *The Sino-Soviet Rift*. Cambridge, Mass.: The MIT Press, 1964.

Hao Yufan and Zhai Zhihai, "China's Decision to Enter the Korean War: History Revisited," *The China Quarterly* No. 121 (March 1990), pp. 94–115.

Horelick, Arnold. "The Soviet Union's Asian Collective Security Proposal: A Club in Search of Members." *Pacific Affairs* (Fall 1974), no. 47: 269–285.

Jacobsen, C. G. *Sino-Soviet Relations Since Mao*. New York: Praeger, 1981.

Kiste, Robert and Richard Herr. *The Potential for Soviet Penetration of the South Pacific Islands: An Assessment.]* Paper prepared for the U.S. Department of State, December 1984.

Kovalenko, Ivan. *Soviet Policy for Asian Peace and Security*. Moscow: Progress Publishers, 1979.

Liu Xiao. *Chu Shi Sulian ba nian* [Eight Years as Ambassador to the Soviet Union]. Beijing: Zhonggong dangshi ziliao chuban she, 1986.

MccGwire, Michael. "The Geopolitical Importance of Strategic Waterways in the Asia-Pacific." *Orbis* (Fall 1975), 19 (3): 1058–1076.

MccGwire, Michael. *Military Objectives in Soviet Foreign Policy*. Washington, D.C.: The Brookings Institution, 1985.

McGregor, Charles. *The Sino-Vietnamese Relationship and the Soviet Union*. Adelphi Papers no. 232. London: International Institute for Strategic Studies, Autumn, 1988.

Menon, Rajan. "New Thinking and Northeast Asian Security Problems." *Problems of Communism* (March-June 1989), 38 (2): 1–32.

Nelson, Harvey. *Power and Insecurity: Beijing, Moscow, and Washington 1949–1988*. Boulder: Lynne Rienner Publishers, 1989.

Nie Rongzhen Huiyilu (Memoirs of Nie Rongzhen). Beijing: People's Liberation Army Press, 1984.

Niiseki, Ninya, ed. *The Soviet Union in Transition*. Boulder, Colo.: Westview, 1987.

Odom, William. "Soviet Military Doctrine." *Foreign Affairs* (Winter 1988–1989), 67 (2): 114–134.

Pike, Douglas. *Vietnam and the Soviet Union*. Boulder, Colo.: Westview, 1987.

Polomka, Peter. *The Two Korea's: Catalyst for Conflict in East Asia?* Adelphi Papers no. 208. London: International Institute for Strategic Studies, Summer 1986.

Robertson, Myles. *Soviet Policy Towards Japan: An Analysis of Trends in the 1970s and 1980s*. Cambridge: Cambridge University Press, 1988.

Robinson, Thomas W. "The Sino-Soviet Border Dispute: Background, Development, and the March 1969 Clashes." *American Political Science Review* (December 1972), 66 (4): 1175–1202.

Segal, Gerald. *Defending China*. London: Oxford University Press, 1985.

Segal, Gerald, ed. *The Soviet Union in East Asia: Predicaments of Power*. London/Boulder, Colo.: Heinemann/Westview, 1983.

Sokolovskiy, V.D. *Soviet Military Strategy*. London: MacDonald and Jane's, 1975.

"Statement by the Spokesman of the Chinese Government." *Beijing Review* (September 6, 1963), 6 (36): 7–16.

Talbot, Strobe, ed. and trans. *Khrushchev Remembers: The Last Testament*. Boston and Toronto: Little, Brown, 1974.

Thakur, Ramesh and Carlyle A. Thayer, eds. *The Soviet Union as an Asian-Pacific Power*. Boulder, Colo.: Westview, 1987.

Tritten, J. J. *Soviet Naval Forces and Nuclear Warfare*. Boulder, Colo.: Westview, 1986.

Ulam, Adam. *Expansion and Coexistence*, 2d ed. New York: Praeger, 1974.

U.S. Department of Defense. *Soviet Military Power: Prospects for Change 1989*. Washington, D.C.: USGPO, 1989.

van Oudenaren, John. *Deterrence, Warfighting and Soviet Military Doctrine*. Adelphi Papers no. 210. London: International Institute for Strategic Studies, Summer 1986.

Whence the Threat to Peace, 4th ed. Moscow: Novosti Press Military Publishing House, 1987.

Wich, Richard. *Sino-Soviet Crisis Politics*. Cambridge, Mass.: Harvard University Press, 1980.

Zagoria, Donald Z., ed. *Soviet Policy in East Asia*. New Haven: Yale University Press, 1982.

4. ASPIRING PLAYER II: THE PEOPLE'S REPUBLIC OF CHINA

Barnett, A. Doak. *China and the Major Powers in East Asia*. Washington, D.C.: The Brookings Institution, 1977.

Bedeski, Robert E. *The Fragile Entente: The 1978 Japan-China Peace Treaty in a Global Context*. Boulder, Colo.: Westview, 1983.

Boorman, Scott. *The Protracted Game*. London: Oxford, 1969.

Chang Pao-min. "The Sino-Vietnamese Conflict and Its Implications for ASEAN." *Pacific Affairs* (Winter 1987–88), 60 (4): 629–648.

Cheng, J. Chester, ed. *The Politics of the Chinese Red Army: A Translation of the Bulletin of Activities of the People's Liberation Army*. Stanford: Hoover Institution Publications, 1966.

Chong-Pin Lin. *China's Nuclear Weapons Strategy: Tradition Within Evolution*. Lexington, Mass./Toronto: Lexington Books, 1988.

Committee on Foreign Relations, United States Senate and the Congressional

Research Service. *The Implications of U.S.-China Military Cooperation.* 98th Cong., 1st Sess., January 1982.

Garrett, Banning and Bonnie Glaser. "Chinese Perspectives on the Strategic Defense Initiative." *Problems of Communism* (March-April 1986), 35 (2): 28–44.

Godwin, Paul H. B., ed. *The Chinese Defense Establishment: Continuity and Change in the 1980s.* Boulder, Colo.: Westview, 1983.

Godwin, Paul, H. B. *Development of the Chinese Armed Forces.* Maxwell Air Force Base, Alabama: Air University Press, June 1988.

Harding, Harry and Melvin Gurtov. *The Purge of Lo Jui-ch'ing: The Politics of Chinese Strategic Planning.* R-548-PR. Santa Monica: The RAND Corporation, February 1971.

Harding, Harry and Yuan Ming, eds. *Sino-American Relations 1945–1955: A Joint Reassessment of a Critical Decade.* Wilmington, Del.: Scholarly Resources, Inc., 1989.

Henning, Stanley. "Chinese Defense Strategy: A Historical Appraisal." *Military Review* (May 1979), 59 (5): 60–67.

Hinton, Harold. *Communist China in World Politics.* Boston: Houghton Mifflin, 1966.

Hsieh, Alice Langley. *Communist China's Strategy in the Nuclear Era.* Englewood Cliffs, N. J.: Prentice-Hall, 1962.

Jencks, Harlan. "China's 'Punitive War' on Vietnam: A Military Assessment." *Asian Survey* (August 1979), 19 (8): 801–815.

Jencks, Harlan. *From Muskets to Missiles: Politics and Professionalism in the Chinese Army 1945–1981.* Boulder, Colo.: Westview, 1982.

Jiang Siyi. *Zhanlue Xingde Da Zhuanbian—Goufang Xiandaihua Lun Gang* (The Big Strategic Change—Fundamentals on the Modernization of National Defense). Beijing: PLA Publishing House, 1987.

Joffe, Ellis. *The Chinese Army After Mao.* Cambridge, Mass.: Harvard University Press, 1987.

Johnson, Chalmers. "The Patterns of Japanese Relations With China, 1952–1982." *Pacific Affairs* (Fall 1986), 59 (3): 402–428.

Johnston, Alastair. "Chinese Nuclear Force Modernization: Implications for Arms Control. *Journal of Northeast Asian Studies* (June 1983), 2 (2): 13-28.

Kierman, Frank, Jr. and John K. Fairbank. *Chinese Ways of Warfare.* Cambridge: Harvard University Press, 1974.

Klintworth, Gary. *China's Modernization: The Strategic Implications for the Asia-Pacific Region.* Canberra: Australian Government Publishing Service, 1989.

Liu Huaqiu. *China and the Neutron Bomb.* Stanford: Center for International Security and Arms Control, June 1988.

Mao Zedong. *Selected Military Writings.* Beijing: Foreign Languages Press, 1967.

Marwah, Onkar and Jonathan D. Pollack, eds. *Military Power and Policy in Asian States: China, India, Japan.* Boulder/Folkestone: Westview/Dawson, 1980.

Military Science Academy Military Planning and Analysis Group. *Guo jixing yu Guo Fang Zhan Lue* (The International Situation and Strategies of National Defense). Beijing: Military Science Press, 1987.

Naughton, Barry. "The Third Front: Defense Industrialization in the Chinese Interior." *The China Quarterly* (September 1988), no. 115, pp. 351-386.

Office of Technology Assessment, U. S. Congress. *Technology Transfer to China*. Washington, D.C.: USGPO, July 1987.

Overholt, William, ed. *Asia's Nuclear Future*. Boulder: Westview, 1977.

Paribatra, Sukhumbhand. *From Enmity to Alignment: Thailand's Evolving Relations with China*. Bangkok: ISIS Thailand, 1987.

Pollack, Jonathan D. *The Lessons of Coalition Politics: Sino-American Security Relations*. R-3133-AF. Santa Monica: The RAND Corporation, February 1984.

Roberts, Moss. *Three Kingdoms: China's Epic Drama*. New York: Pantheon, 1976.

Ryan, Mark. "Early Chinese Attitudes Toward Civil Defense Against Nuclear Attack." *The Australian Journal of Chinese Affairs* (January 1989), no. 21, pp. 81-101.

Scalapino, Robert and Chang Sik-Lee. *Communism in Korea*. Berkeley and Los Angeles: University of California Press, 1972.

Segal, Gerald. *Defending China*. Oxford and New York: Oxford University Press, 1985.

Segal, Gerald. *Sino-Soviet Relations After Mao*. Adelphi Paper no. 202. London: International Institute for Strategic Studies, Autumn 1985.

Segal, Gerald, and William T. Tow, eds. *Chinese Defense Policy*. Urbana and Chicago: University of Illinois Press, 1984.

Song Shilun. "Mao's Military Thinking Is the Guide to Our Armies Victories." *Hongqi* (August 16, 1981), no. 16, 5-15.

Strode, Dan L. "Soviet China Policy in Flux." *Survival* (July/August 1988), 30 (4): 332-350.

Stuart, Douglas T. and William T. Tow, eds. *China, the Soviet Union, and the West*. Boulder, Colo.: Westview, 1982.

Sun Zi. *Art of War*. Samuel B. Griffith, ed. and trans. London: Oxford, 1963.

Tow, William T. "Science and Technology in China's Defense." *Problems of Communism* (July-August 1985), 34 (4): 15-31.

Whiting, Allen S. *China Eyes Japan*. Berkeley: University of California Press, 1989.

Whiting, Allen S. *The Chinese Calculus of Deterrence: India and Indochina*. Ann Arbor: University of Michigan Press, 1965.

Whitson, William, ed. *The Military and Political Power in China in the 1970s*. New York: Praeger, 1972.

Wortzel, Larry M, ed. *China's Military Modernization*. Westport, Conn.: Greenwood Press, 1988.

Xu Xianqian. "Striving to Achieve Modernization in National Defense." *Honqi* (October 2, 1979), no. 10, pp. 28-33.

Yang, Richard H., ed. *SCPS Yearbook on PLA Affairs 1988*. Kaohsiung, Taiwan: National Sun Yat-sen University, 1988.

5. ASEAN AS A "RELUCTANT PLAYER"

Alagappa, Muthiah, "The Major Powers and Southeast Asia." *International Journal* (Summer 1989), 44 (3): 541-597.

Alagappa, Muthiah. *The National Security of Developing States: Lessons from Thailand*. Dover, Mass: Auburn House, 1987.

Alagappa, Muthiah. "A Nuclear-Weapons-Free-Zone in Southeast Asia: Problems and Prospects." *Australian Outlook* (December 1987), 41 (3): 173-180.

Alagappa, Muthiah. *U. S.-ASEAN Security Cooperation: Limits and Possibilities*. Kuala Lumpur: Institute of Strategic and International Studies, 1989.

Ayoob, Mohammed and Chi-anan Sumudavanija. *Leadership Perceptions and National Security*. Singapore: Institute of Southeast Asia Studies, 1989.

Berry, William E., Jr. *U. S. Bases in the Philippines: The Evolution of the Special Relationship*. Boulder, Colo.: Westview, 1989.

Billings-Yun, Melanie. *Decision Against War: Eisenhower and Dienbienphu, 1954*. New York: Columbia University Press, 1988.

Brown, Leslie H. *American Security Policy in Asia*. Adelphi Paper no. 132. London: International Institute for Strategic Studies, Spring 1977.

Buszynski, Leszyk. *SEATO: The Failure of an Alliance Strategy*. Singapore: University of Singapore Press, 1983.

Chin Kin Wah. *The Defense of Malaysia and Singapore: The Transformation of a Security System*. Cambridge: Cambridge University Press, 1983.

Colbert, Evelyn. *Southeast Asia in International Politics 1941-1956*. Ithaca: Cornell University Press, 1977.

Djiwandono, J. Soedjati. *Southeast Asia as a Nuclear-Weapons-Free Zone*. IISS ASEAN Series. Kuala Lumpur: Institute of Strategic and International Studies, 1986.

Garcia, Ed and Francisco Nemenzo. *The Sovereign Quest: Freedom From Foreign Military Bases*. Quezon City: Claretian, 1988.

George, Alexander L., David K. Hall, and William E. Simons. *The Limits of Coercive Diplomacy*. Boston: Little, Brown, 1971.

Greene, Fred, ed. *The Philippine Bases: Negotiations for the Future*. New York: Council on Foreign Relations, 1988.

Halberstam, David. *The Best and the Brightest*. New York: Random House, 1972.

Henry, Donald Putnam, Keith Crane, and Katherine Watkins Webb. *The Philippines Bases: Background for Negotiations*. R-3876411-USSDP/DOS. Santa Monica: The RAND Corporation, August 1989.

Herring, George C. and Richard H. Immerman. " 'The Day We Didn't Go to War' Revisited." *Journal of American History* (September 1984), 71 (2): 343-363.

Hilsman, Roger. *To Move a Nation: The Politics of Foreign Policy in the Administration of John F. Kennedy*. Garden City: Doubleday, 1967.

Indorf, Hans. *Impediments to Regionalism in Southeast Asia: Bilateral Constraints Among ASEAN Member States*. Singapore: Institute of Southeast Asian Studies, 1984.

Leifer, Michael. *ASEAN and the Security of Southeast Asia*. London and New York: Routledge, 1989.

Leifer, Michael. *Conflict and Regional Order in Southeast Asia*. Adelphi Paper no. 162. London: International Institute for Strategic Studies, Winter 1980.

Leifer, Michael. *Malacca, Singapore, and Indonesia*. Alphen aan den Rijn, The Netherlands: Sijthoff & Noordhoff, 1978.

Modelski, George. *SEATO: Six Studies*. Melbourne: F. W. Chesire, 1962.

Moertopo, Ali. "Political and Economic Development in Indonesia in the Context of Regionalism in Southeast Asia." *The Indonesian Quarterly* (April 1978), 6 (2): 30-47.

Morrison, Charles E. *Japan, the United States, and a Changing Southeast Asia*. Lanham: University Press of America, 1985.

Morrison, Charles E. and Astri Suhrke. *Strategies of Survival: The Foreign Policy Dilemmas of Small States*. New York: St. Martin's Press, 1978.

Nair, K. K. *ASEAN-Indochina Relations Since 1975: The Politics of Accommodation*. Canberra Papers on Strategy and Defense no. 30. Canberra: The Strategic and Defense Studies Center, The Research School of Pacific Studies, The Australian National University, 1984.

Office of the Secretary of Defense, Vietnam Task Force. *United States-Vietnam Relations 1945-1967 (The Pentagon Papers)*. Washington, D.C.: USGPO, 1971.

Randolph, R. Sean. *The United States and Thailand: Alliance Dynamics 1950-1985*. Berkeley: University of California, Institute of East Asian Studies, 1986.

Rotter, Andrew. *Origins of the American Commitment to Southeast Asia*. Ithaca: Cornell University Press, 1987.

Scalapino, Robert A. and Jusuf Wanadi, eds. *Economic, Political, and Security Issues in Southeast Asia in the 1980s*. Berkeley: University of California, Institute of East Asian Studies, 1982.

Schlesinger, Arthur M. Jr. *A Thousand Days: John F. Kennedy in the White House*. Boston: Houghton Mifflin, 1965.

Simon, Sheldon. *Asian Neutralism and U. S. Policy*. Washington, D.C.: American Enterprise Institute, August 1975.

Stevenson, Charles A. *The End of Nowhere: American Policy Toward Laos Since 1954*. Boston: Beacon Press, 1972.

Tilman, Robert O. *Southeast Asia and the Enemy Beyond: ASEAN Perceptions of External Threats*. Boulder, Colo.: Westview, 1986.

U.S House of Representatives. Hearing before the Subcommittee on Asian and Pacific Affairs. *Our Commitments in Asia*. 93d Cong., 2d Sess., March 13, 1974.

United States Senate. Hearing before the Committee on Foreign Relations. *The Southeast Asia Collective Defense Treaty--Part I*. 83d Cong., 2d Sess., November 11, 1954.

Weatherbee, Donald, ed. *Southeast Asia Divided: The ASEAN-Indochina Crisis*. Boulder, Colo.: Westview, 1985.

Wilson, Dick, *The Neutralization of Southeast Asia*. New York: Praeger, 1975.

6. THE SOUTHWEST PACIFIC

Albinski, Henry S. *ANZUS, the United States and Pacific Security*. Lanham: University Press of America, 1987.

Albinski, Henry S. *Australia's External Policy Under Labor*. Vancouver: University of British Columbia Press, 1977.

Bercovitch, Jacob, ed. *ANZUS in Crisis*. Basingstoke and London: Macmillan, 1988.

Boston, Jonathan and Martin Holland, eds. *The Fourth Labour Government: Radical Politics in New Zealand*. Auckland: Oxford University Press, 1987.

Burnett, Alan. *The A-NZ-US Triangle*. Canberra: Australian National University, Strategic and Defense Studies Center, 1988.

Chesneaux, Jean. *France in the Pacific: A Tentative Analysis*. Australian Peace Research Center Working Paper no. 24. Canberra: The Australian National University, July 1987.

Dorrance, John C. "The Pacific Islands and U. S. Security Interests." *Asian Survey* (July 1989), 29 (7): 698-715.

Gordon, Bernard. *New Zealand Becomes a Pacific Power*. Chicago: The University of Chicago Press, 1960.

Graham, Kennedy. *National Security Concepts of States: New Zealand*. United Nations Institute for Disarmament Research. New York: Taylor & Francis, 1989.

Herr, Richard A. "Regionalism, Strategic Denial and South Pacific Security." *Journal of Pacific History* (October 1986) 21 (4): 170-182.

Jennings, Peter. *The Armed Forces of New Zealand and the ANZUS Split: Costs and Consequences*. Occasional Paper no. 4. Wellington: New Zealand Institute of International Affairs, 1988.

Joint Committee on Foreign Affairs, Defense, and Trade. The Parliament of the Commonwealth of Australia. *Australia's Relations with the South Pacific*. Canberra: Australian Government Publishing Service, March 1989.

Lange, David. "New Zealand's Security Policy." *Foreign Affairs* (Summer 1985), 63 (5): 1009-1019.

Lange, David. "The Oxford Union Debate." *New Zealand Foreign Affairs Review* (January-March 1985), 35 (1): 7-12.

McHenry, Dean E. and Richard N. Rosecrance. "The Exclusion of the United Kingdom from the ANZUS Pact." *International Organization* (Summer 1958), 12 (3): 320-329.

McMillan, Stuart. *Neither Confirm Nor Deny*. Wellington and Sydney: Allen & Unwin/Port Nicholson Press, 1987.

Millar, T. B. *Australia's Foreign Policy*. Sydney: Angus and Robertson, 1968.

Millar, T. B. *Australia in Peace and War*. New York: St. Martin's Press, 1978.

New Zealand Ministry of Defense. *Review of Defense Policy, 1987*. Wellington: V. R. Ward, Government Printer, 1986.

Ovendale, Ritchie. *The English-Speaking Alliance: Britain, the United States, the Dominions, and the Cold War 1945-1951*. London: George Allen & Unwin, 1985.

Power, Paul F. "The South Pacific Nuclear-Weapons-Free Zone." *Pacific Affairs* (Fall 1986), 59 (3): 455-475.

Pugh, Michael C. *The ANZUS Crisis, Nuclear Visiting, and Deterrence*. Cambridge: Cambridge University Press, 1989.

Ravenhill, John, ed. *No Longer an American Lake? Alliance Problems in the South Pacific*. Berkeley: Institute of International Studies, 1989.

Reese, Trevor. *Australia, New Zealand, and the United States: A Survey of International Relations 1941-1968*. London: Oxford University Press, 1969.

Report of the Defense Committee of Inquiry. *Defense and Security: What New Zealanders Want*. Wellington: Private Bag, July 1986.

Siegfried, Andre. *Democracy in New Zealand*. Wellington: Victoria University Press with Price Milburn, 1982.

Starke, J. G. *The ANZUS Treaty Alliance*. London and New York: Melbourne University Press, 1965.

Tanham, George K. *The Soviet Union and the South Pacific*. RAND P-7431. Santa Monica: The RAND Corporation, April 1988.

Templeton, Malcolm. *Defense and Security: What New Zealand Needs*. Wellington: Victoria University Press for the Institute for Policy Studies, 1986.

Thakur, Ramesh. *The Defense of New Zealand*. Boulder: Westview, 1986.

Tow, William T. "The ANZUS Dispute: Testing U. S. Extended Deterrence in Alliance Politics." *Political Science Quarterly* (Spring 1989), 104 (1): 117-149.

U. S. House of Representatives. Hearing before the Subcommittee on Asian and Pacific Affairs. *Developments in the South Pacific Region*. 99th Cong., 2d Sess., 10 September 1986.

U. S. House of Representatives. Hearing before the Subcommittee on Asian and Pacific Affairs. *Security Treaty Between Australia, New Zealand and the United States*. 99th Cong., 1st Sess., 18 March, 1985.

Van Ness, Peter. *China and the Question of Nuclear Ship Visits*. Peace Research Center Working Paper no. 48. Canberra: The Australian National University, July 1988.

Wood, F. L. W. *Defense Perspectives*. Wellington: Price, Milburne, 1972.

Index

Acheson, Dean, 65, 66, 71, 151
Admiralty islands, 344-345
Aegis air defense system, 129
Afghanistan, Soviet invasion of, 111, 161, 181
Air bases, floating, 494n137
Air-to-air missiles, 184
Alaska, U.S. Army in, 26
Albinski, Henry, 116, 349, 370
Anglo-Malaysian Defense Agreement, 274, 288, 328
Anti-Bases Coalition, 319
Anti-submarine warfare (ASW), 39
ANZAC. *See* Australia New Zealand Army Corps
ANZUS alliance (Australia, New Zealand, U.S.), 12, 58, 59; alternatives to, 348; Britain and, 345-346; escalation control and, 96-98; final break with New Zealand, 369-374; Ford administration and, 98; formation of, 341; geographic scope of, 347; key terms, 356-358; 1984-1986 dispute, 355-374; nuclear-free zone and, 35, 141, 348-349; Pacifist Players and, 350-355; Reagan administration and, 15; response formula, 285; ripple factor and, 374; SEATO and, 347; strategic denial and, 347-348; Truman administration and, 345; U.S. commitments to, 51, 53, 82-83, 113-119
Aquino, Corazón, 168, 320

Arms control, 229; Soviet "new thinking" on, 167-169; verification and, 169. *See also* Intermediate nuclear force (INF) reductions
Asia: Cold War and, 64-71; intermediate nuclear force reductions in, 136; oil supplies and, 177; Soviet influence in, 17. *See also* Asia-Pacific; Association of Southeast Asian Nations; Southeast Asia Treaty Organization; *specific countries*
Asianization, 53, 137
Asia-Pacific: civil wars and, 53; defined, 427n1; economic growth rate, 5; global deterrence planning and, 6; trading cartel, 396. *See also specific countries*
Aspiring Player, 12, 394; China as, 195-268, 403-406; offense versus defense and, 172-180; Soviet Union as, 145-194, 400-403
Association of Southeast Asia, 300, 308
Association of Southeast Asian Nations (ASEAN), 187, 420; Cambodia and, 186, 316-317; collective political defense and, 308-310; communist insurgency movements in, 307; dealing with outside powers and, 331-333; defense self-reliance, 300, 305, 308, 328-331; development aspirations, 490n105; distrust of Soviet Union,

Asso. of Southeast Asian Nations (*Cont.*)
313-314; economic security, 311, 396;
ethnic tensions and, 311-312; formation of, 270-271; global power competition and, 282-283; inconsistent U.S.
strategy and, 274-275; Indochina polarization, 312-313; Indochina reconciliation, 315-317; Indonesia and,
254, 301-302; internal threats to, 273,
307, 311; Japan and, 304, 332; Kampuchea and, 314-315; local deterrence
and, 305, 328-331; maritime deterrence capabilities and, 324-333; neutrality and, 301, 318; Nixon Doctrine
and, 293-298; nuclear-free zone and,
333-339, 375; People's Republic of
China and, 247, 250-254, 314; Philippines basing issue and, 317-324; qualified nonalignment and, 301; Reagan
administration and, 303-307; regional
resilience, 310-312; Reluctant Player
posture, 14, 269-340, 407-408; sea
lane security and, 324-333; Sino-Japanese coalition and, 304; Soviet Union
and, 313-314, 402; U.S. global deterrence and, 272-275; U.S. nuclear
weapons and, 300; U.S. trade and,
28; Vietnam and, 309-310, 314; ZOP-
FAN and, 312-314. *See also* Southeast
Asia
Australia: Air Force, 117; ANZUS and,
341, 360, 371; Asia-Pacific trading
cartel and, 396; communist threat
and, 82-83; Defense Cooperation Program, 142; defense posture, 12, 84,
113-119, 348; Defense White Paper,
118; escalation control and, 96-98;
Five Power Defense Agreement and,
54; forward defense and, 84, 348; intelligence-gathering and, 113-114; listening posts and, 377-378; New Zealand defense ties, 384-385, 386-387;
northern defense threats and, 386-
387; nuclear-free zone and, 97, 116,
349, 366-367; peace movement, 116;
strategic outlook, 62; submarine fleet,
117; Transitional Player posture, 64,
114, 395, 399; U.S. Dominant Player
posture and, 383; U.S. global deterrence and, 59; U.S. security ties with,

10, 53, 64, 82, 141-142; Vietnam War
and, 83
Australian Defense Force, 117
Australia Strategic Basis Paper, 97
Australia New Zealand Army Corps
(ANZAC), 114, 343-345, 348, 356,
376, 384-387

Baikal-Amur Mainline (BAM), 163
Baker, James, 313-314, 373
Bandung Conference (1955), 282
Barents Sea, 72
Barnet, Richard, 17, 18
Belgium, peace movement in, 374, 375
Berlin blockade, 3
Black Bear Island (Heixiaz), 147, 263
Blue zone, 343
Brezhnev, Leonid, 157, 158, 159,
262
Britain: ANZUS and, 345-346; counter-
attack thesis and, 279, 280; Five
Power Defense Agreement and, 54;
intervention in Vietnam and, 279;
Korean War and, 66-67; Laos and,
288; Malaya and, 284, 287, 346; Ma-
laysian arms sales and, 329; Malaysia/
Singapore's security relations with,
273; New Zealand defense ties, 343-
344; nuclear-free zone and, 375; Pa-
cific security role and, 345-346;
SEATO affiliation, 287-288
Brown, Leslie, 269, 296
Brunei, vulnerability of, 331
Bush, George, 1989 journey to Northeast
Asia, 56
Bush, George, administration of, 4, 26;
Asia-Pacific commitments and, 5-6;
Cambodian resistance and, 317;
China ties and, 11-12; Chinese military sales and, 170; defense burden-
sharing and, 122; Dominant Player
posture and, 307; East Asia Strategy
Initiative and, 414; Japanese trade
and, 121; maritime strategy and, 41;
New Zealand and, 373; nuclear weap-
ons and, 420; revisionist-pragmatist
outlook, 391; South Korea and, 105,
107; South Pacific and, 380; Soviet
policy trends and, 150

Cam Ranh Bay, 320; East-West military capabilities and, 31; New Zealand targets and, 354; Sino-Soviet rapprochement and, 186; Soviet force reductions and, 25, 166, 171, 177-178, 186, 187, 320; Soviet presence at, 112, 118, 161, 167, 177, 190; Soviet surge capabilities and, 185; U.S. and, 463n86; vulnerability to U.S. Seventh Fleet, 164, 177

Cambodia: ASEAN and, 186, 316-317; Bush administration and, 317; U.S. operations in, 271; Vietnamese occupation of, 313; Vietnamese withdrawal from, 253, 316, 317

Canberra Agreement (1944), 343-344

Carlucci, Frank, 2, 243, 413

Carrier warfare, 39, 41

Carter, Jimmy, administration of: Asia-Pacific theater and, 50; Japanese self-defense and, 123; Middle East and, 50; national security planning staff, 17; South Korea and, 84, 88-90; swing strategy and, 44, 61; Taiwan and, 96, 111

Carter Doctrine, 50, 303-304

Cheney, Richard ("Dick"), 6, 42, 107, 373

Chiang Kai-shek, 66, 80-81, 95, 155

China National Aero Technology Import-Export Corporation, 240

Chinese formula/Trust Me/Trust Us formula, 356, 362, 363-364, 368, 501n54

Chong-Pin Lin, 196-197, 201, 217, 203

Christmas Island, 117

CINCPAC, 96, 366, 413, 415

Clark Air Base, Philippines, 167, 171, 305, 317, 318, 416

Cocos Island, 117

Cold War, 63-71, 272

Conventional Defense/Balanced Technology Initiative, 127

Cook Islands, New Zealand defense commitments and, 385

Counterattack thesis, 276-277, 279

Crowe, William J., 419-420

Defense Satellite Communications System, 97

de Gaulle, Charles, 35, 381, 393-394

Democratic People's Republic of Korea (DPRK). *See* North Korea

Deng Xiaoping, 197, 263, 404

Denmark, nuclear weapons and, 357, 370-371, 375

Détente, 162, 183, 273, 294

Deterrence: contextual, 461n74; conventional, 38, 40, 71; convergent, 21-22; critics of, 23, 26-27; existential, 70-71, 432n21; general, 33-34, 432n25, 392; proponents of, 23-24, 27; by punishment, 217. *See also* Extended deterrence; *specific countries*

Dibb, Paul, 114-115, 118

Dominant Player posture. *See* U.S. Dominant Player posture

DPRK. *See* North Korea (Democratic People's Republic of Korea)

Dulles, John Foster, 11, 68, 74, 81, 274, 277-278, 279, 280, 282, 285

E-2C early-warning aircraft, 130

Eagleburger, Lawrence, 17, 45

East Asia Strategy Initiative, 6, 107

East China Sea, 84, 95, 112, 177

Eastern Europe, political liberalization in, 5, 47, 147, 263

Eden, Anthony, 279, 283

Eisenhower, Dwight D., administration of, 1; Korean War and, 66-68, 208-209; nuclear deterrence and, 66; Taiwan and, 81, 95; Taiwan Straits crisis and, 68-70; United Action initiative and, 277-278

Escalation, horizontal, 42-43, 102

Escalation control, 6, 37-43, 64-71, 83-98, 433n32; ANZUS and, 96-98; Asia-Pacific vs. Europe, 31-32; Australia and, 96-98; case studies and, 33; existential deterrence and, 70-71; Japan and, 10, 85-87, 100; Korean deterrence strategy and, 79-80; Korean War and, 47, 151; Laos and, 292; Maritime Strategy and, 39-41; People's Republic of China and, 202, 211, 214, 221, 227, 233-234; South Korea and, 10, 88-94; Soviet Union and, 38, 176-177; Soviet-China 1969 clash and, 159; Taiwan and, 47, 80-81, 95-96; U.S. and, 393, 394-395

Escalation dominance, 46
Europe, 1; conventional deterrence and, 34, 47; Dominant Player posture and, 28-32; Flexible Response strategy in, 47; regional security concerns, 45; Soviet influence in, 17; strategic outlook for, 5. *See also* Eastern Europe; *specific countries*
European Security Conference, 420
Existential deterrence, 70-71, 432n21
Extended deterrence, 1-4, 8; as chronic problem, 34-35; consultation between allies and, 115; Dominant Player posture and, 23-57; effectiveness of, 35; general strategy, 33-34, 432n25; immediate strategy, 32-33; management of, 98-113; maritime element, 31; military presence and, 52; NATO and, 11; nuclear context, 47-48, 52; operative requirements of, 34; South Korea and, 137-141; studies on, 33-34. *See also* U.S. extended deterrence

Fallows, James, 121, 124
Fangataufa Island, French nuclear testing and, 381
Federated States of Micronesia, 142
Fiji: nuclear-free zone and, 349; Soviet fishing and, 378
Five Power Defense Agreement, 54, 187, 298, 328, 381
Flexible response, 6, 24, 38, 47, 428n6
Ford, Gerald, administration of: ANZUS and, 98; Pacific Doctrine and, 300-301
Formosa Resolution, 95
Formosa Straits Patrol, 96
France: counterattack thesis and, 279; deterrence approach, 217, 232; Korean War and, 66-67; Laos and, 289, 290; NATO and, 35; nuclear weapons testing, 379, 380-381, 421; Pacific Naval Squadron, 192; U.S. intervention in Indochina and, 278, 279-280
FS-X jetfighter, 92, 108, 128-129, 397
Fuji Heavy Industries, 127

Gaddis, John Lewis, 16-17
Gang of Four, 196, 206
General Dynamics, 128

Glasnost (openness), 149, 170, 403
Global-realist perspective, 16-19, 21, 390
Godwin, Paul, 230
Gorbachev, Mikhail: ASEAN and, 187, 307; Chinese relations and, 174, 262-263; diplomatic initiatives, 13, 56, 146, 149; double-zero proposal, 167; Moscow summit of 1988 and, 184; "new thinking" of, 148, 150, 165-171; nuclear-free zone and, 336; nuclear war and, 148; South Korea economic ties and, 138; South Pacific and, 378
Great Proletarian Cultural Revolution, 196
Greenpeace, 366, 381
Guam, 85, 322, 347, 376

Hawaii, U.S. Army in, 26
Hawke, Bob, 366, 367, 368
Hayden, Bill, 99, 383
Hayden Doctrine, 114
Heixiazi Dao (Black Bear Island), 147, 263
Hellman, Donald, 19-20
Hokkaido, defense of, 102-103
Hong Kong: British responsibilities and, 346; Chinese annexation of, 196
Huntington, Samuel, 38, 119

Imperial overstretch thesis, 18, 26-27, 412
Imperial wars, 27
India: Chinese border skirmish in 1962 with, 199, 255; force levels, 428n11; forward defense posture, 205, 411; maritime power, 31, 396; Sino-Soviet rapprochement and, 264; Soviet Union and, 162
Indian Ocean, 45, 50, 444n85; ANZUS and, 347; PACOM's responsibility for, 44; Soviet navy in, 51, 97, 189, 190; U.S. Navy in, 305
Indigenous Defensive Fighter, 261
Indochina, 5; ASEAN and, 312-313, 315-317; Chinese extended deterrence and, 245-247; SEATO and, 394. *See also specific countries*
Indonesia: ASEAN and, 254, 301-302; border management problems and,

142; China's Aspiring Player approach and, 250, 253-254; collective political defense and, 310; informal security coalitions with, 8; Japanese rearmament and, 304; Malaysia and, 83; national development and, 282; Nixon's visit in 1969 to, 296-297; nuclear-free zone and, 333; *pancasila* philosophy, 310-311; SEATO and, 283-284; Soviet threat to, 328; superpower competition and, 272-273, 283-284; triangular defense community and, 330; Vietnam-Cambodia conflict and, 316; vulnerability of, 331

Integrated Air Defense System, 187
Interalliance transferability, 43-46
Intermediate nuclear force (INF) reductions, 45, 52, 375; in Asia, 136, 146, 229, 259-260; in Europe, 45; Soviet long-range bombers and, 167
International Atomic Energy Agency, 419
Iran: Carter administration and, 50; *Silkworm* sales and, 243
Iran-Iraq war, 134, 241
Iraq: force levels, 428n11; invasion of Kuwait, 243-244

Jamieson, Sir Ewan, 354, 361
Japan, 5, 6, 8; ASEAN and, 304, 332, 396; Bush and, 121; Carter and, 123; China's Aspiring Player posture and, 257; China's exploitation of war guilt and, 258-259; Chinese economy and, 258; comprehensive security and, 125; constitution, 72; control of Okinawa and, 99-100; conventional deterrence and, 34; defense budget, 123-124, 127-128; defense burden-sharing and, 120-126; defense capabilities, 7, 131; defense research and development, 127-128; defense spending, 449n143; Defense White Paper, 130, 131; dual technology and, 397; economic competition with, 28; economic development and, 18, 66; escalation control and, 10, 85-87, 100; global-realists and, 16; Indonesia and, 304; industrial complex, 73; INF positions, 136; international security policy, 132-133; Korean War and, 73-

74; local deterrence posture, 131; Malaysia and, 304-305; maritime strategy, 31, 131, 396; National Defense Program Outline, 126; NATO involvement, 134, 135; NATO parallel, 30; New Zealand nuclear-free zone posture and, 375; nonnuclear principles, 76, 86, 104, 357, 362, 416; nuclear weapons in, 85-87; oil supplies, 134; peace constitution, 362; politico-strategic influence, 180; rearmament and, 18, 31, 49, 74, 104, 122, 160; revisionist-pragmatists and, 20; sea lanes of communication and, 124; security threats to, 59; Self Defense Force, 76, 102, 104, 124; South Korea and, 106, 257; Soviet Aspiring Player posture and, 401; Soviet military threat to, 121-122; Soviet neutralization of, 179-180; as Transitional Player, 11, 395, 397-398; U.S. commitment to, 10, 30, 71-76, 83-84; U.S. escalation control and, 85-87; U.S. forward development strategy and, 129-132; U.S. global security interests and, 134; U.S. military technology relations with, 126; U.S. nuclear commitment to, 103; U.S. nuclear weapons and, 86-87, 362-363; U.S. strategic doctrine changes and, 100-101; U.S. trade and, 11, 121
"Japanese Formula," 356-376, 362-263, 368, 501n54
Jencks, Harlan, 214, 217
Johnson, Lyndon, 290, 293
Johnston, J. Bennett, 107

Kalayaan Island Group, 319
Kamchatka peninsula, 72, 163
Kampuchea, ASEAN and, 314-315
Kelly, James, 243, 359
Kennan, George, 16-17, 410
Kennedy, Paul, 26, 403
Kennedy, John F., administration of, Laos and, 286-287, 290, 291-293
Khmer Rouge, Chinese support for, 246, 248-249, 252-253, 316
Khrushchev, Nikita, 70, 151, 153, 154-156, 205, 211
Kim Il-sung, 151, 182-184, 254, 257

Kiribati, 192, 378
Kissinger, Henry, 17, 45, 50, 122, 294, 304
Korean War, 1, 277; Britain and, 66-67, 71; China and, 58, 95, 151-152, 199, 205, 208-210; escalation control and, 47, 151; France and, 66-67; Japan and, 73-74; nuclear weapons and, 85; Soviet Union and, 208-210; United Nations Command Headquarters for, 73-74; U.S. escalation of, 45, 71, 85
Kuala Lumpur Declaration (1971), 271
Kurile islands, 419
Kurth, James R., 6
Kuwait, Iraq's invasion of, 243-244

Lange, David, 14, 350, 351, 353-354, 360, 361-362, 365, 367, 368-370, 372-373, 387, 408-409
Laos, 49; Britain and, 288; escalation control and, 292; France and, 289, 290; Kennedy and, 286-287, 290, 291-293; neutrality crisis, 14, 286-293; Soviet supplies and, 286; U.S. reticence to intervene in, 286
Latin America, nuclear-free zone and, 338, 382
Launch-on-warning strategy, 41
Layne, Christopher, 19, 20
Lewis, John, 201, 210, 212, 216
Libya, South Pacific nationalism and, 191
Lin Biao, 213, 215
Li Peng, 170, 174, 248, 263

Malaya: Britain and, 284, 287, 346; communist insurgency and, 283, 288
Malaysia, 8; British security relations with, 273; China and, 250, 253-254; Five Power Defense Agreement and, 54; Indonesia and, 83; Japanese rearmament and, 304-305; maritime defense and, 328-329; nuclear-free zone and, 333, 337; PERISTA Plan, 329; Philippines territorial dispute and, 297; Soviet threat to, 328; triangular defense community and, 330; vulnerability of, 331
Malik, Adam, 308-309, 310
Manila Conference, 282

Manila Declaration (1987), 336
Manila Pact, 54, 290
Manila Treaty, 50, 299
Mansfield Amendment, 295-296
Manus Island dispute (1945-1946), 344-345
Mao Zedong, 207, 404; Korean War and, 209-210; military science and, 223-224; military strategy and, 204; Moscow visit in 1949, 150, 151; mutual assured destruction and, 457n21; nuclear weapons and, 210-212; Soviet Union and, 507n14; Taiwan crisis and, 155
Maritime Strategy, 18, 100-102
Marshall Islands, 192, 347
Mayaguez affair (May 1975), 302
Mearsheimer, John, 39, 46, 235
Mediterranean, U.S. offshore military presence in, 2
Mekong River deltas, 274
Melanesian subregion, domestic threats to, 379
Menetrey, Louis, 90, 93
Micronesia, base structure in, 322
Middle East: Carter administration and, 50; New Zealand ground forces and, 346; U.S. containment in, 3. *See also* Persian Gulf; *specific countries*
Misawa air base, 103
Mitsubishi Heavy Industries, 127
Mobile Operational Large Island Airbases, 494n137
Mongolia: Soviet alliance with, 162; Soviet force reductions and, 25, 169, 262, 263
Monroe Doctrine approach, collective defense and, 75-76
Morgan, Patrick, 48, 200
Muldoon, Robert, 98
Mururoa Atoll, French nuclear testing at, 379, 380-381
Mutual assured destruction, 217, 457n21
Mutual security treaties, 71-83

Nakasone, Yasuhiro, 123, 127, 136, 259, 397-398
NATO. *See* North Atlantic Treaty Organization
Neo-isolationists, 19

Netherlands, peace movement in, 374, 375

New Caledonia, 348

New Zealand, 28; ANZUS and, 35, 341, 367-374; Australian defense ties, 384-385, 386-387; British defense ties, 343-344; Bush administration and, 373; common security and, 352; Corner Report, 386; defense commitments, 385-386; deterioration of U.S. relationship, 365-367; economic problems, 141; Exclusive Economic Zone, 354; Five Power Defense Agreement and, 54; foreign policy and, 341; forward defense and, 348, 385; infantry training in Singapore and, 332-333; Labour government and, 342, 348, 350; local deterrence responsibility, 354; nuclear-free zone and, 14-15, 97, 348-355; nuclear power and, 35; as Pacifist Player, 14, 408-409; self-defense capabilities, 384-385; Soviet credibility and, 169; U.S. commitment to, 53, 82; U.S. Foreign Assistance Act and, 372; Western defense isolation, 371, 384, 386

Nie Rongzhen, 209, 210-211, 213

Niue, New Zealand defense commitments and, 385

Nixon, Richard: China visit in 1972 and, 160; Indonesia visit in 1969 and, 296-297; Thailand visit in 1969 and, 297

Nixon, Richard, administration of: Asia-Pacific retrenchment, 61; Chinese nuclear threat and, 473n85; Dominant Player posture and, 306; global strategy, 4, 275; national security planning staffs, 17; one-and-a-half war strategy, 295; SEATO commitment and, 294-296; South Korea and, 90; Taiwan and, 99; Vietnam and, 294-295

Nixon Doctrine, 48, 49, 52, 99, 173, 270, 413, 428n7; ASEAN and, 293-298; defense burden-sharing and, 3; Japan and, 20, 160; one-and-a-half war commitment and, 100, 109; revisionist-pragmatists and, 19-20; Sino-Soviet rift and, 109; Thailand and, 290, 309; U.S. policy errors and, 306

Nonaligned Summit Conference (1970), 271

"Nordic solution," 357, 370-371

North Atlantic Treaty Organization (NATO), 2, 59, 76; extended deterrence and, 11, 45; force planning, 60; France and, 35; Japanese parallel, 30; Japanese participation in, 134, 135; Korean War and, 67; nuclear weapons and, 47; People's Republic of China and, 160-161, 162; response formula, 282; U.S. commitment to, 48; U.S. deterrence strategy and, 5; U.S. ground forces and, 392

North China Industries Corporation, 240

Northern Marianas, 322, 376

North Korea (Democratic Peoples Republic of Korea), 63, 146, 398; air force capabilities, 93; Chinese support of, 202, 256-257; Cold War and, 65; conventional force superiority, 88; force levels, 428n11; nuclear reactors and, 140; persistent threat from, 106-107; repression in, 5; Sino-Soviet ideological dispute and, 182, 183; Soviet commitments to, 180-185, 401-402; Soviet overflight rights, 106, 174; Soviet support during Korean War and, 151-152; surprise attack capability, 92; U.S. land forces and, 20

North Vietnam: Chinese relations with, 186-188; U.S. bombing raids against, 215. *See also* Vietnam

Norway, nuclear weapons and, 357, 370-371

Nuclear-free zone: Southeast Asia and, 167, 254; Soviet Union and, 166, 167, 400. *See also* South Pacific Nuclear-free Zone

Nuclear weapons: immorality argument and, 350-353; inappropriate, 26; global parity, 59; land-based trip wire, 100; NATO and, 47; "neither confirm nor deny" policy, 349, 351, 353, 354, 355, 359-366, 368, 416; as policy ends, 18; Taiwan Straits crisis and, 68-69. *See also specific countries*

Nuclear Free Philippines Coalition, 320

Nunn, Sam, 44

Nunn-Warren Act, 1989, 5-6

Odom, William, 147
Okinawa, 49; Japanese control, 99-100; Kadena Air Base, 132; nuclear weapons in, 85; reversion agreement, 90
Olsen, Edward, 20-21
Omnibus Trade Act, 121
O'Neill, Robert, 99, 377
Operation Barbarossa, 161
Overseas Development Assistance, 135, 136

Pacific Command (PACOM), 25-26, 51
Pacific Doctrine, 270, 300-301
Pacific Economic Cooperation Conference, 396
Pacific Economic Cooperation Council, 148
Pacifist Player posture: ANZUS dispute and, 355-374; New Zealand and, 408-409; Southwest Pacific and, 350
Pago Pago, 376
Palau Islands, 376, 382-383
Palmer, Geoffrey, 367, 369, 373
Papua New Guinea, 118; Australia and, 142; nuclear-free zone and, 349
People's Republic of China (PRC), 8; air defense and, 236-237; ASEAN and, 247, 250-254, 314; Aspiring Player posture, 12-13, 195-268, 403-406; ballistic missile delivery system, 213; ballistic missile submarines, 226; Bush administration and, 11-12, 170; calculated irrationality and, 220-222; changing strategic posture, 215-220; communications systems and, 224, 234; conventional deterrence and, 235-244; dual-use technology and, 160; Eastern Europe liberalization and, 263; escalation control and, 202, 211, 214, 221, 227, 233-234; force levels, 428n11; Four Modernizations, 196, 206, 217-218, 239; H-bomb and, 213; ICBMs and, 163, 231; Indian border skirmish in 1962 with, 199, 255; India's forward policy and, 205; Indochina and, 245-247; Indonesia and, 250, 253-254; intermediate-range ballistic missiles, 215-216, 222, 223, 231; Iran-Iraq war and, 241; Japanese military expansion and, 259; Japanese strategic relations with, 257-260; Japanese war guilt and, 258-259; Khmer Rouge support, 246, 248-249, 252-253, 316; Korean War and, 58, 95, 151-152, 199, 205, 208-210; land-based missiles, 206; land forces, 31; local war strategy, 219-220; Malaysia and, 250, 253-254; medium-range ballistic missiles, 215, 223, 231; Middle East arms sales, 196, 243; military history, 202-207; military modernization and, 13, 61, 207-208, 217-219, 236-241, 404; military spending, 112; NATO and, 160-161, 162; naval power, 31, 163, 226, 234, 396; North Korea and, 137, 138, 182, 202, 256-257; nuclear capabilities, 31, 210-213, 215-217, 222-227, 229-235, 403, 469n51; nuclear-free zone and, 254; prodemocracy movement and, 12, 195, 196, 206, 260, 314, 405; psychological dimension of nuclear deterrence and, 199, 200, 201, 205; rapid response strategy, 199; regional image, 244; regional deterrence, 244, 405; regional nuclear forces, 222; relaxing of Soviet tensions, 400-401; Saudi Arabian missile sales and, 243; Second Artillery Corps, 215; second-strike capability, 159-160, 165, 173, 223; *Silkworm* sales and, 243; South Korean trade with, 138-139, 257; South Pacific nationalism and, 191; Soviet alliance in 1950s, 145, 150, 207-212; Soviet Aspiring Player posture and, 400-401; Soviet geopolitical power struggle with, 158-160; Soviet ICBM targets, 163, 228; Soviet military technology and, 170, 211-212; Soviet military threat and, 197, 262; Soviet nuclear assistance and, 154, 155, 156, 211; Soviet nuclear threat and, 158-159, 164; Soviet rift with, 153-157, 181, 211, 213, 392; Soviet summit in 1989 with, 169-170, 241, 249, 263; Soviet threat assessments and, 228-229; Soviet-U.S. INF Treaty and, 52; Soviet-Vietnamese relations and, 186, 187, 188; strategic deception and, 205-206, 216, 222,

225; strategic interests and, 196-202; superpower nuclear competition and, 60; Taiwan Straits crises and, 68-70, 210; Taiwan reunification and, 260; technology gap and, 237-238; Thailand's security and, 54, 247-249, 316, 405; Third Front, 213; trading corporations, 240; U.S. extended deterrence and, 10, 109-111, 207, 242-244; U.S. military relations with, 170, 241-242; U.S. nuclear weapons and, 363-364; U.S. reconciliation with, 49-50, 392; U.S. technology relations and, 265; U.S. threat assessment and, 229-230; Vietnamese clash off Spratly Islands and, 251-252; Vietnamese negotiations on Cambodia with, 253; Vietnamese war in 1979 with, 199, 218, 219, 221, 245-246; Vietnam-Thailand conflict and, 249; Vietnam War and, 157, 215, 245; Western deterrence concepts and, 200-201. *See also* Sino-Soviet border
People's War, 198, 207, 213-215
People's War Under Modern Conditions, 198-199, 218-219, 224-225
Perestroika, 170, 401, 403
Persian Gulf, 45, 50; Soviet navy in, 177, 190; U.S.-Japanese relations and, 134-135; U.S. Navy in, 2, 305; U.S.-South-Korean relations and, 135
Philippine Marshall Plan, 135
Philippines, 8, 132; basing issue and, 168, 317-324, 408; domestic security problems, 319; economic plight, 319; force reductions, 6; hostility to U.S. deterrence mission, 7; Laos crisis and, 290; Malaysian territorial dispute and, 297; mutual security treaties with, 8; national development and, 282; nonnuclear policy and, 336; regional security interests, 54; SEATO and, 50, 284-285, 299; South Korea and, 135-136; Spratlys and, 331; U.S. extended deterrence and, 54, 273, 284-285, 301; U.S. nuclear weapons in, 320; U.S. policy on Laos and, 289
Polytechnologies Corporation, 240
Port Arthur, 154

Precision guided munitions, 94, 224, 475n110
Preventive war thesis, 276
Pye, Lucian, 110-111

Qian Sanqiang, 209, 213

Radford, Arthur, 81, 276
Radford-Collins Act, 142
Radford-Collins Agreement (1951), 118
Rainbow Warrior, 366, 381
Reagan, Ronald, administration of, 29; ANZUS dispute and, 15; ASEAN and, 303-307; Chinese-Japanese diplomacy and, 52; Commission On Integrated Long-Term Strategy, 422; Dominant Player posture and, 302-307; extended deterrence and, 4, 42-43; forward defense strategy, 18; global deterrence and, 51; horizontal escalation and, 42-43; Japanese self-defense and, 123; Maritime Strategy and, 39-41, 61; military spending and, 165, 197; Moscow summit of 1988 and, 184; New Zealand and, 372; offensive retaliation and, 39; pillar approach to regional security, 14; six pillar defense strategy, 303; South Korea and, 90; Taiwan military sales and, 261
Reed Bank, 319
Reluctant Player posture, ASEAN and, 14, 269-340, 407-408
Republic of Korea (ROK). *See* South Korea
Revisionist-idealists, 17-19, 21, 390
Revisionist-pragmatists, 19-21, 21, 35, 391
Roh Tae Woo, 104-105, 106, 138
Rusk, Dean, 82, 289, 290
Rusk-Thanat Communique, 8, 309
Ryukyu Islands, 76

Saudi Arabia, Chinese ballistic missile sales to, 243
Scalapino, Robert, 53, 137, 184, 256, 413-414
Schelling, Thomas, 37, 46
Scowcroft, Brent, 17
Sea lane security, ASEAN and, 324-333

Sea lanes of communication (SLOCS): Japanese, 72, 179; Singapore and, 331; U.S. supply lines and, 40

Sea-launched cruise missiles, 61, 168

Sea of Japan, 42, 61, 176, 179

Sea of Okhotsk, 72, 163, 418

Segal, Gerald, 178, 203-204, 229

Sense and Destroy Armor, 224

Shevardnadze, Eduard, 166, 169, 178, 180

Shultz, George, 51-52, 261, 360, 362, 367, 368, 369-370, 381, 382

Siabu air weapons testing and practice range, 330

Siberia: bomber deployments in, 163; ICBM fields in, 228

SIGINT (Signals Intelligence), 116, 358, 371

Silkworm crisis, 242, 243

Singapore: British security relations with, 273; Five Power Defense Agreement and, 54; informal security coalitions with, 8; international marketplace and, 5; naval shipping and, 324; regional security objectives, 332; sea lanes of communication and, 331; triangular defense community and, 330; U.S. basing in, 321-322

Sino-Soviet border, 230; horizontal escalation of U.S.-Soviet conflict and, 42; military buildup along, 157; 1969 conflict, 159, 205, 221, 225; 1987-1990 discussions on, 262-263, 264; Soviet troop reductions and, 25, 169, 174, 405

Sino-Soviet New Defense Technical Accord (1957), 154, 211

Sino-Soviet Treaty of Friendship, Alliance, and Mutual Assistance, 207

Smoke, Richard, 37-38

Solarium Task Force C, 277

Solomons, New Zealand defense commitments and, 386

South China Sea, 82; ASEAN-wide joint patrolling of, 326; Soviet navy in, 190; Soviet threat assessment and, 179; U.S. navy in, 81

Southeast Asia: alternatives to Dominant Player role in, 307-314; Chinese Aspiring Player posture and, 254; nuclear-free zone and, 254, 333-339; security reorganization in, 301-302; strategic land-ridge, 269; U.S. global deterrence and, 272-275. *See also* Association of Southeast Asian Nations (ASEAN); Southeast Asia Treaty Organization (SEATO)

Southeast Asia Treaty Organization (SEATO), 50, 58, 158, 269, 281-286; ANZUS and, 347; British affiliation, 287-288; Indochina and, 394; Indonesia and, 283-284; Laos crisis and, 290; Nixon and, 294-296; Philippines and, 284-285, 299; purpose of, 282; response formula, 282, 285; Thailand and, 285, 289-290, 298, 299; U.S. skepticism of, 299-300

Southeast Asian Association for Regional Cooperation, 309

South Korea (Republic of Korea), 65; air force capabilities, 92-93; anti-Americanism in, 107; Bush and, 105, 107; Carter and, 84, 88-90; Chinese trade with, 138-139, 257; Cold War and, 65-68, 272; conventional deterrence and, 34; economic growth in, 5, 398; escalation control and, 10, 88-94; extended deterrence and, 137-141; force strength, 91-92; forward defense posture, 91-92; FX jetfighter and, 92-93; geographic vulnerability of, 63; Japan and, 106; military modernization, 92, 93; military spending, 91; national imperatives, 79; nationalism, 137; Nixon and, 90; Nunn-Warren Act and, 6; oil access, 135; Philippines and, 135-136; Reagan and, 90; Soviet economic ties, 107, 138; technology transfer to, 105; as Transitional Player, 11, 395, 398-399; Truman administration and, 66; U.S. air wing and, 88-89; U.S. Army in, 26; U.S. defense commitment to, 6, 8, 10, 20, 53, 58, 63, 76-80, 104-109, 416; U.S. force expenditures and, 105, 106; U.S. force reductions in, 88-90, 107-109; U.S. nuclear weapons deployment from, 10, 80, 89, 90, 94, 139-140, 398-399; U.S. trade with, 105

South Pacific: Bush administration and,

380; Dominant Player posture and, 376; economic enterprise zone, 379; post-ANZUS era and, 384-387; regional stability, 141-142; Soviet Union and, 191-192, 377; upgraded Australian presence in, 117-118; U.S. relations and, 379-380. *See also* AN-ZUS; *specific countries*
South Pacific Forum, 358
South Pacific island-states: affiliations of, 142; domestic threats to, 379; exploitation of, 342
South Pacific Nuclear-free Zone, 15, 114, 141, 169, 333, 338, 348, 350, 358, 366, 380-383
South Vietnam, ANZUS and, 347
South Vietnamese Rangers, 49
Southwest Pacific: Pacifist Players and, 350; regional threat assessments and, 377-380; strategic denial and, 341-349
Soviet Union, 2; air force reorganization, 172; ASEAN and, 313-314, 332, 402; Asian collective security pact and, 158; Aspiring Player posture, 12-13, 145-194, 400-403; bastion doctrine, 176; China's security objectives and, 208; Chinese alliance in 1950s, 145, 150, 207-212; Chinese ICBM targets and, 163, 228; Chinese military technology and, 170, 211-212; Chinese nuclear assistance, 154, 155, 156, 211; Chinese rift with, 153-157, 181, 211, 213, 392; Chinese summit in 1989 with, 169-170, 241, 249, 263; Chinese surgical strikes, 213, 214; Chinese threat assessments and, 228-229; Chinese trade with, 241; confidence-building proposals and, 136; contexualist diplomacy and, 400; deterrence phases, 149-171; doctrinal shifts and, 147-149; economic development and, 18; economic diplomacy and, 192; escalation control and, 38, 176-177; expansionism and, 172; Eurocentric bias, 171; Far East military buildup, 103-104; force levels, 428*n*11; force reductions, 25, 169; forward projection strategy, 411; fuel shortages and, 178; geopolitical power struggle with China and, 158-160;

ground forces, 31, 158; image concerns, 170-171; India and, 162; Indonesia and, 328; internal crises and, 418; Japanese military threat and, 121-122, 401; Korean War and, 151-153, 208-210; Laos crisis and, 286-287; Manchurian ports and, 156; Mao and, 507*n*14; military buildup in Asia, 161-165; Mongolian alliance, 162; Mongolian force reductions, 25, 169, 262, 263; multifront conflict and, 42-43; NATO-Chinese-Japanese coalition and, 146, 160-161, 162; neutralization of Japan and, 179; nuclear parity and, 412; "1941" complex and, 160; 1950-1957 deterrence, 150-153; 1960s deterrence, 157; 1970s deterrence, 147, 157, 160; 1980s deterrence, 147-148, 160; North Korea military overflights and, 106; North Korea nuclear energy program and, 140; North Korean relations, 146, 180-185, 401-402; nuclear force modernization, 50; nuclear-free zones and, 166, 167, 400; Philippine bases and, 320; Philippine missile targeting and, 321; regional disarmament and, 166, 167, 168; relaxing of Chinese tensions, 400-401; second strike capability and, 173, 176; short-war scenarios and, 38; Siberian military traffic, 130; smile diplomacy and, 147; South Korean economic ties, 107, 138; South Pacific diplomatic ties and, 378; South Pacific interdiction capabilities and, 377; South Pacific nationalism and, 191-192; SSBNs, 39, 72; supply lines, 176, 190; Taiwan Straits crises and, 210; Tonga and, 347; U.S.-Australian defense operations and, 114; U.S. Dominant Player strategy and, 173-174; Vietnam commitment and, 171, 180-181, 185-189; Vietnamese tensions and, 178-179; Vietnam treaty with, 146, 178; Vietnam War and, 157; weaknesses of, 174-180. *See also* Sino-Soviet border
Soviet Union, navy of, 112, 167, 189-192, 465*n*119; Asia-Pacific military operations, 189-192; Chinese ports

Soviet Union *(Continued)*
  and, 154; Chinese targets, 163, 177;
  cutbacks in, 118, 174; in Indian
  Ocean, 51, 97, 189, 190; North Ko-
  rea and, 182; Persian Gulf and, 177;
  protracted war and, 191; sea lanes of
  communication and, 72, 118; in
  South China Sea, 190; Vietnamese
  bases, 171; Vladivostok and, 72, 182;
  weaknesses of, 176. *see also* Cam
  Ranh Bay
Spratly Islands, 251-252, 319, 331, 420
Stalin, Joseph, 150, 152, 208, 209
Straits of Japan, 419
Straits of Malacca, 190, 324
Strategic Defense Initiative (SDI), 114,
  164-165, 192, 229
Subic Bay, Philippines, 167, 171, 177,
  317, 318, 320, 416
Sun Zi, 202, 204, 205, 210, 221
Sunda Straits, 190, 191
Surface-to-air missiles, 127, 184
Swing strategy, 44, 61, 100, 131, 434n52
Syngman Rhee, 80

Taiwan, 8; ANZUS and, 347; Carter
  and, 96, 111; China's prodemocracy
  movement and, 260; Chinese claim
  to, 260-262, 406; Cold War and, 68-
  70; escalation control and, 47, 80-81,
  95-96; international marketplace and,
  5; military modernization and, 260-
  261; Nixon and, 99; nuclear weapons
  program, 260-261; self-reliant deterrence posture, 62; strategic utility of,
  65-66; as Transitional Player, 11, 399;
  Truman administration and, 66; U.S.
  Dominant Player strategy and, 63-64;
  U.S. ending of ties with, 111-113;
  U.S. military sales to, 261; U.S. security relationship, 10, 60, 80-82; Vietnam War and, 84
Taiwan Relations Act (1979), 8, 96, 113,
  262
Taiwan Straits crises (1955, 1958), 47,
  63, 68-70, 150, 154, 200, 210, 211,
  221
Thailand, 8; Chinese deterrence and, 54,
  247-250, 405; Chinese's support
  against Vietnam and, 249; front-line

status, 259; Khmer Rouge assistance
  and, 316; national development and,
  282; Nixon Doctrine and, 297, 309;
  Nixon's visit in 1969 to, 297; regional
  serurity and, 329-330; SEATO and,
  50, 285-286, 289-290, 298, 299; su-
  perpower competition and, 272-273;
  U.S. military advisors in, 298; U.S.
  military sales to, 305; U.S. policy on
  Laos and, 289; U.S. security ties, 5,
  54, 301, 330
Thanat Khoman, 289-290, 308-310
Third World, decolonization of, 16
Tienanmen Square massacre (1989), 170,
  238, 254
Tokelau, New Zealand defense commit-
  ments and, 385
Tonga, Soviet Union and, 347
Toshiba, 127
Total Defense doctrine, 330-331
Trans-Siberian Railway systems, 163
Transitional Player, 11; Australia as, 64,
  114, 395, 399; dominant player ver-
  sus, 62-64; Japan as, 395, 397-398;
  South Korea as, 395, 398-399; Tai-
  wan as, 399; United States and, 10-
  12; U.S. allies as, 61
Treaty of Rarotonga, 169, 254, 350, 358,
  366, 380, 382-383, 421
Treaty of Tlatelolco, 382
Tripartite Treaty, 75. *See also* ANZUS
Truman, Harry S, administration of, 1,
  68; ANZUS and, 345; South Korea
  and, 66
Tuna fishing, 379

United Action initiative, 277-279
United Nations Security Council, 16
United Nations Special Session on Disarmament (May/June 1988), 169
United States: Air Force, 51, 97, 107;
  ANZAC and, 344; ANZUS and, 82-
  83, 97, 113-119, 356; ASEAN trade
  with, 28; China reconciliation, 49-50;
  China support for Khmer Rouge and,
  252-253; China's prodemocracy movement and, 405; Chinese reunification
  and, 406; French presence in Indochina and, 278; Japanese economic
  threat and, 120-121; Japanese trade

relations with, 11; Military Assistance
Advisory Group (MAAG), 95; New
Zealand's deteriorating relationship
with, 365-367; South Korean trade
with, 105; South Pacific nuclear testing and, 381-382
U.S. Dominant Player posture, 8-10, 17,
22, 350-374; alternatives to, 307-314,
395; Asia-Pacific allies and, 49-54;
Bush and, 307; effectiveness of, 27-
28; escalation control and, 83-98, 320;
Europe and, 28-32; existential deterrence and, 70-71; extended deterrence
strategy and, 23-57; interalliance
transferability and, 43; global versus
local deterrence and, 272; long-term
viability of, 28-29; Nixon and, 306;
one-and-a-half war strategy, 119; outmoded, 391-395; Reagan and, 302-
307; revising, 410-425; South Pacific
and, 376; Taiwan and, 63-64; Tran-
sistional Player posture versus, 62-64
U.S. extended deterrence strategy, 4-7;
Asia-Pacific basing alternatives, 321;
Australia defense relations, 12, 59,
64, 113-119, 141-142; Australian listening posts and, 377-378; Cam Ranh
Bay and, 164, 177, 463*n*86; Cambodian military operations, 271; case
studies, 275-286, 306-307; China and,
109-111, 242-244; China's regional security agenda and, 250; Chinese military relations with, 241-242; Chinese
technology relations and, 265;
Chinese threat assessment and, 229-
230; conventional forces, 60; convergent deterrence, 421-425; counterattack thesis, 393; contending regional
security postures and, 22; credibility
of, 393-394; defense burden-sharing
and, 414; escalation control and, 393,
394-395; force levels, 428*n*11; forward
deployed forces, 24-25, 59, 394; forward development strategy, 129-132;
global deterrence and, 15-21, 40, 59,
351-353; implementing strategic reassurance, 417-421; inconsistent Southeast Asian strategy, 274-275; interalliance transferability and, 393;
Japanese defense burden-sharing and,

30, 120-126; Japanese commitment
and, 62, 71-76, 83-84; Japanese military technology relations, 126; Japanese nuclear commitment, 103; Joint
Chiefs of Staff and, 24; land forces,
25-26; Laos crisis and, 292-293; New
Zealand port visitations, 349; nuclear-
free zones and, 333, 336-337, 351-
353; nuclear weapons deployment,
209, 300; offensive versus defensive,
413; offshore cruise missile capabilities, 172; outmoded, 391-394; Pacific
sea lanes of communication and, 411;
Pacifist Players and, 350-374; Philippines' bases and, 168, 317-324, 408;
Philippines relations and, 54, 273,
284-285, 301; post-SEATO era, 299-
301; reactive deployment, 331-332;
regional change in Asia-Pacific and,
52-53; SEATO and, 281-282, 299-
300; Seoul headquarters for Army,
25-26; Singapore bases and, 321-322;
South Korean commitment, 63, 76-
80, 104-109, 272, 398-399, 416; South
Korean military command and, 30;
South Pacific basing options, 376;
South Pacific relations, 379-380; strategic denial and, 342-349; swing strategy and, 44, 61, 100, 131, 434*n*52;
Taiwan commitment, 10, 60, 63-64,
80-82, 111-113; Taiwan military sales
and, 261; Thailand military sales and,
305; Thailand security ties and, 5, 54,
298, 301, 330; theory and practice,
32-35; Treaty of Rarotonga and, 380;
vital interests, 410-417
U.S.-Japan Mutual Security Treaty
(1951), 20, 53, 72, 122, 362,
398
U.S. Navy, 2, 44-45, 51; Antarctic supply depot, 372; carrier force, 41; defensive sea control, 20; in Indian
Ocean, 305; "neither confirm nor
deny" policy and, 349, 351, 353, 354,
355, 359-366, 368, 416; protracted
conflicts and, 40, 188; Seventh Fleet,
155, 177, 189-190, 192, 305, 318,
323; Sixth Fleet, 46, 190; in South
China Sea, 81; SSBN strike force,
189-190; swing strategy and, 44

U.S.-Philipines Military Bases Agreement 1947, 284
U.S.-Philippines Mutual Defense Treaty, 54, 75
U.S.-South Korea Mutual Defense Treaty (1953), 11, 79
U.S.-Taiwan Mutual Defense Treaty, 59, 84, 99
USS *Pueblo*, 183
USS *Ticonderoga*, 441*n*59
Ulam, Adam, 152, 154

Vanuatu, 192, 378
Very low frequency American transmitters, 444*n*83
Vietnam, 1, 18; ASEAN and, 309-310, 314; China's support of Thailand against, 249; China's war of 1979 with, 218, 219, 221, 245-246; Chinese clash off Spratly Islands and, 251-252; force levels, 428*n*11; occupation of Cambodia, 313; withdrawal from Cambodia, 253, 316-317; Soviet Union and, 171; Soviet Union and, 162; Soviet deterrence commitment to, 171, 180-181, 185-189; Soviet tensions and, 178-179; Soviet treaty with, 146, 178
Vietnam War, 47, 49, 275, 294-295; Australia and, 83; Johnson and, 293; People's Republic of China and, 215, 245; Soviet Union and, 157; Taiwan

and, 84, 95-96; U.S. containment strategy and, 270. *See also* Nixon Doctrine
Vladivostok, 72, 182

Warsaw Pact, 47, 150, 154
Weinberger, Caspar, 43, 51-52, 303, 307, 367, 368
Weisner, Maurice F., 51
Western Pacific islands, Japanese assistance to, 136
Western Samoa, New Zealand defense commitments and, 386
West New Guinea, ANZUS and, 347
Whiting, Allen, 155, 173, 199, 204, 259
Wonson air control center, 184
Wu Xiuquan, 197

Xue Litai, 210, 212, 216

Yahuda, Michael, 251
Yokohama, 132
Yoshida, Shigeru, 11, 74
Yoshida Doctrine, 74

Zagoria, Donald, 147, 400
Zarsky, Lyuba, 18
Zhang Aiping, 218-219, 238-240
Zone of Peace, Freedom, and Neutrality (ZOPFAN), 254, 271, 299, 312-314, 326, 337, 420